www.ingramcontent.com/pod-product-compliance
Lightning Source LLC
Chambersburg PA
CBHW030311100426
42812CB00002B/663
9781952895357

TIMES *of* ELEVATION

VOLUME 1

Rosh Hashanah - Simchat Torah

Kabbalah Centre Publishing is a registered DBA of The Kabbalah Centre International, Inc.

For further information:
The Kabbalah Centre
155 E. 48th St., New York, NY 10017
1062 S. Robertson Blvd., Los Angeles, CA 90035

1.800.Kabbalah www.kabbalah.com

Printed in China, September 2024

ISBN: 978-1-952895-35-7

Times of Elevation, Volume 1, First Edition

Cover Design: HL Design (Hyun Min Lee) www.hldesignco.com
Graphic Layout: Shlomit Heymann

TIMES *of* ELEVATION

Secrets of the Zohar on the Most Powerful Days of the Year

Edited by Rav Michael Berg

VOLUME 1

Rosh Hashanah - Simchat Torah

TABLE OF CONTENTS

INTRODUCTION BY RAV MICHAEL BERG

It is with tremendous appreciation that we present to you *Times of Elevation: Secrets of the Zohar on the Most Powerful Days of the Year.*

One of the great blessings we receive from the wisdom of Kabbalah is that we are awakened to the incredible Light that is available to us during the year. However, more important than the awareness is the knowledge we receive of how to capture the great Light and blessings present in these unique windows of time. Without this wisdom we could go about our lives throughout the year, missing so many opportunities.

There is no tool more powerful than the revelation, Light, and Wisdom of the Zohar, to assist us in understanding how to use these most powerful days of the year.

Therefore, what you now hold in your hands is all the wisdom and energy that you need to make your year blessed and filled with Light.

The kabbalists explain that the Zohar is both a book of wisdom and a great source of Light. Keeping this in mind, I would like to share with you how I use the Zohar in preparing for the most important days of the year:

— I recommend that you study the section relating to the days that you are preparing for, to deepen your consciousness as well as your understanding, as the Light that is available to us is dependent on our understanding and consciousness.

— As important, if not more important, is to use the section of the Zohar as a meditation, a prayer to draw down the Light. In reading and studying the Zohar, find and make note of a specific part of the Zohar that shines for you, that inspires you. It is even more powerful if you can learn some of the Aramaic words in that section. And then, in the days leading up to and on the days of connection, meditate upon that section over and over. You will feel a new and deeper awakening of Light greater than you have ever felt on those days. I can tell you from my own work that this will bring new Light and connections more profound then you have had before.

I would also like to share with you the very special place these sections of Zohar hold in my heart. My spiritual foundation, that which has carried me through and continues to push me forward in life, was established in the times I studied with my father, Rav Berg (the Rav). From about the age of the thirteen, almost every night from 1:00 am to 5:00 am, I would learn with the Rav, the Ten Luminous Emanations—the foundational teachings of Kabbalah and the Kabbalistic System. And before each of these days of the year, we would add to our studies the sections from the Zohar found here, as well as the writings of the Ari about them. My father would never enter into these times without this study, year after year.

It was always inspiring for me to see how, even though my father the Rav had been studying these sections for many years, nonetheless, every year there was a renewed zeal, inspiration, and revelation that happened when examining these words.

I bless all of us that in delving more deeply into this book we are endlessly inspired to unlimited connection and growth.

Wishing great connection and blessings,
Rav Michael Berg

ROSH HASHANAH

Vayera

28. Rosh Hashanah and Yom haKippurim

A Synopsis

Through the Zohar, various secrets about Rosh Hashanah and Yom Kippur are revealed. The penetrating sound of the Shofar has the power to confuse the negative angel called Satan, who acts as prosecutor during these Days of Judgment and repentance. The ten days that fall between Rosh Hashanah and Yom Kippur are likened to a great gift. This time frame provides us with the chance to remove all the negativity and decrees of Judgment that we have brought down upon ourselves through our wrongful actions over the prior year. The prerequisite for accomplishing this goal is accountability and genuine permanent change in our character.

The Relevance of this Passage

The act of repentance is a profound tool available to each of us anytime we truly choose to change our ways. The energy radiating from the verses revealing the hidden secrets of Rosh Hashanah and Yom Kippur, allow us to continually draw upon the forces of purification throughout the entire year.

On Rosh Hashanah, Israel need to arouse the Shofar and awaken a sound.

381. תָּא חֲזֵי, כְּגַוְונָא דָא, בְּיוֹם ר"ה, וְיוֹם הַכִּפּוּרִים, דְּדִינָא אִשְׁתְּכַח בְּעָלְמָא, אִיהוּ קָאִים לְקַטְרְגָא, וְיִשְׂרָאֵל בָּעְיָין לְאִתְעָרָא בְּשׁוֹפָר, וּלְאַתְעָרָא קוֹל, דְּכָלִיל בְּאֶשָׁ"א וּבְמַיָּ"א וְרוּחָ"א, וְאִתְעֲבִידוּ חָד, וּלְאַשְׁמָעָא הַהוּא קוֹל, מִגּוֹ שׁוֹפָר.

381. Come and see, the same applies for Rosh Hashanah and Yom Hakippurim, when Judgment hovers over the world and the Satan **is there to prosecute. The children of Israel should be awakened by the Shofar, to awaken a sound that is comprised of water, fire, and**

air, which are Chesed-Gevurah-Tiferet, **which become one** by it, **and sound that voice from within the Shofar.**

Explanation: The twelve months of the year are the correction of Malchut from Her beginning to Her end and because Her end is not complete until the Final Correction, we need to go back and correct Her every year. Therefore every Rosh Hashanah we begin from the beginning of the correction of Malchut, namely as She was emanated on the Fourth Day of Creation, when She was in the secret of "And God made the two great luminaries..." (Genesis 1:16). At that stage, Malchut had the complete Upper Three Sefirot of the Left, which is the secret of the Illumination of Shuruk, namely Chochmah without Chasadim. Therefore the moon complained "it is impossible for two kings to use one crown" (Tractate Chullin 60b), as She could not stand to be without Chasadim. This was also the secret of the denouncement of Satan, whose complaint latched onto Malchut to draw judgments as long as the Upper Three of the Left shone in Her. And we need to remove the grip and denouncement of Satan from Malchut at that time. This is the meaning of "Satan **is there to prosecute"** since every Rosh Hashanah the Upper Three Sefirot of the Left are revealed, which causes Satan to denounce Malchut.

This is the meaning of **"The children of Israel should be awakened by the Shofar, to awaken a sound that is comprised of water, fire, and air"** because to remove the denouncement of Satan here we also need to do an action to nullify the Upper Three of the Upper Three of the Illumination of the Left, just like what was done with the breaking of the heifer's neck and by the elders saying " '...our eyes did not see'" (Deuteronomy 21:7) in the secret of the second Tikkun that was there. This action is the secret of the voice (sound) we raise up through the Shofar. It is known that in general there are two kinds of voices. The first is the voice of Malchut that is not sweetened by Binah, and the second is the voice of Binah, or Malchut sweetened by Binah whose voice is like the voice of Binah. He says here that this voice that we raise up to nullify the Upper Three of the Upper Three is the voice of Binah. This is the meaning of **"and sound that voice from within the Shofar,"** namely Binah called Shofar, which is the secret of the Masach of Chirik, from which emerges the Central Column that unites the two Columns, Right and Left, together. This is the meaning of **"a sound that is comprised of water, fire, and air,"** namely a sound that includes the three Columns, which are nicknamed "water, fire, air," "which become one" since with this Masach the Three Columns become one, which causes the diminishment of the Upper Three of the Upper Three of the Left. Then, the denouncement of Satan on Malchut goes away.

The sound of the Shofar Below awakens the sound of the Shofar Above.

382. וְהַהוּא קוֹל, סָלְקָא עַד אֲתַר, דְּכָרְסְיָיא דְּדִינָא יָתְבָא, וּבָטַשׁ בָּהּ, וְסָלְקָא, כֵּיוָן דְּמָטָא הַאי קוֹל מִתַּתָּא, קוֹל דְּיַעֲקֹב אִתְתַּקַּן לְעֵילָּא, וְקוּדְשָׁא בְּרִיךְ הוּא אִתְעַר רַחֲמֵי, דְּהָא כְּגַוְונָא דְּיִשְׂרָאֵל מִתְעָרֵי לְתַתָּא, קוֹל חַד, כָּלִיל בְּאֶשָׁ"א וְרוּחָ"א וּמַיָ"א, דְּנָפְקֵי כַּחֲדָא, מִגּוֹ שׁוֹפָר, הָכֵי נָמֵי אִתְעַר לְעֵילָּא שׁוֹפָר, וְהַהוּא קוֹל דְּכָלִיל בְּאֶשָׁ"א וּמַיָ"א וְרוּחָ"א אִתְתַּקַּן, וְנָפַק דָּא מִתַּתָּא, וְדָא מֵעֵילָּא, וְאִתְתַּקַּן עָלְמָא, וְרַחֲמֵי אִשְׁתְּכָחוּ.

382. And this voice rises up to where the Throne of Judgment resides, namely to the Upper Three of the Left, on which the denouncement depends, **strikes it,** namely it diminishes the Upper Three of the Upper Three that is there, **and** Malchut **rises** from the Throne of Judgment to the Throne of Mercy. **After this voice from Below has reached, then the voice of Jacob is established Above**, which is the secret of the stature of Chasadim that emerges from the mentioned Masach, which is the secret of the Central Column called Tiferet, Jacob, and Mercy. Then **the Holy One, blessed be He, is awakened with Mercy. Just as Israel awaken a voice from Below through the Shofar that includes fire, water, and air, so is a voice corresponding to them awakened Above through the** Supernal **Shofar,** which is Binah. The power to blow the Shofar is fire, and the voice is formed by the air, and the air also produces sweat and hot breath, which are the secret of water. These arouse the Upper Three Columns of Binah, from where the Mochin are drawn down to Zeir Anpin and Malchut. **And this voice that consists of fire, water, and air,** which has risen from Below, namely the Masach, **is established, and this** Masach **emerges from Below, and another emerges from Above,** namely the stature of Chasadim that comes out of the Masach, **so the world,** which is Malchut, **is established and Mercy prevails.**

When the sound of the Shofar is roused,
the world receives Mercy from the Central Column.

383. וְהַהוּא מְקַטְרְגָא אִעַרְבֵּב, דַּהֲוָה חָשִׁיב לְשַׁלְטָאָה בְּדִינָא, וּלְקַטְרְגָא בְּעָלְמָא, וְחָמֵי דְּמִתְעָרֵי רַחֲמֵי, כְּדֵין אִעַרְבֵּב, וְאִתְּשַׁשׁ חֵילֵיהּ, וְלָא יָכֵיל לְמֶעְבַּד מִדֵּי, וְקוּדְשָׁא בְּרִיךְ הוּא דָּאִין עָלְמָא בְּרַחֲמֵי, דְּאִי תֵּימָא דְּדִינָא אִתְעֲבֵיד, לָאו הָכֵי, אֶלָּא אִתְחַבָּרוּ רַחֲמֵי בְּדִינָא, וְעָלְמָא אִתְדָּן בְּרַחֲמֵי.

383. Now the prosecutor is confused because he thought to govern Judgment and punish the world. He did not think that the Upper Three of the Left will be diminished, causing his control and denouncement to disappear. **But when he realizes that Mercy was aroused, he is perplexed, his strength fails, and he is unable to do anything. Then the Holy One, blessed be He, judges the world with Mercy. You may say that Judgment has been executed,** namely that the Upper Three of the Left Column were diminished by the sound of the Shofar, **but it is not so. Rather, Judgment and Mercy were joined, and the world is judged mercifully.** Meaning that the sound of the Shofar that rises from Below, which is the secret of the elevation of Female Waters of the Masach of Chirik, causes a stature of Chasadim to emerge on the Masach, and this stature is the secret of the Central Column, which is called Jacob and is called Mercy, and the world receives Mercy from the Central Column. Therefore, the diminishment of the Upper Three of the Left is not considered Judgment because without this diminishment there would be no Mercy in the world.

When there is Light present, outside forces try to take from the Light of Wisdom.

384. תָּא חֲזֵי, כְּתִיב תִּקְעוּ בַחֹדֶשׁ שׁוֹפָר בַּכֶּסֶה לְיוֹם חַגֵּנוּ דְּאִתְכַּסְיָא סִיהֲרָא, דְּהָא כְּדֵין, שָׁלְטָא הַאי חִוְיָא בִּישָׁא, וְיָכִיל לְנַזְּקָא עָלְמָא, וְכַד מִתְעָרֵי רַחֲמֵי, סָלְקָא סִיהֲרָא, וְאִתְעֲבָרַת מִתַּמָּן, וְאִיהוּ אִתְעַרְבֵּב, וְלָא יָכִיל לְשַׁלְטָאָה, וְאִתְעֲבַר, דְּלָא יִתְקְרַב תַּמָּן, וְעַל דָּא, בְּיוֹם ר״ה, בָּעֵי לְעַרְבְּבָא לֵיהּ, כְּמַאן דְּאִתְעַר מִשִּׁנְתֵיהּ, וְלָא יְדַע כְּלוּם.

384. Come and see, it is written: "Blow a Shofar in the renewal [of the moon], at the appointed time (*bakeseh*, lit. in the covering) for the day of our festival" (Psalms 81:4) when the moon, which is Malchut, **is covered because at that time,** as a result of the Illumination of the Left, **that evil Serpent prevails and may bring harm to the world. But when Mercy is aroused** by blowing the Shofar, **the moon rises and moves away** from the Illumination of the Left, due to the diminishment of the Upper Three caused by the sound of the Shofar. Thus the Satan **is confused and loses control. Then he is removed** from the moon **and never comes near again** because once the Upper Three of the Left is diminished he has nothing to nourish from Her or prosecute. **This is why on Rosh Hashanah we need to confuse** the Satan **like one who has just woken up from his slumber and doesn't know anything.**

On Rosh Hashanah, the Satan is confused and powerless once he sees Mercy aroused from Below.

385. בְּר״ה בָּעֵי לְנַיְיחָא, וּלְמֶעְבַּד לֵיהּ נַיְיחָא דְּרוּחָא, בְּשָׂעִיר דְּקָרְבִין לֵיהּ, וּכְדֵין אִתְהַפַּךְ סַנֵּיגוֹרְיָא, עֲלַיְיהוּ דְּיִשְׂרָאֵל, אֲבָל בְּיוֹמָא דְּר״ה, אִתְעַרְבֵּב, דְּלָא יָדַע וְלָא יָכִיל לְמֶעְבַּד כְּלוּם. חָמֵי אִתְעֲרוּתָא דְּרַחֲמֵי סָלְקִין מִתַּתָּא,

וְרַחֲמֵי מִלְּעֵילָא, וְסִיהֲרָא סָלְקָא בֵּינַיְיהוּ, כְּדֵין אִתְעַרְבֵּב וְלָא יָדַע כְּלוּם, וְלָא יָכֵיל לְשַׁלְטָאָה.

385. On Yom haKippurim, we need to deal with **the Satan** with ease **and give him appeasement through the goat** to Azazel **that we sacrifice for him** by sending it to the desert, which is his place. **Then he will become a defender for Israel. But on Rosh Hashanah he is confused—as he does not know nor is he able to do anything—as he sees Mercy aroused from Below and bestowed from Above. And the moon,** which is Malchut, **rises in between them. This is when he is perplexed and no longer knows anything. Thus he loses his power.**

The Mercy of the Ten Days of Repentance.

386. וְקוּדְשָׁא בְּרִיךְ הוּא דָּן לְהוֹ לְיִשְׂרָאֵל בְּרַחֲמֵי, וְחָיֵיס עֲלַיְיהוּ, וְאִשְׁתַּכַּח לְהוֹ זִמְנָא כָּל אִינּוּן י׳ יוֹמִין, דְּבֵין ר״ה לְיוֹם הַכִּפּוּרִים, לְקַבְּלָא כָּל אִינּוּן דְּתָיְיבִין קַמֵּיהּ, וּלְכַפָּרָא לוֹן מֵחוֹבַיְיהוּ, וְסָלֵיק לוֹן לְיוֹמָא דְּכִפּוּרֵי.

386. Then the Holy One, blessed be He, judges Israel with Mercy and has compassion for them and gives them time—the ten days between Rosh Hashanah and Yom haKippurim—to accept those who repent before Him, and atone for their sins. Then He raises them up to the sanctity of **Yom haKippurim.**

Everything depends on action and words.

387. וְעַל דָּא, בְּכֹלָּא קוּדְשָׁא בְּרִיךְ הוּא פַּקֵּיד לוֹן לְיִשְׂרָאֵל, לְמֶעְבַּד עוֹבָדָא, בְּגִין דְּלָא יִשְׁלוֹט עֲלַיְיהוּ, מַאן דְּלָא אִצְטְרִיךְ, וְלָא יִשְׁלוֹט עֲלַיְיהוּ דִּינָא, וִיהוֹן כֻּלְּהוֹן זַכָּאִין בְּאַרְעָא, כִּרְחִימוּ דְּאַבָּא עַל בְּנִין, וְכֹלָּא בְּעוֹבָדָא וּבְמִלִּין תַּלְיָא, וְהָא אוֹקִימְנָא מִלִּין.

387. Therefore, to correct **everything the Holy One, blessed be He, commanded Israel to perform the Precept** of the Blowing of the

Shofar **so that they will not have any unnecessary dominion over them,** meaning to abolish the Satan and his denouncement, and **so that Judgment will not rule over them,** rather Mercy will reside on them, **and so that they will be worthy** of His Mercy **on earth, which is like the Mercy of a father towards his children. All this depends on** the arousal of the Lower Beings **through action and words. And all this has already been explained.**

Vayikra

44. The Blowing of the Shofar

A Synopsis

Rav Elazar tells about the Blowing of the Shofar on Rosh Hashanah and on Yom Kippur, and about the day that Isaac was bound. On that day God elevated Abraham, teaching us that the Right was constructed and perfected by binding the Left. God told Israel that they should not be afraid of the Judgments of the Left Column, for He detains those Judgments from emerging. When the sound of the Shofar rises up, the prosecutors Above are pushed aside by the sound and cannot prevail. Rav Elazar talks about the worthiness of the messenger, saying that a Priest and a Levite should be examined before they begin their service to be sure they are worthy of it. Then they shall put incense on the altar so that everything is perfumed, and so that blessings will prevail in all the Worlds.

Rav Shimon bar Yochai would purify his Shofar blower for three days.

302. רִבִּי אֶלְעָזָר וְרִבִּי אַבָּא הֲווֹ יַתְבֵי. א"ר אֶלְעָזָר, וַחֲמֵינָא לְאַבָּא בְּיוֹמֵי דְּרֹאשׁ הַשָּׁנָה וְיוֹם הַכִּפּוּרִים, דְּלָא בָּעֵי לְמִשְׁמַע צְלוֹתָא מִכָּל בַּר נָשׁ, אֶלָּא אִי קָאִים עֲלֵיהּ תְּלָתָא יוֹמִין קוֹדֶם, לְדַכְאָה לֵיהּ. דְּרִבִּי שִׁמְעוֹן הֲוָה אָמַר הָכִי, בִּצְלוֹתָא דְּהַאי בַּר נָשׁ דַּאֲנָא מְדַכֵּינָא, אִתְכַּפַּר עָלְמָא. וְכָל שֶׁכֵּן בִּתְקִיעָה דְּשׁוֹפָר, דְּלָא מְקַבֵּל תְּקִיעָתָא דְּב"נ דְּלָאו אִיהוּ חַכִּים לְמִתְקַע בְּרָזָא דִּתְקִיעָה.

302. Rav Elazar and Rav Aba were sitting. Rav Elazar said: "I saw that on the day of Rosh Hashanah and on Yom Kippur, my father refused to listen to the prayer of a man, unless he was with him three days in advance to purify him. As Rav Shimon used to say, 'Through the prayer of the man whom I purify, the world is atoned for.' All the more so with the blowing of the Shofar, for he did not accept the Shofar Blowing of a man who was not wise to blow with the intention of the secret of Blowing (Teki'ah)."

Teru'ah is Soft Judgment and Shevarim is Harsh Judgment.

303. דְּתָנֵינָן, ר' יֵיסָא סָבָא אָמַר, הָנֵי תְּקִיעָתָא כְּסִדְרָן. קַדְמָאָה, כְּלִילָא מִכֹּלָּא. תִּנְיָינָא, וְחָדָא כְּסִדְרָא וַחֲדָא כְּסִדְרָא, גְּבוּרָה גְּדוֹלָה בֵּינַיְיהוּ. תְּלִיתָאָה, חַד הָכָא וְחַד הָכָא גְּבוּרָה בֵּינַיְיהוּ. פּוּסְקָא סַלְקָא, קוּמַטְרָא נַחְתָּא. חַד תַּקִּיפָא וְחַד רַפְיָא. וְהָא אוּקְמוּהָ. וְאִינּוּן עֲשָׂרָה. וְאִינּוּן תֵּשַׁע. חַד כְּלָלָא דְּכֹלָּא.

303. We have learned that Rav Yesa Saba said that this is the order of the Shofar Blowings: The first order **includes all of them;** meaning it includes Shevarim and Teru'ah, and the order is: Teki'ah, Shevarim-Teru'ah, Teki'ah. **The second** order is **one** Teki'ah **duly** in the beginning, **one** Teki'ah **duly** in the end, **and a Great Gevurah,** namely Shevarim **in between.** The order is Teki'ah, Shevarim, Teki'ah. **The third** order is **one** Teki'ah **on one side** in the beginning, and **one** Teki'ah **on another side** in the end, and a Regular **Gevurah,** which is Teru'ah **in between. The Shevarim ascends** to Gevurah, **and the Teru'ah descends** to Malchut. **One is Harsh** Judgment, namely Shevarim, **and the other is Soft** Judgment, namely Teru'ah. **This has already been explained. There are ten sounds:** Teki'ah, Shevarim-Teru'ah, Teki'ah; Teki'ah, Shevarim, Teki'ah; Teki'ah, Teru'ah, Teki'ah. **Yet they are only nine sounds,** since **one** in the middle of the first order, namely Shevarim-Teru'ah, is not two sounds but **is inclusive;** namely, one sound that includes two, and therefore there are no more than nine sounds.

Explanation: There are two types of Gevurah: one is the Left Column of Zeir Anpin called Isaac, and the other is Malchut, which is built with the Left Column, and She is also Gevurah. Therefore, Gevurah of Zeir Anpin is called a Great Gevurah and Malchut is called a Regular Gevurah. And in general, the Shofar Blowings correspond to the Three Columns, meaning that they are to correct the Left Column, which is Judgment [Isaac], with the two Columns—Right and Central—called Abraham and Jacob, which are Kindness and Mercy. This is the secret of the two Blowings, one in the beginning of the order corresponding to Abraham, and one in the end of the order corresponding to Jacob, where between them is Isaac, the Left Column, which gets sweetened and fragranced.

However, there are two aspects of the Left, which are the Gevurah of Zeir Anpin called Isaac and Regular Gevurah that is Malchut, and both need to be sweetened. Therefore we need three orders because Shevarim corresponds to the Great Gevurah and Teru'ah corresponds to regular Gevurah. Therefore, in the first order we combine both Gevurahs together. This is the meaning of **"The first includes all of them"** and therefore we blow Teki'ah, Shevarim-Teru'ah, Teki'ah. In the second order we sweeten only the Great Gevurah, which is Shevarim, with the two times Teki'ah, therefore it says **"The second, one duly and one duly, and a Great Gevurah in between"** meaning that we blow Teki'ah, Shevarim, Teki'ah. In the third order we sweeten only the Regular Gevurah with the two times Teki'ah, thus **"The third, one on one side, one on another side, Gevurah in between them."** It does not say here "Great Gevurah" but just "Regular Gevurah," which is Malchut, which is Teru'ah. Here we blow Teki'ah, Teru'ah, Teki'ah.

The Shofar blowing is the secret of the Binding of Isaac.

304. וּבְהַאי יוֹמָא מִתְעַטְּרָא יִצְחָק, וְהוּא רֵישָׁא לַאֲבָהָן. בְּהַאי יוֹמָא כְּתִיב, פָּחֲדוּ בְצִיּוֹן חַטָּאִים. בְּהַאי יוֹמָא יִצְחָק אִתְעֲקָד, וְעָקִיד כֹּלָּא, וְשָׂרָה מְיַלֶּלֶת וְקוֹל שׁוֹפְרָא תַּקִּיף לַחֲדָא. זַכָּאָה חוּלָקֵיהּ, מַאן דְּעָבַר בֵּינַיְיהוּ, וְאִשְׁתְּזִיב מִנַּיְיהוּ. א"ר אַבָּא, בְּגִ"כ קָרֵינָן פַּרְשְׁתָּא דְּיִצְחָק בְּהַאי יוֹמָא, דִּבְהַאי יוֹמָא אִתְעֲקַד יִצְחָק לְתַתָּא, וְאִתְקְשַׁר בְּהַהוּא דִּלְעֵילָּא. אֵימָתַי אִתְקְשַׁר. בְּשַׁעֲתָא דִּכְתִּיב וַיַּעֲקוֹד אֶת יִצְחָק בְּנוֹ וְגוֹ'.

304. On this day, Isaac, who is Gevurah and the Left Column, **is adorned and is the head of the Patriarchs. On this day it is written: "The sinners in Zion are afraid…." (Isaiah 33:14) On this day Isaac was bound, and he bound everything. Sarah wails and the sound of**

the Shofar grows very strong. Happy is the portion of he who passes between them and escapes them. Rav Aba said: "This is why we read the portion of the binding **of Isaac on this day, since on this day Isaac was bound Below, and he is tied to the one Above." When was he tied? At the time that it is written: "...and he bound Isaac his son...." (Genesis 22:9)**

Explanation: On Rosh Hashanah the Worlds revert to their original state, namely, as Malchut was on the Fourth Day of Creation, when She clothed the Left Column of Binah and Zeir Anpin [clothed] the Right Column of Binah. At that point, the Right and Left did not yet unite together, and Chochmah was without Chasadim, thus unable to shine, as Chochmah cannot shine without Chasadim. This is the secret of the Judgments and the complaint of the moon. To remedy this, the Holy One, blessed be He, gave the [Precept of the] Blowing of the Shofar. Through the sound that comes out of the Shofar we awaken the force of the Masach of Chirik in Zeir Anpin, which is the secret of the Central Column, and through the Masach of Chirik He diminishes the Left Column from [containing] the Upper Three [Sefirot]. Then the Left is subdued to the Right and unites with it. The Six Corners of Chochmah that remains in the Left is clothed by Chasadim, and then they shine. All this was written earlier (Zohar, Vayera 381).

Thus, on Rosh Hashanah, the Left Column is corrected through the Shofar and is able to shine due to it being clothed by the Chesed of the Right. This is as it says: **"On that day, Isaac is adorned,"** as Isaac, who is the Left Column, is adorned through him being clothed in Chasadim, and he shines in the aspect of the Six Corners of the Upper Three, which is called Adornment. **"and is the head of the Patriarchs,"** since the aspect of the head, which is the secret of the Upper Three that exists in the Chesed-Gevurah-Tiferet of Zeir Anpin, which are called Patriarchs, come from Isaac. [This is] because his Six Corners of Chochmah are the secret of the Upper Three and the Head. But the Right Column, the secret of Abraham, is the secret of Chasadim, which lacks the Upper Three, as the Upper Three only come from Chochmah.

On that day it is written: "The sinners in Zion are afraid...." (Isaiah 33:14) The sinners who wish to only cleave to the Upper Three of the Left, which awakens Judgment in the world, are now in fear since the Masach of Chirik that is awakened by the sound of the Shofar diminishes these Upper Three.

Know that the Blowing of the Shofar and the Binding of Isaac is the same idea. The Binding of Isaac means that Abraham awakened the Masach of Chirik in the Central Column Above, through which he bound his son Isaac, namely that he diminished the Upper Three of Chochmah that are in the Left Column, which are the Aspect of Isaac. Through this diminishment the Left became included in the Right Column Above, which is the secret of Abraham, and so too Isaac Below became included in Abraham, by which they were both perfected.

This is as it says: **"On this day Isaac was bound,"** because the sound of the Shofar diminishes the Upper Three of the Left Column, which is considered as the Binding of Isaac. **"And he bound everything,"** since all aspects of the Left Column Above were bound, and even the Left Column of Binah. **"Sarah wails"** since Binah that is called Sarah wails, which is a diminishment, due to Her Left Column being diminished. He explains why all this is done and says it is because **"the sound of the Shofar grows very strong,"** the strong sound of the Shofar caused all this diminishment, as mentioned earlier. This is as it says: **"Isaac was bound Below, and he is tied to the one Above,"** he was tied unified with the Right and Left Above due to the the Binding, and he merited for his Six Corners of Chochmah to be clothed in Chasadim, which is the Aspect of his Upper Three and [the Upper Three] of the rest of the grades.

The Right is completed by the Binding of the Left.

305. אָמַר רִבִּי אֶלְעָזָר, בְּהַאי יוֹמָא אַעְטָר יִצְחָק לְאַבְרָהָם, דִּכְתִּיב וְהָאֱלֹהִים נִסָּה אֶת אַבְרָהָם. מַאי נִסָּה. כד"א, וְאֶל עַמִּים אָרִים נִסִּי. וַיִּקְרָא שְׁמוֹ יְיָ' נִסִּי. מַאי קָמ"ל. בְּגִין דְּאִשְׁתְּכְלִיל יְמִינָא וְאִשְׁתְּלִים. הה"ד וְהָאֱלֹהִים נִסָּה אֶת אַבְרָהָם. וְהָאֱלֹהִים דַּיְיקָא, וְדָא הוּא וּפַחַד יִצְחָק.

305. Rav Elazar said: "On this day of the Binding of Isaac, **Isaac crowned Abraham** with the Mochin of the Upper Three that are called Crown, in the secret of the verse: '...with the crown with which his mother crowned him...' (Song of Songs 3:11) **as is written, '...and God tested (*nisa*) Abraham....' (Genesis 22:1) What is *nisa*? It is as it said: '...and lift up My ensign (*nisi*) to the peoples....' (Isaiah 49:22) '...and he called its Name Adonai-Nisi (lit. the Lord is my banner).' (Exodus 17:15)"** It is the language of elevation and exaltation, not of testing, for in the Binding of Isaac, he raised and elevated Abraham. He asks: **"What does this teach us?"** He answers: "It teaches us **that the right was founded and perfected** by binding the Left. Before the Right Column, the secret of Abraham, was included in the Left, which is Isaac, it [the Right] only has the Six Corners without the Upper Three. After it is included in the Left it has the Upper Three just like the Left, as mentioned in the previous paragraph. This fusion happens by means of the Binding of Isaac. It is found that the Right is established and perfected through the Binding. **Hence, it is written '...and God tested Abraham...' (Genesies 22:1)** meaning that he increased him with the Upper Three. **It is accurate to use 'and God,' which is the fear of Isaac,** namely the attribute of Gevurah, the Left Column, as this attribute increased him with the Upper Three. This happened with him being included in [the Left] by the Binding of Isaac."

The sweetening and perfuming of the world.

306. רִבִּי אַבָּא אָמַר, כְּתִיב כִּי אֱלֹהִים שׁוֹפֵט זֶה יַשְׁפִּיל וְזֶה יָרִים. כִּי אֱלֹהִים שׁוֹפֵט, אִלְמָלֵא דְּאַעְבַּר דִּינָא דְּיִצְחָק, בַּאֲתַר דְּיַעֲקֹב שָׁארֵי, וְאִתְבְּסָם תַּמָּן, וַוי לְעָלְמָא דְּיֶעְרַע בְּדִינֵיהּ, וְרָזָא דְּמִלָּה, כִּי בָאֵשׁ יְיָ' נִשְׁפָּט. וְדָא הוּא אִתְבַּסְּמוּתָא דְעָלְמָא.

306. Rav Aba said: "It is written, 'For God (Elohim) is the judge: He puts one down, and lifts up another.' (Psalms 75:8) 'For God (Elohim) is the judge': 'Elohim' is Gevurah, and 'the judge' is Tiferet called sentence (*mishpat*). The meaning of this is that **if the Judgment of Isaac,** the secret of Gevurah and the Left Column, **did not pass through the place where Jacob,** who is the secret of Tiferet and the Central Column, **dwells, and** was not **perfumed there, woe to the world who meets his Judgment.** Jacob, the Central Column, diminishes the Left Column through the Masach of Chirik, by which the Left unites with the Right and the Harsh Judgments of the Left are perfumed, as mentioned earlier. **This is the secret of the words: 'For by fire will the Lord (Yud-Hei-Vav-Hei) execute Judgment....' (Isaiah 66:16)** The fire of the Left is judged by Yud-Hei-Vav-Hei, the Central Column, Which joins it with the Right. **This is the perfuming of the world.**

Jacob cools off the intense Judgment of Isaac.

307. וְכֵיוָן דְּעָאל בְּאַתְרָא דְּיַעֲקֹב, וְיַעֲקֹב אָחִיד בֵּיהּ, כְּדֵין שָׁכִיךְ אֶשָּׁא, וְאִצְטַנְּנוּ גּוּמְרֵיהּ. כְּבַ"נ, דַּהֲוָה רָגִיז, וְחָגַר וְזַיִין גַּרְמֵיהּ, וְנָפַק בְּרוּגְזֵיהּ לְקַטְלָא לִבְנֵי נָשָׁא. חַד חַכִּימָא קָם עַל פִּתְחָא, וְאָחִיד בֵּיהּ, אָמַר אִלְמָלֵא לָא אָחִיד בִּי וְאִתְתַּקַּף בִּי, הָא קְטוֹלָא בִּבְנֵי נָשָׁא אִשְׁתְּכַח. בְּעוֹד דְּאִתְתַּקְּפוּ דָּא בְּדָא, וְאָחִיד דָּא בְּדָא, אִצְטַנַּן רוּגְזֵיהּ עַל דְּנָפַק לְקַטְלָא. נָפַק לְאוֹכָחָא, מַאן סָבִיל רוּגְזָא וְתוּקְפָּא דְּדִינָא דְּהַהוּא ב"נ. הֱוֵי אֵימָא, דָּא דְּקָאִים אַפִּתְחָא.

307. "Since Isaac, the Left Column, **enters the place of Jacob,** the Central Column, **and Jacob holds on to him,** by virtue of the Masach of Chirik in him, **the fire is appeased and his coals cool,** namely the Judgments of the Left Column. This is like **a man who got angry and armed himself and in his anger, went out to kill people. A wise man stood by his door, seized him** and did not let him go out. The angry man **said to him: 'Were it not for you who held me and opposed me, there would be killing in the world.' As they were arguing with each other and seizing each other, his anger with his desire to kill cooled off.** The wise man **thus proved who endures the anger and the harshness of that man's rage; namely, whoever stands by the door** to detain him from coming out.

Israel gives strength to the Creator by blowing the Shofar.

308. כַּךְ אָמַר קוּדְשָׁא בְּרִיךְ הוּא לְיִשְׂרָאֵל, בָּנַי, לָא תִּדְחֲלוּן, הָא אֲנָא קָאֵים עַל פִּתְחָא, אֲבָל אִזְדָּרְזוּ בְּהַאי יוֹמָא וְהָבוּ לִי חֵילָא. וּבְמָה. בְּשׁוֹפָר. דְּאִי אִשְׁתְּכַח קוֹל שׁוֹפָר כַּדְקָא יָאוּת, וּמְכַוְּונֵי בֵּיהּ לְתַתָּא, הַהוּא קָלָא סָלִיק, וּבֵיהּ מִתְעַטְּרֵי אֲבָהָן, וְקַיְימֵי בְּמַשְׁכְּנֵיהּ דְּיַעֲקֹב. וְע"ד בָּעֵי לְאִזְדַּהֲרָא בְּשׁוֹפָרָא, וּלְמִנְדַּע בְּהַהוּא קָלָא וּלְכַוְּונָא.

308. "Thus said the Holy One, blessed be He, the secret of the Central Column, **to Israel: 'My children, do not be afraid** of the Judgments of the Left Column, **for I stand by the door** to detain the Judgments from coming out. **Be encouraged on this day and give me strength. With what? With the Shofar.'** Through the sound of the Shofar the Central Column rouses the Masach of Chirik (as explained in paragraph 304), which is its entire ability to diminish the Left Column and sweeten it with the Right. Without it, no power can unite the Left with the Right. **If the sound of the Shofar is found as it should be and is meditated upon Below, the sound rises** and awakens the Masach of Chirik in the Central Column and joins the Right and Left, **with which the fathers are crowned.** By including the Right with the Left they acquire Mochin of the Upper Three, and through this Isaac is crowned and Abraham is crowned. And since all this is caused by Jacob, he is also crowned because whatever Mochin are revealed in the Upper due to the Lower are also received by the Lower. It is found that the Patriarchs, Abraham and Isaac **are in Jacob's abode** because he brings about this unification. **One should therefore be careful with the Shofar, to know that sound and meditate on it."**

The sound of the Shofar awakens the Masach of Chirik to nullify the Judgments.

309. וְלֵית לָךְ קָלָא בְּשׁוֹפָרָא, דְּלָא סָלִיק רְקִיעָא חַד. וְכָל אִינּוּן אוּכְלוֹסִין דְּהַהוּא רְקִיעָא, יָהֲבִין אֲתַר לְהַהוּא קָלָא, וּמַאי קָא אָמְרֵי. וַיְיָ' נָתַן קוֹלוֹ לִפְנֵי חֵילוֹ וְגוֹ'. וְקָאִים הַהוּא קָלָא בְּהַהוּא רָקִיעַ, עַד דְּאָתֵי קָלָא אָחֳרָא, וְאִתְעַתְּדוּ כַּחֲדָא, וְסַלְקִין בְּזִוּוּגָא לִרְקִיעָא אָחֳרָא. וְעַל דָּא תָּנֵינָן, אִית קוֹל דְּסָלִיק קוֹל, וּמַאי אִיהוּ. הַהוּא קָלָא דִּתְקִיעָתָא דְּיִשְׂרָאֵל דְּתַתָּא.

309. There is no sound of the Shofar that does not ascend to a certain Firmament, and all the crowd in that Firmament gives room to this sound. And what do they say? "And the Lord utters His voice before His army...." (Joel 2:11) That sound stands in that Firmament until another sound comes and they assemble and rise, joined to another Firmament. We therefore learned that there is a sound that raises a sound. What is it? It is the sound of the Blowing of Israel Below.

Explanation: You already know that the sound of the Shofar ascends upward and awakens the Masach of Chirik in the Central Column, to diminish the Upper Three of the Left and to unite it with the Right. However, there are two types of action in this Masach of Chirik before it diminishes the Left and unites it with the Right. The first is that it reveals the Masach of the First Contraction (Tzimtzum Alef) that is unsweetened by Binah, which is called Man'ula (Lock), and from here it receives its main power to diminish the Left Column. The second is that it reveals the Masach of the Malchut sweetened by Binah, called Maftecha (Key), and from here it also has the Vessels to receive the Mochin of the Six Corners of the Upper Three. Therefore, two distinguished sounds awaken the Masach of Chirik. The first sound awakens the Masach of Chirik from the aspect of the Malchut of the First Contraction (Tzimtzum Alef) that is unsweetened by Binah, and the second sound awakens the Masach of Chirik from the aspect of the Malchut that is sweetened by Binah, and the second sound is the main objective of the Blowing of the Shofar. These two actions in the Masach of Chirik are called two Firmaments here in the Zohar.

When it says: **"There is no sound of the Shofar that does not ascend to a certain Firmament,"** it means that even the sound from the aspect of the Masach of the unsweetened Malchut that comes out of the Shofar also has one Firmament that performs its action there to diminish the Upper Three of the Left. When it says: **"and all the crowd in that Firmament gives room to this sound,"** it means that they receive the sound and act on it. **"And what do they say? 'And the Lord utters His voice before His army, for His camp is very great, for he who executes his word is strong...' (Joel 2:11)"** because that sound from the Malchut of the attribute of Judgment that is unsweetened is very great and strong and no one can stand before it, and therefore it has the power to diminish the Left Column. This is why they proclaim this verse during their action. However, if this sound of the attribute of Judgment would stay, no one would be worthy anymore to receive any Mochin, even the Six Corners of the Upper Three. This is why we need the second sound of the Masach of Malchut that is unsweetened by Binah, as they both join together, except that the first sound is concealed and is idle, and only the second sound is active, and therefore we are worthy to receive Mochin.

"That sound stands in that Firmament until another sound comes," meaning until the sound of the Masach of Malchut sweetened by Binah comes, **"and they assemble and rise, joined to another Firmament,"** since the two sounds unify together and ascend to the second Firmament, where only the Masach of Malchut sweetened by Binah is active, and the unsweetened Masach is attached to it in concealment to give it strength. **"We therefore learned that there is a sound that raises a sound,"** because the first unsweetened sound raises and gives strength to the second sound that is sweetened by Binah so that it can contain the Left Column to [have only] the Six Corners of the Upper Three, and therefore we need both of them together, and this is **"the sound of the Blowing...."**

The Shofar overthrows the Throne of Judgment.

310. וְכֵיוָן דְּמִתְחַבְּרָן כָּל אִינּוּן קָלִין דִּלְתַתָּא, וְסַלְקִין לְהַהוּא רְקִיעָא עִלָּאָה דְּמַלְכָּא קַדִּישָׁא שָׁארֵי בֵּיהּ, מִתְעַטְּרָן כֻּלְּהוּ קָמֵי מַלְכָּא, וּכְדֵין כּוּרְסְוָון רְמִיוּ וְכוּרְסְיָיא אָחֳרָא דְּיַעֲקֹב קָאִים וְאִתְתָּקַן.

310. Once all these sounds Below are joined, and they rise to the Supernal Firmament in which the Holy King, the Central Column, **abides, they are all adorned before the King. Then the thrones** of Judgment **are overthrown and another throne of Jacob,** the Central Column, **is established and fixed.**

When the sound of the Shofar rises, the prosecutors are pushed aside.

311. עַל דָּא אַשְׁכַּחְנָא בְּסִפְרָא דְּרַב הַמְנוּנָא סָבָא, בְּאִינּוּן צְלוֹתֵי דר"ה, דַּהֲוָה אָמַר, צְלוֹתָא וְקֹל שׁוֹפָרָא דְּאַפִּיק הַהוּא זַכָּאָה, דְּאִשְׁתְּכַח מֵרוּחֵיהּ וּמִנַּפְשֵׁיהּ בְּהַהוּא שׁוֹפָרָא, דְּהַהוּא קוֹל סָלִיק לְעֵילָּא. וּבְהַהוּא יוֹמָא קַיְּימִין וּמִשְׁתַּכְחֵי מְקַטְרְגִין לְעֵילָּא. וְכַד סָלִיק הַהוּא קָלָא דְּשׁוֹפָרָא, כֻּלְּהוּ אִתְדַּחְיָין קָמֵיהּ, וְלָא יַכְלִין לְקַיְּימָא. זַכָּאָה חוּלָקֵיהוֹן דְּצַדִּיקַיָּיא, דְּיַדְעִין לְכַוְּונָא רְעוּתָא לְקָמֵי מָארֵיהוֹן, וְיַדְעִין לְתַקְּנָא עָלְמָא בְּהַאי יוֹמָא, בְּקָל שׁוֹפָרָא. וְעַל דָּא כְּתִיב, אַשְׁרֵי הָעָם יוֹדְעֵי תְרוּעָה. יוֹדְעֵי, וְלָא תּוֹקְעֵי.

311. Therefore I have found in the book of Rav Hamnuna Saba, concerning the prayers of Rosh Hashanah, where he said that the

prayer and the sound of the Shofar a Righteous person emits with the Shofar, which comes out from his Spirit (Ruach) and Soul (Nefesh), rises up. On that day, prosecutors stand ready Above. But when the sound of the Shofar rises, they are all pushed aside by it and cannot prevail. Happy is the portion of the Righteous who know how to direct their desire before their Master, and who know how to mend the world on that day through the sound of the Shofar. It is therefore written: "Happy is the people that know the joyful note (*Teru'ah*)...." (Psalms 89:16) "Know" not "blow."

The need to find a Chazan who knows the ways of the Holy King.

312. בְּהַאי יוֹמָא, בָּעֵי עַמָּא לְאִסְתַּכְּלָא בב"נ שְׁלִים מִכֹּלָּא, דְּיָדַע אָרְחוֹי דְּמַלְכָּא קַדִּישָׁא, דְּיָדַע בִּיקָרָא דְּמַלְכָּא, דְּיִבְעֵי עָלַיְיהוּ בָּעוּתָא בְּהַאי יוֹמָא. וּלְזַמְנָא קָל שׁוֹפָרָא בְּכָלְהוּ עָלְמִין, בְּכַוָּונָה דְּלִבָּא, בְּחָכְמְתָא, בִּרְעוּתָא, בִּשְׁלִימוּ. בְּגִין דְּיִסְתָּלַק דִּינָא עַל יְדוֹי מִן עָלְמָא. וַוי לְאִינּוּן דִּשְׁלִיחָא דִּלְהוֹן לָא אִשְׁתְּכַח כַּדְקָא יָאוּת, דְּהָא חוֹבֵי עָלְמָא אַתְיָין לְאַדְכָּרָא בְּגִינֵיהּ. הה"ד, אִם הַכֹּהֵן הַמָּשִׁיחַ יֶחֱטָא, דְּהוּא שְׁלִיחָא דְּכָל יִשְׂרָאֵל, לְאַשְׁמַת הָעָם הוּא, בְּגִין דְּדִינָא שַׁרְיָא עָלַיְיהוּ.

312. On that day, the people should see that a man who is perfect in every way, who knows the ways of the Holy King and the glory of the King, says the prayer for them on that day and introduces the sound of the Shofar to every world with the concentration of the heart, wisdom, desire and completion, so that Judgment will be removed from the world. Woe to those whose messenger is found unworthy, for the sins of the world will be remembered because of him. As it says, "If it is the anointed priest who has incurred guilt..." who is the messenger of all of Israel, "...that blame falls upon the people..." (Leviticus 4:3) because Judgment rests on the people.

When a proper Chazan is found, all of the nation's prayers are accepted.

313. וְכַד שְׁלִיחָא הוּא זַכָּאָה כַּדְקָא יָאוּת, זַכָּאִין אִינּוּן עַמָּא, דְּכָל דִּינִין מִסְתַּלְּקִין מִנַּיְיהוּ עַל יְדֵיהּ, כ"ש כַּהֲנָא, דְּעָלֵיהּ מִתְבָּרְכָאן עִלָּאֵי וְתַתָּאֵי. א"ר אֶלְעָזָר, וְעַ"ד, כֹּהֵן וְלֵוִי עַד לָא יִסְלַק לְפוּלְחָנָא, בַּדְקִין אֲבַתְרֵיהּ, וְיָדְעִין אָרְחוֹוי וְעוֹבָדוֹי, וְאִי לָא, לָא סָלִיק לְפוּלְחָנָא, וְכֵן בְּסַנְהֶדְרִין לְמֵידָן דִּינָא.

313. Happy are the people when the messenger of the congregation is Righteous, as he should be, for all Judgments are removed from them by him. All the more so for the Priest, for whose sake the Upper and lower beings are blessed. Rav Elazar said: "A priest and a Levite should therefore be examined before they begin their service, to search their ways and actions. Otherwise, they may not rise to the service. So too with the Sanhedrin who execute a judgment," no man is accepted to become a member of the Sanhedrin before he is checked to see whether he is worthy of it.

The Priest and the Levite do not go up to work until they are tested.

314. וְאִי אִשְׁתְּכַח כַּדְקָא יָאוּת, יָהֲבִין עָלֵיהּ חוּמְרָא דְּמַקְדְּשָׁא. וְאִי לָא, לָא סָלִיק לְפוּלְחָנָא. הה"ד, וּלְלֵוִי אָמַר תּוּמֶּיךָ וְאוּרֶיךָ לְאִישׁ חֲסִידֶךָ. מִפְּנֵי מַה זָּכָה לְאוּרִים וּלְתוּמִּים, וּלְמִפְלַח פּוּלְחָנָא. הֱוֵי אוֹמֵר אֲשֶׁר נִסִּיתוֹ וְגוֹ'. הָאוֹמֵר לְאָבִיו וּלְאִמּוֹ לֹא רְאִיתִיו וְגוֹ'. וְכֵיוָן דְּאִשְׁתְּכָחוּ בְּאִלֵּין דַּרְגִּין, כְּדֵין יוֹרוּ מִשְׁפָּטֶיךָ לְיַעֲקֹב וְגוֹ', יָשִׂימוּ קְטוֹרָה וְגוֹ'. לְשַׁכְּכָא רוּגְזָא, וּלְזַמְנָא שְׁלָמָא. וְכָלִיל עַל מִזְבְּחֶךָ, בְּגִין דְּיִתְבַּסְּמוּן כֹּלָּא, וְיִשְׁתַּכְחוּן בִּרְכָאן בְּכֻלְּהוּ עָלְמִין, כְּדֵין בָּרֵךְ יְיָ' חֵילוֹ וְגוֹ'.

314. If the Priest or the Levite **is found worthy, a restrictive measure** [due to the greater import] **of the Temple is put on him, but if not, he does not rise to the service. As it says, "And of Levi he said: Let Your Tummim and Your Urim be with Your pious one...." (Deuteronomy 33:8) Why is he worthy of the Urim and Tummim and of performing service? We conclude this from: "...Whom you**

did prove at Massah..." (Ibid.) because you tested him before and found him worthy. **"Who said of his father and of his mother, I have not seen him...." (Deuteronomy 33:9) When he is found in these grades, then "They shall teach Jacob Your Judgments... they shall put incense..." (Deuteronomy 33:10)** as they shall offer incense **to sooth the anger and incite peace. "...and whole burnt sacrifice upon Your altar" (Ibid.) so that everything will be perfumed and blessings will prevail in all the worlds. Then, "Bless, Lord, his substance...." (Deuteronomy 33:11)**

Emor

32. Blowing the Shofar

A Synopsis

Rav Yitzchak tells us that God did Israel a great kindness by drawing them to Himself from afar. When the Upper and Lower Beings are gathered for Judgment, the Blowing of the Shofar causes the attribute of Judgment to turn to Mercy. The sound of the Shofar Below causes the Supernal Shofar to resound to awaken Mercy. By the sounds Below, Israel give strength Above. We hear about what happens to the wholly Wicked, to the wholly Righteous, and to the Middling.

Abraham was chosen from beyond the river.

187. בַּחֹדֶשׁ הַשְּׁבִיעִי בְּאֶחָד לַחֹדֶשׁ, ר' יִצְחָק פָּתַח, תִּקְעוּ בַחֹדֶשׁ שׁוֹפָר בַּכֶּסֶה לְיוֹם חַגֵּנוּ. זַכָּאִין אִינּוּן יִשְׂרָאֵל, דְּקוּדְשָׁא בְּרִיךְ הוּא קָרִיב לוֹן לְגַבֵּיהּ, מִן כָּל אוּמִּין עע"ז, וְאִתְרְעֵי בְּהוּ, וּמֵאֲתַר רְחִיקָא קָרִיב לוֹן לְגַבֵּיהּ, הה"ד, וַיֹּאמֶר יְהוֹשֻׁעַ אֶל כָּל הָעָם כֹּה אָמַר ה' אֱלֹהֵי יִשְׂרָאֵל בְּעֵבֶר הַנָּהָר יָשְׁבוּ אֲבוֹתֵיכֶם מֵעוֹלָם. לְאַחֲזָאָה, דְּהָא מֵאֲתַר רְחִיקָא אִתְרְעֵי בְּהוּ, וְקָרִיב לוֹן לְגַבֵּיהּ, וּכְתִיב, וָאֶקַּח אֶת אֲבִיכֶם אֶת אַבְרָהָם מֵעֵבֶר הַנָּהָר וְגו'. הָנֵי קְרָאֵי אִית לְאִסְתַּכְּלָא בְּהוּ, וְכִי כָּל יִשְׂרָאֵל לָא הֲווּ יַדְעֵי דָּא, וְכָל שֶׁכֵּן יְהוֹשֻׁעַ.

187. "In the seventh month, on the first day of the month...." (Leviticus 23:24) Rav Yitzchak opened: "Blow a Shofar in the renewal [of the moon], at the appointed time for the day of our festival." (Psalms 81:4) Happy are Israel whom the Holy One, blessed be He, drew near from all the nations in the world, and chose them. From afar He drew them near. As it is said, "And Joshua said to all the people, 'Thus says the Lord, God of Israel: "Your fathers dwelt on the other side of the river in old time..."'" (Joshua 24:2), to indicate that He desired them from a distant place and drew them

near Him. It is also written: "And I took your father Abraham from the other side of the river...." (Joshua 24:3) We have to examine these verses. Did not all the Israelites know this, and surely Joshua? Why did it need to say: "...'Thus says the Lord....'" (Ibid.)

The Creator did a great act of kindness by choosing the Patriarchs and making them Chariots.

188. אֶלָּא אוֹרַיְיתָא כּוּלָּהּ סָתִים וְגַלְיָא, כְּמָה דִשְׁמָא קַדִּישָׁא סָתִים וְגַלְיָא, בְּגִין דְאוֹרַיְיתָא כּוּלָּהּ שְׁמָא קַדִּישָׁא הִיא, וְעַל דָּא אִיהִי סָתִים וְגַלְיָא. אִי יִשְׂרָאֵל וִיהוֹשֻׁעַ הֲווֹ יַדְעֵי, אֲמַאי כְּתִיב כֹּה אָמַר יְיָ'. אֶלָּא וַדַּאי סְתִימָא דְמִלָּה, טִיבוּ סַגֵּי עֲבַד קוּדְשָׁא בְּרִיךְ הוּא בְּיִשְׂרָאֵל, דְאִתְרְעֵי בְּהוּ בַּאֲבָהָתָא, וְעָבֵיד לוֹן רְתִיכָא קַדִּישָׁא עִלָּאָה לִיקָרֵיהּ, וְאַפִּיק לוֹן מִגּוֹ נַהֲרָא עִלָּאָה יַקִּירָא קַדִּישָׁא, בּוּצִינָא דְכָל בּוּצִינִין, בְּגִין דְיִתְעַטַּר בְּהוּ. הֲדָא הוּא דִכְתִיב, כֹּה אָמַר יְיָ' בְּעֵבֶר הַנָּהָר יָשְׁבוּ אֲבוֹתֵיכֶם מֵעוֹלָם. הַנָּהָר: הַהוּא נָהָר דְאִשְׁתְּמוֹדַע, וְאִתְיְידַע.

188. Rather, the whole Torah is both hidden and revealed just like the Holy Name, which is hidden and revealed, spelled as Yud-Hei-Vav-Hei but pronounced Adonai. **This is because the whole Torah is the Holy Name, which is why it is hidden and revealed.** We asked: **"If Israel and Joshua knew this, why is it written: '..."Thus says the Lord..."'?"** (Joshua 24:2) He answers: **"Surely the secret meaning is that the Holy One, blessed be He, did great kindness with Israel in choosing the Patriarchs, making them into a lofty Holy Chariot for His Glory. He brought them from the Supernal, precious and Holy River, the luminary of all luminaries,** namely Binah, **in order to be adorned by them. As it is said: "Your fathers dwelt on the other side of the river in old time...." (Joshua 24:2) "the river"** namely **that River that was made known and is known,** namely Binah.

Explanation: The Patriarchs are the secret of Chesed-Gevurah-Tiferet of Zeir Anpin, and it is known that the Mochin that these Chesed-Gevurah-Tiferet have come from the ascension of Zeir Anpin to Binah.

[Originally,] the Binah-Tiferet-Malchut of Binah fell to Zeir Anpin during the Katnut [Smallness/Immaturity] of Binah, and in Gadlut [Greatness/Maturity] of Binah—when [Binah] brought back these Binah-Tiferet-Malchut to its level—the Chesed-Gevurah-Tiferet of Zeir Anpin also came with them and ascended to Binah. Thus, Chesed-Gevurah-Tiferet of Zeir Anpin are found cleaved there to Binah, in its Left Column, which is the Binah-Tiferet-Malchut that returned to their level.

This is the secret of the verse: **"Your fathers dwelt on the other side of the river... [and they worshipped other Gods]" (Joshua 24:2)** because the Left Column of Binah was then in dispute with the Right Column and was drawing Chochmah from above downward, which is how idol worship and other gods nourish. However, afterwards, Zeir Anpin elevated the Masach of Chirik, by which He diminished the Left Column of Binah and united it with the Right, thus making peace between the Columns. But then Zeir Anpin was distanced and came out of the Upper Three of Chochmah that is in the Left of Binah because before He united the two Columns, and the Left Column was in dispute, Zeir Anpin had the Upper Three of Chochmah from the Left Column. But now that He mediated and united Right and Left together, Zeir Anpin no longer has [the Upper Three] but only the Six Corners of Chochmah, due to the diminishment of the Left Column.

This is [the meaning of] what it says (in verse 187): **"to indicate that He desired them from a distant place...and it is written: "And I took your father Abraham from the other side of the river..." (Joshua 24:3)** Before then, when [Zeir Anpin] was close to the Chochmah of the Left of Binah he could not receive from there because the Left Column was in dispute, and because the abundance from the Left was from above downward and the other gods had [access to] nourish [from there]. Now that [Zeir Anpin] distanced Himself from this Chochmah of the Left and diminished to [only] the six corners of Chochmah He is able to receive all the Mochin and greatness in them. This is [the meaning of] what it says (in verse 188): **"He brought them from the... River... to be adorned by them"** because when the Chesed-Gevurah-Tiferet of Zeir Anpin were cleaved to the Left Column of this River, Binah, they could not receive anything. Only after they exited and distanced themselves from there and diminished to [have only] the Six Corners of Chochmah could they be adorned by the Mochin of that River.

Abraham was removed from the Left Column of Binah since he was Right Column.

189. מֵעוֹלָם, מַאי קָא בָּעֵי הָכָא. אֶלָּא לְאַחֲזָאָה וְחָכְמְתָא. מֵעֵבֶר הַנָּהָר מֵעוֹלָם, אֶלָּא הַהוּא נָהָר עוֹלָם אִקְרֵי. וְעַל דָּא, בְּעֵבֶר הַנָּהָר יָשְׁבוּ אֲבוֹתֵיכֶם מֵעוֹלָם, לְאַחֲזָאָה טִיבוּ וּקְשׁוֹט דְּעָבֵד קוּדְשָׁא בְּרִיךְ הוּא לְיִשְׂרָאֵל. וָאֶקַּח אֶת אֲבִיכֶם אֶת אַבְרָהָם מֵעֵבֶר הַנָּהָר מַאי קָא מַיְירֵי. אֶלָּא אַבְרָהָם לָא אִתְדְּבַק בֵּיהּ בְּהַהוּא נָהָר, כְּמוֹ יִצְחָק דְּאִתְדְּבַק בֵּיהּ בְּסִטְרֵיהּ לְאִתְתַּקְּפָא.

189. The verse says: **"...in old time (*me'olam,* lit. from the world)...." (Joshua 24:2)** He asks: **"What does this want to convey?"** He answers: **"This indicates Chochmah. '...from the other side of the river...'** means **from the world, since that River is called 'World.'** Binah is also called "World," and hence "from the world" has the same meaning as "across the river." **Hence** it says: **"Your fathers dwelt on the other side of the river in old time (lit. from the world)," (Ibid.) to show the kindness and truth the Holy One, blessed be He, did for Israel** in this, since **'...I took your father Abraham from the other side of the river...' (Joshua 24:3)"** and He took him out of the Left Column of Binah, as written in the previous paragraph. He asks: **"What does** the verse **teach us** in saying: '...and I took your father Abraham from the other side of the river..." and not: 'And I took Isaac'?" He answers: **"Rather, Abraham,** who is Chesed of Zeir Anpin and Right Column, **did not cleave to that river,** the Left Column of Binah, **like Isaac,** the Left Column of Zeir Anpin, **who was attached to his own aspect to**

draw strength," namely to the Left Side of Binah, which is the side of Isaac.

Explanation: Isaac is still attached to the portion of the Left Column of Binah, as he receives from it the Six Corners of Chochmah of the Left. But Abraham, who is Right Column and Chasadim, went out of there completely. Therefore, it says: **"I took your father Abraham,"** and it does not say: **"and I took Isaac."** This is [the meaning of]: **"who was attached to his own aspect to draw strength"** namely, to receive the Six Corners of Chochmah.

Replacing the Throne of Judgment with the Throne of Mercy.

190. תָּא וַחֲזֵי, הַאי נָהָר, אַף עַל גַּב דְּלָאו אִיהוּ דִּינָא, דִּינִין נָפְקֵי מִסִּטְרֵיהּ, וְאִתְתַּקְּפוּ בֵּיהּ. וְכַד יִצְחָק אִתְתַּקַּף בְּדִינוֹי, כְּדֵין עִלָּאִין וְתַתָּאִין מִתְכַּנְּשֵׁי לְדִינָא, וְכוּרְסְיָיא דְּדִינָא אִתְתַּקַּן, וּמַלְכָּא קַדִּישָׁא יָתִיב עַל כּוּרְסְיָיא דְּדִינָא, וְדָאִין עָלְמָא, כְּדֵין, תִּקְעוּ בַחֹדֶשׁ שׁוֹפָר בַּכֶּסֶה לְיוֹם חַגֵּנוּ. זַכָּאִין אִינּוּן יִשְׂרָאֵל, דְּיַדְעִין לְסַלְּקָא כּוּרְסְיָיא דְּדִינָא, וּלְתַקְּנָא כּוּרְסְיָיא דְּרַחֲמֵי. וּבְמָּה. בַּשּׁוֹפָר.

190. Come and see, [regarding] this River, which is Binah, **even though it is not Judgment,** as Binah is the attribute of Mercy, nevertheless **Judgments come out from its side,** namely from the Left side in it, while it is Chochmah without Chasadim, and Judgments **are strengthened in it. When Isaac grows strong in his Judgments** from there, while he is there [as] Chochmah without Chasadim, **the Upper and Lower Beings are gathered for Judgment; the Throne of Judgment,** which is Malchut from the aspect of its Judgment, **is prepared, and the Holy King,** Zeir Anpin, **sits on the Throne of Judgment and sentences the world. Then, "Blow a Shofar in the renewal [of the moon], at the appointed time for the day of our festival." (Psalms 81:4)** Through the Shofar the attribute of Judgment turns into the attribute of Mercy. **Happy are Israel who know how to remove the Throne of Judgment**

and prepare the Throne of Mercy. [He asks:] **"How** do they do it?" [He answers:] **"With the Shofar."**

The Shofar alludes to Binah.

191. רִבִּי אַבָּא הֲוָה יָתִיב קַמֵּיהּ דְּרִבִּי שִׁמְעוֹן, אָמַר לֵיהּ, הָא זִמְנִין סַגִּיאִין שָׁאִילְנָא עַל הַאי שׁוֹפָר, מַאי קָא מַיְירֵי, וְעַד כָּאן לָא אִתְיַשַּׁבְנָא בֵּיהּ. אָמַר לֵיהּ, וַדַּאי הַאי הוּא בְּרִירָא דְּמִלָּה, דְּיִשְׂרָאֵל בָּעְיָין בְּיוֹמָא דְּדִינָא, שׁוֹפָר, וְלָא קֶרֶן. בְּגִין דְּקֶרֶן הָא אִתְיְידַע בְּאָן אֲתַר אִיהוּ, וּלְאִתְדַּבְּקָא דִּינָא לָא בָּעֵינָא. אֲבָל הָא תָּנֵינָן, בְּמִלִּין וּבְעוֹבָדָא, בָּעֵינָן לְאַחֲזָאָה וּלְאִתְעָרָא מִלִּין סְתִימִין.

191. Rav Aba was sitting before Rav Shimon. He said to him, "I have asked many times 'What is it all about?' concerning this Shofar, and until now I still am not settled about it." He said to him, "Surely this is its clear meaning. On the Day of Judgment Israel need a Shofar and not a horn, for the place of origin of the horn is known, as it indicates Malchut, which is the aspect of Judgment, **and we should not arouse Judgment.** It is not so with the Shofar that alludes to Binah, which is Mercy. **However, we learned that through words and action we need to indicate and rouse hidden things,"** namely, by the Blowing of the Shofar and its blessing.

When Binah does not shine onto the children,
judgments are awakened in the world.

192. תָּא חֲזֵי, כַּד הַהוּא שׁוֹפָר עִלָּאָה, דִּנְהִירוּ דְּכֹלָּא בֵּיהּ, אִסְתַּלַּק וְלָא נָהִיר לִבְנִין, כְּדֵין דִּינָא אִתְּעַר, וְכֻרְסְוָון אִתְתְּקָנוּ לְבֵי דִינָא, וְדָא שׁוֹפָר, אִילוּ דְּיִצְחָק אִקְרֵי, תּוּקְפֵיהּ דְּיִצְחָק, תּוּשְׁבַּחְתֵּיהּ דְּאַבְהָן, כַּד אִסְתַּלַּק הַהוּא שׁוֹפָר גָּדוֹל, דְּלָא יָנְקָא לִבְנִין, כְּדֵין יִצְחָק אִתְתַּקַּף, וְאִתְתְּקַן לְדִינָא בְּעָלְמָא.

192. Come and see, [regarding] the Supernal Shofar, in which are the Lights of all, namely Binah when its Three Columns are united with each other, as all the Mochin of Zeir Anpin and Nukva of Atzilut, and [all of] Briyah, Yetzirah, and Asiyah come from it, **if it is gone and does not shine upon the children,** Zeir Anpin and Malchut, **Judgment is roused and Thrones are prepared for the courthouse. This Shofar,** the secret of Binah, **is called Isaac's ram (*eylo shel yitzchak*),** namely **Isaac's strength,** since [the Hebrew word] *ayil* (ram) can also mean "strength," as in "...and the mighty of the land (*eylei ha'aretz*) he took away" (Ezekiel 17:13), **and it is the praiseworthiness of the Patriarchs,** which are Chesed-Gevurah-Tiferet who receive all their praiseworthiness from that Shofar, Binah. **When this Great Shofar is gone and does not shine on the children,** Zeir Anpin and Malchut, namely when there is no unification in Zeir Anpin and Malchut, rather Zeir Anpin nourishes from the Right Column of Binah and Malchut from the Left Column of Binah, and since the Left of Binah is without Right, the Mochin of Binah leave Zeir Anpin, **Isaac,** the Left Column, **grows strong,** due to the dominion of the Left Column of Binah, **and prepares himself to judge the world** because when Chochmah of the Left is without Chasadim, Harsh Judgment is drawn to the world (see the secret of the Blowing of the Shofar in Zohar, Vayikra 302-312).

The Lower Shofar awakens the Supernal Shofar.

193. וְכַד אִתְעַר הַאי שׁוֹפָר וְכַד בְּנֵי נָשָׁא תַּיְיבִין מֵחַטָּאֵיהוֹן, בַּעְיָין לְנַגְדָא קוֹל שׁוֹפָר מִתַּתָּא, וְהַהוּא קָלָא סָלִיק לְעֵילָּא, כְּדֵין אִתְעַר שׁוֹפָרָא אָחֳרָא עִלָּאָה, וְאִתְעַר רַחֲמֵי, וְאִסְתַּלַּק דִּינָא. וּבְעֵינָן לְאַחֲזָאָה עוֹבָדָא בְּשׁוֹפָר, לְאִתְעָרָא שׁוֹפָרָא אָחֳרָא, וּלְאַפָּקָא בְּהַאי שׁוֹפָר לְתַתָּא, אִינּוּן קָלֵי, לְאַחֲזָאָה דְּכָל אִינּוּן קָלִין דִּלְעֵילָּא, דִּכְלִילָן כֻּלְּהוּ בְּהַהוּא שׁוֹפָר עִלָּאָה, יִתְעֲרוּן לְנַפְקָא.

193. When this Shofar is roused, and when the people repent of their sins, the sound of the Shofar should resound from Below, and the sound ascends up, and then another, Supernal Shofar is roused, which is Binah. **Mercy is awakened and Judgment is gone. A deed must be displayed by** the Blowing of **the Shofar, in order to awaken another Shofar,** Binah, **and to emit from the Lower Shofar all those**

sounds, Teki'ah, Shevarim, Teru'ah, Teki'ah, and so on, **to show that all the Celestial sounds that are included in the Supernal Shofar,** which are the Three Columns and their subcategories that are all included in Binah, **will be roused to emerge** from Binah to Zeir Anpin and Malchut.

Explanation of the matter: Every Rosh Hashanah the world comes back to its original state as it was on the Fourth Day of Creation, when Malchut was diminished. Malchut is called "year," and the 12 months of the year are the stages of Her correction, from Her beginning until the Final Correction. If the year is completed and we did not finish Her correction it is up to us to correct Her in the next year, and again we need to begin from the start of Her existence as She was on the Fourth Day of the Workings of Creation. This happens every single year until the Final Correction. On the Fourth Day of the Workings of Creation it says: "And God made the two great luminaries..." (Genesis 1:16) as Malchut was as big as Zeir Anpin, since then Zeir Anpin clothed the Right Column of Binah and Malchut the Left Column of Binah. These two Columns of Binah were separated from each other, and therefore the Left Column of Binah was with Chochmah without Chasadim, [a state] where Harsh Judgments come from the Left Column of Binah, which is darkness and not Light since Chochmah cannot shine without Chasadim.

Therefore, it is considered then that the Holy One, blessed be He, sits on the Throne of Judgment and judgments are drawn to the world. [This is] because we only receive from the Malchut, which is called a Throne to Zeir Anpin, and if Malchut is in the Left of Binah separated from the Right, when [She is] full of Judgment, it is found that Malchut bestows Judgment to the world. This is [the meaning of] what it said (in verse 192): **"When this great Shofar is gone and does not shine on the children,"** namely when the two Columns of Binah are separated from each other, "**Isaac grows strong and prepares himself to judge the world,"** then the Left called Isaac prevails and bestows judgments to

Malchut, and from Malchut to the world. Then the Precept of Blowing the Shofar was given to us.

Two corrections are made by the Blowing of the Shofar. The first correction is [that it] elevates Mayin Nukvin (Female Waters) to awaken a Unification (Zivug) on the Masach of Chirik that is in Zeir Anpin, who is in the place of Binah. This diminishes the Left Column and unites it with the Right, thus producing the Three Columns in Binah, which are the secret of Chochmah-Binah-Da'at. This is [the meaning of] what it said (in verse 193): **"the sound of the Shofar should resound from Below, and the sound ascends up."** The sound of the Shofar ascends in the secret of Mayin Nukvin and awakens the sound from Above, the secret of Zeir Anpin called "Sound," who is above in Binah. Thus, **"then another, Supernal Shofar is roused,** which is Binah. **Mercy is awakened,"** meaning that the Central Column, the secret of Mercy, is awakened and unites the two Columns of Binah together. Then **"and Judgment is gone,"** because after the Left Column is included with the Right, all the Judgments leave the Left. This is the first correction made by the Blowing of the Shofar.

The second correction is [that it] brings out the sounds from Binah, which are the Three Columns that emerged in [Binah] through Zeir Anpin called "Sound," and it draws them to Zeir Anpin in His place Below. In the secret of [the concept] that since the Three Columns of Binah emerged by one, Zeir Anpin, then one is found with three—Zeir Anpin also merits the Three Columns. All the Mochin that the Lower causes the Upper, the Lower merits as well. However, we need an action Below to awaken this Above (as mentioned in verse 191) **"through words and action we need to indicate and rouse hidden things"** and this is done through the order of the sounds: Three sets of Teki'ah, Shevarim-Teru'ah, Teki'ah, three sets of Teki'ah, Shevarim, Teki'ah, and three sets of Teki'ah, Teru'ah, Teki'ah, which we blow, as he explains presently.

Awakening strength on high.

194. וּבְהָנֵי קָלִין דִּלְתַתָּא, יָהֲבִין יִשְׂרָאֵל חֵילָא לְעֵילָּא, וְעַל דָּא בָּעֵינָן לְזַמְּנָא שׁוֹפָר בְּיוֹמָא דָּא, וּלְסַדְּרָא קָלִין, לְכַוְּונָא בֵּיהּ בְּגִין לְאַתְעֲרָא שׁוֹפָר אָחֳרָא, דְּבֵיהּ כְּלִילָן קָלֵי לְעֵילָּא.

194. With the sounds Below, Israel give strength Above. Therefore, a Shofar needs to be summoned on that day, to arrange the sounds, namely the sets of Teki'ah, Shevarim-Teru'ah, Teki'ah, and so on, **to meditate on it so as to awaken another Shofar,** Binah, **in which all the Upper sounds,** Chesed-Gevurah-Tiferet of Zeir Anpin, **are included.**

The meditations of the first set of Teki'ah, Shevarim-Teru'ah, Teki'ah.

195. סִדְרָא קַדְמָאָה, קָלָא נָפִיק, וּמִתְעַטְּר לְעֵילָּא, סָלִיק רְקִיעִין, וְאִתְבְּקַע בֵּין טוּרֵי רָמָאֵי, וּמָטֵי לְגַבֵּיהּ דְּאַבְרָהָם, וְשַׁרְיָא בְּרֵישֵׁיהּ, וְאִתְעַטָּר, וְאִתְּעַר הוּא, וְאַתְקִין לְכוּרְסְיָּיא. וּבְסִפְרָא דְּאַגַּדְתָּא תָּנֵינָן, בְּשַׁעְתָּא דְּהַהוּא קָלָא קַדְמָאָה סָלִיק, אִתְּעַר וְאִתְעַטָּר אַבְרָהָם, וְאַתְקִין לְכוּרְסְיָּיא, פַּקְדִין עָלֵיהּ אַבָּא.

195. The first set of the three sets of Teki'ah, Shevarim-Teru'ah, Teki'ah. **A sound emerges and is adorned Above,** in Binah. **It rises through Firmaments to be cleft between the High Mountains,** between the two Columns of Binah. From there **it reaches Abraham,** Chesed of Zeir Anpin, **and resides on his head and he is adorned. He is awakened and prepares the Throne** to be a Throne of Mercy. **In the Book of Agadah, we learned that when the first sound rises, Abraham is awakened, adorned and prepares the Throne, and Aba is summoned upon him.**

Explanation of the matter: You already know the two corrections made through the Blowing of the Shofar. The first one is to awaken the Central Column within Binah that unites the two Columns [Right and Left] together. The second is after the Three Columns emerge in Binah and are included together, we draw them to the place of Zeir Anpin. However, you need to remember with all this that the main objective of the Blowing of the Shofar is to diminish the Left Column from having the Upper Three and to nullify its Harsh Judgments that come from these Upper Three of the Left. The sounds we raise are forces of Judgment that diminish the Left Column from having these Upper Three, thus revealing the Unification (Zivug) of the Three Columns from the aspect of Mercy.

In general, there are three types of Judgments, in the secret of three sowings: Cholam, Shuruk, and Chirik. The Judgments of Cholam, Right Column, emerge from the ascension of Malchut to Binah, which diminishes Binah to [a state of] Six Corners without a Head. This is the secret of Judgments of the Female. The Judgments of Shuruk, Left Column, emerge from the returning of the Upper Three to Binah, which happens to the Left Column of Binah. It is known that since it is Chochmah without Chasadim, Harsh Judgments are drawn from it. Because these Judgments come from the completion of the Upper Three of the Left they are called the Judgments of the Male. There is also the Judgments of Chirik, the Central Column, which are comprised of two aspects: Lock (*Man'ula*) and Key (*Maftecha*). They, too, are Judgments of the Female.

Know that the Judgments of the Female are called Teru'ah and the Judgments of the Male are called Shevarim. Through the [order of the] Blowings, we awaken all these Judgments in the Left column, to diminish its Upper Three so that it unites with the Right.

There is a difference between the Judgments of the Female in the Right Column and the Judgments of the Female in the Central Column. [Concerning] the Judgments of the Female of the Right, even though they fight the Left Column, they nevertheless cannot diminish it. It is found that two aspects of Judgment prevail in the Right Column: its own

Female Judgment and the Male Judgment of the Left Column. They fight with each other and one cannot overpower the other, except with the help of the Central Column, [only then is] the Left subdued. This is not the case with the Judgments of the Female in the Central Column, as they overpower the Left Column and diminish its Upper Three, and with the diminishment of the Upper Three, all the Judgments of the Male disappear. It is found that there are no Judgments of the Male at all in the Central Column, rather only Judgments of the Female. And in the Left Column surely there are no Judgments of the Female at all, only Judgments of the Male, since if Judgments of the Female prevailed in it then its Upper Three would be nullified.

Thus, Shevarim-Teru'ah, which are the secret of the Judgments of the Female with the Judgments of the Male, applies to the Right. Shevarim alone—the secret of the Judgments of the Male—applies to the Left. In the Central is Teru'ah alone, which are the Judgments of the Female alone without the Judgments of the Male, Shevarim. However, all these Judgments that we awaken with these sounds, we only direct to the Left Column to diminish it. The Shevarim-Teru'ah to the Left Column that is included in the Right, the Shevarim to the Left column of the Left, and Teru'ah to the Left Column of the Central. In other words, there are three differentiations in the awakening of the Judgments of the Left, according to the arrangement of the Three Columns.

In the origin of the Three Columns there is no need for them to have more than nine aspects, as they must be included within each other. Three Columns in the Right, Three Columns in the Left, and Three Columns in the Central, thus nine aspects. However because there are three differentiations in the Left Columns of the Three Columns—since in the Left of the Right there is Shevarim-Teru'ah, in the Left of the Left there is Shevarim, and in the Left of the Central there is Teru'ah, as previously mentioned—therefore three more inclusions are needed. One inclusion of nine aspects in the Right Column by itself, namely Three

Columns that each include Teki'ah, Shevarim-Teru'ah, Teki'ah. Similarly, nine aspects in the Left, which are Three Columns that each include Teki'ah, Shevarim, Teki'ah. And similarly, nine aspects in the Central, which are Three Columns that each include Teki'ah, Teru'ah, Teki'ah.

This is: **"The first set,"** namely the first set of Three Columns in the Right Column, or the first set of Teki'ah, Shevarim-Teru'ah, Teki'ah of the three sets of Teki'ah, Shevarim-Teru'ah, Teki'ah. **"A sound emerges,"** namely the first Teki'ah that awakens the Right Column of this set, **"and is adorned Above,"** namely Shevarim-Teru'ah that awaken the Left Column of this set, since "adorn" alludes to the Upper Three of the Left. **"It rises through Firmaments to be cleft between the High Mountains,"** namely the second Teki'ah that awakens the Central Column whose Masach of Chirik pierces the grades. It elevates the Masach of Malchut to the place of Binah and the grade splits to Keter-Chochmah Above and Binah-Tiferet-Malchut descend Below.

After the first Three Columns of the Right of Binah are awakened, they need to be drawn to the Right of Zeir Anpin called Abraham. This is: **"it reaches Abraham"** and Three Columns are also awakened in him, which are Teki'ah, Shevarim-Teru'ah, Teki'ah, as mentioned earlier. **"...and resides on his head"** namely the Right Column, the secret of Keter-Chochmah, **"and he is adorned"** is the secret of Binah-Tiferet-Malchut that returned and became the Upper Three and the Left Column. **"He"** the Central Column, **"is awakened and prepares the Throne,"** it prepares the Throne of Mercy by virtue of the unification of the Three Columns. These Three Columns are drawn from Chochmah of Israel-Saba and Tevunah, which is the secret of Aba. This is: **"Aba is summoned upon him,"** namely Aba of Israel-Saba and Tevunah. Until here are the meditations of the first set of Teki'ah, Shevarim-Teru'ah, Teki'ah of the three sets of Teki'ah, Shevarim-Teru'ah, Teki'ah. This set of Teki'ah, Shevarim-Teru'ah, Teki'ah is under the control of the Teki'ah, namely the Right Column of Three Columns of the Right.

The Shofar blower needs to direct his heart to subdue the prosecutor, in the merit of Abraham.

196. אַדְהָכִי, סַלְקָא תִּנְיָינָא, תַּקִּיפָא לְתַבְרָא תּוּקְפֵּי רְגִיזִין. וְדָא סִדְרָא תִּנְיָינָא, הַהוּא קָלָא תְּבִירָא בְּתוּקְפוֹי. וּכְדֵין סַלְקָא, וְכָל דִּינִין דְּאִתְעֲרַעַן קָמֵיהּ אִתְבָּרוּ, עַד דְּסָלִיק לְאַתְרֵיהּ דְּיִצְחָק. כֵּיוָן דְּיִצְחָק אִתְעַר, וְחָמֵי לְאַבְרָהָם מְתַקֵּן לְכוּרְסְיָיא לְקַיְּימָא קַמֵּיהּ, כְּדֵין אִתְכַּפְיָא, וְתָבַר תּוּקְפָּא קַשְׁיָא. וּבְהַאי, בָּעֵי מַאן דְּתָקַע, לְכַוְּונָא לִבָּא וּרְעוּתָא, בְּגִין לְתַבְרָא חֵילָא וְתוּקְפָּא דְּדִינָא קַשְׁיָא, הֲדָא הוּא דִּכְתִּיב, אַשְׁרֵי הָעָם יוֹדְעֵי תְרוּעָה, יוֹדְעֵי תְרוּעָה וַדַּאי.

196. In the meantime the second sound rises, namely the first Teki'ah of the second set of the Right. **It is strong to break Harsh Judgments. This is the second set** of Teki'ah, Shevarim-Teru'ah, Teki'ah, which is under the control of the Left of the Right, which is Shevarim-Teru'ah as mentioned. **The sound breaks,** Shevarim, **with its strength,** Teru'ah. **It rises** to Binah **and all Judgments** from the Upper Three of the Left **that meet** there **are broken before it, until they rise to the place of Isaac,** who is in Zeir Anpin. **Once Isaac,** the Left Column of this set, **is roused** by the second Teki'ah of this set, which is the Central Column of this second set, **and sees Abraham,** the Right Column of this set, **preparing the Throne** of Mercy **to stand before it, he is then subdued and breaks the Harsh Judgment** that comes from the Upper Three of the left. **Whoever blows needs to direct his heart and desire upon this, in order to break the power,** to diminish the Upper Three of the Left, **and the strength of the Harsh Judgment** that comes from the Upper Three of the Left. **As it is written: "Happy is the people that know the joyful note (*Teru'ah*)..." (Psalms 89:16) assuredly they "know Teru'ah" precisely** since Teru'ah is derived from breaking, as in "...break them (*tero'em*) with a metal rod...." (Psalms 2:9)

Explanation: Here [the Zohar] explains the second set of Teki'ah, Shevarim-Teru'ah, Teki'ah, which is under the control of the Left of the Right but includes within it all Three Columns, which is why we blow

Teki'ah, Shevarim-Teru'ah, Teki'ah in it. Even though we said that in the Left Column there are no Judgments of the Female, which is Teru'ah, but only Judgments of the Male, which is Shevarim, this is only said about the Left of the Left Column, which is brought later (in verse 199). But here it [speaks about] the three sets in the general set of the Right (as said in verse 195), and therefore even the second set here is not like the actual Left in its place, but rather the Left that is included in the Right. Therefore, it can include within it the Judgments of the Female as well, which is the aspect of Shevarim-Teru'ah. What it says: **"he is then subdued and breaks the Harsh Judgment"** is only the beginning but the main nullification and subduing of the Upper Three of the Left is in the Central Column, which is in the third set of Teki'ah, Shevarim-Teru'ah, Teki'ah that is spoken about in the next paragraph, which says: **"Then they both hold...."** Thus the meditations of the second set of the three sets of Teki'ah, Shevarim-Teru'ah, Teki'ah has been explained.

The meditations of the third set of Teki'ah, Shevarim-Teru'ah, Teki'ah.

197. סִדְרָא תְּלִיתָאָה, קָלָא נָפִיק, וְסָלִיק, וּבָקַע כָּל אִינּוּן רְקִיעִין, וְרַחֲמֵי מִתְעָרִן, וּמָטֵי הַהוּא קָלָא לְרֵישֵׁיהּ דְּיַעֲקֹב וְיַעֲקֹב אִתְּעַר, וְחָמֵי לְאַבְרָהָם מִתְתַּקַּן בְּגִיסָא אָחֳרָא, כְּדֵין אֲחִידָן תַּרְוַויְיהוּ בֵּיהּ בְּיִצְחָק, דָּא מֵהַאי סִטְרָא, וְדָא, מֵהַאי סִטְרָא וְלָא יַכְלִין תּוּקְפוֹי לְנָפְקָא לְבַר. וְהָנֵי תְּלָתָא סִדְרִין, כֻּלְּהוּ סִדְרָא חַד.

197. The third set of Teki'ah, Shevarim-Teru'ah, Teki'ah is under the control of the Central Column of the Right, the secret of the second Teki'ah. **A sound emerges,** namely the first Teki'ah of this set, **and rises,** namely the Shevarim-Teru'ah of this set. **It pierces all Firmaments,** namely the second Teki'ah of this set, **and mercy is aroused.** All this occurs in Binah, and from there **that sound** of the entire Teki'ah Shevarim-Teru'ah, Teki'ah, which are under the control of the second Teki'ah, **reaches Jacob's head,** namely in the place of Zeir Anpin. **Jacob,** the Central Column of this set, **wakes up and sees Abraham,** the Right

Column of this set, **preparing on the other side,** namely the Right Side of this set. **Then they both hold Isaac,** the Left Column of this set, **from one side,** the Right, **and the other,** the Center, **and the power** of the Judgment of the Left **cannot come out,** since its Upper Three become diminished (as mentioned in verse 195). **All these three sets,** namely the three mentioned Teki'ah, Shevarim-Teru'ah, Teki'ah, **are all one set.** They are all the set of Blowings of the Blowings that apply to the Right Column, namely the nine aspects of the Right Column, whose Left Column aspect includes Shevarim-Teru'ah together (as mentioned in verse 195). Thus the meditations of the third set of the three sets of Teki'ah, Shevarim-Teru'ah, Teki'ah has been explained.

The first set of Teki'ah, Shevarim, Teki'ah.

198. סִדְרָא אָחֳרָא, קָלָא נָפִיק, וְסָלִיק, וְנָטִיל לְאַבְרָהָם מֵאַתְרֵיהּ, וְנָגִיד לֵיהּ לְתַתָּא, לַאֲתַר דְּתוּקְפֵיהוֹן דְּיִצְחָק שַׁרְיָין וְקַיְימָן לֵיהּ לְאַבְרָהָם בְּגַוַּויְיהוּ.

198. The other set, is the nine aspects that are the three times Teki'ah, Shevarim, Teki'ah, which are in the Left Column. This first set of Teki'ah, Shevarim, Teki'ah is under the control of the Right of the Left, which is the first Teki'ah. **A sound emerges,** namely the first Teki'ah, **rises,** namely Shevarim that shines from below upward, **takes Abraham from his place,** namely in the second Teki'ah, **and draws him down to the place where the strengths of Isaac dwell.** It draws its Illumination that is below the chest of Zeir Anpin because all these nine aspects in this set are drawn below the chest of Zeir Anpin since they are all under the control of the Left Column, which is the secret of the Illumination of Chochmah that only shines in the place below the chest of Zeir Anpin. Above the chest is the aspect of Chasadim that are covered from Chochmah, and the Left Column has no control there. **They maintain Abraham among them.** In other words, this entire set is under the control of the Right of Left, the aspect of Abraham of that is in Isaac. Thus, the meditations of the first set of the three sets of Teki'ah, Shevarim, Teki'ah, has been explained.

The second set of Teki'ah, Shevarim, Teki'ah.

199. סִדְרָא תִּנְיָינָא, נָפִיק קָלָא תְּבִירָא, לָא תַּקִּיפָא כְּקַדְמָאָה, לָא דְּחָלִישׁ הַהוּא קָלָא דְּתָקַע, אֶלָּא דְּהַהוּא קָלָא לָאו אִיהוּ לְגַבֵּי יִצְחָק בְּקַדְמֵיתָא, דְּתַמָּן תּוּקְפָּא תַּקִּיפָא שַׁרְיָא, אֶלָּא לְגַבֵּי אִינּוּן בֵּי דִּינָא דִּלְתַתָּא, דְּאִינּוּן רְפוּיִין יַתִּיר, וְכֻלְּהוּ חָמָאן לְאַבְרָהָם לְגַבַּיְיהוּ, וְאִתְכַּפְיָין קַמֵּיהּ.

199. The second set of Teki'ah, Shevarim, Teki'ah is under the control of the Left of Left, which is Shevarim. **A broken sound emerges,** Shevarim (lit. breaks), **not as strong as the first,** namely it does not have Teru'ah like the Left of the nine aspects of the Right but only Shevarim. **It is not because the sound he blew is weak but it is not directed at Isaac** that is above the chest of Zeir Anpin **as before, where there is great strength,** as the Left Column cannot be revealed at all there, and the Left Column there needs to be completely subdued (as mentioned in verse 196). **But** this sound **is meant for the Lower Courthouse,** namely to the Illumination of the Left Column that is below the chest of Zeir Anpin, which is the aspect of Malchut called the Lower Courthouse, where Judgments **are more lax,** as the Illumination of below the chest only shines from below upward. **They all see Abraham**, who is the Right Column, **and are subdued before him.** Here the Zohar does not explain all Three Columns, Teki'ah, Shevarim, Teki'ah, like in the first ones, as it relies on what it explained in the first ones, and it is understood on its own. He only explained the new aspect in it, namely the reason why here there is Shevarim without Teru'ah.

The third set of Teki'ah, Shevarim, Teki'ah.

200. אַדְּהָכִי, סִדְרָא תְּלִיתָאָה, קָלָא נָפִיק, וְסָלִיק, וְאִתְעַטָּר בְּרֵישֵׁיהּ דְּיַעֲקֹב, וְנָגִיד לֵיהּ לְתַתָּא לְהַהוּא אֲתַר דְּאִינּוּן גְּבוּרָאן שַׁרְיָין, וְקָאֵים לָקֳבְלַיְיהוּ, אַבְרָהָם

מֵהַאי סִטְרָא, וְיַעֲקֹב מֵהַאי סִטְרָא, וְאִינּוּן בְּאֶמְצָעִיתָא. כְּדֵין אִתְכַּפְיָין כֻּלְּהוּ, וּמִשְׁתַּכְחִין בְּאַתְרַיְיהוּ. וְהָנֵי כֻּלְּהוּ סִדְרָא אָחֳרָא תִּנְיָינָא.

200. Then comes the third set of Teki'ah, Shevarim, Teki'ah, which is under the control of the Central Column of the Left, which is the second Teki'ah. **A sound emerges,** namely the first Teki'ah, **and rises,** namely Shevarim. **It is crowned on the head of Jacob,** namely the second Teki'ah, **and draws him down to where the Gevurot of the Left dwell,** namely to the place below the chest of Zeir Anpin, where all the nine aspects of the Left Column reside. **Before them stand Abraham on the one side,** the Right Side, the first Teki'ah, **and Jacob on the other,** from the Central side, the second Teki'ah. **They,** the Gevurot, namely Shevarim, which is the secret of Isaac, **are among the two of them. Then all** the Gevurot of the Left **are subdued, and they are found** shining **in their place,** namely only from below upward, and they are not drawn below their place. **All these** three sets, the three times Teki'ah, Shevarim, Teki'ah, **are another** collective **set** that includes the nine aspects of the Left Column, as the Left aspect in them includes Shevarim without Teru'ah. Thus, the meditations of the three sets of Teki'ah, Shevarim, Teki'ah were explained.

The meditations of Teki'ah, Teru'ah, Teki'ah.

201. סִדְרָא בַּתְרָאָה, דְּבַעְיָיא לְסַלְּקָא לוֹן לְאַתְרַיְיהוּ, וּלְיַישְׁבָא בֵּינַיְיהוּ לְיִצְחָק כְּמִלְּקַדְּמִין. בְּגִין דְּהַאי בָּעֵי לְיַשְּׁרָא לֵיהּ בְּאַתְרֵיהּ, וְלָא יִפּוֹק בְּתוּקְפוֹי לְבַר, כְּדֵין דִּינִין כֻּלְּהוּ אִתְכַּפְיָין, וְרַחֲמִין אִתְּעֲרוּ.

201. The last collective **set,** namely nine aspects that are three times Teki'ah, Teru'ah, Teki'ah, which is in the Central Column. **These** nine aspects **need to raise** the Illumination of the Left that shine below the chest **to their place,** above the chest, **and settle Isaac among them as before.** In other words, to cover the Illumination of the Left called Isaac just like it was covered before during the shining of the nine aspects of the Right Column that shine above the chest, which happens due to the power of the Judgments of Teru'ah that control the Left of these nine aspects. This is **because they need to put him,** the Left, Isaac, **in his place** in such a way **that he will not come out with his intensity** of the Gevurot. **Then, all Judgments are subdued and Mercy awakens.** Here the Zohar does not detail the three times Teki'ah, Teru'ah, Teki'ah like in the other sets because the meditation follows in the same manner of the previous ones, except for what he added here that we need to meditate in every Teru'ah to raise the Illumination of the Left back to its place and cover it.

Directing the Shofar sounds with our consciousness.

202. עַל דָּא בָּעֵי לְכַוְּונָא לִבָּא וּרְעוּתָא בְּהָנֵי קָלֵי, וּלְמֶהְדַּר בְּתִיּוּבְתָּא קָמֵי מָארֵיהוֹן. כְּדֵין כַּד יִשְׂרָאֵל מִתְקְנֵי וּמְסַדְּרֵי קָלִין בִּרְעוּתָא דְּלִבָּא כַּדְקָא יָאוּת, בְּשׁוֹפָרָא דָּא, אַהְדָּר הַהוּא שׁוֹפָר עִלָּאָה, וְכַד אַהְדָּר, מְעַטְּרָא לֵיהּ לְיַעֲקֹב, וְאִתְתָּקַּן כֹּלָּא. וְכוּרְסְיָיא אָחֳרָא רְמִיוּ, וּכְדֵין חֵידוּ אִשְׁתְּכַח בְּכֹלָּא, וְקוּדְשָׁא בְּרִיךְ הוּא מְרַחֵם עַל עָלְמָא. זַכָּאָה חוּלָקֵיהוֹן דְּיִשְׂרָאֵל, דְּיַדְעִין לְנַגְּדָא וּלְאַמְשָׁכָא לְמָארֵיהוֹן, מִדִּינָא לְרַחֲמֵי, וּלְתַקְּנָא כֻּלְּהוּ עָלְמִין עַל יְדַיְיהוּ.

202. Therefore, it behooves us to direct the heart and desire in these sounds, the three times Teki'ah, Shevarim-Teru'ah, Teki'ah, three times Teki'ah, Shvarim, Teki'ah, and three times Teki'ah, Teru'ah, Teki'ah. **And they need to repent before their Master. Then, when Israel ready themselves and arrange these sounds with their heart's desire as is proper with this** Lower **Shofar, the Upper Shofar,** Binah, **returns** to shine again. **When it returns** to shine, **it adorns Jacob,** Zeir Anpin, **and everything is established. A different Throne,** the Throne of Mercy, **is placed. Joy abounds everywhere and the Holy One, blessed be He, has Mercy upon the world. Happy is the lot of Israel, who know how to guide and draw their Master from Judgment to Mercy, and establish the Worlds by their handiwork.**

Three sets of blowings for the three books that are open on Rosh Hashanah.

203. ת"ח, לְקָבֵל דָּא, תְּלָתָא סִפְרִין פְּתִיחִין בְּיוֹמָא דָא, וּכְמָה דִּרְחֲמִין מִתְעָרִין, וְדִינִין קַשְׁיָין אִתְכַּפְיָין וְעָאלִין לְדוּכְתַּיְיהוּ. כַּךְ הוּא לְתַתָּא כְּגַוְונָא דִלְעֵילָא, דִּינִין קַשְׁיָין אִתְכַּפְיָין וְאִתְעֲבָרוּ מֵעָלְמָא. וּמַאן אִינּוּן. אָלֵין אִינּוּן רְשָׁעִים גְּמוּרִים, דְּאִינּוּן דִּינִין קַשְׁיָין דְּאִתְכַּפְיָין וְאִתְעֲבָרוּ מֵעָלְמָא. וְעַל דָּא נִכְתָּבִים וְנֶחְתָּמִים וְכוּ'. אָ"ר אַבָּא, וַדַּאי דָּא הוּא בְּרִירָא דְמִלָּה, בְּרִיךְ רַחֲמָנָא דְּשָׁאִילְנָא וְרַוַוחְנָא בְּהָנֵי מִילֵי.

203. Come and see, correpsonding to this—the three sets of the Shofar, the Three Columns—**three books are open on this day.** One is for the Completely Righteous, the secret of the Right Column, one for the Completely Evil, the secret of the Harsh Judgment on the Left Column, and one for the In-Betweener, the secret of the Central Column. **Just as** through the Blowing of the Shofar **Mercy awakens and Harsh Judgments are subdued and go to their place, so it is Below like it is Above. The Harsh Judgments** Below **are subdued and removed from the world. Who are they? They are the completely wicked, who are Harsh Judgments. They are subdued and removed from the world. Therefore, they are immediately written and sentenced to death.** The Completely Righteous, the Chariot to the Right, are written to life immediately. The In-Betweeners, who are the Chariot to the Central Column, are in suspense until Yom Kippur, when the Central Column is complete, in the secret of the Illumination of Chochmah in Binah, the secret of the Light of Life. **Rav Aba said: "Surely this is the clear meaning of the matter. Blessed is the Merciful One that I have asked and attained these matters."**

A memorial of blowing.

204. אָ"ר יְהוּדָה, כְּתִיב זִכְרוֹן תְּרוּעָה, זִכְרוֹן עֲבִדֵינָן, לְכַוְּונָא לִבָּא וּרְעוּתָא, יִשְׂרָאֵל עַבְדִין זִכְרוֹן לְתַתָּא, בְּמָה. בְּעוֹבָדָא, בְּגִין דְּיִתְעַר מִלָּה כְּהַהוּא גַּוְונָא לְעֵילָא.

204. Rav Yehuda said: "It is written, '...a memorial of blowing....' (Leviticus 23:24) which means **we are reminded to direct the heart and desire** in the manner mentioned earlier. **With what do Israel perform a memorial below? By the deed** of Blowing the Shofar **so that a similar thing will be roused above,"** as mentioned in the previous paragraphs in the order of the meditations.

Sins cover the Light; repentance and the Shofar uncovers the Light.

205. אָמַר ר' אֶלְעָזָר, כְּתִיב בַּכֶּסֶה לְיוֹם חַגֵּנוּ דְּאִתְכַּסְיָא בֵּיהּ סִיהֲרָא. וְהֵיךְ אִתְכַּסְיָא. אֶלָּא, כַּד קַיְּימָא עֵיבָא, וְשִׁמְשָׁא לָא נָהִיר, כְּדֵין סִיהֲרָא אִתְכַּסְיָא, וְלָא נָהִיר. וְעַל דָּא, מִקַּמֵּי עֵיבָא שִׁמְשָׁא לָא נָהִיר, כ"ש סִיהֲרָא דְּאִתְכַּסְיָא וְלָא נְהִירָא. וְעַל דָּא בַּכֶּסֶה לְיוֹם חַגֵּנוּ, בְּהֵ"א, דְּאִתְכַּסְיָא סִיהֲרָא. וּבְמָּה נָהִיר. כֹּלָּא בִּתְיוּבְתָּא, וּבְקָל שׁוֹפָרָא, דִּכְתִיב אַשְׁרֵי הָעָם יוֹדְעֵי תְרוּעָה כְּדֵין יְיָ' בְּאוֹר פָּנֶיךָ יְהַלֵּכוּן.

205. Rav Elazar said: "It is written, '...at the appointed time (*bakeseh*: lit. in the covering) for the day of our festival.' (Psalms 81:4) This is because **the moon,** Malchut, **was covered on it,** for on Rosh Hashanah the moon is hidden." He asks: **"How is it covered?"** He answers: **"When there is a cloud** underneath the sun, **and the sun,** which is Zeir Anpin, **does not shine, the moon is covered,** which means **it does not shine,** since there is no one from whom to receive Light, for whatever Malchut has She receives from Zeir Anpin. **Therefore, if because of the cloud,** which indicate Judgments, **the sun,** Zeir Anpin, **cannot shine, the moon is all the more hidden and does not shine. Hence, in "...at the covering (*bakeseh*) of the day of our festival," (Psalms 81:4)** *bakeseh* (בכסה) is spelled with **Hei** (ה)at the end, to indicate that **the moon is covered** because of Judgments. **How can everything,** both Zeir Anpin and Malchut, **shine? Through repentance and the sound of the Shofar, as it is written: "Happy is the people that know the joyful note..." (Psalms 89:16) then, "...they shall walk, Lord, in the light of Your Countenance." (Ibid.)**

Emor

33. Rosh Hashanah

A Synopsis

We learn that the day of Rosh Hashanah is a day when the moon is hidden and the world is under Judgment. God allotted the prosecutor a specific day in which to demand all the punishments in the world so that the fear of God would increase. He wants the world to know that there is Judgment and there is a Judge. Witnesses come on the Day of Judgment and testify about all the deeds of everyone in the world. These witnesses are called the eyes of the Lord that see everything. We are told how everything is put down in writing, and how someone's verdict can be torn up if he repents. God prefers people to be saved from punishment; His love for His children overcomes His love of Judgment. We hear the explanation of Isaac's blessing of Jacob instead of Esau, and of how this relates to the days between Rosh Hashanah and Yom Kippur.

The Shofar opens previously closed Gates.

רעיא מהימנא

206. בַּחֹדֶשׁ הַשְּׁבִיעִי בְּאֶחָד לַחֹדֶשׁ וְגו'. פִּקּוּדָא דָא, לִתְקוֹעַ שׁוֹפָר בְּרֹאשׁ הַשָּׁנָה, דְּהוּא יוֹמָא דְּדִינָא לְעָלְמָא, כְּמָה דְּאוֹקִימְנָא. וְהָא אוֹקְמוּהָ דִּכְתִּיב, תִּקְעוּ בַחֹדֶשׁ שׁוֹפָר בַּכֶּסֶה לְיוֹם חַגֵּנוּ. וְהָא אִתְּמַר. דְּהַאי אִיהוּ יוֹמָא דְּסִיהֲרָא אִתְכַּסֵּי בֵּיהּ, וְקָאִים עָלְמָא בְּדִינָא בְּגִין, דְּהַהוּא מְקַטְרְגָא, חָזֵי וְכַסֵּי וְאַנְעַל פִּתְחָא עַל מַלְכָּא, אֲתַר דְּדִינָא שַׁרְיָא, לְמִתְבַּע דִּינָא עַל עָלְמָא.

Ra'aya Meheimna (Faithful Shepherd)

206. "... 'In the seventh month, on the first day of the month....'" (Leviticus 23:24) This Precept is to blow the Shofar on Rosh Hashanah, which is the Day of Judgment for the world, as we established. They already established it, as it is written: "Blow a Shofar in the renewal [of the moon], at the appointed time (*bakeseh*,

lit. in the covering) for the day of our festival." (Psalms 81:4) We already learned that this day is a day when the moon, Malchut, **is covered and the world is under Judgment** (as mentioned in verse 193). **For the prosecutor covers, hides and locks the entrance to the King,** who is Zeir Anpin, and the moon is **a place where Judgment abides to demand justice from the world.**

The Angel of Death was created so that there will be reverance in the world.

207. וְאִי תֵּימָא, אֵיךְ אִתְיְיהִיב לֵיהּ רְשׁוּ לְהַהוּא מְקַטְרְגָא לְחַפָּאָה וּלְמִתְבַּע דִּינָא. אֶלָּא וַדַּאי בִּידָא דְהַאי מְקַטְרְגָא, שַׁוֵּי קוּדְשָׁא בְּרִיךְ הוּא לְמִתְבַּע דִּינָא עַל כָּל עָלְמָא, וְשַׁוֵּי לֵיהּ יוֹמָא יְדִיעָא, לְמִתְבַּע קַמֵּיהּ כָּל דִּינִין דְעָלְמָא, דְּהָא קוּדְשָׁא בְּרִיךְ הוּא עָבֵד לֵיהּ וְשַׁוֵּי לֵיהּ קַמֵּיהּ, לְמֶהֱוֵי דְּחִילוּ דְקוּדְשָׁא בְּרִיךְ הוּא סַלְקָא, וְשַׁרְיָא עַל כֹּלָּא. וְרָזָא דָּא, וְהָאֱלֹהִים עָשָׂה שֶׁיִּרְאוּ מִלְּפָנָיו. מַאי עָשָׂה. עָשָׂה לְהַאי מְקַטְרְגָא, וְאַתְקִין לֵיהּ קַמֵּיהּ, לְמֶהֱוֵי סַיְיפָא שְׁנָנָא עַל כָּל עָלְמָא. וְכָל דָּא בְּגִין דְּיִדְחֲלוּן מִקַּמֵּי קוּדְשָׁא בְּרִיךְ הוּא כֹּלָּא. וְדָא אִיהוּ סַנְטִירָא, דְּתָבַע חוֹבֵי בְּנֵי נָשָׁא, וְתָבַע דִּינָא, וְתָפִיס בְּנֵי נָשָׁא וְקָטִיל לוֹן וְאַלְקֵי לוֹן, כֹּלָּא כְּמָה דְּנָפִיק מִן דִּינָא.

207. You may wonder: "How was the prosecutor given permission to cover the Light of Malchut **and demand punishment?"** He answers: **"Surely the Holy One, blessed be He, allowed the prosecutor to demand justice from the whole world. He allotted him a specific day in which to demand all the punishments in the world, for the Holy One, blessed be He, made him and placed him before Himself, so that the fear of the Holy One, blessed be He, will increase and reside on everyone." This is the secret of: "...and God (Elohim) has brought to pass that men fear Him." (Ecclesiastes 3:14) What is "brought"?** It means that **He brought this prosecutor and established him before Himself to be a sharp sword over the whole world. All this so that all will fear the Holy One, blessed be He. This is the supervisor that prosecutes the sins of people, demands punishment,**

seizes people, kills them and strikes them; all just as it was decided in the Courthouse.

Permission was granted to the one appointed over the Lower Courthouse to demand justice.

208. כְּגַוְונָא דְּהַהוּא מְמוּנֶּה בֵּית דִּין דִּלְתַתָּא, דְּאִתְיְיהִיב לֵיהּ רְשׁוּ לְאַדְכְּרָא קַמֵּי בֵּי דִּינָא, פְּלוֹנִי עֲבַד כַּךְ, וּפְלוֹנִי עָבַר עַל כַּךְ, וּלְמִתְבַּע עָלַיְיהוּ דִּינָא. וּתְנָן, רְשׁוּ אִתְיְיהִיב לְהַהוּא מְמוּנֶּה בֵּית דִּין, לְאַנְעֲלָא עַל בֵּי דִּינָא פִּתְחָא, עַד דְּיִגְזְרוּן דִּינָא עַל כָּל מַה דְּאִיהוּ תָּבַע, וְלֵית רְשׁוּ לְבֵית דִּין לְדַחְיָיא לֵיהּ. בְּגִין כִּי אֲנִי יְיָ' אוֹהֵב מִשְׁפָּט. וְאִיהוּ בָּעֵי דְּעָלְמָא יִתְקַיֵּים בְּדִינָא, וּלְמִנְדַּע דְּאִית דִּין וְאִית דַּיָּין.

208. It is **like the one appointed over the Lower Courthouse, who was given permission to mention before the Courthouse that so-and-so did this, and so-and-so transgressed that, and to demand punishment. We learned that the minister appointed over the Courthouse was given permission to lock the entrance to the Courthouse until verdicts will be meted out to all until they sentence a decree for all that he prosecuted them. The Courthouse is not allowed to decline him, because, "For I the Lord love justice..." (Isaiah 61:8), and He wants the world to be maintained by Judgment, so as to make known that there is Judgment and there is a Judge.** All this applies to the Lower Courthouse.

The prosecutor has permission to cover Malchut until he exacts Judgment on the wicked.

209. כְּהַאי גַּוְונָא שַׁוֵּי קוּדְשָׁא בְּרִיךְ הוּא קַמֵּיהּ לְהַאי, דְּאִיהוּ תָּבַע דִּינָא קַמֵּי מַלְכָּא, עַל כָּל בְּנֵי עָלְמָא. וּבְהַאי יוֹמָא אִתְיְיהִיב לֵיהּ רְשׁוּ, לְכַסָּאָה פִּתְחָא דְּמַלְכָּא, וְסִיהֲרָא אִתְחַפְיָיא לְגוֹ, עַד דְּיִתְגְּזַר דִּינָא עַל כָּל בְּנֵי עָלְמָא. וְאַף עַל גַּב דְּכֹלָּא אִתְגְּלֵי קַמֵּי קוּדְשָׁא בְּרִיךְ הוּא, לָא בָּעֵי אֶלָּא בְּדִינָא.

209. The Holy One, blessed be He, did the same. He placed before Him that prosecutor **who demands punishment before the King for all the people in the world. On that day, he is given permission to cover the entrance of the King,** Zeir Anpin, **and the moon,** Malchut, **is hidden inside until punishment is meted out to all the people in the world. Though everything is revealed before the Holy One, blessed be He, nevertheless He only wants it with Judgment.**

On Rosh Hashanah, witnesses go up to demand Judgment on the people of the world.

210. כֹּלָּא כְּגַוְונָא חֲדָא עֵילָּא וְתַתָּא, אַתְקִין כּוּרְסְיָא דְּדִינָא בְּהַאי יוֹמָא, וְסַנְטִירָא אָתָא, וְתָבַע דִּינָא עַל כָּל עוֹבָדֵי בְּנֵי עָלְמָא, כָּל חַד וְחַד כְּפוּם אָרְחוֹי, וּכְפוּם מַה דְּעָבַד. וְסָהֲדִין אַתְיָין וְסָהֲדֵי עַל כָּל עוֹבָדֵי בְּנֵי עָלְמָא. וְאִלֵּין אִינּוּן עֵינֵי יי', דְּאִינּוּן מְשַׁטְטֵי בְּכָל עָלְמָא. וְכַמָּה אִינּוּן עֵינֵי יְיָ', דְּלֵית לוֹן חוּשְׁבָּנָא, דְּקָא אַזְלֵי וּמְשַׁטְטֵי בְּכָל עָלְמָא, וְחָמָאן כָּל עוֹבָדֵי בְּנֵי עָלְמָא.

210. Everything operates in the same way Above and Below. On that day, the Holy One, blessed be He, **fixes the Throne of Judgment, and the supervisor comes and demands justice for all the deeds of the people in the world, each according to his ways and deeds. Witnesses come and testify to all the deeds of the people in the world, and these** witnesses **are** called **the eyes of the Lord that roam throughout the whole world and see the deeds of the people in the world.**

There are two angels that bear witness to all of the person's deeds.

211. וַוי לְאִינּוּן דְּלָא מַשְׁגִּיחִין וְלָא מִסְתַּכְּלִין בְּעוֹבָדֵיהוֹן, דְּהָא לְגַבַּיְיהוּ קַיְימִין אִלֵּין סָהֲדֵי מַלְכָּא, וּמַשְׁגִּיחִין וְחָמָאן כָּל מַה דְּאִינּוּן עַבְדִּין, וְקָאַמְרֵי, דְּהָא אִינּוּן סַלְקֵי וְסָהֲדֵי קַמֵּי מַלְכָּא. וְהַאי סַנְטִירָא קָאִים קָמֵּי מַלְכָּא, וְתָבַע דִּינָא, פְּלוֹנִי עָבַר דִּינָא, פְּלוֹנִי עֲבַד כַּךְ. וְהָא הָכָא סַהֲדֵי. וְעַד דְּקוּדְשָׁא בְּרִיךְ הוּא לָא שָׁאִיל לוֹן, לֵית לוֹן רְשׁוּ לְסַהֲדָא. כְּדֵין אִינּוּן סַהֲדֵי סַהֲדוּתָא.

211. Woe to those who do not care and do not observe their doings, for the witnesses of the King stand by them, observe and see whatever they do or say. They ascend and testify before the King. That supervisor stands before the King and demands punishment: "So-and-so transgressed the law and so-and-so did that; here are the witnesses." As long as the Holy One, blessed be He, does not ask them, they have no permission to testify. When He asks them, **they deliver their testimony.**

A person's sentence is written as black fire on white fire.

212. וְכֹלָּא אַכְתִּיב קַמֵּי מַלְכָּא בְּפִתְקָא. בְּבֵי מַלְכָּא אִית חַד הֵיכָלָא. הֵיכָלָא דָּא מַלְיָא אֶשָּׁא חִוָּורָא, וְהַאי אֶשָּׁא מִתְגַּלְגְּלָא בְּפַלְקָא, וְלָהִיט שְׁבִיבִין וְהַאי לָא פָּסִיק לְעָלְמִין. לְגוֹ הַאי הֵיכָלָא, אִית הֵיכָלָא אוּחֲרָא, מַלְיָא אֶשָּׁא אוּכְמָא, דְּלָא פָּסִיק לְעָלְמִין. תְּרֵין סוֹפְרִין קַיְימִין תָּדִיר קַמֵּיהּ מַלְכָּא. בְּשַׁעֲתָא דְּדִינָא, סָהֲדִין כָּל סַהֲדֵי קַמֵּי מַלְכָּא. אִינּוּן סוֹפְרִין נַטְלִין מֵהַהוּא פַּלְקָא דְּאֶשָּׁא חִוָּורָא, וְכַתְבֵי עָלֵיהּ בְּהַהוּא אֶשָּׁא אוּכְמָא.

212. Everything is written before the King in writing. In the King's House there is a certain Chamber full of white fire. This fire rolls in a circle with burning sparks and never ceases. Inside this Chamber there is another Chamber full of black fire, which never ceases. Two scribes stand before the King at all times. During trials, all witnesses testify before the King. The scribes take from the circle of white fire and write the verdict **on it with the black fire.**

The King delays the verdict in case people will repent.

213. וּכְדֵין מַלְכָּא אַוְזְמִין דִּינָא, עַד זִמְנָא יְדִיעָא, דִּלְמָא בֵּין כַּךְ וּבֵין כַּךְ יַהַדְרוּן בִּתְשׁוּבָה. אִי יַהַדְרוּן, פַּתְקִין נַקְרְעִין. וְאִי לָאו, מַלְכָּא יָתִיב, וְכָל אִינּוּן דְּבֵי זְכוּתָא קַיְימֵי קַמֵּיהּ, כָּרוֹזָא קָם וְכָרִיז, פְּלוֹנִי עֲבַד כַּךְ, מַאן יוֹלִיף עָלֵיהּ זְכוּת, אִי אִית מַאן דְּיוֹלִיף עָלֵיהּ זְכוּת, יָאוּת. וְאִי לָאו הָא אִתְמְסַר לְסַנְטִירָא.

213. The King then holds the verdict for some time, in case they will repent in the meantime. If they returned in repentance, **the writings are torn up. If not, the King sits and all the defenders stand before Him. The crier stands and announces, "So-and-so did this; who shall defend him?" If there is someone to defend him, it is well. Otherwise, he is given to the supervisor** to be punished.

The Holy One, blessed be He, judges humanity through Judgment and justice.

214. וְכֹלָּא יָדַע קוּדְשָׁא בְּרִיךְ הוּא, אַמַּאי אִצְטְרִיךְ לְכָל דָּא. אֶלָּא בְּגִין דְּלָא, יְהֵא פִּטְרָא דְּפוּמָא לִבְנֵי עָלְמָא. אֶלָּא לְאַחֲזָאָה דְּכֹלָּא עָבִיד בְּאֹרַח קְשׁוֹט, וְנַיְיחָא קַמֵּיהּ מַאן דְּאִשְׁתְּזִיב מִן דִּינֵיהּ. וְאִי תֵּימָא מְנָלָן. הַאי, אִתְמְסַר לְחַכִּימֵי, וַאֲפִילּוּ לְמַאן דְּלָא יָדְעֵי, מַאן דְּבָעֵי לְאִסְתַּכְּלָא, יַשְׁגַּח בְּמָה דְּאִיהוּ בְּאִתְגַּלְיָא, וְיָדַע בְּמָה דְּאִיהוּ בְּסִתְרָא, דְּהָא כֹּלָּא כְּגַוְונָא חָדָא, כָּל מַה דְּפָקִיד קוּדְשָׁא בְּרִיךְ הוּא בְּאַרְעָא, כֹּלָּא אִיהוּ כְּגַוְונָא דִּלְעֵילָּא.

214. He asks: **"Yet the Holy One, blessed be He, knows everything, why does He need all this?"** He answers: **"Rather, this is so that people will have no excuse, and to show that He does everything in the way of Truth, and He prefers it when one is saved from His punishment. You may ask: 'From where do we know this?'** This **was given to the sages. And even those who do not know, whoever wants to see, may see what is revealed** Below in this world, **and thus know what is** Above in **concealment, since everything follows the same pattern. For whatever the Holy One, blessed be He, does in the ways of the world, is in the likeness of Above."**

The Creator's love of His children overcomes His love of Judgment.

215. יוֹמָא דר"ה, אִיהוּ יוֹמָא דְּדִינָא, וּמַלְכָּא יָתִיב בְּכוּרְסְיָיא דְּדִינָא, סַנֵּיגוֹרָא קָא אָתֵי וְחָזֵי פִּתְוָא דְּמַלְכָּא, וְתָבַע דִּינָא. וְאַף עַל גַּב דְּקוּדְשָׁא בְּרִיךְ הוּא רָחִים לֵיהּ לְדִינָא, כְּמָה דְּאַתְּ אָמֵר, כִּי אֲנִי יְיָ' אוֹהֵב מִשְׁפָּט. נָצַח רְחִימוּ דִּבְנוֹי,

לִרְחִימוּ דְּדִינָא. וּבְשַׁעֲתָא דְּסַנְטִירָא קָם לְמִטְעַן מִלִּין עֲלַיְיהוּ, פָּקִיד לְמִתְקַע בַּשּׁוֹפָר, בְּגִין לְאִתְעָרָא רַחֲמֵי מִתַּתָּא לְעֵילָּא, בְּהַהוּא שׁוֹפָר.

215. The day of Rosh Hashanah is Judgment Day, and the King sits on the Throne of Judgment. The supervisor comes and covers the entrance to the King and demands punishment. And even though the Holy One, blessed be He, loves Judgment, as written: "For I the Lord love justice..." (Isaiah 61:8) the love of His children overcomes the love of Judgment. When the supervisor rises to speak about them, the Holy One, blessed be He, **commands the Shofar to be blown in order to rouse love from below upward with that Shofar.**

When the Shofar is awakened, all the claims of the Satan are scrambled.

216. סַלְקָא הַהוּא קָלָא, כְּלִילָא בְּאֶשָּׁא וְרוּחָא וּמַיָּא, וְאִתְעָבֵיד מִנַּיְיהוּ קָלָא חֲדָא, וְאִתְּעַר קָלָא אָחֳרָא לְעֵילָּא, כַּד הַהוּא קָלָא אִתְּעַר מֵעֵילָּא וּמִתַּתָּא, כְּדֵין כָּל טַעֲנוֹת דְּקָא טָעִין הַהוּא מְקַטְרְגָא מִתְעַרְבְּבֵי.

216. The sound rises, comprised of fire, air, and water, which correspond to Chesed-Gevurah-Tiferet **that merge into one sound. Another sound from Above is roused before it,** which is the Central Column that unites Left and Right. **When that sound is roused from Above and from Below, all the charges the prosecutors raise are confused.** This is because the Upper Three of the Left, the source of the Judgments, is diminished, and Mercy that emerges through the unification of the Right and Left is revealed (as explained in Zohar, Vayera 383 in the Sulam).

On Rosh Hashanah, Isaac calls Esau to fetch him all the sins of the world.

217. בְּיוֹמָא דְּרֹאשׁ הַשָּׁנָה, נָפִיק יִצְחָק בִּלְחוֹדוֹי, וְקָרֵי לְעֵשָׂו, לְאַטְעֲמָא לֵיהּ תַּבְשִׁילִין דְּכָל עָלְמָא, כָּל חַד כְּפוּם אוֹרְחוֹי, דְּהָא בְּהַהִיא שַׁעֲתָא וַתִּכְהֶןָ עֵינָיו

מֵרְאוֹת, דְּנָפִיק מִנֵּיהּ מַאן דְּאוּשְׁךְ אַפֵּי בִּרְיָין, וְאִתְפְּרַשׁ, וְשָׁכִיב עַל עַרְסֵיהּ דְּדִינָא, וְקָרֵי לְעֵשָׂו, וְאָמַר וְצוּדָה לִּי צָיִדה וַעֲשֵׂה לִי מַטְעַמִּים וְהָבִיאָה לִּי.

217. On the day of Rosh Hashanah, Isaac comes out alone, namely the Left Column reigns without the Right and without the joining of the Central Column, which are Abraham and Jacob. **He calls Esau,** the Other Side, **to give him to taste of the cooked food of the whole world, according to their deeds,** namely to demand punishment for the actions of all the people in the world. **For at that time, "...his eyes were dim, so that he could not see..." (Genesis 27:1) because he that darkens people's faces comes out from him** namely the prosecutor is drawn from the Left, when it is without the Right. **He is separated** from the Right and Central Columns, **lies on the couch of Judgment and calls Esau,** who is the Other Side and the prosecutor, **and says: "...hunt me some venison... and make me savory food..." (Genesis 27:3-4)** from the evil deeds of people, **"...and bring it to me...." (Ibid.)**

Rivka advises Jacob to awaken prayers and petitions to incorporate the Right with the Left.

218. וְרִבְקָה אָמְרָה אֶל יַעֲקֹב בְּנָהּ, רְחִימָא דְּנַפְשָׁהּ, בְּנָהּ רְחִימָא דְּאִתְמְסַר לָהּ מִיּוֹמָא דְּאִתְבְּרֵי עָלְמָא. וּפַקִּידַת לֵיהּ, לְאִתְעָרָא אִיהוּ בְּאִינּוּן מַטְעַמִּים דִּילֵיהּ. וְיַעֲקֹב אִתְּעַר מִתַּתָּא, וּמִתְלַבַּשׁ בִּצְלוֹתִין וּבָעוּתִין, וְהַקּוֹל קוֹל יַעֲקֹב בְּהַהוּא שׁוֹפָר דְּקָא סָלִיק, וְאִתְּעַר יַעֲקֹב לְגַבֵּיהּ, וְאִתְקְרִיב בַּהֲדֵיהּ, וַיַּגֶּשׁ לוֹ וַיֹּאכַל, וְאִתְכְּלִיל דָּא בְּדָא. כֵּיוָן דְּאִתְכְּלִיל בַּהֲדֵיהּ, וַיָּבֵא לוֹ יַיִן, דָּא יַיִן דְּמִנַּטְרָא, יַיִן דְּהוּא חֲדִידוּ דְּלִבָּא, רָזָא דְּעָלְמָא דְּאָתֵי, כְּדֵין וַיָּרַח אֶת רֵיחַ בְּגָדָיו, צְלוֹתִין דְּסַלְקִין וּבָעוּתִין. וַיְבָרְכֵהוּ, נָח רוּגְזָא, וְחַדֵּי לִבָּא, וְכֹלָּא אִיהוּ רַחֲמֵי.

218. "And Rivkah, who is Malchut, **spoke to Jacob her son..." (Genesis 27:6) the beloved of her soul, her beloved son given to her since the world was created. She orders him to rouse himself with his own dishes. Jacob awakens Below, dons prayers and petitions, and "The voice is Jacob's voice" (Genesis 27:22), with the Shofar that**

he raises. Supernal **Jacob,** who is the Central Column, **awakens toward him,** Isaac, **and approaches him,** meaning he joins him with Abraham, who is the Right. **"...And he brought it near to him, and he did eat..."** **(Ibid. 25),** which means **they were incorporated within each other,** and the Mochin, the secret of eating, shone. **Once** the Central Column **was included in him, "...he brought him wine" (Ibid.), which is the preserved wine,** namely the Illumination of Chochmah that shines from below upwards, fixed by the Central Column, **the wine that gladdens the heart, which is the secret of the World to Come,** namely the Illumination of Chochmah that is drawn from Binah called the World to Come. **Then, "...he smelt the smell of his garments..." (Genesis 27:27)** namely **the ascending prayers and petitions, "...and blessed him..." (Ibid.)** meaning **that anger abated, the heart rejoiced and everything is merciful.**

Once Jacob is incorporated with the Left, all Harsh Judgments are dispersed.

219. כֵּיוָן דְּאִיהוּ אִתְכְּלִיל בְּיַעֲקֹב, כָּל אִינּוּן חַיָּילִין וְתוּקְפִּין וְרוּגְזִין דַּהֲווֹ זְמִינִין, אִתְבַּדְּרוּ, וְלָא אִשְׁתְּכָחוּ תַּמָּן. וְיִשְׂרָאֵל נָפְקִין מִן דִּינָא, בְּחֶדְוָה וּבְבִרְכָאן. וַיְהִי אַךְ יָצֹא יָצָא יַעֲקֹב מֵאֵת פְּנֵי יִצְחָק אָבִיו, בְּיוֹמָא דָא, בְּחֶדְוָה, וּבְבִרְכָאן עִלָּאִין, וְעֵשָׂו אָחִיו בָּא מִצֵּידוֹ, טָעִין טוֹעֲנֵי מֵעוֹבָדֵי דְּעָלְמָא, וַיַּעַשׂ גַּם הוּא מַטְעַמִּים, חַדִּיד לִישָׁנֵיהּ לְמִטְעַן טַעֲנוֹת. אַתְקִין סַהֲדֵי, וַיָּבֵא לְאָבִיו וַיֹּאמֶר יָקוּם אָבִי, יִתְּעַר בְּדִינוֹי, וְיֹאכַל כַּמָּה עוֹבָדִין בִּישִׁין דְּכָל עָלְמָא דְּקָא אַשְׁכַּחְנָא.

219. Once he is incorporated in Jacob all the awaiting powers, Harsh Judgments and anger dispersed and were no longer found there. Israel emerges from Judgment with happiness and blessings. "Jacob had just left the presence of Isaac his father..." on that day, with joy and Celestial blessings, "...when Esau his brother came from his hunting" (Genesis 27:30), loaded with burdens of the deeds of the world to denounce them. **"And he also had made savory food..." (Ibid. 31), sharpening his tongue to give charges and prepare testimony, "...and brought it to his father, and said to his father, 'Let my father**

arise,' rousing himself with his Judgment, "...and eat" (Ibid.) the many evil deeds done **in the whole world that I have found.**

After the prayers of Rosh Hashanah are accepted, the satan has no control except on the rest of the nations.

220. וַיֶּחֱרַד יִצְחָק חֲרָדָה גְּדוֹלָה עַד מְאֹד, דְּהָא לָא יָכִיל לְאִתְפָּרְשָׁא מִכְּלָלָא דְּיַעֲקֹב, דְּאִיהוּ בְּחֶדְוָה. וַיֹּאמֶר מִי אֵפוֹא הוּא הַצָּד צַיִד, בְּכַמָּה צְלוֹתִין וּבָעוּתִין, וָאוֹכַל מִכֹּל בְּטֶרֶם תָּבֹא וָאֲבָרְכֵהוּ גַּם בָּרוּךְ יִהְיֶה. כִּשְׁמוֹעַ עֵשָׂו אֶת דִּבְרֵי יִצְחָק אָבִיו וַיִּצְעַק צְעָקָה וְגוֹ'. דְּחָמֵי דְּהָא צֵידוֹ לָא הֲוָה כְּלוּם. עַד לְבָתַר דְּאָמַר לֵיהּ, הִנֵּה מִשְׁמַנֵּי הָאָרֶץ וְגוֹ' אִלֵּין תַּקִּיפִין וְאוּכְלוּסִין דִּשְׁאָר עַמִּין וְדָא קַשְׁיָא לֵיהּ מִכֹּלָּא. וַיִּשְׂטֹם עֵשָׂו אֶת יַעֲקֹב, לְמֵיזָל אֲבַתְרֵיהּ, וּלְקַטְרְגָא לֵיהּ תָּדִיר.

220. "And Isaac trembled very much..." (Genesis 27:33), for he could not be separated from being incorporated in Jacob, who abides in joy, "...and said: 'Who then is he that has taken venison...' by many prayers and petitions, '...and I have eaten of all before you came, and have blessed him? Moreover, he shall be blessed.' And when Esau heard the words of his father, he cried with a great and exceedingly bitter cry" (Ibid. 33-34) because he saw that his venison was worthless. Eventually he said to him, "Behold, your dwelling shall be of the fatness of the earth..." (Ibid. 39), who are the mighty men and the multitudes of the other nations. This was hardest for him, "And Esau hated Jacob..." (Ibid. 41) following him and constantly denouncing him.

Between Rosh Hashanah and Yom Kippur, Esau is ready to prosecute Israel, until Jacob sends him a gift.

221. וְיַעֲקֹב אָזִיל בְּאִינּוּן יוֹמִין דְּבֵין ר"ה לְיוֹם הַכִּפּוּרִים, עָרִיק לְאִשְׁתְּזָבָא מִנֵּיהּ. תָּב בִּתְיוּבְתָּא, שַׁוֵּי גַּרְמֵיהּ בְּתַעֲנִיתָא, עַד דְּאָתֵי יָ"ה, כְּדֵין יַדְעֵי יִשְׂרָאֵל דְּעֵשָׂו בָּא, וְעִמּוֹ אַרְבַּע מֵאוֹת אִישׁ, כֻּלְּהוּ מְקַטְרְגֵי זְמִינִין לְקַטְרְגָא לוֹן, מִיַּד וַיִּירָא יַעֲקֹב מְאֹד וַיֵּצֶר לוֹ וְאַסְגֵּי בִּצְלוֹתִין וּבָעוּתִין. וַיֹּאמֶר יַעֲקֹב אֱלֹהֵי אָבִי

אַבְרָהָם וֵאלֹהֵי אָבִי וְגוֹ'. עַד דְּנָטִיל עֵיטָא וְאָמַר, כִּי אָמַר אֲכַפְּרָה פָנָיו בַּמִּנְחָה הַהוֹלֶכֶת לְפָנָי וַיִּקַּח מִן הַבָּא בְיָדוֹ מִנְחָה וְגוֹ', עִזִּים מָאתַיִם וּתְיָשִׁים עֶשְׂרִים רְחֵלִים מָאתַיִם וְגוֹ'.

221. On these days between Rosh Hashanah and Yom Kippur Jacob goes and flees so as to be saved from him. He repents and places himself in fasting until Yom Kippur arrives. Then Israel knows that Esau comes with four hundred people, all prosecutors ready to denounce them. Immediately, "Jacob was greatly afraid and distressed..." (Genesis 32:8), and raises many prayers and petitions, "And Jacob said: 'God of my father Abraham, and God of my father..." (Ibid. 10), until he takes advice and says, "...For he said: 'I will appease him with the presents that goes before me..." (Ibid. 21) "...and took of that which came to his hand these presents... two hundred she-goats, and twenty he-goats, two hundred ewes...." (Ibid. 14-15) By giving a gift to the Other Side the prosecutor becomes the defender.

A camel and a snake allude to Satan.

222. גְּמַלִּים וְגוֹ', כַּךְ הוּא סִטְרָא דִילֵיהּ. גְּמַלִּים הוּא נָחָשׁ, כְּמִין גָּמָל, בְּשַׁעֲתָא דְפַתֵּי סָמָאֵ"ל לְאָדָם, אַרְכִּיב עַל נָחָשׁ כְּמִין גָּמָל. תָּנֵינָן, מַאן דְחָזֵי גָּמָל בְּחֶלְמֵיהּ, מִיתָה נִקְנְסָה עָלֵיהּ מִלְּמַעְלָה, וְאִשְׁתְּזִיב מִינָּהּ. וְכֹלָּא חַד.

222. "Camels...." (Genesis 32:16) Such is his side, like camels. **Camels are the** primordial **Serpent** that was **like a camel. When** the angel **Sama"el tempted Adam** to eat of the Tree of Knowledge of Good and Evil, **he was riding on a camel-like Serpent. We learned that whoever sees a camel in his dream was punished by death from Above but was saved from it. It is all one,** meaning that the camel and the Serpent that delivered death to the world are the same idea.

After Neila the prosecutor parts from Israel, and the Holy One, blessed be He, rejoices with His children during Sukkot.

223. וּכְדֵין, אַהֲדַר עֵשָׂו אַפּוֹטְרוֹפּוֹסָא דְּיַעֲקֹב, וְיַעֲקֹב לָא בָּעָא דּוּבְשֵׁיהּ וְעוּקְצֵיהּ. יַעֲבָר נָא אֲדוֹנִי לִפְנֵי עַבְדּוֹ. כְּדֵין וַיָּשָׁב בַּיּוֹם הַהוּא עֵשָׂו לְדַרְכּוֹ. אֵימָתַי. בְּשַׁעַת נְעִילָה, דְּהָא אִתְפָּרַשׁ מֵעַמָּא קַדִּישָׁא. וְקוּדְשָׁא בְּרִיךְ הוּא שָׁבִיק לְחוֹבֵיהוֹן, וְכַפֵּר עֲלַיְיהוּ. כֵּיוָן דְּהַהוּא מְקַטְרְגָא אָזַל בְּהַהוּא דּוֹרוֹנָא, וְאִתְפָּרַשׁ מִנַּיְיהוּ, בָּעֵי קוּדְשָׁא בְּרִיךְ הוּא לְמֶחֱדֵי בִּבְנוֹי, מַה כְּתִיב, וְיַעֲקֹב נָסַע סֻכֹּתָה וַיִּבֶן לוֹ בָּיִת וְגוֹ'. עַל כֵּן קָרָא שֵׁם הַמָּקוֹם סוּכּוֹת, כֵּיוָן דְּיָתְבֵי בְּסֻכּוֹת, הָא אִשְׁתְּזִיבוּ מִן מְקַטְרְגָא, וְקוּדְשָׁא בְּרִיךְ הוּא חַדֵּי בִּבְנוֹי. זַכָּאָה חוּלָקֵיהוֹן בְּהַאי עָלְמָא וּבְעָלְמָא דְּאָתֵי.

ע"כ רעיא מהימנא.

223. Esau then reverted to be Jacob's defender, yet Jacob wanted neither his honey nor his sting, but said: **"Let my master, I pray you, pass over before his servant…." (Genesis 33:14) Then, "Esau returned that day on his way to Seir." (Ibid. 16) When** does this happen? **During the Neilah prayer, since then he parts from the Holy Nation, and the Holy One, blessed be He, forgives their iniquities and atones for them. Once the prosecutor leaves with the gift and separates from them, the Holy One, blessed be He, wishes to rejoice with His children. It is then written: "And Jacob journeyed to Sukkot, and built himself a house… therefore the name of the place is called Sukkot." (Ibid. 17) Since Israel dwelt in Sukkot, they were saved from the prosecutor, and the Holy One, blessed be He, rejoiced in His children. Happy is their lot in this world and in the World to Come.**

End of Ra'aya Meheimna (Faithful Shepherd)

Pinchas

8. From Rosh Hashanah to the last day of Sukkot

A Synopsis

Rav Elazar explains to Rav Chiya the significance of the days mentioned in the title of this section. We hear that it has to do with the order in which God lifts up his Right Arm and extends it to embrace Malchut and unite with her. It includes the purification and fasting that the children of Israel do at this time.

The Relevance of this Passage

This passage expounds upon the deep secrets underlying the days between Rosh Hashanah and Sukkot. The words of Rav Chiya and Rav Elazar ignite the unification and cleansing powers of these cosmic instruments.

These spiritual influences uproot all immoral qualities from our nature in a merciful, softhearted fashion. They cleanse all the iniquities of humanity, our sins, and our misdeeds, purifying and preparing us for union with the Light of Creator. Judgments are overturned. Sentences are repealed. The Right, Left, and Central Columns are balanced and perfected. All the Worlds are refined and corrected.

And because the Zohar is above time and place, outside the laws of physics; because this mystical tome deals with the secrets of the soul and the secrets of secrets, the effect and results are all-embracing, universal, macrocosmic, and in the Now. Our actions here are the ultimate atonement, bringing forth our Final Redemption and unification with the Light, thanks to the righteousness and power of the friends cited throughout this ancient Holy Book.

The order from Rosh Hashanah until the last day of Sukkot is known to the wise sages.

27. אָמַר רִבִּי חִיָּיא לְרִבִּי אֶלְעָזָר, אִלֵּין יוֹמִין, מֵרֹאשׁ הַשָּׁנָה עַד יוֹמָא בַּתְרָאָה דְּחַג, בָּעֵינָא לְמֵיקָם עֲלַיְיהוּ. א"ר אֶלְעָזָר, הָא אִתְּמַר וְחַבְרַיָּיא אִתְּעָרוּ בְּהוּ. א"ר חִיָּיא, וַדַּאי הָכִי הוּא, אֲבָל אֲנָא שְׁמַעְנָא לְבוּצִינָא קַדִּישָׁא עִלָּאָה מִלָּה בְּהוּ. אָמַר לֵיהּ, אֵימָא הַהוּא מִלָּה. א"ל עַד לָא קָאִימְנָא בֵּיהּ. א"ר אֶלְעָזָר, אַף עַל גַּב דְּחַבְרַיָּיא אוֹקְמוּ מִלָּה, וְשַׁפִּיר הוּא, אֲבָל סִדּוּרָא דְּהָנֵי יוֹמֵי, רָזָא דְּחָכְמְתָא הוּא, בֵּין מְחַצְּדֵי חַקְלָא.

27. Rav Chiya said to Rav Elazar: "I would like to settle these days from Rosh Hashanah until the last day of Sukkot." Rav Elazar said: "But we have already studied them, and the friends have made their comments about them." Rav Chiya said: "Of course, but I heard something about them from the Supernal Holy Luminary, Rav Shimon.**" He said to him: "Tell us that thing." He said to him: "I still am not settled in it** and it is not as clear as it should be.**" Rav Elazar said: "Although the friends have already discussed this matter, and it is beautiful, the order of these days is the secret of wisdom among the reapers in the field,"** namely among those scholars who have already completed all the refinements of Malchut called "a field."

His Holy arm is the Left Column, on which salvation depends.

28. ת"ח, הָא אִתְּמַר סִדּוּרָא דְּיִחוּדָא כֹּלָּא בְּחַד הֵיךְ הֲוֵי. וְהָא אִתְּמַר. פָּתַח וְאָמַר, חָשַׂף יְיָ' אֶת זְרוֹעַ קָדְשׁוֹ, דָּא דְּרוֹעָא חֲדָא, דְּבֵיהּ תַּלְיָא יְשׁוּעָה, דְּבֵיהּ תַּלְיָא נוּקְמָא, דְּבֵיהּ תַּלְיָא פּוּרְקָנָא. וְלָמָּה, לְמֵיקָם לָהּ לכנ"י מֵעַפְרָא, וּלְקַבְּלָא לָהּ לְגַבֵּיהּ, לְאִזְדַּוְּוגָא כַּחֲדָא. וְכַד הַאי אִתְּעַר לְקַבְּלָהּ, כַּמָּה דְּחֵילוּ שַׁרְיָא בְּעָלְמָא, עַד דְּיָנַח הַהוּא דְּרוֹעָא תְּחוֹת רֵישָׁהָא לְאִתְחַבְּרָא. כְּמָה דְּאַתְּ אָמַר, שְׂמֹאלוֹ תַּחַת לְרֹאשִׁי וְגוֹ', וּכְדֵין נַיְיחָא דִּינָא, וּמְכַפֵּר חוֹבִין.

28. Come and see, we have already learned how the order of unifying all into one goes. It was already said. He opened and said, "The

Lord has made bare His Holy arm...." (Isaiah 52:10) This is one arm, which is the Left Column, **on which are dependent salvation, vengeance, and redemption. But why** did the Lord make bare this Holy arm of His? **It was to raise up the Congregation of Israel,** namely Malchut, **from the dust and to welcome Her with Him so as to unite as one. When that** arm **is raised up toward Her, there is much fear present in the world, until He rests that arm under Her head to unite with Her, as it is said: "His left hand is under my head...." (Song of Songs 2:6) And then Judgment rests and He atones the sins.**

When Malchut is connected with the Central Column,
it is the completion and joy of all.

29. לְבָתַר אָתֵי יְמִינָא לְחַבְּקָא, כְּדֵין חֶדְוָותָא שַׁרְיָיא בְּעָלְמָא, וְכָל אַנְפִּין נְהִירִין. לְבָתַר אִזְדַּוְּוגַת בְּגוּפָא, וּכְדֵין כֹּלָּא אִקְרֵי אֶחָד, בְּלָא פֵּרוּדָא, כְּדֵין הוּא שְׁלִימוּ דְּכֹלָּא, וְחֶדְוָותָא דְּכֹלָּא, וְאִתְאַחֲדוּ וַדַּאי, מַה דְּלָא אִשְׁתְּכַח הָכִי בִּשְׁאַר זִמְנֵי.

29. Afterwards, the Right Column **comes to embrace Her. Then joy resides in the world, and all countenances shine. Subsequently, She,** Malchut, **unites with the body,** the Central Column, **and then everything is considered one without separation,** as the Central Column includes the Right and the Left. **Then everything is perfect and everything is joyous, and they,** Zeir Anpin and Malchut, **certainly unite, which is not the case at other times.**

Immersing in water before Yom Kippur.

30. כְּגַוְונָא דְּהַאי, סִדּוּרָא דְּהָנֵי יוֹמִין, מֵרֹאשׁ הַשָּׁנָה עַד יוֹמָא בַּתְרָאָה דְּחַג. בְּרֹאשׁ הַשָּׁנָה, אִתְּעַר דְּרוֹעָא דִּשְׂמָאלָא, לְקַבְּלָא לָהּ לְמַטְרוֹנִיתָא, וּכְדֵין כָּל עָלְמָא בִּדְחִילוּ בְּדִינָא, וּבָעֵי הַהוּא זִמְנָא בִּתְיוּבְתָּא שְׁלִים, לְאִשְׁתַּכְּחָא עָלְמָא קַמֵּי קוּדְשָׁא בְּרִיךְ הוּא. לְבָתַר אֲתִיאַת מַטְרוֹנִיתָא, וּבַעְיָין בְּנֵי הֵיכָלָא בְּתִשְׁעָה לְיַרְחָא, לְמֶעְבַּד חֶדְוָותָא, וּלְמִטְבַּל בְּנַהֲרָא, לְדַכְאָה גַּרְמַיְיהוּ בְּזִוּוּגָא

דְּמַטְרוֹנִיתָא, בְּיוֹמָא אַחֲרָא, הוּא זִוּוּגָא דִּילָהּ לְשַׁוָּאָה שְׂמָאלָא תְּחוֹת רֵישָׁהָא, כְּמָה דְּאַתְּ אָמַר שְׂמֹאלוֹ תַּחַת לְרֹאשִׁי.

30. Likewise is the order of these days from Rosh Hashanah until the last day of Sukkot. On Rosh Hashanah, the Left arm is awakened, namely the Left Column of Zeir Anpin**, to welcome the Queen. The whole world is then in fear of Judgment, and the whole world has to be in complete repentance before the Holy One, blessed be He. Afterwards, the Queen comes on the ninth of the month, and the members of the Palace,** the children of Israel, **need to make merry and immerse themselves in the river to purify themselves** to be worthy of **the union of the Queen** with Zeir Anpin **on the other day,** namely the tenth of the month, Yom Kippur. **For her union is** accomplished **by** Zeir Anpin **placing his Left under her head, as you say, "His left hand is under my head...." (Song of Songs 2:6)**

The Light of Chochmah is revealed on Yom Kippur.

31. וּכְדֵין יִשְׂרָאֵל בְּתַעֲנִיתָא עַל חוֹבַיְיהוּ, וּמִכַּפְּרָא לְהוּ. דְּהָא אִימָּא עִלָּאָה אַנְהִירַת אַנְפָּהָא לְמַטְרוֹנִיתָא בְּזִוּוּגָהָא, וּמִתְכַּפְּרִין כָּל בְּנֵי הֵיכָלָא. כֵּיוָן דִּשְׂמָאלָא מְקַבְּלָה לָהּ בְּהַאי יוֹמָא, דְּרֵישָׁא דְּמַטְרוֹנִיתָא שַׁרְיָיא עַל שְׂמָאלָא.

31. Then Israel fast for their sins and are forgiven. For Supernal Ima, Binah, **shines Her face on Malchut in the union,** for on Yom Kippur Malchut rises and clothes Binah, **and makes atonement for all of the members of the Palace,** Israel, **since the Left** of Zeir Anpin **welcomes her on this day, as the head of Malchut rests on the Left.**

Explanation: Then the Illumination of Chochmah is revealed from the Left of Zeir Anpin, which draws from the Left of Binah, as the Illumination of Chochmah atones sins, as explained earlier (Zohar, Vayera 381-387).

Wherever the Right resides, there must be joy all around.

32. בְּיוֹמָא קַדְמָאָה דְּחַג, יִתְעַר יְמִינָא לְקַבְּלָהּ, בְּגִין לְחַבְּקָהּ וּכְדֵין כָּל חֶדְוָוא וְכָל אַנְפִּין נְהִירִין, וְחֶדְוָותָא דְּמַיִם צְלִילָן, לְנַסְּכָא עַל מַדְבְּחָא. וּבָעְיָין בְּנֵי נָשָׁא לְמֶחֱדֵי בְּכָל זִינִין דְּחֶדְוָה, דְּהָא יְמִינָא גָּרִים. בְּכָל אֲתַר דְּשָׁארֵי יְמִינָא, חֶדְוָותָא אִצְטְרִיךְ בְּכֹלָּא, כְּדֵין חֶדְוָותָא הִיא לְאִשְׁתַּעְשְׁעָא.

32. On the first day of Sukkot, the Right Column of Zeir Anpin **begins to move toward** Malchut **to embrace Her** in the secret of the verse: "...and his right hand embraces me." (Song of Songs 2:6) **Then everyone rejoices and all countenances shine. There is joy in pouring pure water on the altar. People should be happy by rejoicing in many different ways, since the Right causes this. Wherever the Right side,** Chasadim **resides, there has to be joy everywhere. Then there is joy with which to be happy.**

On Simchat Torah the Creator is exclusively with Israel.

33. לְבָתַר בְּיוֹמָא תְּמִינָאָה, חֶדְוָותָא דְּאוֹרַיְיתָא הוּא, דְּהָא כְּדֵין זִוּוּגָא דְּגוּפָא, הוּא זִוּוּגָא דְּכֹלָּא, לְמֶהֱוֵי כֹּלָּא חַד, וְדָא הוּא שְׁלִימוּ דְּכֹלָּא, וְדָא יוֹמָא דְּיִשְׂרָאֵל אִיהוּ וַדַּאי, וְעַדְבָא דִּילְהוֹן בִּלְחוֹדַיְיהוּ, דְּלֵית בֵּיהּ חוּלָקָא לְאַחֲרָא. זַכָּאִין אִינּוּן יִשְׂרָאֵל בְּעָלְמָא דֵּין, וּבְעָלְמָא דְּאָתֵי, עֲלַיְיהוּ כְּתִיב כִּי עַם קָדוֹשׁ אַתָּה לַיְיָ' אֱלֹהֶיךָ וְגוֹ'.

33. Later, on the day of Shmini Atzeret, is the joy of the Torah, as then the unification of the body, namely of the Central Column called "body" **takes place. This is the union of all,** for it includes both the unification of the Left of Rosh Hashanah and Yom Kippur, as well as the unification of the Right of the holiday of Sukkot, since the Central Column includes Right and Left **to make everything as one. This is the completion of everything. This surely is the day of Israel and their lot alone, as it has no portion for any other,** unlike the festival of Sukkot when seventy bulls are sacrificed for the seventy nations, because the nations have no part in Shmini Atzeret. **Happy are Israel in this world and in the World to Come. About them it is written: "Because you are a holy people for the Lord your God...." (Deuteronomy 14:2)** (See Zohar, Tzav 116)

Pinchas

128. Rosh Hashanah

A Synopsis

Rav Shimon uses the story of Isaac and Jacob and Esau to illustrate the meaning of the two Days of Judgment and the need for the burnt offering.

Satan is fueled by the Upper Three of the Left.

881. וּבַחֹדֶשׁ הַשְּׁבִיעִי, כְּמָה דְּאִתְּמַר, יוֹמָא דר"ה, דִּינָא דְּכָל עָלְמָא, דִּינָא תַּקִּיפָא, וְדִינָא רַפְיָא. וַעֲשִׂיתֶם עוֹלָה, וְהִקְרַבְתֶּם מִבָּעֵי לֵיהּ, כִּשְׁאָר כָּל יוֹמִין, מַאי וַעֲשִׂיתֶם. אֶלָּא בְּיוֹמָא דָּא, וַעֲשֵׂה לִי מַטְעַמִּים כְּתִיב. כַּמָּה מַטְעַמִּים וְתַבְשִׁילִים עָבְדוּ יִשְׂרָאֵל בְּהָנֵי יוֹמֵי, בְּעוֹד דִּמְקַטְרְגָא אָזִיל לְפַשְׁפְּשָׁא בְּחוֹבִין דְּעָלְמָא. וע"ד לָא כְּתִיב וְהִקְרַבְתֶּם, אֶלָּא וַעֲשִׂיתֶם עוֹלָה. וְלָא אִשֶּׁה עוֹלָה. וְכֵן בְּכָל שְׁאָר יוֹמִין, לָא כְּתִיב אִשֶּׁה, דְּלֵית לוֹן חוּלָקָא בְּכָל הָנֵי יוֹמֵי. כ"ש בְּהַאי יוֹמָא, דְּאִנּוּן עַבְדִּין מַטְעַמִּים וְתַבְשִׁילִים בְּלָא דַּעְתָּא דְּסִטְרָא אַחֲרָא, דְּהָא יִצְחָק מְשַׁדֵּר לֵיהּ לָצוּד צֵידָה דְּחוֹבִין דִּבְנֵי עָלְמָא, וּלְאַיְיתָאָה לְגַבֵּיהּ.

881. "And in the seventh month, on the first day of the month...." **(Numbers 29:1) This is as we have learned, that Rosh Hashanah is the Day of Judgment for the whole world: Harsh Judgment** on the first day **and Soft judgment** on the second day. He asks: "It is written, **'And you shall make a burnt offering** (*olah*)**..." (Numbers 29:2) whereas it should have been written: "And you shall offer a burnt offering" as on all the other days. What is the meaning of 'And you shall make...'?"** He answers, **"On this day** of Rosh Hashanah **it is written: 'And make me savory food...' (Genesis 27:4)** which is what Isaac said to Esau, who is the Accuser. **And during these days, Israel make many savory foods and dishes,** namely, with precepts and prayers, **while the Accuser goes to search for the sins of the world,** to make them into savory foods for the prosecution. **It is therefore not written:**

'And you shall offer a burnt offering' but 'And you shall make a burnt offering...' (Numbers 29:2) namely, make and prepare savory foods. **And** it is **not** written: **'...a burnt offering by fire (*isheh olah*)....' Also on all the other Festival Days, days in which there is no part** for the Other Side, **it is not written '...by fire (*isheh*)...'** as in Shavuot and Yom Kippur, **and certainly not on this Day when we make savory foods and dishes without the knowledge of the Other Side, for he had been sent by Isaac to hunt game, which is the iniquities of men, and to bring them to him."**

Explanation: In each of the sacrifices we give a portion to the Other Side. But on this day of Rosh Hashanah it is the opposite, as through the Blowing of the Shofar we confuse the mind of Satan. This means that through the Blowing of the Shofar the Upper Three of the Left, which is where the vitality of the Other Side comes from, get nullified. On Rosh Hashanah, the first condition of Malchut reigns, and it is the secret of what Isaac, the Left column, says to Esau "...and hunt me some game." (Genesis 27:3) He gave him permission to draw the Upper Three of the Left and awaken all the Judgments that come with it, which is the secret of "And Isaac was seized with very violent trembling...." (Genesis 27:33) These Judgments start being awakened on Rosh Hashanah. However in the midst of it, **"on the way, Israel take advice from Rivkah... and prepare a Shofar and sound it"** as it says in the next verse [882]. This means that through the Blowing of the Shofar the Upper Three of the Left get diminished, which are all the Mochin of the Other Side, and with this the Other Side gets confused. It is found that not only does [the Other Side] not have a portion in the Sacrifices of Rosh Hashanah, as it does in the other sacrifices but it also loses all its grasp and its mind gets confused. (See Zohar, Emor 187-224)

This is: **"and certainly not on this Day when we make savory foods and dishes without the knowledge of the Other Side,"** not only do we not give him energy from the sacrifices but we also confuse his mind,

"for he had been sent by Isaac to hunt game that is the iniquities…" because it is the first condition of Malchut when Isaac, the Left Column, sits on the Throne of Judgment and wishes for his reign to prevail. He sent Esau to hunt game, meaning to draw the Upper Three of the Left, and since he gave him permission, Judgments are immediately awakened, which judge the world unfavorably. And as it says in the next verse [882]: **"And while he is yet on the way,"** namely before [Esau] has a chance to reveal the Judgments of the Upper Three of the Left, **"[Israel] prepare a Shofar and sound it in order to awaken Mercy"** because through the Blowing of the Shofar, the Upper Three of the Left get nullified and the Other Side can no longer draw them, and its mind is confused. In their place, the savory dishes of Jacob are drawn, which are Mercy.

Israel do the work of Rosh Hashanah, and then get blessed by Isaac.

882. וּבְעוֹד דְּאִיהוּ אָזִיל, יִשְׂרָאֵל נַטְלֵי עֵיטָא בְּרִבְקָה, וְעַבְדִין כָּל אִינּוּן פּוּלְחָנִין, כָּל אִינּוּן צְלוֹתִין, מְזַמְּנֵי שׁוֹפָר וְתַקְעִין לֵיהּ, בְּגִין לְאַתְעָרָא רַחֲמֵי. וְהָא אוֹקִימְנָא, וַיָּבֵא לוֹ יַיִן וַיֵּשְׁתְּ, דְּאָתֵי מֵרָחוֹק, מִגּוֹ אֲתָר דְּחַמְרָא עַתִּיקָא, וְשָׁתֵי. וְאַטְעִים לֵיהּ, וְחַדֵי. וְאַחַר כָּךְ מְבָרֵךְ לֵיהּ בְּכַמָּה בִּרְכָאן, וְאַעְבַּר עַל חוֹבוֹי. מַה כְּתִיב, וַיְהִי אַךְ יָצוֹא יָצָא יַעֲקֹב וְעֵשָׂו אָחִיו בָּא מִצֵּידוֹ, טָעִין מִכַּמָּה טוּעֲנֵי כְּמָה דְּאִתְּמַר, וְהָא אוֹקִימְנָא מִלָּה.

882. And while he is yet on the way, Israel takes advice from Rivkah and does all these rituals and all these prayers, and prepares a Shofar and sounds it in order to awaken Mercy. And we have already learned: "…and he brought him wine, and he drank" (Genesis 27:25) for he came from afar, from Binah, **from that place where the wine is old,** which is the secret of the Illumination of Chochmah of the Six Corners [Sefirot] of the Left, after the nullification of the Upper Three of the Left, which is called "old wine." **And he drank, found it delicious, and rejoiced. And after that** Isaac, who is the Left Column, **blessed him with a number of blessings and removed his iniquities**, as the Illumination of Chochmah atones iniquities. **It is then written: "Jacob**

had just left the presence of Isaac his father, when Esau his brother came back from his hunting" (Genesis 27:30) namely, he was **carrying with him a number of burdens** of iniquities, **as has been stated, and we have already learned these matters.** (See Zohar, Emor 218-219)

With one goat we bribe the Satan to atone for nullifying his Upper Three of the Left.

883. ובג"כ אִיהוּ יוֹמָא דְּיַבָּבָא, וְקָרְבְּנָא אִיהוּ עוֹלָה. אַיִל אֶחָד, כְּמָה דְּאִתְּמַר, בְּגִין אֵילוֹ דְּיִצְחָק. וּשְׂעִיר עִזִּים אֶחָד לְחַטָּאת, שׂוֹחַד לְסַמָּאֵל לְכַפָּרָה אַנְפּוֹי, בְּהַהוּא בְּכִיָּה דְּאִיהוּ בָּכֵי בְּהַאי יוֹמָא, כֵּיוָן דְּחָמֵי דְּלָא אִתְעֲבִיד רְעוּתֵיהּ, וְהָא לְמַגָּנָא צָד צֵידָה. כְּמָה דְּאִתְּמַר. כְּגַוְונָא דָּא יוֹמָא דְּכִפּוּרֵי, וְהָא כְּתִיב בפ' אֱמוֹר.

883. And this is why it is a "...day of Teru'ah" (Numbers 29:1), and the sacrifice is a burnt offering (*olah*). "...One ram..." (Ibid. 2) is, as we have learned, because of the ram of Isaac. The "...one hairy goat for a sin offering..." (Ibid. 5) is a bribe to Sama"el, as only from this sacrifice does he get some energy from the aspect of the Six Corners of Chochmah, **to atone for his face for having wept on that day when he realized that his will had not been done and he had gone hunting for nothing**, as his Upper Three of the Left got nullified, which is his entire strength, and the diminishment of the Upper Three is called "weeping," **as we have learned. This is similar on Yom Kippur, as written in the [Zohar] portion of Emor [227-257].**

Beresheet

49. "Sin crouches at the door"

A Synopsis

A verse in the Torah states that negativity and evil forces hover by doorways, openings, and beginnings of all kinds. This idea is related to the secret and power of a seed. If one plants a defective apple seed, it will yield a defective apple tree. Doorways and beginnings represent the seed level. The door to the home is the seed of the entire house. Negative forces attack at the seed level so as to influence all the future stages and developments. They cling to all entranceways to infect the seed with negativity. The Mezuzah, or doorpost ornament, not only cancels this negative force, but also transforms negative energy into positive energy. The Mezuzah contains a piece of parchment bearing the Hebrew letters Shin, Dalet, and Yud שדי. This is a powerful Name of God that brings us protection.

These passages bring protection to all the starts or beginnings in our lives, including marriage, business ventures, or any other area of activity.

On Rosh Hashanah, the barren women are attended to.

461. תָּא וַחֲזֵי, בְּרֹאשׁ הַשָּׁנָה אִתְיְלִיד אָדָם, בְּרֹאשׁ הַשָּׁנָה, וַדַּאי רָזָא לְעֵילָּא וְתַתָּא ר״ה לְעֵילָּא, ר״ה לְתַתָּא. בְּרֹאשׁ הַשָּׁנָה עֲקָרוֹת נִפְקָדוֹת, מְנָלָן דִּבְרֹאשׁ הַשָּׁנָה הֲוָה, דִּכְתִּיב וַה׳ פָּקַד אֶת שָׂרָה, וַה׳ דַּיְיקָא, דָּא רֹאשׁ הַשָּׁנָה, וּבְגִין דְּנָפִיק אָדָם מֵרֹאשׁ הַשָּׁנָה נָפִיק בְּדִינָא, וְעָלְמָא קַיְּימָא בְּדִינָא, וּבְגִינֵי כָּךְ לַפֶּתַח וַדַּאי. חַטָּאת רוֹבֵץ בְּגִין לְאִתְפָּרְעָא מִינָּךְ, וְאֵלֶיךָ תְּשׁוּקָתוֹ, עַד דְּתִשְׁתֵּיצֵי.

461. Come and behold: on Rosh Hashanah Adam was born. Rosh Hashanah is the secret of the upper and lower, referring to the Male and Female principles, who are called the supernal man, and to the lower man. **There is Rosh Hashanah Above,** which is Zeir Anpin and his

Female principle when they are in a state of judgment, **and there is a Rosh Hashanah Below,** in the frame of time, which is the Sixth Day of Creation, the day when lower man was created. This teaches us that man was created by the secret of Judgment, for he was created on lower Rosh Hashanah. This is connected to the aspect of Above, upper Rosh Hashanah, which is Zeir Anpin and his Female principle in a state of Judgment. **On Rosh Hashanah, the barren women are attended to. How do we know this happens on Rosh Hashanah? Because it is written: "And the Lord attended to Sarah...." (Genesis 21:1) The reference to the term "And the Lord (VaHashem; ויהוה)...")Ibid) is precise** to indicate that **it was on Rosh Hashanah** that she was attended to. Whenever the scripture uses the term "And the Lord," it alludes to Zeir Anpin and his Courthouse, which is the upper Rosh Hashanah. **Because Adam was born on Rosh Hashanah, he was born under the influence of Judgment that then prevailed in the world. Thus, it is precisely so that "...sin crouches at the door..." (Genesis 4:7)** alluding to the Angel of Death, **to exact payment from you. And the verse: "...and to you is its desire..." (Ibid)** means that the Angel of Death desires to punish you **until he destroys you.**

Bo

2. "And it was on that day... and the Adversary came also among them"

A Synopsis

Rabbi Elazar begins by talking about Rosh Hashanah, Judgment Day. He says there are messengers who are appointed by God to watch over the actions of people, and at Judgment Day these messengers accuse those whose actions were improper. When Israel sin, they weaken God, but when they perform good actions they give might and power to Him. Rabbi Elazar speaks about "The Adversary also came among them," and recounts the conversation between God and Satan, wherein God distracts Satan from his accusation of Israel, by asking him if he has considered His servant Job. Satan always requests justice from God. We read that Job was judged as he had judged Israel, since he had been one of Pharaoh's advisors. The Satan was given permission to afflict Job's bones and flesh, but not to kill him. We are told that God does not want to destroy the whole world on the word of the Accuser, since the Accuser's desire is always to destroy.

The discussion turns to "The End of all Flesh," which is the Satan, and "the end of days" that is in Holiness. On Rosh Hashanah those who come before God with repentance deserve to be written on the side of Life; those who come with evil actions are written on the Other Side, which is Death. We are told then of the balance, where the world is half Life and half Death, and the actions of one Righteous man or one wicked person can tip the balance so that all the world is written to Life or Death.

A person should not be set apart by himself because he can be noticed and accused from above. Job, who was set apart, and who was tested severely, did not even then join the Other Side. He should, however, have given a part of his sacrifice to the Other Side because then the Other Side would have removed himself from the Temple. The conclusion of this section is that God judged Job, giving him first good and then bad and then good again; thus it is proper for a person to know good and bad, and to return himself to good.

Vayehi hayom always refers to Rosh Hashanah.

5. רִבִּי אֶלְעָזָר פָּתַח, וַיְהִי הַיּוֹם וַיָּבֹאוּ בְּנֵי הָאֱלֹהִים לְהִתְיַצֵּב עַל יְיָ' וַיָּבֹא גַם הַשָּׂטָן בְּתוֹכָם. וַיְהִי הַיּוֹם: דָּא רֹאשׁ הַשָּׁנָה, דְּקוּדְשָׁא בְּרִיךְ הוּא קָאִים לְמֵידָן עָלְמָא. כְּגַוְונָא דָא, וַיְהִי הַיּוֹם וַיָּבֹא שָׁמָּה. הַהוּא יוֹמָא יוֹם טוֹב דְּרֹאשׁ הַשָּׁנָה הֲוָה.

5. Rav Elazar opened the discussion, saying: "'And it was on that day (vayehi hayom) when the sons of God (Elohim) came to stand by the Lord, and the Adversary came also among them.' (Job 1:6) 'Now there was a day...' (Ibid.) refers to Rosh Hashanah, the day that the Holy One, blessed be He, rises to judge the world. Similarly, 'And the day came (vayehi hayom) and he went there.' (II Kings 4:11) That day was the holiday of Rosh Hashanah.

The actions of Israel are more watched than any other nation.

6. וַיָּבֹאוּ בְּנֵי הָאֱלֹהִים, אִלֵּין רַבְרְבִין מְמַנָּן שְׁלִיחָן בְּעָלְמָא, לְאַשְׁגָּחָא בְּעוֹבָדִין דִּבְנֵי נָשָׁא. לְהִתְיַצֵּב עַל ה': כְּמָה דְּאַתְּ אָמֵר, וְכָל צְבָא הַשָּׁמַיִם עוֹמְדִים עָלָיו מִימִינוֹ וּמִשְּׂמֹאלוֹ. אֲבָל לְהִתְיַצֵּב עַל ה' בְּהַאי קְרָא אַשְׁכַּחְנָא רְחִימוּתָא דְּקוּדְשָׁא בְּרִיךְ הוּא עֲלַיְיהוּ דְּיִשְׂרָאֵל. בְּגִין, דְּהָנֵי שְׁלִיחָן, דְּאִינּוּן מְמַנָּן לְאַשְׁגָּחָא עַל עוֹבָדִין דִּבְנֵי נָשָׁא, אַזְלִין וְשָׁאטִין וְנַטְלִין אִינּוּן עוֹבָדִין כֻּלְּהוּ, וּבְיוֹמָא דְּקָאֵי דִּינָא לְמֵיקָם, לְמֵידָן עָלְמָא, אִתְעֲבֵידוּ קַטֵּיגוֹרִין לְמֵיקָם עֲלַיְיהוּ דִּבְנֵי נָשָׁא. וְתָא חֲזֵי, מִכָּל עַמִּין דְּעָלְמָא, לָא קַיְימִין לְאַשְׁגָּחָא בְּעוֹבָדַיְיהוֹן, בַּר בְּיִשְׂרָאֵל בִּלְחוֹדַיְיהוּ, בְּגִין דְּאִלֵּין בְּנִין לְקוּדְשָׁא בְּרִיךְ הוּא.

6. "And the sons of God (Elohim) came...." (Job 1:6) These are the appointed ministers whose mission in the world is to observe the actions of people. "...to stand by the Lord..." (Ibid.) as is written: "...

and all the Hosts of Heaven standing by Him on His right hand and on His left" (I Kings 22:19). But in the passage, "...to stand by the Lord...." (Job 1:6) I have found the love of the Holy One, blessed be He, toward Israel. These messengers who are appointed to observe the actions of people wander around in the world **and take all these actions, and on the day that Judgment rises to judge the world, they become Accusers and stand to** denounce **mankind. Come and behold, of all the nations in the world,** the ministers **stand to watch over the activities of Israel only, because they are the children of the Holy One, blessed be He.**

Israel gives strength, so to speak, to the Creator through their good deeds.

7. וְכַד לָא אִשְׁתְּכָחוּ עוֹבָדִין דְּיִשְׂרָאֵל כַּדְקָא יָאוּת, כִּבְיָכוֹ"ל אִינּוּן מְמָנָן שְׁלִיחָן, כַּד בָּעָאן לְקַיְּימָא עַל אִינּוּן עוֹבָדִין דְּיִשְׂרָאֵל, עַל ה' וַדַּאי קַיְימִין, דְּהָא כַּד יִשְׂרָאֵל עַבְדִּין עוֹבָדִין דְּלָא כַּשְׁרָן, כִּבְיָכוֹ"ל מַתִּישִׁין חֵילָא דְּקוּדְשָׁא בְּרִיךְ הוּא. וְכַד עַבְדִּין עוֹבָדִין דְּכַשְׁרָן, יַהֲבִין תּוּקְפָּא וְחֵילָא לְקוּדְשָׁא בְּרִיךְ הוּא. וְעַל דָּא כְּתִיב, תְּנוּ עֹז לֵאלֹהִים. בְּמָה. בְּעוֹבָדִין דְּכַשְׁרָן. וְעַל דָּא, בְּהַהוּא יוֹמָא, כֻּלְּהוּ רַבְרְבָן מְמָנָן אִתְכְּנָשׁוּ עַל ה'. עַל ה' וַדַּאי, דְּהָא כֵּיוָן דְּעַל יִשְׂרָאֵל אִתְכְּנָשׁוּ, עָלֵיהּ אִתְכְּנָשׁוּ.

7. When the actions of the children of Israel are found to be improper, then when these appointed messengers want to stand against these actions of Israel, they stand against the Lord, so to speak. For when the children of Israel perform actions that are not good, they weaken, so to speak, the strength of the Holy One, blessed be He. When they perform good actions, they give might and power to the Holy One, blessed be He. Of this, it is written: "Give strength to God...." (Psalms 68:35) How is strength given? **By good actions. Therefore, on that day all the appointed ministers gathered against (lit. upon) the Lord. "Upon" the Lord most certainly, because since they gathered** to bring accusations **upon Israel,** it is like they **gathered against the Lord** to weaken His strength, so to speak.

Two sides are open on Rosh Hashanah: life and death.

21. ות"ח, וַיְהִי הַיּוֹם וַיָּבוֹאוּ בְּנֵי הָאֱלֹהִים לְהִתְיַצֵּב עַל יְיָ'. כְּמָה דְּאִתְּמַר. וְהַהוּא יוֹמָא, קַיְּימִין תְּרֵין סִטְרִין, לְקַבְּלָא בְּנֵי עָלְמָא. כָּל אִינּוּן דְּאַתְיָין קָמֵי קוּדְשָׁא בְּרִיךְ הוּא בִּתְיוּבְתָּא וּבְעוֹבָדִין טָבִין, אִינּוּן זַכָּאן לְמֶהֱוֵי כְּתִיבִין לְגַבֵּיהּ דְּהַהוּא סִטְרָא דְּאִיהוּ חַיִּים, וְאַפִּיק תּוֹצְאוֹת חַיִּים. וּמַאן דְּאִיהוּ מִסִּטְרֵיהּ, אִכְתִּיב לְחַיִּים. וְכָל אִינּוּן דְּאַתְיָין בְּעוֹבָדִין בִּישִׁין, אִינּוּן כְּתִיבִין לְהַהוּא סִטְרָא אַחֲרָא דְּאִיהוּ מוֹתָא, וְאִקְרֵי מָוֶת, וּבֵיהּ שַׁרְיָא מוֹתָא.

21. Come and behold, "And it was on that day when the sons of God (Elohim) came to stand by the Lord" (Job 1:6) as explained that it was on Rosh Hashanah. **For on that day, two sides are before the world. All those who come before the Holy One, blessed be He, with repentance and good deeds, merit to be written on that side, which is Life, which brings out the effects of life. And whoever is from its side is recorded for Life. All those who come with evil actions are written on the Other Side, which is Death. It is called "death," and in it death dwells,** to kill people.

One righteous or wicked individual can tip the scales.

22. וּבְהַהוּא יוֹמָא, קַיְּימִין אִלֵּין תְּרֵין סִטְרִין: חַיִּים, וּמָוֶת. אִית מַאן דְּאִכְתִּיב לְסִטְרָא דְּחַיִּים. וְאִית מַאן דְּאִכְתִּיב לְסִטְרָא דְּמָוֶת. וּלְזִמְנִין דְּעָלְמָא שַׁרְיָא בְּאֶמְצָעִיתָא, אִי קַיְּימָא חַד זַכָּאָה בְּעָלְמָא, דְּאַכְרַע עָלַיְיהוּ, כֻּלְּהוּ קַיְּימִין וְאִכְתִּיבוּ לְחַיִּים. וְאִי חַד חַיָּיבָא אַכְרַע עָלְמָא, כֻּלְּהוּ אִכְתִּיבוּ לְמִיתָה.

22. On that day these two sides exist, Life and Death. Some are written to the side of Life, and some are written to the side of Death. Sometimes the world is in the middle, meaning half worthy and half guilty. **If there is one righteous man to tip the balance in the world, they all stand and are written to Life, but if one wicked person ever balances the world, they are all written to Death.**

At the time of Job, the world was in the middle.

23. וְהַהוּא זִמְנָא, עָלְמָא הֲוָה קַיְּים בְּאֶמְצָעִיתָא, וְהַהוּא מְקַטְרְגָא בָּעָא לְאַסְטָאָה. מִיָּד מַה כְּתִיב, הֲשַׂמְתָּ לִבְּךָ עַל עַבְדִּי אִיּוֹב כִּי אֵין כָּמוֹהוּ בָּאָרֶץ וְגוֹ'. כֵּיוָן דְּאִשְׁתְּמוֹדַע אִיהוּ בִּלְחוֹדוֹי, מִיַּד אַתְקִיף בֵּיהּ מְקַטְרְגָא. וע"ד תָּנֵינָן, דְּלָא אִצְטְרִיךְ לֵיהּ לְבַר נָשׁ לְאִתְפָּרְשָׁא מִכְּלָלָא דְּסַגִּיאִין, בְּגִין דְּלָא יִתְרְשִׁים אִיהוּ בִּלְחוֹדוֹי, וְלָא יְקַטְרְגוּן עָלֵיהּ לְעֵילָּא.

23. At that particular time the world was in the middle, meaning half guilty and half worthy, **and the Prosecutor wanted to accuse** and to tip the world to the scale of guilt. **Immediately, it is written: "Have you considered my servant Job, that there is none like him on earth..." (Job 1:8). As soon as he was set apart, the Accuser immediately attacked him. Therefore, we learn that a person should not remove himself from the community so that he will not be noted apart, and he will not be accused from above.**

Beshalach

1. "And Elisha passed to Shunem"

A Synopsis

Rav Shimon opens by talking about Habakkuk but then discusses the entire story recounted in II Kings about Elisha and the Shunamite woman who had fed him bread when he passed by and prepared for him a "small upper chamber...with walls...a bed and table and chair and a lamp." We are told that on the day Elisha came to the Shunamite and promised her that she would bear a son it was Rosh Hashanah, when the barren women of the world were remembered. We are told that one must not be alone on the Day of Judgment because one might be noticed on his own and more subject to judgment, and the Mercies of God are always present over the whole people together.

Rav Shimon says that when Elisha asked the woman if she would be spoken for to the king, he was offering to beseech the Supernal King on her behalf, but she did not want to separate from her people. We hear that the reason the child born to her later died was because he was from the Female side, since he was given to her and not her husband. Elisha was not told by the Holy One, blessed be He that the boy would die so that he would not try to save him through prayer. His servant Gehazi was not worthy of the miracle being performed through him, so the Shunamite woman insisted that Elisha come with her. When Elisha lay upon the boy to bring him back to life he reconnected him to a different high place, the place where life is found.

Rav Shimon returns now to Habakkuk, with whom this passage began, and says that Habakkuk means "two embraces"; one from his mother and one from Elisha, one from the Female area and one from the Male. He tells us that there were various types of praises available to the prophets to cause the Spirit of Prophecy to dwell upon them, and that all prophets need pleasantness in order to draw that Spirit upon themselves. Only for Moses was this unnecessary. Rabbi Shimon ends by saying that the children of Israel only tasted death when they departed from Egypt but that God healed them.

Elisha the Prophet was hosted by the Shunamite woman on Rosh Hashanah.

‫9. וַיְהִי הַיּוֹם וַיָּבוֹא שָׁמָּה. וַיְהִי הַיּוֹם, מַאן הוּא יוֹמָא דָּא. אֶלָּא כְּמָה דְּאוּקְמוּהָ.‬
‫ות״ח. הַהוּא יוֹמָא, יוֹמָא טָבָא דְּרֹאשׁ הַשָּׁנָה הֲוָה, דְּאִתְפַּקְדוּ בֵּיהּ עֲקָרוֹת‬
‫דְּעָלְמָא, וְאִתְפַּקְּדָן בֵּיהּ בְּנֵי עָלְמָא. קָרָא לַשּׁוּנַמִּית וְאָמַר, הִנֵּה חָרַדְתְּ אֵלֵינוּ‬
‫אֵת כָּל הַחֲרָדָה הַזֹּאת. בְּגִינֵי כַּךְ, אִצְטְרִיכְנָא לְעַיְּינָא יוֹמָא דָּא בְּדִינֵי דְּעָלְמָא,‬
‫דְּקוּדְשָׁא בְּרִיךְ הוּא דָּאִין בְּיוֹמָא דָּא לְעָלְמָא, וּבְגִין דְּאִתְפָּרַשְׁנָא בִּלְחוֹד בַּאֲתַר‬
‫דָּא, אִצְטְרִיכְנָא לְאִסְתַּכְּלָא בְּרִגְזוּ דְּעָלְמָא.‬

9. **"And the day came and he went there...."** (II Kings 4:11) He asks: **"And the day came."** What day was it? He answers: **It is as we explained. Come and behold, that day was the holiday of Rosh Hashanah when the barren women of the world and the inhabitants of the world were remembered. He called the Shunamite and said, "Behold, you have been careful to take all this trouble for us...."** (Ibid. 13) **Therefore, I must study the Judgments of the world today, because today the Holy One, blessed be He, judges the world, and because I separated myself to be alone in this place,** in the enclosed Upper Chamber that was prepared for me, **I must look into the judgments of the world.** Namely, as it says later on that whoever separates to be alone on the Day of Judgment is snared first, though he may be guiltless.

Elisha offered to give a good word to the King of the World on her behalf.

‫10. וּמֶה לַעֲשׂוֹת לָךְ הֲיֵשׁ לְדַבֶּר לָךְ אֶל הַמֶּלֶךְ אוֹ אֶל שַׂר הַצָּבָא. וְכִי מִלָּה‬
‫דָּא לְמָה אִצְטְרִיכָא לְגַבֵּי אִתְּתָא, דְּלָא נַפְקַת וְלָא אַזְלַת וְלָא עָאלַת בְּהֵיכְלָא‬
‫דְּמַלְכָּא. אֶלָּא, יוֹמָא דָּא הֲוָה גָּרִים, דְּכָל בְּנֵי עָלְמָא יַתְבִין בְּדִינָא, וּבְהַהוּא‬

יוֹמָא אִקְרֵי קוּדְשָׁא בְּרִיךְ הוּא מֶלֶךְ. הַמֶּלֶךְ הַמִּשְׁפָּט. אָמַר לָהּ, אִי אַתְּ אִצְטְרִיךְ לָךְ לְגַבֵּי מַלְכָּא עִלָּאָה, עַל עוֹבָדִין דִּי בִּידָךְ.

10. "What can be done for you? Should we speak to the king on your behalf, or to the general of the army?" (II Kings 4:13) He asks: **"Is this necessary for a woman who never goes out nor goes to the king's palace?"** He answers: **"Rather, this day caused all the inhabitants of the world to await Judgment, and on that day the Holy One, blessed be He, is called a King, the King of Judgment. He said to her, 'If you need the Supernal King** to forgive you **for your actions,** I will speak and beseech on your behalf.'

When Judgment prevails, one should not isolate or single themselves out.

11. וַתֹּאמֶר בְּתוֹךְ עַמִּי אָנֹכִי יֹשָׁבֶת. מַאי קָאַמְרַת. אֶלָּא בְּשַׁעֲתָא דְּדִינָא תַּלְיָא בְּעָלְמָא, לָא יִתְפְּרַשׁ בַּר נָשׁ בִּלְחוֹדוֹי, וְלָא יִתְרְשִׁים לְעֵילָּא, וְלָא יִשְׁתְּמוֹדְעוּן בֵּיהּ בִּלְחוֹדוֹי, דְּהָא בְּזִמְנָא דְּדִינָא תַּלְיָא בְּעָלְמָא, אִינּוּן דְּאִשְׁתְּמוֹדְעוּן וּרְשִׁימִין בִּלְחוֹדַיְיהוּ, אע"ג דְּזַכָּאִין אִינּוּן, אִינּוּן אִתְפְּסָן בְּקַדְמֵיתָא. וְעַל דָּא, לָא לִבְעֵי לֵיהּ לְאִינִישׁ, לְאִתְפָּרְשָׁא מִבֵּין עַמָּא לְעָלַם, דִּבְכָל זִמְנָא רַחֲמֵי דְּקוּדְשָׁא בְּרִיךְ הוּא עַל עַמָּא כֻּלְּהוּ כְּחַד. וּבְגִינֵי כַּךְ אָמְרָה, בְּתוֹךְ עַמִּי אָנֹכִי יֹשָׁבֶת, וְלָא בְּעֵינָא לְאִתְפָּרְשָׁא מִנַּיְיהוּ, כְּמָה דַּעֲבַדְנָא עַד יוֹמָא דֵּין.

11. "And she answered, 'I dwell among my people.' (II Kings 4:11)" He asks: **"What does she mean?"** He answers: **"At the time when Judgment prevails over the world, a person should not separate himself from the general community and be apart. Then he will not be singled out Above, and will not be noticed on his own. For at the time when Judgment prevails over the world, those who were distinctly known and recorded apart are caught first, even though they may be righteous. Therefore, a person should never separate to be apart from the people, for the Mercies of the Holy One, blessed be He, are always present over the whole people together. Therefore,**

she said, 'I dwell among my people' (Ibid.) and I do not want to be separate from them, as I have done until this day.

The Shunamite bore a child that later died since he was from the side of the Female.

12. וַיֹּאמֶר גֵּחֲזִי אֲבָל בֵּן אֵין לָהּ וְגוֹ'. אָמַר לָהּ אֱלִישָׁע. הָא וַדַּאי שַׁעֲתָא קַיְּימָא, דְּהָא יוֹמָא גָּרִים. וַיֹּאמֶר לַמּוֹעֵד הַזֶּה כָּעֵת חַיָּה אַתְּ חוֹבֶקֶת בֵּן. וַתַּהַר הָאִשָּׁה וַתֵּלֶד בֵּן לַמּוֹעֵד הַזֶּה כָּעֵת חַיָּה אֲשֶׁר דִּבֶּר אֵלֶיהָ אֱלִישָׁע. לַמּוֹעֵד וַדַּאי. לְבָתַר מִית. מַאי טַעֲמָא מִית. אֶלָּא בְּגִין דְּאִתְיְהִיב לָהּ, וְלָא לְבַעְלָהּ. וּמֵאֲתַר דְּנוּקְבָא אִתְקְשַׁר, וּמַאן דְּאִתְקְשַׁר בְּנוּקְבָא, מוֹתָא אִזְדַּמְּנַת קַמֵּיהּ. מְנָא לָן דִּלָהּ אִתְיְהִיב, דִּכְתִּיב אַתְּ חוֹבֶקֶת בֵּן.

12. "And Gehazi answered, 'Verily she has no child....' (II King 4:14) Elisha said to her, 'Certainly, the time is favorable for you to redeem yourself with a son, **because the day induces it,'** for on Rosh Hashanah, barren women are remembered. **'And he said, "About this time, in the coming year, you shall embrace a son"... And the woman conceived and bore a son in the season of which Elisha had spoken to her.' (Ibid. 16-17) 'About this time' is exact, and afterwards he died."** He asks: **"What is the reason that he died?"** He answers: **"Because the child was given to her and not to her husband, and he was bound to the Female place. Death awaits one who is bound to the Female."** He asks: **"Whence do we know that he was given to her?"** He answers: **"Because it is written, '...and you shall embrace a son.' (Ibid. 16)"**

Terumah

29. Nefesh, Ruach, Neshamah

A Synopsis

This section explains the three levels of the soul of man and the corresponding three levels in the Supernal Realm. These levels are Nefesh, Ruach, and Neshamah. The Nefesh is present in the grave until the body decays into dust. The Ruach is the one that enters the terrestrial Garden of Eden and is shaped there in the form of the body belonging to this world. Neshamah ascends immediately to her place, the place from whence she emerged, Malchut. We learn that until the Neshamah ascends to and becomes attached to the Throne, the Ruach does not become crowned in the Garden of Eden of the Earth and the Nefesh does not settle in its place. As soon as the Neshamah ascends, they all can rest. When people pray at the cemetery, the Nefesh awakens, then floats to awaken Ruach, who ascends and awakens the Neshamah. Then the Holy One has mercy on the world. We read how the three are bonded as one: the Nefesh is the throne for the Ruach, while Neshamah takes out the Ruach, gives it power, dominates it and illuminates it with the light of life.

After death, at the time that the Neshamah becomes adorned above in the Holy Crown, the Ruach is standing in the supernal Light during Shabbat, New Moons and Festivals. Then when the Ruach descends from the supernal Light to dwell in the Garden of Eden, the Nefesh stands on the grave and becomes attired in the form that the body had originally, and praises the Holy One. If people gave themselves permission they could see these forms on the graves thanking and praising the Holy One. During the day of Rosh Hashanah when the world is being judged and the Throne of Judgment stands by the supernal King to judge the world, every single Nefesh hovers and beseeches Mercy for the living. Sometimes they notify the living of their verdicts in a vision at night, and then the living repent.

The text goes on to tell how Yedomi"am is the appointed angel who oversees the taking of souls. Then we read of the correspondence between these three levels of soul in man and the three levels in the four worlds of Asiyah, Yetzirah, Briyah and Atzilut. The moon is the Nefesh of Atzilut, and it illuminates all the chariots and camps of the three lower worlds even as the Nefesh of man illuminates the limbs and bones of the body. The text says, Happy are the righteous to merit three rests in the World to Come.

The Relevance of this Passage

This profound portion raises our consciousness to the highest level of our souls (Neshamah). The ascension assures a peaceful and merciful transition into the World to Come. Our meditation awakens the force of mercy, causing supernal compassion to spill down upon creation. Transformation of our nature and positive change in the world is achieved through a path of Mercy as opposed to one of torment.

All Judgments are hereby rescinded upon the merit of the righteous throughout history.

On Rosh Hashanah, our souls investigate our verdict
and inform us so we can repent.

295. בְּיוֹמָא דְּר"ה, דְּעָלְמָא אִתְדָּן, וְכָרְסְיָא דְּדִינָא קַיְּימָא, לְגַבֵּי מַלְכָּא עִלָּאָה, לְמֵידָן עָלְמָא. כָּל נֶפֶשׁ וְנֶפֶשׁ מְשַׁטְטָן, וּבָעָאן רַחֲמֵי עַל חַיֵּי. בְּלֵילְיָא דְּנָפְקָא יוֹמָא דְּדִינָא, אַזְלִין וְקָא מְשַׁטְטִין לְמִשְׁמַע וּלְמִנְדַּע מַאן הוּא דִּינָא דְּאִתְדָּן עַל עָלְמָא, וּלְזִמְנִין דְּקָא מוֹדִיעִין בְּחֶזְוָוא לְחַיָּיא, כד"א בַּחֲלוֹם חֶזְיוֹן לַיְלָה בִּנְפוֹל תַּרְדֵּמָה עַל אֲנָשִׁים וְגוֹ', אָז יִגְלֶה אֹזֶן אֲנָשִׁים וּבְמוֹסָרָם יַחְתּוֹם. מַאי מוֹסָרָם. דָּא נֶפֶשׁ, דְּאִיהִי קַיְּימָא וְחָתִים לִבְנֵי נָשָׁא מִלִּין, לְקַבְּלָא מוּסָר.

295. During the day of Rosh Hashanah, when the world is judged and the Throne of Judgment stands by the supernal King to judge

the world, every single Nefesh hovers and beseeches Mercy for the living people. **During the night of the end of the Day of Judgment, they go and hover to hear and know the verdict that was decided for the world. Sometimes they notify the living in a vision, as it is written: "In a dream, in a night vision when a deep sleep falls upon men... then He opens the ears of man, and with discipline seals their instruction." (Job 33:15-16)** He asks, **"What is 'with discipline'?"** He answers, **"This is the Nefesh who stands and establishes things for people so that they should accept discipline,"** meaning that it notifies them of their verdict in a vision at night and then they repent.

Tetzaveh

9. The bread of the first fruits

A Synopsis

We learn that two types of bread were eaten by Israel: when they left Egypt they ate matzah, the bread from Malchut; when they were in the wilderness they ate manna, the bread from heaven, Zeir Anpin. The question is asked, why, now that Israel merited the higher bread, was leavened bread not abolished entirely? Why was the offering of the first fruits called leavened bread? Rav Shimon explains that as soon as Israel had eaten Matzah, leavened bread could no longer harm them. The Chametz is burned on the altar and can have no power over Israel. When God gave the Torah to Israel He had them taste the Supernal Bread, Manna, through which they knew and observed the teachings of the Torah. After these explanations Rav Shimon and his companions meet an old man holding a boy by the hand.

Rav Shimon and the friends meet an old man holding a young boy.

79. ר' שִׁמְעוֹן וְרִבִּי אֶלְעָזָר בְּרֵיהּ, הֲווֹ אַזְלֵי בְּאָרְחָא, וַהֲווֹ אַזְלִין עִמְּהוֹן, רִבִּי אַבָּא וְרִבִּי יוֹסֵי, עַד דַּהֲווֹ אַזְלֵי אִעֲרָעוּ בְּחַד סָבָא, וַהֲוָה אָחִיד בִּידֵיהּ וְחַד יַנּוּקָא, זָקַף עֵינוֹי רִבִּי שִׁמְעוֹן וְחָמָא לֵיהּ, אָמַר לֵיהּ לְרִבִּי אַבָּא וַדַּאי מִלִּין חַדְתִּין אִית גַּבָּן בְּהַאי סָבָא.

79. Rav Shimon and Rav Elazar, his son, were traveling on the road accompanied by Rav Aba and Rav Yosi. While they were walking, they met an old man who was holding a young boy by the hand. An old man alludes to the Mochin of the Face, and a young boy alludes to the Mochin of the Back. **Rav Shimon raised his eyes and saw him. He said to Rav Aba: "Assuredly this old man has new ideas for us."**

The old man came from the wilderness to civilization for Sukkot.

80. כַּד מָטוֹ לְגַבֵּיהּ, אָמַר רִבִּי שִׁמְעוֹן, בְּמָטוֹל דְּקוּפְטְרָךְ בְּגַבָּךְ קָא אָתֵית, מַאן אַנְתְּ. אָמַר לֵיהּ, יוּדָאי אֲנָא. אָמַר, מִלִּין חַדְתִּין וַדַּאי יוֹמָא דָא לְגַבָּךְ, אָמַר לֵיהּ לְאָן הוּא אַרְעָךְ. אָמַר לֵיהּ, דִּיוּרִי הֲוָה בְּאִינּוּן פְּרִישֵׁי מַדְבְּרָא, דַּהֲוֵינָא, מִשְׁתַּדַּל בְּאוֹרַיְיתָא, וְהַשְׁתָּא אֲתֵינָא לְיִשּׁוּבָא, לְמֵיתַב בְּצִלָּא דְּקוּדְשָׁא בְּרִיךְ הוּא, בְּאִלֵּין יוֹמֵי דְּיַרְחָא שְׁבִיעָאָה דָא.

80. When they reached him, Rav Shimon said to him: "Why do you come with a load tied to your back… meaning, do you not have a donkey to carry your load? This alludes to the Mochin of the Back that he is holding on to, which are like a burden for him. **…who are you?" He said to him: "I am a Jew."** Rav Shimon **said to him: "You must definitely have certain new matters with you today."** Rav Shimon **said to him: "Where is your country?" He said to him: "I used to live among those who retired to the wilderness for I was endeavoring there in the Torah. Now, I have come to civilization to sit in the shadow of the Holy One, blessed be He, during the days of this seventh month."**

Rav Shimon asks the old man to reveal secrets regarding Tishrei.

81. חַדֵּי ר' שִׁמְעוֹן, אָמַר, נָתִיב דְּוַדַּאי קוּדְשָׁא בְּרִיךְ הוּא שַׁדְּרָךְ לְגַבָּן. אָמַר לֵיהּ, וְחַיֶּיךָ דְּנִשְׁמַע מִלָּה מִפּוּמָךְ, מֵאִינּוּן מִלִּין חַדְתִּין עַתִּיקִין, דִּנְטַעְתּוּן תַּמָּן בְּמַדְבְּרָא, מֵהַאי יַרְחָא שְׁבִיעָאָה. וַאֲמַאי אִתְפְּרַשְׁתּוּן הַשְׁתָּא מִמַּדְבְּרָא, לְמֵיתֵי לְיִשּׁוּבָא. אָמַר לֵיהּ הַהוּא סָבָא, בְּשְׁאֶלְתָּא דָא, יַדְעְנָא דְּחָכְמְתָא גַּבָּךְ, וּמִילָּךְ מָטוֹ לִרְקִיעֵי דְּחָכְמְתָא.

81. Rav Shimon rejoiced and said: "Let us sit because certainly the Holy One, blessed be He, has sent you to us." He said to him: "upon your life, we shall hear a word from your mouth of those new yet old matters that you planted there in the wilderness concerning this seventh month. Why did you leave the wilderness to come to

civilization?" The old sage said to him: From this question I know that you possess wisdom and your words reach the firmament of Wisdom."

10. "And in the wilderness, where you have seen"

A Synopsis

The old sage speaks about the reason that God led Israel into the powerful wilderness, the domain of Sama"el, when they left Egypt. Had they not sinned, God would have crushed Sama"el so he would have had no power but because they sinned they spent forty years in the wilderness to fulfill the verse, "And you shall bruise his heel." We are told that the only light is that light that comes out of the darkness. There is no service of God except from out of darkness, and no good except from out of evil. Overall perfection is good and evil together that rise to the good afterward.

The old man dwelt in the wilderness to subdue the Negative Side.

87. וַאֲנָן, עַד הַשְׁתָּא יָתִיבְנָא תַּמָּן, כָּל יוֹמֵי שַׁתָּא, בְּגִין לְאַכְפְּיָא בְּמַדְבְּרָא לְהַהוּא סִטְרָא. הַשְׁתָּא דְּמָטָא זִמְנָא דְּפוּלְחָנָא קַדִּישָׁא, דְּסִטְרָא דִּקְדוּשָּׁא, אַהֲדַרְנָא לְיִשּׁוּבָא דְּתַמָּן אִיהוּ פּוּלְחָנָא דִּילֵיהּ. וְתוּ, דְּהַשְׁתָּא בְּר"ה מָטָא זִמְנָא דְּהַהוּא חִוְיָא, לְמִתְבַּע דִּינָא מִקָּמֵי קוּדְשָׁא בְּרִיךְ הוּא, וְתַמָּן אִיהוּ שַׁלִּיט. וּבְגִין כַּךְ נָפַקְנָא מִתַּמָּן וַאֲתֵינָא לְיִשּׁוּבָא.

87. We have dwelt there throughout the year until now in order to subdue that Side in the wilderness. Now that the time for the holy service of the side of Holiness has come, we return to civilization, for the service of the Holy One, blessed be He, **is there. Furthermore, now, during Rosh Hashanah, the time has arrived for that Serpent to request Judgment before the Holy One, blessed be He. He rules there in the wilderness. Therefore, we left it and came to civilization.**

11. "Blow a Shofar at the New Moon"

A Synopsis

The old sage continues by saying that at the New Moon, on the feast day, Harsh Judgment awakens and strengthens the Other Side; then the whole world is under Judgment, as the moon, Malchut, radiates no light. All the acts of correction that preserve the worlds arise from the Lower Beings if their deeds are correct; if they are not, Malchut remains without Illumination until the wicked are separated from the righteous, and then Judgment awakens. We learn that God gave the Shofar to Israel in order to break the covering on the moon that prevents it from shining; the sound of the Shofar arouses Mercy below and Binah above. The Upper World, Binah, always gives to the lower world, Malchut, according to its present state, so human gladness below draws supernal gladness. The old sage says that on Yom Kippur Malchut lights up with a Supernal Illumination from the Light of the World to Come, Binah.

When Harsh Judgments are awakened,
the Other Side grows strong and covers the moon.

88. פָּתַח הַהוּא סָבָא וְאָמַר, תִּקְעוּ בַחֹדֶשׁ שׁוֹפָר בַּכֶּסֶה לְיוֹם חַגֵּנוּ, הַשְׁתָּא אִיהוּ זִמְנָא, לְאִתְעָרָא דִּינָא עִלָּאָה תַּקִּיפָא, וְכַד אִיהוּ אִתְּעַר סִטְרָא אַחֲרָא אִתְתָּקַף בַּהֲדֵיהּ, וְכֵיוָן דְּאִיהוּ אִתְתָּקַף, סָלִיק וְחַפְיָא לְסִיהֲרָא, דְּלָא נָהִיר נְהוֹרָא, וְאִתְמַלְיָא מִסִּטְרָא דְּדִינָא. כְּדֵין כָּל עָלְמָא אִיהוּ בְּדִינָא, עִלָּאִין וְתַתָּאִין, וְכָרוֹזָא כָּרִיז בְּכֻלְּהוּ רְקִיעִין, אַתְקִינוּ כּוּרְסְיָא דְּדִינָא, לְמָארֵיהּ דְּכֹלָּא, דְּאִיהוּ בָּעֵי לְמֵידָן.

88. The old sage opened the discussion, saying: "Blow a Shofar at the New Moon, at the full moon (lit. the covering) on our feast day." (Psalms 81:4) Now is the time for the supernal Harsh Judgment to awaken. When it awakens, the Other Side is strengthened by it. Once the Other Side grows strong, it rises and covers the moon, which is Malchut, **so it does not radiate any light but is filled from the**

aspect of Judgment. Then the whole world is under Judgment, both higher and lower beings, and a proclamation is issued throughout all the firmaments: 'Prepare the Throne of Judgment for the Master of all, for He wishes to Judge.'

The world is sustained by the good deeds of the Lower Beings.

89. וְרָזָא הָכָא, וְאִתְנְהִיר לוֹן בְּמַדְבְּרָא, אֲמַאי אִתְעַר דִּינָא עִלָּאָה בְּיוֹמָא דָּא. אֶלָּא כָּל רָזִין וְכָל קִדּוּשִׁין יַקִּירִין, כֻּלְּהוּ תַּלְיָין בִּשְׁבִיעָאָה. וְהַהוּא שְׁבִיעָאָה עִלָּאָה, עָלְמָא עִלָּאָה, דְּאִקְרֵי עָלְמָא דְּאָתֵי. מִנֵּיהּ נַהֲרִין כָּל בּוּצִינִין, וְכָל קִדּוּשִׁין, וְכָל בִּרְכָאן. וְכַד מָטֵי זִמְנָא, לְחַדְּתוּתֵי בִּרְכָאן וְקִדּוּשִׁין לְאַנְהֲרָא, בָּעָא לְאַשְׁגָּחָא בְּכָל תִּקּוּנָא דְּעָלְמִין כֻּלְּהוּ, וְכָל אִינּוּן תִּקּוּנִים לְאִתְקַיְּימָא כֻּלְּהוֹן, סַלְּקִין מִגּוֹ תַּתָּאֵי, אִי אִינּוּן כַּשְׁרָאן. וְאִי לָא כַּשְׁרָאן, כְּדֵין קַיְּימָא דְּלָא נָהִיר, עַד דְּאִתְפָּרְשָׁן חַיָּיבִין מִגּוֹ זַכָּאִין, כְּדֵין אִתְעַר דִּינָא.

89. "There is a secret here, which shone upon us in the wilderness. Why did supernal Judgment awaken on this day?" He answers: **"All the secrets and all the precious sanctities stem from the seventh,** which is Malchut. **And that Supernal Seventh, which is the Supernal World that is called the World to Come,** namely Binah, **from it all the candles, sanctities and blessings shine** on Malchut. **When the time arrives to renew the blessings and sanctities so they will shine, one should observe the corrections of all the worlds,** in order to renew the blessings and sanctifications. **All the corrections that sustain the worlds rise from the lower beings, if their deeds are straight. If they are not straight,** Malchut **remains without Illumination until the wicked are separated from the righteous, and then Judgment awakens.**

The Accuser wants to take the wicked people.

90. וּמֵהַהוּא דִּינָא, אִתְתָּקַּף סִטְרָא אַחֲרָא, וְאִשְׁתְּכַח מְקַטְרְגָא, בְּגִין דְּיִנָּתְנוּן לֵיהּ אִינּוּן, חַיָּיבַיָּא. בְּגִין דְּעָלֵיהּ כְּתִיב, וּלְכָל תַּכְלִית הוּא חוֹקֵר. וְחַפְיָא לְסִיהֲרָא,

אֲמַאי לָא מָסְרָא לוֹן בִּידָא דִּמְקַטְרְגָא. בְּגִין דְּלֵית תֵּיאוּבְתֵּיהּ דְּקוּדְשָׁא בְּרִיךְ הוּא, לְאוֹבָדָא לְעוֹבָדֵי יְדוֹי.

90. "From that Judgment, the Other Side is strengthened, and the Accuser is present so that the wicked be given over to him, for it is written of him: 'And searches out all perfection' (Job 28:3), and covers the moon so it will not shine. Why does He not give over the wicked **to the Accuser? Because the Holy One, blessed be He, does not wish to destroy the works of His hands.**

Only the Shofar can break the unbreakable Klipah.

91. וְהַהוּא סִטְרָא אַחֲרָא, קַיְּימָא קְלִיפָּא תַּקִּיפָא, דְּלָא יָכִיל לְאִתְּבָרָא, בַּר בְּהַהוּא עֵיטָא דְּקוּדְשָׁא בְּרִיךְ הוּא יָהִיב לְיִשְׂרָאֵל, דִּכְתִּיב תִּקְעוּ בַחֹדֶשׁ שׁוֹפָר בַּכֶּסֶה לְיוֹם חַגֵּנוּ. בְּגִין לְתַבְרָא הַהוּא כִּסֵּה דְּאִתְחַפְיָא סִיהֲרָא, וְלָא נָהִיר.

91. "In the Other Side there is a hard Klipah that is impossible to break, except with the counsel the Holy One, blessed be He, gave the children of Israel, as written: 'Blow a Shofar at the new moon, at the full moon (lit. the covering) on our feast day' (Psalms 81:4) in order to break that cover with which the moon, Malchut, **is covered and does not shine.**

The Shofar brings forth an awakening of Mercy.

92. וְכַד מִתְעֲרֵי יִשְׂרָאֵל לְתַתָּא בְּשׁוֹפָר, הַהוּא קָלָא דְּנָפִיק מִשּׁוֹפָר, בָּטַשׁ בַּאֲוִירָא, וּבָקַע רְקִיעִין, עַד דְּסַלְקָא לְגַבֵּי הַהוּא טִנָּרָא תַּקִּיפָא, דְּחָפֵי לְסִיהֲרָא, אַשְׁגַּח, וְאַשְׁכַּח אִתְעֲרוּתָא דְּרַחֲמֵי, כְּדֵין הַהוּא דְּסָלִיק וְקַיְּימָא לְעֵילָא, אִתְעַרְבָב. כְּדֵין הַהוּא קָלָא קַיְּימָא, וְאַעְבַּר הַהוּא דִּינָא, וְכֵיוָן דִּלְתַתָּא אַתְעָרוּ רַחֲמֵי, הָכִי נָמֵי לְעֵילָא, אִתְּעַר שׁוֹפָרָא אַחֲרָא עִלָּאָה, וְאַפִּיק קָלָא דְּאִיהוּ רַחֲמֵי, וְאִתְעָרְעוּ קָלָא בְּקָלָא, רַחֲמֵי בְּרַחֲמֵי, וּבְאִתְעָרוּתָא דִּלְתַתָּא, אִתְּעַר הָכִי נָמֵי לְעֵילָא.

92. "When the children of Israel awaken below by the blow of the Shofar, the sound that emanates from the Shofar blasts the air and splits Firmaments until it rises to that hard rock, namely the Other Side, **that covers the moon. It observes and brings forth an awakening of Mercy. Then** the Other Side **that rises and remains above** covering the moon **is confounded. That sound stands and removes that Judgment** from Malchut. **Since Mercy has awakened below,** in Malchut, **another Supernal Shofar also awakens above,** which is Binah, **and produces a sound,** namely the Mochin of Zeir Anpin that is called 'sound,' **which is Mercy. Sound meets sound, mercy meets mercy, because by the awakening below there is also an awakening above."**

Explanation: On Rosh Hashanah, the original awakening of the Fourth Day of Creation returns to the world, where the Nukva is attached to the Left Column without the Right, and then Judgments issue forth from Her to the world, for She cannot shine when She is with Chochmah without Chasadim. This is considered that the Other Side covers Her, due to the actions of the Lower Beings that are not proper, who are the wicked that cleave to the Left Column. [In verse 89] this is: "**If they are not straight,** Malchut **remains without Illumination....**" The secret of the blowing of the Shofar is the secret of the raising of Mayin Nukvin from the Masach of Chirik, by which the power of Left is diminished and unites with the Right. This is the secret of the sound of Shofar, since sound alludes to Zeir Anpin called "sound," which is the secret of the Central Column that is comprised of three columns—Fire, Water and Wind. Thus, the Other Side, which covers Malchut with power of the Left Column, is confounded since the Left Column was diminished and lost its Upper Three, and surely the Other Side that draws its power from there.

This is: "**Then** the Other Side **that rises and remains above** covering the moon **is confounded,"** as its Illumination has left it, "**then that sound**

stands and removes that Judgment," of the Left that does not wish to unite with the Right, and now it is subdued and receives Chasadim from the Right, and Mercy is revealed in Malchut. This is: **"Since Mercy has awakened Below, another Supernal Shofar also awakens Above and produces a sound, which is Mercy."** Binah awakens and births the Mochin of Zeir Anpin called "sound," which is the secret of the Central Column that draws the Mochin of Binah, in the secret of "three emerge from one, one is sustained by three," and they are drawn to Malchut.

This is: "**Sound meets sound, Mercy meets Mercy.**" The sound and Mercy from Binah meet the Central Column and Mercy that emerged in Malchut via the lower awakening of the Shofar's sound. **"...by the awakening Below"** of the Shofar's sound **"there is also an awakening Above,"** since the Mochin of Binah are drawn to Zeir Anpin, and from Zeir Anpin to Malchut. These Mochin are the awakening from Above in the secret of the sound of the Shofar, as the Shofar Above is the secret of Binah, and its sound is the Mochin of the Three Columns that are drawn from it, which are called Fire, Water and Wind.

The Upper World gives to the Lower World according to how it stands.

93. וְאִי תֵּימָא, הֵיךְ יָכִיל קָלָא דִּלְתַתָּא, אוֹ אִתְעָרוּתָא דִּלְתַתָּא לְאַתְעֲרָא, הָכִי נָמֵי. תָּא וַחֲזֵי, עָלְמָא תַּתָּאָה, קַיְּימָא לְקַבְּלָא תָּדִיר, וְהוּא אִקְרֵי אֶבֶן טָבָא. וְעָלְמָא עִלָּאָה לָא יָהִיב לֵיהּ, אֶלָּא כְּגַוְונָא דְּאִיהוּ קַיְּימָא. אִי אִיהוּ קַיְּימָא בִּנְהִירוּ דְּאַנְפִּין מִתַּתָּא, כְּדֵין הָכִי נַהֲרִין לֵיהּ מִלְעֵילָּא. וְאִי אִיהוּ קַיְּימָא בַּעֲצִיבוּ, יַהֲבִין לֵיהּ דִּינָא בְּקָבְלֵיהּ.

93. You may ask how a sound below or an awakening below awaken that which corresponds to it above. **Come and see, the Lower World,** which is Malchut, **is always ready to receive and is called a "precious stone." The Upper World,** which is Binah, **gives it according to how it stands. If it stands with an illuminated face, then they shine**

to it as such. And if it stands in sadness, it is correspondingly given Judgment.

Gladness Below draws gladness Above.

94. כְּגַוְונָא דָא, עִבְדוּ אֶת יְיָ' בְּשִׂמְחָה. חֶדְוָה דְּבַ"נ, מָשִׁיךְ לְגַבֵּיהּ חֶדְוָה אַחֲרָא עִלָּאָה. הָכִי נָמֵי הַאי עָלְמָא תַּתָּאָה, כְּגַוְונָא דְּאִיהִי אִתְעַטְּרַת, הָכִי אַמְשִׁיךְ מִלְּעֵילָּא. בג"כ מַקְדִּימֵי יִשְׂרָאֵל, וְאַתְעֲרֵי בַּשּׁוֹפָר קָלָא דְּאִיהוּ כָּלִיל בְּאֶשָּׁא וּמַיָּא וְרוּחָא, וְאִתְעָבֵיד חַד, וְסַלְּקָא לְעֵילָּא, וּבָטַשׁ בְּהַאי אֶבֶן טָבָא, וְאִצְטְבַע בְּאִינּוּן ג' גַּוְונִין דְּהַאי קָלָא, וּכְדֵין כְּמָה דְּאִתְחַזְּיָאת, הָכִי מָשִׁיךְ מִלְּעֵילָּא.

94. Similarly, "Serve the Lord with gladness" (Psalms 100:2), because gladness of man draws another, supernal gladness. Thus, just as the Lower World, namely Malchut, **is crowned, so it draws from above. Therefore, the children of Israel are early to rouse with the Shofar a sound, which is combined of fire, water and air,** namely, the Central Column, which is combined of three Columns. **They become one, which rises and strikes that precious stone,** namely that it diminishes its Left Column, **and it is colored with these three colors,** which are white, red, and green, which are three Columns combined **in this sound, and then it draws from above as it is worthy of.**

When Mercy resides on Malchut, the Other Side is confounded.

95. וְכֵיוָן דְּאִתְתַּקְנַת בְּהַאי קָלָא. רַחֲמֵי נָפְקֵי מִלְּעֵילָּא, וְשַׁרְיָין עָלָהּ, וְאִתְכְּלִילָא בְּרַחֲמֵי, מִתַּתָּא וּמִלְּעֵילָּא. וּכְדֵין אִתְעַרְבַּב סִטְרָא אַחֲרָא. וְאִתְחַלָּשׁ תָּקְפֵּיהּ, וְלָא יָכִיל לְקַטְרְגָא. וְהַאי אֶבֶן טָבָא, קַיְּימָא בִּנְהִירוּ דְּאַנְפִּין, מִכָּל סִטְרִין, בִּנְהִירוּ דִּלְתַתָּא, וּבִנְהִירוּ דִּלְעֵילָּא.

95. Once Malchut **has been perfected with this sound** from below, **Mercy emerges from above and dwells upon Her, and She becomes included in Mercy from Below and Above. Then the Other Side is confounded, and its power is weakened and it cannot accuse. This**

precious stone, which is Malchut, **remains with radiant countenance in every direction, with Illumination from below and Illumination from Above.**

On Yom Kippur, Malchut is found with the Illumination from Binah.

96. אֵימָתַי קַיְּימָא בִּנְהִירוּ דִּלְעֵילָּא, הֲוֵי אוֹמֵר בְּיוֹמָא דְּכִפּוּרֵי. וּבְיוֹמָא דְּכִפּוּרֵי אִתְנְהִיר הַהוּא אֶבֶן טָבָא, בִּנְהִירוּ דִּלְעֵילָּא, מִגּוֹ נְהִירוּ דְּעָלְמָא דְּאָתֵי, וּכְדֵין מִתַּקְנִין יִשְׂרָאֵל לְתַתָּא חַד שָׂעִיר, וּמְשַׁדְּרִין לְהַאי מַדְבְּרָא תַּקִּיפָא, דְּאִיהוּ שַׁלְטָא עָלֵיהּ.

96. When does She remain with the Illumination from above? On Yom Kippur, for on Yom Kippur that precious stone is lit up, namely Malchut, **with a supernal Illumination from the light of the world to come,** which is Binah. **Then the children of Israel prepare a goat and send it to this tough wilderness, which rules over it.**

Pekudei

57. The Fourth Chamber of the Other Side, Debt—gruesome mud and a stumbling stone

A Synopsis

We learn that this Chamber has to do with balancing the merits and sins of a person. The Fourth Chamber on the Holy Side is called Merit and holds a man's precepts or good deeds; the Fourth Chamber on the Other Side is called Debt and holds his sins. Then the scales are balanced on Rosh Hashanah, and one side or the other wins. If the scales tip to Merit, the person is given life. If the scales tip to Debt, he is delivered to death. If he is on the side of Holiness, God answers when he calls to Him. If he is on the side of defilement, he has no one to answer him and he is far away from God. In this Fourth Chamber of the Other Side the strange Elohim are found, and also everyone who incites men to prostitution and adultery. Rav Shimon tells us about the spirits called "plague" and "plague and pestilence." He talks about how the Unholy Side is strengthened if the tables are not prepared properly on Shabbat eve. We learn that in this Fourth Chamber there are no children, no longevity and no sustenance. Rav Shimon reveals that those who curse arouse the Serpent called "Leviathan, the crooked Serpent," bring curses on the world.

On Rosh Hashanah, we are written to the side of Holiness or defilement, life or death.

885. וְאִי נַצְחָן חוֹבִין, הַאי סִטְרָא אַחֲרָא מִסְאֲבָא, דְּאִקְרֵי חוֹבָה וּמָוֶת, אָחִיד בֵּיהּ, אָמַר הַאי דִּידִי הוּא, וְדִידִי הֲוֵי, וּכְדֵין אִכְתּוּב דְּאִיהוּ דִּילֵיהּ. וְדָא הוּא דְּתָנֵינָן, דְּהָא בְּיוֹמָא דָּא דר"ה, אִכְתּוּב ב"נ, אוֹ לְחַיִּים אוֹ לְמִיתָה. אִי אִכְתּוּב בְּסִטְרָא דִּקְדוּשָּׁה, אִכְתּוּב לְחַיִּים, וְאִתְקַיָּים תַּמָּן, וְאִתְדַּבַּק בֵּיהּ. וְאִי אִכְתּוּב בְּסִטְרָא אַחֲרָא, אִתְקַיָּים בְּסִטְרָא דִּמְסָאֲבוּתָא, וְדָבִיק בֵּיהּ, וְדָא הוּא הֵן לְחַיִּים הֵן לְמָוֶת. וְאִתְמְשַׁךְ בְּהַאי סִטְרָא אוֹ בְּהַאי סִטְרָא.

885. If the sins win, the unholy Other Side called Debt and Death grasps him and says: "This is mine, and was mine." And then it is written that the man is his. This is what we learned, that on the day of Rosh Hashanah, a man is written to life or death. If he is written to the side of holiness, he is written to life. He abides there and cleaves to it. If he is written upon the Other Side, he abides by the side of defilement, and clings to it, which is death. **It is either to life or death,** namely **it is drawn from either this or that side.**

When we cleave to Holiness, the Creator answers when we call.

886. כָּל זִמְנָא דְּאִיהוּ קַיְּימָא בְּסִטְרָא דָּא דִּקְדוּשָּׁה, כָּל קְדוּשִּׁין וְכָל דַּכְיָין מִתְדַּבְּקִין בֵּיהּ. יִקְרָא וְקוּדְשָׁא בְּרִיךְ הוּא יָתִיב וְיִשְׁמַע לֵיהּ, עָלֵיהּ כְּתִיב יִקְרָאֵנִי וְאֶעֱנֵהוּ עִמּוֹ אָנֹכִי בְצָרָה אֲחַלְּצֵהוּ וַאֲכַבְּדֵהוּ אוֹרֶךְ יָמִים אַשְׂבִּיעֵהוּ וְאַרְאֵהוּ בִּישׁוּעָתִי. וְכָל זִמְנָא דְּאִיהוּ קַיְּימָא בְּסִטְרָא אַחֲרָא דִּמְסָאֲבָא, כָּל מִסְאֲבוּ, וְכָל חוֹבָה, וְכָל בִּישִׁין מִתְדַּבְּקָן בֵּיהּ. יִקְרָא, וְלֵית מַאן דְּיִשְׁמַע לֵיהּ. מְרַחֲקָא אִיהוּ מִקּוּדְשָׁא בְּרִיךְ הוּא, עָלֵיהּ כְּתִיב רָחוֹק מֵרְשָׁעִים יְשׁוּעָה וּכְתִיב גַּם כִּי תַרְבּוּ תְפִלָּה אֵינֶנִּי שׁוֹמֵעַ.

886. Whenever he is on the side of Holiness, all sacredness and purity cleave to him. He calls and the Holy One, blessed be He, sits and listens. Of him says the verse, "He shall call upon Me, and I will answer him; I will be with him in trouble; I will deliver him, and honor him. With long life I will satisfy him, and show him My salvation." (Psalms 91:15) As long as he is on the unholy Other Side, all defilement, all sins and evils cling to him. He calls and there is no one to listen to him. He is far away from the Holy One, blessed be He. Of him it is written: "Salvation is far from the wicked" (Psalms 119:155), and "even when you make many prayers, I will not hear." (Isaiah 1:15)

Pinchas

57. Now there was a day when the sons of God came to present themselves before the Lord

A Synopsis

Rav Shimon talks about Rosh Hashanah, when Harsh Judgment is present in the world. We learn that "the sons of Elohim" are the Supreme Court, the seventy officials who always surround the King, and that everyone must take care to honor the Holy Name to avoid judgment.

The Relevance of this Passage

The power of Rosh Hashanah is available to us. Reading this portion with great remorse sweetens and annuls Judgments otherwise in store for us, by awakening Mercy. And because this secret of Rosh Hashanah is revealed through the Zohar—the soul and essence of the Torah and the world—the effect is cosmic. The entire world is sweetened with Mercy as Judgments are repealed. The Supreme Court is permanently adjourned, and our adversaries—the prosecuting attorneys Satan and Lili"t—are relieved of their duties.

Vayehi denotes anguish, and Vayehi hayom denotes Rosh Hashanah.

351. אָמַר רִבִּי יְהוּדָה, לֵימָא לָן מֹר, מִלִּין מְעַלְּיָיתָא דְּרֹאשׁ הַשָּׁנָה. פָּתַח רִבִּי שִׁמְעוֹן וְאָמַר וַיְהִי הַיּוֹם. בְּכָל אֲתַר דִּכְתִיב וַיְהִי, אִיהוּ צַעַר, וַיְהִי בִּימֵי צַעַר. וַדַּאי, וַיְהִי הַיּוֹם, יוֹמָא דְּאִית בֵּיהּ צַעַר, וְדָא הוּא רֹאשׁ הַשָּׁנָה, יוֹמָא דְּאִית בֵּיהּ דִּינָא קַשְׁיָא עַל עָלְמָא. וַיְהִי הַיּוֹם וַיַּעֲבֹר אֱלִישָׁע אֶל שׁוּנֵם, יוֹמָא דְּרֹאשׁ הַשָּׁנָה הֲוָה. וּבְכָל אֲתַר וַיְהִי הַיּוֹם, דָּא רֹאשׁ הַשָּׁנָה. וַיְהִי הַיּוֹם וַיָּבֹאוּ בְּנֵי הָאֱלֹהִים, יוֹם רֹאשׁ הַשָּׁנָה הֲוָה.

351. Rav Yehuda said to Rav Shimon, "**Let my master say some beautiful things about Rosh Hashanah." Rav Shimon began by**

quoting: "'Now there was (*vayehi*) a day....' (Job 1:6) Wherever it is written: *vayehi*, it is a term of **anguish. 'Now there was a day' refers to anguish. Certainly 'Now there was a day' refers to a day on which there is anguish, and this is Rosh Hashanah, a day on which there is Harsh Judgment on the world.** Similarly: **'And it happened one day (*vayehi*), that Elisha passed to Shunem...' (II Kings 4:8) was on the day of Rosh Hashanah. And wherever it is said 'And it happened one day (*vayehi*)' the day referred to is Rosh Hashanah.** Consequently, **'Now there was a day when the sons of the God (Elohim) came...' (Job 1:6) refers to the day of Rosh Hashanah.**

Rosh Hashanah is two days so that the Left Column will include Judgment and Mercy.

352. בְּכָל זִמְנָא תְּרֵין יוֹמִין אִינּוּן, מַאי טַעֲמָא. בְּגִין, דִּלְהֱוֵי יִצְחָק כָּלִיל דִּינָא וְרַחֲמֵי, תְּרֵין יוֹמִין וְלָא חַד. דְּאִלְמָלֵא יִשְׁתְּכַח יְחִידָאי, יַחֲרִיב עָלְמָא. וְעַל דָּא כְּתִיב תְּרֵין זִמְנִין, וַיְהִי הַיּוֹם וַיְהִי הַיּוֹם.

352. "Rosh Hashanah always lasts for two days. What is the reason for this? It is so that Isaac, who is the Left Column, which is the aspect of Rosh Hashanah, **should be composed of Judgment and Mercy,** which are **two days, and** Isaac will **not** be just **one. For** were Isaac to be **just one,** without the inclusion of Mercy, **he would destroy the world, and this is why it is written** in Job **twice: 'Now there was a day....' (Job 1:6; 2:1)**

The first to be judged is the one who does not honor the Holy Name, the Torah, and His servants.

353. וַיָּבֹאוּ בְּנֵי הָאֱלֹהִים, אִלֵּין ב"ד רַבְרְבָא. בְּנֵי הָאֱלֹהִים וַדַּאי, בְּנוֹי דְּמַלְכָּא קְרִיבִין לְגַבֵּיהּ. וְאִינּוּן שַׁבְעִין מְמָנָן, דְּסַחֲרִין תְּדִירָא לְמַלְכָּא. וְאִינּוּן נַחְתִּין דִּינָא עַל עָלְמָא. לְהִתְיַצֵּב עַל יְיָ', וְכִי עַל יְיָ' קַיְימֵי. אֶלָּא, בְּשַׁעֲתָא דְּאִלֵּין קַיְימֵי עַל דִּינָא, דִּינָא קַדְמָאָה דְּכֹלָּא בֵּיהּ, מַאן הוּא. דְּלָא יוֹקִיר לִשְׁמָא דְּקוּדְשָׁא בְּרִיךְ

הוּא, וּדְלָא יוֹקִיר לְאוֹרַיְיתָא וּלְעַבְדוֹי. אוּף הָכִי, מַאן הוּא דְלָא חָיֵישׁ עַל יְקָרָא דִשְׁמָא קַדִּישָׁא, דְלָא יִתְחַלֵּל בְּאַרְעָא. מַאן הוּא דְלָא חָיֵישׁ לִיקָרֵיהּ דְקוּדְשָׁא בְּרִיךְ הוּא, מַאן הוּא דְלָא שַׁוֵּי יְקָר לִשְׁמָא דָא. וַיָּבֹא גַם הַשָּׂטָן בְּתוֹכָם, גַּם, לְרַבּוֹת הַהִיא נוּקְבָא דִילֵיהּ. אוּף הָכִי לְהִתְיַצֵּב עַל יְיָ, דְאִיהוּ חָיֵישׁ נָמֵי לִיקָרָא דִשְׁמָא דָא.

353. "'...the sons of God (the Elohim) came...' (Job 1:6) are certainly the Supreme Court. "...the sons of God (the Elohim)...' (Ibid.) before whom the children namely Israel **of the King draw near. And they are the seventy officials who always surround the King, and they decree sentences on the world. '...to present themselves before (lit. upon) the Lord.'" (Ibid.)** He asks, **"Do they stand upon the Lord?"** He answers, **"No, but when they stand to judge** the world, **the first to be judged is the one who does not honor the Holy Name and does not respect the Torah and His servants. So, too, whoever is not concerned about the honor of the Holy Name,** which is the Shechinah, **that it be not desecrated on earth, and whoever is not concerned over the honor of the Holy One, blessed be He,** who is Zeir Anpin, **he does not give honor to this Name. '...and the Adversary came also among them' (Ibid.): 'also' adds the female of the Adversary,** Lili"t. **And so it is here: '...to present themselves before the Lord...' means that the Satan, too, was concerned for the honor of this Name,** which is to say, he came to incite against it."

58. The righteous man suffers and the wicked man thrives

A Synopsis

Rav Hamnuna tells Elijah that a righteous man whose sins are few is punished in this world, but a man with many sins and a few good deeds is rewarded in this world. He goes on to say that people must confess their own sins to God and then He will hear, judge, and forgive him.

The Relevance of this Passage

When we confess our own sins, absolutely, to the Creator, as opposed to having our Accuser (Satan) present them as an indictment against us, the Zohar states:

> "…**The heavenly court leaves alone the person who expounds his own sins** and does not find him guilty."

This passage is our opportunity to confess and procure a favorable verdict concerning that sins we have committed. Acknowledging our misdeeds is the key to activating the power of this passage.

Why some righteous suffer and some wicked prosper.

354. הָכָא אַפְלִיגוּ עַמּוּדִין קַדְמָאִין דְּעָלְמָא. חַד אָמַר, אִיּוֹב מֵחֲסִידֵי אוּמּוֹת הָעוֹלָם הֲוָה. וְחַד אָמַר, מֵחֲסִידֵי יִשְׂרָאֵל הֲוָה. וְאִלְקֵי, לְכַפָּרָא עַל עָלְמָא. דְּהָא יוֹמָא חַד אַשְׁכְּחֵיהּ רַב הַמְנוּנָא לְאֵלִיָּהוּ. א"ל, וַדַּאי תָּנֵינָן דְּאִית צַדִּיק וְרַע לוֹ, רָשָׁע וְטוֹב לוֹ. אָמַר, צַדִּיק, כָּל שֶׁמְּמוּעָטִין לוֹ חוֹבוֹתָיו נוֹתְנִין לוֹ בָּעוֹלָם הַזֶּה חוֹבוֹ, וְעַל כֵּן צַדִּיק וְרַע לוֹ. וְכָל שֶׁמְּרוּבִּין עֲוֹנוֹתָיו, וּמְמוּעָטִין זְכִיּוֹתָיו, נוֹתְנִין לוֹ שְׂכָרוֹ בָּעוֹלָם הַזֶּה, רָשָׁע וְטוֹב לוֹ. א"ל, דִּינוֹי דְּמָארֵי עָלְמָא, עֲמִיקִין אֲבָל בְּשַׁעֲתָא דְּבָעֵי קוּדְשָׁא בְּרִיךְ הוּא לְכַפָּרָא חוֹבִין דְּעָלְמָא, אַלְקֵי בִּדְרוֹעָא דִּלְהוֹן, וְאָסֵי לְכוּלְּהוּ מִתַּל לְאַסְיָיא, דְּאַלְקֵי לִדְרוֹעָא, לְשֵׁיזָבָא לְכָל שַׁיְיפִין. כְּמָה דִּכְתִיב, וְהוּא מְחוֹלָל מִפְּשָׁעֵינוּ וְגוֹ'.

354. Here the ancient pillars of the world were divided. One said: "Job was one of the pious of the nations of the world," and another said, "Job was one of the pious of Israel, but was smitten in order to atone for the world." One day, Rav Hamnuna found Elijah and said to him, "We have definitely learned that there is a righteous man who suffers and a wicked man who prospers." Rav Hamnuna explained and **said, "A righteous man is one whose sins are few and who pays the price for them in this world, and thus the righteous man suffers. But if his sins are many and his good deeds few, then he receives his reward in this world,** and thus **is a wicked man who**

prosper.s" He said to him, "The judgments of the Master of the World are profound but when the Holy One, blessed be He, wants to make atonement for the sins of the generation, He smites their arm and through this action the generation is healed. It can be likened to a doctor who smites, namely lets blood in **the arm in order to save all the parts, as it is written: 'But he was wounded because of our transgressions....' (Isaiah 53:5)"**

One who confesses his sins is judged only by the Creator.

355. כְּמָה דְּאִתְּמַר, בְּהַהוּא יוֹמָא שֶׁל רֹאשׁ הַשָּׁנָה, דְּקַיְימִין שַׁבְעִין קַתֶּדְרָאִין לְמֵידָן דִּינָא לְעָלְמָא, כַּמָּה אִינּוּן מָארֵי תְּרִיסִין, קַטֵּיגוֹרִין, דְּקַיְימֵי לְעֵילָּא. אִלֵּין מִיַּימִינִין לִזְכוּ וְאִלֵּין מִשְּׂמָאלִין לְחוֹבָא, לְאַדְכְּרָא חוֹבִין דְּעָלְמָא, וְחוֹבִין דְּכָל חַד וְחַד. וְעַל דָּא אִצְטְרִיךְ לב"נ, לְפָרְשָׁא חוֹבוֹי, כָּל חַד וְחַד כְּמָה דְּאִיהוּ בְּגִין דְּמַאן דִּמְפָרֵשׁ וְחֶטְאוֹי, לָא אִתְמְסַר דִּינֵיהּ, אֶלָּא בִּידָא דְּמַלְכָּא קוּדְשָׁא בְּרִיךְ הוּא בִּלְחוֹדוֹי. וּמַאן דְּדָאִין לֵיהּ קוּדְשָׁא בְּרִיךְ הוּא, אִיהוּ לְטָב. וע"ד בָּעָא דָּוִד מַלְכָּא, שָׁפְטֵנִי אֱלֹקִים, אַנְתְּ, וְלָא אַחֲרָא. וְכֵן שְׁלֹמֹה אָמַר, לַעֲשׂוֹת מִשְׁפַּט עַבְדּוֹ, הוּא, וְלָא אַחֲרָא, וְכָל ב"ד בְּדִילִין מִמֶּנּוּ.

355. As we have learned, on that day of Rosh Hashanah, seventy seats of justice arise to judge the world, many for the defense and many for the prosecution standing on high, those on the right for innocence and those on the left for guilt, to recall the sins of the world and the sins of each individual. A man has therefore to confess and **specify his sins—each one just as it is—for whoever expounds his sins** before the Holy One, blessed be He, **Judgment is passed on him by the Holy One, blessed be He, and by no other. And whoever is judged by the Holy One, blessed be He, it is for his good. This is why King David requested: "Judge me, God..." (Psalms 43:1) You and none other. Similarly, Solomon said, "...to do justice to His servant...." (I Kings 8:59) He and no other. And the** Heavenly **Court leaves him.**

The Heavenly Court leaves alone the person who expounds his own sins.

356. וע"ד אִצְטְרִיךְ לוֹן לְפָרְשָׁא חוֹבִין דְּכָל שַׁיְיפָא וְשַׁיְיפָא, וְכָל מַה דְּעָבֵיד בִּפְרָט. הה"ד, חַטָּאתִי אוֹדִיעֲךָ וְגוֹ'. לְבָתַר וְאַתָּה נָשָׂאתָ עֲוֹן חַטָּאתִי סֶלָה. מְנָלָן. מִמּשֶׁה, דִּכְתִיב אָנָּא חָטָא הָעָם הַזֶּה וְגוֹ'. בְּיִשְׂרָאֵל כְּתִיב, חָטָאנוּ כִּי עָזַבְנוּ אֶת יְיָ', דְּאִי תֵּימָא הַאי בְּיָחִיד, אֲבָל בְּצִבּוּר לָא. הָא כְּתִיב קְרָא דָא. וְאִי תֵּימָא הָא בְּצִבּוּר, אֲבָל שְׁלִיחָא דִּלְהוֹן לָא, הָא כְּתִיב וַיָּשָׁב משֶׁה אֶל יְיָ' וְגוֹ'. וּכְתִיב וַיַּעֲשׂוּ לָהֶם וְגוֹ'. מ"ט. מַאן דִּמְפָרֵשׁ חוֹבֵיהּ, בֵּי דִּינָא בְּדֵילִין מִינֵּיהּ, בְּגִין דב"נ קָרִיב לְגַרְמֵיהּ, וְלָא אִתְדָּן עַל פּוּמֵיהּ.

356. This is why the sins of every limb have to be expounded, and everything that he did in detail, as it is written: "I acknowledge my sin to You." (Psalms 32:5) And this same verse concludes: "and You forgave the iniquity of my sin. Sela." How do we know this? We know it from Moses, for it is written: "This people has sinned a great sin." (Ibid. 31) **And about Israel is written: "We have sinned because we have forsaken the Lord." (I Samuel 12:10) Should you suggest** that the verse about Moses **refers to an individual alone, while in public one does not** have to specify one's sins, **then the other verse** "We have sinned because we have forsaken the Lord" **comes to teach the opposite,** for it is said in public. **And should you agree that it is to be in public, but that it is not the cantor** who has to detail the sins, **the opposite is suggested, as it is written: "And Moses returned to the Lord and said: 'This people has sinned a great sin… and have made them an God of gold.'" What is the reason? It is because the Heavenly Court leaves alone the person who expounds his own sins** and does not find him guilty. **Because a man is his own relative,** and a relative is unacceptable as a witness. Therefore **he is not judged according to his** own **testimony.**

Confession leaves no room for the prosecutor to use anything against us.

357. וְתוּ, לָא שָׁבִיק לְמְקַטְרְגָא לְאוֹלְפָא עָלֵיהּ חוֹבָא מוּמָא. דְּבַר נָשׁ יַקְדִּים וְיֵימָא, וְלָא יָהִיב דּוּכְתָּא לְאַחֲרָא לְמֵימַר. כְּדֵין קוּדְשָׁא בְּרִיךְ הוּא מָחִיל לֵיהּ, הה"ד, וּמוֹדֶה וְעוֹזֵב יְרוּחָם.

357. Moreover, he does not let the prosecutor teach guilt and fault about him, because the person himself comes first and tells all, leaving nothing for anyone else to mention. Then the Holy One, blessed be He, forgives him, as it is written: "But whoever confesses and forsakes them shall have mercy." (Proverbs 28:13)

59. Rosh Hashanah

A Synopsis

We learn why Rosh Hashanah lasts for two days and that when people are coming to be judged Israel comes in first. It is important that we know the meaning of the blowing of the Shofar that arouses leniency and mercy.

The Relevance of this Passage

Rosh Hashanah is commonly known as the Jewish New Year. Traditionally, it is also a time of Judgment, when the Creator takes a reckoning of our deeds during the previous year. But according to Kabbalah, both these depictions of Rosh Hashanah are inaccurate.

Kabbalah teaches that the Force we call God does not preside over a Heavenly Court, deciding who will be forgiven and who will be punished. And Rosh Hashanah actually occurs in the seventh month of the Hebrew Calendar, so it does not signify a new year.

Science offers us some insight into the true significance of Rosh Hashanah. A principle of physics states that for every action there is an equal reaction. Rosh Hashanah is also built upon this foundation—the universal law of cause and effect.

Though we may not be aware of it, when we behave in a contemptuous, uncivil, or rude manner, we arouse negative forces. When we cheat, lie, steal, insult, embarrass, or harm other people, a negative energy force is brought into existence. These negative forces are the unseen cause behind all the things that just "happen" to go wrong in our lives, be it illness, emotional pain, or financial adversity.

Rosh Hashanah is our opportunity to confront the negative energy aroused through the wrongful acts we have committed during the preceding year. At this special time, the spiritual cycle of the universe is structured so that the consequences of our careless misdeeds, intolerant behavior, and hurtful words return to us. These repercussions of our own actions stand in judgment before us. The court of Cause and Effect stands in session.

Moreover, this self-confrontation is not exclusive to the children of Israel. According to the Zohar, the experience of cause and effect is shared by all mankind.

Put in simple terms, Kabbalah teaches that reality is like a mirror. Look into a mirror and smile, and the image smiles back. If one curses at the mirror, the image curses back. When we perform a negative act in our world, the cosmic mirror—our universe—reflects that negative energy.

The Creator never stands in judgment of us, and we are never required to stand in judgment in front of the Creator.

Crime and punishment

There is only one Force, one energy source for the entire cosmos, just as there is but one electrical force flowing through your home. This Force is good, positive, and infinitely compassionate.

Consider this: Electricity enriches human life by providing power for an entire nation. But this same force can also be used destructively. Placing one's finger into a light socket will cause electrocution. But the nature of the electricity never changed, and it would be senseless to say that the electricity "punished" you.

In the same way, the Creator never punishes us. We ourselves have chosen to place our finger in the socket through wrongful conduct.

We always have the free choice of how we react to life's challenges. Even when we know something is wrong, we sometimes choose to do it anyway. And when we know something is right, we may forsake it for a negative option. The choice is always ours.

Crimes and misdemeanors

Negative activity and sin can materialize in ways both large and small. Consider the sins of murder, evil speech, and adultery:

Murder

- We can kill someone physically, or we may also kill someone emotionally and spiritually.
- We can assassinate a person's body, or we may also assassinate a person's character.
- We can destroy someone's relationships, or we may also ruin their livelihood.

Kabbalah teaches that the sin of "spilling blood" is not limited to physical violence. Spilling blood can refer to the shame and embarrassment we may cause to others, forcing the blood to rush to their faces out of humiliation.

Evil Speech

According to Kabbalah, any form of malicious speech—even about someone we have never met—is one of the most serious crimes a person can commit.

Speech has tremendous powers. When we speak badly of others, we not only damage their lives, we also damage ourselves and even the entire world. At Rosh Hashanah, our damaging words come back to haunt us. Evil speech, therefore, is a no-win situation. According to the wisdom of the sages, people should be more concerned with what comes out of their mouths than what goes into their mouths.

Adultery

The concept of adultery is not limited to extramarital affairs. One can also covet another person's business, children, or material possessions. Envy and adultery occur when we fail fully to appreciate all that we have. And this lack of appreciation occurs when we gain our possessions through egocentric, destructive behavior.

Requesting a pardon

Now that we understand that there are real repercussions associated with our negative behavior, we may be tempted to ask for a pardon or seek exoneration through ignorance of the law of cause and effect. But ignorance of the law is no excuse, and natural laws of the universe cannot be violated without consequences. You cannot plead ignorance of the force of gravity while you are plunging a thousand feet toward the ground.

However, it is *also* a spiritual law of the universe that when a person achieves a remarkable change in his or her own nature, the universe must respond and reflect that miraculous energy back to us. We can then use that energy to alter our destiny and deflect judgments.

The first thing we must do in order to bring about change is to admit that we are guilty. Accept responsibility. Become accountable for our actions (that, perhaps, is the hardest thing to do). Then, with all our heart and soul, we make every attempt to change our ways during the time frame of Rosh Hashanah. This internal change begins with a mighty and majestic blast of a horn!

The secret of the Shofar

Most people associate the blowing of the Shofar with tradition. It's viewed as ceremonial activity—symbolic act of commemoration. However, symbolism and traditional rituals offer no practical benefit to our daily lives, according to the Kabbalist.

But because we have remained ignorant as to the true purpose of the Shofar, its effect in our lives, throughout history, has been negligible. Two thousand years of pain and suffering are evidence to that harsh truth.

The Shofar's power can only be expressed when knowledge of its true purpose is instilled within our consciousness. Knowing why we sound the Shofar is the electrical current that turns it on.

The sound emanating from the horn operates like a spiritual laser beam that dissolves all the blockages of negative energy that we have created. The mystical sound also acts as a cleansing agent that permeates every crack and crevice in our being, removing negative residues and purifying our soul. Once these blockages are removed, the Judgments have lost their targets. The evidence is destroyed.

The "prosecuting attorney," the Accuser Satan, stands before the "court"—universal law of cause and effect—without a shred of evidence. Case dismissed!

Here we ignite the sounds and secrets of the Shofar. The negative energy created by the sins of man is dissolved away and all Judgments are annulled.

Two days of Rosh Hashanah for Upper Judgment and Lower Judgment.

358. בְּיוֹמֵי דר״ה, מִתַּקְּנִין בֵּי דִּינָא כּוּרְסְיָיא לְמַלְכָּא, לְמֵידָן כָּל עָלְמָא. וְיִשְׂרָאֵל עָאלִין בְּקַדְמֵיתָא בְּדִינָא קַמֵּיהּ, דְּלִיפוּשׁ רַחֲמֵי. תְּנָן וּמִשְׁפַּט עַמּוֹ יִשְׂרָאֵל דְּבַר יוֹם בְּיוֹמוֹ, יוֹם בְּיוֹמוֹ מַאי הוּא. אֶלָּא הָנֵי תְּרֵי יוֹמִין דר״ה. אֲמַאי

תְּרֵי יוֹמִין. בְּגִין דְּאִינּוּן תְּרֵי בֵּי דִּינָא, דְּמִתְחַבְּרָן כַּחֲדָא. דִּינָא עִלָּאָה, דְּאִיהוּ קַשְׁיָא, בְּדִינָא תַּתָּאָה, דְּאִיהוּ רַפְיָא, וְתַרְוַויְיהוּ מִשְׁתַּכְחֵי.

358. On the days of Rosh Hashanah, the court prepares a throne for the King to judge the whole world. Israel come in first to be judged before Him, so that Mercy will multiply, namely before anger is aroused at the sinners of the world. **It is written: "...and the justice of His people, Yisrael, fulfilling the need of each day, on that day." (I Kings 8:59) What is "...of each day, on that day"?** The meaning is **the two days of Rosh Hashanah.** He asks: **"And why are there two days?"** He answers: **"Because they are two courts joined together. There is the Upper Judgment, which is harsh, and the Lower Judgment that is lenient, and both of them exist."**

Explanation: The secret of the Shofar blowing is to awaken the Judgments of the Masach of Chirik of the Central Column, to unite both the Right and Left Columns together. This Masach of Chirik does two actions to the Left Column. The first action is in the secret of the Man'ula (Lock), which is Harsh Judgment, and the second action is in the secret of Maftecha (Key), which is Soft Judgment. The Man'ula is hidden in the Upper Three of every grade and the Maftecha is in the Lower Six of each grade. This is why the Man'ula is called the Upper Courthouse and Maftecha the Lower Courthouse. And they always shine one within the other because they need each other. The Maftecha receives the force of Judgment from Man'ula, and the Man'ula receives a sweetening Illumination from Maftecha.

This is: **"they are two courts joined together. There is the Upper Judgment, which is harsh,"** which is the secret of the Man'ula that is hidden in the Upper Three, **"and the Lower Judgment that is lenient,"** which is the secret of the Maftecha that is in the Lower Six, **"and both of them exist,"** since they shine within each other, as mentioned. Therefore the first day of Rosh Hashanah is the aspect of the Upper Three, where the Man'ula rules, which is Harsh Judgment, and the second day of Rosh Hashanah is the aspect of the Lower Six, where the Maftecha rules.

We blow both the Shevarim and Teru'ah because both are needed.

359. וְעַל דָּא לָא יַדְעֵי הָנֵי בַּבְלָאֵי, רָזָא דִּיבָבָא וִילָלוּתָא, וְלָא יַדְעֵי דְּתַרְוַויְיהוּ אִצְטְרִיכוּ, יְלָלוּתָא דְּאִיהוּ דִּינָא תַּקִּיפָא. תְּלַת תְּבִירִין דְּאִיהוּ דִּינָא רַפְיָא, גְּנוּחֵי גָּנַח רַפְיָא. אִינּוּן לָא יַדְעֵי, וְעַבְדִין תַּרְוַויְיהוּ. וַאֲנָן יַדְעִינָן, וְעַבְדֵינָן תַּרְוַויְיהוּ. וְכֹלָּא נָפְקִין לְאֹרַח קְשׁוֹט.

359. This is why the Babylonians did not know the secret of the Shevarim and Teru'ah and that both of them are required. The Teru'ah is strict Judgment. The three notes of the Shevarim are Soft Judgment, and it is like **someone who groans** from his heart, **which is soft. They did not know** which of the two was required, and **they** therefore **had both of them. But we know** both, that both of them are required, **and do both** of them. **And everything goes by the way of truth.**

Soft Judgment-Maftecha, and Harsh Judgment-Man'ula.

360. פָּתַח וְאָמַר, תִּקְעוּ בַחֹדֶשׁ שׁוֹפָר בַּכֶּסֶה לְיוֹם חַגֵּנוּ. תִּקְעוּ בַחֹדֶשׁ שׁוֹפָר, מַאי בַחֹדֶשׁ. דָּא בֵּי דִּינָא רַפְיָא, דְּאִקְרֵי חֹדֶשׁ. בַּכֶּסֶה: דָּא דִּינָא קַשְׁיָא, פַּחַד יִצְחָק. דִּינָא דְּאִתְכַּסְיָיא תָּדִיר, דְּלָאו אִיהוּ דִּינָא בְּאִתְגַּלְיָיא. כִּי חֹק, דָּא דִּינָא רַפְיָא. וּמִשְׁפָּט, דָּא דִּינָא בְּרַחֲמֵי. וְתַרְוַויְיהוּ אִינּוּן כַּחֲדָא. בג"כ תְּרֵין יוֹמִין, וְתַרְוַויְיהוּ בְּרָזָא חֲדָא.

360. He began by quoting: "Blow the Shofar at the New Moon, in concealment for our feast day. For it is a statute for Israel, an ordinance of the God of Jacob." (Psalms 81:4-5) He asks: **"What is 'Blow the Shofar at the New Moon'?"** He answers: **"It means Soft Judgment that is called 'New Moon.'"** He asks: **"And what is 'in concealment'?"** He answers: "**This is Harsh Judgment, which is** also termed **'the fear of Isaac'. It is a Judgment that is always concealed,** namely the Man'ula (Lock), **which is not revealed Judgment. 'For it is a statute' (Ibid.) refers to Soft Judgment,** which is the secret of Maftecha, which is revealed. **'and an ordinance' refers to Judgment** included **with Mercy, and the two of them are there together, and this is why there are two days** of Rosh Hashanah, **and they are both in the same secret."**

Those who know the Teru'ah merit to walk in the Light of the Countenance of the Creator.

361. אַשְׁרֵי הָעָם יוֹדְעֵי תְרוּעָה וְגוֹ', לָא כְּתִיב שׁוֹמְעֵי, אוֹ תּוֹקְעֵי תְרוּעָה, אֶלָּא יוֹדְעֵי תְרוּעָה. בְּגִין וַחֲכִימִין דְּדַיְירִין בַּאֲוִירָא דְאַרְעָא קַדִּישָׁא, אִינּוּן יָדְעֵי תְרוּעָה. רָזָא דִתְרוּעָה, כְּמָה דִכְתִיב תְּרוֹעֵם בְּשֵׁבֶט בַּרְזֶל. מַאן עַמָּא כְּיִשְׂרָאֵל, דְּיַדְעִין רָזִין עִלָּאִין דְּמָארֵיהוֹן, לְמֵיעַל קַמֵּיהּ, וּלְאִתְקַשְּׁרָא בֵּיהּ. וְכָל אִינּוּן דְּיַדְעֵי רָזָא דִתְרוּעָה, יִתְקָרְבוּן לְמֵיהַךְ בְּאוֹר פָּנָיו דְקוּדְשָׁא בְּרִיךְ הוּא. וְדָא אוֹר קַדְמָאָה דְּגָנִיז קוּדְשָׁא בְּרִיךְ הוּא לְצַדִּיקַיָּיא. וע"ד אִצְטְרִיךְ לְמִנְדַּע לָהּ.

361. "Happy is the people that know the joyful note (Teru'ah)" (Psalms 89:15). It does not say that "hear," nor does it say "that blow the sounds of a Teru'ah," **but "that know." This is because** only **the sages who dwell in the atmosphere of the Holy Land are the ones who know Teru'ah. The secret of the Teru'ah is as it is written: "You shall break them (tero'em) with a rod of iron…." (Psalms 2:9) What people is there like Israel, who know the Heavenly secrets of their Master, enter in before Him, and associate with Him? And all those who know the secret of the Teru'ah will draw near and walk in the Light of the Countenance of the Holy One, blessed be He, because this is the first Light that the Holy One, blessed be He, hid for the righteous. This is why it is necessary to know it,** the Teru'ah.

60. The appendage of the liver, gall, trachea, esophagus, and the Shofar

A Synopsis

Rav Hamnuna talks about the iniquity of Lili"t and Sama"el, saying that they are the liver and the appendix, and that from them emerge the gall that is the sword of the Angel of Death. On Rosh Hashanah the gall wanders the world collecting up sins, and all of Israel are in trouble; this is when they blow the Shofar.

The Relevance of this Passage

Extraordinary notions relating to heart disease, human behavior, healing, and world peace emerge from this ancient passage. According to the Zohar, our reactive emotions, notably anger and rage, manifest in our liver and its appendage.

A remarkable insight is then presented in paragraph 364:

> **"From the liver and the appendage,** which are Sama"el and Lili"t, **emerges the gall, which is the sword of the Angel of Death, from which come bitter drops to kill human beings."**

In paragraph 365, the Zohar says that the gall:

> **"overcomes the arteries of the heart and all the arteries in the limbs of the body"**

Interestingly, gall is defined as both "bile" and "bitterness of spirit" or "rancor." This definition reinforces the kabbalistic viewpoint that a vital connection exists between human behavior and physical health. Moreover, it is the liver that secretes gall (bile), and its primary component is cholesterol. High levels of cholesterol are a major cause of atherosclerosis, the hardening and blockage of arteries, one of the most frequent causes of heart disease and death.

All the anger and negative reflexive emotions that we have expressed throughout the year are used by the negative angel Lili"t during Rosh Hashanah as an indictment against us. The ensuing Judgment manifests as illness and heart-related diseases. The Shofar is used to purify us, and to remove the force of Satan from our arteries and cardiovascular system. Metaphysically, it works like this:

The esophagus is spelled Vav-Shin-Tet (*Veshet*; ושט). However, the Zohar explains that when we are overly self-indulgent, allowing our ego and selfish desires to grow incessantly, the letter Vav (ו) also grows and extends into the letter Nun (ן). The letters that spell esophagus are now rearranged to spell Satan (Sin-Tet-Nun; שטן). This effect is rooted in an event that took place in the Torah, in the Book of Numbers. The children of Israel were given Manna from Heaven, a spiritual substance that could taste like the finest meal one could imagine. However a consciousness of certainty in the Manna's power was the prerequisite. The Israelites did not possess this state of mind and could therefore not connect to this spiritual energy. They demanded and received physical meat. The Satan infiltrated their bodies while the meat was in their teeth, indicating their total connection to physicality.

The Zohar states that when our own physical desires run rampant and we choose the physical world over the spiritual, the Satan again overcomes "all the limbs and the arteries" for all the 365 days of the solar year.

There is, however, recourse for the repentant heart—and it is found in the instrument of the Shofar, the trachea, and the event of Yom Kippur.

The trachea is a windpipe, just like the Shofar, which is a musical windpipe. The Shofar correlates to the realm of Binah, where there is so much pleasure and fulfillment that there is no need for food and drink. Like the Shofar, the trachea is not utilized when we eat or drink; only air enters our trachea.

On Yom Kippur, there is also no eating and drinking, signifying Binah and the unimaginable spiritual nourishment that it provides. Second, the numerical value of the "the Satan" (השטן) is 364, which is one number short of the 365 days of the year. Yom Kippur is the one day of the year when Satan is banished from our world.

Blowing the Shofar and observing Yom Kippur reestablishes our connection to Binah. The Nun (ן) in the word Satan is reduced in size—just as we reduce our desire to consume food and drink on Yom Kippur—and it reverts back into a Vav (ו) to again spell *Veshet* (ושט), esophagus in Hebrew. Satan and the force of death are now extracted from our arteries and limbs.

This splendid passage recalls the energy of Yom Kippur and it sounds the Shofar on our behalf to heal our hearts, liver, arteries, trachea, esophagus, and limbs. Good cholesterol levels rise while bad cholesterol levels decrease. Our blood is cleansed of toxins. The arteries are cleared of deadly deposits and plaque.

Israel, the cosmic counterpart of the human heart, also functions as the heart of humankind. Israel's relationship to the rest of the world is like the heart's arteries that carry blood and oxygen to the rest of the body. The nations of the world correspond to the body's organs and limbs. Hence, the same way that the heart now supplies purified blood to nourish the body, Israel furnishes Light to aid all the nations of the world because of our meditation. Furthermore, conflicts and barriers between Israel and all nations are henceforth eliminated, clearing the way for global harmony and lasting peace.

As Satan is absent from the world on Yom Kippur, the Light generated from this passage now banishes Satan from the other 364 days of the solar calendar, paving the way for the Messiah to arrive in our day.

The appendage of the liver alludes to Lili"t, the female of Sama"el.

362. כְּתִיב הַיּוֹתֶרֶת מִן הַכָּבֵד. וּכְתִיב וְאֶת הַיּוֹתֶרֶת עַל הַכָּבֵד. יוֹתֶרֶת מִן הַכָּבֵד, דָּא אֵשֶׁת זְנוּנִים, דְּאַזְלָא וְנָפְקָא מִן הַכָּבֵד, לְאַסְטָאָה בְּנֵי עָלְמָא, וּלְאַסְטְנָא עֲלַיְיהוּ. וְשַׁבְקַת לִדְכוּרָא, לְמֶעְבַּד זְנוּנִים. וּבג"ד הַיּוֹתֶרֶת מִן הַכָּבֵד, יוֹתֶרֶת עַל הַכָּבֵד. בָּתַר דְּעַבְדַת נִיאוּפָא, אִסְתָּלְקַת עָלֵיהּ. מֵצַח אִשָּׁה זוֹנָה. אִתְגַּבְּרַת עַל בַּעְלָהּ דְּאִיהוּ כָּבֵד, בְּכַעַס דְּמָרָה, אֵשֶׁת מְדָנִים, וָכַעַס, דְּשַׁלְטָא אִיהִי עַל דְּכוּרָא דִּילָהּ. מֵצַח אִשָּׁה זוֹנָה שַׁלְטָא עַל הַכָּבֵד, אֵשֶׁת מְדָנִים וָכַעַס.

362. It is written: "…the appendage of the liver…" (Leviticus 9:10), and also "…the appendage above the liver…." (Leviticus 3:4) "the appendage of the liver" means **a woman of harlotry,** that is Lili"t, **who comes out and emerges from the liver,** that is Sama"el, **to mislead people and denounce them, and she leaves the male to practice prostitution. And that is why** it is written: **"the appendage of the liver"; "the appendage above the liver"** means that, **after her fornications, she rises above him. She has "a harlot's forehead (brazenness)" (Jeremiah 3:3) and subdues her husband, who is** Sama"el, who is called **"liver," with the anger of the gall, being a quarrelsome and anger-prone wife who rules over her male.** Thus **"The harlot's forehead" has control over the liver,** which is Sama"el, because she is **a quarrelsome, angry woman** and is therefore called "the appendix above the liver."

The female Klipah commits adultery.

363. יוֹתֶרֶת מִן הַכָּבֵד, מִן הַכָּבֵד נָפְקָא לְאַבְאָשָׁא לְכָל עָלְמָא, וּלְמֶעְבַּד נִיאוּפִין עִם כֹּלָּא. לְבָתַר אִיהִי סַלְקָא לְגַבֵּי דְּכוּרָא, מֵצַח אִשָּׁה זוֹנָה, בְּעַזּוּתָא דְּאַנְפִּין, וּכְדֵין אִיהִי עַל הַכָּבֵד. וְעוֹד, יוֹתֶרֶת מִן הַכָּבֵד אִתְקְרִיאַת מִסִּטְרָא אַחֲרָא, בָּתַר דְּנַפְקַת לְנָאֲפָא עִם כֹּלָּא, יְהִיבַת שִׁיּוּרִין לְבַעְלָהּ, וְהַאי אִיהִי יוֹתֶרֶת מִן הַכָּבֵד.

363. "the appendage of the liver:" Because she **emerges from the liver,** who, as explained above, is Sama"el her husband, **in order to harm the whole world and practice adultery with all. She then mounts the male, with "a harlot's forehead," audaciously, and she is then above the liver. Also, she is called "the appendix of the liver," from another point of view, for after she has gone out to play prostitute with all, she gives the leftovers to her husband, and this is the meaning of "the appendix (*yoteret*) of the liver,"** *yoteret* means additional, namely leftovers.

Explanation: The appendage of the liver is from the aspect of Sama"el, which is the Male Judgments, but because she prostitutes with others also the Female Judgments are mixed in as well.

The gall is the sword of the Angel of Death,
which prowls through the world on Rosh Hashanah.

364. מִגּוֹ כָּבֵד, וְיוֹתֶרֶת דִּילָהּ, נַפְקַת מָרָה, וְאִיהִי חַרְבָּא דְּמַלְאָךְ הַמָּוֶת, דְּנַפְקוּ מִנָּהּ טִפִּין מְרִירָן לְקַטְלָא בְּנֵי נָשָׁא. הה"ד, וְאַחֲרִיתָהּ מָרָה כַלַּעֲנָה. וְאִיהִי תַּלְיָא בְּכָבֵד, כָּל מַרְעִין וּמוֹתָא בֵּיהּ תַּלְיָין. וְהַהוּא יוֹמָא דר"ה מְשַׁטְּטָא בְּעָלְמָא, לְמִכְנַשׁ כָּל חוֹבֵי עָלְמָא וּכְדֵין כָּל אֵבָרִין דְּאִינּוּן יִשְׂרָאֵל, אִינּוּן בְּעָאקוּ, דְּאִינּוּן אֵבָרֵי דְּמַטְרוֹנִיתָא, נֵר יְיָ' נִשְׁמַת אָדָם, שְׁכִינְתָּא קַדִּישָׁא. וּכְדֵין כָּל יִשְׂרָאֵל בְּעָאקוּ, וְנַטְלֵי שׁוֹפָר לְאִתְעָרָא בֵּיהּ הַהוּא תְּקִיעָה וּשְׁבָרִים וּתְרוּעָה.

364. From the liver and its appendage, which are Sama"el and Lili"t, **emerges the gall, which is the sword of the Angel of Death, from which come bitter drops to kill people. It is written: "Her end is bitter (marah) as wormwood." (Proverbs 5:4) And** the gall (*marah*) **is hanging over the liver, all sickness and death coming from it,** from the Klipah that is called "gall." **And on that day of Rosh Hashanah, she prowls through the world, collecting up all the sins that are in the world. And then all the parts, which are Israel, are in trouble,** for Israel **are the parts of the Shechinah,** as it is said, **"The soul of**

man is the candle of the Lord" (Proverbs 20:27), which means that the soul of man is derived from the candle of the Lord, **which is the Holy Shechinah. And then,** on Rosh Hashanah, **all Israel are in trouble, so they take a Shofar to awaken with it those calls: Teki'ah, Shevarim, Teru'ah.**

A Synopsis

Moses talks about the participation of the body—the trachea, the lungs, the arteries, the breath, the esophagus, and the mouth—in the blowing of the Shofar. He says that the Satan has no control on Yom Kippur, the Day of Atonement. Israel's strength is in the voice, not in eating and drinking like everyone else in the world, and it is necessary to awaken the voice with the ten Shofar verses.

The Shofar is likened to the trachea, which blows goodness to the body.

רעיא מהימנא

365. אָמַר רַעְיָא מְהֵימְנָא, וַדַּאי בָּתַר דְּאֵבָרִים וְעַרְקִין דְּלִבָּא, דְּדַמְיָין לְיִשְׂרָאֵל, אִינּוּן בְּעָאקוּ. צְרִיכִין לְאַתְעָרָא בְּקָנֶה, דְּאִיהוּ שׁוֹפָר. וְדָא קָנֶה דְּרֵיאָה. בָּתַר דְּכַנְפֵי רֵיאָה לָא יַכְלִין לְשַׁכְּכָא רוּגְזָא דְּמָרָה דְּאִתְגַּבְּרַת עַל עַרְקִין דְּלִבָּא, וְעַל כָּל עַרְקִין דְּאֵבָרִים דְּגוּפָא. הַהוּא רוּחָא דְּנָשִׁיב בְּהוֹן, סָלִיק בְּקָנֶה, דְּאִיהוּ שׁוֹפָר, עָלְמָא דְּאָתֵי. דְּהָכִי אוֹקְמוּהָ, וֶשֶׁט, דּוֹמֶה לְעָלְמָא דֵּין, דְּבֵיהּ אֲכִילָה וּשְׁתִיָּה. קָנֶה, דּוֹמֶה לְעָלְמָא דְּאָתֵי, דְּלֵית בֵּיהּ אֲכִילָה וּשְׁתִיָּה.

Ra'aya Meheimna (Faithful Shepherd)

365. The Faithful Shepherd said, "Certainly, after the limbs and the arteries of the heart, which are likened to Israel, are in trouble, they have to awaken in the trachea pipe, which is the secret of the Shofar, this being the windpipe connected to the lung. Since the lobes of the lung are unable to quiet the anger of the gall, which overcomes the arteries of the heart and all the arteries in the limbs of the body, that breath, which is the secret of Chasadim **that blows in them, rises in the trachea, which is a Shofar, namely the World to Come.** For the

Shofar is the secret of Binah that is called the 'World to Come.' **And so it has been taught: The esophagus is like this world,** which is the secret of Malchut, **within which is eating and drinking,** namely the Mochin of Chasadim and Chochmah that are termed eating and drinking. **The trachea is likened to the World to Come,** which is Binah, **for there is no eating and drinking in it,** for those Mochin are not revealed there in Binah but in Malchut.

When the esophagus wanders off, it becomes Satan.

366. וּלְבָתַר דְּשָׁט ו' מִן וֶשֶׁט, בְּרִבּוּי אֲכִילָה דְּגָזֵל אִתְאֲרַךְ וְאִתְעֲבִיד שָׂטָן. וּמַאן גָּרִים דָּא. שָׁטוּ הָעָם וְלָקְטוּ שְׁטוּתָא דִּלְהוֹן, דְּאִתְעָרְבוּ בְּעֶרֶב רַב שַׁטְיָין, דְּתַאֲוָה דִּלְהוֹן אֲכִילָה וּשְׁתִיָּה דְּגָזֵל וְחָמָס, דְּשׁוֹד עֲנִיִּים וְאֶנְקַת אֶבְיוֹנִים. בְּנוּן כְּפוּפָה שַׁטְיָין, דְּאַכְלִין בְּלָא טְחִינָה. מַה כְּתִיב בְּהוּ, הַבָּשָׂר עוֹדֶנּוּ בֵּין שִׁינֵּיהֶם טֶרֶם יִכָּרֵת וְאַף יְיָ' חָרָה בָעָם. אִתְפְּשַׁט ו' דְּשָׁטוּ, אִיהוּ דְּרוּחֵיהּ כָּפוּף, וְאִיהוּ נ'. וְדָא גָּרַם דְּאִתְפְּשַׁט שָׂטָן בַּאֲכִילָה וּשְׁתִיָּה, וְאִתְגַּבַּר עַל כָּל אֵבָרִין וְעַרְקִין בְּשַׂ"ה לֹא תַעֲשֶׂה. כְּחוּשְׁבַּן הַשָּׂטָ"ן חָסֵר חַד, דָּא יוֹם הַכִּפּוּרִים, דְּלֵית בֵּיהּ אֲכִילָה וּשְׁתִיָּה.

366. "And after the Vav (ו) of esophagus (*veshet*; Vav-Shin-Tet; ושט) has wandered off (*shat*; Shin-Tet; שט) because of the great amount of eating that it robbed, it grew longer, and the Vav (ו) **became a final Nun and becomes the Satan** (Sin-Tet-Nun; שטן)**. Who caused that? 'The people wandered about (*shatu*) and gathered....' (Numbers 11:8)** *shatu* can be derived from the word *shtut* (stupidity). For this **brought about their stupidity in that they intermingled with the foolish mixed multitude whose craving was for food and drink and robbery and violence, 'For the violence done to the poor, for the sighing of the needy' (Psalms 12:6). They went astray with a bent Nun (נ), for they ate without grinding it. And what is written about them? 'And while the meat was yet between their teeth, before it was chewed, the wrath of the Lord was inflamed against the people....' (Numbers 11:33) For the Vav (ו) of *shatu* (Shin-Tet-Vav;**

שׂטו) **expanded** and became a final Nun (ן), thus making Satan (שׂטן). **And he whose spirit is hunched is as a** bent **Nun,** meaning that the Holiness had become a bent Nun, but the Other Side a straight final Nun. **And the result of this was that the Satan spread through eating and drinking and overcame all the limbs and the arteries with the 365 negative precepts,** for all 365 days of the solar year. **And this is as the numerical value of *haSatan* (the Satan; השׂטן), minus one, which is** the day of **Yom Kippur** that he does not have, **on which there is no eating and drinking.** Thus the Satan has no control on Yom Kippur, and is short one day of the full 365."

Explanation: The incorporation of Chochmah with Chasadim in Netzach and Hod is called "grinding," in the secret of the Firmament called *shechakim* where manna is ground for the Righteous. The Mixed Multitudes amplify the Left and draw their eating and drinking from the Left without the Right, which is considered without grinding. This is: **"They went astray with a bent Nun, for they ate without grinding it."** Since they ate without grinding, the Satan cleaved to them and the Holiness in them became a bent Nun, since the Holy Spirit departed from them.

One who sees a trachea in a dream merits Chochmah and Binah.

367. וְאִיהוּ כְּגַוְונָא דְקָנֶה, וְאִיהוּ ו' בֶּן יָ"ה, מִן בִּינָה. וּבְגִינֵיהּ אוּקְמוּהָ מָארֵי מַתְנִיתִין, הָרוֹאֶה קָנֶה בַּחֲלוֹם, זוֹכֶה לַחָכְמָה. הה"ד, קְנֵה חָכְמָה קְנֵה בִינָה. דְּלֵית קָנֶה דְּאִיהוּ פָּחוֹת מִתַּרְוַויְיהוּ, דְּאִינּוּן י' חָכְמָה, ה' בִּינָה. וּבג"ד, צָרִיךְ לְאִתְעָרָא בַּשּׁוֹפָר, דְּאִיהוּ קָנֶה, עָלְמָא דְאָתֵי, עוֹלָם אָרוֹךְ, אֶרֶךְ אַפַּיִם, דְּמִשְׁתַּכְּחֵי מִינֵּיהּ י"ג מְכִילָן דְּרַחֲמֵי, כְּחוּשְׁבַּן וָא"ו, א' אֶרֶךְ, ו' ו' אַפַּיִם.

367. And Yom Kippur **is like the trachea (*kaneh;* קָנֶה)** of the lung, which is Binah and the World to Come, as above. **And it is Vav, the son of Yud-Hei (*ben* Yud-Hei; בן יה) of Binah (בינה). And in respect thereof, the sages of the Mishnah taught: "He who sees a reed**

(***kaneh***; **קָנֶה**) **in a dream, attains wisdom, for it says "Get (*k'neh*; קְנֵה) wisdom, get understanding....' (Proverbs 4:5) For there is no *kaneh* that is less than both, namely Yud-Chochmah, Hei-Binah,** for there is no Binah without Chochmah and no Chochmah without Binah. **And this is why they should awaken the Shofar, which is a trachea,** as mentioned, **which is the World to Come—a long world** that receives from Arich Anpin (Long Face) **from whom come the Thirteen Attributes of Mercy that equals Vav-Alef-Vav in numerical value, where the Alef is** the secret of ***erech*** **(long), and the two Vavs are** the secret of ***apayim*** **(suffering; lit. two noses)."**

The blasts of the Shofar correspond to the Patriarchs and Malchut that links them.

368. וְאִימָּא עִלָּאָה אִיהִי תְּקִיעָה, מִסִּטְרָא דְּאַבְרָהָם. שְׁבָרִים, מִסִּטְרָא דְּיִצְחָק. תְּרוּעָה, מִסִּטְרָא דְּיַעֲקֹב. שְׁכִינְתָּא תַּתָּאָה, קֶשֶׁר דְּכֻלְּהוּ. דְּהַיְינוּ: ק' תְּקִיעָה. ש' שְׁבָרִים. ר' תְּרוּעָה. וְכֻלְּהוּ מְשַׁלְּשִׁין לְגַבֵּי שְׁכִינְתָּא, הה"ד, קְדוּשָּׁה לְךָ יְשַׁלֵּשׁוּ. דְּלֵית קָלָא יָכִיל לְנָפְקָא לְבַר, אֶלָּא מִן הַפֶּה. אוּף הָכִי, לֵית לְאַפְרְשָׁא שְׁכִינְתָּא מִן קוּדְשָׁא בְּרִיךְ הוּא. דְּקוּדְשָׁא בְּרִיךְ הוּא אִתְּמַר בֵּיהּ, קוֹל יְיָ' חוֹצֵב לַהֲבוֹת אֵשׁ. וּשְׁכִינְתָּא תְּפִלַּת כָּל פֶּה. וְאִינּוּן סִימָנִין, קֶשֶׁ"ר קְשׁ"ק קְר"ק.
עַד כָּאן רַעְיָא מְהֵימְנָא

368. And Supernal Ima is Teki'ah from the side of Abraham, who is Chesed. **Shevarim are from the side of Isaac,** who is Gevurah. **Teru'ah is from the side of Jacob,** who is Tiferet. **The lower Shechinah,** which is Malchut, **is the link (Kof-Shin-Resh; קֶשֶׁר) between them all,** for she receives them all. And the word *kesher* is formed from the initial letters of Teki'ah, Shevarim, Teru'ah, where **Teki'ah is Kof, Shevarim is Shin, and Teru'ah is Resh. And all of them are sounded thrice in the Shechinah, as it is written: "They proclaim You thrice Holy." (from the Nakdishach) For the voice cannot come out** of the body **other than through the mouth. So here, too, the Shechinah must not be separated from the Holy One, blessed be He, for about the**

Holy One, blessed be He, it is said: "The voice of the Lord hews out flames of fire." (Psalms 29:7) And the Shechinah is "the prayer of every mouth." And these are the mnemonics: Kof-Shin-Resh-Kof, Kof-Shin-Kof, Kof-Resh-Kof. And the explanations of the blowings are explained in Zohar Emor 195.
End of Ra'aya Meheimna (Faithful Shepherd)

Teki'ah and Teru'ah are blown together to incorporate Harsh and Soft Judgments together.

369. נַטְלִין שׁוֹפָר, לְאִתְעֲרָא בֵּיהּ, תְּרוּעָה וּתְקִיעָה, דִּינָא קַשְׁיָא בְּרַחֲמֵי, וּשְׁבָרִים דִּינָא רַפְיָא בְּרַחֲמֵי וּכְדֵין הָכִי יִתְעֲרוּ לְעֵילָּא לְאִתְעָרְבָא דָא בְּדָא.

369. The Shofar is taken in order to awaken with it Teru'ah and Teki'ah, which are **Harsh Judgment with Mercy,** for the Teru'ah is harsh Judgment, and Teki'ah is Mercy. **And Shevarim** Teki'ah **means Soft Judgment with Mercy,** since Shevarim is Soft Judgment and Teki'ah is Mercy. **And then they thus awaken on high and intermingle with each other,** that is, Judgment with Mercy and Mercy with Judgment.

The strength of Israel is through their voice.

רעיא מהימנא

370. וּבְחִבּוּרָא קַדְמָאָה, אָמַר רַעְיָא מְהֵימְנָא, בְּהַאי אִתְבְּסַם שָׂטָן, וְקָמִיט נו"ן מִן וָשֵׂט, מַה דַּהֲוָה שָׂטָן לְפָנִים, תָּב לַאֲחוֹרָא, וְאִתְהֲדַר וָשֵׂט, כִּדְבְקַדְמֵיתָא. בְּגִין דְּהַקּוֹל קוֹל יַעֲקֹב. יִשְׂרָאֵל לֵית חֵילֵיהוֹן בַּאֲכִילָה וּשְׁתִיָּה, כִּשְׁאַר עַמִּין, דְּיַרְתִּין עָלְמָא דֵּין, דְּחֵילֵיהוֹן בַּאֲכִילָה וּשְׁתִיָּה. אֶלָּא חֵילֵיהוֹן בְּקוֹל דָּא, דְּאִיהוּ עָלְמָא דְּאָתֵי, עוֹלָם אָרוֹךְ, דְּאִתְבְּרֵי בְּאָת יו"ד, וּבְגִין דְּקוֹל שׁוֹפָר מִנֵּיהּ נָפִיק, אָמְרוּ רַבָּנָן אֵין פּוֹחֲתִין מֵעֲשָׂרָה שׁוֹפָרוֹת. וּבְאוֹת י' וַדַּאי, אִתְעֲבִיד עוֹלָם אָרוֹךְ, דְּאִיהוּ ו' עָלְמָא דְּאָתֵי וּבְאָת ה', בָּרָא עָלְמָא דֵּין, דְּאִיהִי ה' זְעֵירָא, דְּבָהּ אֲכִילָה וּשְׁתִיָּה דְּאוֹרַיְיתָא.

Ra'aya Meheimna (Faithful Shepherd)

370. And in the first compilation, the Faithful Shepherd said, "Through this the Satan is mitigated and the final Nun (ן) of *veshet* (esophagus; Vav-Shin-Tet; ושט) was folded and it returned to be a Vav (ו). **Where** the esophagus **became the Satan, it is now put back and becomes an esophagus again, as it was. This is because 'the voice is the voice of Jacob' (Genesis 27:22) for Israel have no power through eating and drinking, as do the other nations who inherit this world, whose strength lies in eating and drinking. But** as for Israel, **their strength is in the voice, which is the World to Come, a long world that was created with the letter Yud. And since the voice of the Shofar,** which is the secret of the Mochin of Zeir Anpin that are called Voice, which receives from Shofar, which is Binah, **emerges from it,** from the Yud which is Chochmah, **the sages said: one may not blow less than... ten Shofar verses,'** namely corresponding to the letter Yud (10). **For with the letter Yud a long world is certainly made, which is Vav, the World to Come,** namely that receives Mochin of the World to Come, as mentioned. **And with the letter Hei, He created this world, which is small Hei,** namely Malchut, **in which there is eating and drinking of the Torah,** namely the Mochin of Chochmah and Chasadim that are called 'eating' and 'drinking.'

Yud and Vav are able to nullify the decree that was sentenced in the two Courthouses, Hei and Hei.

371. וְעוֹד רָזָא אַחֲרָא, בָּתַר דְּאִתְגְּזַר גְּזֵרָה בִּתְרֵין אַתְוָון, דְּאִינּוּן ה' ה', תְּרֵין בָּתֵּי דִּינִין, מַאן יָכִיל לְבַטְלָא גְּזֵרָה דִּתְרַוַויְיהוּ. י"ו. דְּאָת הֵ"א אִימָּא עִלָּאָה. י' אַב. וּמַה כְּתִיב, כָּל נֵדֶר וְכָל שְׁבוּעַת אִסָּר לְעַנּוֹת נָפֶשׁ, דְּאִיהִי ה', אִישָׁהּ יְקִימֶנּוּ וְאִישָׁהּ יְפֵרֶנּוּ. וּבג"ד, צָרִיךְ לְאַתְעָרָא קָלָא דְּאִיהוּ ו', בַּעֲשָׂרָה שׁוֹפָרוֹת, דְּאִינּוּן י'. וְעִקָּרָא דִּלְהוֹן בִּנְשִׁימָה אַחַת, כָּל סִימָן וְסִימָן, בַּפֶּה, דְּאִיהִי י' מֵעֲשָׂרָה.

371. "And there is yet another secret. For after the decree is enacted in the two letters Hei-Hei, which are the two courts, Binah and

Malchut, **who is able to rescind the decree of both of them**, if not Yud-Vav of Yud-Hei-Vav-Hei? **For the letter Hei** of Yud-Hei-Vav-Hei **is Supernal Ima,** Binah, **and Yud is father,** Chochmah." He asks: **"And what is written?"** He answers: **"Every vow and every binding oath to afflict the soul," which is Hei** called 'soul' (*Nefesh*), **'...her husband may let it stand or her husband may make it void.' (Numbers 30:14) Here Yud is the husband of the first Hei, which is Binah, and Vav is the husband of the second Hei, which is Malchut. Thus the Yud and Vav can rescind the decree of the two Heis. It is thus necessary to awaken the voice, which is Vav,** which is Zeir Anpin, **with the ten Shofar verses that are Yud**, so as to annul the Judgments of the two Heis, Binah and Malchut. **And the main thing is that each of the Shofar sequences should be sounded in one breath, in the mouth, which is the tenth** part **of ten** (the sequences being Teki'ah, Shevarim-Teru'ah, Teki'ah; Teki'ah, Shevarim, Teki'ah; Teki'ah, Teru'ah, Teki'ah)."

Rav Shimon and the friends awaken appreciation
for being able to hear secret directly from Moses.

372. מִיַּד דְּשָׁמְעוּ מִלִּין ר"ש וְכָל חַבְרַיָּיא, אָמְרוּ, בְּרִיךְ אֱלָהָא דְּזָכֵינָא לְמִשְׁמַע מִלִּין, מֵהַהוּא דְּאִתְקְרֵי רַבָּן שֶׁל נְבִיאִים, רַבָּן דַּחֲכָמִים, רַבָּן דְּמַלְאֲכֵי הַשָּׁרֵת, דְּקוּדְשָׁא בְּרִיךְ הוּא וּשְׁכִינְתֵּיהּ מְדַבֵּר עַל פּוּמוֹי, וְכָתַב עַל יְדוֹי רָזִין אִלֵּין, דְּלָא אִשְׁתְּמָעוּ כְּוָותַיְיהוּ מִמַּתַּן תּוֹרָה, וְעַד כְּעַן.

372. Immediately upon hearing these matters, Rav Shimon and the friends exclaimed, "Blessed be God that we have been privileged to hear such matters from him who is called the Master of all the Prophets, Master of all the Sages, Master of all the Ministering Angels, [and] through whose mouth the Holy One, blessed be He, and His Shechinah speak, and by whose hands He wrote these secrets—the likes of which have not been heard since the revelation of the Torah until now."

The Faithful Shepherd asked Rav Shimon to continue speaking his words.

373. א"ל, בּוֹצִינָא קַדִּישָׁא, אַשְׁלִים מִלּוֹלֵי דְּרָזִין דְּחִבּוּרָא קַדְמָאָה, לְפָרְשָׁא לוֹן, דְּהָא כָּל מָארֵי מְתִיבְתָּאן דִּלְעֵילָּא, וּמָארֵי מְתִיבְתָּאן דִּלְתַתָּא, כֻּלְּהוּ מְזוּמָנִין לְמִשְׁמַע מִלִּין אִלֵּין מִפּוּמָךְ, וּפֵירוּשִׁין דִּילָךְ. דְּהָא חֶדְוָה וּפוּרְקָנָא, יִתְּעַר בְּהוֹן לְעֵילָּא וְתַתָּא. אַל תִּתְּנוּ דֳּמִי, לָא אַנְתְּ, וְכָל סִיעָתָא דִּילָךְ.
עד כאן רעיא מהימנא

373. The Faithful Shepherd **said** to Rav Shimon, **"Holy Luminary, complete the matters of the secrets of the first compilation, by expounding on them, for the heads of all of the Yeshivot Above and the heads of all the Yeshivot Below are waiting to hear these words from your mouth, with your clarifications. For thereby will rejoicing and redemption awaken in Heaven Above and on the Earth Below. 'And give no rest…' (Isaiah 62:7), neither you nor any of your friends."**
End of Ra'aya Meheimna (Faithful Shepherd)

61. The liver and the heart

A Synopsis

Rav Shimon says that the heart (God) takes from the liver only that which is pure and clean, leaving all the foulness for Sama"el, who distributes it to the idol worshipping nations.

The Relevance of this Passage

Once again, we discover how the spiritual worlds mirror the function of the physical body, shedding further light on the ultimate origins of disease. In essence, when we listen to and respond to selfish impulses (reactive behavior), we succumb to the prodding of our evil adversaries: the angels Satan/Sama"el and Lili"t. Each time we are responsive to their provocations—the rush to judgment, the urge to scream, the need to mistreat another person, the impulse to lie and deceive—their strength and hold over our body and our life increases.

Their stronghold, the Zohar tells us, is the liver. Physically, the liver filters our blood and then sends it, cleaned and purified, to the heart.

This medical truth is revealed by the Zohar's cryptic language:

> **"...everything that the liver is holding it sacrifices to the heart, which is the King, to nourish him... He takes everything that is clear and pure,** namely **all the merits and the good deeds...."**

This last statement alludes to the relationship among a good liver, purified blood, a healthy heart, and our positive behavior. The bile of the liver absorbs fat as well as waste and toxic matter from the blood. This function is encoded into the following text of Zohar:

> **"...all the foulness, the filth and the dirt, which are the bad deeds, He leaves for the liver,** which is Sama"el."

Our selfish impulses come from Sama"el. If we allow our selfish impulses to guide us in life, then Sama"el has the power to send impurities of the blood from the liver to the heart. In other words, our reactive, stress-induced behavior creates negative energy that manifests physically in our body as heart disease. **This truth is found in the following verse:**

> **"And the iniquities of His people are in the arteries** and sinews **that pulsate in the heart."**

Research shows that heart disease kills twice as many people as cancer and is one of the leading causes of death. The Zohar passage that we are now discussing provides us with spiritual Light that removes stress and anxiety from our being. We are imbued with the strength to resist reactive emotions and desires, and with the ability to resist heart disease.

Our blood is cleansed. Fatty deposits, also called plaque, are extracted from the walls of our arteries and dissolved away. The entire cardiovascular system is cleared and regenerated. Heart-related illnesses and diseases are treated and cured as the Light extinguishes the dark influences of the negative adversaries.

In paragraph 375, the Zohar explains that skin sores, boils, and leprosy are rooted in the liver and toxins that remain in our body. In addition to heart disease, these Zohar verses also heal all skin-related diseases.

The blasts of the Shofar return the sins to the liver and its arteries.

374. בִּתְרוּעָה וּתְקִיעָה וּשְׁבָרִים, אִתְבְּסַם כֹּלָּא דָּא בְּדָא. וְכָל מַה דְּהַהוּא כָּבֵד נָקִיט, אַקְרִיב לְגַבֵּי לֵב, דְּאִיהוּ מַלְכָּא, לְזַיְינָא. וְהַהוּא לֵב, לָאו אוֹרְחֵיהּ, וְלָאו תִּיאוּבְתֵּיהּ, בַּעֲכִירוּ דְּעוֹבָדִין דְּעַמֵּיהּ. אֶלָּא נָקִיט כָּל בְּרִירוּ, וְכָל צָחוּתָא, וְכָל זַכְיָין, וְכָל עוֹבָדִין טָבִין. וְכָל הַהוּא עֲכִירוּ וְטִנּוּפִין וְלִכְלוּכָא דְּאִינּוּן עוֹבָדִין בִּישִׁין, אַנַּח לְכָבֵד. דְּאִתְּמַר בֵּיהּ, עֵשָׂו אִישׁ שָׂעִיר. וְכָל עַרְקִין דִּילֵיהּ, דְּאִינּוּן שְׁאַר עַמִּין עכו"ם. הה"ד, וְנָשָׂא הַשָּׂעִיר עָלָיו אֶת כָּל עֲוֹנוֹתָם. מַאי עֲוֹנוֹתָם. עֲוֹנוֹת תָּם. דְּאִתְּמַר בֵּיהּ, וְיַעֲקֹב אִישׁ תָּם. וְחוֹבִין דְּעַמֵּיהּ דְּאִינּוּן עַרְקִין וְדַפְקִין דְּלִבָּא.

374. With Teru'ah, Teki'ah, and Shevarim, everything is perfumed, one with the other, for all of the Judgments are mitigated, **and everything that the liver holds it sacrifices to the heart, which is the king, to nourish it. And it is neither the way of the heart, nor does it desire the foulness of the deeds of its people, rather it takes everything that is clear and pure,** namely **all the merits and the good deeds, while all the foulness, the filth and the dirt that are the bad deeds it leaves for the liver,** which is Sama"el, **about whom it is said:**

"…Esau is a hairy (*sa'ir*) man…." (Genesis 27:11) And all its arteries, which are the other idol-worshipping people, are as it is written: "And the goat (*se'ir*) shall bear upon him all their iniquities…." (Leviticus 16:22) What is meant by "their iniquities" (*avonotam*)? *Avonot tam,* namely the iniquities of a *tam,* a complete man, the reference being to the same one about whom it is said, "…and Jacob was a complete man (*ish tam*)…." (Genesis 25:27) And the iniquities of its people are in the arteries and sinews **that pulsate in the heart.**

Shoftim

3. "At the mouth of two witnesses... shall the matter be established"

A Synopsis

Rav Shimon tells the Faithful Shepherd that the children of Israel are dry wood, connected to secular fire, and that they do not deserve to have miracles performed for them. But as soon as Moses descends on them with the Torah, the Tree of Life descends on them as well, and so does the *mitzvah* that is the candlelight of God—all for the sake of Moses. Through this candlelight, the heathen nations of the world will be burned. Rav Shimon talks about the two witnesses necessary in any trial, and says that even the walls of one's house will bear witness; the walls of one's house are said to be the inner walls of the heart, and the members of one's household are the 248 organs and limbs. Rav Shimon says that a wicked person's sins are even engraved on his bones. We learn that the reason sins are engraved on the bones is because the bones are white and the black script is easily recognizable. This is like the Torah with the white parchment and the black ink—black and white being darkness and light. In addition to this reason for the sins being carved into the bones, the body is destined to be reinstated with its bones, so all its merits and demerits are engraved there. If it is not worthy, it will not be resurrected from the dead. Returning to the issue of the two witnesses, Rav Shimon calls them the Seeing Eye and the Hearing Ear. He says that even the sun and moon testify about a person, and he speaks a good deal about those who give testimony.

The moon covers itself so that it cannot testify against Israel.

14. וְלָא עוֹד, אֶלָּא תְּרֵין סָהֲדִין אִינּוּן עַל ב"נ, עַיִן רוֹאָה וְאוֹזֶן שׁוֹמַעַת, וּב"ד סוֹפֵר, וְדָן חוֹבוֹי. וְלֹא עוֹד, אֶלָּא שִׁמְשָׁא וְסִיהֲרָא סָהֲדִין עַל ב"נ, כְּמָה דְּאוֹקְמוּהָ תִּקְעוּ בַחֹדֶשׁ שׁוֹפָר בַּכֶּסֶה לְיוֹם חַגֵּנוּ. מַאי בַּכֶּסֶה. בְּיוֹמָא דְסִיהֲרָא מִתְכַּסְּיָא. וַאֲמַאי מִתְכַּסְּיָא. בְּגִין דְּכַד מָטֵי רֹאשׁ הַשָּׁנָה, יֵיתֵי סָמָאֵל לְמִתְבַּע

דִּינָא לִבְנוֹי קַמֵּי קוּדְשָׁא בְּרִיךְ הוּא, וְהוּא יֵימָא לֵיהּ דְּיֵיתֵי סָהֲדִין. וְהוּא יֵיתֵי לְשִׁמְשָׁא עִמֵּיהּ. אָזַל לְמַיְיתֵי סִיהֲרָא, וְהִיא מִתְכַּסְיָא. בְּאָן אֲתָר מִתְכַּסֵּית. אֶלָּא סְלִיקַת, לְהַהוּא אֲתָר, דְּאִתְּמַר בֵּיהּ בַּמְכוּסֶּה מִמְּךָ אַל תַּחְקוֹר, לְפַיְּיסָא לֵיהּ עַל בְּנָהָא.

14. Furthermore, there are two witnesses on man: a Seeing Eye and a Hearing Ear. And the court counts and judges his iniquities. Furthermore, even the sun and moon testify about the person, as we explained: "Blow a Shofar at the New Moon, at the full moon (lit. 'on the covering') on our feast day." (Psalms 81:4) He asks: **"What is the meaning of 'covering'?"** He answers: **"That is the day when the moon,** which is Malchut, **is covered."** He asks: **"Why is it covered?"** He answers: **"That is because when Rosh Hashanah arrives, Sama"el will approach to demand punishment against her children,** meaning Israel, who are the children of Malchut, **before the Holy One, blessed be He. And He will tell him to bring forth the witnesses, so he will bring with him the sun. As he is about to bring the moon, she is covered."** He asks: **"At which place is she covered?"** He answers: **"She goes up to that place regarding which it is said: 'Do not investigate into what is hidden from you,' in order to reconcile the Holy One, blessed be He, with her children."**

A person needs to connect his iniquities to Keter.

15. וְהַאי הוּא דְּאָמַר קְרָא, תִּקְעוּ בַחֹדֶשׁ שׁוֹפָר בַּכֶּסֶה לְיוֹם חַגֵּנוּ. לַאֲתָר דְּבֵיהּ סְלִיקַת שְׁכִינְתָּא, דְּאִתְּמַר בֵּיהּ וּבַמְכוּסֶּה מִמְּךָ אַל תַּחְקוֹר. וְחוֹבִין בְּאִתְכַּסְיָיא, תַּמָּן צָרִיךְ לְמֵידָן בֵּינוֹ לְבֵין קוֹנוֹ. וְחוֹבִין דְּאִתְגַּלְיָיא דְּעָבֵד לוֹן, אִתְּמַר מְכַסֶּה פְּשָׁעָיו לֹא יַצְלִיחַ. דִּשְׁכִינְתָּא מִסִּטְרָא דְּכֶתֶר אִיהִי עָלְמָא דְּאִתְכַּסְיָא, וְאוֹקְמוּהָ מָארֵי מַתְנִיתִין, דְּצָרִיךְ ב"נ לְחַבְּרָא לָהּ לְהַהוּא אַתְרָא, בְּהַהוּא זִמְנָא מָטֵי זִמְנָא דְּרַחֲמֵי, וְאַעְבַּר דִּינָא. וּבְג"ד לְחַבְרֵיהּ אָמַר לְזַכָּאָה לֵיהּ בְּעֵדוּתֵיהּ. אֲבָל לְרָשָׁע אֵין מְזַכִּין לוֹ.

15. That is what the scripture says: "Blow a Shofar at the New Moon, at the covering on our feast day" (Psalms 81:4) meaning the area to which the Shechinah ascended. Regarding this, it is said, "Do not investigate into what is hidden from you." The iniquities that are in concealment need to be judged there between himself and his Creator. About the iniquities he committed in public it is written: "He that covers up his sins shall not prosper…." (Proverbs 28:13) The Shechinah from the side of Keter is the hidden world and the sages of the Mishnah have explained that a person needs to connect his iniquities **to that place,** which is Keter. **At that time, a period of Mercy arrives and Judgment passes away. Therefore, he recommends to connect** one's iniquities to Keter, **to free him from the testimony** of Malchut. **However, the wicked is not acquitted.**

Explanation: On Rosh Hashanah the world goes back its original state, and Malchut reverts to the first state it was in on the Fourth Day of Creation, namely the aspect of the "two great luminaries" (Genesis 1:16) where Zeir Anpin and Nukva clothe Binah, Zeir Anpin the Right Column of Binah and Malchut the Left Column. It is known that the Illumination of the Left without the Right is darkness, and the Right without the Left is Six Sefirot without Mochin. Therefore, then Zeir Anpin was in Dormita (Sleep State), as one who sleeps without their consciousness (Mochin), and Nukva was in Darkness. Then Sama'el came to demand Judgment, and he was told to be two witnesses—Zeir Anpin and Malchut—where the Heavens, Zeir Anpin, does not produce rain, meaning does not bestow to Malchut, and the Earth, Malchut, does not yield its produce to the Lower Beings.

However, Sama"el only brought with him one witness, which is the Heavens, Zeir Anpin who was in Dormita and did not bestow to Malchut. Once he came to bring Malchut, so that She will not yield Her produce to the Lower Beings, then Malchut covered Herself, namely She minimized Her Nine Lower Sefirot and remained only with her point of Keter. This diminishment is done by the blowing of the Shofar, since through the sound that comes from the Shofar, the force of the Masach of Chirik is awakened in Zeir Anpin, the Central Column, and through the Masach of Chirik, He diminishes the Left Column of Binah and unites there the Right and Left of Binah together. This awakens Mercy in the world with the power of this unification of Right and Left. Once the Left Column of Binah is diminished, all the Nine Lower Sefirot departed from Malchut, Whose entire foundation was from this Left Column then, and She remained with the point of Keter. This is the secret of: **"Blow a Shofar at the New Moon,"** which causes **"the covering on our feast day" (Psalms 81:4),** as the moon, Malchut, is covered in the secret of its point of Keter, and through this, Judgment is covered and Mercy is revealed in Judgment.

[In verse 14] this is: **"Why is it covered... and he will bring with him the sun,"** namely the fact that Zeir Anpin has no Mochin and does not bestow. **"As he is about to bring the moon...,"** namely to show Her darkness, **"...She goes up to that place... Do not investigate into what is hidden from you,"** namely She minimized Herself from all Her Sefirot and only Keter remained in Her, of which it is said, "Do not investigate into what is hidden from you" and then Mercy was formed in the world, as mentioned. [In verse 15] this is: **"The iniquities that are in concealment need to be judged there between himself and his Creator,"** because once the Left Column has been diminished and the attribute of Mercy emerged, there is no more room for Sama"el to grasp Malchut, and the Judgments of man are between himself and his Creator, without the harassment of Sama"el, and therefore the Creator has compassion on him. But as long as the Left Column is in control, **"the iniquities he committed in public,"** where the sins of man are grasped in the revealed world, Malchut, it is said "**He that covers up his sins shall not prosper...." (Proverbs 28:13)** since he cannot cover the sins in a way that Sama"el would not have a grasp on Malchut.

"**The Shechinah from the side of Keter is the hidden world**" since when the Shechinah is in the aspect of Her Keter, She is the concealed world since Keter is called "what is hidden from you," and Sama'el has no grasp there. This is: "**a person needs to connect them to that place. At that time, a period of Mercy arrives,**" as then the Right is unified with the Left via the Central Column, and Mercy is revealed. **"Therefore, he recommends to connect** one's iniquities to Keter, **to free him from the testimony,"** namely the wicked thinks to connect his sins to the aspect of Keter to free himself from its testimony, namely so that it cannot testify that Malchut is hidden there. **"However, the wicked is not acquitted."** And therefore it says "shall not prosper." But after Zeir Anpin diminishes the Left, by which Malchut elevates until her Keter that remains, the attribute of Mercy is revealed.

Zeir Anpin and Malchut give constant testimony.

16. וְעוֹד, קוּדְשָׁא בְּרִיךְ הוּא וּשְׁכִינְתֵּיהּ סָהֲדִין עַל ב"נ, הה"ד הַעִדוֹתִי בָכֶם הַיּוֹם אֶת הַשָּׁמַיִם וְאֶת הָאָרֶץ. אֶת הַשָּׁמַיִם, הַהוּא דְּאִתְּמַר בֵּיהּ וְאַתָּה תִּשְׁמַע הַשָּׁמַיִם. וְאֶת הָאָרֶץ, הַהוּא דְּאִתְּמַר בָּהּ וְהָאָרֶץ הֲדוֹם רַגְלָי. וְעוֹד, תְּרֵין סָהֲדִין: עַמּוּדָא דְּאֶמְצָעִיתָא, וְצַדִּיק. וְאִינּוּן ע"ד, מִן אֶחָד. עֵד, מִן בָּרוּךְ שֵׁם כְּבוֹד מַלְכוּתוֹ לְעוֹלָם וָעֶד.

16. Furthermore, the Holy One, blessed be He, and His Shechinah give constant **testimony about the person** and not only on Rosh Hashanah, as mentioned. **This is what is written: "I call Heaven and Earth to witnesses against you this day...." (Deuteronomy 4:26) "Heaven" is the one about which it is written: "Hear You (in) Heaven" (I Kings 8:32),** That is Zeir Anpin. **"Earth" is the one about which is written: "...and the earth is My footstool..." (Isaiah 66:1),** that is Malchut. **In addition, the two witnesses are the Central Column,** Zeir Anpin, **and the Righteous,** Yesod. **They are Ayin (ע) and Dalet (ד) of Shema (שמע) and Echad (one; אחד),** namely Ayin from the spelling of Shema, and Dalet from Echad. This is the witness

(*Ed;* עֵד; Ayin-Dalet) from the aspect of Zeir Anpin; **there is another witness from, "Blessed is the Name of the glory of His Kingdom forever and ever (va'ed; וָעֶד),"** namely *Ed* (עֵד) from the word *va'ed,* which is a witness from the aspect of Yesod in Zeir Anpin, which is included in Malchut.

Testimony against the side of death must be with two or more witnesses.

17. עַל פִּי שְׁנַיִם עֵדִים אוֹ שְׁלֹשָׁה עֵדִים יוּמַת הַמֵּת, דָא סָמָאֵל, מֵת מֵעִקָּרוֹ וַיִּשָּׂאוּהוּ בַמּוֹט בִּשְׁנָיִם. לֹא יוּמַת עַל פִּי עֵד אֶחָד, דְלָא יְהֵא לֵיהּ חוּלָקָא בְּאֵל אֶחָד.

17. "At the mouth of two witnesses or three witnesses, shall the dead be put to death...." (Deuteronomy 17:6) That is Sama"el, who is essentially dead: "...they carried it between two on a pole...." (Numbers 13:23) "...he shall not be put to death by the mouth of one witness" (Deuteronomy 17:6), meaning he shall have no portion in the one God.

Explanation: It was explained that on Rosh Hashanah, Malchut exists as the Left without the Right, and then Sama'el grasps Her. This happens until the blowing of the Shofar, which is the secret of Zeir Anpin that diminishes the Upper Three of the Left Column in Binah Above, through the Judgments of the Masach of Chirik that diminish Malchut to the point of Keter, which causes Sama"el to separate from Malchut. There are two witnesses here in the distancing of Sama"el from the Left Column of Malchut. The first is Her darkness, for when She cleaved to the Left without the Right all her Lights froze and she became darkness, yet Sama"el did not separate from Her and he nourished from Her. Thus She could not unite with Zeir Anpin, due to him. This is: **"...he shall not be put to death by the mouth of one witness" (Deuteronomy 17:6)** But afterwards, when the blowing of the Shofar awakens the Judgments of the Masach of Chirik in Zeir Anpin and diminishes the Upper Three of the Left through those Judgments, and the Lower Nine Sefirot of Malchut depart and she remains with Keter, then Sama"el separates from Malchut and She can be rebuilt and connect with Zeir Anpin and unite with him Face-to-Face. Once the Judgment of the Masach of Chirik is added to the Judgment of the darkness, then the "two witnesses" validate the testimony and Sama"el separates from Malchut.

This is: **"At the mouth of two witnesses or three witnesses, shall the dead be put to death…." (Deuteronomy 17:6) That is Sama"el,"** since it should have said "shall the living be put to death," not "the dead." Rather, it alludes to Sama"el who is **"essentially dead."** He cannot be put to death with one witness, namely the Judgment of the darkness, but only two witnesses, which are the Judgment of the darkness and the Judgment of the Masach of Chirik. This is the secret of: **"…they carried it between two on a pole…." (Numbers 13:23)** namely two witnesses. **"…he shall not be put to death by the mouth of one witness" (Deuteronomy 17:6)** which is the Judgment of darkness alone, and this is so that **"he shall have no portion in the one God."** The Judgments of darkness are very Holy, and they are the secret of the Dalet of Echad, and they are vital for the unification of the Alef-Chet of Echad with the Dalet of Echad. Therefore we do not lower them to wage war with Sama"el, and we wait for the second witness, which is the Judgment of the Masach of Chirik. And when it says: **"or three witnesses"** it is because in the Masach of Chirik there are two types of Judgments—Man'ula and Maftecha. Thus there are three Judgments: Darkness, Man'ula, and Maftecha. In essence, two witnesses suffice, which are Darkness and Maftecha, yet at first Man'ula needed to emerge and then it is stored away. This is why we count only two witnesses, even though in the sequence of actions three witnesses emerged. This is why the verse says "At the mouth of two witnesses or three witnesses…" namely it alludes that two are enough but there are three witnesses and before their testimony, he [Sama"el] is not nullified from Malchut.

Zohar Chadash: Beresheet

47. "Let there be lights"

Every action is judged on Rosh Hashanah.

587. בְּרֹאשׁ הַשָּׁנָה דָּן כָּל הָעוֹלָם כֻּלּוֹ, גּוּפוֹת בְּנֵי אָדָם וְהַנְּשָׁמוֹת, וּפוֹקֵד אוֹתָם, וְדָן אוֹתָם עַל כָּל מַה שֶּׁעָשׂוּ כָּל הַשָּׁנָה כֻּלָּהּ. וְתָאנָא, אֲפִילּוּ צְעָדָיו שֶׁל אָדָם נִמְנִין וּבָאִין בַּדִּין בְּאוֹתוֹ הַיּוֹם, הֲדָא הוּא דִכְתִיב, וְכָל צְעָדַי יִסְפּוֹר.

587. On Rosh Hashanah, He judges the whole world, the bodies and souls of people. He remembers them and judges them for everything they did during the whole year. We have learned that even man's steps are counted and brought to justice on that day. Hence, it says "…and count my steps." (Job 31:4)

Three classes of people: Righteous, Evil, and Mediocre.

588. תָּאנֵי רַבִּי יוֹסֵי, שָׁלֹשׁ כִּתּוֹת נִכְנָסִין לְיוֹם הַדִּין. כַּת צַדִּיקִים גְּמוּרִים. כַּת רְשָׁעִים גְּמוּרִים. כַּת בֵּינוֹנִים. וּכְנֶגְדָּן שָׁלֹשׁ כֹּחוֹת בָּאָדָם. כֹּחַ הַנְּשָׁמָה הַקְּדוֹשָׁה. וְכֹחַ הַמִּתְאַוָּה. וְכֹחַ הַמְּנִיעָה. מַאי כֹּחַ הַמְּנִיעָה, אָמַר רַבִּי יְהוּדָה, כֹּחַ הַמְגַדֶּלֶת וְהַמְּנִיעַ אֶת הַגּוּף בְּכָל צְרָכָיו.

588. Rav Yosi taught that three classes are brought to Judgment on that day: the class of the absolutely Righteous, the class of the absolutely Evil and the class of the Mediocre. These correspond to the three forces within man: the force of the Holy Soul, the desiring force and the driving force. He asks: **"What is the driving force?" Rav Yehuda said, "The force that nourishes and drives the body in all its needs."**

The Creator's Mercy is that He gave us advice to be saved from Judgment.

589. רַבִּי יוֹסֵי בֶּן פָּזִי אוֹמֵר, בֹּא וּרְאֵה רַחֲמָנוּתוֹ שֶׁל הַקָּדוֹשׁ בָּרוּךְ הוּא, אַף עַל פִּי שֶׁבֵּית דִּין שֶׁל מַעְלָה בָּאִין לַעֲמֹד בַּדִּין, וְלָדוּן אֶת הַבְּרִיּוֹת, וּלְהוֹרוֹת לִפְנֵי הַקָּדוֹשׁ בָּרוּךְ הוּא זְכוּת וְחוֹבָה שֶׁל בְּנֵי אָדָם. דְּתָאנֵי ר' יוֹסֵי בֶּן פָּזִי, שָׁלֹשׁ כִּתּוֹת שֶׁל מַלְאֲכֵי הַשָּׁרֵת עוֹמְדִין עַל הַדִּין בְּיוֹם רֹאשׁ הַשָּׁנָה. יֵשׁ מֵהֶם שֶׁהֵם מוֹרִים זְכוּת לְטוֹבָה. וְיֵשׁ מֵהֶם חוֹבָה לְרָעָה. וְתָא חֲזֵי, רַחֲמָנוּתוֹ שֶׁל הַקָּדוֹשׁ בָּרוּךְ הוּא, שֶׁנָּתַן עֵצָה לְהִנָּצֵל מִן הַדִּין.

589. Rav Yosi ben Pazi says: "Come and see the Mercy of the Holy One, blessed be He, despite the Celestial Court that comes to give Judgment, judge humans, and argue for or against people before the Holy One, blessed be He." For as Rav Yosi ben Pazi taught, three classes of ministering angels stand to judge on Rosh Hashanah; some of them argue to merit favorably and some argue **guilt unfavorably. "Come and see the Mercy of the Holy One, blessed be He, who gives advice how to be saved from Judgment."**

When we awaken the Shofar we are saved from our enemies.

590. דְּתַנְיָא מַהוּ דִּכְתִיב, זִכְרוֹן תְּרוּעָה לָא אַשְׁכַּחְנָא זְכִירָה לִתְרוּעָה, אֶלָּא הַאי דְּאָמַר רַבִּי יוֹסֵי, כְּתִיב וְכִי תָבֹאוּ מִלְחָמָה בְּאַרְצְכֶם עַל הַצַּר וְגוֹ' וַהֲרֵעֹתֶם וְגוֹ', וְזֵכֶר לִתְרוּעָה זוֹ, אָמַר הַקָּדוֹשׁ בָּרוּךְ הוּא, הָרִיעוּ לְפָנַי בִּתְרוּעָה זוֹ, שֶׁתְּהֵא זִכְרוֹן אוֹתָהּ הַתְּרוּעָה, מִיָּד, וְנוֹשַׁעְתֶּם מֵאֹיְבֵיכֶם.

590. We have learned the words "...a memorial of blowing of horns." (Leviticus 23:24) We have found no memorial of blowing of horns save this, as Rav Yosi said, "It is written, 'And if you go to war in your land against the enemy... then you shall blow....' (Numbers 10:9) As a memorial of this blow the Holy One, blessed be He, said, 'blow this blowing before Me, a memorial of that blow. Straightway, '... you shall be saved from your enemies.' (Ibid.)"

Even if we have one in a thousand angels to point out our merit we are saved.

591. מָאן אִינּוּן, אִלֵּין הֵם הַמּוֹרִים חוֹבָתָם שֶׁל בְּנֵי אָדָם. דְּתַנְיָא אָמַר רַבִּי יוֹחָנָן, מַלְאָכִים יֵשׁ הַמּוֹרִים חוֹבָתָן שֶׁל בְּנֵי אָדָם. וּמַלְאָכִים יֵשׁ הַמּוֹרִים זְכוּתָן. וַאֲפִילּוּ אֶחָד מִנִּי אֶלֶף מוֹרֶה זְכוּתוֹ, שֶׁבּוֹקִין לוֹ. הֲדָא הוּא דִּכְתִיב, אִם יֵשׁ עָלָיו מַלְאָךְ מֵלִיץ אֶחָד מִנִּי אָלֶף. וּכְתִיב בַּתְרֵיהּ, וַיְחֻנֶּנּוּ וַיֹּאמֶר פְּדָעֵהוּ מֵרֶדֶת שַׁחַת וְגוֹ'.

591. He asks: **"Who are** 'your enemies'?" He answers: **"These are** the angels **that point out men's guilt, for we learned that Rabban Yochanan said: 'Some angels point out the guilt of men and some their merit, and even if one out of a thousand speaks of his merit, he is released.' Hence it says 'If there be an angel over him, an interpreter, one among a thousand...' (Job 33:23) followed by 'and says, "...deliver him from going down to the pit...."' (Ibid. 24)**

There are angels in charge of pointing out man's flaws.

592. וְכִי יֵשׁ מַלְאָךְ מַשְׂטִין זְכוּתוֹ שֶׁל אָדָם, אָמַר רַבִּי שִׁמְעוֹן, חַס וְשָׁלוֹם שֶׁמַּלְאָךְ מַשְׂטִין זְכוּת. אֶלָּא, יֵשׁ מַלְאָכִים מְמוּנִּים לְעַיֵּין וּלְהוֹרוֹת בְּחוֹבָתוֹ שֶׁל אָדָם, בְּכָל שָׁעָה שֶׁיַּעֲבוֹר, וְהֵם מוֹרִים אוֹתוֹ דָּבָר שֶׁנִּצְטַוּוּ.

592. He asks: **"Could an angel accuse and distort a man's merit?" Rav Shimon said, "Heaven forbid that an angel should speak ill of a merit, but some angels are in charge of searching and pointing out a man's guilt, any time he sins, and they instruct as they were commanded,** namely to speak of men's sins."

Right and Left represent merit and guilt.

593. כְּיוֹצֵא בַּדָּבָר וְכָל צְבָא הַשָּׁמַיִם עוֹמֵד עָלָיו מִימִינוֹ וּמִשְּׂמֹאלוֹ. מַאי עָלָיו, עָלָיו שֶׁל אַחְאָב. שֶׁהָיוּ מְעַיְּינִים בְּדִינוֹ. מִימִינוֹ וּמִשְּׂמֹאלוֹ, וְכִי יֵשׁ יָמִין וכו', אִלּוּ הַמְיַמִּינִים לִזְכוּת, וְאִלּוּ הַמַּשְׂמְאִילִים לְכַף חוֹבָה.

593. Similarly "... 'and all the Host of Heaven standing by Him on His right hand and on His left." (I Kings 22:19) He asks: **"What is 'by Him'?"** He answers: **"It is about Ahab, whose sentence was pondered on his right and left."** He asks: **"Is there right** and left above?" He answers: "It is only that **some turn right for merit and some turn left to the scale of guilt."**

Adam's body and soul were created on Rosh Hashanah.

594. אָמַר רַב יְהוּדָה אָמַר רַב, מִפְּנֵי מָה בְּרֹאשׁ הַשָּׁנָה דִּין הַגּוּף וְהַנְּשָׁמָה, מִפְּנֵי שֶׁבּוֹ נוֹלַד אָדָם הָרִאשׁוֹן, וּבוֹ בַּיּוֹם נַעֲשָׂה גוּף, וְנִזְרְקָה בוֹ נְשָׁמָה, וּבוֹ בַּיּוֹם נִידּוֹן וְנִקְבַּע הַדִּין לְדוֹרוֹת.

594. Rav Yehuda said, "Rav said: 'Why is the judgment of body and soul on Rosh Hashanah?' The reason is that Adam was born on it, and on the very day a body has been made and a soul put in it, on that day was he judged and Judgment was fixed for generations."

YOM KIPPUR

Tetzave

13. Two goats

A Synopsis

The old sage wonders why Israel sent two goats for sacrifice: one for Azazel in the wilderness, and one for God. Rav Shimon explains that the Slanderer will think he ate from His meal and will not know of the other joyous meal prepared for God and those He loved. Even when Israel are in exile, when they pray, Malchut ascends before God on Yom Kippur and asks for Mercy for Her children; then God declares all His vengeance against Edom, and the Slanderer is removed from the world. Because of this, the children of Israel are free and joyful. Rav Shimon tells why a young goat is sacrificed rather than a grown one. He speaks about atonement (Kippur) and says that it is so called because it cleanses all impurity from a person so that God forgives him. We read that there are five deprivations on Yom Kippur—eating and drinking, washing, anointing, wearing shoes, and having marital relations. These deprivations are so that the person may be helped by the five Supernal aspects—Chesed, Gevurah, Tiferet, Netzach, and Hod.

Why was one goat for the Lord?

100. תָּא חֲזֵי, הַהוּא שָׂעִיר דְּמְשַׁדְּרִין יִשְׂרָאֵל לַעֲזָאזֵל, לְהַהוּא מַדְבְּרָא, בְּגִין לְמֵיהַב חוּלָקָא לְהַהוּא סִטְרָא אַחֲרָא, לְאִתְעַסְּקָא בַּהֲדֵיהּ. וְאִי תֵּימָא, תְּרֵין שְׂעִירִין אַמַּאי הָכָא, חַד לַיְיָ' וְחַד לְהַהוּא סִטְרָא אַחֲרָא. תִּינַח הַהוּא שָׂעִיר דְּסִטְרָא אַחֲרָא. לַיְיָ' אַמַּאי.

100. He asks: **"Come and behold: Israel sent the goat to Azazel, to the wilderness, so as to give a portion to the Other Side with which to be occupied** (see Zohar, Noach 105 Sulam Commentary). **You may ask why there are two goats here, one for the Lord and one for the**

Other Side. It is understandable to send **the goat of the Other Side** to Azazel, **but why the goat to the Lord?"**

The King, the son, the bailiff, and the butler.

101. אֶלָּא לְמַלְכָּא דַּהֲוָה אַרְגִּיז עַל בְּרֵיהּ, קָרָא לְסַנְטִירָא, הַהוּא דְּעָבֵיד דִּינָא בִּבְנֵי נָשָׁא תָּדִיר, בְּגִין דְּיִזְדַּמַּן לְמֶעְבַּד דִּינָא בִּבְרֵיהּ. הַהוּא סַנְטִירָא חַדֵּי, וְעָאל בְּבֵי מַלְכָּא לְמֵיכַל תַּמָּן, כֵּיוָן דְּאַשְׁגַּח בֵּיהּ בְּרֵיהּ, אָמַר, וַדַּאי לָא עָאל סַנְטִירָא דָּא בְּבֵי אַבָּא, אֶלָּא בְּגִין דְּאַרְגִּיז מַלְכָּא עָלַי. מָה עָבֵד, אָזַל וְאִתְפָּיֵּיס בַּהֲדֵיהּ. כֵּיוָן דְּאִתְפָּיֵּיס בַּהֲדֵיהּ, פָּקִיד מַלְכָּא לְמֶעְבַּד סְעוּדָתָא עִלָּאָה לֵיהּ וְלִבְרֵיהּ, וּפָקִיד דְּלָא יָדַע בֵּיהּ הַהוּא סַנְטִירָא. לְבָתַר עָאל הַהוּא סַנְטִירָא. אָמַר מַלְכָּא הַשְׁתָּא אִי יִנְדַּע דָּא, מִסְּעוּדָתָא עִלָּאָה דְּאַתְקִינִית לִי וְלִבְרִי, יִתְעַרְבֵּב פָּתוֹרָא. מָה עֲבַד. קָרָא לִמְמַנָּא עַל סְעוּדָתָא, אָמַר לֵיהּ, אַתְקִין מִדִּי, וּתְשַׁוֵּי קַמָּאי, וּתְשַׁוֵּי קַמֵּיהּ דְּהַהוּא סַנְטִירָא, בְּגִין דְּיַחְשִׁיב דִּסְעִיד קַמָּאי מִדִּילִי, וְלָא יִנְדַּע בְּהַהִיא סְעוּדָתָא יַקִּירָא דְּחֶדְוָה דִּילִי וְדִבְרִי, וְיִטּוֹל הַהוּא חוּלָקָא וְיֵיזִיל לֵיהּ, וְיִתְפְּרַשׁ מֵחֶדְוָה דִּסְעוּדָתָא דִּילָן. וְאִי לָאו דְּמַלְכָּא עָבִיד הָכִי, לָא יִתְפְּרַשׁ הַהוּא סַנְטִירָא מִבֵּי מַלְכָּא.

101. He answers: "It is similar **to a king who was angry with his son. He summoned a bailiff, who regularly meted out justice to people, to come and punish his son. The bailiff rejoiced and entered the king's palace to eat there. As soon as the son saw him, he thought, 'Certainly, the only reason this bailiff has come to my father's palace is that the king is angry with me.' So what did he do? He tried to please him. Once he pleased him, the king ordered a magnificent feast for himself and his son, and commanded that the bailiff would not know of it. Afterward, the bailiff came. The king thought, 'Now if he knows of the grand feast that I prepared for my son and myself, there will be confusion at the table.' So what did he do? He called the butler in charge over the feast and told him, 'Prepare something to put before me and the bailiff, so that the bailiff would think that he dined with me and would not know about that other precious feast for me and my son. He would then take that portion and leave,**

and disengage from our joyous feast.' If the king had not done this, that bailiff would not have left the king's palace.

The goat to Azazel distances the Slanderer so that he is not present when Israel receive blessings from Binah.

102. כַּךְ אָמַר קוּדְשָׁא בְּרִיךְ הוּא לְיִשְׂרָאֵל, אַזְמִינוּ תְּרֵין שְׂעִירִין, חַד לִי וְחַד לְהַהוּא דִּלְטוֹרָא, בְּגִין דְּיַחְשִׁיב דְּמִסְעוּדָתָא דִּילִי קָאֲכִיל, וְלָא יִנְדַּע בִּסְעוּדָתָא דְּחֶדְוָה אַחֲרָא דִּילָן, וְיִסַּב הַהוּא חוּלָקָא, וְיֵיזִיל לְאָרְחֵיהּ, וְיִתְפְּרַשׁ מִבֵּיתִי. כֵּיוָן דְּאִמָּא עִלָּאָה, עָלְמָא דְּאָתֵי, אָתֵי לְמִשְׁרֵי גּוֹ הֵיכְלָא דְּעָלְמָא תַּתָּאָה, לְאַשְׁגְּחָא עָלָהּ בִּנְהִירוּ דְּאַנְפִּין, דִּין הוּא דְּלָא יִשְׁתְּכַּח הַהוּא דִּלְטוֹרָא, וְלָא מָארֵי דְּדִינִין לְקַמֵּיהּ, כַּד אַפִּיק כָּל בִּרְכָאן, וְאַנְהִיר לְכֹלָּא. וְכָל הַהוּא חֵירוּ יִשְׁתְּכַּח, וְיִשְׂרָאֵל נַטְלֵי מֵאִינּוּן בִּרְכָאן.

102. "So too did the Holy One, blessed be He, say to Israel: 'Prepare two goats, one for Me and one for that Slanderer, namely the Other Side, **so that he will think that he ate from My meal and will not know of the other—our own joyous meal. Let him take that portion and go his way and depart from My house.' Since Supernal Ima, which is the World to Come,** namely Binah, **came to dwell in the Sanctuary of the Lower World, to observe it with a radiant face, it is only right that the Slanderer would not be present, nor the plaintiffs, when He takes out all the blessings and illuminates everything. And all manner of freedom is available** in Malchut, **and Israel receive those blessings.**

Explanation: On Rosh Hashanah, Malchut returns to its original state, where Judgments and destruction emanate from Her, since the Other Side is attached to Her in the aspect of the middle point of the world's desolation, and She prosecutes the world and wishes to nullify the Right column completely. Then the Creator gave the advice to blow the Shofar, to awaken the Masach of Chirik of the Central Column from Below and diminish the Upper Three [Sefirot] of the Left Column. Through this the Other Side, whose entire power stems from the Left Column, is mixed up and the world is saved from Judgments and destruction. However, after the Upper Three of the left is nullified, the Other Side has a grip on the place of lack. Therefore, we need a second correction to remove the Other Side from the place of lack in a way that it will completely be separated from the Holiness. This takes place on Yom Kippur, when we give a portion to the Other Side with this goat that we send to the wilderness.

On Yom Kippur, Malchut elevates to Binah and receives from It the Supernal point, which is the root for both destruction and habitation (as mentioned in Tetzaveh 98), where the Upper Three of the Left return, and there is also the correction of the Central Column that draws Chochmah clothed with Chasadim. From this aspect we give two goats—one for the Creator and one for Azazel in the desert—and the Azazel goat is the secret of drawing the Upper Three of the Left, which we draw from the point of Binah, to remove the Other Side from the place of lack. This is the secret as to why we send it to the desert, which is a place of desolation—like what issues forth from the Left. It is found that the Holiness Itself gives a portion to the Other Side to its detriment, to remove it from Holiness and to give the great Mochin of Chochmah and Chasadim together to Israel.

With this you will understand what is written (see Zohar, Vayera 384) **"On Rosh Hashanah we need to confuse him,"** namely to nullify the Upper Three of the Left, which confuses the Satan and makes him lose dominion. **"On Yom haKippurim, we need to** deal with **the Satan** with ease **and give him appeasement through the goat..."** namely we draw back the Upper Three that were nullified on Rosh Hashanah, by which the Other Side acquires dominon and receives appeasement, and study there (Zohar, Vayera 387). However, it is to his detriment. This is the meaning of what it says here (in verse 102): **"Prepare two goats, one for Me and one for that Slanderer... Let him take that portion,"** namely the Upper Three of the Left that we send toward the desert to the place of destruction to return his dominion to the aspect of the middle point of the world's desolation, **"and go his way,"** to the place of destruction and desolation, **"and depart from My house,"** since through this he is separated from the Holiness, as he has no more space of lack to hold on to.

This is: " **Since Supernal Ima, which is the World to Come, came to dwell in the Sanctuary of the Lower World,"** since on Yom Kippur Malchut clothes Binah, which is the secret of the middle point of the whole world, whether for desolation or for habitation, **"it is only right that the Slanderer would not be present,"** namely since we complete the aspect of lack of the Holiness, and the Other Side has no more place of lack to hold on to, **"nor the plaintiffs,"** because there is no more fear of what the Judgments of the Upper Three of the Left cause once we send the goat to the place of destruction and desolation, since Holiness is only in the place of Habitation, and the Other Side separated from the Holiness. Then Supernal Ima bestows from the aspect of It being the middle point of the world's habitation as well; It "**illuminates everything,"** namely Chochmah and Chasadim together. **"And all manner of freedom is available, and Israel receive those blessings."** This explains the rest of the article.

On Yom Kippur, Malchut rejoices in the feast of Binah,
and all the worlds are blessed.

103. דְּהָא כַּד עָלְמָא דְּאָתֵי, עָאל לְהֵיכָלָא דְּעָלְמָא תַּתָּאָה, וְאִשְׁכַּח דְּחַדֵּי עָלְמָא תַּתָּאָה עִם בְּנוֹי בְּהַהִיא סְעוּדָתָא עִלָּאָה, כְּדֵין אִיהוּ בָּרִיךְ פָּתוֹרָא, וְעָלְמִין כֻּלְּהוּ מִתְבָּרְכִין, וְכָל חֵידוּ וְכָל נְהִירוּ דְּאַנְפִּין אִשְׁתְּכָחוּ תַּמָּן. הה"ד לִפְנֵי יְיָ' תִּטְהָרוּ.

103. "When the World to Come, which is Binah, **enters the Sanctuary of the Lower World,** which is Malchut, **and the Lower**

World rejoices in its children in that magnificent feast that is drawn from Binah, **then** Binah **blesses the table. All the worlds are blessed and every kind of joy and shining face are present there. This is the meaning of: "...before (lit. the face of) the Lord will you be purified." (Leviticus 16:30)**

The Slanderer is excited for the goat,
and does not realize it is to his detriment.

104. כְּתִיב וְנָתַן אַהֲרֹן עַל שְׁנֵי הַשְּׂעִירִים גּוֹרָלוֹת גּוֹרָל אֶחָד לַיְיָ' וְגוֹרָל אֶחָד לַעֲזָאזֵל. דָּא אִיהוּ הַהוּא חֶדְוָה דְּהַהוּא דִּלְטוֹרָא, בְּגִין דְּקוּדְשָׁא בְּרִיךְ הוּא יָטִיל עִמֵּיהּ גּוֹרָל, וְזַמִּין לֵיהּ, וְלָא יָדַע דְּנוּר דָּלִיק אַטִּיל עַל רֵישֵׁיהּ, וְעַל עַמָּא דִּילֵיהּ, כד"א כִּי גֶחָלִים אַתָּה חוֹתֶה עַל רֹאשׁוֹ.

104. It is written: "And Aaron shall cast lots on the two goats; one lot for the Lord and the other lot for Azazel." (Leviticus 16:8) This is the joy of the Slanderer that the Holy One, blessed be He, casts lots with him and invites him to take the scapegoat. **But he does not realize that He pours a flaming fire on his head and on his people, as it is written: "For You will heap coals of fire upon his head...." (Proverbs 25:22)**

An allusion to Yom Kippur in the story of Purim.

105. וְסִימָנָךְ, אַף לֹא הֵבִיאָה אֶסְתֵּר הַמַּלְכָּה עִם הַמֶּלֶךְ אֶל הַמִּשְׁתֶּה אֲשֶׁר עָשָׂתָה כִּי אִם אוֹתִי. וּכְתִיב, וַיֵּצֵא הָמָן בַּיּוֹם הַהוּא שָׂמֵחַ וְטוֹב לֵב. בְּהַהוּא חוּלָקָא דְּנָטִיל, וְאָזִיל לֵיהּ. וּלְבָתַר כַּד אָתֵי מַלְכָּא עִלָּאָה, לְבֵי מַטְרוֹנִיתָא, מַטְרוֹנִיתָא תַּבְעַת עָלָהָא, וְעַל בְּנָהָא, וְעַל עַמָּא מִן מַלְכָּא.

105. A mnemonic for this is in the verse: "**... 'Even Esther the queen let no one come in with the king to the banquet that she prepared but myself...'" (Esther 5:12) and "Then Haman went out that day joyful and with a glad heart" (Esther 5:9) with that portion that he**

received, and went his way. Afterwards, when the Supernal King came to the Queen's palace, the Queen asked for Herself, for Her children, and for the people of the King.

On Yom Kippur it is decreed how the Slanderer will be removed from this world.

106. וַאֲפִילּוּ בִּזְמְנָא דְיִשְׂרָאֵל בְּגָלוּתָא, וְצַלּוּ צְלוֹתִין בְּכָל יוֹמָא, אִיהִי סַלְקַת בְּיוֹמָא דָא, לְקָמֵי מַלְכָּא עִלָּאָה, וְתַבְעַת עַל בְּנָהָא. וּכְדֵין אִתְגְּזָרוּ, כָּל אִינּוּן נוּקְמִין, דְזַמִּין קוּדְשָׁא בְּרִיךְ הוּא לְמֶעְבַּד עִם אֱדוֹם, וְאִתְגְּזַר הֵיךְ זַמִּין דַּלְטוֹרָא דָא לְאִתְעַבְּרָא מֵעָלְמָא, כד"א בִּלַּע הַמָּוֶת לָנֶצַח.

106. Even when the children of Israel are in exile and pray daily, Malchut **ascends on this day,** Yom Kippur, **before the King and asks for Her children. Then all vengeance that the Holy One, blessed be He, is going to bring against Edom are decreed, and it is decreed how this Slanderer will be removed from this world, as it is written: "Death will be swallowed up forever…." (Isaiah 25:8)**

When Israel is in exile the Great Name of the Creator is blemished.

107. וְסִימָנָךְ, בִּזְמְנָא דְגָלוּתָא כִּי נִמְכַּרְנוּ אֲנִי וְגוֹ'. כִּי אֵין הַצָּר שֹׁוֶה בְּנֵזֶק הַמֶּלֶךְ. מַאי בְּנֵזֶק הַמֶּלֶךְ. כד"א, וְהִכְרִיתוּ אֶת שְׁמֵנוּ מִן הָאָרֶץ וּמַה תַּעֲשֶׂה לְשִׁמְךָ הַגָּדוֹל. דְהָא שְׁמָא עִלָּאָה, לָא אִתְקַיַּים בְּקִיוּמֵיהּ, וְדָא אִיהוּ בְּנֵזֶק הַמֶּלֶךְ.

107. A mnemonic for this is that about the time of exile it is written: **"For we have been sold, I and my people… but the oppressor takes no account of the king's loss." (Esther 7:4)** He asks: **"What is 'the king's loss?"** He answers: **"It is as you say, '…and cut off our name from the earth, and what will You do for Your Great Name?' (Joshua 7:9) because the Great Name will no longer be maintained, and this is the king's loss.**

From Yom Kippur onward, freedom and joy openly rule over Israel.

108. וּכְדֵין וְהָמָן נִבְעָת מִלִּפְנֵי הַמֶּלֶךְ וְהַמַּלְכָּה כְּדֵין, נְהִירוּ דְּאַנְפִּין, וְכָל חֵידוּ אִשְׁתְּכַח, וְיִשְׂרָאֵל נַפְקֵי לְחֵירוּ, בְּהַהוּא יוֹמָא. כְּדֵין מֵהַהוּא יוֹמָא וּלְהָלְאָה, חֵירוּ וְחֶדְוָה בְּאִתְגַּלְיָא, לְשַׁלְטָאָה עֲלַיְיהוּ, כְּדֵין בָּעֵי לְמֶחֱדֵי עִמְּהוֹן, מִכָּאן וּלְהָלְאָה, כְּמָה דְּיָהֲבוּ לֵיהּ חוּלָקָא לְאִתְפָּרְשָׁא מִנְּהוֹן, הָכִי נָמֵי יַהֲבִין לִשְׁאָר עַמִּין, לְאִתְפָּרְשָׁא מִנְּהוֹן לְתַתָּא.

108. "Then, '…And Haman, who is the Other Side, was struck with terror before the king and the queen.' (Esther 7:6) Then every shining face and every joy is present, and the children of Israel go out free on that day—Yom Kippur. From that day and onward, freedom and joy openly rule over them and He wishes to rejoice with them. From here on, just as a portion is given to the Other Side so that he shall depart from Israel, a portion is also given to the other nations, so that they depart from Israel Below."

What is the spiritual significance of a young goat?

109. תָּא חֲזֵי, מַה הוּא רָזָא דְּקָרְבְּנָא, לְקָרְבָּא שָׂעִיר, וְלָא מִלָּה אַחֲרָא. וְאַמַּאי שָׂעִיר בְּרֵאשׁ חֹדֶשׁ, וְהָכָא נָמֵי שָׂעִיר. אֶלָּא אִי תֵּימָא בְּגִין דְּאִיהוּ סִטְרָא דִּילֵיהּ יֵאוֹת. אַמַּאי לָא הֲוֵי עֵז.

109. He asks: "Come and behold, what is the secret meaning of offering a goat rather than something else? Why is it that on the first day of the month we offer a goat, and also here on Yom Kippur? If you say that it is because the goat is of its aspect, it is well, but why not an adult goat (ez), but a young goat (se'ir), which is small?"

The Other Side has affinity with things that do not produce fruit.

110. אֶלָּא מִלָּה דָּא אִצְטְרִיךְ, וְאִיהִי אִשְׁתְּכַחַת לְמָארֵיהוֹן דְּחַרְשִׁין, דְּכָל עוֹבָדַיְיהוּ בְּמָה דְּלָא אִתְחַבַּר בְּנוּקְבָּא. וְע״ד שָׂעִיר לָא אִתְחַבַּר בְּנוּקְבָּא,

בְּסִטְרִין דִּילֵיהּ כֻּלְּהוּ. עֵז כַּד אִתְחַבַּר בְּנוּקְבָא. וּבְגִין דְּאִיהוּ מַלְכָּא, יַהֲבִין לֵיהּ בְּגִין יְקָרָא דִּילֵיהּ, הַאי דְּלָא אִתְחַבַּר בְּנוּקְבָא, וְלָא יָהִיב חֵילֵיהּ לְאַחֲרָא. וְדָא אִשְׁתְּמוֹדַע לְאִינּוּן חָרָשִׁין, דְּמִשְׁתַּמְּשִׁין בְּהָנֵי עוֹבָדֵי. וּבְגִינֵי כַּךְ, שָׁרְיָין עַל הַהוּא שָׂעִיר, כָּל אִינּוּן חַטָּאֵיהוֹן.

110. He answers: **"This is needed,** namely just a goat, **and it is known to all those who perform witchcraft, who perform it only with that which has not yet mated with a female. Therefore, all the young goats, which have not yet mated with a female, are among its species** of the Other Side. And the reason is that the Other Side is sterile and produces no fruit. **But a grown goat has already mated with a female** and produced fruit. Therefore, it is not in the portion of the Other Side. **Since** the Other Side **is a king,** as it is written, 'An old and foolish king' (Ecclesiastes 4:13), **in its honor,** a young goat **is given, one that never mated with a female, and did not give of his strength to another,** of his own kind, as mentioned. **And each sorcerer who performs these functions knows this. Therefore, they lay all their sins on that young goat.**

The young goat is given to the other side because its impurity is not as severe.

111. ות"ח, אע"ג דְּאִיהוּ חוּלָקָא לְהַהוּא סִטְרָא אַחֲרָא, רָזָא הָכָא, כָּל הָנֵי סִטְרִין אַחֲרָנִין דִּלְתַתָּא, כֻּלְּהוּ מִסְאֲבִין יַתִּיר. וְכָל מַה דְּנַחְתִּין דַּרְגִּין תַּתָּאִין, הָכִי מִסְאֲבוּ דִּלְהוֹן יַתִּיר. וּבְגִין כַּךְ, בָּעֵז יַתִּיר חוּלָקְהוֹן, בְּגִין דְּשַׂעֲרָא דִּילֵיהּ תַּלְיָא יַתִּיר מִבְּעִירָא אַחֲרָא, כְּמָה דְּדִינָא דִּלְהוֹן תַּלֵּי לְתַתָּא בְּמִסְאֲבוּ. אֲבָל הַאי מַלְכּוּ וַחֲיָיבְתָא אַחֲרָא, מַלְכָּא דְּכֹלָּא בְּהַהוּא סִטְרָא, בָּרוּר אִיהוּ יַתִּיר מִסְאֲבוּ דִּילֵיהּ, וְלָא מִסְאֲבוּ שְׁלִים כְּהָנֵי תַּתָּאֵי. וְעַל דָּא שָׂעִיר, דְּשֵׂעָר דִּילֵיהּ לָא תַּלְיָא, וְלָא שְׂעִיעַ. לָא שְׂעִיעַ, בְּגִין דְּהַהוּא מִסְאֲבוּ דִּילֵיהּ. וְלָא תַּלְיָא, בְּגִין דְּלָא יִתְתַּקַּף בֵּיהּ מִסְאֲבוּ כְּהָנֵי תַּתָּאֵי, וְעַל דָּא וַדַּאי שָׂעִיר וְלָא אַחֲרָא.

111. "Come and behold, even though the young goat is the portion of the Other Side, there is a secret here, for in the Side of Impurity **the lower the aspects, the greater their impurity, and the more the**

lower grades descend, the greater is their impurity. Therefore, the portion of the Other Side **is greater in a grown goat, because its hairs hang** down **more than any other animal, just as their Judgments stem below in impurity. The impurity of this evil kingdom, which is the king of the entire Other Side is clearer** and more refined, **and is not as completely impure as the lower ones. Therefore, it is given a young goat (seir; lit. hairy) whose hair does not hang** down, **and is not smooth. It is not smooth because of its impurity, but the hair does not hang downward, so that the impurity shall not grow strong, like these lower** grades of the Other Side. **Therefore, it is surely a young goat, and nothing else."**

Explanation: An adult goat, whose hairs hang down, indicates the Upper Three of the Left that are drawn from above downward, which is severe impurity. And a young goat that has hairs but they do not hang down indicates slight impurity from the aspect of the Lower Six of the Left, which are drawn a bit but not down. And since the goat to Azazel is sent to the King of the Other Side, whose impurity is only from the Lower Six of the Left, we therefore send a young goat and not an adult goat. This is an additional reason of the mentioned reason.

Yom Kippur is a day of cleansing.

112. כִּפּוּר, אֲמַאי אִקְרֵי כִּפּוּר, אֶלָּא בְּגִין דְּנָקֵי כָּל מְסָאֲבוּ, וְאַעְבַּר לֵיהּ מִקַּמֵּיהּ, בְּהַהוּא יוֹמָא. וְעַל דָּא, יוֹם כִּפּוּר: יוֹמָא דְּנִקְיוּתָא, וְהָכִי קָרֵינָא לֵיהּ. כְּתִיב כִּי בַיּוֹם הַזֶּה יְכַפֵּר עֲלֵיכֶם לְטַהֵר אֶתְכֶם, כִּי הַיּוֹם הַזֶּה מִבָּעֵי לֵיהּ, מַאי כִּי בְּיוֹם הַזֶּה. אֶלָּא בְּגִין דְּאִתְדְּכֵי מַקְדְּשָׁא לְעֵילָּא, וְאִתְנְהִיר, כְּתִיב כִּי בַיּוֹם הַזֶּה יְכַפֵּר עֲלֵיכֶם, יְכַפֵּר וִינַקֵּי בְּקַדְמֵיתָא בַּיּוֹם הַזֶּה, בְּגִין דְּיִתְדְּכֵי, וּלְבָתַר עֲלֵיכֶם.

112. He asks: **"Why is it called 'atonement' (*kippur*)?"** He answers: **"Because it cleanses all impurity and removes it from before Him on this day. Therefore, it is called Yom Kippur,** which means **a day of cleansing. Thus we call it. It is written: "For on this day He shall**

atone for you to cleanse you." **(Leviticus 16:30)** He asks: **"Why does it say, 'for on this day'? It should have said, 'for this day.'** He answers: **"Because the Celestial Temple,** which is Malchut, **was purified and lit up. Therefore it is written: "For on this day He shall atone for you to cleanse you,"** which means **He shall forgive and cleanse first this day,** namely Malchut, **so that He may purify and forgive you afterwards.**

Malchut needs to be cleansed because of us.

113. תּוּ, יְכַפֵּר בַּיּוֹם הַזֶּה, וְיַנְקֵי לֵיהּ בְּקַדְמֵיתָא, וְכָל דָּא עֲלֵיכֶם, בְּגִינְכוֹן אִצְטְרִיךְ לְנַקָּאָה לֵיהּ, וּלְדַכְּאָה לֵיהּ בְּקַדְמֵיתָא. יְכַפֵּר, מַאן יְכַפֵּר. אֶלָּא דָּא הוּא עָלְמָא עִלָּאָה, דְּנָהִיר וְנַקֵּי לְכֹלָּא. וְע"ד כֻּלְּהוּ סִטְרִין בִּישִׁין, דְּאִקְרוּן מְצוּלוֹת יָם, אִתְעֲבָרוּ. וּכְמָה דְּאִינּוּן מְצוּלוֹת יָם תַּלְיָין, הָכִי נָמֵי תַּלְיָיא שַׂעֲרָא דִּילֵיהּ, דְּהוּא סִטְרָא דִּלְהוֹן, וְשַׂעֲרָא דְּהַהוּא סִטְרָא לָא שְׁעִיעַ.

113. "Another explanation is: **He shall atone on that day,** which is Malchut, **and cleanse it first. The only reason it needs to be cleansed is 'you,' that is, for your sake it needs to be cleansed and purified first. He shall atone."** He asks: **"Who shall atone?"** He answers: **"It is the Upper World,** which is Binah **that illuminates and cleanses everything. Therefore, all the evil aspects, which are called 'the depths of the sea,' are removed. As these depths of the sea are drooping down, so are the hairs** of the young goat, **which pertains to its side,** namely the Other Side. **The hairs of that Side are not smooth** but are coarse, which alludes to Judgments."

Five deprivations corresponding to the five Sefirot.

114. כְּגַוְונָא דָּא כְּתִיב, וְכִפֶּר עַל הַקֹּדֶשׁ מִטֻּמְאֹת בְּנֵי יִשְׂרָאֵל וּמִפִּשְׁעֵיהֶם לְכָל חַטֹּאתָם. דְּלָא יָכִיל מְקַטְרְגָא לְשַׁלְטָאָה עֲלַיְיהוּ וְעַל דָּא בְּיוֹמָא דְּכִפּוּר, דְּאִיהוּ קְנוּחָא דְּכָל חוֹבִין, וְנַקְיוּ דִּלְהוֹן. בָּעְאן יִשְׂרָאֵל לְנַקָּאָה גַּרְמַיְיהוּ, וּלְמֵיהַךְ יְחֵפֵי רַגְלִין, כְּמַלְאָכֵי עִלָּאִין. וַחֲמֵשׁ עִנּוּיִין, בְּגִין לְאִסְתַּיְּיעָא בְּחָמֵשׁ סִטְרִין עִלָּאִין, דְּיוֹמָא דְּכִפּוּרֵי אַפִּיק לוֹן, וְאִינּוּן תַּרְעִין דִּילֵיהּ.

114. Similarly, it is written: "And he shall make atonement for the Holy Place because of the uncleanness of the children of Israel, and because of their transgression in all their sins" (Leviticus 16:16), meaning that the Accuser will not have power over them. Therefore, on Yom Kippur, which is the wiping away of all the sins and their cleansing, Israel should purify themselves and walk barefoot like the lofty angels. There are **five deprivations** on Yom Kippur, which are eating and drinking, washing, anointing, wearing shoes and marital relations, **in order to be helped by five Supernal aspects,** which are Chesed, Gevurah, Tiferet, Netzach, and Hod, **which Yom Kippur,** which is Binah, **brought forth, and which are its gates.**

The sixth deprivation represents Yesod.

115. וְאִי שְׁתִיָּה קָא חָשִׁיב, דְּאִיהוּ מִסִּטְרָא דְּיִצְחָק, הָא שִׁית, וְאע"ג דְּבִכְלָל אֲכִילָה אִיהוּ, וּכְדֵין אִינּוּן שִׁית, וְעִנּוּיָא בַּתְרָאָה תַּשְׁמִישׁ הַמִּטָּה אִיהוּ, וּבְדַרְגָּא שְׁתִיתָאָה שְׁכִיחַ, וְלָקֳבְלֵיהּ אֲנָן עָבְדִין עִנּוּיָא דָא.

115. If drinking is considered as a separate deprivation, then there are six deprivations because drinking is from the side of Isaac, which is Gevurah, and eating is from the side of Abraham, which is Chesed. This is why they are two, **even though drinking is included in eating, so then they are six. The last deprivation is marital relations and is located in the sixth level,** which is Yesod, **and corresponding to it we perform this deprivation.**

14. "On the tenth day of this seventh month"

A Synopsis

The Old Sage explains why the Yom Kippur is on the tenth day. We learn of the seventy years that apply to everyone. We learn that on Yom Kippur, one must not reveal his sins to another because the Accusers may use it against him, and besides, it is shameless to reveal one's sins; it is a desecration of God's Holy Name. The seventh month is God's but He gave it to Israel as a revelation. This entire month is from the Upper World, Binah; therefore it is covered because the Upper World is in concealment. On the fifteenth day of the month, it is revealed, since everything becomes revealed with the fullness of the moon. From this day the Sefirot descend to the secret of the Lower World, Malchut. The Old Sage and Rav Shimon discuss the question of who passed Judgment on the world on Rosh Hashanah, and why Malchut judges only those who are twenty years of age or older.

The Ten Sefirot rest upon Malchut on Yom Kippur.

116. כְּתִיב וּבֶעָשׂוֹר לַחֹדֶשׁ הַשְּׁבִיעִי הַזֶּה, וּכְתִיב אַךְ בֶּעָשׂוֹר לַחֹדֶשׁ. בֶּעָשׂוֹר בָּעֲשִׂירִי מִבָּעֵי לֵיהּ, מַאי בֶּעָשׂוֹר. אֶלָּא, בְּגִין דְּהַשְׁתָּא בְּיוֹמָא דָא, כָּל דַּרְגִּין עִלָּאִין, אַתְיָין אִלֵּין עַל אִלֵּין, לְמִשְׁרֵי עַל סִיהֲרָא, וּלְאַנְהֲרָא לָהּ. וְכֻלְּהוּ בְּרָזָא דְעֶשֶׂר, עַד דְּסַלְקָא לְמֵאָה. וְכַד קַיְּימָא בְּרָזָא דְמֵאָה, כְּדֵין כֹּלָּא חַד, וְאִקְרֵי יוֹם הַכִּפּוּרִים. וְעַל דָּא בֶּעָשׂוֹר, כְּמָה דְּאַתְּ אָמֵר זָכוֹר שָׁמוֹר דְּכֻלְּהוּ אַתְיָין בְּגִין לְעַשְּׂרָא וּלְאַנְהָרָא בְּרָזָא דְעֶשֶׂר.

116. It is written: "On the tenth day (*be'asor*) of this seventh month…" (Numbers 29:7) and "Indeed on the tenth day of this month…." (Leviticus 23:27) He asks: "Why it is written ***'be'asor'*** (on **day ten) when it should say 'tenth.' Why 'ten?'** He answers: **"It is because now, on this day, all the high grades come upon each other,** meaning that the ten Sefirot that have the Upper Three are drawn from Ima, **to rest upon the moon,** which is Malchut, **to shine on it. And they all pertain to the secret of ten so they add up to a hundred,** because ten times ten equals a hundred. **When it is based on the secret of a hundred,** meaning that it has the Upper Three Sefirot, **then it is all one,** for Malchut is one with Ima. **And** both **are called the Day of Atonement. Therefore it is written, 'on day ten (*asor*),'** which represents the source, **as it is written, 'Remember' (Exodus 20:8) and 'Keep.' (Deuteronomy 5:12)** This is because 'tenth' (*asiri*) alludes to Malchut only, which is the tenth Sefirah, but 'ten,' which represents the source number, indicates all ten Sefirot together. **For they all come** from Ima **to multiply** each Sefirah **by ten and shine by means of ten,** namely also including the Upper Three Sefirot."

Where does one hundred come from?

117. אַהֲדַר הַאי סָבָא רֵישֵׁיהּ לְקַבְלֵיהּ דְּר"ש, וְאָמַר לֵיהּ, הָא יָדַעְנָא דִּשְׁאֶלְתָּא תִּבְעֵי בְּהַאי, בֶּעָשׂוֹר לַחֹדֶשׁ הַשְּׁבִיעִי. א"ל ר"ש וַדַּאי, בֶּעָשׂוֹר יָאוֹת הוּא. אִי הָכִי הוּא, אַמַּאי סָלִיק לְמֵאָה, וְהָא מִקְּרָא לָא אִתְחָזֵי, אֶלָּא דְּסָלִיק לְשַׁבְעִין, מַשְׁמַע דִּכְתִּיב בֶּעָשׂוֹר לַחֹדֶשׁ הַשְּׁבִיעִי, וְכַד מְעַשְּׂרֵי לְשִׁבְעָה עֶשֶׂר זִמְנִין, הָא וַדַּאי סָלִיק לְשַׁבְעִין. א"ל, עַל דָּא אַהֲדַרְנָא רֵישָׁא לְגַבָּךְ, דְּהָא יָדַעְנָא דְּחַכִּימָא אַנְתְּ.

117. The Old Sage turned toward Rav Shimon and said to him, "I know that you have a question about this passage, 'On the tenth day of this month….' (Numbers 29:7) Rav Shimon said to him, "Certainly, what you said that **'on day ten,'** points to ten **is fitting. But if it is so, why does it add up to a hundred? From the passage, it seems that it all adds up only to seventy, for it is written, 'On day ten of this seventh month…' (Ibid.) And when you multiply seven by ten, it equals seventy." He said to him, "For this did I turn to you because I know you are a wise man."**

The level of seventy and the level of a hundred.

118. ת"ח, תְּרֵין רָזִין הָכָא, חַד דְּהָא סִיהֲרָא חֹדֶשׁ הַשְּׁבִיעִי אִקְרֵי, וּבג"כ אִקְרֵי חֹדֶשׁ הַשְּׁבִיעִי עָשׂוֹר, בְּגִין דְּקָא מְנַהֲרִין לָהּ עֶשֶׂר זִמְנִין, הָא מֵאָה. וְתוּ, הַאי מִלָּה דְּקָאַמְרַת, וַדַּאי לְשַׁבְעִין סְלִיקָא בְּהַאי יוֹמָא, וּבְדַרְגָּא דְּשַׁבְעִין אִיהוּ, וּבְדַרְגָּא דְּמֵאָה אִיהוּ. לְדַרְגָּא דְּמֵאָה לְאַשְׁלְמָא וּלְאַנְהָרָא. וּבְהַאי דַּרְגָּא דְּשַׁבְעִין, דְּהָא בְּיוֹמָא דָּא נָטִיל לְכָל עַמָּא דְּיִשְׂרָאֵל לְמֵידָן, וְכֻלְּהוּ קַיְימִין בְּנִשְׁמְתָא יַתִּיר מִגּוּפָא, דְּהָא בְּיוֹמָא דָּא עִנּוּיָא דְּנַפְשָׁא אִיהוּ, וְלָא מִגּוּפָא, כְּמָה דְּאַתְּ אָמַר וְעִנִּיתֶם אֶת נַפְשֹׁותֵיכֶם כִּי כָל הַנֶּפֶשׁ אֲשֶׁר לֹא תְעֻנֶּה. וְהַאי יוֹמָא

נָטִיל לְכָל נַפְשָׁאן וַהֲווֹ בִּרְשׁוּתֵיהּ, וְאִי לָא קַיְּימָא בְּרָזָא דְּשַׁבְעִין, לֵית לֵיהּ רְשׁוּ בְּנַפְשָׁאן, דְּקִיּוּמָא דְּנַפְשָׁאן בְּרָזָא דְּשַׁבְעִין, כד"א יְמֵי שְׁנוֹתֵינוּ בָּהֶם שִׁבְעִים שָׁנָה וְגוֹ'.

118. "Come and behold, there are two secrets here. The first is that the moon, which is Malchut, **is called 'the seventh month' and therefore the seventh month is called 'ten'** as it says, 'on day ten of this seventh month....' (Numbers 29:7) **This is because they shine on it tenfold,** meaning ten Sefirot, and ten times ten **equals a hundred.** There is **another** secret here, **because you said** that 'ten' indicates multiplying seven by ten, **which assuredly amounts to seventy on that day** in such a manner **that it is both in the level of seventy and in the level of a hundred.** It is **in the level of a hundred so as to make it whole** with the Upper Three Sefirot **and shine on it;** and it is **in the level of seventy because on this day** Malchut **takes the entire nation of Israel so as to judge them. They all stand with soul more than with body because on this day the soul is afflicted but not the body, as it is written: '...and you shall afflict your souls...' (Leviticus 23:27) and '...for whatever person (lit. 'soul') shall not be afflicted....' (Ibid. 29) For that day takes all the souls, and they are under its authority. Had it not been of the secret of seventy, it would not have authority over the souls because souls are maintained by means of seventy, as it is written: 'The days of our years are seventy....' (Psalms 90:10)**

Explanation: It was explained earlier (in verse 98) that on Yom Kippur, Malchut elevates to Ima, whence she first receives Ima's point, which is the root for both the desolate and habitable parts of the world, where from this aspect we perform the correction of one goat for God and one goat for Azazel. Afterwards, Malchut receives from Ima the complete Mochin of the Face, which are the Upper Three. These complete Mochin of the Face are the level of "one hundred" that Malchut is on this day. These Mochin that Malchut receives in the point of Binah are the aspect of the Mochin of the Lower Six, since they are from the aspect of the Left Column of Ima alone. This is why we were commanded to have five deprivations related to the Left Column of Binah before the Central Column comes to unite the Columns.

These mochin of the Lower Six are the secret of "seventy," which indicates the lack of the Upper Three of the Face. These Mochin are the completion of the Nefesh, which is why it says "…for whatever Nefesh shall not be afflicted…," (Leviticus 23:29) because the Chochmah of the Left is only revealed in Malchut, and the Light of Malchut is the Light of Nefesh. This is: **"souls are maintained by means of seventy,"** since the completion of the Nefesh is specifically from the Mochin of Malchut that are in the aspect of seventy, which she receives by the five deprivations because the Mochin that are the aspect of "one hundred," which are the Upper Three of the Face, no longer have the aspect of seventy, which is Chochmah of the Left.

Children who pass away are also under the jurisdiction of Malchut.

119. וְאִי תֵּימָא נַפְשָׁאן דְּרַבְיֵי דְּלָא אַשְׁלִימוּ לְשַׁבְעִין שְׁנִין לָא שַׁלְטָא בְּהוּ. וַדַּאי שַׁלְטָא בְּהוּ, אֲבָל לָא בִּשְׁלִימוּ, כְּמַאן דְּזָכֵי יוֹמִין סַגִּיאִין לְפִקּוּדֵי אוֹרַיְיתָא, וְעִכ"ד בְּכֻלְּהוּ שַׁבְעִין שְׁנִין אַזְלָא. וְעַל דָּא תָּנֵינָן אֶחָד הַמַּרְבֶּה וְאֶחָד הַמַּמְעִיט. מַאן אֶחָד. בְּיִחוּדָא דְּשַׁבְעִין שְׁנִין, מַאן דְּאַסְגֵּי, וּמַאן דְּאַמְעִיט.

119. "You may argue that the souls of the children have not completed seventy years, and say **that** Malchut **has no power over them."** He answers: **"She definitely has power over them,** since the Mochin of the Lower Six are the secret of the Small Face, which represent children, **but not completely, as over one who merited the commandments of the Torah for many days. Even so, the seventy years apply to everyone,** both children and old people. **Of this we learned 'One who increases and one who decreases.' (Tractate Berachot 5b)"** He asks: **"What is 'one'?"** He answers: **"It is the unification of seventy years of he who increases,** namely the old, **and he who decreases,** namely the child**."**

Explanation: The "seventy years" that Malchut receives on Yom Kippur from Ima, in the secret of the five deprivations happens when She also has the Mochin of the Face, which are the secret of one hundred—ten times ten—as mentioned. Therefore, even the Mochin of the Left that she receives in the secret of the affliction of the Nefesh become many Lights in the secret of seventy years. And the Mochin of the Left that children receive are the aspect of the Small Face, namely Left without Right, which is drawn from the first State of Nukva, and these Mochin only shine a little bit. This is: **"She definitely has power over them, but not completely, as over one who merited the commandments of the Torah,"** because one who merited the commandments of the Torah, which is the Central Column called Torah, contains the Illumination of even the Mochin of the Left in a corrected way, and therefore he merits many days.

This is what is alluded to in: **"One who increases and one who decreases. What is 'one'? It is the unification of seventy years."** The Mochin of the Chochmah of the Left is the secret of One, and they contain two aspects. "One who increases" is the secret of the elder that uses these Mochin of the Left as Malchut does on Yom Kippur, which produces increased Light; and "one who decreases" is the secret of the child, namely the Small Face, which does not have the Mochin of the Face but only these Mochin of the Left alone, whose Illumination is very decreased. With this you will understand the allusion mentioned in verse 79: **"they met an old man who was holding a young boy by the hand."** Rav Shimon recognized in him that he is an elder and has the Mochin of the Face, yet he was holding in his hands a young boy, the secret of the Mochin of the Lower Six, which are the aspect of the Back. However, a great Light shone in him since he also had the Mochin of the Face, which is the secret of the elder, and he was in the aspect of "one who increases." The entire discussion of the old man was about these two aspects of Mochin.

The prayer of an individual who did not clean his soul descends to the Klipot.

120. וְעַל דָּא, בְּיוֹמָא דְּכִפּוּרֵי אַעְבַּר בְּכֻלְּהוּ שַׁבְעִין, וְאִשְׁתְּלִים הַאי דַּרְגָּא בְּכֻלְּהוּ, וְכָל נִשְׁמָתִין סַלְּקִין קָמֵיהּ, וְדָאִין לְהוֹן בְּדִינָא, וְקוּדְשָׁא בְּרִיךְ הוּא חַיִּיס עֲלַיְיהוּ דְּיִשְׂרָאֵל בְּיוֹמָא דָא, מַאן דְּלָא אַעֲבַר טִינָא מִרוּחֵיהּ לְכַפָּרָא עָלֵיהּ, כַּד סָלִיק צְלוֹתֵיהּ בְּהַאי יוֹמָא, טָבַע בְּהַהוּא אֲתַר דְּאִקְרֵי רֶפֶשׁ וָטִיט, וְאִיהוּ מְצוּלוֹת יָם וְלָא סָלִיק לְאִתְעַטְּרָא בְּרֵישָׁא דְּמַלְכָּא.

120. "Therefore on Yom Kippur, Malchut **passes through all these seventy,** which are the mentioned Mochin of the Left, **and this level** of Chochmah **is completed with all** the Sefirot, since each Sefirah of the seven Sefirot acquired the aspect of the Upper Three Sefirot and they become Ten Sefirot. Yet it is still lacking the general Upper Three Sefirot, and thus they are only seventy. **All the souls ascend before Him and He judges them with Judgment,** since the Mochin of seventy years are in the secret of Judgment, as mentioned. **The Holy One, blessed be He, has Mercy on the children of Israel on that day,** and bestows to the Mochin of the aspect of one hundred, as mentioned. **Whoever has not removed the filth from his soul to cleanse it, when his prayer ascends on that day it sinks into that place that is called 'mud' and 'clay,'** which are Sama"el and Lili"t, **and it is the depths of the sea.** His prayer **does not ascend to adorn the Head of the King.**

We do not disclose our sins to others on Yom Kippur.

121. בְּיוֹמָא דָא לָא אִצְטְרִיךְ בַּר נָשׁ לְפָרְשָׁא חֲטָאוֹי קָמֵי אַחֲרָא, בְּגִין דְּכַמָּה אִינּוּן דְּנַטְלֵי הַהִיא מִלָּה, וְסַלְּקֵי לָהּ לְעֵילָּא, וְאִית סָהֲדִין בְּהַהִיא מִלָּה. וּמִמִּשּׁוֹכֶבֶת חֵיקֶךָ שְׁמוֹר פִּתְחֵי פִּיךָ, כָּל שֶׁכֵּן אִינּוּן דְּאַזְלֵי וְעַיְינֵי לְקַטְרְגָא לוֹן, וְסָהֲדֵי עָלֵיהּ. וְכָל שֶׁכֵּן דְּחָצִיפוּ אִיהוּ לְקָמֵי כֹּלָּא, וְזִלְזוּל שְׁמָא דְּקוּדְשָׁא בְּרִיךְ הוּא. וְעַ"ד כְּתִיב, אַל תִּתֵּן אֶת פִּיךָ לַחֲטִיא אֶת בְּשָׂרֶךָ.

121. "On this day, a person should not reveal his sins before another because there are many Accusers **who take this word that he has revealed and bring it up and testify against that word. If** it is written: **'…from her that lies in your bosom, guard the doors of your mouth' (Micah 7:5) then surely these** Accusers go after him **and study** how **to accuse him and testify against him.** But in addition to this, **he is shameless toward everyone,** who is not abashed to reveal his sins, **which is a desecration of the Name of the Holy One, blessed be He. Therefore, it is written, 'Do not let your mouth cause your flesh to sin….' (Ecclesiastes 5:5)"**

The first month is for Israel but the seventh month is for the Creator.

122. פָּתַח וְאָמַר, הַחֹדֶשׁ הַזֶּה לָכֶם רֹאשׁ חֳדָשִׁים וְגוֹ', וְכִי כֻּלְּהוּ זִמְנִין וְיַרְחִין לָאו אִינּוּן דְּקוּדְשָׁא בְּרִיךְ הוּא. אֶלָּא הַחֹדֶשׁ הַזֶּה לָכֶם, דִּילִי אִיהוּ, אֲבָל אֲנָא מָסְרִית לֵיהּ לְכוֹן, דִּלְכוֹן אִיהוּ בְּאִתְגַּלְיָא, אֲבָל שְׁבִיעָאָה דִּילִי אִיהוּ, וְעַ"ד אִיהוּ בַּכֶּסֶה, וְלָא בְּאִתְגַּלְיָא. יַרְחָא דִּלְכוֹן, אִיהוּ בְּסִדּוּרָא, כְּסֵדֶר דְּאַתְוָון אָבִיב, דְּאִיהוּ אב"ג. י"ב אִיהוּ רָזָא דְּג'. אֲבָל יַרְחָא שְׁבִיעָאָה דִּילִי אִיהוּ מִסּוֹפָא דְּאַתְוָון. מַאי טַעֲמָא. אַתּוּן מִתַּתָּא לְעֵילָּא, וַאֲנָא מֵעֵילָּא לְתַתָּא.

122. He opened the discussion, saying, "This month shall be to you the beginning of months…." (Exodus 12:2) He asks: **"Do not all the holidays and months belong to the Holy One, blessed be He?** Why does it say, 'This month shall be to you'?" He answers: **"'This month shall be to you,'** means **it is Mine but I gave it over to you. 'To you,'** means **that it is revealed,** meaning that the lights are revealed in it for Israel, **but the seventh month is Mine. Therefore, it is covered and not revealed,** as it is written: '…at the full moon (lit. covered) of our feast day….' (Psalms 81:4) The idea of the Lights being revealed or concealed refers to the Illumination of Chochmah. **Your month is according to the sequence** of the alphabet, **in the order of Aviv (lit. Spring),** because Nissan is called the month of Aviv (Alef-Bet-Yud-Bet; (**אביב**). **This is Alef-Bet-Gimel (אב"ג), because Yud-Bet (י"ב)** of Aviv is the

secret of Gimel (ג), because the reduced numerical value of Yud is one. Thus the letters of Aviv numerically equal Alef-Bet-Gimel (6). **But the seventh month is Mine; therefore** its name starts **with the last letters** of the alphabet, namely Tishrei (Tav-Shin-Resh-Yud; **תשרי**)." He asks: **"What is the reason?"** He answers: **"You are** in forward sequence Alef-Bet-Gimel, which is **from below upward,** namely, the letters increase in numerical value, first Alef (1) then Bet (2), and so on. **But I am** in backward order Tav-Shin-Resh-Yud, which is **from above downward** because the letters decrease in value, first Tav (400), then Shin (300) and then Resh (200)."

Explanation: The Partzuf of Malchut is called year, which contains 12 months. Six months are from the Chest up, which are Chesed, Gevurah, Tiferet, Netzach, Hod, and Yesod, which are from Tishrei until Adar. And six months are from Her Chest down, which are Chesed, Gevurah, Tiferet, Netzach, Hod, and Yesod, which are from Nissan until Elul. Even though the Chest up is Chesed, Gevurah, and Tiferet, and the Chest down is Netzach, Hod, and Yesod, they each include each other. This is why there is Chesed, Gevurah, Tiferet, Netzach, Hod, and Yesod Above, and so Below. It is known that Malchut from the Chest up is the aspect of Binah, and there she is concealed, and from the Chest down is considered the aspect of Malchut itself, and there she is revealed.

This is: **"To you** means **that it is revealed"** since the Month of Nissan, which is from the chest down is revealed, namely that the Lights are revealed. **"but the seventh month is Mine. Therefore, it is covered and not revealed,"** because the month of Tishrei is from the chest up, the aspect of Binah, and there She is concealed. This lasts until the month of Adar. However since the beginning of concealment is in Tishrei it only mentions Tishrei. So too the revelation of the month of Nissan lasts until Elul. However since the beginning of revelation is in it, scripture only mentions Nissan. This is why it is called the first of the months of the year, namely the first for revealed Lights, as the Zohar says in the next paragraph regarding the fifteenth of Tishrei being the first for revelation.

The meaning of: **"Your month… Alef-Bet-Gimel… but the seventh month is Mine, from the last letters"** is that when the letters are in their order, it alludes to the revelation of Lights where they consecutively grow, but when the letters are backwards like in Tishrei it alludes to the covering of Lights as they gradually diminish in number. Just as it is in general so it is in particular, meaning in each of the twelve months the first half of the month is the aspect of above the Chest, where the Lights are concealed, and from the fifteenth day on it is below the Chest, where the Lights are revealed, as it goes on to explain.

The Lights are covered in the first half of Tishrei.

123. הַאי דִּילִי. בְּרֵישָׁא דְּיַרְחָא, אֲנָא אִיהוּ בְּאִתְכַּסְיָיא. בַּעֲשָׂרָה דְּיַרְחָא, אֲנָא אִיהוּ, בְּגִין דַּאֲנָא בְּחָמֵשׁ קַדְמָאֵי, וּבְחָמֵשׁ אַחֲרָנִין, וּבְחָמֵשׁ תְּלִיתָאֵי. בְּקַדְמֵיתָא דְּיַרְחָא אֲנָא אִיהוּ, בְּגִין חֲמִשָּׁא יוֹמִין. בַּעֲשָׂרָה דְּיַרְחָא אֲנָא אִיהוּ, בְּגִין חֲמֵשׁ יוֹמִין אַחֲרָנִין. בט"ו דְּיַרְחָא אֲנָא אִיהוּ, בְּגִין חֲמֵשׁ תְּלִיתָאֵי.

123. "This seventh month **is Mine. At the beginning of the month, I am covered. On the tenth of the month, I am** covered **because I am so during the first five days** of the month, **during the other five days, and during the third set of five days. At the beginning of the month, I am so because it is of the five first days. During the tenth day of the month, I am so because it is part of the other five days. During the fifteenth day of the month, I am so because it is part of the third five days."**

Explanation: The month is also divided into two on the Chest, just like the twelve months of the year, as mentioned earlier. It has Three Columns above the Chest, which is Binah and is concealed, and Three Columns below the Chest, which is Malchut Itself and is revealed. And because the Columns come from Binah, which includes five Sefirot—Chesed, Gevurah, Tiferet, Netzach, and Hod—therefore each Column contains five Sefirot. This is: **"At the beginning of the month, I am so"** namely I am concealed and it is not revealed for you, **"because it is of the five first days,"** since they are five day of the Right Column above the Chest, which are Chesed, Gevurah, Tiferet, Netzach, and Hod. **"During the tenth day of the month, I am so"** in concealment and it is not yours in a revealed way, **"because it is part of the other five days,"** which are the second set of Chesed, Gevurah, Tiferet, Netzach, and Hod, which are the Left Column above the Chest. **"During the fifteenth day of the month, I am so,"** namely until the fifteenth day I am in concealment and it is not yours in a revealed way, **"because it is part of the third five days,"** which are the third set of Chesed, Gevurah, Tiferet, Netzach and Hod, which are the Central Column above the Chest. Therefore, until the fifteenth day the Lights are concealed and they are not yours. But from the fifteenth day on the Lights are revealed, because the fifteenth day is the secret of the point of the Chest, whence the reveleation of Lights begin, as it goes on to say.

Tishrei is covered because it comes from Binah.

124. מ"ט כּוּלֵי הַאי. בְּגִין דְּכָל יַרְחָא דָּא מֵעָלְמָא עִלָּאָה אִיהוּ, וְעָלְמָא עִלָּאָה בְּרָזָא דְּחָמֵשׁ אִיהוּ, בְּכָל זִמְנָא וְזִמְנָא, וּבְגִינֵי כַּךְ יַרְחָא דָּא אִיהוּ בְּכִסֵּה, וְלָא בְּאִתְגַּלְיָא, בְּגִין דְּעָלְמָא עִלָּאָה בְּכִסֵּה אִיהוּ, וְכָל מִלּוֹי בְּאִתְכַּסְיָּא. וְיַרְחָא דָּא דְּקוּדְשָׁא בְּרִיךְ הוּא אִיהוּ בִּלְחוֹדוֹי. כֵּיוָן דְּמָטָא יוֹמָא דְּחָמֵיסַר, כְּדֵין זֵלְיָּא. כֹּלָּא אִיהוּ מָטָא בְּוַחֲדוּתָא דְּסִיהֲרָא, וְסִיהֲרָא אִשְׁתְּכְלִימַת, וְאִתְנְהִירַת מֵאִימָּא עִלָּאָה, וְקַיְימָא לְאַנְהָרָא לְתַתָּאֵי מִגּוֹ נְהוֹרָא דִּלְעֵילָּא, וְעַ"ד אִקְרֵי רִאשׁוֹן, כְּדַ"א וּלְקַחְתֶּם לָכֶם בַּיּוֹם הָרִאשׁוֹן. עַד הַשָּׁתָא קַיְימֵי כָּלְּהוּ יוֹמִין בְּרָזָא עִלָּאָה, מִכָּאן נַחְתִּין לְרָזָא תַּתָּאָה.

124. He asks: **"What is the reason it is so** covered, that is, until the fifteenth day of the month?" He answers: **"Because this entire month is from the Upper World,** meaning from Binah, since the first six months are from Binah, **and the Upper World is in the secret of five at any time**, meaning that in each Column there are five Sefirot, Chesed, Gevurah, Tiferet, Netzach, and Hod. **Therefore, this month is covered rather than revealed because the Upper World is in concealment and all its aspects are covered. This month is for the Holy One, blessed be He, alone** and is not for you. **Upon the fifteenth day** of the month, which is the secret of the point of the Chest, **it is revealed** because from the Chest down, whether from the aspect of the entirety of the year (Nissan) or the aspect of the the month (the fifteenth day), it is considered the aspect of Malchut itself and the Light are revealed. **Everything reaches the renewal of the moon,** since all the Lights that were concealed above the Chest come from the Chest down at the renewal of the moon, which is Malchut, since from the Chest down it is already the aspect of the moon itself and not Binah. Therefore, **the moon is full and shines from Supernal Ima,** which is Binah, **and is ready to shine down from the Lights Above. Therefore,** the fifteenth day of the month **is called** by the name **'first,' as it is written: 'And you shall take for yourselves on the first day....' (Leviticus 23:40) Until now,** meaning until the fifteenth day, all the Sefirot **were based on the secret of the Upper** World, which is Binah. **From** the fifteenth day, **the Sefirot descend to the secret of the Lower** World, which is Malchut, which is why the Lights are revealed. And since the fifteenth day is the first for revealed Light it is called 'the first day.' (Ibid.)"

The Judgments in Binah and the Judgments in Malchut.

125. תּ"ח, מִיּוֹמָא עִלָּאָה הֲווֹ אִלֵּין יוֹמִין קַדְמָאִין, רָזָא דְעָלְמָא עִלָּאָה, מַאן דָּאִין דִּינָא דְעָלְמָא, דְּהָא דִּינָא לָא אִשְׁתְּכַח בְּהַאי עָלְמָא, אֶלָּא מִדִּינָא תַּתָּאָה, דְּדָא אֱלֹהֵי כָל הָאָרֶץ יִקָּרֵא. דְּאִי תֵּימָא דִּינָא דְעָלְמָא דָּאִין לְעֵילָּא, א"ה לָא אִתְקְרֵי עָלְמָא דְחֵירוּ, עָלְמָא דִּנְהִירוּ דְּכָל עָלְמִין. עָלְמָא דְּכָל חַיִּין, עָלְמָא דְּכָל חֵירוּ. וְאִי תֵּימָא מִדִּינָא דְּיִצְחָק. אִי אִיהוּ אִתְּעַר דִּינָא לְגַבֵּי הַאי עָלְמָא, לָא יַכְלִין כָּל עָלְמָא לְמִסְבַּל, דְּהַהוּא אֶשָּׁא תַּקִּיפָא עִלָּאָה, לָא אִית מַאן דְּסָבִיל לֵיהּ, אֶלָּא אֶשָּׁא דִּלְתַתָּא, דְּאִיהוּ אֶשָּׁא דְסָבִיל אֶשָּׁא.

125. "Come and behold. The first days before the fifteenth of the month **came from the Supernal Day,** namely Binah, **as it is the secret of the Upper World**, Binah." He asks: "If so, **who passed Judgment on the world** on Rosh Hashanah? **For there is no Judgment in this world, except the Judgment of the Lower** World, **'...Who is called "God of the whole earth"....' (Isaiah 54:5) If you say that the Judgment of the world is passed Above,** in Binah, **then** Binah **would not be called the World of Freedom, 'a world** that contains **the Lights of all the worlds,' 'the world** that contains **all life,' 'the world of all liberty.'** Since Binah is called by all these names, how can you say that it contains the Judgment to judge the whole world? **If you say it is derived from the Judgment of Isaac,** namely the Left Column of Binah, this is impossible **because if it aroused Judgment for this world, then the whole world could not bear it. For no one can bear this strong Supernal fire** of the Left Column of Binah **except for the lower fire,** which is Malchut, **which is a fire that bears fire."**

Explanation: Any awakening of the Left Column of Binah, the secret of Isaac, is considered as drawing Chochmah from above downward due to It being in the place of the Upper Three, thus making it very Harsh Judgment that the world cannot endure. This is not the case with Malchut, where even though it too is drawn from the Left Column of Binah, which is strong fire, nevertheless since it is the Light of the Female, which is below upward, its Judgment is not as strong and the world can bear it. It is found that the fire of the Left Column of Binah is only awakened to Malchut, which is the fire Below, and Malchut can bear it since It is Female Light. This is: **"For no one can bear this strong Supernal fire except for the lower fire,"** since it becomes [in Malchut] a Female Illumination that only shines from below upward, which is not as strong, and the world can bear it. And since Rosh Hashanah is from above the Chest, which is Binah, he asks "who judges the world?" For Binah itself is the World of Freedom, and if only Its Left Column is awakened the world could not bear it.

The Judgments of Rosh Hashanah is from Malchut that ascended to Binah.

126. אֶלָּא, כְּמָה דְּעָלְמָא דָא עָלְמָא תַּתָּאָה דְּכֻלְּהוּ עָלְמִין. הָכִי נָמֵי כָּל דִּינוֹי מֵעָלְמָא תַּתָּאָה, דֶּאֱלֹהִים שׁוֹפֵט. וְדָא אִקְרֵי דִּינָא עִלָּאָה עַל הַאי עָלְמָא, וּבְגִין דְּאִיהוּ דַּרְגָּא שְׁבִיעָאָה, לָא גָּזֵיר גְּזֵרָה עַל בַּר נָשׁ, אֶלָּא מֵעֶשְׂרִין שְׁנִין וּלְעֵילָא.

126. He answers: "**Just as this world** of ours **is the lowest of all Worlds, so are all its Judgments from the lowest World** in Atzilut, which is Malchut, that is called '**God (Elohim) the Judge.**' And Her Judgments **are considered Supernal Judgment in relation to this** Lower **World of** ours. Therefore, they are considered in relation to us like the Judgments of Binah, **and because She is the seventh level** of Zeir Anpin, **a decree is only issued against a man who is twenty years and older.**"

Rav Shimon's question to the Old Man.

127. אַשְׁגַּח הַאי סָבָא בְּר' שִׁמְעוֹן, וְחָמָא לֵיהּ דְּזַלְגִּין עֵינוֹי דִּמְעִין. אָמַר רַבִּי שִׁמְעוֹן, אִי הִיא שְׁבִיעָאָה, אַמַּאי מֵעֶשְׂרִין שְׁנִין וּלְעֵילָא. אָמַר לֵיהּ, זַכָּאָה מַאן דְּמַלִּיל עַל אוּדְנִין דְּשַׁמְעִין.

127. That Old Sage looked at Rav Shimon and saw that his eyes were shedding tears. Rav Shimon said: "If She is seventh, why does She judge the person **of twenty years of age and older?"** He said to him: **"Blessed is he who speaks to ears that hear.**

The Terrestrial Court judges from age 13,
the Celestial Court judges from age 20.

128. ת"ח, בֵּי דִּינָא דִּלְתַתָּא בְּאַרְעָא, לָא גָּזְרִין דִּינָא עַל בַּר נָשׁ, עַד תְּלֵיסַר שְׁנִין. מַאי טַעְמָא. בְּגִין דְּשַׁבְקִין שֶׁבַע שְׁנִין לְשָׁבְעָאָה, אֱלֹהֵי כָּל הָאָרֶץ יִקָּרֵא. וְלֵית רְשׁוּ לְבַר נָשׁ בְּאִינּוּן שֶׁבַע. וְאִינּוּן שֶׁבַע, לָא עָדְראן אֶלָּא עַל תְּלֵיסַר דִּלְתַתָּא, דְּאִינּוּן כֻּרְסְיָיא לְגַבֵּיהּ, וּבְגִין כַּךְ, כָּל גְּזֵרִין, וְכָל דִּינִין דִּלְתַתָּא, מֵאִינּוּן שֶׁבַע שְׁנִין דִּלְתַתָּא, כֻּלְּלָא דְּעֶשְׂרִין שְׁנִין אִיהוּ.

128. "Come and behold: the Lower, Terrestrial Courthouse does not pass Judgment against a person until he is thirteen years of age." He asks: **"What is the reason?"** He answers: **"It is because they leave seven years for the seventh, 'The God of the whole earth shall He be called' (Isaiah 54:5) A person has no authority over these seven, and these seven do not reside except upon the thirteen Below, which are a throne for it. Therefore, all the decrees and all the Judgments of Below come from these lower seven years, which add up to twenty years."**

Explanation: In any state of Malchut where there is Judgment She is called a Courthouse. Malchut has two states of Katnut [Immaturity], which are Judgment. The first is when She receives only from the aspect of the Cholam Vowel, as then she has the Nefesh and Ruach of Katnut, and these Judgments are the aspect of the Female Judgments. Malchut is then called the Lower Courthouse. The second state is when She receives from the aspect of the Shuruk Vowel, where She ascends and clothes the Left Column of Binah, and She is then in the aspect of Chochmah without Chasadim. She thus receives the Neshamah of Katnut. These Judgments are called the Male Judgments, and Malchut is then called the Upper Courthouse, since these Judgments are drawn from the Upper Three, namely from the Neshamah of Katnut.

Malchut is called "seven," as mentioned earlier, and thus Her Nefesh, Ruach, and Neshamah are three times seven. Therefore, in the first state of Katnut, where she only has Nefesh and Ruach of Katnut, She has two times seven, which is 14. And in the second state of Katnut, where she also has Neshamah, she has three times seven, which is 21. This is the secret of why the Lower Courthouse, which is drawn from the first state of the Katnut of Malchut, does not punish until [the individual is] thirteen years and one day, as one day of the year is considered a year. There is two times seven there, which is 14, just like the Lower Courthouse, which is Nefesh and Ruach of the Katnut of Malchut.

But the Upper Courthouse, which is the aspect of the Neshamah of Katnut, does not punish until 20 years and a day, as one day of the year is considered a year, and there is three times seven there, which is 21.

[In verse 126] this is: **"Just as this world is the lowest of all Worlds, so are all its Judgments from the lowest World,"** as our world can only receive from Malchut, and not from Binah, **"and this is considered Supernal Judgment in relation to this world."** Even though the Judgment of Rosh Hashanah comes from Malchut, it is considered as Supernal Judgment that comes from Binah in relation to this world of ours, for this Judgment of Rosh Hashanah is due to Malchut clothing the Left Column of Binah, which is Male Judgments and the aspect of the Neshamah of Katnut of Malchut. This is why it is considered for us as the aspect of Binah, since then Malchut ascends to Binah and is actually considered like Binah in relation to us. This answers the question of how there are judgments if the first day of Rosh Hashanah is Binah. The answer is that the Judgments are from Malchut that ascended to Binah, which for us is like Binah Itself.

This is: **"the Lower, Terrestrial Courthouse does not pass Judgment against a person until he is thirteen years of age,"** namely the first state of the Katnut of Malchut, which is only the Nefesh and Ruach of Katnut, which is two times seven, fourteen, namely thirteen years and a day, as mentioned. **"What is the reason?" "It is because they leave seven years for the seventh, 'The God of the whole earth shall He be called'" (Isaiah 54:5)** The Lower Courthouse only has a hold on the two times seven of the Nefesh and Ruach of Katnut, and the third set of seven of the Neshamah of Katnut they leave for Malchut called "God of the whole earth." **"A person has no authority over these seven,"** as one has no permission to take hold of these Judgments of the third set of seven, since they are drawn from the ascent of Malchut to Binah, and man cannot grasp or control there. **"and these seven do not reside except upon the thirteen Below, which are a throne for**

it." The third set of seven, which is the Neshamah of Katnut cannot be revealed unless Malchut first attains the thirteen years from the Nefesh and Ruach of Katnut, which are considered a throne for the third set of seven. "**Therefore, all the decrees and all the Judgments of Below,"** namely the decrees and judgments that are drawn to humankind Below **"come from these lower seven years,"** which are the secret of the Upper Courthouse, namely the third set of seven of Malchut, the lower World, which is the Neshamah of Katnut of Malchut, **"which add up to twenty years,"** since the third set of seven necessarily includes the two times seven of the Nefesh and Ruach as well, as mentioned earlier, and it includes 20 years. That is when the Upper Courthouse, namely the Neshamah of Katnut of Malchut, punishes, as explained.

Malchut receives assistance from the Lower Beings.

129. **וְדִינָא דְעָלְמָא בְּר"ה, עַל יְדָא דְהַאי דַּרְגָּא אִיהוּ, דְּאִיהוּ מַמָּשׁ קַיְּימָא בְּדִינָא עַל בְּנוֹי בְּהַאי עָלְמָא, בְּגִין לְאִתְדַּכְּאָה לְגַבֵּי עָלְמָא עִלָּאָה, בְּגִין דְּלֵית לֵיהּ סִיוּעַ לְסַלְּקָא וּלְאִתְדַּכְּאָה אֶלָּא מִגּוֹ תַּתָּאֵי.**

129. "The Judgment of the world on Rosh Hashanah is carried through this level, namely the Neshamah of Katnut of Malchut, which is the third set of seven, **which actually stands in Judgment over Her children in this world so as to be purified for the Upper World,** namely to receive the Mochin of Gadlut from Binah **because She has no assistance to rise and be purified except through the Lower Beings,** when they do Teshuvah and raise Mayim Nukvin (Female Waters)."

Acharei Mot

1. "After the death of the two sons of Aaron"

A Synopsis

Rav Yehuda and Rav Shimon discuss the words "spoke" and "said" in "The Lord spoke to Moses" and "The Lord said to Moses," and we learn that they are from two levels, Judgment and Mercy, which are from the same source, that is Zeir Anpin. Rav Yitzchak says that one verse says to serve the Lord in fear and another says to come before Him with singing, and that these two verses seem contradictory. Rav Shimon explains that if one shows awe and reverence, he will then deserve the joy and singing. One should not rejoice too much over worldly matters so that he will be able to perform the precepts with gladness. We are told that fear of God is the beginning of service to Him. We read of the several reasons that Nadab and Abihu died while giving the offering, and that they were still under the authority of their father Aaron at the time. Rav Chiya tells how he encountered two men studying the Torah in a cleft in the mountain, and of how they were discussing poems and Psalms and songs, and speaking about the sons of Korah who did not die. They say that every time a righteous person dies it brings forgiveness for the sins of the whole generation. The memory of the two sons of Aaron serves as atonement for Israel while they are in exile because Nadab and Abihu are each considered equal to the seventy members of the Sanhedrin who served before Moses.

The death of the righteous atones for the generation.

9. תּוּ פָּתְחוּ וְאָמְרוּ. בְּכָל זִמְנָא דְּצַדִּיקַיָּא מִסְתַּלְּקֵי מֵעָלְמָא, דִּינָא אִסְתַּלָּק מֵעָלְמָא, וּמִיתַתְהוֹן דְּצַדִּיקַיָּא מְכַפֶּרֶת עַל חוֹבֵי דָּרָא. וְעַל דָּא פַּרְשְׁתָּא דִּבְנֵי אַהֲרֹן, בְּיוֹמָא דְּכִפּוּרֵי קָרֵינָן לָהּ, לְמֶהֱוֵי כַּפָּרָה לְחוֹבֵיהוֹן דְּיִשְׂרָאֵל. אָמַר קוּדְשָׁא בְּ"ה, אִתְעַסְּקוּ בְּמִיתָתְהוֹן דְּצַדִּיקַיָּא אִלֵּין, וְיִתְחַשֵּׁב לְכוּ כְּאִלּוּ אַתּוּן מְקָרְבִין קָרְבָּנִין בְּהַאי יוֹמָא לְכַפָּרָא עֲלַיְיכוּ. דְּתָנֵינָן, כָּל זִמְנָא דְּיִשְׂרָאֵל

יְהוֹן בְּגָלוּתָא, וְלָא יְקָרְבוּן קָרְבְּנִין בְּהַאי יוֹמָא, וְאִינּוּן תְּרֵין שְׂעִירִין לָא יַכְלִין לְקָרְבָא, יְהֵא לְהוֹ דִּכְרָנָא, דִּתְרֵי בְּנֵי אַהֲרֹן, וְיִתְכַּפֵּר עֲלַיְיהוּ.

9. Furthermore, they said: "Every time that the righteous depart this world, there is likewise annulled from this world all the harsh decrees, and the death of the righteous brings forgiveness for the sins of the generation. Therefore, we read the portion dealing with the sons of Aaron on Yom Kippur to bring forgiveness for the sins of Israel. The Holy One, blessed be He, says, 'Deal with the death of these Tzadikim, and it will be accredited for you as if you offered sacrifices this day to atone for you.' For we have learned that as long as Israel are exile and do not bring offerings on this day and cannot offer the two goats, they will have the remembrance of the two sons of Aaron and it will serve as atonement for them."

The superiority of Nadab and Abihu.

י. דְּהָכִי אוֹלִיפְנָא, דִּכְתִּיב וְאֵלֶּה שְׁמוֹת בְּנֵי אַהֲרֹן הַכֹּהֲנִים וְגוֹ'. וּכְתִיב, הַבְּכוֹר נָדָב וַאֲבִיהוּא אֶלְעָזָר וְאִיתָמָר. וְאֶלְעָזָר וְאִיתָמָר מִבָּעֵי לֵיהּ, מַהוּ אֶלְעָזָר וְאִיתָמָר. אֶלָּא שָׁקוּל הֲוָה אֲבִיהוּא כִּתְרֵי אֲחוֹי. וְנָדָב כְּכֻלְּהוּ.

10. We have learned that it is written: "These are the names of the sons of Aaron, the priests…" (Numbers 3:3) and also "the firstborn Nadab, and Abihu, Elazar and Itamar." (Numbers 3:2) He asks: **"It should read: 'And Elazar and Itamar'** just like it says 'and Abihu,' **so why write 'Elazar and Itamar'?"** Why delete the connecting 'and' from Elazar? He answers: **"Abihu was equal to his two brothers.** The verse thus reads as 'And Abihu is like Elazar and Itamar,' **and Nadab is equal to all the others.**

There were none like Nadab and Abihu in Israel.

11. וְאִית דְּמַתְנֵי הַבְּכוֹר נָדָב, דָּא בִּלְחוּדוֹי, וַאֲבִיהוּא בִּלְחוּדוֹי, וְכָל חַד אִתְחֲשִׁיב בְּעֵינֵיהּ, כִּתְרַוַויְיהוּ, כְּאֶלְעָזָר וְאִיתָמָר. אֲבָל נָדָב וַאֲבִיהוּא בִּלְחוּדַיְיהוּ, שְׁקוּלִין הֲווֹ לְקָבֵל שַׁבְעִין סַנְהֶדְרִין, דַּהֲווֹ מְשַׁמְּשִׁין קָמֵי מֹשֶׁה. וּבְגִין כָּךְ, מִיתָתְהוֹן מְכַפְּרָא עַל יִשְׂרָאֵל. וְעַל דָּא כְּתִיב, וַאֲחֵיכֶם כָּל בֵּית יִשְׂרָאֵל יִבְכּוּ אֶת הַשְּׂרֵפָה. וְאָמַר ר׳ שִׁמְעוֹן, הַבְּכוֹר נָדָב, כְּלוֹמַר, הַהוּא, דְּכָל שְׁבָחָא וִיקָרָא דִּילֵיהּ. נָדָב וַאֲבִיהוּא, עַל אַחַת כַּמָּה וְכַמָּה, דְּהָנֵי תְּרֵי, לָא אִשְׁתְּכָחוּ כְּוָתַיְיהוּ בְּיִשְׂרָאֵל.

11. "There are those who learn as follows: 'the firstborn Nadab' is on its own 'and Abihu' is on its own, and afterwards 'Elazar and Itamar' are read as joined together to teach **that each one,** Nadab and Abihu, **is considered in the eyes** of scripture **as both Elazar and Itamar** together. **But** both **Nadab and Abihu by themselves are each considered equal to the seventy members of the Sanhedrin who served before Moses. For this reason, their deaths atoned for Israel. Therefore, it is written, 'But let your brethren, the whole house of Israel bewail the burning.' (Leviticus 10:6) Rav Shimon said:** "Therefore the verse specifies **'Nadab the firstborn,' meaning the one who all praise and honor are his. How much more so with Nadab and Abihu** together, **because there were none among Israel like these two."**

3. Nadab and Abihu

A Synopsis

Rav Shimon says that in a way Nadab and Abihu died twice, once before God when offering the sacrifice and once because they left no children, since someone who does not merit children is considered as though dead. We learn that Nadab and Abihu died physically but did not die spiritually because they reincarnated in Pinchas. The reason they were reincarnated together in one body was because they had not married and so were only considered a half body each. Their sin was later corrected by Pinchas' action in slaying the foreign woman. The two sons of Aaron and Zimri had essentially committed the same sin, which is, bringing near something that was far from holiness. Rav Shimon talks about the covenant of peace. We learn that Rav Yosi had said that people have their sins forgiven when they feel compassion for afflictions visited upon the just. Therefore during Yom Kippur, people read about the death of the two sons of Aaron, and they feel distress for them so that their own sins are forgiven. Also, they are reassured that their own children will not die during their lifetimes.

Why we read about the death of Nadab and Abihu on Yom Kippur.

28. תָּאנָא א"ר יוֹסֵי, בְּהַאי יוֹמָא דְּכִפּוּרֵי, אִתְתַּקַּן לְמִקְרֵי פָּרְשְׁתָּא דָּא, לְכַפְּרָא לְיִשְׂרָאֵל בְּגָלוּתָא, בְּגִין דָּא, סִדְרָא דְּיוֹמָא דָּא, הָכָא אִתְסָדַּר, וּבְגִין דְּמִיתַתְהוֹן דִּבְנֵי אַהֲרֹן, מְכַפְּרָא עַל יִשְׂרָאֵל.

28. We have learned that Rav Yosi said, "It was established to read this portion of the sons of Aaron **on this day of Yom Kippur so as to bring atonement for Israel in exile** who are unable to offer sacrifices. **For this reason, the order** of the sacrifices **for this day,** Yom Kippur, **was established here** in the portion about the sons of Aaron, and reciting it replaces the sacrifice. Furthermore, **the deaths of the sons of Aaron atone for Israel.**

Crying over the death of the righteous.

29. מִכָּאן אוֹלִיפְנָא, כָּל הַהוּא ב"נ דְּיִסּוּרֵי דְּמָארֵיהּ אַתְיָין עָלֵיהּ, כַּפָּרָה דְּחוֹבוֹי אִינּוּן. וְכָל מַאן דְּמִצְטָעַר עַל יִסּוּרֵיהוֹן דְּצַדִּיקַיָּא, מַעֲבִירִין חוֹבַיָּא דִּלְהוֹן מֵעָלְמָא. וְעַ"ד בְּיוֹמָא דָּא, קוֹרִין, אַחֲרֵי מוֹת שְׁנֵי בְּנֵי אַהֲרֹן, דְּיִשְׁמְעוּן עַמָּא, וְיִצְטַעֲרוּן עַל אֲבוּדְהוֹן דְּצַדִּיקַיָּא, וְיִתְכַּפֵּר לְהוֹן חוֹבַיְיהוּ. וְכָל דְּמִצְטָעַר עַל אֲבוּדְהוֹן דְּצַדִּיקַיָּא, אוֹ אָחִית דִּמְעִין עָלַיְיהוּ, קָבְ"ה מַכְרִיז עָלֵיהּ וְאוֹמֵר, וְסָר עֲוֹנֶךָ וְחַטָּאתְךָ תְּכוּפָּר. וְלֹא עוֹד, אֶלָּא דְּלָא יְמוּתוּן בְּנוֹי בְּיוֹמוֹי. וְעָלֵיהּ כְּתִיב, יִרְאֶה זֶרַע יַאֲרִיךְ יָמִים וְגוֹ'.

29. From here we learn that every person who has affliction visited upon him from his Master, these serve as atonement for sins. And anyone who is in pain for the afflictions of the righteous will have their sins pass away from this world. For this reason, on this day, Yom Kippur, **we read about, "After the death of the two sons of Aaron..." (Leviticus 16:1) so that the congregation listens and feels pain for the rightous who were lost, so that their sins be forgiven. Of him, who feels sorrow for the righteous who perished, or sheds tears for them, the Holy One, blessed be He, announces, "...and your iniquity is taken away, and your sin is purged." (Isaiah 6:7) Furthermore, he is reassured that his children will not die during his lifetime and it is written about him, "...He shall see his seed, he shall prolong his days...." (Isaiah 53:10)**

19. "And Aaron shall cast lots upon the two goats"

A Synopsis

Rav Aba wonders what the "lots" in the title verse were for. Rav Shimon begins his explanation by talking about why Shimon was the brother chosen by Joseph to be taken away and bound. Shimon was from the aspect of Harsh Judgment, and he had allied himself with Levi who was also from the side of Judgment. We learn of two spirits who pursue Judgment, and who spy on the land every day. We are reminded how Israel is beloved of God above all other nations, and that God gave them one day a year to purify themselves so that they will rule over all the prosecutors and spirits. Rav Shimon says that one of the goats mentioned was for The Lord and one for Azazel. If both goats had been for Azazel the world would not have been able to bear it. The goat cannot slander the children of Israel on Yom Kippur because it finds them doing good deeds, and in fact it becomes their defender. As a result of the sacrifice of the goat, Judgment no longer rules over Israel.

Rav Aba asks about the Yom Kippur service.

111. אָתָא רִבִּי אַבָּא וְשָׁאִיל, כְּתִיב וְנָתַן אַהֲרֹן עַל שְׁנֵי הַשְּׂעִירִים גּוֹרָלוֹת וְגוֹ׳. הָנֵי עַדְבִין לָמָּה. וְאַהֲרֹן לָמָּה לֵיהּ לְמֵיהַב עַדְבִין. וּפַרְשָׁתָא דָא לָמָּה. וְהָא אוֹלִיפְנָא קַמֵּי דְּמַר סִדְרָא דְּיוֹמָא, וְהַאי בְּעֵינָא לְמִנְדַּע.

111. Rav Aba came and asked: "It is written, 'And Aaron shall cast lots upon the two goats...' (Leviticus 16:8) What where those lots for? Why did it require Aaron to place the lots? What is this Torah **portion for? I have learned before my master the order** of the Yom Kippur **service,** and also **this matter I wish to know."**

Shimon is always the opening for Judgment.

112. פָּתַח ר״ש וְאָמַר, וַיִּקַּח מֵאִתָּם אֶת שִׁמְעוֹן וַיֶּאֱסוֹר אוֹתוֹ לְעֵינֵיהֶם. וְכִי מַה חָמָא יוֹסֵף לְמֵיסַב לְשִׁמְעוֹן עִמֵּיהּ יַתִּיר מֵאֲחוֹהִי. אֶלָּא, אָמַר יוֹסֵף, בְּכָל אֲתַר שִׁמְעוֹן פְּתִיחוּתָא דְּדִינָא אִיהוּ, וְהַהִיא שַׁעֲתָא דַּאֲזִילְנָא מֵאַבָּא לְגַבַּיְיהוּ דְּאֶחָי, שִׁמְעוֹן פָּתַח בְּקַדְמֵיתָא בְּדִינָא, הה״ד וַיֹּאמְרוּ אִישׁ אֶל אָחִיו הִנֵּה בַּעַל הַחֲלוֹמוֹת הַלָּזֶה בָּא וְעַתָּה לְכוּ וְגוֹ׳. לְבָתַר בִּשְׁכֶם, וַיִּקְחוּ שְׁנֵי בְנֵי יַעֲקֹב שִׁמְעוֹן וְלֵוִי, כֻּלְּהוּ בְּדִינָא הֲווֹ. טַב לְמֵיסַב דָּא, וְלָא יִתְעַר קְטָטוּתָא בְּכֻלְּהוּ שִׁבְטִין.

112. Rav Shimon opened and said, "...and he took Shimon from them, and bound him before their eyes." (Genesis 42:24) He asks: **"For what reason did Joseph see fit to take Shimon with him rather than any one of the** other **brothers?"** He answers: **"Joseph said 'Shimon is always the opening for Judgment, and at that time when I went from my father to my brothers, Shimon opened with Judgment first, as the verse says, 'And they said one to another, "Behold, this dreamer comes. Come now therefore...."' (Genesis 37:19-20) Later in Shechem, '...that two sons of Jacob, Shimon and Levi....' (Genesis 34:25) All these actions pertain to Judgment.** Therefore **it is better to take this one and not allow him to arouse quarreling among all the tribes."**

Shimon and Levi need to be separated, lest the world be destroyed.

113. וְתָנֵינָן, מַאי קָא חָמָא שִׁמְעוֹן לְאִזְדַּוְּוגָא בְּלֵוִי יַתִּיר מִכֹּלָּא. וְהָא רְאוּבֵן הֲוָה אָחוּהָ וְסָמִיךְ לֵיהּ, אֶלָּא שִׁמְעוֹן חָמָא וְיָדַע דְּלֵוִי מִסִּטְרָא דְּדִינָא קָא אָתֵי, וְשִׁמְעוֹן מִסִּטְרָא דְּדִינָא קַשְׁיָא יַתִּיר אִתְאַחָד. אָמַר נִתְעָרֵב חַד בְּחַד וְאֲנָן נֶחֱרִיב עָלְמָא. מָה עָבַד קוּדְשָׁא בְּרִיךְ הוּא, נָטַל לֵיהּ לְחוּלָקֵיהּ לְלֵוִי, אָמַר מִכָּאן וּלְהָלְאָה שִׁמְעוֹן לֵיתִיב בְּקוּפְטִירָא בְּהֲדֵיהּ בִּלְחוֹדוֹי.

113. [He asks:] **"We have learned, 'What did Shimon see in attaching himself to Levi more than to the others? Reuven was also his brother and close to him,** just as Levi, so why did he not stick with Reuven?'" He answers: **"Shimon saw and realized that Levi was of the aspect of Judgment and Shimon was attached to even harsher Judgment. So he said: 'Let us join one with the other and we could destroy the world.'"** [He asks:] **"What did the Holy One, blessed be He, do?"** [He answers:] **"He took Levi aside to His place and said: 'From this point on, let Shimon stay bound with ropes alone.'"**

Two spirits who pursue Judgment on the land by foot.

114. תָּאנָא בְּסִטְרָא דְּאִימָא, תְּרֵין גַּרְדִּינֵי טְהִירִין אִתְאַחֲדָן בִּידָא שְׂמָאלָא, וְהָא אוֹקִימְנָא דְּאִינּוּן מְאַלְלֵי אַרְעָא בְּכָל יוֹמָא וְיוֹמָא, וְהַיְינוּ רָזָא דִּכְתִיב שְׁנַיִם אֲנָשִׁים מְרַגְּלִים.

114. We have learned that from the aspect of Ima there are two spirits who pursue Judgment attached to the left hand. We have established that they spy on the land, Malchut, **on foot daily,** meaning they nourish from Netzach-Hod-Yesod of Malchut, referred to as "feet." **This is the secret of, "...two men to spy [on foot]...." (Joshua 2:1)**

Out of His excessive love, the Creator gave the Israelites one day a year to be purified.

115. וְתָאנָא, זַכָּאָה חוּלָקֵיהוֹן דְּיִשְׂרָאֵל יַתִּיר מִכָּל עַמִּין עע"ז דְּקוּדְשָׁא בְּרִיךְ הוּא בָּעֵי לְדַכְּאָה לְהוּ, וּלְרַחֲמָא עֲלַיְיהוּ, דְּאִינּוּן חוּלָקֵיהּ וְעַדְבֵיהּ, הה"ד כִּי חֵלֶק יְיָ' עַמּוֹ וְגוֹ', וּכְתִיב יַרְכִּיבֵהוּ עַל בָּמֳתֵי אָרֶץ. עַל בָּמֳתֵי אֶרֶץ דַּיְיקָא. דְּהָא אִינּוּן אִתְאַחֲדָן לְעֵילָּא לְעֵילָּא. וְעַ"ד קוּדְשָׁא בְּרִיךְ הוּא רְחִימוּתָא דִּילֵיהּ אִתְדְּבַק בְּהוּ, הה"ד אָהַבְתִּי אֶתְכֶם אָמַר יְיָ', וּכְתִיב כִּי מֵאַהֲבַת יְיָ' אֶתְכֶם וְגוֹ', וּמִגּוֹ רְחִימוּתָא יַתִּירָא דְּרָחִים לְהוּ, יָהַב לוֹן יוֹמָא חַד בְּשַׁתָּא לְדַכְּאָה לְהוּ, וּלְזַכָּאָה לְהוּ מִכָּל חוֹבֵיהוֹן, דִּכְתִיב כִּי בַיּוֹם הַזֶּה וְגוֹ'. בְּגִין דִּיהוֹן זַכָּאִין בְּעָלְמָא דֵּין, וּבְעָלְמָא דְּאָתֵי, וְלָא יִשְׁתְּכַח בְּהוּ חוֹבָא. וְעַ"ד בְּיוֹמָא דָּא, מִתְעַטְּרִין יִשְׂרָאֵל, וְשַׁלְטִין עַל כֻּלְּהוּ גַּרְדִּינִין, וְעַל כֻּלְּהוּ טְהִירִין.

115. We have learned: praiseworthy is the lot of Israel more than all the other idolatrous nations, as the Holy One, blessed be He, desired to purify them and have mercy on them as they are His portion and inheritance. It is written: "For the Lord's portion is His people..." (Deuteronomy 32:9) and "He made him ride on the high places of the earth...." (Ibid. 13) "...on the high places of the earth" exactly, as they attach themselves higher and higher to Zeir Anpin. **Therefore, the love of the Holy One, blessed be He, clings to them, as it is written: "'I have loved you,' says the Lord..." (Malachi 1:2) and "But because the Lord loved you...." (Deuteronomy 7:8) From this excessive love, He gave them one day during the year to purify them and clear them from their sins, as is written: "For on this day..." (Leviticus 16:30) so that they may be meritorious in this world and in the World to Come, and that no sin may be found in them. Consequently on this day, Israel are crowned and rule over the prosecutors and all spirits.**

Aaron stems from the aspect of Chesed and is thus able to perfect Malchut.

116. תָּאנָא וְנָתַן אַהֲרֹן עַל שְׁנֵי הַשְּׂעִירִים גּוֹרָלוֹת. וְנָתַן אַהֲרֹן, בְּגִין דְּאָתֵי מִסִּטְרָא דְּחֶסֶד. עַל שְׁנֵי הַשְּׂעִירִים, עַל דַּיְיקָא, בְּגִין דְּתִתְבַּסֵּם מַטְרוֹנִיתָא. גּוֹרָל אֶחָד לַיְיָ' וְגוֹרָל לַעֲזָאזֵל וְהָא תְּרֵין שְׂעִירִין אִינּוּן, אַמַּאי חַד לַיְיָ'. אֶלָּא אָמַר קֻבָּ"ה, יָתִיב הַאי גַּבָּאי, וְחַד יֵזִיל וְיָשׁוּט בְּעָלְמָא, דְּאִלְמָלֵי תַּרְוַויְיהוּ מִזְדַּוְּוגָן, לָא יָכִיל עָלְמָא לְמִסְבַּל.

116. We have learned: "And Aaron shall cast lots upon the two goats...." (Leviticus 16:8) [He asks:] **"'And Aaron shall cast...'** why specifically Aaron?" [He answers:] **"Because he stems from the aspect of Chesed,** and thus is able to perfect Malchut with Chasadim. **'Upon the two goats,' 'upon' precisely,** alluding to Malchut that is above the two goats, **so as to give fragrance to the Matron,** Malchut. **"...one lot for the Lord, and the other lot for Azazel." (Leviticus 16:8)** He asks: **"These two goats** symbolize Judgments, **so why should one of them be for the Lord?"** He answers: **"The Holy One, blessed be He, said: 'Let one** goat **stay with Me and let the other wander around in the world, for if both joined together, the world would not be able to bear it.'"**

The goat cannot slander when Israel are seen performing the work of Yom Kippur.

117. נָפַק הַאי, אָזִיל וְשָׁאט בְּעָלְמָא, וְאַשְׁכַּח לְהוּ לְיִשְׂרָאֵל, בְּכַמָּה פּוּלְחָנִין, בְּכַמָּה דַּרְגִּין, בְּכַמָּה נִמּוּסִין טָבָן, לָא יָכִיל לְהוּ, כֻּלְּהוּ שְׁלָמָא בֵּינַיְיהוּ, לָא יָכִיל לְמֵיעַל בְּהוּ בְּדַלְטוֹרָא. הַאי שְׂעִירָא שַׁלְחִין לֵיהּ בְּמַטּוּלָא דְּכָל חוֹבַיְיהוּ דְּיִשְׂרָאֵל.

117. This goat **comes out and roams around the world. It finds Israel performing various kinds of worship on various levels and a variety of good practices and it cannot overcome them. Among them all, peace reigns and** the goat **cannot commence to slander them,** meaning to instigate against them. **This goat is sent with the burden of all the sins of Israel.**

The prosecutor becomes the defense attorney.

118. תָּאנָא, כַּמָּה חֲבִילֵי טְרִיקִין מִזְדַּמְנָן, דְּאִינּוּן תְּחוֹת יְדֵיהּ, וּמִמְנָן לְאַלְכָּא אַרְעָא, עַל כָּל אִינּוּן דְּעָבְרִין עַל פִּתְגָּמֵי אוֹרַיְיתָא. וְהַהוּא יוֹמָא, לָא שְׁכִיחַ דִּלְטוֹרָא לְמַלְּלָא בְּהוּ בְּיִשְׂרָאֵל. כַּד מָטָא הַאי שְׂעִירָא לְגַבֵּי טוּרָא, כַּמָּה חֶדְוּ עַל חֶדְוּ מִתְבַּסְמִין כֻּלְּהוּ בֵּיהּ. וְהַהוּא גַּרְדִּינָא דְּנָפִיק, אַהְדָּר וְאָמַר תּוּשְׁבַּחְתָּא דְּיִשְׂרָאֵל, קַטֵּיגוֹרָא אִתְעֲבֵיד סַנֵּיגוֹרָא.

118. We have learned that numerous bands of destroyers are ready under the authority of this goat, **prepared to spy out the land against all those transgressing the Torah, but on that day,** Yom Kippur, **it is unable to find words of slander against Israel. When this goat** of Azazel **arrives at the mountain, much joy upon joy is sweetened through it to all. That judgment pursuer that emerged,** namely the Supernal goat, **recants and speaks praise of Israel. The prosecutor has become the defense attorney,** meaning the denouncer has now become the champion spokesman.

Explanation of the article: Rav Aba asked Rav Shimon three questions [in verse 111]. The first is: **"What were those lots for?"** The second is: **"Why did it require Aaron to place the lots,** and not anyone else?" The third is: **"What is this portion for?"** Meaning, why is this portion specifically read on Yom Kippur? For [Rav Shimon] to answer these three questions [of Rav Aba], he brings here three matters: the matter of Shimon and Levi, the matter of the two spies, and the matter of the two goats. The root of [all three] are equal in terms of their Judgments.

You already know that there are two types of Judgments that are the root of all the Judgments and sins in the world—the Judgments of the Male that come from the Left Column, and the Judgments of the Female that come from the Curtain (Masach). When the Judgments of the Female emerge due to the Correction (Tikkun), namely from the Central Column, they then negate the Judgments of the Female and cancel them out. However, if the Judgments of the Female do not emerge due to the Tikkun but rather from the Judgments themselves, then they not only cancel out the Judgments of the Male but they are further added to them and destroy the world.

Shimon and Levi were both in the aspect of Judgments. Shimon was from the aspect of the Judgments of the Male that came from the Left Column, and Levi had the aspect of the Judgments of the Female that came from the Masach. [In verse 113] this is: **"Shimon saw and realized... Let us join one with the other and we could destroy the world,"** because the Female Judgments in Levi would destroy the world had it been added to the Male Judgments of Shimon. **"What did the Holy One, blessed be He, do? He took Levi aside,"** meaning that he elevated him to the aspect of his Tikkun, which is the Central Column, and thus he negates the Male Judgments and effaces from it its Upper Three of the Left, as is the way of the Central Column. **"From this point on, let Shimon stay bound with ropes alone,"** meaning that his Upper Three of the Left will be diminished and he will remain with the Six Corners [Sefirot] of Chochmah, which is considered for him as if he is bound with ropes due to the Female Judgments in Levi. This also answers what he asked [in verse 112] about: **"'And he took Shimon from them, and bound him before their eyes' (Genesis 42:24) For what reason did Joseph see fit...?"** because Yosef is the aspect of Yesod, which is the Central Column below the chest, and therefore the aspect of the Corrected Female Judgments in the Central Column bound up Shimon, by diminishing the Upper Three of the Left within Shimon, from where come all Judgments and arguments.

[In verse 114] this is: **"from the aspect of Ima there are two spirits who pursue Judgment attached to the left hand,"** which are the Judgments of the Female and the Judgments of the Male that are mentioned, and both are drawn from Ima to Malchut. The Judgments of the Female are added on and cleave to the Judgments of the Male, which are from the left hand of Ima. **"We have established that they spy on the land on foot daily,"** as they are attached to the Netzach-Hod-Yesod of Malchut that are called "feet," and Malchut is called "land," and therefore they are called "foot-spies of the land." They are awakened every single day, and their correction is through the Illumination of the Central Column every single day. This is the secret of, "...two men to spy [on foot]...." (Joshua 2:1)

[In verse 116] this is: **"Why should one of them be for the Lord?"** He answers: **"The Holy One, blessed be He, said: 'Let one** goat **stay with Me,"** namely the goat of the sin-offering. The two goats in their root Above are also the two aspects of Judgments that were mentioned earlier. The goat of the sin-offering is the Judgments of the Female and the goat to Azazel is the Judgments of the Male. The Holy One, blessed be He, who is the Central Column, says that the goat of the sin-offering should "stay with me," meaning that its Judgments should be corrected by the aspect of the Central Column that diminishes the Upper Three of the Left Column. **"...and let the other wander around in the world,"** meaning that the goat for Azazel, which is from the Judgments of the Male, should wander around in the world alone, as mentioned with Shimon and Levi that: **"He took Levi aside to His place and said: 'From this point on, let Shimon stay bound with ropes alone... for if both joined together, the world would not be able to bear it,'"** for had they joined together they would destroy the world. If the Judgments of the Female are not drawn via the correction of the Central Column, they are added onto the Judgments of the Male and destroy the world. Therefore, He took the goat of the sin-offering to Him.

However, to properly understand the concept of the goat for Azazel, we need to expound on this. It says in the Zohar (Vayera 384-385): **"This is why on Rosh Hashanah we need to confuse the Satan... On Yom haKippurim, we need to** deal with **the Satan** with ease **and give him appeasement... Then he will become a defender."** The explanation is that on Rosh Hashanah the world reverts to the way it was on the Fourth Day of Creation, namely that the Upper Three of Chochmah return and are revealed, and then the Other Side awakens to draw Judgments of the Left onto the world. The correction for this is the Blowing of the Shofar that diminishes the Upper Three from the Worlds, thus [they remain] with Six Corners [Sefirot] without a head. [This] confuses Satan, as his entire grasp is in the Upper Three of the Left, and now they have disappeared due to the Blowing of the Shofar.

However now that the Upper Three have disappeared, a lack is created in the Worlds, and the Other Side rises and grasps the place where the Upper Three is lacking and causes the Created Beings to sin, which is the secret of the In-Betweeners being in suspense until Yom Kippur. Therefore, a second correction is made on Yom Kippur, which is that we return to draw the Illumination of Chochmah and with all this, a correction is made where the Other Side will not grab hold of the Left to cause the world to sin by drawing Chochmah downward. This is the Correction [Tikkun] that is mentioned in many places that whenever Chochmah is revealed Harsh Judgments that punish the wicked are revealed with it, and with this the Chochmah is guarded so the wicked cannot draw it from above downward.

Know that the source of this correction is done on Yom Kippur via the goat given to Azazel. On Yom Kippur, Chochmah is revealed through Malchut clothing Binah. Then, **"And Aaron shall cast lots upon the two goats...." (Leviticus 16:8)** One goat is the secret of the Judgments of the Female and the other goat is the Judgments of the Male that are drawn from the Upper Three of Chochmah. **"...one lot for the Lord" (Ibid.)** namely through the Blowing of the Shofar, the goat that has the Judgments of the Female elevates to the Lord, the Central Column, and receives the Illumination of Chochmah in the aspect of the Six Corners [Sefirot], as is the way of Holiness. **"...and the other lot for Azazel" (Ibid.)** namely the Upper Three of Chochmah is revealed on the goat that has the Judgments of the Male, since it draws the Illumination of Chochmah from above downward, as is the way of the Other Side. Then, "and he sends the goat to the wilderness" (Leviticus 16:22) namely that it experiences all the punishments that are drawn to those who cleave to it, since they must follow it to the wilderness and the destruction.

Then the two Judgments are corrected: the Judgments of the Female are corrected by their lot going up to the Lord, the Central Column, which corrected them to be the Illumination of the Six Corners of Chochmah. And so that the Other Side will not grab onto the vacant space of the Upper Three of Chochmah, a goat for Azazel was given to him, which draws the Upper Three of Chochmah with all the Judgments and punishments. Then (verse 118), **"The prosecutor becomes the defense attorney,"** because he would not want to grab onto the vacant space of the Upper Three of Chochmah so as to not ruin his own Upper Three that he nourishes from the goat to Azazel. There also is no concern that he will cause the world to sin by drawing it from above downward, due to all the Judgments that rest on it by sending it to the wilderness. This is: **"When this goat arrives... all are fragranced through it,"** namely all the Judgments, both Male and Female, as explained.

[In verse 116] this is: **"Let one stay with Me..."** namely, the one that is from the aspect of the Judgments of the Female will stay with Me and receive the Six Corners of Chochmah like the way of Holiness, **"...and let the other wander around the world"** to entice the people of the world to draw for him the Upper Three from above downward as he likes. Then the Other Side goes and misleads people to draw to him the Illumination of Chochmah from above downward. This is: **"This** goat **comes out and roams around the world. It finds Israel performing various kinds of worship..."** namely through the lots, which clarifies the advantage of the goat designated by lot to the Lord, namely its great Illuminations and Mochin that are drawn from it, and corresponding to it the many Judgments and punishments that are revealed with the goat designated by lot to Azazel. Then all of Israel cleave to the Creator with all their soul, and the Other Side **"cannot commence to slander them"** in fear of the Judgments that are revealed with it.

It is known that the two mentioned Judgments are the root of all sins and iniquities, and once these two root Judgments are corrected, we are confident that the house of Israel will no longer sin. This is: **"This goat is sent with the burden of all the sins of Israel,"** as it is said: "Thus the goat shall carry on it all their iniquities to an inaccessible region" (Leviticus 16:22) as Israel are made certain that they will no longer sin due to the Judgments that are revealed with the goat that is sent to an inaccessible region, and then it atones for them. This explains well the question Rav Aba asked [in verse 111]: **"What where those lots for?"** What he asked: **"Why did it require Aaron to place the lots"** is as it says [in verse 116] **"'Aaron shall cast,' because he stems from the aspect of Chesed"** and therefore he was fit to draw the abundance of Chasadim on the goat designated by lot to the Lord and to unite the Right and Left of Malchut together. What he asked: **"What is this portion for?"** meaning why is it read on Yom Kippur? [The answer is] as it is written [in verse 115]: **"From this excessive love, He gave them one day during the year to purify them and clear them from their sins."**

Through the two goats, Israel pacifies all agents of Judgment.

119. ות"ח, לָאו דָּא בִּלְחוֹדוֹי הוּא, אֶלָּא בְּכָל אֲתַר דְּבָעְיָין יִשְׂרָאֵל לְאִתְדַּכְאָה מֵחוֹבַיְיהוּ, קֻבְּ"ה יָהִיב לוֹן עֵיטָא לְקַשְּׁרָא מָארֵי דְּדִינָא, וּלְבַסְּמָא לְהוּ בְּאִינּוּן קָרְבְּנִין וְעִלָּוִון, דְּקָרְבִין קָמֵי קֻבְּ"ה, וּכְדֵין לָא יַכְלִין לְאַבְאָשָׁא. וְהַהוּא יוֹמָא יַתִּיר עַל כֹּלָּא, כְּמָה דְּמִבַּסְּמִין יִשְׂרָאֵל לְתַתָּא לְכֹלָּא, הָכִי מְבַסְּמִין לְכָל אִינּוּן דְּאִית לְהוּ לְטוֹרָא וְכֹלָּא קָרְבְּנָא הוּא וּפוּלְחָנָא דְּקֻבְּ"ה.

119. Come and see, not only this alone but wherever Israel need to be cleansed of their sins, the Holy One, blessed be He, gives them

advice to bind the agents of Judgment so they will not accuse, **and pacify them through the means of sacrifices and burnt offerings that they offer before the Holy One, blessed be He, and then they are unable to cause harm. And on that day,** Yom Kippur, **more than any other day, just as Israel below sweeten everything,** through the two goats, **so do they pacify all the Accusers. All of this is the sacrifice and the service of the Holy One, blessed be He.**

The priest's offerings Below awaken the ones Above.

120. תָּאנָא, בְּהַהִיא שַׁעֲתָא דִּכְתִּיב, וְלָקַח אַהֲרֹן אֶת שְׁנֵי הַשְּׂעִירִם וְגוֹ', מִתְעָרִין אִינּוּן בְּהַהוּא יוֹמָא לְעֵילָּא, וּבַעְיָין לְשַׁלְטָאָה וּלְמֵיפַּק בְּעָלְמָא. כֵּיוָן דְּכַהֲנָא מְקָרֵב אִלֵּין לְתַתָּא, מִתְקָרְבִין אִינּוּן לְעֵילָּא. כְּדֵין עַדְבִין סַלְקִין בְּכָל סִטְרִין, כַּהֲנָא יָהַב עַדְבִין לְתַתָּא, כַּהֲנָא יָהִיב עַדְבִין לְעֵילָּא. כְּמָה דְּחַד אִשְׁתְּאַר בֵּיהּ בְּקוּדְשָׁא בְּרִיךְ הוּא לְתַתָּא. וְחַד אַפְּקִין לֵיהּ לְהַהוּא מַדְבְּרָא, הָכִי נָמֵי לְעֵילָּא, חָד אִשְׁתְּאַר בֵּיהּ בְּקוּדְשָׁא בְּרִיךְ הוּא, וְחַד נָפִיק וְשָׁט בְּעָלְמָא, לְהַהוּא מַדְבְּרָא עִלָּאָה, וְחַד בְּחַד מִתְקַשַּׁר.

120. We have learned: at that time when it is written "And Aharon shall take the two goats..." (Leviticus 16:7), on that day these two goats, which are the Female and Male Judgments, **are awakened Above and wish** to join together, as mentioned, **to rule and to set out into the world. When the Priest offers** the two goats **down below** in the Temple, **the ones Above are offered. And then the lots are spread in every direction. The Priest casts lots down Below, the Priest,** who is Chesed, **casts the lots Above. Just as Below one remains with the Holy One, blessed be He,** referring to the one goat allotted to the Lord, **and one,** namely the goat of Azazel, **is brought out to the desert, so it is Above. One remains with the Holy One, blessed be He,** in the Central Column, **and one goes out and wanders in the world into the wilderness Above,** meaning the Judgments that become revealed with the emergence of Chochmah, which are considered of the aspect of desert and foreboding wilderness. **The one joins with the other,** meaning they shine one upon the other, and thus the two types of Judgments, both the Judgments of the Female and the Judgments of the Male, cancel each other out, as mentioned earlier at length.

Aaron's hands over the head of the goat.

121. כְּתִיב וְסָמַךְ אַהֲרֹן אֶת שְׁתֵּי יָדָיו עַל רֹאשׁ הַשָּׂעִיר הַחַי וְהִתְוַדָּה עָלָיו וְגוֹ'. בְּגִ"כ וְסָמַךְ אַהֲרֹן אֶת שְׁתֵּי יָדָיו, דְּקוּדְשָׁא בְּרִיךְ הוּא יִסְתַּכַּם עַל יְדוֹי. עַל רֹאשׁ הַשָּׂעִיר הַחַי, הַחַי דַּיְיקָא, לְאַכְלְלָא הַהוּא דִּלְעֵילָּא.

121. It is written: "And Aaron shall lay both his hands upon the head of the live goat and confess over it…." (Leviticus 16:21) Therefore it is written: "And Aaron shall lay both his hands…" which are the secret of the Right and Left Columns **so that the Holy One, blessed be He,** the Central Column, **will harmonize his hands. In "…upon the head of the live goat,"** [the words] **"the live" is precise** as it comes **to include the goat Above**, on which the Upper Three of Chochmah with Judgments are revealed, and Chochmah is called "live."

Confession—transferring the sins to the goat.

122. וְהִתְוַדָּה עָלָיו אֶת כָּל עֲוֹנוֹת, כְּמָה דִּכְתִיב וְהִתְוַדָּה אֲשֶׁר חָטָא עָלֶיהָ. וְאוֹקִימְנָא עָלֶיהָ, דְּאִתְדְּכֵי ב"נ וְאִשְׁתְּאַר עָלֶיהָ כָּל הַהוּא חוֹבָא. אוֹף הָכִי וְהִתְוַדָּה עָלָיו, בָּתַר דְּאוֹדֵי כַּהֲנָא בְּגִינַיְיהוּ דְּיִשְׂרָאֵל, עָלָיו: כְּלוֹמַר, יִשְׁתַּאֲרוּן כֻּלְּהוּ עָלָיו.

122. "…and confess over it all the iniquities" (Leviticus 16:21) is similar to "…he shall confess having sinned on it." (Leviticus 5:5) We established that "on it" means that the person becomes cleansed and that sin rests on it, on the sheep. **So also here "…and confess over it," implies that after the Priest makes a confession on behalf of Israel over it,** all the sins **will rest "over it."**

Sacrificing to the Creator and not to the goat.

123. א"ל ר' אַבָּא, אִי הָכִי וְהָא כְּתִיב וְלֹא יִזְבְּחוּ עוֹד אֶת זִבְחֵיהֶם לַשְּׂעִירִים, אָמַר לֵיהּ שָׁאנֵי הָכָא, דְּהָתָם לַשְּׂעִירִים הֲווֹ קָרְבִין קָרְבְּנָא, ובג"כ לָא כְּתִיב וְלֹא יִזְבְּחוּ עוֹד אֶת זִבְחֵיהֶם שְׂעִירִים, אֶלָּא לַשְּׂעִירִים, דְּהָתָם לַשְּׂעִירִים הֲווֹ עַבְדֵי פּוּלְחָנָא, וְשׁוּלְטָנוּתָא. וְהָכָא וְנָשָׂא הַשָּׂעִיר עָלָיו אֶת כָּל עֲוֹנוֹתָם, וְקָרְבְּנָא לָא אִתְעֲבֵיד אֶלָּא לְקוּדְשָׁא בְּרִיךְ הוּא. ת"ח, דִּבְגִינֵי קָרְבְּנָא מִתְבַּסְמָן עִלָּאִין וְתַתָּאִין, וְדִינָא לָא שַׁרְיָא וְשַׁלְטָא עֲלַיְיהוּ דְּיִשְׂרָאֵל.

123. Rav Aba said to him: "If so, behold it is written, 'And they shall no more offer their sacrifices to the demons (lit. goats)" (Leviticus 17:7) so how can you say that the goat of Azazel corresponds with the goat Above?" **He answered him: "Here it is different, as there they used to offer sacrifices to the goats, thus it is not written: 'And they shall no more offer their sacrifices goats,' but rather 'to the goats' as they worshipped goats** and gave them **authority. Here** only **"And the goat shall bear upon it all their iniquities..." (Leviticus 16:22) and the sacrifice was made only for the Holy One, blessed be He. Come and see, as a result of a sacrifice, those Above and those Below are sweetened, and Judgment neither dwells nor rules upon Israel.**

22. A goat to Azazel

A Synopsis

The goat is dispatched to Azazel so that the Other Side will be separated from Israel and will not testify against Israel before God. We are told that every single thing in the world, whether good or bad, is needed, even the Angel of Death. The entire remedy depends on this, not to arouse the secret of Judgment Above and thus intensify this Judgment to annihilate humankind. That Judgment is aroused through the sins of humankind.

Sending the goat separates the Other Side from the Holy Nation.

רַעְיָא מְהֵימְנָא

134. פִּקּוּדָא דָא, לְמִפְלַח כַּהֲנָא רַבָּא פּוּלְחָנָא דְהַהוּא יוֹמָא כְּמָה דְאִצְטְרִיךְ, וּלְמִשְׁלַח שָׂעִיר לַעֲזָאזֵל. רָזָא דָא כד"א, בְּגִין לְאִתְפָּרְשָׁא מֵעַמָּא קַדִּישָׁא, וְלָא יִתְבַּע חוֹבֵיהוֹן קָמֵי מַלְכָּא. וְלָא יְקַטְרֵג עָלַיְיהוּ, דְהָא לֵית לֵיהּ תְּקִיפוּ וְשׁוּלְטָנוּ, בַּר כַּד אִתְתַּקַף רוּגְזָא מִלְעֵילָּא, וּבְהַהוּא דוֹרוֹנָא אִתְהַפָּךְ לְבָתַר אַפּוֹטְרוֹפּוֹסָא עָלַיְיהוּ, וְעַל דָא אִתְדַּחְיָיא מִקַּמֵּי מַלְכָּא. וְהָא אוֹקִימְנָא, בְּגִין דְאִיהוּ קֵץ כָּל בָּשָׂר.

Ra'aya Meheimna (Faithful Shepherd)

134. This Precept is that the High Priest should perform the service of that day as need be, and send the goat to Azazel. The secret is as you have said: so that the Other Side **is separated from the Holy nation and cannot make demands for their sins before the King. He should not accuse them, as he has neither strength nor authority except when anger is intensified Above. With this gift** of the goat to Azazel, **he is then transformed to become their guardian. As a result he is banished from before the King. We have learned that this is so because he is the end of all flesh.**

Explanation: It was explained in Zohar, Noach 130 that [the Other Side] is called "the end of all flesh" because its desire is always for flesh. We explained there in the Sulam that "flesh" is the secret of the Illumination of Chochmah of the Left, and the Other Side desires this Light immensely, study there its reason and its details. The secret of the goat to Azazel is the drawing of Chochmah of the Left (as mentioned in verse 118), and therefore when the Israelites draw to it this Light, it becomes a defender and advocates for them.

The Other Side becomes our advocate.

135. וְעַמָּא קַדִּישָׁא יָהֲבִין לֵיהּ כְּמָה דְּאִצְטְרִיךְ לֵיהּ שָׂעִיר, וְרָזָא דָּא הֵן עֵשָׂו אָחִי אִישׁ שָׂעִיר. כְּמָה דְּאִיהוּ בִּסְטָר דִּקְדוּשָּׁה דְּכַר וְנוּקְבָא, אוּף הָכִי בִּסְטָר מְסָאֲבוּ דְּכַר וְנוּקְבָא. מַתְלָא אַמְרֵי, לְכַלְבָּא אַרְמֵי לֵיהּ גַּרְמָא, יְלַחֵךְ עַפְרָא דְּרַגְלָךְ.

135. The Holy nation gives to him what is needed for him, namely **a goat** (*sa'ir*)**. This is the secret of "... 'Behold, Esau my brother is a hairy** (*sa'ir*) **man...'" (Genesis 27:11)** as he is an aspect of the Other Side. It contains Male and Female, **since just as in the side of Holiness there is Male and Female, so too in the side of defilement there exists Male and Female. A parable people say is: "Throw a bone to a dog and he will lick the dust off your feet;"** here too, we give to the Other Side a goat and he becomes an advocate.

Everything in the world is needed.

136. שָׁאֲלוּ לְבֶן זוֹמָא, מַהוּ לְסָרוּסֵי כַּלְבָּא. אָמַר לָהֶם, וּבְאַרְצְכֶם לֹא תַעֲשׂוּ, כָּל שֶׁבְּאַרְצְכֶם לֹא תַעֲשׂוּ. כְּמָה דְּאִצְטְרִיךְ עָלְמָא לְהַאי, הָכִי אִצְטְרִיךְ עָלְמָא לְהַאי. וְעַל דָּא אִתְּמַר, וְהִנֵּה טוֹב מְאֹד דָּא מַלְאַךְ הַמָּוֶת. לֵית לְבַטְּלָא לֵיהּ מִן עָלְמָא, עָלְמָא אִצְטְרִיךְ לֵיהּ, אע"ג דִּכְתִיב בֵּיהּ, וְהַכְּלָבִים עַזֵּי נֶפֶשׁ לֹא יָדְעוּ שָׂבְעָה וְגוֹ', לָא יִתְבַּטְּלוּן מִן עָלְמָא. כֹּלָּא אִצְטְרִיךְ טוֹב וָרָע.

136. They asked ben Zoma: "Is it permissible for us **to emasculate a dog?" He replied: "...Neither shall you do thus in your land." (Leviticus 22:24)** meaning: **you shall not do thus to anything in your land,** even to a dog, **because just like the world needs this, so does the world need that,** meaning that there is nothing in the world that is not needed. **Therefore we learned that "...and, behold, it was very good" (Genesis 1:31) refers to the Angel of Death, which should not be blotted from the world** because **the world needs him. Even though about him,** the Angel of Death, **it is written: "Moreover the dogs are**

greedy, they never have enough...." **(Isaiah 56:11) it is not** good **that they should become extinct from the world. Everything is needed,** both **good and bad.**

Occupying the Accuser.

137. וּבְגִינֵי כַּךְ אִית לָן בְּיוֹמָא דָא לְמִרְמֵי לֵיהּ גַּרְמָא לְכַלְבָּא, עַד דְּאִיהוּ גָּרִיר, יֵיעוֹל מַאן דְּיֵיעוֹל לְגַבֵּי הֵיכָלָא דְּמַלְכָּא, וְלֵית מַאן דְּיִמְחֵי בִּידוֹי. לְבָתַר יְכַשְׁכֵּשׁ לֵיהּ בִּזְנָבֵיהּ.

137. Therefore on this day, we need to throw a bone to the dog, meaning the goat of Azazel. **While he is dragging** the bone, **he who will enter will enter the palace of the King and there is no one to stop him,** for the Accuser is preoccupied with his gift. **Afterwards, he will further be wagging his tail,** meaning he will become a defender.

The Accuser testifies to the Creator that Israel are clear of sins.

138. מַה כְּתִיב וְהִתְוַדָּה עָלָיו אֶת כָּל עֲוֹנוֹת בְּנֵי יִשְׂרָאֵל, וּכְתִיב וְנָשָׂא הַשָּׂעִיר עָלָיו אֶת כָּל עֲוֹנוֹתָם. כֵּיוָן דְּאִיהוּ חָמֵי הַאי שָׂעִיר. תִּיאוּבְתֵּיהּ לְגַבֵּיהּ, וּלְאִשְׁתַּכְלְלָא בַּהֲדֵיהּ, וְלָא יָדַע מֵאִינּוּן חוֹבִין דְּהָא נָטִיל שָׂעִיר. תָּב לְגַבַּיְיהוּ דְּיִשְׂרָאֵל, וְחָמֵי לוֹן בְּלָא חוֹבִין, בְּלָא פִּשְׁעִין, דְּהָא כֻּלְּהוּ שָׁרָאן בְּרֵישָׁא דְּשָׂעִיר, סָלִיק לְעֵילָּא, וְשַׁבַּח לוֹן קָמֵי קוּדְשָׁא בְּרִיךְ הוּא. וְקוּדְשָׁא בְּרִיךְ הוּא וְחָמֵי סַהֲדוּתָא דְּהַהוּא מְקַטְרְגָא, וְהוֹאִיל וְתִיאוּבְתֵּיהּ לְרַחֲמָא עַל עַמֵּיהּ, אע״ג דְּאִיהוּ יָדַע כָּל עוֹבָדָא, וְחָס עֲלַיְיהוּ דְּיִשְׂרָאֵל.

138. It is written: "...and confess over it all the iniquities of the children of Israel..." (Leviticus 16:21) and "...the goat shall bear upon it all their iniquities..." (Ibid. 22) When the Other Side **sees this goat, his desire toward it** is aroused **to be with it, and he does not know which of the sins the goat took upon himself. He then returns to Israel and sees that they are free and clear of sins and blemishes since all sins are upon the head of the goat. He ascends and praises**

them before the Holy One, blessed be He. The Holy One, blessed be He, pays attention to the testimony of the Accuser and, since His desire is to have mercy on His people, He extends Mercy to Israel even though He is aware of all that has transpired.

Harsh Judgment is awakened by the sins of humankind.

139. וְכֹלָּא שַׁרְיָא בְּדָא, בְּגִין דְּלָא יִתְעַר רָזָא דְּדִינָא מִלְעֵילָּא, וְיִתְתַּקַּף הַאי וְיִשְׁתֵּצוּן בְּנֵי עָלְמָא, דְּהָא דָּא מִסִּטְרָא דְּדִינָא קַשְׁיָא קָא אָתֵי. וְאִי יִתְעַר הַאי, בְּחוֹבֵי בְּנֵי אִינָשָׁא אִתְעַר. דְּהָא לֵית לֵיהּ אִתְעָרוּ לְסַלְּקָא לְעֵילָּא לְאִתְעָרָא דִּינָא קַשְׁיָא בַּר בְּדִיל חוֹבֵי בְּנֵי נָשָׁא. דְּהָא בְּשַׁעֲתָא דְּב"נ עָבִיד חוֹבָא, אִתְכְּנַשׁ הַאי, וְכַמָּה אֲלַף סַיְיעָן דִּילֵיהּ, וּמִתְכַּנְּפֵי תַּמָּן, וְנַטְלֵי לֵיהּ, וְסַלְקֵי לְעֵילָּא רַחֲמָנָא לִישֵׁזְבָן. וְעַל כֹּלָּא יָהַב קוּדְשָׁא בְּרִיךְ הוּא עֵיטָא לְיִשְׂרָאֵל לְאִשְׁתְּזָבָא מִכָּל סִטְרִין. וְעַ"ד כְּתִיב, אַשְׁרֵי הָעָם שֶׁכָּכָה לּוֹ אַשְׁרֵי הָעָם שֶׁיְיָ' אֱלֹהָיו.
ע"כ רַעְיָא מְהֵימְנָא

139. The entire remedy **depends upon this, so that the secret of the Supernal Judgment will not be awakened, be intensified and annihilate the people of the world, as this comes from Harsh Judgment. If this** Judgment **is awakened, it is awakened by the sins of humankind, since it has no awakening to ascend Above to awaken Harsh Judgment if not for the sins of humankind. When a person commits a sin, it gathers and joins other thousands that assist it. They assemble there and ascend upward, may the Merciful One protect us. For all of this, the Holy One, blessed be He, gave counsel to Israel to be saved from all angles, as is written: "Happy are the people who have it so. Happy are the people whose God is the Lord." (Psalms 144:15)**

Explanation of the article: You already know that from the point of view of the Malchut of Tzimtzum Alef, called Man'ula (Lock), the Malchut and the Lower Beings that come from it are not worthy of receiving the Supernal Light. This is because the force of the Tzimtzum (Contraction) and the Masach (Curtain) is mounted on it so as to not receive any Light. The Holy One, blessed be He, saw that the world could not exist, so He therefore elevated Malchut to the attribute of Mercy, Binah, and [Malchut] got sweetened by [Binah]. This sweetened Malchut is called Maftecha (Key) and from its aspect, Malchut and the Lower Beings that come from it are able to receive Supernal Lights.

However, even after Malchut got corrected with the Vessels of Maftecha, the point of Man'ula does not disappear completely but only gets hidden in it. This is why Malchut is called the Tree of Knowledge of Good and Evil, **"if he merits, it is good" (Zohar, Prologue 123)** and Man'ula is stored away and hidden, and Maftecha rules Her. Then She receives all the Lights and shines them to the Lower Beings. **"If he does not merit"** and he sins, **"it is evil" (Ibid.)** then the Man'ula returns and becomes revealed in the root of the sinner in Malchut, and thus the Light departs due to Her, and from this the sinner dies.

One may ask: "If the Holy One, blessed be He, wanted the world to exist and thus corrected the Malchut with the point of Maftecha, then would it have been appropriate for Him to completely cancel out the Man'ula so that it cannot return and be awakened by the sinner? To this it says (verse 136): **"'and, behold, it was very good' (Genesis 1:31) refers to the Angel of Death, which should not be blotted from the world; the world needs him..."** Even though the point of Man'ula causes death, nevertheless the world needs it and it should not be canceled out before the Final Correction. **"Therefore on this day, we need to throw a bone to the dog,"** namely the goat to Azazel, since through the work of Israel, the Upper Three of Chochmah of the Left together with its Harsh Judgments is revealed on [the goat], and the Other Side takes great pleasure in it for the reason it mentions (in verse 134) **"because he is the end of all flesh,"** study there. Therefore, this is considered as if we throw a bone to a dog.

All this is done so that the Other Side will not denounce Israel nor awaken Above the revelation of Man'ula due to the sins of Israel since now **"while he is dragging"** the bone we threw to him, **"he who will enter will enter the palace of the King,"** namely that the High Priest will draw Lights and all kind of goodness from the Palace of the King, **"and there is no one to stop him"** because the Other Side will not denounce him and reveal the Man'ula that banishes the Lights because then he too will lose the gift of the goat of Azazel that he acquired due to the work of Israel. Not only that but **"he will further be wagging his tail"** meaning that he will praise Israel for this, as it explains.

He further explains (in verse 138): **"It is written: '...and the goat shall bear....' (Leviticus 16:22)"** He clarifies how the goat bears all the iniquities of the house of Israel and says: **"When he sees this goat, his desire towards it** is aroused **to be with it..."** because he only desires flesh, which is the Chochmah of the Left that is revealed on the head of the goat. **"...and he does not know which of the sins the goat took upon himself,"** as all these Lights of Chochmah of the Left are revealed in Malchut only because the point of Man'ula is hidden within it, and only the point of Maftecha is used in a revealed way. It turns out that the point of Man'ula, which banishes these Lights is included within this goat in a concealed way but the Other Side is not aware of this since it is concealed. And because he is busy with his goat and does not want to lose his Lights, **"He then returns to Israel and sees that they are free and clear of sins... and he praises them before the Holy One, blessed be He,"** as he wants Israel to be meritorious and the Man'ula to not be revealed, so that he too can hold onto his goat.

"The Holy One, blessed be He, pays attention... He extends Mercy to Israel even though He is aware of all that transpired." Even though the Holy One, blessed be He, knows that the Man'ula is concealed, His knowledge does not cause the Lights to depart because the Holy One, blessed be He, is compassionate toward Israel, which is why He concealed the Man'ula and revealed the attribute of Mercy. As long as the Other Side does not denounce this, no Judgment will be awakened due to the Creator's knowledge of this. This is: **"so that the secret of the Supernal Judgment will not be awakened. If it is awakened,"** if Judgment is awakened and the Man'ula is revealed, **"it is awakened by the sins of humankind,"** as the sin gives the Other Side the power to awaken the Man'ula, as mentioned earlier. **"...since it has no awakening to ascend Above to awaken Harsh Judgment,"** the secret of Man'ula, **"...if not for the sins of mankind,"** as we mentioned earlier: **"If he does not merit, it is evil." (Zohar, Prologue 123)** But if the Other Side does not reveal, even though the Holy One, blessed be He knows, it does not hurt at all. This is because the Holy One, blessed be He, intentionally stored away the attribute of Judgment of Man'ula and revealed in it the Maftecha, which is the secret of joining Mercy with Judgment, as mentioned earlier, so that the world can exist with the attribute of Mercy. **End of Ra'aya Meheimna (Faithful Shepherd)**

32. "From all your sins before the Lord, that you may be clean"

A Synopsis

We learn that the High Priest is capable of bringing atonement on the people because he is a Chariot to Zeir Anpin; he is the voice of Zeir Anpin. We read about God's forgiveness of sins. We read about the High Priest when he enters the Holy of Holies and hears the sounds of the Cherubs' wings. Because of his actions, there is joy Above and Below.

Only the High Priest says, "You will be purified."

194. קָלָא מִתְקַשֵּׁר עִמֵּיהּ דְּכַהֲנָא, וְהוּא אָתִיב לְגַבַּיְיהוּ. וְאָמַר תִּטְהָרוּ. תִּטְהָרוּ לָא אַמְרִין שְׁאָר כַּהֲנֵי וְעַמָּא, בַּר כַּהֲנָא רַבָּא, כַּד אִתְקַשַּׁר בֵּיהּ הַהוּא קָלָא.

194. The voice, namely Zeir Anpin, the Central Column, **joins with the Priest,** meaning the Priest becomes a Chariot to Zeir Anpin. **He says to them, "...you will be purified." (Leviticus 16:30)** As a Chariot to the Central Column, he can bring on them the Illumination of Chochmah that brings atonement of sins and purification. **Neither the people nor any other priest say, "...you will be purified." (Ibid.) except the High Priest when the voice is attached to him,** meaning Zeir Anpin, for then he is capable of bringing atonement on them, and he proclaims, "... you will be purified." (Ibid.)

The Face of the Lord is the Illumination of Chochmah.

195. תָּאנָא, מִכֹּל חַטֹּאתֵיכֶם לִפְנֵי יְיָ', כֵּיוָן דִּכְתִיב מִכֹּל חַטֹּאתֵיכֶם, אֲמַאי לִפְנֵי יְיָ'. אֶלָּא א"ר יִצְחָק, לִפְנֵי יְיָ' מַמָּשׁ.

195. We have learned "...from all your sins before the Lord." (Leviticus 16:30) He asks: **"If he already wrote,** 'to cleanse you **from all your sins,' (Ibid.) why** write 'that you may be clean **before the Lord'?" Rav Yitzchak said:** "...'that you may be clean **before (lit. in the face of) the Lord,' literally,** meaning the Illumination of the face of the Lord because the Illumination of the Lord's face, which is the secret of the Illumination of Chochmah, in the secret of the verse, "a man's wisdom will light his face..." (Ecclesiastes 8:1) cleanses sins and brings purity.

Awakening excitement for when the Creator will sit on the Throne of Mercy.

196. דְּתַנְיָא, מֵרֵישָׁא דְּיַרְחָא סִפְרִין פְּתִיחִין, וְדַיָּינֵי דַּיְינִין. בְּכָל יוֹמָא וְיוֹמָא בָּתֵּי דִּינִין אִתְמַסְרָן, לְאִתְפַּתְחָא בְּדִינָא, עַד הַהוּא יוֹמָא דְּאִקְרֵי תִּשְׁעָה לְיַרְחָא. בְּהַהוּא יוֹמָא, סַלְקִין דִּינִין כֻּלְּהוּ לְמָארֵי דְּדִינָא, וּמִתַקְּנֵי כּוּרְסְיָיא עִלָּאָה דְּרַחֲמֵי, לְמַלְכָּא קַדִּישָׁא. בְּהַהוּא יוֹמָא בָּעָאן יִשְׂרָאֵל לְתַתָּא, לְמֶחֱדֵי בְּחֶדְוָותָא לְקַדְמוּת מָארֵיהוֹן, דְּזַמִּין לְיוֹמָא אָחֳרָא, לְמֵיתַב עֲלַיְיהוּ בְּכוּרְסְיָיא קַדִּישָׁא דְּרַחֲמֵי, בְּכוּרְסְיָיא דְּוַותְרָנוּתָא.

196. We have learned that from the New Moon, meaning Rosh Hashanah, **the books are opened and the judges judge. Every single day the Courthouses are allowed to open in Judgment until that day known as the ninth day of the month. On that day, all Judgments go up to the judge, and they prepare a Supernal Throne of Mercy for the Holy King. On this day, Israel need to rejoice in joy before their Master who is destined on the following day to sit on a Throne of Mercy for them, His Throne of Absolution,** meaning forgiveness of sins.

Explanation: Malchut is called "Throne," and every Rosh Hashanah the world, which is Malchut, reverts to its original state, namely as it was in the Fourth Day of Creation. At that time, Malchut emanated as "the two great luminaries," where Zeir Anpin clothed the Right Column of Binah, which is Chasadim, and Malchut the Left Column of Binah, which is Chochmah without Chasadim. Then Judgments come from Her and She is called the Throne of Judgment. This is the secret [of what the Sages say] that the Creator, Zeir Anpin, sits on the Throne of Judgment, which means that Malchut bestows Judgments and judges the world.

Through the blowing of the Shofar and through all the Judgments that are drawn from the Upper Three of the Left until Yom Kippur, the Left is subdued and unites with the Right via the Central Column. Then Malchut ascends to Binah, after the Left Column already united with the Right via the Central Column, which is the secret of Mercy that unites Kindness and Judgment. Once Malchut receives from the Left Column that is already sweetened by the Central Column She is called the Throne of Mercy. Thus it is found that the Creator sits on the Throne of Mercy and the Worlds receive from the Throne of Mercy. Thus all those Judgments that emerged from the Left Column from Rosh Hashanah until the night of the ninth of the month forced the Left

Column to be incorporated with the Right, thus preparing the Throne of Mercy on Yom Kippur.

This is: **"On that day, all Judgments go up to the judge,"** namely to the Left Column of Binah the source of all Judgments, and through this the Left unites with the Right via the Central Column on Yom Kippur. This is: **"and they prepare a Supernal Throne of Mercy,"** since the Judgments force the Left Column to be incorporated with the Right via the Central Column, which is Mercy, and Malchut becomes the Throne of Mercy since She receives from the Left that is incorporated with the Right. However the correction of Malchut Herself to be able to receive from this corrected Left is on Yom Kippur. This is: **"who is destined on the following day to sit on a Throne of Mercy for them,"** since on Yom Kippur Malchut becomes the Throne of Mercy, **"His Throne of Absolution"** as then the corrected Illumination of Chochmah, which atones sins, is revealed in Malchut.

When the High Priest unifies the Holy Name, a voice comes down and causes him to say, "Will you be purified."

197. וְכָל אִינּוּן סִפְרִין דִּפְתִיחִין קָמֵיהּ, וּכְתִיבִין קָמֵיהּ כָּל אִינּוּן חוֹבִין, הוּא מְזַכֵּי לוֹן, וּמַדְכֵּי לוֹן מִכָּלְהוּ, הה"ד מִכֹּל חַטֹּאתֵיכֶם לִפְנֵי יְיָ' תִּטְהָרוּ. לִפְנֵי יְיָ' מַמָּשׁ, אִינּוּן דְּאַמְרֵי קְרָא, עַד הָכָא אַמְרִין, וְלָא יַתִּיר. וְלֵית רְשׁוּ לְאָחֳרָא דִּילְמָא תִּטְהָרוּ, אֶלָּא כַּהֲנָא רַבָּא, דְּפָלַח פּוּלְחָנָא, וְקָשַׁר שְׁמָא קַדִּישָׁא בְּפוּמֵיהּ, וְכַד הֲוָה אִתְקְשַׁר וּמִתְבָּרֵךְ בְּפוּמֵיהּ, הַהוּא קָלָא נָחִית וּבָטַשׁ בֵּיהּ, וְאִתְנְהִיר מִלָּה בְּפוּמֵיהּ דְּכַהֲנָא, וְאוֹמֵר תִּטְהָרוּ. פָּלַח פּוּלְחָנָא, וּמִתְבָּרְכִין כָּל אִינּוּן עִלָּאִין דְּאִשְׁתָּאֲרוּ.

197. All these books are open before Him and all these sins recorded before Him. He credits them and cleanses them from all sins, as it is written: "...from all your sins before the Lord will you be purified." (Leviticus 16:30) "...before the Lord (lit. the face of the Lord)..." (Ibid.) literally, namely the Illumination of the face of the Lord, the secret of the Illumination of Chochmah that forgives all sin. **Those that recite this verse only do so until this point,** namely until "...before the Lord..." (Ibid.) **but no more, as no one else is permitted to announce "...will you be purified" (Ibid.) except for the High Priest** alone, **who performs the service and unifies the Holy Name with his mouth. When he unifies and blesses** the Holy Name **with his mouth, that voice,** namely Zeir Anpin, **comes down, strikes him and causes the word to glow in the mouth of the Priest and says, "...will you be purified." (Ibid.) He performs his service and thus the rest of the supernal beings are blessed.**

Three rows surround the High Priest as he enters the Holy of Holies.

198. וּלְבָתַר אַסְחֵי גּוּפֵיהּ, וְקַדֵּשׁ יְדוֹי, לְאַעֲלָא בְּפוּלְחָנָא אָחֳרָא קַדִּישָׁא. עַד דְּיִתְכַּוֵּון לְמֵיעַל לַאֲתַר אָחֳרָא עִלָּאָה, קַדִּישָׁא מִכֹּלָּא. ג' שׁוּרִין סַחֲרִין לֵיהּ, כַּהֲנֵי אָחוֹי, וְלֵיוָאֵי, וּמִכָּל שְׁאָר עַמָּא כֻּלְּהוּ. זַקְפִין יְדִין עָלֵיהּ בִּצְלוֹתָא וְקִטְרָא דְּדַהֲבָא זַקְפָא בְּרַגְלֵיהּ.

198. Afterwards, he washes his body and sanctifies his hands to enter into another Holy Service. Then he aims to enter another most Holy, lofty place; namely, the Holy of Holies. **Three rows surround** the High Priest, **his priestly colleagues, the Levites, and the rest of the people.** They represent the Three Columns, Priest and Levite represent Right and Left and Israel represents the secret of the Central Column. **They raise their hands towards him in prayer. A knot** of **of gold** rope **hangs from his leg,** from fear perhaps he would die in the Holy of Holies, and they would need to pull him out with this rope.

The sound of the Cherubs in the Holy of Holies.

199. נָטִיל ג' פְּסִיעָן, וְכֻלְּהוּ קַיְימִין בְּקִיּוּמַיְיהוּ, וְלָא נַטְלִין בַּתְרֵיהּ נָטִיל ג' פְּסִיעָן אָחֳרָן, אַסְחַר לְדוּכְתֵּיהּ. נָטִיל ג' פְּסִיעָן, אַסְתִּים עַיְינִין, וְאִתְקַשַּׁר לְעֵילָּא. עָאל

לַאֲתַר דְּעָאל, שָׁמַע קוֹל גַּדְפֵּי דִּכְרוּבַיָּיא מְזַמְּרִין, וְאַקִּישָׁן גַּדְפִּין פְּרִישָׁאן לְעֵילָּא. הֲוָה אַקְטִיר קְטוֹרֶת, מִשְׁתַּכְּכָא קוֹל גַּדְפַּיְיהוּ וּבִלְחִישׁוּ אִתְדַּבְּקָן.

199. He takes three steps, but the others remain where they are and do not follow. He takes another three steps and returns to his place. He takes three steps, closes his eyes, and connects to that Which is Above. He enters where he enters, namely the Holy of Holies, **and hears the sound of wings of the Cherubs singing and fanning their upstretched wings. When he would offer the incense, the sound of their wings quieted and they were silently clasped together.**

When the High Priest smells pure Supernal balsam he is settled.

200. אִי כַּהֲנָא זָכֵי, דְּהָא לְעֵילָּא בְּחֶידוּ אִשְׁתְּכַח, אוּף הָכָא בְּהַהִיא שַׁעֲתָא נָפִיק רַעֲוָא דִּנְהוֹרָא, מִתְבַּסְּמָא מֵרֵיחִין דְּטוּרֵי אֲפַרְסְמוֹנָא דַּכְיָא דִּלְעֵילָּא, וְאַזְלָא בְּכָל הַהוּא אֲתַר, אָעִיל רֵיחָא בִּתְרֵי נוּקְבֵי דְּחוֹטָמֵיהּ, וְאִתְיַישְּׁבָא לִבָּא. כְּדֵין כֹּלָּא הוּא בִּלְחִישׁוּ, וּפִטְרָא לָא אִשְׁתְּכַח תַּמָּן. פָּתַח כַּהֲנָא פּוּמֵיהּ בִּצְלוֹתָא בִּרְעוּתָא בְּחֶדְוָותָא, וְצַלֵּי צְלוֹתֵיהּ.

200. If the Priest merits, then once joy prevails Above, here too Below **the goodwill of Light is manifested at that time and scented with the fragrance of mountains of the pure Supernal balsam, whose fragrance spreads throughout that place. The smell enters the two nostrils of the Priest and his heart is settled. Then everything is silent with no fault to be found. The priest opens his mouth in prayer willingly and with joy, and he utters his prayer.**

The Priest knows the prayer was accepted when he hears the Cherubs sing.

201. בָּתַר דְּסַיֵּים, זַקְפִּין כְּרוּבַיָּיא כְּמִלְּקַדְּמִין גַּדְפַּיְיהוּ, וּמְזַמְּרִין. כְּדֵין יָדַע כַּהֲנָא דִּרְעוּתָא הֲוֵי, וְעִידָּן חֶדְוָותָא לְכֹלָּא, וְעַמָּא יַדְעִין דְּאִתְקַבֵּל צְלוֹתֵיהּ, כְּמָה דִּכְתִיב אִם יִהְיוּ חֲטָאֵיכֶם כַּשָּׁנִים כַּשֶּׁלֶג יַלְבִּינוּ. וְהוּא תָּב לַאֲחוֹרֵיהּ, וְצַלֵּי צְלוֹתֵיהּ. זַכָּאָה חוּלָקֵיהּ דְּכַהֲנָא, דְּהָא עַל יְדוֹי חֵידוּ עַל חֵידוּ אִשְׁתְּכַח הַהוּא

יוֹמָא לְעֵילָּא וְתַתָּא, עַל הַהִיא שַׁעֲתָא כְּתִיב, אַשְׁרֵי הָעָם שֶׁכָּכָה לּוֹ, אַשְׁרֵי הָעָם שֶׁיְיָ' אֱלֹהָיו.

201. After he completes his prayer, **the Cherubs raise their wings as before and sing. At that point, the Priest realizes that goodwill prevails, a time of joy for all. The people know that his prayer was accepted, as the verse reads, "...though your sins be like scarlet, they shall be as white as snow." (Isaiah 1:18)** The Priest **steps back and utters his prayer. How fortunate is the lot of the Priest. Because of him, there is joy upon joy that day on high and low. Concerning that hour, it is written: "Happy is that people, who have it so; happy is that people, whose God is the Lord." (Psalms 144:15)**

37. Nefesh and Ruach

Body and soul surrender on Yom Kippur to be atoned.

223. תְּעַנּוּ אֶת נַפְשׁוֹתֵיכֶם, נַפְשׁוֹתֵיכֶם קָאָמַר, בְּגִין דְּיִשְׂרָאֵל מִשְׁתַּכְחִין קָמֵי מַלְכָּא קַדִּישָׁא זַכָּאִין, וִיהֵא רְעוּתָא דִּלְהוֹן לְגַבֵּי קֻבָּ"ה, וּלְאִתְדַּבְּקָא בֵּיהּ, בְּגִין דְּיִתְכַּפֵּר לְהוּ חוֹבַיְיהוּ. וְעַל דָּא, מַאן דְּאָכַל וְשָׁתֵי בְּתִשִׁיעָאָה, וּמְעַנְּגָא נַפְשֵׁיהּ בְּמֵיכְלָא וּמִשְׁתְּיָיא, אִשְׁתְּכַח בַּעֲשִׂירָאָה עִנּוּיָא דְּנַפְשָׁא בִּתְרֵין חוּלָקִין, וְאִשְׁתְּכַח כְּאִלּוּ אִתְעַנֵּי תְּשִׁיעָאָה וַעֲשִׂירָאָה. אֶת נַפְשׁוֹתֵיכֶם: לְאַכְלְלָא כֹּלָּא, גּוּפָא וְנַפְשָׁא, וּלְאִתְכַּנְּעָא בְּהַאי יוֹמָא, לְאִתְכַּפָּרָא עַל חוֹבֵיהוֹן.

223. "...you shall afflict your souls...." (Leviticus 16:29) It says "... your souls..." (Ibid.) so that Israel be found meritorious before the Holy King and their desire be toward the Holy One, blessed be He, to cleave to Him, so that all their sins may be forgiven. Therefore, whoever eats and drinks on the ninth day and pleasures his soul with food and drink is found with double affliction on the tenth day, and it will be considered as if he fasted on the ninth and tenth. "...your souls..." (Ibid.) includes all, body and soul, to surrender on this day so that their sins be atoned for.

40. "You shall afflict your souls"

A Synopsis

Rav Shimon tells us that one should eat and drink on the ninth of the month more than any other day. On the tenth day, the Judgments cause wisdom to be revealed. We read that the children of Israel were only exiled because they renounced God, and He forgives them on the Day of Atonement.

The affliction of the Nefesh.

236. בַּחֹדֶשׁ הַשְּׁבִיעִי בֶּעָשׂוֹר לַחֹדֶשׁ. בֶּעָשׂוֹר דַּיְיקָא, כְּמָה דְּאוֹקִימְנָא. תְּעַנּוּ אֶת נַפְשׁוֹתֵיכֶם, וַדַּאי הָכִי הוּא, וְהָא אִתְּמַר נַפְשׁוֹתֵיכֶם וַדַּאי. דְּהָא בְּנַפְשָׁא תַּלְיָא מִלְּתָא, וּבְגִין כָּךְ, אֲכִילָה וּשְׁתִיָּה מִתְּשִׁיעָאָה, יַתִּיר מִיּוֹמָא אָחֳרָא. ואע"ג דְּהַאי מִלָּה אִתְּמַר בְּגַוְונָא אָחֳרָא, וְכֹלָּא שַׁפִּיר, וְהַאי וְהַאי מִלָּה חֲדָא, וְכָל חַד בְּאַתְרֵיהּ, וְהָכִי הוּא.

236. "...In the seventh month, on the tenth day of the month...." (Leviticus 16:29) Tenth is exact, as we have learned tenth denotes Malchut. **"...you shall afflict your souls...." (Ibid.) This is exact. We have learned "your souls (*Nefashot*)" (Ibid.) indeed, as it all depends upon Nefesh,** as the Light of Malchut is called Nefesh and Nefesh always denotes Malchut. **For this reason, one should eat and drink from the ninth** of the month, which is Yesod, **more than any other day. Even though we learned this in a different way, it is all well, as they are both one, each one in its place. This is how it should be.**

Explanation: You already know that Chochmah cannot be revealed until Harsh Judgment accompany it to rain on the heads of the wicked, lest they draw Chochmah from above downward. This is the secret of the five afflictions of Yom Kippur, from which Judgment flows to the heads of the wicked, as only then can Chochmah be revealed. This is the secret of "For any person (Nefesh) who will not be afflicted on this very day shall be cut off from his people." (Leviticus 23:29) If he does not accept these five afflictions to distance the wicked, then Chochmah cannot appear in the Nefesh, and the Light of Chochmah is the Light of Life. Therefore, "...shall be cut off from his people." (Ibid.)

This is: **"'on the tenth day of the month' (Leviticus 16:29) Tenth is exact,"** which is Malchut, the place of the revelation of Chochmah, since Chochmah is not revealed in any Sefirah except the Sefirah of Malchut alone. Therefore we need to set this correction there, so that Judgments flow from Her to the heads of the wicked when Chochmah is revealed in Her. This is: **"'your souls (Nefashot)' (Ibid.) indeed,"** since we need to awaken the five afflictions in Malchut, where these Judgments flow from, **"as it all depends upon Nefesh,"** which is the aspect of Malchut, the only place Chochmah is revealed in. Therefore, when the Judgments are revealed in Her She is able to receive Chochmah from the Yesod of Zeir Anpin, since there is no more risk of the wicked nourishing from it. This is: **"For this reason, one should eat and drink from the ninth more than any other day,"** as for this reason Malchut can receive the Mochin of the Illumination of Chochmah, which is termed eating and drinking, from Yesod more than any other day, since Malchut can only receive from Yesod. This is the secret behind the need to increase our eating and drinking the day before Yom Kippur, which is the ninth of the month, namely Yesod. The accepting of the afflictions on Yom Kippur enables Her to be able to receive eating and drinking from Yesod. It is such that the affliction of the Nefesh of Yom Kippur shines through the eating and drinking of the ninth day of the month, as She is protected from the wicked. This is the secret of the sages who say, "One who eats and drinks on the ninth, the verse ascribes him credit as if he fasted on both the ninth and the tenth" (Berachot 8b), since the affliction of the Nefesh on the tenth shines on the Mochin that are bestowed on the ninth and protects them.

The five afflictions cause the Light of Chochmah to shine.

237. וְתָאנָא, בְּהַאי יוֹמָא, כָּל חֵידוּ, וְכָל נְהִירוּ, וְכָל וַתְרָנוּתָא דְּעָלְמִין, כֻּלְּהוּ תַּלְיָין בְּאִימָּא עִלָּאָה, דְּכָל מַבּוּעִין נָגְדִין וְנָפְקִין מִנָּהּ. וּכְדֵין נְהִירִין כָּל אִינּוּן בּוֹצִינִין, וְנַהֲרִין בִּנְהִירוּ בְּחֶדְוְותָא, עַד דְּמִתְבַּסְּם כֹּלָּא. וּכְדֵין כָּל אִינּוּן דִּינִין אִשְׁתְּכָחוּ בִּנְהִירוּ, וְדִינָא לָא אִתְעֲבֵיד, וְעַל דָּא תְּעַנּוּ אֶת נַפְשׁוֹתֵיכֶם.

237. We have learned, on this day all joy, all Light and all absolutions in the Worlds, namely forgiveness of sins, **all depend on Supernal Ima. All springs are drawn and flow from it,** meaning both the Illumination of Chochmah and the Illumination of Chasadim. **Then all these candles glow,** the secret of the Lights of fire within Malchut, **and they glow with Light and joy until everything becomes fragrant. At that point, all Judgments are found in Illumination,** since those Judgments drawn from the five afflictions cause Chochmah to shine. If not for them, Chochmah would not become revealed, as mentioned. **And Judgment is not carried out,** but is merely impending. **Therefore, "...you shall afflict your souls," (Ibid.)** to enable the Illumination of Chochmah.

Israel were only exiled for renouncing Malchut.

238. אָמַר רַבִּי אַבָּא, הָא אוֹקִים לָהּ מוֹר, מִן גּוּפָא דְּמַתְנִיתָא, לָא גָּלוּ יִשְׂרָאֵל מֵאַרְעָם, עַד שֶׁכָּפְרוּ בְּקֻבְּ"ה. דִּכְתִּיב, אֵין לָנוּ חֵלֶק בְּדָוִד וְלֹא נַחֲלָה בְּבֶן יִשַׁי, וְהָא אִתְּמַר. קְרָא אַחֲרִינָא אַשְׁכַּחְנָא בְּהַאי, דִּכְתִּיב, רְאֵה בֵיתְךָ דָּוִד. אָ"ל, הָכִי הוּא וַדַּאי, בֵּית דָּוִד אִקְרֵי, כְּמָה דִּכְתִּיב בֵּית יַעֲקֹב לְכוּ וְנֵלְכָה בְּאוֹר יְיָ'. בֵּית יַעֲקֹב, כד"א וּבֵית תִּפְאַרְתִּי אֲפָאֵר. לְכוּ וְנֵלְכָה בְּאוֹר יְיָ', דִּכְתִּיב וְנָהָר יוֹצֵא מֵעֵדֶן לְהַשְׁקוֹת אֶת הַגָּן, וְנָטַע הַאי גַּן לְאִשְׁתַּעְשְׁעָא בֵּיהּ עִם צַדִּיקַיָּיא, דְּבֵיהּ שָׁרְיָין.

238. Rav Aba said, "My master has told us from the text of the Mishnah that Israel were only exiled from their land for renouncing the Holy One, blessed be He, as it is written, '...We have no part

in David, neither have we inheritance in the son of Yishai....' (II Samuel 20:1) David denotes Malchut, so they were saying, 'we have no part in Malchut.' **I have found another verse on this. It is written, '...Now see to your own house, David....' (I Kings 12:16)"** He asks whether the house of David also denotes Malchut. **He said to him: "Certainly** Malchut **is referred to as the house of David, as it is written, 'House of Jacob, come, and let us walk in the Light of the Lord.' (Isaiah 2:5) The house of Jacob is similar to that which is written: '...and I will glorify My House of Glory (*Tiferet*)' (Isaiah 60:7)** for Jacob is Tiferet and the house of Tiferet is Malchut. In the same manner, the house of David points to Malchut. The explanation of the verse, "House of Jacob, **come, and let us walk in the Light of the Lord" (Isaiah 2:5) is** the same **as, 'And a river went out of Eden to water the garden....' (Genesis 2:10)** where 'river' refers to Zeir Anpin that waters the garden that is Malchut. **He planted the Garden to enjoy himself there with the pious ones who dwell within.** Therefore, it is said, 'House of Jacob,' denoting Malchut, 'come, and let us walk in the Light of the Lord,' (Isaiah 2:5) which is Zeir Anpin that waters Malchut.

The matter of afflicting the soul depends on the tenth day.

239. תָּאנָא, כְּתִיב אַךְ בֶּעָשׂוֹר לַחֹדֶשׁ הַשְּׁבִיעִי הַזֶּה יוֹם הַכִּפּוּרִים הוּא וְגוֹ' וְעִנִּיתֶם אֶת נַפְשׁוֹתֵיכֶם. וּכְתִיב וְהָיְתָה לָכֶם לְחֻקַּת עוֹלָם בַּחֹדֶשׁ הַשְּׁבִיעִי וְגוֹ'. אַךְ דִּכְתִּיב מַאי קָא בָּעֵי הָכָא. אָ"ל, לְמִעוּטָא קָא אַתְיָא. דְּכֵיוָן דְּאָמַר וְעִנִּיתֶם אֶת נַפְשׁוֹתֵיכֶם בְּתִשְׁעָה לַחֹדֶשׁ, אָמַר לְבָתַר אַךְ בֶּעָשׂוֹר. אַךְ עָשׂוֹר מִבָּעֵי לֵיהּ, דְּבֶעָשׂוֹר תַּלְיָא מִלְּתָא.

239. "We have learned that it is written, 'But on the tenth day of this seventh month there shall be a Day of Atonement... and you shall afflict your souls....' (Leviticus 23:27) It is also written, 'And this shall be a statute forever to you: In the seventh month, on the tenth day of the month, you shall afflict your souls....' (Leviticus 16:29) In the latter it does not say, 'but on the tenth.'" He asks: **"What is meant by 'But** on the tenth' **that is written in this verse?" He replied to him, "It comes to exclude,** for wherever the word 'but (*ach*)' is written, its purpose is to exclude. **For since it is written, 'And you shall afflict your souls, on the ninth day of the month...' (Leviticus 23:32) it later says, '... but on the tenth day.' It should merely say, 'but the tenth day.'** Rather it comes to teach us **that on the tenth rests the whole matter** of '...you shall afflict your souls...' (Ibid.) not on the ninth day of the month."

Affliction only takes place after the time allotted to eating.

240. א"ל אִי הָכִי, אַךְ בַּיּוֹם הָרִאשׁוֹן תַּשְׁבִּיתוּ שְׂאוֹר מִבָּתֵּיכֶם, וְתָנֵינָן אַךְ חִלֵּק, וֶחֱצְיוֹ אָסוּר בַּאֲכִילַת חָמֵץ, וְחֶצְיוֹ מוּתָּר. אוּף הָכָא אַךְ בֶּעָשׂוֹר לַחֹדֶשׁ, אֵימָא דְּחֶצְיוֹ אָסוּר בַּאֲכִילָה, וְחֶצְיוֹ מוּתָּר. א"ל אוּף הָכָא בְּעִנִּיתֶם אֶת נַפְשׁוֹתֵיכֶם תַּלְיָא, דְּהָא עִנּוּי לָא אִשְׁתְּכַח אֶלָּא מִפַּלְגּוּת יוֹמָא וּלְהָלְאָה, וְשַׁפִּיר הוּא אַךְ חִלֵּק בְּעִנִּיתֶם אֶת נַפְשׁוֹתֵיכֶם.

240. He said to him: "If so, '...but on the first day you shall have put away leaven out of your houses....' (Exodus 12:15) We have learned 'but' sets a dividing line, meaning for a half day the eating of leaven is prohibited and for a half day it is permitted. So too when it says, 'But on the tenth day of the month...' (Leviticus 23:27) we can say that half the day it is prohibited to eat and half permitted." He said to him: "Here too in 'And you shall afflict your souls....' (Leviticus 23:32) there is a separation, since affliction only takes place from midday onward, meaning after the time allotted to eating. **It is found that 'but' divides also applies to "...and you shall afflict your souls...' (Ibid.) as well."**

Binah flows springs to water and satiate everything on Yom Kippur.

241. אָמַר רִבִּי אֶלְעָזָר, כְּתִיב, כִּי בַיּוֹם הַזֶּה יְכַפֵּר עֲלֵיכֶם וְגוֹ'. אֲכַפֵּר עֲלֵיכֶם מִבָּעֵי לֵיהּ. אֶלָּא יְכַפֵּר עֲלֵיכֶם, לְאַכְלְלָא יוֹבְלָא, דְּנָגִיד מַבּוּעֵי לְאַשְׁקָאָה בְּהַאי

יוֹמָא לְכָל עִיבָר, לְאַרְוָאָה כֹּלָּא, וּלְאַשְׁקָאָה כֹּלָּא. וְדָא עֲלֵיכֶם, כְּלוֹמַר, בְּגִינֵיכוֹן לְדַכְּאָה לְכוֹן בְּהַאי יוֹמָא, דִּכְתִּיב לִפְנֵי יְיָ' תִּטְהָרוּ. וְלָא יִשְׁלוֹט עֲלַיְיכוּ דִּינָא.

241. Rav Elazar said, "It is written, 'For on that day will He forgive you....' (Leviticus 16:30) It should say, 'will I forgive you,' as if someone is speaking for himself." He answers, **"'Will He forgive you'** spoken in third person **includes Jubilee,** Binah, **from which flow springs,** the Illumination of Chochmah, **to water on this day all sides, and to water and satiate everything. This is the meaning of 'you,' namely 'for you,' so as to cleanse you this day, as it says, "...before the Lord shall you be purified."** (Ibid.) **and Harsh Judgment will not affect you."**

The Creator desires Israel to be members of His Chamber.

242. רַבִּי יְהוּדָה, אָמַר זַכָּאִין אִינּוּן יִשְׂרָאֵל, דְּקוּדְשָׁא בְּרִיךְ הוּא אִתְרְעֵי בְּהוּ, וּבָעֵי לְדַכְּאָה לְהוּ, דְּלָא יִשְׁתְּכַח בְּהוּ חוֹבָה, בְּגִין דִּיהוֹן בְּנֵי הֵיכָלֵיהּ, וְיִדוּרוּן בְּהֵיכָלֵיהּ. וּלְזִמְנָא דְּאָתֵי כְּתִיב, וְזָרַקְתִּי עֲלֵיכֶם מַיִם טְהוֹרִים וְגוֹ'.

242. Rav Yehuda said: "How happy are Israel that the Holy One, blessed be He, desired them and wished to purify them, so that no sin would be found with them, so that they could be members of His Chamber and dwell in His Palace. Regarding the future to come, it is written: "Then will I sprinkle clean water upon you...." (Ezekiel 36:25)

Emor

34. Yom Kippur

A Synopsis

We are told that on Yom Kippur Malchut is illuminated not from the light of the sun but from supernal light instead. Rav Aba learns from Rav Shimon that Zeir Anpin does not unite with Malchut except when she shines from supernal Aba, at which time Malchut is called holiness. Rav Aba says that Adam stands as an example to all men in that he repented after his sin, and God accepted him and had pity on him.

Two Lights, Binah and Malchut, shine on Yom Kippur.

224. ת"ח, בְּהַאי יוֹמָא אִתְכַּסְיָיא סִיהֲרָא, וְלָא נָהִיר עַד בֶּעָשׂוֹר לַחֹדֶשׁ, דְּיִשְׂרָאֵל תַּיְיבִין כֻּלְּהוּ בִּתְיוּבְתָּא שְׁלֵימָתָא, וְאִימָּא עִלָּאָה תָּאבַת וְנָהֲרַת לָהּ. וְהַאי יוֹמָא נְהִירוּ דְּאִימָּא נַטְלָא, וְאִשְׁתְּכַח חֵידוּ בְּכֹלָּא. וְעַל דָּא כְּתִיב, יוֹם הַכִּפּוּרִים הוּא. יוֹם כִּפּוּר מִבָּעֵי לֵיהּ, מַאן יוֹם הַכִּפּוּרִים. אֶלָּא בְּגִין דִּתְרֵי נְהוֹרִין נָהֲרִין בְּחַד. בּוֹצִינָא עִלָּאָה, נָהִיר לְבוֹצִינָא תַּתָּאָה. וּבְהַאי יוֹמָא מִנְּהוֹרָא עִלָּאָה נָהִיר. וְלָא מִנְּהוֹרָא דְּשִׁמְשָׁא וּבג"כ בַּכֶּסֶה לְיוֹם חַגֵּנוּ כְּתִיב.

224. Come and see, on that day of Rosh Hashanah **the moon,** Malchut, **is covered and does not shine until the tenth day of the month, when all of Israel return in complete repentance, and Supernal Ima,** Binah, **again shines upon it. On that day,** Yom Kippur, Malchut **receives the Illuminations of Ima,** Binah, **and joy abounds everywhere. Hence it is written: "...it is a day of Atonements** (*Yom haKippurim*)**...." (Leviticus 23:28) It should have said "day of atonement" (Yom Kippur); what is the meaning of Yom HaKippurim** in the plural? **Rather, it is because** at that time **two Lights shine together: the Supernal Luminary,** Binah, **shines upon the Lower Luminary,** Malchut. **On that day,** Malchut **shines with Supernal Light,** which is Binah, **instead of from the light of the sun,** Zeir Anpin. **Hence it is written: "at the appointed time (lit. in the covering) for the day of our festival" (Psalms 81:4)** because Malchut does not shine until Yom Kippur.

When does the Congregation of Israel unite with the Holy King?

225. ר' אַבָּא שָׁלַח לֵיהּ לְר"ש, אָמַר, אֵימָתַי זִוּוּגָא דִּכְנֶסֶת יִשְׂרָאֵל בְּמַלְכָּא קַדִּישָׁא. שָׁלַח לֵיהּ, וְגַם אָמְנָה אֲחוֹתִי בַת אָבִי הִיא אַךְ לֹא בַת אִמִּי וַתְּהִי לִי לְאִשָּׁה. אִתְרְגִּישׁ ר' אַבָּא, אָרִים קָלֵיהּ, בָּכָה וְאָמַר, ר' ר' בּוּצִינָא קַדִּישָׁא, וַוי, וַוי לְעָלְמָא כַּד תִּפּוּק מִנֵּיהּ, וַוי לְדָרָא דִּיהוֹן בְּעָלְמָא כַּד תִּסְתָּלַק מִנְּהוֹן וְיִשְׁתַּאֲרוּן יַתְמִין מִנָּךְ. א"ל רִבִּי חִיָּיא לְרִבִּי אַבָּא, הַאי דְּשָׁלַח לָךְ לְקַבְלָךְ. מַאי קָאָמַר.

225. Rav Aba sent a question to Rav Shimon, saying: "When does the union of the Congregation of Israel, Malchut, **with the Holy King,** Zeir Anpin, **occur?" He sent to him, "And yet indeed she is my sister; she is the daughter of my father, but not the daughter of my mother. And she became my wife." (Genesis 20:12) Rav Aba trembled and raised his voice in crying. He said: "Rav, Rav, Holy Luminary, woe, woe to the world when you shall depart from it. Woe to that generation, which will be in the world when you shall leave them and they shall be orphaned from you." Rav Chiya said to Rav Aba: "What does this** verse **he sent you mean?"**

On Yom Kippur Malchut receives from the house of Ima, and thus intercourse is forbidden.

226. אָמַר וַדַּאי לָאו זִוּוּגָא דְּמַלְכָּא בְּמַטְרוֹנִיתָא, אֶלָּא בְּזִמְנָא דְּנַהֲרָא מֵאַבָּא עִלָּאָה, וְכַד אִתְנַהֲרָא מִנֵּיהּ, קָרֵינָן לָהּ קֹדֶשׁ דְּהָא מִבֵּי אַבָּא נַטְלָה הַאי. וּכְדֵין מִזְדַּוְּוגֵי כַּחֲדָא, בְּגִין דְּמַלְכָּא קֹדֶשׁ אִקְרֵי, דִּכְתִיב קֹדֶשׁ יִשְׂרָאֵל לַיְיָ', דְּנָטִיל מֵאֲתַר דְּאִקְרֵי קֹדֶשׁ. כְּדֵין אֲחוֹתִי בַת אָבִי הִיא אַךְ לֹא בַת אִמִּי, דְּהָא מִבֵּי אַבָּא שְׁמָא דָּא, וְלָא מִבֵּי אִימָּא, וְעַל דָּא וַתְּהִי לִי לְאִשָּׁה, לְאִזְדַּוְּוגָא כַּחֲדָא,

בְּזִמְנָא דָא, וְלָא בְּזִמְנָא אָחֳרָא, בְּזִמְנָא דְנַטְלָא מִבֵּי אַבָּא, וְלָא בְּזִמְנָא דְנַטְלָא מִבֵּי אִימָא. וְיוֹם הַכִּפּוּרִים אוֹכַח, דְּתַשְׁמִישׁ הַמִּטָּה אָסוּר, בְּגִין דְּזִוּוּגָא לָא אִשְׁתְּכַח, דְּהָא מִבֵּי אִימָא נַטְלָא, וְלָא מִבֵּי אַבָּא. אָמַר רִבִּי חִיָּיא, וַדַּאי זַכָּאָה דָּרָא דר"ש שָׁארֵי בְּגַוֵּיהּ, זַכָּאִין אִינּוּן דְּקַיְימִין קַמֵּיהּ כָּל יוֹמָא.

226. Rav Aba **said** to him: **"Surely the King does not unite with the Matron,** namely Zeir Anpin with Malchut, **except when she shines from Supernal Aba,** when the Chochmah of Ima is clothed in the Chasadim of Aba. **When she shines from him, she is called Holiness, since she receives it from the abode of** Supernal **Aba,** as Aba is the secret of Holiness. **Then** Zeir Anpin and Nukva **unite together. For the King is called Holiness, as written: 'Israel is holiness to the Lord...' (Jeremiah 2:3) receiving from the place called holiness. Then** Zeir Anpin says, **'My sister; she is the daughter of my father, but not the daughter of my mother,' because that Name,** Holiness, **is from Aba's house, and not from my mother's house,** not from Binah. **Therefore 'And she became my wife,' to unite as one during that time but on no other time,** namely **when she receives from the House of Aba but not when she receives from the House of Ima. Yom Kippur proves that, as intercourse is forbidden on it, since then there is no coupling** of Zeir Anpin and Malchut, **since on** Yom Kippur **she receives from the House of Ima and not from the House of Aba." Rav Chiya said: "Certainly, happy is the generation amongst whom dwells Rav Shimon. Happy are those who stand before him daily."**

Repentance transforms Judgment to Mercy.

227(1). אָמַר רִבִּי אַבָּא, בְּרֹאשׁ הַשָּׁנָה נִבְרָא אָדָם, וְקָאִים בְּדִינָא קַמֵּי מָארֵיהּ, וְתָב בְּתִיּוּבְתָּא, וְקַבִּיל לֵיהּ קוּדְשָׁא בְּרִיךְ הוּא. א"ל, אָדָם, אַנְתְּ תְּהֵא סִימָנָא לִבְנָךְ לְדָרֵי דָּרִין, בְּהַאי יוֹמָא קַיְימִין בְּדִינָא, וְאִי יְתוּבוּן אֲנָא אֲקַבֵּל לוֹן, וְאֵיקוּם מִכּוּרְסְיָּיא דְדִינָא, וְאִתְקַיֵּים עַל כּוּרְסְיָּיא דְּרַחֲמֵי, וַאֲרַחֵם עֲלַיְיהוּ. וְדָוִד אָמַר, אָהַבְתִּי כִּי יִשְׁמַע יְיָ' אֶת קוֹלִי תַּחֲנוּנָי. וְעַל דָּא כְּתִיב, כִּי עִמְּךָ הַסְּלִיחָה לְמַעַן תִּוָּרֵא. וּכְתִיב, כִּי עִמְּךָ מְקוֹר חַיִּים בְּאוֹרְךָ נִרְאֶה אוֹר.

227(1) Rav Aba said: "Adam was created on Rosh Hashanah and stood on trial before his Master for eating of the Tree of Knowledge of Good and Evil. **He repented and the Holy One, blessed be He, accepted him." He said to him, "Adam, you shall serve as a symbol for your descendants for generations, who are sentenced on this day. If they shall repent, I shall accept them, rise from the throne of Judgment and sit on the throne of Mercy and have pity on them. David used to say, 'I love the Lord who hears my voice and my supplications.' (Psalms 116:1) Hence it is written: 'But there is forgiveness with You, that You may be feared' (Psalms 130:4) and 'For with You is the fountain of life. In Your light we see light.' (Psalms 36:10)"**

A Synopsis

We learn that it is a commandment to be afflicted on Yom Kippur, to subjugate body and soul.

Five grades of Yom Kippur.

רעיא מהימנא

227(2). פִּקּוּדָא דָא, לְאִתְעַנָּאָה בְּיוֹמָא דְּכִפּוּרֵי, לְאַכְנְעָא גּוּפָא וְנַפְשָׁא, בְּרָזָא דְּחָמֵשׁ עִנּוּיִין, דְּחָמֵשׁ דַּרְגִּין דְּיוֹמָא דְּכִפּוּרֵי. דְּהָא מְקַטְרְגָא קָא אָתֵי לְאַדְכְּרָא חוֹבֵיהוֹן, כְּמָה דְּאִתְּמַר. וְכֻלְּהוּ בְּתִיּוּבְתָּא שְׁלֵימָתָא קַמֵּי אֲבוּהוֹן. כֹּלָּא, כְּמָה דְּאִתְּמַר בְּכַמָּה דּוּכְתֵּי.

ע"כ רעיא מהימנא

Ra'aya Meheimna (Faithful Shepherd)

227b. This Precept is to fast on Yom Kippur, to subjugate body and soul by means of the five afflictions, the five grades of Yom Kippur, which are Chesed, Gevurah, Tiferet, Netzach, and Hod, **for the denouncer comes to mention their sins, as we learned. And they are**

all, all of Israel, **repenting wholly before their Father, as we learned in different places.**

End of Ra'aya Meheimna (Faithful Shepherd)

A Synopsis

Rav Chiya tells us about the ten kinds of songs in the book of Tehilim. He speaks about a *maskil* (understanding) that bestows wisdom; from it comes forgiveness and freedom. He says that a man who repents before God has his sins hidden but if he will not repent then his sins shall be made known before everyone. Rav Aba explains what happens to the good deeds that were done by a man who is on balance judged to be evil, and what happens to the sins that were done by a man who is on balance judged to be worthy. He talks about the depths of the sea, where all the sins are found, and about the lot that chooses the goat for Azazel. We are told how God distracted the prosecutor from accusing Israel by giving him Job to occupy himself with; this left Israel free to cross the sea and escape from the Egyptians. The offering on Yom Kippur is for the same purpose, allowing God to forgive Israel without interference from the prosecutor. Rav Aba talks about the ritual counting of the Priest as he sprinkles the blood of the offering, the purpose of which is to draw and guide the one that is Supernal Ima through specific grades and to draw the deep rivers upon the Congregation of Israel. Rav Yitzchak and Rav Aba tell us about the High Priest as he enters the Holy of Holies and hears the wings of the Cherubs singing. Rav Shimon says that Malchut is only able to join with Zeir Anpin when her children Israel are judged to be worthy.

There are ten kinds of songs in Psalms, the highest being Halleluyah.

228. אַךְ בֶּעָשׂוֹר לַחֹדֶשׁ הַשְּׁבִיעִי הַזֶּה יוֹם הַכִּפּוּרִים הוּא מִקְרָא קֹדֶשׁ יִהְיֶה לָכֶם. ר' חִיָּיא פָּתַח, לְדָוִד מַשְׂכִּיל אַשְׁרֵי נְשׂוּי פֶּשַׁע כְּסוּי חֲטָאָה. לְדָוִד מַשְׂכִּיל, הָא תָּנֵינָן בְּי' זִינֵי זִמְרָא אִתְקְרֵי סֵפֶר תְּהִלִּים, בְּנִצּוּחַ, בְּנִגּוּן, בְּמַשְׂכִּיל, בְּמִכְתָּם, בְּמִזְמוֹר, בְּשִׁיר, בְּאַשְׁרֵי, בִּתְפִלָּה, בְּהוֹדָאָה, בְּהַלְלוּיָהּ, וְעִלָּאָה מִכֻּלְּהוּ הַלְלוּיָהּ, וְהָא אוּקְמוּהָ.

228. "Only on the tenth day of this seventh month there shall be a Day of Atonement; A holy calling shall it be for you…." (Leviticus 23:27) Rav Chiya opened with, "Of David, a maskil (understanding). Blessed is he whose transgression is forgiven, whose sin is covered." (Psalms 32:1) "Of David, a maskil…." We learned that the Book of Psalms is recited with ten kinds of songs: by the Chief Musician (Nitzu'ach), by a melody (Niggun), by Understanding (Maskil), by a Poem (Michtam), by a Psalm (Mizmor), by a Song (Shir), by "Blessed" (Ashrei), by Prayer (Tefilah), by Acknowledgment (Hoda'ah), by Halleluyah. The highest is Halleluyah, as we already explained.

Understanding (Maskil) bestows wisdom, goodness, and forgiveness.

229. הָכָא מַשְׂכִּיל, אַתְרֵיהּ יְדִיעַ, מַהוּ מַשְׂכִּיל, מַיָּא דְּאַחְכִּימוּ לְאִינּוּן דְּשָׁתוּ לְהוּ, הַהוּא אֲתַר דְּאִקְרֵי מַשְׂכִּיל, כד"א, מַשְׂכִּיל עַל דָּבָר יִמְצָא טוֹב. וּבְגִין דְּאִקְרֵי הָכֵי, תַּלְיָא בֵּיהּ סְלִיחָה, וְחֵירוּ דְּחֵירִין. הה"ד אַשְׁרֵי נְשׂוּי פֶּשַׁע כְּסוּי חֲטָאָה.

229. Here, Maskil; its place is known, which is Yesod of Binah. **What is this** that is called **Maskil? It is that its water makes wise those who drink from it,** namely, it bestows Chochmah. **The place called Maskil is as you say, "He who considers (*maskil*) his words shall find good…." (Proverbs 16:20)** If Maskil bestows on something, there will be good in it, which is the Illumination of Chochmah clothed in Chasadim. **Since it is so called, forgiveness and the freedom of freedom depend on it,** since forgiveness and freedom are bestowed from the Chochmah in Binah. **This is: "Blessed is he whose transgression is forgiven, whose sin is covered" (Psalms 32:1)** since his transgression is forgiven by the abundance of Chochmah.

When one sins repeatedly and does not repent,
their sins are eventually revealed to all.

230. מַאי כְּסוּי חֲטָאָה. הָא אוּקְמוּהָ, דְּהוּא כְּסוּי מִבְּנֵי נָשָׁא, הַהוּא חֲטָאָה דְּחָב לְקוּדְשָׁא בְּרִיךְ הוּא, וְאוֹדֵי קַמֵּי קוּדְשָׁא בְּרִיךְ הוּא. אֲבָל ת"ח, כַּד בַּר נָשׁ חָטֵי, וְחָב זִמְנָא חֲדָא, וּתְרֵין וּתְלָתָא, וְלָא אַהְדָר בֵּיהּ, הָא חוֹבוֹי בְּאִתְגַּלְיָא אִינּוּן וּמְפַרְסְמֵי לוֹן לְעֵילָּא, וּמְפַרְסְמֵי לוֹן לְתַתָּא. וְכָרוֹזֵי אָזְלִין קַמֵּיהּ וּמַכְרְזֵי, אִסְתַּלָּקוּ מִסְּחֲרָנֵיהּ דִּפְלַנְיָא, נָזִיף הוּא מִמָּארֵיהּ, נָזִיף הוּא לְעֵילָּא, נָזִיף הוּא לְתַתָּא, וַוי לֵיהּ דְּפָגִים דְּיוּקְנָא דְּמָארֵיהּ, וַוי לֵיהּ דְּלָא חָיִישׁ לִיקָרָא דְּמָארֵיהּ, קוּדְשָׁא בְּרִיךְ הוּא גַּלֵּי חוֹבֵיהּ לְעֵילָּא, הה"ד, יְגַלּוּ שָׁמַיִם עֲוֹנוֹ וְאֶרֶץ מִתְקוֹמָמָה לוֹ. וְכַד בַּר נָשׁ אָזִיל בְּאוֹרְחָא דְּמָארֵיהּ, וְאִשְׁתַּדַּל בְּפוּלְחָנֵיהּ, וְאִזְדַּמַּן לֵיהּ חֲטָאָה חַד, כֹּלָּא מְכַסִּין עֲלוֹי, עִלָּאִין וְתַתָּאִין, דָּא אִקְרֵי כְּסוּי חֲטָאָה.

230. He asks: **"What is** the meaning of **'...whose sin is covered'? (Psalms 32:1)"** He answers: **"It was explained that the sin he committed before the Holy One, blessed be He, is covered from people, and he confessed it before the Holy One, blessed be He. Yet come and see, when a man sins, sinning once, twice, and thrice, and does not repent, his sins become public** because **they are made known Above and made known Below. Criers walk before him and announce: 'Get away from around so-and-so. He is chided by his Master, chided Above and chided Below. Woe to him for blemishing his Master's image. Woe to him, who has no fear for his Master's glory.' The Holy One, blessed be He, reveals his iniquity Above. This is the meaning of: 'The heaven shall reveal his iniquity; and the earth shall rise up against him.' (Job 20:27) When a man walks the path of his Master and busies himself with His service and happens to sin, everyone covers it, the Upper and Lower Beings. This is called, 'whose sin is covered.' (Psalms 32:1)"**

Why "whose sin is a covering" instead of "covered sin."

231. א"ל ר' אַבָּא, עַד כְּעַן לָא מָטִית לְעִקָּרָא דְּמִלָּה. וְשַׁפִּיר קָאַמְרַתְּ. וְהַאי דְּקָאָמְרוּ חַבְרַיָּיא שַׁפִּיר. אֲבָל אִי הָכִי, מְכוּסֶּה חַטָּאָה מִבָּעֵי לֵיהּ, מַהוּ כְּסוּי חַטָּאָה.

231. Rav Aba said to him: "You have not yet reached the crux of the matter. You spoke well, and whatever the friends said is **fine. But if this is so, it should have said: 'covered sin.' Why does it say, 'whose sin is covered (lit. a covering)' (Psalms 32:1)?"**

Regretting former good deeds.

232. אֶלָּא תְּרֵי מִלֵּי דְּחָכְמְתָא אִית בֵּיהּ, וְתַרְוַויְיהוּ הָכִי. חַד כְּמָה דְּתָנֵינָן, דְּעוֹבָדִין טָבִין דְּבַר נָשׁ עָבֵיד בְּהַאי עָלְמָא, עָבְדִין לֵיהּ בְּהַהוּא עָלְמָא לְבוּשָׁא יַקִּירָא עִלָּאָה, לְאִתְלַבְּשָׁא בְּהוּ. וְכַד ב"נ אַתְקִין עוֹבָדִין טָבִין, וְגַבְרִין עָלֵיהּ עוֹבָדִין בִּישִׁין, וְאַשְׁגַּח בֵּיהּ קוּדְשָׁא בְּרִיךְ הוּא, וְעוֹבָדוֹי בִּישִׁין סַגִּיאִין, וְאִיהוּ רָשָׁע, דְּאִשְׁתְּכַח חַטָּאָה קַמֵּי מָארֵיהּ, וְתוֹהֵא עַל אִינּוּן טָבָאן דַּעֲבַד בְּקַדְמֵיתָא, הָא אִתְאֲבִיד הוּא מִכֹּלָּא, מֵהַאי עָלְמָא, וּמֵעָלְמָא דְּאָתֵי. מַה עָבֵיד קוּדְשָׁא בְּרִיךְ הוּא מֵאִינּוּן טָבָאן דַּעֲבֵיד הַאי חַטָּאָה בְּקַדְמֵיתָא.

232. Rav Aba answers: **"There are two matters of wisdom here,** in the verse, '…whose sin is covered,' (Psalms 32:1) **as follows: The first is as we learned that from the good deeds man performs in this world a costly garment is made in that world for him to wear. When man does good deeds, yet the evil deeds overpower him, and the Holy One, blessed be He, sees that his evil deeds are more numerous** than his good deeds, then **he is evil because he is guilty before his Master,** since there are more misdeeds than good deeds. **He repines and regrets the good deeds he performed in the past. Then he is entirely lost from this world and the World to Come."** He asks: **"What does the Holy One, blessed be He, do from the good deeds the sinner performed before this?"**

The good deeds of an evil person can be transferred to the Righteous.

233. אֶלָּא קוּדְשָׁא בְּרִיךְ הוּא, אַף ע"ג דְּהַהוּא רָשָׁע וְחַטָּאָה אִתְאֲבִיד. אִינּוּן טָבָאן וְזַכְיָין לָא אִתְאֲבִידוּ. אִית צַדִּיק דְּאָזִיל בְּאָרְחוֹי דְּמַלְכָּא עִלָּאָה, וְאַתְקִין לְבוּשׁוֹי מֵעוֹבָדוֹי, וְעַד לָא אַשְׁלִים לְבוּשׁוֹי, אִסְתָּלַּק. קוּדְשָׁא בְּרִיךְ הוּא אַשְׁלִים לֵיהּ, מֵאִינּוּן עוֹבָדִין דַּעֲבַד הַאי רָשָׁע וְחַטָּאָה, וְאַשְׁלִים לְבוּשׁוֹי, לְאִתְתַּקְּנָא בְּהוּ בְּהַהוּא עָלְמָא, הה"ד, יָכִין וְצַדִּיק יִלְבַּשׁ. הַהוּא וְחַטָּאָה אַתְקִין, וְצַדִּיק אִתְחֲפֵי מִמָּה דְּאִיהוּ תַּקִּין הה"ד כְּסוּי וְחַטָּאָה, וְעַל דָּא לָא כְּתִיב מְכוּסֶּה, אֶלָּא כְּסוּי.

233. He answers: **"Rather, even though the wicked man is lost,** through **the Holy One, blessed be He, the good deeds and merits he committed are not lost. For there is a Righteous Man who walks the ways of the Supernal King and fixed garments from his** good **deeds, but before completing** his garments **he departed** from the world. **The Holy One, blessed be He, finishes** his garments **for him from the** good **deeds the evil sinner has committed and completes his garment for him to be fixed in that world. This is the meaning of:** the evil **'may prepare it, but the Righteous shall put it on....' (Job 27:17) The evil man made it and the Righteous Man covers himself with what he made. This is the meaning of: '...whose sin is a covering' (Psalms 32:1);** the covering, namely his garment, comes from the sinner. **Hence it is not written that it is "covered" but that is it "a covering"** because it refers to a garment.

A worthy person's sin is cast to the depths of the sea.

234. וַחַד, דְּאִתְחֲפֵי הַהוּא וְחַטָּאָה דְּהַאי זַכָּאָה, בְּאִינּוּן דְּאִקְרוּן מְצוּלוֹת יָם, דְּהָא מַאן דְּנָפִיל בִּמְצוּלוֹת יָם, לָא אִשְׁתְּכַח לְעָלְמִין בְּגִין דְּמַיִין חָפִין עֲלַיְיהוּ. כְּמָה דְּאַתְּ אָמֵר, וְתַשְׁלִיךְ בִּמְצוּלוֹת יָם כָּל חַטֹּאתָם. מַאן מְצוּלוֹת יָם. אֶלָּא רָזָא יַקִּירָא הוּא, וְהָא אוּקְמֵיהּ ר' שִׁמְעוֹן, וְאָמַר, כָּל אִינּוּן דְּאָתוּ מִסִּטְרָא תַּקִּיפָא, וְאִתְאֲחָדוּ בְּזִינִין בִּישִׁין, בְּכִתְרִין תַּתָּאִין, כְּגוֹן עֲזָאזֵל בְּיוֹמָא דְּכִפּוּרֵי, דָּא אִקְרֵי מְצוּלוֹת יָם. כְּזוּפְטָא דְּכַסְפָּא, כַּד בַּחֲנִין לֵיהּ בְּנוּרָא, הֲדָא הוּא דִּכְתִיב הָגוֹ סִיגִים מִכָּסֶף.

234. The second explanation **is that the sin a worthy** man **has committed is covered inside what is called the Depths of the Sea. For whatever fell into the Depths of the Sea is never found, since the water covers it. This is the meaning of, "...and You will cast all their sins into the depths of the sea." (Micah 7:19)** [He asks:] **"What are the depths of the sea?"** He answers: **"This is a precious secret, which Rav Shimon explained. He said: 'All those coming from the harsh side and holding onto evil species and the Lower Sefirot, like Azazel on Yom Kippur, is considered the Depths of the Sea, like the oars of silver refined by fire, as in: "Separate the dross from the silver...." (Proverbs 25:4)**

On Yom Kippur, the Depths of the sea descends
and takes the filth of the body.

235. כַּךְ הַאי, מֵאִינּוּן מְצוּלוֹת יָם הוּא, וּמְצוּלוֹת יָם אִקְרֵי, מְצוּלוֹת מֵהַהוּא יָם קַדִּישָׁא, מְצוּלוֹת, זוּהֲמָא דְּכַסְפָּא. וְעַל דָּא, כָּל אִינּוּן חֲטָאִין דְּיִשְׂרָאֵל שַׁרְיָין לְגַוֵּיהּ, וְהוּא קַבִּיל לוֹן, וְיִשְׁתַּאֲבוּן בְּגַוֵּיהּ. מַאי טַעֲמָא. בְּגִין דְּאִיהוּ חַטָּאָה אִקְרֵי. מַאי חַטָּאָה. גְּרִעוּנָא. וְעַל דָּא הוּא גְּרִעוּנָא דְּכֹלָּא, וְנָטַל גְּרִעוּנָא דְּגוּפָא וְדִנַפְשָׁא. בְּהַאי יוֹמָא נָחִית הַאי מְצוּלוֹת יָם, זוּהֲמָא דְּנַפְשָׁא, וְנָטִיל זוּהֲמָא דְּגוּפָא. מַאן הוּא זוּהֲמָא דְּגוּפָא. דָּא אִינּוּן חוֹבִין דְּאִתְעֲבִידוּ עַל יְדֵי דְּיֵצֶר הָרַע, דְּאִקְרֵי מְזוֹהָם מְנוּוָל.

235. So too is this Azazel **from the depths of the sea and is called the Depths of the Sea,** namely **the Depths of that Holy Sea. The "depths"** refer to **the filth of silver. Therefore all the sins of Israel dwell in it; it receives them and they are drawn into it. The reason is that** Azazel **is called "sin."** [He asks:] **"What is sin?"** [He answers:] **"Deficit. Hence it is the deficit of all, and it takes the deficit of the body and the soul. On this day,** Yom Kippur, **this Depths of the Sea descends, which is the filth of the soul, and takes the filth of the body."**[He asks:] **"What is the filth of the body?"** [He answers:] **"It is the sins done by the Evil Inclination that is called filthy and disgraceful."**

Explanation: Malchut is called the Tree of Knowledge of Good and Evil because it has two points. One is the point sweetened by Binah, and from its side it receives all its Lights. The second is the point of the attribute of Judgment of Tzimtzum Alef, and from its side it is not worthy of receiving the Supernal Light. If a person merits, only the first point called Maftecha (Key) is revealed, and the second point is stored away. Then the Malchut receives all the Supernal Lights for him. If he does not merit, then the second point called Man'ula (Lock) is revealed in Malchut, and all the Lights in Malchut depart. Besides these Judgments of Man'ula that are concealed in Malchut called the Judgments of the Female, there is also further Judgments from the power of the Illumination of Chochmah in the Left column from above downward, which [Malchut] has from the time it was in the situation of Achorayim (Back), which are called the Judgments of the Male, and these Judgments are very harsh. Malchut is called "sea," and under Her there are two types of Judgments in the aspect of filth. They are called the Depths of the Sea, namely the filth in the seabed.

This is: "**So too is this** goat for Azazel, **from the depths of the sea...**" because it is from the aspect of the Judgments of the Male that is on the seabed. **"...the Depths of that Holy Sea,"** which is the filth, namely the refuse in the bottom of Malchut called the Holy Sea. **"The depths** refer to **the filth of silver,"** meaning the depths also contain the filth of the silver that is in the bottom of Malchut, which are the Judgments of the Female that were mentioned earlier. **"Therefore, all the sins of Israel dwell in it... and they are drawn into it"** and therefore the Azazel goat draws to it all the sins of Israel, both the sins that come from the Judgments of the Male and the Judgments of the Female. **"The reason is that it is called 'sin'";** the Judgments of Azazel are called "sin" because they come from the sin drawn of the Chochmah of the Left from above downward. **"What is sin? Deficit."** Sin means deficit and lack, namely the filth of the Judgments of the Male. **"Hence it is the deficit of all..."** because since it already has the lack of the Judgments of the Male called the "filth of the soul," it also has the lack of the Judgments of the Female called the "filth of the body." This is: **"...it takes the deficit of the body and the soul"** because lack begets lack, so the Judgments of the Female also cleave to Azazel.

"On this day, Yom Kippur, **this Depths of the Sea descends, which is the filth of the soul..."** namely the Judgments of the Male in Azazel, **"...and takes the filth of the body,"** which is the Judgments of the Female aspect in the Depths of the Sea, and they too are included in Azazel. Therefore scripture says: "And the goat shall bear upon it all their iniquities to an inaccessible region..." (Leviticus 16:22) as it even bears the Judgments of the Female, since lack begets lack. Once Israel are separated from the Judgments of the Male through sending the Azazel to the wilderness—as sending it to the wilderness indicates that Israel removed their hands from this sin called Azazel, which is the drawing of the Left from above downward, and with this all the sins that come from the Judgments of the Male are atoned for —then also the sins that come from the Judgments of the Female are also atoned for. Although this does not depend directly on sending the Azazel to the wilderness, as it does not have Judgments of the Female at all, it is only because deficit causes deficit that the Judgments of the Female cleave to it as well.

This is the secret of: "...whose sin is covered" (Psalms 32:1) as Azazel called "sin," namely deficit, covers the deficit of the Judgments of the Female and all their sins are forgiven. The way you read the verse is: **"...Blessed is he whose transgression (*pesha*) is forgiven..." (Psalms 32:1)** happy is he who is even forgiven for his transgressions rooted in *pesha,* the secret of the Judgments of the Female, **"...whose sin is covered" (Ibid.)** as the sin—Azazel—covered those Judgments.

We give Samech-Mem a portion that day so he does not speak negatively of Israel.

236. אָמַר רִבִּי יוֹסֵי, תָּנֵן וְנָתַן אַהֲרֹן עַל שְׁנֵי הַשְּׂעִירִים גּוֹרָלוֹת, אִי הָכִי יְקָרָא הוּא דַּעֲזָאזֵל, וַחֲמִיתוּן עַבְדָּא דְּשַׁדֵּי עַדְבִין בְּמָארֵיהּ, אוֹרְחוֹי דְּעָלְמָא דְּעַבְדָּא לָא נָטֵל אֶלָּא מַה דְּיָהִיב לֵיהּ מָארֵיהּ. אֲבָל, בְּגִין דְּסָמָאֵ"ל זַמִּין הַאי יוֹמָא בִּדְלְטוֹרָא, וּבְגִין דְּלָא יְהֵא לֵיהּ פִּטְרָא יָהֲבִין לֵיהּ חוּלָקָא בְּהַאי.

236. Rav Yosi said: "We learned, 'And Aaron shall cast lots upon the two goats....' (Leviticus 16:8) If this is so, it is an honor to Azazel, for have you ever seen a servant casting lots on equal footing **with his master? It is the way of the world that a servant receives only what his master gives him.** He answers: **"Rather it is because Sama"el is ready on that day to speak negatively** of Israel, **and so that he will not have an opportunity to open his mouth, he is given a portion.**

The lot of Azazel comes up on its own accord.

237. וְהַאי עַדְבָא מִגַּרְמֵיהּ הוּא דְּסָלִיק בֵּיהּ, דְּאָמַר רִבִּי יְהוּדָה אָמַר ר' יִצְחָק, מִלָּה עִלָּאָה אַשְׁכַּחְנָא בְּעַדְבָא. עַדְבָא דִּיהוֹשֻׁעַ, כְּתִיב בֵּיהּ, עַל פִּי הַגּוֹרָל, עַל פִּי הַגּוֹרָל וַדַּאי, דְּאִיהוּ אָמַר דָּא חוּלָקָא דִּיהוּדָה, דָּא דְּבִנְיָמִין וְכוּ', וְכֵן כֻּלְּהוּ. אוּף הָכָא, כֵּיוָן דְּכַהֲנָא שַׁוֵּי יְדוֹי, אִינּוּן עַדְבִין מְדַלְּגֵי וְסַלְּקִין בִּידָא דְּכַהֲנָא, וְשָׁארָן בְּאַתְרַיְיהוּ. הֲדָא הוּא דִּכְתִיב, וְהַשָּׂעִיר אֲשֶׁר עָלָה עָלָיו הַגּוֹרָל, עָלָה עָלָיו וַדַּאי.

237. This lot reaches it on its own accord, as Rav Yehuda said in the name of Rav Yitzchak: "I found a Supernal matter in that lot. It is written of the lot of Joshua, '...according to the lot (lit. by mouth of the lot)....' (Numbers 26:56) '...by mouth of the lot' precisely, as the lot said: 'this is the portion of Judah, this is the portion of Benjamin, and so on.' Here too, once the Priest put his hands, the lots were jumping and climbing the hand of the Priest and come to their places. This is the meaning of, 'But the goat, for which the lot

of Azazel came up…' (Leviticus 16:10); 'came up' precisely on its own accord.

Giving the prosecutor something to be occupied with leaves Israel alone on this day.

238. וְלָא דָא בִּלְחוֹדוֹי, אֶלָּא בְּכָל זִמְנָא דִּדְלָטוֹרָא זַמִּין, וְאִתְיְיהִיב לֵיהּ רְשׁוּתָא, בָּעֵינָן לְשַׁוָּואָה לְקַבְלֵיהּ בְּמָה דְּיִתְעַסַּק, וְשָׁבִיק לוֹן לְיִשְׂרָאֵל. בְּהַאי יוֹמָא דִּלְטוֹרָא זַמִּין לְאַלְלָא אַרְעָא. הה"ד וַיֹּאמֶר יְיָ' אֶל הַשָּׂטָן מֵאַיִן תָּבֹא. וְהָא תָּנֵינָן, מִשּׁוּט בָּאָרֶץ, מַאי הוּא. אֶלָּא הַאי הוּא דִּלְטוֹרָא רַבָּא מְקַטְרְגָא דְּיִשְׂרָאֵל.

238. "Not only that, but as long as the prosecutor is ready and has permission, something should be put before him to be occupied with so he leave Israel alone. On this day of Yom Kippur, **the prosecutor is ready to spy out the land, as it is written: 'And the Lord said to the adversary, "From where do you come?"….' (Job 1:7) We have already learned what is: '…From going to and fro in the earth' (Ibid.) This is the great prosecutor that denounces Israel."**

The Prosecutor said that at the splitting of the Red Sea the Israelites were not worthy of entering Israel.

239. וְהָא אִתְּעָרוּ חַבְרַיָּיא, בְּהַהִיא שַׁעְתָּא דַּהֲווֹ זְמִינִין יִשְׂרָאֵל לְמֶעְבַּר יַמָּא, וּלְאִתְפָּרְעָא מִמִּצְרָאֵי, אָמַר, אֲנָא אַעְבַּרְנָא בְּאַרְעָא קַדִּישָׁא, וַחֲמֵינָא דְּלָא אִתְחֲזוּן אִלֵּין לְמֵיעַל, בְּגַוָּוהּ, אִי אַנְתְּ דָּאִין דִּינָא, דִּינַיְיהוּ הָכָא כְּמִצְרָאֵי, מַה שַּׁנְיָין אִלֵּין מֵאִלֵּין, אוֹ יְמוּתוּן כֻּלְּהוּ כַּחֲדָא, אוֹ יַהְדְּרוּן כֻּלְּהוּ לְמִצְרַיִם. וְלָאו אַנְתְּ הוּא דְּאֲמַרְתְּ, וַעֲבָדוּם וְעִנּוּ אוֹתָם ד' מֵאוֹת שָׁנָה, וְהָא לָא סְלִיקוּ מֵחוּשְׁבְּנָיא אֶלָּא רד"ו, וְלָא יַתִּיר.

239. The friends remarked that when Israel were ready to cross the sea and take revenge on the Egyptians, the prosecutor **said: "I have passed the Holy Land and I see that these are not worthy of entering it. If You mete out punishment, their punishment here** is like **the Egyptians. What is the difference between them? Either they will all die together or they will all return to Egypt. Was it not You, who said: '...and shall serve them; and they shall afflict them four hundred years' (Genesis 15:13); yet from the reckoning only 210 years have passed, no more."**

It was proposed that Job occupy the Prosecutor so the Israelites will be left alone.

240. אָמַר קוּדְשָׁא בְּרִיךְ הוּא, מַאי אַעְבִּיד, אִשְׁתַּדְּלוּתָא בַּעְיָא הָכָא, לְאַיְיתָאָה קְרָבָא לְקַבְלֵיהּ, יָהִיבְנָא לֵיהּ בְּמָה דְּיִתְעֲסָק, וְיִשְׁבּוֹק בְּהוּ לִבְנַי, וְהָא אִשְׁתְּכַח בְּמַאן דְּיִתְעֲסָק, מִיַּד אָמַר לֵיהּ, הֲשַׂמְתָּ לִבְּךָ אֶל עַבְדִּי אִיּוֹב כִּי אֵין כָּמוֹהוּ בָּאָרֶץ. מִיַּד פָּלַג לֵיהּ דַּלְטוֹרָא בְּמִלִּין, וַיַּעַן הַשָּׂטָן אֶת יְיָ' וַיֹּאמַר הַחִנָּם יָרֵא אִיּוֹב אֱלֹהִים.

240. The Holy One, blessed be He, said: "What shall I do? Occupation is needed to be brought here and brought close to him. I shall give him something to be occupied with, so he will leave My children. Let us find someone for him to be busy with." Immediately He said: "Have you considered My servant Job, that there is none like him on earth...." (Job 1:8) He interrupted the prosecutor with words. "Then the adversary answered the Lord, and said: 'Does Job fear God for naught?'" (Ibid. 9)

Giving the biggest sheep to occupy the wolf and save the flock.

241. לְרַעְיָא דְּבָעֵי לְאַעְבְּרָא עָאנֵיהּ בְּחַד נַהֲרָא, אַעְבָּר זְאֵבָא לְקַטְרְגָא לֵיהּ בְּעָאנֵיהּ, רַעְיָא הֲוָה חַכִּים, אָמַר מַאי אַעְבִּיד, דִּבְעוֹד דַּאֲנָא אַעְבָּר לְטַלְיָיא, יְקַטְרֵג הוּא בְּעָאנֵי. זָקַף עֵינוֹי, וְחָמָא בֵּין עָאנָא, חַד תַּיְישָׁא מֵאִלֵּין תַּיְישֵׁי בָּרָא, דַּהֲוָה רַב וְתַקִּיף. אָמַר, אַשְׁדֵּי דָּא לְקַבְלֵיהּ, וּבְעוֹד דִּמְקַטְרְגֵי דָּא בְּדָא, אַעְבָּר לְכָל עָאנָא, וְיִשְׁתֵּזְבוּן מִנֵּיהּ.

241. This is likened **to a shepherd who wanted to pass his flock across a river. A wolf passed by and afflicted his flock. The wise shepherd said: "What shall I do? He might destroy the flock while I move the lambs across." He raised his eyes and saw a wild goat, big and strong among the flock. He said: "I shall throw him before the wolf. While they do battle with each other, I shall remove all the flock and they shall be saved from him."**

Job was used to distract as the Israelites were left alone.

242. כַּךְ קוּדְשָׁא בְּרִיךְ הוּא. אָמַר, וַדַּאי הָא תַּיְישָׁא חַד רַב וְתַקִּיף וְאַלִּים, אַשְׁדֵּי לְקָבְלֵיהּ, וּבְעוֹד דְּהוּא יִשְׁתַּדַּל בֵּיהּ, יַעַבְרוּן בָּנַי, וְלָא יִשְׁתְּכַּח קַטֵּיגוֹרָא לְגַבַּיְיהוּ. מִיַּד, וַיֹּאמֶר יְיָ' אֶל הַשָּׂטָן הֲשַׂמְתָּ לִבְּךָ. עַד דְּקוּדְשָׁא בְּרִיךְ הוּא זָוִוג לְהוּ כַּחֲדָא, דִּכְתִּיב הִנּוֹ בְיָדֶךָ. בְּעוֹד דְּהוּא אִשְׁתַּדַּל בֵּיהּ, שָׁבִיק לוֹן לְיִשְׂרָאֵל, וְלָא אִשְׁתְּכַּח קַטֵּיגוֹרָא לְגַבַּיְיהוּ.

242. This is what the Holy One, blessed be He, did. He said: "I shall certainly send a big, strong, and mighty goat, Job, **his way, and while he will be occupied with it, My children shall cross** the sea, **without a prosecutor over them." Immediately, "And the Lord said to the adversary, 'Have you considered…'" (Job 1:8) Eventually, the Holy One, blessed be He, joined them together, as it is written: "… 'Behold, he is in your hand….'" (Job 2:6) While he was busy with him, he left Israel alone, and uttered no denouncement on them.**

Giving an offering to Satan keeps him preoccupied to leave Israel alone.

243. אוּף הָכִי בְּהַאי יוֹמָא, דִּלְטוֹרָא זַמִּין לְאַלְקָא אַרְעָא, וּבָעֵינָא לְשַׁדְּרָא לְקָבְלֵיהּ בְּמָה דְּיִתְעֲסָק, וּבְעוֹד דְּאִיהוּ אִשְׁתָּדַּל בֵּיהּ, שָׁבִיק לוֹן לְיִשְׂרָאֵל. וּמַתְלָא אַמְרֵי לִזְלְזוּלָא דְּבֵי מַלְכָּא, הַב לֵיהּ זְעֵיר חַמְרָא, וְיִשַׁבְּחָךְ קַמֵּי מַלְכָּא. וְאִי לָאו יֵימָא לְמַלְכָּא מִלָּה בִּישָׁא. לִזְמְנִין נַטְלִין לָהּ לְהַהִיא מִלָּה, עָלָאֵי דְּבֵי מַלְכָּא, וּמַלְכָּא עָבִיד דִּינָא בְּגִינֵיהּ.

243. Similarly, on this day of Yom Kippur, **the Satan is ready to spy out the land, and we should send something before him with which to be busy. While he is busy with it, he will leave Israel alone. There is an allegory about the lowliest in the king's house,** [which says:] **"Give him a little wine, and he will praise you before the king, otherwise he will speak evil words** about you **before the king." Sometimes the superiors in the king's house receive** that evil **speech and the king punishes that man.**

Giving the prosecutor a gift intoxicates him so he can only say praises.

244. רִבִּי יִצְחָק אָמַר, לְשַׁטְיָא דְקָאֵים קָמֵי מַלְכָּא, הַב לֵיהּ חַמְרָא, וּלְבָתַר אֵימָא לֵיהּ, וְאַחְזֵי לֵיהּ, כָּל אִינּוּן טַעֲוָון דַּעֲבַדְתְּ, וְכָל אִינּוּן בִּישִׁין, וְהוּא יֵיתֵי וִישַׁבְּחָךְ, וְיֵימָא דְּלָא יִשְׁתְּכַח בְּעָלְמָא כְּוָותָךְ. אוּף הָכָא, הָא קָאֵים דַּלְטוֹרָא תָּדִיר קַמֵּי מַלְכָּא, יִשְׂרָאֵל יָהֲבִין לֵיהּ הַאי דּוֹרוֹן, וּבְהַאי דּוֹרוֹן פִּתְקָא, לְכָל בִּישִׁין, וּלְכָל טַעֲוָון, וּלְכָל חוֹבִין דַּעֲבְדוּ יִשְׂרָאֵל, וְהוּא אָתֵי וּמְשַׁבַּח לְהוּ לְיִשְׂרָאֵל, וְאִתְעֲבִיד סַנֵּיגוֹרָא עֲלַיְיהוּ, וְקוּדְשָׁא בְּרִיךְ הוּא אַהְדָּר כֹּלָּא לְרֵישָׁא דְּבִישֵׁי דְּעַמֵּיהּ, בְּגִין דִּכְתִיב כִּי גֶּחָלִים אַתָּה חוֹתֶה עַל רֹאשׁוֹ.

244. Rav Yitzchak said: "This is likened **to a fool who is in the king's presence. Give him a little wine and then tell him and show him all the abominable things you have done and all the evil, yet he will praise you and say there is none in the world like you. Here too, the prosecutor is constantly in the King's presence. Israel give him this offering** of the goat to Azazel. **In this offering there is a note** where all is written down **of the evil things, the abominable things, and the iniquities Israel has done. Yet he comes and praises Israel and becomes their defender. And the Holy One, blessed be He, returns everything upon the heads of the wicked of his people, since it is written, 'You shall heap coals of fire upon his head....' (Proverbs 25:22)"**

These iniquities will then actually befall the other side.

245. א"ר יוֹסֵי, וַוי לוֹן לְעַמָּא דְעֵשָׂו, בְּשַׁעֲתָא דְהַאי שָׂעִיר מְשַׁדְּרֵי לְהַהוּא דִּלְטוֹרָא מְמֻנָּא דְעָלַיְיהוּ, דִּבְגִינֵיהּ אָתֵי לְשַׁבְּחָא לוֹן לְיִשְׂרָאֵל, וְקוּדְשָׁא בְּרִיךְ הוּא אַהֲדַר כָּל אִינּוּן חוֹבִין לְרֵישָׁא דְעַמֵּיהּ, בְּגִין דִּכְתִּיב דּוֹבֵר שְׁקָרִים לֹא יִכּוֹן לְנֶגֶד עֵינָי. א"ר יְהוּדָה, אִלְמָלֵי הֲווֹ יַדְעֵי אוּמּוֹת הָעוֹלָם מֵהַאי שָׂעִיר, לָא שַׁבְקִין לוֹן לְיִשְׂרָאֵל, יוֹמָא חַד בְּעָלְמָא.

245. Rav Yosi said: "Woe to the people of Esau, when that goat is sent to that slanderer who is appointed over them, namely Sama"el, the minister of Esau **that comes to praise Israel for its sake. The Holy One, blessed be He, returns all those iniquities on the head of his people because it is written, '...he that tells lies shall not remain in my sight.' (Psalms 101:7)" Rav Yehuda said: "If the idolaters knew of this goat, they would not let Israel live one day in the world."**

This prosecutor is transformed into a defender and speaks praise of Israel.

246. תָּא חֲזֵי, כָּל הַהוּא יוֹמָא מִשְׁתַּדֵּל אִיהוּ בְּהַהוּא שָׂעִיר, וּבְגִ"כ קוּדְשָׁא בְּרִיךְ הוּא מְכַפֵּר לְהוּ לְיִשְׂרָאֵל, וְדָכֵי לוֹן מִכֹּלָּא, וְלָא אִשְׁתְּכַח קַטֵּגוֹרְיָא קַמֵּיהּ. לְבָתַר, הוּא אָתֵי וּמְשַׁבַּח לְהוּ לְיִשְׂרָאֵל. וּכְדֵין שָׁאִיל לֵיהּ, כד"א, וַיֹּאמֶר יְיָ' אֶל הַשָּׂטָן מֵאַיִן תָּבֹא, אָתִיב בְּתוּשְׁבַּחְתַּיְיהוּ דְּיִשְׂרָאֵל, וְקַטֵּיגוֹרָא אִתְעֲבֵיד סַנֵּיגוֹרָא וְאָזִיל לֵיהּ.

246. Come and see, All that day he busies himself with that goat. Then the Holy One, blessed be He, forgives Israel and cleanses them in every respect, and there is no prosecutor in His presence. He then comes and praises Israel. The Holy One, blessed be He, **then asks him, as it is written: "And the Lord said to the adversary, 'From where do you come?'..." (Job 1:7) and he answers by praising Israel. The prosecutor transforms into a defender and goes his way.**

The Prosecutor accepts all the sins on himself.

247. כְּדֵין קוּדְשָׁא בְּרִיךְ הוּא אָמַר לְשַׁבְעִין שָׂרִין דְּסַחֲרִין כּוּרְסְיָּיא, חֲמִיתוּן הַאי דִּלְטוֹרָא, הֵיאַךְ קָאִים עַל בְּנַי תָּדִיר, הָא שְׂעִירָא חֲדָא דְּאִשְׁתְּכַח גַּבֵּיהּ, בְּפִתְקָא דְּכָל חוֹבַיְיהוּ וְכָל טָעֲוָתַיְיהוּ, וְכָל מַה דְּחָטוּ וְחָבוּ קַמָּאי, וְהוּא קַבִּיל לוֹן. כְּדֵין אִסְתַּכָּמוּ כֻּלְּהוּ, דְּיִהַדְרוּן אִינּוּן חוֹבִין עַל עַמֵּיהּ.

247. The Holy One, blessed be He, then says to the seventy ministers that surround His **Throne,** the secret of the Supernal Courthouse, **"Have you seen this slanderer, how he is always about** to slander **My children? Behold, there is a goat with him, with a note containing all their iniquities, all their abominable acts, and all that they sinned and transgressed before Me. But he accepted them** upon himself." **They all agree then that these iniquities go back on his** [Azazel's] **people.**

The Priest is adorned with crows, and atones for all of Israel.

248. ר' אַבָּא אָמַר, כָּל אִינּוּן חוֹבִין וְחַטָּאִין מִתְדַּבְּקִין בֵּיהּ, כְּמָה דִּכְתִּיב, וְתַשְׁלִיךְ בִּמְצוּלוֹת יָם כָּל חַטֹּאתָם. וּלְבָתַר, כֻּלְּהוּ מִתְהַדְּרָן בְּרֵישַׁיְיהוּ דְּעַמֵּיהּ, הה"ד וְנָשָׂא הַשָּׂעִיר עָלָיו אֶת כָּל עֲוֹנֹתָם אֶל אֶרֶץ גְּזֵרָה. בְּהַאי יוֹמָא מִתְעַטַּר כַּהֲנָא בְּעִטְרִין עִלָּאִין, וְהוּא קָאִים בֵּין עִלָּאֵי וְתַתָּאֵי, וּמְכַפֵּר עָלֵיהּ וְעַל בֵּיתֵיהּ, וְעַל כַּהֲנֵי, וְעַל מַקְדְּשָׁא, וְעַל יִשְׂרָאֵל כֻּלְּהוּ.

248. Rav Aba said: "All the iniquities and sins first **are attached to him, as it is written, '…and You will cast all their sins into the depths of the sea.' (Micah 7:19) Then they return upon the heads of his people, as it is written: "and the goat shall bear upon it all their iniquities to a barren land…." (Leviticus 16:22) On that day, the Priest is adorned with lofty Crowns and is situated between the Upper and Lower. He atones for him, for his household, for the Priests, the Temple and the whole of Israel.**

Explanation of the article: All the punishments in the world come from two types of Judgments. The first is the Judgments of the Male, which stem from the drawing of the Illumination of Chochmah of the Left from above downward. The second is the Judgments of the Female, which stem from the revelation of Man'ula (Lock) Above in Malchut, in the secret of **"If he does not merit, it is evil." (Zohar, Prologue 123)** By means of prayers, repentance, and the Holiness of the day, the Israelites merit to be purified from all the Judgments and punishments. Their purification is set for them by sending the Azazel to the wilderness. The secret of the lots draws to them the Illumination of the Left, as the goat for the sin-offering is the secret of drawing Holiness, which is from below upward, and this is the portion of Israel. And the goat to Azazel is the secret of the drawing of the Other Side, which is from above downward, which we awaken with the lot to Azazel and send it to a barren land—namely to the place where Sama"el and the nation of Esau, who draw Chochmah from above downward, reign, and from whom great punishments are drawn. Once the Israelites' repentence is set through this, to be separated from the deeds of the wicked, all the Judgments of the Male in them are nullified and they draw all the Holy Mochin in the secret of the goat of the sin-offering.

However first it is necessary to attach the Judgments of the Female to Azazel as well, in the secret of **"...and You will cast all their sins into the depths of the sea," (Micah 7:19)** since lack attracts lack (as mentioned in verse 235). Then, we send it off to a barren land so that the Judgments will be separated from Israel and fall on those who draw the Illumination of Chochmah from above downward, which are Sama"el and his people, the nation of Esau. This is: **"All the iniquities and sins are attached to him,"** as all the iniquities and sins must first be attached to it—both those that come from the Judgments of the Male as well as those that come from the Judgments of the Female—in the secret of deficit attracting deficit, **"as it is written, '...and You will cast all their sins into the depths of the sea." (Micah 7:19) Then they return upon**

the heads of his people." Afterwards, we send it to a barren land, to the domain of Sama"el and his nation who are attached to Azazel and whose way is to draw from above downward. Then all the Judgments fall on their heads, both the Judgments of the Female and the Judgments of the Male.

However, the denouncer can still denounce Israel and reveal the point of Man'ula (Lock) in their root, in Malchut, which banishes all the Lights. This is especially true on Yom Kippur, when the denouncer is given permission to reveal this, as on Rosh Hashanah the Man'ula (Lock) was already revealed, in the secret of the Blowing of the Shofar, which gave him permission to mention this. [In verse 236] this is: **"Rather, it is because Sama"el is ready on that day to speak negatively,"** as it was already revealed on Rosh Hashanah, **"and so that he will not have an opportunity to open his mouth he is given a portion,"** namely the goat of Azazel. This is because the other side is called "the end of all flesh," (Genesis 6:13) since his desire is always for flesh, which means that all he desires and wants is to draw Chochmah of the left from above downward. Therefore, when we awaken for him the goat of Azazel and send it to him, it is a very important gift. And if he denounces Israel and reveals the Man'ula in Malchut, then all the lights in Malchut will depart, and also his own portion of Azazel will depart and be lost. In fear of this happening, he is afraid to open his mouth. Not only that, but so that he is secure in his light he even praises Israel. This is [in verse 244]: "this is **likened to a fool who is in the king's presence. Give him a little wine and... he will praise you and say there is none in the world like you"** because he is afraid of losing the intoxicating wine you gave him, which is the secret of the Illumination of Azazel, as mentioned earlier. This is [in verse 245]: **"If the idolaters knew of this goat,"** namely that this Illumination we give to their minister draws to them all the mentioned Judgments that were supposed to go to Israel, **"they would not let Israel live one day in the world."**

Sprinkling the blood on the Curtain.

249. תָּאנָא, בְּשַׁעְתָּא דְּעָאל בְּדָמָא דְּפָר, מְכַוֵּין בְּרֵישָׁא דִּמְהֵימְנוּתָא וְאַדֵּי בְּאֶצְבְּעֵיהּ, כְּמָה דִּכְתִיב, וְהִזָּה אוֹתוֹ עַל הַכַּפֹּרֶת וְלִפְנֵי הַכַּפֹּרֶת וְהֵיךְ עָבֵיד. בָּסִים בְּקִפְטָא דְּאֶצְבְּעָא, וְאַדֵּי כְּמַצְלִיף, בְּטִיפִּין דְּאֶצְבְּעָא, לִסְטְרֵי קַפּוּתְרָא, אַדֵּי וְאִתְכַּוַּון, וְשָׁארֵי לְמִמְנֵי אַחַת, אַחַת וְאַחַת. אַחַת בִּלְחוֹדָהָא, אַחַת דְּכָלִיל כֹּלָּא, אַחַת שְׁבָחָא דְּכֹלָּא, אַחַת דְּכֹלָּא אֲהַדְרָן לְקָבְלָהּ, אַחַת רֵישָׁא דְּכֹלָּא. לְבָתַר אַחַת וְאַחַת, דְּאִינּוּן שַׁרְיָין כַּחֲדָא, בִּרְעוּתָא בְּאַחֲוָותָא, וְלָא מִתְפָּרְשָׁן לְעָלְמִין.

249. We learned that when the priest **entered with the bullock's blood, he would meditate on the head of Faith,** namely on the Upper Three [Sefirot]—Keter-Chochmah-Binah, **and sprinkle it with his finger, as it is written: "...and sprinkle it upon the covering, and before the covering" (Leviticus 16:15)** namely one Above and seven Below. [He asks:] **"How did he do that?"** [He answers]: **"He dipped the fingertip in blood and sprinkled the drops as if swinging a whip at the side of the Ark covering.** He did not let the drops fall on the covering itself but at its side, and the drops fell on the ground. **He sprinkled and concentrated and started counting, 'one,' which includes everything, one which is the most valuable, one to which everything turns, one that is at the top,** namely the Sefirah of Keter. **Next is 'one and one,'** which are Chochmah and Binah **that dwell together willingly in brotherhood, and never separate** from each other.

The sprinkling draws Light from Binah to the Lower Sefirot.

250. בָּתַר דְּמָטָא לְהַאי וְאַחַת, דְּהִיא אִימָּא דְּכֹלָּא. מִכָּאן שָׁארֵי לְמִמְנֵי בְּזִוּוּגָא, וּמָנֵי וְאָמַר, אַחַת וּשְׁתַּיִם. אַחַת וְשָׁלֹשׁ. אַחַת וְאַרְבַּע. אַחַת וְחָמֵשׁ. אַחַת וָשֵׁשׁ. אַחַת וָשֶׁבַע. בְּגִין לְאַמְשָׁכָא וּלְנַגְּדָא לְהַאי אַחַת, דְּהִיא אִימָּא עִלָּאָה, בְּדַרְגִּין יְדִיעָן, לְכִתְרָא דְּאִימָּא תַּתָּאָה. וּלְאַמְשָׁכָא נְהִירִין עֲמִיקִין מֵאַתְרַיְיהוּ לכ"י. וְעַ"ד, יוֹמָא דָּא תְּרֵין נְהוֹרִין נַהֲרִין כַּחֲדָא, אִימָּא עִלָּאָה נַהֲרָא לְאִימָּא תַּתָּאָה. וְעַל דָּא כְּתִיב יה"כ, כְּמָה דְּאִתְּמַר.

250. "Upon reaching 'and one,' which is the Mother of everything, namely Binah, **he starts counting from here,** from Binah, **by joining, counting and saying, 'one and two,'** namely joining Binah with two, Chesed and Gevurah, **'one and three,'** joining Binah to Chesed, Gevurah, and Tiferet, **'one and four,'** joining Binah to Chesed, Gevurah, Tiferet, and Netzach, **'one and five,'** joining Binah to Chesed, Gevurah, Tiferet, Netzach, and Hod**, 'one and six,'** joining Binah to Chesed, Gevurah, Tiferet, Netzach, Hod and Yesod, **'one and seven,'** joining Binah to Chesed, Gevurah, Tiferet, Netzach, Hod, Yesod, and Malchut, **in order to draw and guide the one, which is Supernal Ima,** namely Binah, **through the specific grades** mentioned earlier, **to the Keter of Lower Ima,** which is Malchut, **and draw the deep rivers,** the Lights of Binah, **from their place to the Congregation of Israel,** which is Malchut. **Therefore on this day, two Lights shine together,** which are **Supernal Ima that shines to Lower Ima,** Binah to Malchut. **Hence it is written Yom haKippurim (Day of Atonements)** in the plural, **as we said** [in verse 224]."

The High Priest entered the Holy of Holies on this day.

251. א"ר יִצְחָק קִפְטְרָא וְחָדָא קְשִׁירָא בְּרַגְלוֹי דְּכַהֲנָא, בְּשַׁעֲתָא דַּהֲוָה עָאל, דְּאִי יָמוּת הָתָם, יַפְּקוּהוּ מִלְּבַר. וּבְמָּה יַדְעֵי. בְּהַהוּא זְהוֹרִיתָא אִתְיְידַע וְאִשְׁתְּמוֹדַע, כַּד לָא יְהָפֵךְ גַּוְונוֹי. בְּהַהִיא שַׁעֲתָא אִשְׁתְּמוֹדַע, דְּכַהֲנָא אִשְׁתַּכַּח לְגוֹ בְּחַטָּאָה. וְאִי יִפּוּק בִּשְׁלָם, בְּזְהוֹרִיתָא אִתְיְידַע וְאִשְׁתְּמוֹדַע, דְּיִהֲפֵךְ גַּוְונוֹי לְחִוָּור. כְּדֵין חֶדְוְותָא הֲוָה בְּעִלָּאֵי וְתַתָּאֵי. וְאִי לָאו כֻּלְּהוּ אִשְׁתְּכָחוּ בְּצַעֲרָא, וַהֲווֹ יַדְעֵי כֹּלָּא, דְּלָא אִתְקַבָּלוּ צְלוֹתְהוֹן.

251. Rav Yitzchak said: "A chain was tied to the feet of the High Priest when he entered the Holy of Holies, **so that if he dies they can take him out,** since it is forbidden to enter there." [He asks:] **"How did they know** whether he was alive or not?" [He answers]: **"By a crimson colored strap. If its color did not turn** white, **it was known at that time that the Priest was there in sin. And if he came out in peace, it**

was known and recognized by the crimson strap that turned white. Then there was joy among the Upper and Lower Beings. If not, they were all in sorrow and all knew that their prayer was not accepted."

How the Priest would know that the work was accepted.

252. אָמַר רִבִּי יְהוּדָה, כֵּיוָן דַּהֲוָה עָאל, וְטַמְטֵם עֵינוֹי דְּלָא לְאִסְתַּכְּלָא בְּמָה דְּלָא אִצְטְרִיךְ, וַהֲוָה שָׁמַע קָל גַּדְפֵּי כְּרוּבַיָּיא מְזַמְּרֵי וּמְשַׁבְּחֵי. הֲוָה יָדַע כַּהֲנָא, דְּכֹלָּא הֲוָה בְּחֶדְוָה, וְיִפּוּק בִּשְׁלָם. וְעִם כָּל דָּא בִּצְלוֹתֵיהּ הֲוָה יָדַע, דְּמִלִּין נָפְקִין בְּחֶדְוָותָא, וּמִתְקַבְּלָן וּמִתְבָּרְכָן כִּדְקָא יָאוּת, וּכְדֵין חֶדְוָותָא הִיא בְּעִלָּאֵי וְתַתָּאֵי.

252. Rav Yehuda said: "Once he entered, he closed his eyes so as not to look where he should not. When he heard the sound of the wings of the Cherubs singing and praising, the Priest would know that everything is in joy and exit in peace. With all that, through his prayer he would know, since the words came out of his mouth in joy and were properly accepted and blessed. Then joy abounded among the Upper and Lower Beings."

Malchut ascends to Binah on Yom Kippur.

253. רִבִּי אֶלְעָזָר שָׁאַל לְר"ש אֲבוֹי, א"ל, הַאי יוֹמָא אֲמַאי הוּא בְּהַאי אֲתַר תָּלֵי, וְלָא בְּדַרְגָּא אָחֳרָא, דְּיָאוּת הוּא לְמֶהֱוֵי בְּדַרְגָּא דְּמַלְכָּא שָׁארֵי, יַתִּיר מִכֹּלָּא. אָמַר לֵיהּ ר' שִׁמְעוֹן אֶלְעָזָר בְּרִי, הָכִי הוּא וַדַּאי, וְיָאוּת שָׁאַלְתְּ.

253. Rav Elazar asked Rav Shimon his father: "Why does this day of Yom Kippur **originate in that place,** Binah, as Malchut ascends to Binah, the secret of the Left, **instead of from another place? It would have been appropriate for it to be of the grade where the King dwells the most,** namely that She would unite with Her husband Zeir Anpin, the secret of the Right." **Rav Shimon said to him: "My son Elazar, surely it is so** that it should come from Binah, **and you have asked well.**

The Matron is permitted to join with the Holy King if She is worthy, otherwise She returns to exile.

254. ת"ח, מַלְכָּא קַדִּישָׁא, שָׁבִיק הֵיכָלֵיהּ וּבֵיתֵיהּ בִּידָא דְּמַטְרוֹנִיתָא, וְשָׁבַק לִבְנוֹי עִמָּהּ, בְּגִין לְדַבְּרָא לוֹן, וּלְאַלְקָאָה לוֹן, וּלְמִשְׁרֵי בְּגַוַויְיהוּ. דְּאִי זַכָּאן מַטְרוֹנִיתָא עָאלַת בְּחֶדְוָותָא בִּיקָרָא לְגַבֵּי מַלְכָּא. וְאִי לָא זַכָּאן, הִיא וְאִינּוּן, אִתְהֲדָרוּ בְּגָלוּתָא. וְהָא אוֹקִימְנָא, כְּמָה דִּכְתִּיב, מְשַׁדֶּד אָב יַבְרִיחַ אֵם. וּכְתִיב, וּבְפִשְׁעֵיכֶם שֻׁלְּחָה אִמְּכֶם.

254. "Come and see, the Holy King left His Palace and Abode in the hand of the Matron, Malchut, **and left His children with her, in order for her to guide them, strike them and dwell among them. If they are worthy, the Matron enters joyfully and honorably to the King. If they are not worthy, she and they are returned into exile. We already explained this, as it is written:** 'A son who causes shame and disgrace **shall ruin his father, and drive his mother away' (Proverbs 19:26)** chasing her into exile **and: '...for your transgressions was your mother put away.' (Isaiah 50:1)**

On Yom Kippur, Malchut rises up to Binah without Zeir Anpin.

255. וְעַל דָּא אִית יוֹמָא וַחַד בְּשַׁתָּא, לְאַשְׁגָּחָא בְּהוּ, וּלְעַיְּינָא בְּהוּ. וְכַד אִזְדַּמַּן הַאי יוֹמָא, אִימָּא עִלָּאָה דְּכָל חֵירוּ בִּידָהָא, אִזְדַּמַּן לְקַבְלֵיהּ, לְאִסְתַּכְּלָא בְּהוּ בְּיִשְׂרָאֵל. וְיִשְׂרָאֵל אִזְדָּרְזוּ בְּהַאי יוֹמָא, בְּכַמָּה פּוּלְחָנִין, בְּכַמָּה צְלוֹתִין, בְּכַמָּה עִנּוּיִין, כֻּלְּהוּ בְּזַכְוּתָא. כְּדֵין אִזְדַּמַּן לְהוּ חֵירוּ, מֵאֲתַר דְּכָל חֵירוּ בִּידָהָא דְּמַטְרוֹנִיתָא. בְּנֵי מַלְכָּא בְּנָהָא, דְּאִתְפְּקָדָן בִּידָהָא, כֻּלְּהוּ זַכָּאִין, כֻּלְּהוּ בְּלָא חֲטָאָן, בְּלָא חוֹבִין, כְּדֵין אִזְדַּוְּוגַת לְגַבֵּי מַלְכָּא, בִּנְהִירוּ, בְּחֶדְוָה, בִּשְׁלִימוּ, בִּרְעוּתָא. דְּהָא רַבִּיאַת בְּנִין לְמַלְכָּא עִלָּאָה כַּדְקָא יָאוּת.

255. "Therefore there is one day in the year to look at them and observe their deeds. **When that day comes, Supernal Ima,** Binah, **in whose hands are all kinds of freedom,** namely the Mochin of the Illumination of Chochmah clothed in Chasadim, the secret of Freedom, which banish and subdue all the Klipot. **She is readied toward** that day **to observe Israel,** namely to bestow upon them, **and Israel hasten on that day with many kinds of worship and prayers, and many afflictions, all of them meritorious. Then freedom comes upon them from the place where all freedom exists in the hand of the Matron,** Malchut. This means that Malchut rises to Binah, and receives all freedom from Binah. **The King's children,** Israel below, **who are Her children who were trusted in Her hands, are all meritorious without sins or iniquities. She then joins the King with Light, joy, completion and desire because she raised proper children for the King,** namely she cleaves to the Right. However, before Israel receive purity and freedom from Binah, Malchut cannot unite with Zeir Anpin and receive from the Right." This settles the question of his son Rav Elazar.

Either Israel is not worthy and there is no freedom
or Israel is saved and purified.

256. וְכַד הַאי יוֹמָא לָא אִשְׁתְּכָחוּ כַּדְקָא יָאוּת, וַוי לוֹן, וַוי לִשְׁלוּחֵיהוֹן, וַוי דְּהָא מַטְרוֹנִיתָא אִתְרַחֲקַת מִן מַלְכָּא, וְאִימָא עִלָּאָה אִסְתַּלָּקַת, וְלָא נָפִיק מִנָּהּ חֵירוּ לְעָלְמִין. זַכָּאִין אִינּוּן יִשְׂרָאֵל, דְּקוּדְשָׁא בְּרִיךְ הוּא אוֹלִיף לוֹן אוֹרְחוֹי, בְּגִין לְאִשְׁתְּזָבָא מִן דִּינָא, וְיִשְׁתַּכְחוּן זַכָּאִין קַמֵּיהּ. הה"ד, כִּי בַיּוֹם הַזֶּה יְכַפֵּר עֲלֵיכֶם. לְטַהֵר אֶתְכֶם. וּכְתִיב, וְזָרַקְתִּי עֲלֵיכֶם מַיִם טְהוֹרִים וּטְהַרְתֶּם מִכֹּל טֻמְאוֹתֵיכֶם וְגוֹ'.

256. When that day is not proper, woe to them, to Israel, **woe to their messenger,** the High Priest, **woe that the Matron is distanced from the King and that Supernal Ima,** Binah, **is gone and no freedom comes from Her to the worlds. Happy are Israel, whom the Holy One, blessed be He, taught His ways so as to be saved from Judgment and to be meritorious before Him. This is the meaning of, "For on this day atonement shall be made for you to purify you..." (Leviticus 16:30) and "Then will I sprinkle clean water upon you, and you shall be clean... from all your impurities." (Ezekiel 36:25)**

Balak

29. "And he lifted up his eyes, and saw the women and the children"

A Synopsis

Rav Shimon explains the title verse, wherein he says that the Accuser sees Israel anguished from fasting and believes that they are fasting because they are afraid of him. We read how and why God protects innocent children during Yom Kippur, so that they are not punished for the sins of Israel. The innocent children are the Torah scholars, to whom God has told His secrets. No evil eye can have any power over them. Next, we hear that the three trees that are sheltering the rabbis bend down individually over their heads immediately after Rav Shimon says that the three trees are the secret of the Patriarchs.

Sending a present to the Accuser so that he becomes our advocate.

326. וַיִּשָּׂא אֶת עֵינָיו וַיַּרְא אֶת הַנָּשִׁים. הַאי קְרָא, בְּרָזָא דְּחָכְמְתָא אִתְּמַר, בְּיוֹמָא דְּכִפּוּרֵי, דִּבְנֵי עָלְמָא קַיְימֵי בְּדִינָא, וְיִשְׂרָאֵל תַּיְיבִין בְּתִיוּבְתָּא קַמֵּי קוּדְשָׁא בְּרִיךְ הוּא, לְכַפָּרָא עַל חוֹבַיְיהוּ. וְהַהוּא מְקַטְרְגָא קַיְימָא עֲלַיְיהוּ, דְּחָשִׁיב לְאוֹבָדָא לוֹן עַל חוֹבַיְיהוּ, שַׁלְחֵי לֵיהּ הַהוּא דּוֹרוֹנָא, וּכְדֵין כְּתִיב, כִּי אָמַר אֲכַפְּרָה פָנָיו בַּמִּנְחָה הַהוֹלֶכֶת לְפָנָי. לְבָתַר דִּמְקַבֵּל הַהוּא מְקַטְרְגָא לְהַהוּא דּוֹרוֹנָא, אִתְהַפָּךְ לְהוּ סַנֵּיגוֹרָא.

326. "And he lifted up his eyes, and saw the women and the children." (Genesis 33:5) This verse was said in the secret of wisdom. On Yom Kippur, when people stand for trial, and Israel repent before the Holy One, blessed be He, to be forgiven for their iniquities and the Accuser standing over them, planning to destroy them due to their iniquities, they send him that gift, meaning the goat for Azazel. **Then it is written: "For he said, 'I will appease him with the present that**

goes before me.'" (Genesis 32:21) After the Accuser receives this gift, he reverses himself and becomes his advocate.

The Accuser thinks we are fasting out of fear of him.

327. זָקִיף וְחָמֵי לוֹן לְיִשְׂרָאֵל, כֻּלְּהוּ מִתְעַנָּן בְּתַעֲנִיתָא, יְחֵפֵי רַגְלִין. חָמֵי נָשִׁין, וְחָמֵי יַנּוּקִין, כֻּלְּהוּ בְּתַעֲנִיתָא, כֻּלְּהוּ נְקִיִּים בִּנְקִיו. וַיֹּאמֶר מִי אֵלֶּה לָּךְ. שְׁמָא קַדִּישָׁא לָךְ. מִי אֵלֶּה לָךְ. שָׁאִיל עַל יַנּוּקֵי, וְאָמַר הַיְלָדִים אֲשֶׁר חָנַן אֱלֹהִים אֶת עַבְדֶּךָ. וְכִי אֲמַאי אִצְטְרִיךְ לְאָתָבָא לֵיהּ כְּלוּם. אֶלָּא כֵּיוָן דִּמְקַבֵּל הַהוּא שׁוֹחַד, אִתְהַפָּךְ לְהוּ סַנֵּיגוֹר. זָקִיף עֵינוֹי, וְחָמֵי לוֹן לְיִשְׂרָאֵל כְּגַוְונָא דָא, וְחָשִׁיב דִּבְגִין דְּחִילוּ דִּילֵיהּ אִינּוּן קַיְּימִין כַּךְ.

327. The Accuser **raises** his eyes **and sees Israel are fasting and are bare footed. He sees women and he sees children; all are fasting, all are clean with purity. "And he said, 'Who (*mi*) are those (*eleh*) with you?'…" (Genesis 33:5),** meaning **the Holy Name** Elohim (אלהים) that is derived from *Mi Eleh* (מי אלה); they are **with you,** Israel. **He asked about the children, and "…he replied, 'The children that God (Elohim) has graciously given your servant.'" (Genesis 33:5)** He asks: **"Did he need to answer him anything?"** He replies: **"Since he accepted that bribe,** meaning the scapegoat, **he turned to be a good advocate for them. He raised his eyes and saw Israel in this way and thought that due to the fear of him,** lest he make accusations about them, **they were in such a state** of fasting and repentance.

Children who pass away without sin.

328. שָׁאִיל עַל יַנּוּקֵי, וְאָמַר מִי אֵלֶּה לָּךְ. מַהוּ מִי אֵלֶּה לָךְ. אֶלָּא אָמַר, תִּינַּח אַתּוּן דְּחַבְתּוּן קַמֵּי מַלְכָּא. אֲבָל אִלֵּין יַנּוּקֵי, אֲמַאי קַיְּימִין הָכִי, מִי אֵלֶּה לָךְ. וַיֹּאמַר הַיְלָדִים, רוּחַ קֻדְשָׁא אָמַר, וְעַ"ד זָקִיף טַעֲמָא. וַיֹּאמַר הַיְלָדִים. בְּאַרְחַ סָתִים אֲשֶׁר חָנַן אֱלֹהִים אֶת עַבְדֶּךָ, וְכִי רוּחַ הַקֹּדֶשׁ אָמַר אֶת עַבְדֶּךָ. אֶלָּא רוּחַ קֻדְשָׁא אָמַר, אִלֵּין אִינּוּן יַנּוּקֵי דְּלָא חָאבוּ, וְלָא טָעִימוּ טַעֲמָא דְּחָטְאָה, וּמָסַר

לוֹן קוּדְשָׁא בְּרִיךְ הוּא, בִּידָא דְהַהוּא מְמָנָא דִילָךְ, וְקָטִיל לוֹן בְּלָא חוֹבָא, כד"א וּמִיַּד עוֹשְׁקֵיהֶם כֹּחַ. וְדָא הוּא אֶת עַבְדֶּךָ.

328. "Another explanation: He asked about the children and said, 'Who are these with you?' (Genesis 33:5)" He asks: **"What is the meaning of: 'Who are these with you'? (Ibid.)"** He answers: **"Rather, he said 'it befits you** to fast and repent **because you sinned against the King, but why are these children in this state** of fasting? **Who are these with you?' "And he said, 'The children'" (Ibid.)** meaning, **the Holy Spirit said this; therefore, there is a vertical cantillation mark,** Zakef Gadol, on top of **'And he said,'** and on top of **'the children' without specifying,** to indicate that the Holy Spirit spoke so. **'…that God (Elohim) has graciously given your servant' (Ibid.)"** He asks: **"Did the Holy Spirit then say** to Esau, **'your servant'?"** He answers: **"The Holy Spirit said, 'These are the children who have not had a taste of sin** in their first incarnation. **The Holy One, blessed be He, placed them in the hands of your minister and he killed them without them having sinned, as it says, "And on the side of their oppressors there was power…." (Ecclesiastes 4:1) That is the meaning of, 'your servant.'** So the verse reads: 'that God has graciously given your servant,' namely your minister, and gave him the souls of the children that did not experience the taste of sin.

The Accuser awakens the Creator's compassion regarding the children who died without sin.

329. כֵּיוָן דְּשָׁמַע מֵאִינּוּן יַנּוּקֵי, מִיַּד סָלִיק לְגַבֵּי קוּדְשָׁא בְּרִיךְ הוּא, וְאָמַר, מָארֵיהּ דְעָלְמָא, כָּל אָרְחָךְ בְּדִינָא דִקְשׁוֹט, וְאִי דִינָא שַׁרְיָא עַל יִשְׂרָאֵל בְּגִין חוֹבֵיהוֹן אִיהוּ, יַנּוּקִין דִלְהוֹן דְּלָא חָאבוּ לְקָמָךְ, אֲמַאי מַסְרַת לוֹן לְקָטְלָא לוֹן בְּלָא חוֹבָא. וְקוּדְשָׁא בְּרִיךְ הוּא נָטִיל מִלּוֹי בְּכַךְ, וְחָס עֲלַיְיהוּ. וְהַהִיא שַׁעֲתָא, לָא הֲוֵי אַסְכָּרָא בְּתִינּוֹקוֹת.

329. "As soon as he heard about these children, he immediately ascended to the presence of the Holy One, blessed be He, and said, 'Master of the World, all Your ways are just and true. If any Judgment resides upon Israel, it is because of their sins. Why did You hand their children who have not sinned over to be killed?' The Holy One, blessed be He, accepts these words of his and has compassion on them. At that time, in Yom Kippur, **children do not suffer from diphtheria.**

The Accuser takes back the souls of the children from the minister.

330. וְהַהוּא מְקַטְרְגָא נָטִיל קִנְאָה מֵהַהוּא מְמָנָא דִּתְחוֹת יְדֵיהּ. אָמַר, וְכִי לִי יָהִיב קוּדְשָׁא בְּרִיךְ הוּא אִינּוּן דְּמִתְלַבְּשָׁן בְּחָטְאִין וְחוֹבִין, וּלְהַהוּא מְמָנָא דִּילִי מָסַר יַנּוּקִין בְּלָא חוֹבָא, דְּלָא טַעֲמוּן טַעֲמָא דְּחוֹבָה. מִיַּד אָזַל לְאַפָּקָא לוֹן מִתְּחוֹת יְדֵיהּ, וְלָא יִשְׁלוֹט בְּהוּ. וְעַ"ד אַקְדִּים לֵיהּ וְאָ"ל, הַיְלָדִים אֲשֶׁר חָנַן אֱלֹהִים אֶת עַבְדֶּךָ. לְהַהוּא עַבְדֶּךָ, בְּלָא חוֹבָא וּבְלָא חַטָּאָה. וּבְגִין דְּלָא יְהֵא שְׁבָחָא לַמְּמָנָא דִּילֵיהּ יַתִּיר מִנֵּיהּ, בָּעָא לְאַפָּקָא לוֹן מִן יְדוֹי.

330. "The Accuser becomes jealous about this minister appointed under him and says, 'Did the Holy One, blessed be He, give me those who carry upon themselves sins and iniquities, and to the minister He handed children without sin, who do not even know the taste of sin?' He immediately goes and removes them from his hand, so he should not have any control over them. Therefore, the Holy Spirit **proceeded and said, 'The children that God has graciously given your servant,' (Genesis 33:5) to that servant,** meaning He graciously gave him children that are **without taste of any iniquity or sin. And so that the minister shall not have more praise than him, he wishes to remove them from his hand."**

Explanation: there are five aspects of the soul called Nefesh, Ruach, Neshamah, Chayah, and Yechidah, without which man is not complete. However, there are few who achieve all five in one incarnation. There are those who achieve only up to the Upper Three of Ruach alone, and they die and reincarnate to acquire the remaining aspects of the Neshamah. Those souls who died with the Upper Three of Ruach are called children, as these Mochin are Mochin of Yenikah (Suckling), and they are called "the babies and children of the world." (Zohar, Prologue 6) They are considered to have died without sin, since in the Upper Three of Ruach the Chochmah of the Left Column shines and distances from them all sins.

The reason they die is in the secret of the verse: **"And on the side of their oppressors there was power..." (Ecclesiastes 4:1)** where since they were given over to death they acquire power to attain the remaining parts of the soul. When does this happen? It happens on Yom Kippur, since then the Other Side receives the goat for Azazel, which is similar to those Mochin of Yenikah, since the goat for Azazel is the secret of the Upper Three of the Left. And through the death of these children, these Mochin of the Upper Three of the Left are nullified. This is why Sama"el is bothered by his appointed minister who kills these children, since with this he damages the Illumination of the goat to Azazel.

Therefore, the Holy Spirit, the Shechinah, reminds him of these souls of the children. This is: **"The Holy Spirit said, 'These are the children who have not had a taste of sin... and he killed them without them having sinned,"** namely the souls that only attained the Mochin of Yenikah that the Creator gave over to the Other Side to be killed so that they receive power from them, through the prosecutor that becomes the defender on Yom Kippur due to the Illumination of the Azazel [goat] that he received. This is: **"As soon as he heard about these children, he immediately ascended...'Why did You hand their children who have not sinned over to be killed?'"** He felt that through giving these children over to the Other Side to be killed it ruins the Illumination of Azazel that he received, and therefore he becomes their defense attorney. This is: **"And on the side of their oppressors there was**

power…" (Ecclesiastes 4:1) for had they not been delivered to be killed, the general prosecutor would never have become an advocate on their behalf on Yom Kippur. Once the prosecutor becomes an advocate it is found that the oppressors gave strength to these souls to receive all the remaining parts of the soul; and the admission of a litigant is similar to that of one hundred witnesses. This is: "**The Holy One, blessed be He, accepts these words of his and has compassion on them,**" namely He completes them by giving the remaining parts of the Mochin. This is: "**The Accuser becomes jealous about this minister appointed under him,**" since he damages for him the Illumination of the goat of Azazel, and especially since that minister is from the aspect of Harsh Judgments and can overpower him and nullify his Illumination. This is: **"And so that the minister shall not have more praise than him, he wishes to remove them from his hand,"** meaning he needs to save the children from his hands so that he [the minister] does not prevail over him and nullify his Azazel Illumination, thus making him superior to him.

Malchut diminished Herself seven times so She could unite with Zeir Anpin.

331. כַּד סַלְקִין צְלוֹתִין דְּיִשְׂרָאֵל בְּיוֹמָא דָא קַמֵּי קוּדְשָׁא בְּרִיךְ הוּא, מַה כְּתִיב וְהוּא עָבַר לִפְנֵיהֶם. הָא רוּחַ קוּדְשָׁא אַעְבַּר לְקָמַיְיהוּ, כד"א וַיַּעֲבוֹר מַלְכָּם לִפְנֵיהֶם וְהוּא וַדַּאי עָבַר לִפְנֵיהֶם. וַיִּשְׁתַּחוּ אַרְצָה שֶׁבַע פְּעָמִים, רוּחַ קוּדְשָׁא, אַזְעַר גַּרְמֵיהּ לְגַבֵּי עֵילָּא ז' זִמְנִין, לְגַבֵּי ז' דַּרְגִּין עִלָּאִין דְּעָלֵיהּ, וְאַקְטִין גַּרְמֵיהּ, לְאַכְלְלָא לוֹן עִמֵּיהּ כָּל וַחַד וְחָד. עַד גִּשְׁתּוֹ עַד אָחִיו, לְהַהוּא דַּרְגָּא דְּרַחֲמֵי, דְּהָא בֵּן וּבַת אִינּוּן. בֵּן, בְּנֵי בְּכוֹרִי יִשְׂרָאֵל. בַּת, כ"י. רוּחַ קוּדְשָׁא עָבֵיד אַזְעִירוּ דְּגַרְמֵיהּ, עַד גִּשְׁתּוֹ.

331. "When the prayers of Israel ascend on that day to the Holy One, blessed be He, what is written? 'And he passed before them….' (Genesis 33:3) Here, the Holy Spirit, Malchut, **passed before them, as it says, 'And their king passed before them' (Micah 2:13) and he definitely passed before them. '…and bowed himself to the ground seven times…' (Genesis 33:3); meaning the Holy Spirit,** Malchut,

diminished Itself toward the one above, Zeir Anpin, **seven times, corresponding to the seven Supernal grades above it,** Chesed, Gevurah, Tiferet, Netzach, Hod, Yesod, and Malchut of Zeir Anpin, **and diminished itself to include each one of them with it. '...until he came near to his brother' (Ibid.), meaning to that level of Mercy,** which is Zeir Anpin that is considered the brother of the Holy Spirit, Malchut, **since they are son and daughter** to Binah, and therefore, they are brothers. Zeir Anpin is called **'son' as it is said, '..."Israel is My son, My firstborn"' (Exodus 4:22)** namely Zeir Anpin that is called Israel. **Daughter is the Congregation of Israel,** meaning Malchut. **The Holy Spirit caused a diminishing of itself until its approach** to its brother, Zeir Anpin."

Explanation: Malchut was originally as big as Zeir Anpin in the secret of "...two great luminaries...." (Genesis 1:16) Yet at that state, She could not bestow abundance to Israel, so to bestow to Israel She diminished Herself seven times, meaning that she departed from all Her seven great Sefirot and became a dot under Yesod. After this, She is rebuilt and is made worthy to receive all Seven Sefirot of Zeir Anpin. This is: **"diminished itself toward the one above seven times, corresponding to the seven supernal grades above it,"** namely so that She can be rebuilt with the Seven Sefirot of Zeir Anpin, which are Chesed, Gevurah, Tiferet, Netzach, Hod, Yesod, and Malchut. This is: **"The Holy Spirit caused a diminishing of itself until its approach."** Malchut that is called the Holy Spirit diminished Herself until She was able to unite with Zeir Anpin, as mentioned. Had She not diminished herself She would not be able to approach Him.

Zeir Anpin and Nuvka ascend to Ima to request compassion for Israel.

332. כֵּיוָן דְּמָטָא לְגַבֵּיהּ, תָּבַע מִינֵּיהּ, וְאוֹדַע לֵיהּ צַעֲרָא דִּבְנַיְיהוּ לְתַתָּא. וְתַרְוַויְיהוּ עָאלִין לְהֵיכָלָא טְמִירָא גְּנִיזָא דְּיוֹם הַכִּפּוּרִים, אִימָּא דִּלְהוֹן, וְתַבְעִין

עַל יִשְׂרָאֵל לְכַפְּרָא לוֹן, כְּדֵין כְּתִיב כִּי בַיּוֹם הַזֶּה יְכַפֵּר עֲלֵיכֶם לְטַהֵר אֶתְכֶם וְגוֹ'. אֲכַפֵּר עֲלֵיכֶם לָא כְּתִיב, אֶלָּא יְכַפֵּר עֲלֵיכֶם.

332. **"As soon as** Malchut **reached him,** Zeir Anpin, **She beseeched Him and informed Him of the distress of their children below,** in this world. **Both** Zeir Anpin and Malchut **entered the hidden and concealed chamber of Yom Kippur,** which is Binah, **their mother,** since on Yom Kippur, Zeir Anpin and Nukva ascend to Ima **and ask for Israel to be atoned for. Then it says, 'For on this day He shall atone for you to cleanse you....' (Leviticus 16:30) It does not say, 'I shall atone' but rather 'He,'** in the third person hinting at Binah.

The Creator gave the sages the secrets of the Torah to be adorned with.

333. וְהַשְׁתָּא הַיְלָדִים, אִלֵּין וַחַכִּימִין דְּהָכָא, קוּדְשָׁא בְּרִיךְ הוּא יָהַב לוֹן רָזִין דְּאוֹרַיְיתָא, לְאִתְעַטְּרָא בְּהוּ, וּלְאִשְׁתַּדְּלָא בְּהוּ. עֵינָא בִּישָׁא לָא שַׁלְטָא עָלַיְיהוּ, בְּגִין עֵינָא טָבָא, רוּחַ קוּדְשָׁא דְּר' פִּנְחָס, דְּשַׁרְיָא עָלַיְיהוּ. אָתָא ר' פִּנְחָס וּנְשָׁקֵיהּ. אָמַר, אִלְמָלֵא לָא אֲתֵינָא אָרְחָא דָּא, אֶלָּא לְמִשְׁמַע מִלִּין אִלֵּין, דַּי לִי. זַכָּאָה אָרְחָא דָּא דְּאָתֵינָא לְגַבָּךְ.

333. **"Now,** regarding **'...the children...,' (Genesis 33:5) these are the sages present here, whom the Holy One, blessed be He, gave the secrets of the Torah to be adorned with and occupied with. No evil eye has power over them, due to the benevolent eye and the Holy Spirit of Rav Pinchas that dwells upon them." Rav Pinchas approached and kissed** Rav Shimon. **He said: "Had I only gone on this path to listen to these words, it would have been sufficient for me. Praised is this road upon which I came to you."**

Pinchas

63. The scapegoat, the liver, and the heart

A Synopsis

The Faithful Shepherd explains how the goat bears all of Israel's iniquities.

The Relevance of this Passage

The humility embodied by King David rises in our hearts. Since this passage serves as the very scapegoat that absolves us of sin, all of our iniquities are abolished.

Through the Light of paragraph 378, Satan/Sama"el and Lili"t are battered, broken, and banished from our existence. In turn, our hearts and arteries receive the Light of healing, and our livers successfully extract the poisons, toxins, and fats from our system. This cleansing occurs globally as well. The sins of man are cleansed by the "scapegoat." The world's heart, Israel, and the nations of the world are healed as peace and loving-kindness permeate our planet.

The Azazel goat falls due to the heavy load of sins.

378. וְעוֹד וְנָשָׂא הַשָּׂעִיר עָלָיו, כַּד רְעוּתֵיהּ לְמֶעְבַּד קוּרְצְיָא לְקוּדְשָׁא בְּרִיךְ הוּא עִם יִשְׂרָאֵל, דְּאִיהוּ נָשָׂא כָּל חוֹבִין דְּיָכִיל לְמִסְבַּל לוֹן, עַד דְּאִתְעָבֵיד כָּבֵד, כְּמַשָּׂא כָּבֵד יִכְבְּדוּ מִמֶּנּוּ, וְחוֹבִין עַל גַּדְפּוֹי. מָה עָבֵיד, סָלִיק לְטוּרָא עִלָּאָה, כַּחֲמָרָא כַּד אִיהוּ בָּעֵי לְסַלְּקָא לְטוּר גָּבוֹהַ, כְּמַשָּׂא כָבֵד יִכְבַּד עָלֵיהּ. כַּד אִיהוּ לְעֵילָּא, וּבָעֵי לְסַלְּקָא לְפִי מִעוּט דְּאִשְׁתְּאַר לֵיהּ, אִתְיַקַּר עָלֵיהּ מָטוּלָא, וְנָפִיל, וְאַפִּיל גַּרְמֵיהּ לְתַתָּא, וּבְכֹבֶד מַשָּׂא דְּאִתְתַּקַּף עָלֵיהּ, אִתְעֲבִידוּ כָּל אֵבָרִין דִּילֵיהּ פִּסְקוֹת, דְּלָא אִשְׁתְּאַר אֵבֶר שָׁלִים. אוּף הָכָא אִירַע לְסָמָאֵל וְנָחָשׁ, כָּבֵד וְיוֹתֶרֶת הַכָּבֵד, יֵצֶר הָרָע וּבַת זוּגֵיהּ זוֹנָה. מִתַּמָּן כָּל בַּת אֵל נֵכָר זוֹנָה.
ע״כ רעיא מהימנא

378. Furthermore: "And the goat shall bear upon itself all their iniquities..." (Leviticus 16:22), when the Satan **wants to slander Israel before the Holy One, blessed be He, and he bears all the sins that he can carry until he becomes heavy (*kaved*) "...like a heavy burden they are too heavy for" him (Psalms 38:5)** to carry **upon his wings.** He asks: **"What does he do?"** He answers: **"He climbs a high mountain, like a donkey that wants to ascend a tall mountain, and the sins are heavy like a heavy burden. When he gets** near **the top and wants to climb up that little bit more that is left for him, the weight of the burden overcomes him and falls, and he tumbles down to the bottom, and with the weight of the burden pressing on him all his limbs are broken into pieces, until not a single limb in him remains whole. Thus, too, did it happen to Sama"el and the Serpent that are the liver (*kaved*) and the appendage of the liver, the Evil Inclination and its partner, a harlot, whence every daughter of a strange El is** called **'a harlot.'"**

End of the Ra'aya Meheimna (Faithful Shepherd)

The secret of the goat to Azazel was already explained in Zohar, Acharei Mot 116, and here the Faithful Shepherd shares an additional secret. The root of the entire Other Side is Sama"el and the Serpent, which are Male and Female. Sama"el comes from the Male Judgments, which means that he is in charge of all the punishments for the sins that come from the Male Judgments. The Serpent, his female counterpart, is from the Female Judgments, which means that She is in charge of all the punishments for the sins that come from the Female Judgments.

It is known that these two types of Judgment are the root of every type of sin in the world. The Faithful Shepherd says that the secret of the Supernal Azazel is that it is the sum of all the prosecutions that Sama"el and the Serpent carry on them to bring before the Holy One, blessed be He, so that He can give them permission to punish Israel from the two aspects of their Judgment. The Supernal Azazel is likened to a donkey carrying a burden because that is how the Azazel goat carries on itself all the slander of Sama"el and the Serpent, whose root are these two types of Judgment mentioned.

It was explained in Zohar, Acharei Mot 116 that if these two types of Judgment join together, they can destroy the whole world. The solution for them is the Central Column, since through it the Female Judgments cancel out the Male Judgments, by means of its Masach of Chirik that nullifies the Upper Three of the Illumination of the Left; study there well. **"When** the Satan **wants to slander..."** namely when Sama"el and the Serpent send the Supernal Azazel to slander Israel, **"and he bears all the sins that he can carry until he becomes heavy,"** namely both the Male and Female Judgments, which are too heavy to carry, **"what does he do? He climbs a high mountain,"** to awaken the Male Judgments, meaning he ascends to the Left Column, which is called a "high mountain," since the Three Columns are called "mountains." **"When he gets** near **the top,"** and is already in the Left Column but in the aspect of the Lower Six of the Left, **"and wants to climb up that little bit more that is left for him,"** namely that he wants to ascend to the Upper Three of the Left, where there is no union with the Right and where all Male Judgments come from **"the weight of the burden overcomes him and falls,"** meaning that the Female Judgments in his burden become heavy for him in the place of the Upper Three of the Left, to cancel them out. This happens through the Central Column that makes this correction through Israel sending the goat to Azazel below. Then, **"and he tumbles down to the bottom,"** meaning he goes down from the entire Left Column, not even wanting the Lower Six of the Left that the Central Column leaves because the Other Side flees from the Central Column and its corrections.

"Thus, too, did it happen to Sama"el and the Serpent," who are the messengers of Azazel and are **"the Evil Inclination and its partner, a harlot,"** since Sama"el is the Evil Inclination and the Serpent, his partner, is a harlot. Male and Female must always be aligned with their type, and since Sama"el is from the Male Judgments then his partner also should have been from those Judgments. Yet, she is from the Female Judgments. Being that her husband, Sama"el, did not give those judgments to her, where did she get them from? Rather, she fornicates with other Supernal forces and receives the Female Judgments from them. therefore, Sama"el and his partner are called "Evil Inclination and harlot." This is: **"whence every daughter of a strange El is** called **'a harlot.'"** The Female of Sama"el is the root of all harlots of the world, and the daughter of a strange El receives from her.

This is the secret of what it says in Zohar, Pinchas 362: **"'the appendage (lit. additional) above the liver'** means that, **after her fornications, she... subdues her husband,"** because after she fornicates with other forces and receives the Female Judgments from them she then overpowers her husband, Sama"el, as the Female Judgments are harsher than the Male Judgments.

A Synopsis

Rav Pinchas reiterates the information about the role of Sama"el, the liver.

The Accuser must bring some merits so that his slander is established.

379. אָמַר רִבִּי פִּנְחָס, אוֹרְחָא דָּא הֲוָה מִתְקְנָא לִי, לְמִשְׁמַע מִלִּין אִלֵּין מֵעַתִּיק יוֹמִין, זַכָּאָה עָלְמָא דְּאַנְתְּ שָׁארֵי בְּגַוֵּיהּ. וַוי לְעָלְמָא, דְּיִשְׁתַּאֲרוּן יַתְמִין, וְלָא יַדְעִין מִלֵּי דְּאוֹרַיְיתָא כַּדְקָא יָאוֹת. וַדַּאי הָכִי הוּא, דְּכָבֵד נָטִיל כֹּלָּא טַב וּבִישׁ. ואע"ג דְּמִשַּׁטְטָא וְלָקִיט כָּל חוֹבֵיהוֹן דְּיִשְׂרָאֵל, ה"נ זַכְיָין דִּלְהוֹן לָקִיט, בְּגִין לְקַיְּימָא קוּרְצֵיהּ. וְכֹלָּא הַאי וְהַאי מַקְרִיב לְגַבֵּי לֵב. וְאוֹרְחוֹי דְּלֵב, לָא נָטִיל אֶלָּא זְכִיכוּ וּבְרִירוּ וְצָחוּתָא דְּכֹלָּא, כְּמָה דְּאַמָרַת. וּשְׁאַר טִנּוּפָא וְלִכְלוּכָא, אַהֲדָר לְכָבֵד, וְנָטִיל כֹּלָּא בְּעַל כָּרְחֵיהּ, דִּכְתִיב וְנָשָׂא הַשָּׂעִיר עָלָיו וְגוֹ'. מִלָּה דָּא אַהַדְרְנָא, בְּגִין דְּיִתְבַּסַּם לְפוּמִי כְּמִתְקָא דְּדוּבְשָׁא, זַכָּאָה חוּלָקִי דְּזָכֵינָא לְהַאי, לְמֶחֱמֵי דָּא בְּעֵינַי.

379. Rav Pinchas said to Rav Shimon, **"This path was ordained for me to hear these things from Atik Yomin (the Ancient of Days). Happy is the world in which you reside. Woe to the world, who will remain orphans without knowing matters of Torah properly. For it is certainly like that; the liver,** which is Sama"el, **takes everything, good and bad, and although it moves around and gathers in all the sins of Israel, it likewise gathers up their merits, too, to establish its slander,** for the liar has to speak some truth at the beginning for people to believe him. **And it brings everything,** both merits and demerits, **to the heart, and the way of the heart is to take nothing but the purest, clearest, and brightest of all,** namely the merits, **as you have said. And the remaining filth and dirt,** which are the iniquities, **it returns to the liver, who has no choice but to take everything, as it is written: "And the goat shall bear upon itself all their iniquities." I am going over this matter again,** although you have already stated it, **so that it will be sweet in my mouth as the sweetness of honey. Happy is my portion that I have been privileged to see this with my own eyes."**

Pinchas

101. The Yud-Hei-Vav-Heis in the middle

A Synopsis

The Faithful Shepherd tells how the Earth was founded by wisdom and the Heavens were established by understanding.

Daughter and father on the Right, mother and son on the Left.

רעיא מהימנא

678. אָמַר ר"מ, וַדַּאי בְּנֵי שָׁנָה אִתְקְרִיאוּ עַל שֵׁם חַמָּה, אִימָּא קַדִּישָׁא, דְּאִתְּמַר בָּהּ פְּנֵי מֹשֶׁה כִּפְנֵי חַמָּה. שָׁנָה אִית בָּהּ שס"ה יוֹמִין, כְּחוּשְׁבַּן שס"ה לֹא תַעֲשֶׂה. וְאִיהוּ עֵד לִשְׂמָאלָא. אִימָּא עִלָּאָה, סִיהֲרָא בִּימִינָא. אֲסוּרָה בְּרַתָּא לְאַבָּא דְּאִיהוּ לִימִינָא חֶסֶד. וְאִיהִי כְּלִילָא מרמ"ח פִּקּוּדִין. אִשְׁתְּכַח ו' עִם אִימָּא לִשְׂמָאלָא. בְּרַתָּא עִם אַבָּא לִימִינָא דְּחֶסֶד. וְרָזָא דְּמִלָּה, בְּחָכְמָה יָסַד אֶרֶץ. חָכְמָה אַבָּא. אֶרֶץ בְּרַתָּא. כּוֹנֵן שָׁמַיִם דְּאִיהוּ בְּרָא, עִם אִימָּא דְּאִיהוּ תְּבוּנָה, וְהַאי אִיהוּ ידד"ו, הֲוָיוֹת בְּאֶמְצַע.

Ra'aya Meheimna (Faithful Shepherd)

678. The Faithful Shepherd said: "Certainly the lambs **are called one-year-old after the sun, which is Holy Ima,** Binah, **about which it is said: 'The face of Moses is as that of the sun,** meaning that he has the Upper Three called 'Face,' from Binah called 'sun.' **A year (*shanah,* 355) contains 365 days,** that is, together with the ten days from Rosh Hashanah to Yom Kippur, **which is the same number as the 365 Negative Precepts. It is a witness to the Left and is Supernal Ima. The moon,** Malchut, **is on the Right side, for the daughter is tied to Aba, which is Chesed on the Right Side. And She,** Malchut, **is composed of the 248 Positive Precepts. It is found that the Vav (ו),** which is Zeir Anpin, **is with Ima on the Left Side,** in the secret of the 365 Negative Precepts, **and the daughter is with Aba on the Right Side, which is Chesed. And the secret of the matter is** in the verse: **'The Lord founded the earth by wisdom....' (Proverbs 3:19) Wisdom refers to Aba,** namely, Chochmah of the Right, which is Chesed. **'Earth is the daughter,** namely, Malchut, and thus the daughter is tied to Aba. **'He established the heavens,' (Ibid.) which is the son,** namely, Zeir Anpin, **with Ima, which is Tevunah. And this results in** the permutation of **Yud-Hei-Hei-Vav, which is the secret of the 'beings' in the middle (יההו).**"

Explanation: Here the Zohar gives a different explanation for the seven lambs from what it explained in verse 675, as there it said that they are the Seven Sefirot of the moon and here it says that they correspond to the Seven Sefirot of the sun, which is Zeir Anpin. This is: **"the** lambs **are called one-year-old after the sun, which is Holy Ima,"** namely Zeir Anpin called the Light of the sun, which receives from Holy Ima, as He is called "sun," from the point of view of the Light of the Left He receives from Holy Ima. This is: **"about which is said: The face of Moses**, who is Zeir Anpin, **is as that of the sun,"** for when he receives from Ima his face is considered as the sun in its might. "**A** solar **year contains 365 days, like the number of the 365 negative precepts,"** as the 365 Negative Precepts are the secret of the Mochin of the Left. **"It is a witness to the Left,"** since the Mochin are referred to as "Eden" (עדן) and as "*ed*" (עד; witness), thus the Mochin of the 365 days of the solar year are a witness to the Left, namely the Illumination of Chochmah of the Left. **"and is Supernal Ima,"** as they are drawn from Supernal Ima.

The seven one-year-old lambs that are brought correspond to the Seven Sefirot of Zeir Anpin, as they draw down to Him the Illumination of Chochmah of the Left from Ima. This is why they are one-year-old, namely from the 365 solar days, which are the Mochin of the Left of Ima. But **"the moon,** which is Malchut, **the daughter is tied to Aba, which is Chesed on the Right Side."** Malchut is tied with the Mochin of Aba, which is Chochmah of the Right, which is the Light of Chasadim, since its own Chochmah was stored away and hidden, and it only shines with the Light of Chesed.

"And she, Malchut, **is composed of the 248 Positive Precepts,"** which are Chesed. It is found that through the sacrifice of Rosh Chodesh, each one receives what it lacks. Zeir Anpin, whose source is Chasadim without Chochmah, receives now through the sacrifice the Chochmah of the Left, which is from Ima. Malchut, whose source is Chochmah of the Left and only lacks Chasadim, receives Chasadim from Supernal Aba. This is: **"It is found that the Vav (ו),** which is Zeir Anpin, **is with Ima on the left side,"** as He receives from Ima the Chochmah of the Left, which he lacked. **"The daughter is with Aba on the Right Side, which is Chesed."** The daughter is found with Aba, the Chochmah of the Right, which is Chesed that She lacks.

"This results in the permutation of **Yud-Hei-Hei-Vav,"** where the lower Hei, Malchut, is after the Yud, which is Aba; and the upper Hei, Ima, is before the Vav, which is Zeir Anpin [so the order is Aba, Malchut, Ima, Zeir Anpin].

"'...beings' in the middle (יההו)." Usually the four portions of the Tefilin are in the order of the Yud-Hei-Vav-Hei. Yud is "Sanctify to Me..." (Exodus 13:1–10); the upper Hei is "It shall be when the Lord brings you..." (Exodus 13:11–16); Vav is "Hear, Israel ..." (Deuteronomy 6:4–9); and the lower Hei is "It shall be if you observe My Commandments...." (Deuteronomy 11:13-21) However, in the previously mentioned order of "Father establishes the daughter," (Zohar, Pinchas 841) the two "beings" are in the middle, meaning the two portions that begin with "It shall be" (Exodus 13:11 and Deuteronomy 11:13), for they are the secret of the two Heis, and "Sanctify to Me" that is Yud is in the beginning, and "Hear, Israel" that is Vav is at the end, namely in the order of Yud-Hei-Hei-Vav.

102. A he-goat to Azazel

A Synopsis

Moses says that the goat for Azazel is a bribe to assuage Sama"el's anger and to prevent him from drawing near the Temple and making accusations against Israel.

He also tells us why the goat is sent by the hand of a crippled man, and how the goat bears all of Israel's iniquities.

The Azazel goat is a bribe to break Sama"el's anger.

679. וְעוֹד וּשְׂעִיר עִזִּים אֶחָד, תְּרֵין שְׂעִירִין אִינּוּן, דְּאִתְּמַר עֲלַיְיהוּ וְלָקַח אֶת שְׁנֵי הַשְּׂעִירִים וְגוֹ' גּוֹרָל אֶחָד לַיְיָ' וְגוֹרָל אֶחָד לַעֲזָאזֵל. שְׂעִיר לַיְיָ', בְּגִין מִיעוּט סִיהֲרָא, וְאִיהוּ שְׂעִיר אֶחָד לַיְדֹוָ"ד לְחַטָּאת. אֶחָד: מִסִּטְרָא דְּיִחוּדָא. אֲבָל שְׂעִיר דַּעֲזָאזֵל, לָא כְּתִיב בֵּיהּ אֶחָד, לָא קָרְבָּן, וְלָא אִשֶּׁה, וְלָא עוֹלָה. אֶלָּא וְשִׁלַּח בְּיַד אִישׁ עִתִּי הַמִּדְבָּרָה. וְשִׁלַּח, כְּדְאָמַר יַעֲקֹב מִנְחָה הִיא שְׁלוּחָה לַאדֹנִי לְעֵשָׂו. אוּף הָכִי שׁוֹחַד, לְתַבְרָא רוּגְזָא דְּסָמָא"ל, דְּלָא יִתְקְרִיב לְמַקְדְּשָׁא לְקַטְרְגָא.

679. "Another explanation for: **'…one he-goat….' (Numbers 29:11) There are two goats, about which it is said: "And he shall take the two goats… one lot for the Lord, and the other lot for Azazel.' (Leviticus 16:7-8) The goat that is for the Lord** is an atonement **for the diminishment of the moon, and it is 'one he-goat for a sin offering to the Lord….' (Numbers 28:15)** It is therefore referred to as **'one'** because it is **from the side of unity. But the goat for Azazel is not referred to as 'one,' neither is it called 'a sacrifice,' 'a fire offering,' nor 'a burnt offering,' but '…shall send him away by the hand of an appointed man into the wilderness.' (Leviticus 16:21) '…and shall send away…' (Ibid.) is as Jacob said,** '**…it is a present sent to my lord Esau….' (Genesis 32:19) Likewise,** the goat for Azazel **is a bribe to**

break Sama"el's anger so that he should not draw near the Temple, to denounce it.

Transforming the enemy to an advocate.

680. לְכַלְבָּא דְּאִיהוּ רָעֵב, וּמַאן דְּבָעֵי דְּלָא נָשִׁיךְ לֵיהּ, יָהִיב לֵיהּ בִּשְׂרָא לְמֵיכַל, אוֹ נַהֲמָא, וְיַשְׁקֵי לֵיהּ מַיָּא. וְרָזָא דְּמִלָּה, אִם רָעֵב שׂוֹנַאֲךָ הַאֲכִילֵהוּ לֶחֶם וְגוֹ'. וּבְדָא יִתְהַדַּר רְחִימוּ דב"נ, דְּלָא דַּיי דְּלָא נָשִׁיךְ לֵיהּ בְּכַמָּה יִסּוּרִין, אֶלָּא אִתְהַדַּר לְמֶהֱוֵי לֵיהּ סַנֵּיגוֹרָא, וְאִתְהַדַּר רְחִימוֹי.

680. "It is like **a hungry dog; whoever does not want to be bitten by it gives it meat or bread to eat and water to drink. And the secret of the matter is contained in the verse: 'If your enemy be hungry, give him bread to eat; and if he be thirsty, give him water to drink.' (Proverbs 25:21) He thereby becomes friendly toward the person, and not only does it not bite him with many afflictions, but it becomes an advocate for him and loves him."**

Anything from the Other Side is defective and full of blemishes.

681. וַאֲמַאי הֲווֹ שַׁלְחִין לֵיהּ בְּיַד אִישׁ עִתִּי, פָּגִים. בְּגִין דִּסְטְרִין אַחֲרָנִין כֻּלְּהוּ מָארֵי מוּמִין, וְאִתְקְרִיאוּ שְׂעִירִים, דִּכְתִּיב וּשְׂעִירִים יְרַקְּדוּ שָׁם. וְאִתְּמַר בְּהוֹן, וְלֹא יִזְבְּחוּ עוֹד אֶת זִבְחֵיהֶם לַשְּׂעִירִים. דַּעֲלַיְיהוּ אִתְּמַר, יִזְבְּחוּ לַשֵּׁדִים לֹא אֱלוֹהַּ. וּבְשָׂעִיר דָּא, אִתְפְּרַשׁ מִכֹּלָּא, וְנוֹשֵׂא כָּל חוֹבִין דְּיִשְׂרָאֵל עָלֵיהּ, כד"א, וְנָשָׂא הַשָּׂעִיר עָלָיו אֶת כָּל עֲוֹנוֹתָם. וְעוֹד, בָּתַר דְּנָטִיל אִיהוּ וְנָשָׂא. קוּדְשָׁא בְּרִיךְ הוּא נוֹשֵׂא עָוֹן. מַאי בֵּין נוֹשֵׂא לְנָשָׂא. נָשָׂא: מְטוּלָא. נוֹשֵׂא: סְלִיקוּ דִּמְטוּלָא.
עַד כָּאן רַעְיָא מְהֵימְנָא

681. He asks, **"Why is** the goat **sent** to Azazel **by the hand of an appointed man who is crippled?"** He answers, **"Because all of the Other Sides are defective, and are called 'goats' (*se'irim*), as it is written: '…and demons (*se'irim*) shall dance there.' (Isaiah 13:21) And about them it is said: 'And they shall no more offer their**

sacrifices to the demons (*se'irim*)...' (Leviticus 17:7) and also 'They sacrificed to powerless spirits....' (Deuteronomy 32:17) And with this goat to Azazel, Sama"el **is separated from everything and bears all the transgressions that are in Israel upon him, as it is written: 'And the goat shall bear upon it all their iniquities....' (Leviticus 16:22) And furthermore, after that** Azazel **takes all** the transgressions **and bears them,** namely, that the Holy One, blessed be He, shall bear and forgive, **the Holy One, blessed be He, is called '... forgiving (bearing) iniquity... (Exodus 34:7),** and about the goat for Azazel it is written: 'And the goat shall bear upon it all their iniquities...' (Leviticus 16:22)" He asks: **"What is the difference between these two types of bearing?"** He answers: **"'Bear' means** carrying **a burden, while 'bearing'** means **the removal of the burden,** namely that He atones for the iniquities. And all of this is explained above.

End of Ra'aya Meheimna (Faithful Shepherd)

120. Yom Kippur

A Synopsis

The Zohar tells us that Yom Kippur is from the Tree of Life, where no evil has any part. On that day, even those people who are under a sentence of Judgment are forgiven. We hear about the difference between vows and oaths, and about the iniquities of Israel that are purified or whitened through repentance. We learn that on Yom Kippur, a Shofar raises up a voice for freedom. There are three grades of worship on that day: thought, speech, and deed.

The tenth day is Yud and the five prayers are Hei to unite Chochmah with Binah.

807. וּבֶעָשׂוֹר לַחוֹדֶשׁ הַשְּׁבִיעִי, דְּאִיהוּ תִּשְׁרֵי. מִקְרָא קֹדֶשׁ יִהְיֶה לָכֶם, דָּא יוֹם הַכִּפּוּרִים. דְּאִיהוּ עֲשִׂירִי י', כָּלִיל מֵעֲשֶׂרֶת יְמֵי תְּשׁוּבָה. וְתַקִּינוּ בֵּיהּ ה' צְלוֹתִין,

לְחַבְּרָא עִם ה'. מַאי מִקְרָא קֹדֶשׁ. לְאַפְרְשָׁא לֵיהּ מִשְּׁאַר יוֹמִין, דְּאִית בְּהוֹ פּוּלְחָנָא דְּחוֹל. וּבְגִין דָּא, כָּל מְלֶאכֶת עֲבוֹדָה לֹא תַעֲשׂוּ.

807. "On the tenth day of the same seventh month..." (Numbers 29:7) which is the month of Tishrei, "...a calling of holiness shall there be for you." (Ibid.) This is Yom Kippur, which is the tenth, which is Yud, which is comprised of the Ten Days of Repentance. Five prayer services were ordained for it in order to join the Yud (י; 10) with the Hei (ה; 5), namely Chochmah with Binah. [He asks:] **"What is the meaning of 'a calling of holiness'?"** [He answers]: **It is to differentiate it from other days when secular work is permitted, and because of this: '...you shall not do any work.' (Ibid.)**

Only the Tree of Life reigns on Yom Kippur.

808. דְּיוֹמִין דְּאִית בְּהוֹן מְלֶאכֶת חוֹל, אִינּוּן מִסִּטְרָא דְּעֵץ הַדַּעַת טוֹב וָרָע. דְּאִתְהַפָּךְ מִמַּטֶּה לְנָחָשׁ, וּמִנָּחָשׁ לְמַטֶּה. לְכָל חַד כְּפוּם עוֹבָדוֹי, וְדָא מְטַטְרוֹן מַטֶּה, נָחָשׁ, סָמָאֵל. אֲבָל בְּהַאי יוֹמָא דְּאִיהוּ יוֹם הַכִּפּוּרִים דְּאִתְקְרֵי קֹדֶשׁ, שַׁלְטָא אִילָנָא דְּחַיֵּי, דְּלָא אִשְׁתַּתַּף עִמֵּיהּ שָׂטָן וּפֶגַע רָע. וּמִסִּטְרֵיהּ לֹא יְגֻרְךָ רָע. וּבְגִין דָּא, בֵּיהּ נַיְיחִין עַבְדִּין בְּאִילָנָא דְּחַיֵּי, וּבֵיהּ נָפְקִין לְחֵירוּת, בֵּיהּ נָפְקֵי מִשַּׁלְשְׁלֵיהוֹן.

808. "Because those days on which secular work may be done are from the side of the Tree of Knowledge of Good and Evil, which flips from a rod to a Serpent and from a Serpent to a rod, for each person according to his deeds. Metatr"on is the Rod (*Mateh*), and **Sama"el** is the **Serpent. But on this day, which is Yom Kippur that is called 'Holy,' the Tree of Life is in control, and no evil adversary and harm joins with it, and from its side "...nor shall evil dwell with You" (Psalms 5:5)** and it is entirely good. **And this is why in it, in the Tree of Life, the slaves find rest and go out to freedom, and emerge from their chains."**

Explanation: The days of the week are Chesed, Gevurah, Tiferet, Netzach, Hod, and Yesod of Metatr"on, who is drawn from the side of the Tree of Knowledge of Good and Evil, which is Malchut. Therefore on the weekdays, Good and Evil reign. If one merits, he cleaves to Metatr"on called "Rod (*Mateh*)." If one does not merit, he cleaves to Sama"el who is Evil and is called a "Serpent." And so it controls man based on his deeds, which is the secret of the rod turning into a Serpent, as the deeds determine if Good or Evil control. But on Yom Kippur, which is called "Holy," the Tree of Life that is Zeir Anpin controls, which is entirely Good and has no place for Satan and Sama"el to have access. One who merits to cleave to Yom Kippur, which is the secret of the Tree of Life, already leaves the Realm of the shifting of the Rod to the Serpent and merits to be cleaved to it eternally, and thus no Evil can control him. This is the secret of the verse: **"...nor shall evil dwell with You" (Psalms 5:5)** which is said about the one who merits to cleave to the Tree of Life. This is: **"in it they go out to freedom and emerge from their chains"** because then they become free from the battle of Good and Evil, and they emerge from the chains of the Other Side forever.

The purpose of Kol Nidrei on Yom Kippur.

809. אִינּוּן דְּאִית עָלַיְיהוּ גְּזַר דִּין, בְּנֶדֶר וּבִשְׁבוּעָה, וּבְגִין דָּא תַּקִּינוּ לְמֵימַר בֵּיהּ, כָּל נִדְרֵי וְאֵיסָרֵי וְכוּ', כּוּלְּהוֹן יְהוֹן שְׁבִיתִין וּשְׁבִיקִין לָא שְׁרִירִין וְלָא קַיָּימִין. וּבְגִין דָּא נֶדֶר דַּיְדֹוָ"ד, דְּאִיהוּ תִּפְאֶרֶת. וּשְׁבוּעָה דַּאֲדֹנָי, דְּאִיהוּ מַלְכוּת. דְּעַבְדוּ עַל גָּלוּתָא דִּלְהוֹן, בְּחָכְמָה וּבִינָה יְהוֹן שְׁבִיקִין וּשְׁבִיתִין לָא שְׁרִירִן וְלָא קַיָּימִין, וְנִסְלַח לְכָל עֲדַת בְּנֵי יִשְׂרָאֵל. דְּחֶסֶד אִיהוּ מַיִם. גְּבוּרָה אֵשׁ. תִּפְאֶרֶת אֲוִיר. וּבְגִין דָּא אוּקְמוּהָ מָארֵי מַתְנִיתִין, הֶתֵּר נְדָרִים פּוֹרְחִים בַּאֲוִיר.

809. [Concerning] **those over whom there is a verdict,** a verdict not to be changed **under vow or oath, it was decreed for this reason that the following shall be recited: "All vows (*kol nidrei*), bonds... they shall all of them be released and annulled; they shall not be binding, nor shall they have any power."** (Kol Nidrei Prayer) But the verdict shall be voided from them. **And this is why the vow is in the Name of Yud-Hei-Vav-Hei (יהוה), which is Tiferet, while the oath is in the Name of Alef-Dalet-Nun-Yud (אדני), which is Malchut, for they caused their own exile** through their sins. And now, **by means of Chochmah and Binah, "they… will be released and annulled; they shall not be binding, nor shall they have any power'. (Kol Nidrei Prayer) "And all the congregation of the children of Israel… shall be forgiven…." (Numbers 15:26) Chesed is Water, Gevurah is Fire, and Tiferet is Air,** and since the vows are in Tiferet, which is Air, **the sages of the Mishnah therefore taught: the dissolution of vows flies in the air,** for the dissolution from Chochmah and Binah flies in the air, which is Tiferet, and from there annuls the vow.

The difference between an oath and a vow.

810. וּבְגִין דִּשְׁבוּעָה מִמַּלְכוּת, דְּאִיהִי לְתַתָּא מִינַּיְיהוּ. אוֹקְמוּהָ, נְדָרִים עַל גַּבֵּי שְׁבוּעוֹת עוֹלִים. וְעוֹד אוֹקְמוּהָ, כָּל הַנִּשְׁבָּע כְּאִילּוּ נִשְׁבַּע בַּמֶּלֶךְ עַצְמוֹ. וְכָל הַנּוֹדֵר כְּאִילּוּ נוֹדֵר בְּחַיֵּי הַמֶּלֶךְ. הַמֶּלֶךְ עַצְמוֹ, אֲדֹנָ"י. חַיֵּי הַמֶּלֶךְ, יְדֹוָ"ד. וּבְגִין דָּא כִּי יִדּוֹר נֶדֶר לַיְדֹוָ"ד.

810. And since the oath (*shvu'a*) is from Malchut, which is below the vow (*neder*), which is Tiferet, **they taught that vows are higher than oaths, and they also taught: Everyone who swears an oath it is as though he swears on the King Himself, and everyone who vows a vow it is as though he does so on the life of the King Himself. The King Himself** refers to **Alef-Dalet-Nun-Yud (אדני),** which is Malchut. **The life of the King** refers to **Yud-Hei-Vav-Hei (יהוה),** which is Zeir Anpin, from whom the life flows to the King, which is Malchut. **And for this reason,** it is written: **"If a man vow a vow to the Lord (Yud-Hei-Vav-Hei)…" (Numbers 30:3)** which is Zeir Anpin.

A vow relates to Chochmah, an oath relates to Binah.

811. וְאוּף הָכִי אִית רָזָא אַחֲרָא, חַיֵּי הַמֶּלֶךְ, חָכְמָה. הה"ד הַחָכְמָה תְּחַיֶּה בְעָלֶיהָ. כָּל הַנּוֹדֵר בַּיהֹוָה, דְּאִיהוּ תִּפְאֶרֶת. כְּאִילּוּ נוֹדֵר בַּחָכְמָה, דְּאִיהוּ יו"ד ה"א וא"ו ה"א, חַיֵּי הַמֶּלֶךְ. וְכָל הַנִּשְׁבַּע בַּאדנ"י, כְּאִילּוּ נִשְׁבַּע בַּמֶּלֶךְ עַצְמוֹ. עַצְמוֹ דָּא אִימָּא עִלָּאָה, כְּאִילּוּ נִשְׁבַּע בָּהּ, דְּאִיהִי עֶצֶם הַשָּׁמַיִם לָטוֹהַר. מִסִּטְרָא דְּחֶסֶד, עֶצֶם מֵעֲצָמַי. וּבָשָׂר מִבְּשָׂרִי, מִסִּטְרָא דִּגְבוּרָה, דָּא מַלְכוּת. וּבְחָכְמָה דְּאִיהִי חַיֵּי תִּפְאֶרֶת, אִיהוּ סָלִיק לְאִתְקְרֵי אָדָם, הה"ד כְּתִפְאֶרֶת אָדָם.

811. And here too, there is another secret: The life of the King refers to Chochmah, as it is written: "...wisdom gives life to those who have it." (Ecclesiastes 7:12) Therefore **everyone who vows on Yud-Hei-Vav-Hei, which is Tiferet, it is as if he vowed upon Chochmah** of Zeir Anpin, **which is** Yud-Hei-Vav-Hei spelled out with Alefs, like this: **Yud-Vav-Dalet, Hei-Alef, Vav-Alef-Vav, Hei-Alef (יוד הא ואו הא), which is the Life of the King,** which is the Life of Zeir Anpin. **Whoever swears an oath on Alef-Dalet-Nun-Yud it is as though he swore on the King Himself. This is because Himself (*Atzmo*) is Supernal Ima,** Binah, and it is **as though he had sworn on Her, as She is "... like the heaven itself (*etzem*) for purity" (Exodus 24:10),** namely the Mochin of Malchut. **For from the aspect of Chesed** Malchut is called **"...bone (*etzem*) of my bones...." (Genesis 2:23) But from the aspect of Gevurah Malchut is called "and flesh of my flesh" (Ibid.), and in Chochmah, which is the life of Tiferet,** namely its Mochin, **it,** Tiferet, **rises up to be called "man" (*adam*),** which is 45 in numerical value, **as it is written: "...the beauty (*tiferet*) of a man...." (Isaiah: 44:13)** For Tiferet is called "man" when it has the Mochin of Chochmah, which is the secret of why He is called by Yud-Hei-Vav-Hei spelled out with Alefs, that has the numerical value of 45.

The five afflictions allude to the purification of the Lower Hei in the Upper Hei.

812. וְאִתְּמַר בְּיוֹם הַכִּפּוּרִים. וְעִנִּיתֶם אֶת נַפְשׁוֹתֵיכֶם. וּבֶעָשׂוֹר לַחֹדֶשׁ הַשְּׁבִיעִי הַזֶּה תְּעַנּוּ אֶת נַפְשׁוֹתֵיכֶם. תַּקִּינוּ בֵּיהּ ה' עִנּוּיִים, בְּגִין דְּתִתְלַבֵּן ה' זְעֵירָא בְּה' עִלָּאָה, דְּאִיהוּ ה' צְלוֹתִין. לְקַיֵּים בְּיִשְׂרָאֵל, אִם יִהְיוּ חֲטָאֵיכֶם כַּשָּׁנִים כַּשֶּׁלֶג יַלְבִּינוּ. וְהַאי אִיהוּ רָזָא דְּלָשׁוֹן שֶׁל זְהוֹרִית, בְּגִין דְּכָל חוֹבִין דְּיִשְׂרָאֵל מָטוֹן לְגַבֵּי מַלְכוּת. וּתְשׁוּבָה דְּאִיהִי בִּינָה, מְלַבֶּנֶת לוֹן. בְּגִין דְּאִתְּמַר בָּהּ, הַשּׁוֹכֵן אִתָּם בְּתוֹךְ טוּמְאוֹתָם. וְד' בִּגְדֵי לָבָן, וְד' בִּגְדֵי זָהָב לְמִלְבַּשׁ, יְאֲהדְוֹנָהִי.

812. And it is said about Yom Kippur: "...and you shall afflict your souls..." (**Numbers 29:7**) and also: **"...In the seventh month, on the tenth day of the month, you shall afflict your souls...."** (**Leviticus 16:29**) **And five afflictions were decreed for it, so that the small Hei,** Malchut, **will be whitened by the Upper Hei,** Binah, as the afflictions come from her Left Column, **which are five prayers, to establish in Israel: "...though your sins be like scarlet, they shall be as white as snow...."** (**Isaiah 1:18**) **And this is the secret of the crimson colored strip,** which was tied to the door of the Sanctuary [Holy of Holies] from inside, which, when the he-goat reached the wilderness, turned white. (Tractate Yoma 67a) **All the iniquities of the House of Israel reach to Malchut; and Repentance, which is Binah, whitens them, for about** Malchut **it is written:** I am the Lord **"Who dwells among them in the midst of their uncleanness."** (**Leviticus 16:16**) **And the four garments of white and the four garments of gold for apparel are** the secret of **Yud-Alef-Hei-Dalet-Vav-Nun-Hei-Yud** (**יאהדונהי**), which is the combination of the letters of Yud-Hei-Vav-Hei (**יהוה**) and those of Alef-Dalet-Nun-Yud (**אדני**). For the four garments of white are the secret of the four letters of Yud-Hei-Vav-Hei while the four garments of gold are the secret of the four letters of Alef-Dalet-Nun-Yud.

The Shofar of Yom Kippur.

813. וְתַקִּינוּ לְתְקוֹעַ שׁוֹפָר בְּיוֹם הַכִּפּוּרִים, לְסַלְּקָא קוֹל דְּאִיהוּ ו', לְחֵרוּת. דְּאִתְּמַר בָּהּ, בְּכָל צָרָתָם לוֹ צָר, בְּא', וּבְו', קְרֵי וּכְתִיב. וַעֲבוֹדַת יוֹם הַכִּפּוּרִים אִיהִי בַּאֲרִיכוּת, וְאִיהִי כְּלִילָא מִתְּלַת דַּרְגִּין, בְּמַחֲשָׁבָה דִּבּוּר וּמַעֲשֶׂה.

813. And it was decreed that a Shofar be sounded on Yom Kippur, to raise up a Voice, which is Vav (ו) of Yud-Hei-Vav-Hei, namely Zeir Anpin, **to freedom,** which is Binah, **about which it is said: "In all their troubles He was troubled (*lo tzar;* לוֹ צָר)…." (Isaiah 63:9)** [The word] *lo* is [is spelled] **with Alef (לא) and Vav (לו),** namely **in how it is pronounced and written,** for it is spelled with Alef (לא; not), although pronounced with Vav (לו; He was). For "…in all their troubles…" alludes to the five afflictions and the Judgments whose source is in Binah, in its Left Column. And in the secret of the Shofar Blowing, Zeir Anpin is also raised up there to Binah, and this is why there are two versions of the text, as written and as read, with an Alef (לא צר; He was not troubled) and with a Vav (לו צר; He was troubled), where the Alef alludes to Binah, in the secret of *elaf binah* (teach understanding), and the Vav alludes to Zeir Anpin that ascended to Binah. **And worship on Yom Kippur is conducted at length and comprises three grades: thought, speech, and deed.**

Tikunei HaZohar: Sixth Tikkun

Yom Kippur is likened to Noah's ark

32. וְאִיהִי בְּעַד הַחַלּוֹן נִשְׁקְפָה וַתְּיַבֵּב בִּתְרוּעָה, דְּאִיהוּ יְבָבָא, דְּאִתְּמַר בָּהּ וַיִּפְתַּח נֹחַ אֶת חַלּוֹן הַתֵּבָה אֲשֶׁר עָשָׂה, וְדָא יוֹם הַכִּפּוּרִים, דְּתֵיבַת נֹחַ הִיא אִימָּא עִלָּאָה, חַלּוֹן דִּילָהּ הוּא עַמּוּדָא דְאֶמְצָעִיתָא, דְּבֵיהּ אוֹר, וְתוֹרָה אוֹר, וְאִיהוּ אוֹר הַגָּנוּז. וַיִּפֶן כֹּה וָכֹה, מֵצִיץ מִן הַחֲרַכִּים, אִלּוּ עֲשֶׂרֶת יְמֵי תְּשׁוּבָה. וַיַּרְא כִּי אֵין אִישׁ.

32. And she, Binah: **"Through the window she looked forth, and peered..."** (Judges 5:28) **with a Teru'ah, that is moaning. As is said of** Binah: **"Noah opened the window of the ark that he had made."** (Genesis 8:6) **This refers to Yom Kippur, as Noah's ark is the Supernal Ima,** Binah. **Her window is the Central Column,** Zeir Anpin, **in which there is Light,** according to the secret of: **"...and Torah is Light"** (Proverbs 6:23) since Zeir Anpin is considered Torah. **This is the Hidden Light (Or haGanuz),** in the secret of "the mother lends to her daughter from her own." **"And he looked this way and that (KoH and KoH) way,"** to illuminate the Fifty Gates of Binah. **"He peers through the lattices" are the ten intermediate days of repentance** [between Rosh Hashanah and Yom Kippur], **and "he saw that there was no man."**

The Creator watches us in exile through a window.

33. וְעוֹד, מַשְׁגִּיחַ מִן הַחַלּוֹנוֹת, אִלֵּין חַלּוֹנוֹת דְּבֵי כְנִישְׁתָּא, דְּאַבָּא וּבְנוֹי אִינּוּן בְּבֵית אֲסִירָן וְאִיהוּ בְּכָל יוֹמָא אַשְׁגָּחוּתֵיהּ עֲלַיְהוּ, וְיָהִיב לוֹן מְזוֹנָא. וַיִּפֶן כֹּה וָכֹה, אִם אִית מָאן דְּיִתְעַר בִּתְיוּבְתָּא לְתַבְרָא בֵּית אֲסוּרִין דִּלְהוֹן, הֲדָא הוּא דִכְתִיב לֵאמֹר לַאֲסוּרִים צֵאוּ וְלַאֲשֶׁר בַּחֹשֶׁךְ הִגָּלוּ.

33. It could **also** be explained: **"He looks through the windows," as referring to the windows of the synagogue because the father and**

the children, namely the Holy One, blessed be He, and Israel **are in the jailhouse** during exile. **And He watches over them daily and provides** Israel **their sustenance: "And he looked this way and that"** to see **if there is anyone awakened to repent** in order **to break down their own jailhouse, as is written: "Saying to the prisoners, 'Go forth;' to them that are in darkness, 'show yourselves.'"** (Isaiah 49:9)

Those who bark their prayers in self-interest.

34. וַיִּפֶן כֹּה וָכֹה וַיַּרְא כִּי אֵין אִישׁ. אֶלָּא אִישׁ לְדַרְכּוֹ פָּנוּ, בַּעֲסָקִין דִּלְהוֹן, בְּאוֹרְחִין דִּלְהוֹן. אִישׁ לְבִצְעוֹ מִקָּצֵהוּ, בְּבִצְעָא דְּהַאי עָלְמָא, לְיָרְתָא הַאי עָלְמָא. וְלַאו אִינּוּן מִסִּטְרָא דְּאִלֵּין, דְּאִתְּמַר בְּהוֹן, אַנְשֵׁי חַיִל יִרְאֵי אֱלֹקִ"ים אַנְשֵׁי אֱמֶת שׂוֹנְאֵי בָצַע, אֶלָּא כֻּלְּהוּ צָוְוחִין בִּצְלוֹתִין בְּיוֹמָא דְּכִפּוּרֵי, כְּכַלְבִּים, הַב הַב לָנָא מְזוֹנָא וּסְלִיחוּ וְכַפָּרָה וְחַיֵּי, כָּתְבֵנוּ לְחַיִּים. וְאִינּוּן עַזֵּי נֶפֶשׁ, כְּכַלְבִּים דְּאִינּוּן אוּמִין דְּעָלְמָא, דְּצָוְוחֵי לְגַבֵּיהּ, וְלֵית לוֹן בֹּשֶׁת אַנְפִּין.

34. "And he looked this way and that, and…he saw that there was no man," (Exodus 2:12) **rather, each to his own way, bent on their own business, and their own ways: "each one to their own gain, one and all…."** (Isaiah 56:11) All turn to their gain, from every quarter, **to have profit in this world, in order to inherit this world, and they do not have qualities of these** men **of whom it says: "Able and God-fearing men, men of truth, hating unjust gain…."** (Exodus 18:21) **But they bark their prayers on Yom Kippur, like dogs: "Give, give us sustenance, forgiveness, atonement, and longevity, record us for life." And they are insolent as those idol worshippers that scream to Him and are not ashamed** to pray and plead just for their own benefit.

Kindness with an agenda.

35. דְּלָא אִית מָאן דְּקָרָא לֵיהּ בִּתְיוּבְתָּא, לְמֶהֱדַר לְגַבֵּיהּ. וְאִדַּמְיָין לִכְלָבִים, דְּאִתְּמַר בְּהוֹן וַיִּתְעָרְבוּ בַגּוֹיִם וַיִּלְמְדוּ מַעֲשֵׂיהֶם. וְאִינּוּן עֵרֶב רַב, דְּכָל חֶסֶד דְּעָבְדִין, לְגַרְמַיְיהוּ עָבְדִין.

35. For there is no one who calls to the Holy One blessed be He, **to repent and return to Him. And they are likened to dogs, of whom is said: "But mingled themselves with the nations, and learned their works."** (Psalms 106:35) **These are the mixed multitudes (erev rav),** derived from "mingle," **that any kindness they do is for their own benefit** and not for the sake of their Creator.

Praying for spiritual blessings.

36. וְעוֹד, אִינּוּן שָׁאֲלִין מְזוֹנָא וְכִסוּיָא וְעוֹנָה דְאִיהוּ עוֹנַת זִוּוּגַיְיהוּ, דְאִתְּמַר בָּהּ, שְׁאֵרָהּ כְּסוּתָהּ וְעֹנָתָהּ לֹא יִגְרָע. וְלָא אִית מָאן דְּשָׁאִיל מְזוֹנָא, דְאִיהוּ תוֹרָה, שְׁאֵרָהּ דִּשְׁכִינְתָּא, וְאִיהִי אִימָא עִלָּאָה, דְאִתְּמַר בָּהּ וְאַל תִּטֹּשׁ תּוֹרַת אִמֶּךָ, כְּסוּתָהּ: דָּא כִּסוּיָא דְצִיצִית, וְעַטִּיפוּ דִילֵיהּ. וּתְפִלִּין דְּיָד, דְאִתְּמַר בָּהּ תְּפִלָּה לְעָנִי כִי יַעֲטֹף. וְעוֹנָתָהּ: דָּא קְרִיאַת שְׁמַע בְּעוֹנָתָהּ. דְאִם שְׁלָשׁ אֵלֶּה לֹא יַעֲשֶׂה לָהּ לִשְׁכִינְתָּא, וְיָצְאָה חִנָּם אֵין כָּסֶף, לֵית לֵיהּ כִּסוּפָא מִן שְׁכִינְתָּא, וְחָצוּף אִיהוּ. וְעוֹד אֵין כָּסֶף: לָא יְהֵא לֵיהּ כִּסוּפָא לְעָלְמָא דְאָתֵי.

36. Also, they request and plead for **their food, clothing, and mate [lit. season], meaning their time for mating, as is said "...her food, her clothing, and her conjugal rights, shall he not diminish."** (Exodus 21:10) **But no one requests** spiritual **food, which is the Torah, the sustenance of the Shechinah, who is Supernal Ima,** Binah, **about whom it is said: "And do not forsake the teaching (Torah) of your mother."** (Proverbs 1:8) **"Her clothing" refers to the garment of Tzitzit and its enveloping,** with this fringed Tzitzit blessing: "To envelope in Tzitzit," **and also the arm Tefilin,** which are the Mochin of Malchut in the secret of "weak arm." [See Tikunei Zohar, Introduction 197] **Of it, it is said: "A prayer of the afflicted, when he faints [also: envelops]...."** (Psalms 102:1) **"And her conjugal rights [lit. season]" refers to the Shema reading on time.** Since by the Shema reading, the mating of Aba and Ima is made, in the secret of "her season" because from their union, Mochin flow to Zeir Anpin and Malchut so they could unite during the Amidah prayer, at "Bestow peace" (Sim shalom). **"And if he**

will not do these three to her," to the Shechinah: **"...then she shall go out for nothing, without money (*kesef*)."** (Exodus 21:11) **such a one has no humility before the Shechinah; he is impudent,** likened to impudent dogs. **Money (*kesef*)** can **also** be interpreted as longing (*kisuf*) and craving: **"...he will have no craving for the World to Come."** [See Zohar, Mishpatim 71 and 72]

Tikunei HaZohar: Twenty-First Tikkun

Teshuvah returns the Vav-Hei back to Yud-Hei.

473. וְעוֹד אִיהִי תְּשׁוּבָה, יוֹם הַכִּפּוּרִים, כְּלִילָא מֵעֲשֶׂרֶת יְמֵי תְּשׁוּבָה, דְּאִינּוּן י"ה, יוֹם הַכִּפּוּרִים, דָּא ה', כְּלִילָא מֵחָמֵשׁ צְלוֹתִין. עֲשֶׂרֶת יְמֵי תְּשׁוּבָה, דָּא י'. לְקַבֵּל שָׁבִים דָּא ו"ק, כָּל מָאן דְּהָדַר בִּתְיוּבְתָּא, כְּאִלּוּ הָדַר ו"ה עִם י"ה. וְעִקָּרָא לְסַלְּקָא כֹּלָּא בְּמַחֲשָׁבָה דְּאִיהִי יו"ד ק"א וא"ו ק"א.

473. Furthermore, She, Malchut **is** called **repentance** (see Zohar, Naso 26), and when She ascends to Binah, **She is called Yom haKipurim,** in plural, as is written (Zohar, Emor 224): "Why Yom haKipurim? Because two Lights illuminate together," **consisting of the Ten Days of Repentance** that are from Rosh Hashanah until Yom Kippur, **which are Yud-Hei,** meaning Chochmah and Binah of Binah; because Yud is Chochmah and Hei is in Binah. **Yom Kippur is Hei, consisting of five prayers. The Ten Days of Repentance are Yud. To receive the penitents, this is Vav-Hei,** which are Zeir Anpin and Nukva. **Whoever returns in penitence (*teshuvah*) it is as though he returned Vav-Hei**—which is Zeir Anpin and Nukvah—to unite **with Yud-Hei** because he causes their Mochin that are called Yud-Hei to illuminate in Zeir Anpin and Nukva. **The most important of all** is **to ascend in thought,** which is the Right of Supernal Aba and Ima because "thought" *machshavah* (**מחשבה**) is the letters of *chashav* Mem-Hei (**חשב מה**), and Chochmah is the letters of *ko'ach* Mem-Hei (**כח מה**), **which is** the Name **Yud-Vav-Dalet, Hei-Alef, Vav-Alef-Vav, Hei-Alef** (**יו"ד ה"א וא"ו ה"א**) that numerically equals Mem-Hei (45), which is the secret of the Mochin of Gadlut (Maturity) of Zeir Anpin and Nukva.

Accepting the five afflictions in retribution for the pain we caused Malchut in exile.

475. וְצָרִיךְ בַּר נַשׁ, לְקַבְּלָא עֲלֵיהּ חָמֵשׁ עִנּוּיִין, בְּגִין עִנּוּי דְּגָרִים לַה' זְעֵירָא דְּגָלַת בְּגָלוּתָא, וְאִתְקְרִיאַת עֲנִיָּה סוֹעֲרָה לֹא נוּחָמָה. וְאַבָּא וְאִמָּא אִינּוּן נָחְתֵי בִּימִינָא וּשְׂמָאלָא, לְקַבְּלָא בְּהוֹן ו"ה דְּאִינּוּן תּוֹרָה וּמִצְוָה, וְרָזָא דְּמִלָּה, וָשָׁב וְרָפָא לוֹ, וְדָא אִיהוּ שׁוּבָה יִשְׂרָאֵל עַד יְיָ' אֱלֹקֶי"ךָ.

475. A person needs to accept upon himself five afflictions on Yom Kippur, which are: eating and drinking, bathing, anointing, conjugal relations, and leather shoes **because of the affliction he caused** through his sins **to the smaller Hei,** which is Malchut, **that was banished into exile and is called: "Afflicted one, tossed with tempest, and not comforted…." (Isaiah 54:11) And Aba and Ima,** who are Chochmah and Binah that are called **Yud-Hei, descend to the Right and Left to receive Vav-Hei,** which are Zeir Anpin and Nukva that are called **Torah and Precept (Mitzvah). The secret of the matter is: "… return, and be healed." (Isaiah 6:10) as is written: "Return Israel unto the Lord your God…" (Hosea 14:2)** until the Name of God will be completed through you. (See Zohar, Pinchas 807-813)

In Binah the Tetragrammaton is pronounced how it is written.

500. בְּיוֹם הַכִּפּוּרִים דְּאִיהִי עָלְמָא דְאָתֵי, לָא אִתְקְרֵי יקו"ק בְּאדנ"י דְּאִיהִי דִּין, וְאִיהוּ נַעַל, נְעִילַת דֶּלֶת, וְאֵינוֹ נוֹעֵל הַדֶּלֶת, אֶלָּא אִיהִי פְּתִיחָא לְקַבֵּל שָׁבִים, וּבְגִין דָּא, יוֹם הַכִּפּוּרִים אָסוּר בִּנְעִילַת הַסַּנְדָּל, דְּלֵית יִחוּדָא בֵּיהּ לְקוּדְשָׁא בְּרִיךְ הוּא וּשְׁכִינְתָּא. דִּלְזִמְנִין אִיהִי שְׁכִינְתָּא, וְאִסְתַּלַּק קוּדְשָׁא בְּרִיךְ הוּא, וּלְזִמְנִין קוּדְשָׁא בְּרִיךְ הוּא, וְאִסְתַּלַּק שְׁכִינְתָּא.

500. During Yom Kippur, when Malchut ascends to Binah, **which is the World to Come, Yud-Kei-Vav-Kei is not pronounced Adonai (Alef-Dalet-Nun-Yud), which is judgment, lock, and the locking of the door,** because of the judgments in it that lock the door and guard that the Externals do not draw its sustenance. This is not the case on Yom Kippur, when Malchut ascends to Binah and becomes like Binah since the Lower that ascends to the Upper becomes like it. And in Binah there is no access to the Externals, and Chochmah illuminates in Binah without the clothing of Chasadim. Therefore the Name is pronounced as it is written. **And he does not lock the door but rather it is open to accept the penitent,** who are the intermediate ones who are suspended and wait until Yom Kippur; if they repent they are sealed for life. And the secret of the atonement of sins on Yom Kippur is the secret of drawing the Illumination of Chochmah through the Malchut that ascended to Binah, since atonement for sins is only by the revelation of the Light of Chochmah, which is the secret of the Light of Life, in the secret of: "...wisdom (*chochmah*) preserves the life of its possessors." (Ecclesiastes 7:12) **Therefore,** since Malchut shines on Yom Kippur like Binah, without any restrictions, **it is prohibited to lock a shoe on Yom Kippur because on** Yom Kippur **there is no union** and unification **between the Holy One, blessed be He, and the Shechinah,** which are Zeir Anpin and Nukva, **because sometimes,** meaning when they unite there are times when **the Shechinah,** which is Malchut, **does** shine, since She is the Illumination of Chochmah, **and** the Illumination of **the Holy One, blessed be He,** who is Zeir Anpin that shines Chasadim, **departs. And sometimes the Holy One, blessed be He,** shines with the Light of Chasadim **and** the Illumination of Chochmah of **the Shechinah,** which is Malchut, **departs** because then Malchut turns to receive Chasadim, and the Chochmah becomes hidden in Her.

SUKKOT

Noach

14. The Israelite

The following section reveals the hidden secrets and mysteries concerning the holidays of Rosh Hashanah, Yom Kippur, Sukkot, and the First Day of each new month. The Zohar reveals the process by which we utilize these spiritual tools to cleanse our world, and our souls, of the negative residues from our egotistic behavior. We can help facilitate all these processes as we meditate and intently browse through the ancient text.

The sages meet an Israelite on his way to buy the four species.

94. עַד דַּהֲווֹ אָזְלֵי, חָמוּ חַד יוּדָאי דַּהֲוָה אָתֵי, אֲמַר רַבִּי יוֹסֵי, הַאי בַּר נָשׁ יוּדָאי אִיהוּ, וְאִתְחֲזֵי. כַּד מָטָא גַּבַּיְיהוּ, שְׁאִילוּ לֵיהּ, אֲמַר לוֹן, שְׁלִיחָא דְּמִצְוָה אֲנָא, דְּהָא אֲנָן דַּיְירֵי בִּכְפַר דְּרָאמִין, וּמָטֵי זִמְנָא דְּחַג, וַאֲנַן צְרִיכִין לוּלָב, וְזִינִין דְּעִמֵּיהּ, וַאֲנָא אָזֵיל לְקָטְעָא לוֹן לְמִצְוָה, אָזְלוּ כַּחֲדָא.

94. As they were walking along, they saw an Israelite coming toward them. Rav Yosi said: "This person is an Israelite because he looks like an Israelite.**" When he reached them, they asked him** who he was. **He told them "I am an agent to carry out a Precept. I live in the village of Dramin and the time of Sukkot has arrived. We needed a *Lulav* and its species, and I am on my way to cut them down for the purpose of the Precept." They walked together.**

The friends invite the Israelite to share wisdom regarding the species.

95. אֲמַר לְהוֹ הַהוּא יוּדָאי, הַנֵּי אַרְבַּע מִינִין דְּלוּלָב, דִּבְכֻלְּהוֹ אָתְאָן לְרַצּוּיֵי עָלְמָא, שְׁמַעְתּוּן אַמַּאי אֲנַן צְרִיכִין לוֹן בַּחַג. א"ל כְּבָר אִתְעָרוּ בְּהוֹ חַבְרַיָּיא, אֲבָל אִי מִלָּה חַדְתָּא אִיהוּ תְּחוֹת יְדָךְ אֵימָא לָהּ.

95. The Israelite spoke to them and asked, "Have you heard why we need the four species of the *Lulav* to appease the world during this holiday, but not at any other time?" **They told him, "The friends have already explained** the reason of **this subject, but if you have a new explanation, then say it."**

Sukkot is a time to have dominion over the ministers of the nations.

96. אֲמַר לוֹן, וַדַּאי הַהוּא אֲתַר דַּאֲנַן דָּיְירֵי בֵּיהּ, הוּא זְעֵיר, וְכֻלְּהוֹ עָסְקֵי בְּאוֹרַיְיתָא. וְאִית עֲלָן צוֹרְבָא מֵרַבָּנָן, רַבִּי יִצְחָק בַּר יוֹסֵי מֵחוֹזָאָה שְׁמֵיהּ, וּבְכָל יוֹמָא וְיוֹמָא אֲמַר לָן מִלִּין וַחֲדָתִין בְּאוֹרַיְיתָא. וַאֲמַר, דְּהָא בְּחַג זִמְנָא הוּא, לְשַׁלְטָאָה. אֲזַי עָבַר עַל נַפְשֵׁנוּ הַמַּיִם הַזֵּידוֹנִים, בָּרוּךְ ה' שֶׁלֹּא נְתָנָנוּ טֶרֶף לְשִׁנֵּיהֶם, וְכִי אִית שִׁינַּיִם לְמַיִם. אֶלָּא אִינּוּן שְׁאָר עַמִּין. אִינּוּן רַבְרְבִין מְמַנָּן עַל שְׁאָר עַמִּין עכו"ם וּמִתְבָּרְכָאן מִסִּטְרַיְיהוּ דְּיִשְׂרָאֵל, וְקָרֵינָן לוֹן מַיִם הַזֵּידוֹנִים, כְּמָא דְּאַתְּ אָמֵר הַמַּיִם הַזֵּידוֹנִים.

96. He said to them, "The place where we dwell is indeed a small one, but everyone deals with the Torah. We have a rabbi, who is well known among the Rabbis, whose name is Rav Yitzchak the son of Rav Yosi from Choza'a. He teaches us new explanations of the Torah each and every day. And he said that in this holiday is the time to have dominion, namely that Israel have dominion over the ministers of the seventy nations. So it is written, **'...then the seething waters have gone over our soul. Blessed be the Lord, who has not given us as a prey to their teeth.' (Psalms 124:5-6)** He asks: **"Does water have teeth?"** He answers: **"They,** the seething waters, **refer to the other nations,** and the 'teeth' refer to **the Supernal ministers of these nations, who are worshippers of the planets and constellations. They are blessed through Israel, and they are called seething waters, as it says 'the malicious waters.'"**

The four species awaken the Holy Name.

97. וּבְגִין לְשַׁלְטָאָה עֲלַיְיהוּ אָתֵינָא בִּרְזָא דִשְׁמָא קַדִּישָׁא, בְּאִינוּן אַרְבַּע מִינִין שֶׁבַּלּוּלָב, לְרַצּוּיֵי לֵיהּ לְקֻדְשָׁא בְּרִיךְ הוּא, וּלְשַׁלְטָאָה עֲלַיְיהוּ בִּרְזָא דִשְׁמָא קַדִּישָׁא, וּלְאַתְעָרָא עֲלָן מַיִין קַדִּישִׁין, לְנַסְכָא עַל גַּבֵּי מַדְבְּחָא.

97. To have dominion over the ministers of the nations **we come with the Holy Name that is represented by those four species of the *Lulav*.** The myrtle is the secret of Chesed, Gevurah and Tiferet from the letter Yud, the willow branches are the secret of Netzach and Hod from the first letter Hei, the ***Lulav*** is the secret of Yesod from the letter Vav, and the *Etrog* is the secret of Malchut, the lower Hei. **Together they appease the Holy One, blessed be He, and rule over them by means of the Holy Name. They bring and arouse upon us the Holy Waters,** namely the abundance of the Upper Waters, **to pour on the altar,** which is Malchut, which subdue the seething waters.

On Rosh Hashanah the Lower Courthouse awakens to judge the world.

98. תּוּ אֲמַר לוֹן, בְּר"ה אִתְעֲרוּתָא קַדְמָאָה אִיהוּ בְּעָלְמָא. מַאי אִתְעֲרוּתָא קַדְמָאָה, דָּא בֵּי דִּינָא דִּלְתַתָּא, דְּאִתְעַר לְמֵידַן עַלְמָא, וְקֻדְשָׁא בְּרִיךְ הוּא יָתֵיב עַל עָלְמָא בְּדִינָא, וְדָאִין עָלְמָא.

8. He further said that on Rosh Hashanah the first awakening reoccurs and appears in the world, which is Nukva. In other words, the Nukva returns to its original state it was in on the Fourth Day of Creation. He asks: **"What is this first awakening?"** He answers: **"It is the Lower Courthouse that is aroused to judge the world, and the Holy One, blessed be He, sits on the Throne of Judgment and judges the world."**

Explanation: Nukva is called "house," and on the Fourth Day of Creation, before She was built, She was situated below the Chest of Zeir Anpin behind Him. She was then full of Judgments and thus called "the Lower Courthouse," meaning below the Chest. Therefore, She judges the world in Judgment, and Zeir Anpin too sits then on the Throne of Judgment and judges the world. This situation is called "the first awakening."

On Yom Kippur the prosecuting Serpent is not present in the world.

99. וְשָׁלְטָא הַאי בֵּי דִינָא, לְמֵידַן עָלְמָא, עַד יוֹמָא דְכִפּוּרֵי, דְּנָהֲרִין אַנְפָּהָא, וְלָא אִשְׁתְּכַח חִוְיָא דִּלְטוֹרָא בְּעָלְמָא, דְּאִיהוּ אִתְעַסַּק בַּמֶּה דְּאַתְיָין לֵיהּ הַהוּא שְׂעִיר, דְּאִיהוּ מִסִּטְרָא דְּרוּחַ מְסָאֲבָא, כִּדְקָא חָזֵי לֵיהּ. וּבְגִין דְּאִתְעַסַּק בְּהַהוּא שְׂעִיר, לָא קָרֵיב לְמַקְדְּשָׁא.

99. "This Courthouse rules and judges the world until Yom Kippur, when Her face lights up, namely when She receives the Upper Three called 'Face,' **and the prosecuting Serpent is not present in the world as he is busy with that goat** to Azazel **that is brought to him, which is from the side of the spirit of defilement, as is appropriate for him,** the prosecutor. **And because he is occupied with that goat, he does not approach the Temple,** the Nukva." In other words, he does not approach to prosecute the children of Israel and separate the unification of Zeir Anpin and Nukva.

The goat of Yom Kippur is similar to the goat of Rosh Chodesh.

100. וְשָׂעִיר דָּא כְּהַהוּא שְׂעִיר דְּר"ח דְּאִתְעַסַּק בֵּיהּ, וְאַנְהִירוּ אַנְפָּהָא דְּמַקְדְּשָׁא. וְעַל דָּא יִשְׂרָאֵל כֻּלְּהוּ, מַשְׁכְּחִין רַחֲמֵי קַמֵּי קֻדְשָׁא בְּרִיךְ הוּא, וְאִתְעֲבַר חוֹבַיְיהוּ. וְרָזָא חָדָא, אֲמַר לוֹן, וְלָא אִתְיְיהֵיב רְשׁוּ לְגַלָּאָה, בַּר לַחֲסִידֵי קַדִּישִׁין עֶלְיוֹנִין וְחַכִּימִין. אֲמַר רַבִּי יוֹסֵי מַאן אִיהוּ, אֲמַר לוֹן, עַד לָא בָּדִיקְנָא בְּכוּ.

100. "This scapegoat is like the goat of the sin-offering of Rosh Chodesh, for he is occupied with it, and thus the face of the Temple, which is the Nukva, **lights up. This is how all Israel find Mercy in the**

eyes of the Holy One, blessed be He, and He removes their sins." The Israelite **said to them, "But there is one secret that may not be revealed, except to exceedingly wise, saintly, and pious men." Rav Yosi asked him, "And what is that secret?" He answered: "I have not yet checked you out,** so I cannot tell whether you are fit to hear this secret."

Nukva is first brought close to Zeir Anpin through the Left Column.

101. אָזְלוּ, לְבָתַר אֲמַר לוֹן, כַּד סִיהֲרָא אִתְקְרִיבַת בְּשִׁמְשָׁא, אַתְעַר קֻדְשָׁא בְּרִיךְ הוּא סִטְרָא דְצָפוֹן, וְאָחִיד בָּהּ בִּרְחִימוּ, וּמָשִׁיךְ לָהּ לְגַבֵּיהּ, וְדָרוֹם אִתְעַר מִסִּטְרָא אָחֳרָא, וְסִיהֲרָא סַלְקָא וּמִתְחַבְּרָא בְּמִזְרָח, וּכְדֵין יָנְקָא מִתְּרֵין סִטְרִין, וְנָטִיל בִּרְכָאן בַּחֲשַׁאי, וּכְדֵין אִתְבָּרְכָא סִיהֲרָא, וְאִתְמַלְיָא. וְהָכָא אִתְקְרִיבַת אִתְּתָא בְּבַעֲלָהּ.

101. They proceeded on their way, and after a while he said to them: "When the moon, the Nukva, **is brought close to the sun,** Zeir Anpin, **then the Holy One, blessed be He, stirs up the northern side,** which is the Left Column that comes from the Shuruk vowel, **and He grasps Her lovingly and draws Her toward Himself.** This is the secret of asking permission and appeasement. **Then the southern side,** which is the Right Column, **is aroused from the other side**, the side of the Chirik vowel**. And the moon,** the Nukva, **rises and unites with the east,** which is Zeir Anpin. **Thus She nourishes from both sides,** from the south and from the north, **and receives the blessings**, namely the abundance of the unification, **in silence**, which is the aspect of the Lower Six from the Chirik vowel, which is the secret of "...and her voice was not heard..." (I Samuel 1:13) since voice and speech refer to the Upper Three. **Then the moon is blessed and is filled** with abundance, **and here a woman approaches her husband.** This is a complete unification that bestows complete Mochin to the world. This teaches us that the order of unification is first Zeir Anpin draws the Illumination of the Left Column to Nukva, which is the secret of the verse, "His left hand was under my head..." (Song of Songs 2:6) and then [He draws] the Right Column, which is the secret of the verse "...and his right hand embraced me." (Ibid.) From the Left comes the Illumination of Chochmah and from the Right comes Chasadim, as is known. Now the Zohar will explain how the snake latches on when the Left Column shines.

Left and Right exist in every level and grade.

102. כְּמָה דְאִית רָזָא דְיוֹקְנָא שַׁיְיפֵי דְאָדָם, וְתִיקּוּנוֹי. הָכֵי נָמֵי אִית רָזָא דִדְיוֹקְנֵי דְשַׁיְיפֵי נוּקְבָא, וְתִקּוּנֵי דְנוּקְבָא. וְכֹלָּא פָּרִישׁ בְּגַוָון. הָכֵי נָמֵי אִית לְעֵילָא, אָחִיד בָּהּ, וְאִתְעַר לְקַבֵּל בִּרְחִימוּ, הַ״נ אִית לְתַתָּא, רָזָא וְתִקּוּנָא דְאָדָם תַּתָּאָה אָחֳרָא, תְּחוֹת סִיהֲרָא.

102. "Just as there is the secret of the shape of the body parts of man, Zeir Anpin **and its composition, so too there is the secret of the shape of the body parts of the Nukva** of Zeir Anpin **and its composition. The only difference between them is their color.** The color green is the secret of Zeir Anpin, while red is the secret of the Nukva. Nevertheless, the shapes of their parts are similar. **Similarly, below Atzilut there is the secret and composition of another, lower man**, from the Other Side, **that is below the moon.** He also has the same shape of body parts, namely Left and Right, and so on. What we learn from this is that all the levels are modeled after one another, such that the shapes of the Upper Level carry down to the Lower one. And the arousal of any one of these aspects arouses an opposite aspect in the other levels, as shall further be explained.

Just as Zeir Anpin holds Nukva with His left, so does the Serpent.

103. כְּמָה דִדְרוֹעָא שְׂמָאלָא לְעֵילָא אָחִיד בָּהּ, וְאִתְעַר לְקַבְלָהּ בִּרְחִימוּ, הָכֵי נָמֵי אִית לְתַתָּא, הַאי נָחָשׁ, אִיהוּ דְרוֹעָא שְׂמָאלָא דְרוּחַ מְסָאֲבָא, וְאָחִיד בֵּיהּ מַאן דְרָכִיב בֵּיהּ, וְקָרְבָא לְגַבֵּי דְסִיהֲרָא, וּמָשִׁיךְ לָהּ בֵּינַיְיהוּ דְקוּטְפָּא וְאִסְתָּאֲבַת.

103. "Just as the left arm Above, in Zeir Anpin, **holds the Nukva and awakens lovingly toward her, so too is there Below** the Nukva, **this Serpent, which is the left arm of the spirit of defilement,** and it is the female aspect of defilement, **who is held by he who rides upon** the Serpent. **He then approaches the moon,** the Nukva, **and draws her,** meaning nourishes from Her, **from between the adhesions,** meaning the place of the mating, **and thus, she is defiled.**

Explanation: There are two points in the Nukva. One is of the attribute of Judgment, which is not fit to receive Mochin due to the First Contraction (Tzimtzum Alef), and it is hidden in Her. The other is of the attribute of Mercy from Binah, where She receives all the Mochin and shines to the world, and it is revealed in Her. This is why She is called the Tree of Knowledge of Good and Evil, because "if man merits, it is good, but if man does not merit, it is evil." (Zohar, Prologue 123) The meaning of this is that if man receives the Illumination of the Left with the corrections of Holiness, which is from below upward, then it is good since he receives from it all the Mochin in completion. But if he does not merit, and he draws the Mochin from above downward, the Serpent then draws near the Nukva and exposes Her point of the attribute of Judgment, which is not fit to receive the Mochin and abundance from Zeir Anpin due to the First Contraction (Tzimtzum Alef). Because of this, even the second point of the attribute of Mercy is corrupted. Thus the unification is disrupted and it is considered as if She became defiled and is no longer fit to unite with Zeir Anpin and receive abundance.

This is: **"He then approaches the moon and draws her from between the adhesions, and thus she is defiled,"** namely he exposes the point of the attribute of Judgment that is hidden between the adhesions. Then **"she is defiled,"** meaning that she can no longer have unification and receive abundance for the world, as explained.

The goat of Rosh Chodesh purifies the Nukva from the defilement of the Serpent.

104. וּכְדֵין יִשְׂרָאֵל לְתַתָּא, מְקָרְבִין שָׂעִיר. וְהַהוּא נָחָשׁ, אִתְמְשַׁךְ אֲבַתְרֵיהּ דְּהַהוּא שָׂעִיר, וְסִיהֲרָא אִתְדְּכִיאַת, וְסַלְקָאת לְעֵילָא, וְאִתְקַשְּׁרַת לְעֵילָא, לְאִתְבָּרְכָא, וּנְהִירִין אַנְפָּהָא, מַה דְּאִתְחַשְּׁכַת לְתַתָּא.

104. "Then, Israel below offer the goat on Rosh Chodesh. Through the goat we sweeten Malchut in Binah and draw the Illumination of the Left from below upward. **The Serpent is drawn to that goat**, since its entire craving is for the Illumination of the Left. **Then the moon is purified,** for she is now fit to receive abundance from her husband, Zeir Anpin. **She then ascends up and clings above** to Zeir Anpin **to be blessed. Whereas before, when she was Below** and had not yet united with Zeir Anpin, **she was dark, now her face lights up.** This explains that the goat of Rosh Chodesh comes to purify the Nukva, namely to draw to Her the Vessels of the attribute of Mercy from Binah, with the Illumination of the Left. With this She returns to her purity. And even though the Serpent can still awaken the point of the attribute of Judgment after she was already revealed to him, he does not do so because he does not want to ruin the Illumination of the left, which he so desires. Thus the prosecutor becomes the defender.

On Yom Kippur we also use the goat to free the Nukva from the Serpent.

105. כְּדֵין הָכָא בְּיוֹמָא דְּכִפּוּרֵי, כֵּיוָן דְּהַהוּא חִוְיָא בִּישָׁא, אִתְעַסַּק בְּהַהוּא שָׂעִיר, סִיהֲרָא אִתְפָּרְשַׁת מִנֵּיהּ, וְאִתְעַסְקַת לְאוֹלְפָא עֲלַיְיהוּ סָנֵיגוֹרְיָא, וְסוֹכֶכֶת עֲלַיְיהוּ, כְּאִמָּא עַל בְּנִין, וְקֻדְשָׁא בְּרִיךְ הוּא בָּרִיךְ לוֹן מִלְּעֵילָּא, וּמָחֵיל לוֹן.

105. "The same is true of Yom Kippur, where since that evil Serpent is kept busy with the goat to Azazel, which is also the drawing down of the Illumination of the Left like the goat of Rosh Chodesh, **the moon is separated from** the snake, as it is occupied with the goat and no longer wishes to prosecute her, **and** the Nukva **is occupied with advocating for Israel and hovers over them as a mother over the children. Then the Holy One, blessed be He, blesses Israel from Above and forgives them** for their sins.

On Sukkot, the Right connects to the Nukva,
and She gives a portion to the ministers of the nations.

106. לְבָתַר, יִשְׂרָאֵל כַּד מָטוֹ לְחַג, מִתְעָרֵי סִטְרָא דִּימִינָא לְעֵילָא, בְּגִין דְּיִתְקַשַּׁר בֵּיהּ סִיהֲרָא, וְיִתְנְהִירוּ אַנְפָּהָא כִּדְקָא יָאוּת. וּכְדֵין פַּלְגַת חוּלָקָא דְּבִרְכָאן, לְכָל אִינּוּן מְמַנָּן דִּלְתַתָּא, דְּיִתְעַסְּקוּן בְּחוּלָקְהוֹן, וְלָא יֵיתוּן לְיַנְקָא וּלְקָרְבָא בְּסִטְרָא דְּחוּלָקְהוֹן דְּיִשְׂרָאֵל.

106. "Later, when Israel reach the holiday of Sukkot, **the Supernal Right Side is aroused,** as alluded to in the verse, '…and his right hand embraces me.' (Song of Songs 2:6) **This allows the moon,** who is the Nukva, **to attach herself to Him,** namely to the Right, **and then her face shines as is suitable. Then she shares her blessings with all the ministers Below,** namely the seventy ministers, **so they are kept occupied with their share and do not approach to nourish from Israel's portion.** As is described with the Serpent and the Nukva, where since it is occupied with the goat it does not prosecute the Nukva.

When the nations are blessed, they do not meddle with Israel.

107. כְּגַוְונָא דָּא לְתַתָּא, כַּד שְׁאָר עַמִּין אִתְבָּרְכוּן, כֻּלְּהוֹן אִינּוּן מִתְעַסְּקִין בְּאַחְסָנַת חוּלָקְהוֹן, וְלָא הֲווֹ אַתְיָין לְאִתְעָרְבָא בַּהֲדַיְיהוּ דְּיִשְׂרָאֵל, וּלְחָמְדָא חוּלַק אַחְסַנְתְּהוֹן, וּבְגִין כָּךְ יִשְׂרָאֵל, אִינּוּן מָשְׁכִין בִּרְכָאן לְכָל אִינּוּן מְמַנָּן, בְּגִין דְּיִתְעַסְּקוּן בְּחוּלָקְהוֹן, וְלָא יִתְעָרְבוּן בַּהֲדַיְיהוּ.

107. "The same applies Below in this world. **When all the other nations are blessed, they all become occupied with their portion and do not meddle with Israel or covet their portion.** Just as we described previously—the Serpent with the Nukva and the seventy supernal ministers with Israel—so is the case with the seventy nations and Israel below. **This is why** during Sukkot, when they offer the seventy bulls as a sacrifice, **Israel draw blessings down to all the Supernal ministers** of the seventy nations, **so they will be occupied with their portion and not meddle with them.**

Only Israel nourish from the blessings gathered Above.

108. וְכַד סִיהֲרָא אִתְמְלֵי בִּרְכָאן לְעֵילָּא, כִּדְקָא יָאוּת, יִשְׂרָאֵל אַתְיָין וְיַנְקִין מִנָּהּ בִּלְחוֹדַיְיהוּ. וְעַל דָּא כְּתִיב בַּיּוֹם הַשְּׁמִינִי עֲצֶרֶת תִּהְיֶה לָכֶם, מַאי עֲצֶרֶת, כְּתַרְגּוּמוֹ, כְּנִישׁוּ. כָּל מַה דִּכְנִישׁוּ, מֵאִינּוּן בִּרְכָאן עִלָּאִין, לָא יָנְקִין מִנֵּיהּ עַמִּין אָחֳרָנִין, בַּר יִשְׂרָאֵל בִּלְחוֹדַיְיהוּ, וּבְגִין כָּךְ כְּתִיב, עֲצֶרֶת תִּהְיֶה לָכֶם, לָכֶם וְלָא לִשְׁאָר עַמִּין, לָכֶם וְלָא לִשְׁאָר מְמַנָּן.

108. "When the moon is full of blessings from Above as is suitable, Israel alone come and nourish from Her. That is why it is written: 'On the eighth day you shall have a solemn assembly (*atzeret*)....' (Numbers 29:35) What is this assembly? It indicates the assembling of the blessings from Above, from which only Israel may draw sustenance, and not the other nations. And that is why it is written: 'There shall be a solemn assembly for you,' (Ibid.) referring specifically **to 'you' and not to the other nations; to you and not to the other Supernal ministers.**

The water libations.

109. וְעַל דָּא אִינּוּן מְרַצִּין עַל הַמַּיִם, לְמֵיהַב לוֹן חוּלַק בִּרְכָאן, דְּיִתְעַסְקוּן בֵּיהּ, וְלָא יִתְעָרְבוּן לְבָתַר, בְּחֶדְוָותָא דְּיִשְׂרָאֵל, כַּד יָנְקִין בִּרְכָאן עִלָּאִין. וְעַל הַהוּא יוֹמָא כְּתִיב, דּוֹדִי לִי וַאֲנִי לוֹ, דְּלָא אִתְעָרַב אוּחֲרָא בַּהֲדָן.

109. "This is the reason why Israel **appease** the Holy One, blessed be He, **with water libations** upon the altar, **to give the Supernal ministers**

of the nations **part of the blessings, so that they are occupied with it and do not meddle with the joy of Israel when they come to draw the blessings from above. And of this day, it is written: 'My beloved is mine and I am his' (Song of Songs 2:16),** meaning **that there is no stranger interfering with us.**

The King who wants to rejoice alone with his beloved.

110. לְמַלְכָּא דְּזַמִּין רְחִימוֹי בִּסְעוּדָתָא עִלָּאָה, דַּעֲבִיד לֵיהּ לְיוֹמָא רְשִׁימָא. הָא רְחִימוֹי דְּמַלְכָּא יָדַע, דְּמַלְכָּא אִתְרְעֵי בֵּיהּ. אֲמַר מַלְכָּא הַשְׁתָּא אֲנָא בָּעֵי לְמֶחֱדֵי עִם רְחִימָאי, וְדָחִילְנָא דְּכַד אֲנָא בִּסְעוּדָתָא, עִם רְחִימָאי, יֵעֲלוּן כָּל אִינוּן קַסְטוֹרֵי מְמַנָּן, וְיִתִיבוּן עִמָּנָא לִפְתוֹרָא, לְמִסְעַד סְעוּדָתָא דְּחֶדְוָה, עִם רְחִימָאי. מָה עֲבַד, אַקְדִּים הַהוּא רְחִימוֹי קוֹסְטוֹרִין דִּירוֹקֵי, וּבִשְׂרָא דְתוֹרֵי, וְאַקְרֵיב קַמַּיְיהוּ, דְּאִינוּן קַסְטוֹרֵי מְמַנָּן לְמֵיכַל. לְבָתַר יָתֵיב מַלְכָּא עִם רְחִימוֹי, לְהַהִיא סְעוּדָתָא עִלָּאָה, מִכָּל עִדּוּנִין דְּעָלְמָא. וּבְעוֹד דְּאִיהוּ בִּלְחוּדוֹי, עִם מַלְכָּא, שָׁאִיל לֵיהּ כָּל צָרְכוֹי, וְיָהִיב לֵיהּ. וְאַחֲדֵי מַלְכָּא עִם רְחִימוֹי, בִּלְחוּדוֹהִי, וְלָא אִתְעָרְבִין אָחֳרָנִין בֵּינַיְיהוּ. כָּךְ יִשְׂרָאֵל, עִם קֻדְשָׁא בְּרִיךְ הוּא, בְּגִין כָּךְ כְּתִיב בַּיּוֹם הַשְּׁמִינִי עֲצֶרֶת תִּהְיֶה לָכֶם.

110. "This is comparable to a king who invited his beloved to a feast he is making on a specific day, so that the beloved of the king will know that the king is pleased with him. The king thinks to himself: 'Now I wish to rejoice with my beloved alone but I fear that during my feast all the other ministers will come and join us at our table to be together and take part in the festive meal that I have prepared for my beloved and myself.' So what does the king do? He first regales his governors and ministers with dishes of vegetables and beef. Only after they are satisfied can he sit in peace with his friend and enjoy the Supernal banquet with the world's finest delicacies spread before them. And while alone with the king, his friend puts before him all his petitions and requests, which the king grants. So just as the king enjoys the company of his beloved alone, with no stranger disturbing them, the Holy One, blessed be He, enjoys Israel. Hence

it is written: 'On the eighth day you shall have a solemn assembly....' (Numbers 29:35)"

Tetzaveh

16. "You shall dwell in booths"

A Synopsis

We read that verse 134 refers to the Supernal World, Binah, and that this verse was said when the world was created. We read about the Supernal Tabernacle formed as Supernal Chochmah emerged from the unknown and unseen place, and of the Lower Tabernacle, Malchut, that is like a lantern displaying Light. Israel should sit under the shade of the Tabernacle of Peace in the secret of Faith. During Sukkot, Malchut takes the souls of Israel and elevates them to Zeir Anpin, as She descends and holds all the blessings that Israel draw down during the whole seven days through the actions and sacrifices offered to Her. Then on the eighth day, She descends to be close to Her children and make them happy; this is Shmini Atzeret, the Eighth Day of Convocation.

Sukkot is the secret of Faith.

134. כְּתִיב בַּסֻּכֹּת תֵּשְׁבוּ שִׁבְעַת יָמִים, דָּא הוּא רָזָא דִּמְהֵימְנוּתָא, וְהַאי קְרָא עַל עָלְמָא עִלָּאָה אִתְּמַר, וְהָכִי תָּנֵינָן, כַּד אִתְבְּרֵי עָלְמָא, אִתְּמַר הַאי קְרָא.

134. It is written: "You shall dwell in booths (*sukkot*) seven days…." (Leviticus 23:42) This is the secret of Faith, which is Malchut, as in the secret of this verse She receives all Her Mochin. **This verse refers to the Supernal World,** which is Binah, **as we have learned. When the world was created, this verse was said.**

The Curtain, which is the roof of the Sukkah,
enables the Light to be revealed.

135. כַּד שָׁרָא וְחָכְמָה לְנָפְקָא, מֵאֲתַר דְּלָא יְדִיעַ וְלָא אִתְחֲזֵי, כְּדֵין נָפִיק וַחַד מִשְׁחָתָא, וּבָטַשׁ, וְהַהִיא וְחָכְמְתָא עִלָּאָה, נָצִיץ וְאִתְפָּשַׁט לְכָל סִטְרִין, בְּרָזָא

דְּמַשְׁכְּנָא עִלָּאָה. וְהַהוּא מַשְׁכְּנָא עִלָּאָה, אַפִּיק שִׁית סִטְרִין, וּכְדֵין הַהוּא נְצִיצוּ דְּמִשְׁחֲתָא נָהִיר לְכֹלָּא, וְאָמַר בַּסֻּכֹּת תֵּשְׁבוּ שִׁבְעַת יָמִים.

135. When Chochmah, namely Supernal Aba and Ima that are called Aba and Chochmah, **started to emerge from the unknown and unseen place,** namely from the Head of Arich Anpin, **then a Curtain emerged and struck. That Supernal Chochmah sparkled and spread in all directions in the secret of the Supernal Tabernacle,** which is Israel-Saba and Tevunah that is called Binah and Ima. **That Supernal Tabernacle brought forth Six Corners,** which are Zeir Anpin, **and then the sparkling of the Curtain Illuminated everything and said: "You shall dwell in booths seven days…." (Leviticus 23:42)**

The seven days of Sukkot are Seven Lights of Binah shining to Malchut.

136. מַאן סֻכֹּת חָסֵר ו'. דָּא מַשְׁכְּנָא תַּתָּאָה, דְּאִיהוּ כְּעֶשְׁשִׁיתָא, לְאַחֲזָאָה לְכָל נְהוֹרִין, וּכְדֵין אָמַר, בַּסֻּכֹּת תֵּשְׁבוּ שִׁבְעַת יָמִים. מַאן שִׁבְעַת יָמִים. מֵעָלְמָא עִלָּאָה לְתַתָּאָה, דְּכֻלְּהוּ קַיְימֵי בְּקִיּוּמָא, לְאַנְהָרָא לְהַאי סֻכֹּת. וּמַאן אִיהִי. דָּא סֻכַּת דָּוִד הַנֹּפֶלֶת. סֻכַּת שָׁלוֹם. וּבָעֵי עַמָּא קַדִּישָׁא לְמֵיתַב תְּחוֹת צִלָּהָא, בְּרָזָא דִּמְהֵימְנוּתָא, וּמַאן דְּיָתִיב בְּצִלָּא דָּא, יָתִיב בְּאִינּוּן יוֹמִין עִלָּאִין.

136. Why is *sukkot* (סכת) spelled without the Vav (ו)? This is the Lower Tabernacle, Malchut, **which is like a lantern** that is a glass utensil into which a candle is placed to shine, **to show all Lights. Then** the glittering of the curtain **said: "You shall dwell in booths (*sukkot*) seven days…." (Leviticus 23:42) Who are the "seven days"? They are from the Supernal World,** which is Binah, **to the Lower** World, which is Malchut, **for all** the seven days, which are Chesed, Gevurah, Tiferet, Netzach, Hod, Yesod, and Malchut of Binah, **maintain their existence to shine on this Tabernacle (*Sukkah*). What is it? It is "… the Tabernacle of David that is fallen…" (Amos 9:11) the Tabernacle of Peace,** namely Malchut. **And the Holy Nation should sit under its**

shade in the secret of Faith, which is Malchut. **One who sits in this shade, sits among these Supernal Days** of Binah.

Explanation: In the beginning the world was created with the attribute of Judgment, which is Malchut of Tzimtzum Alef (First Contraction). [The Creator] saw that the world cannot exist because the Vessels that come from the Malchut of the attribute of Judgment are not fit to receive within them the Supernal Light, so He stood and paired the attribute of Mercy with it. This means that He raised Malchut to the place of Binah, which is the attribute of Mercy. Then all the levels split into two halves. Keter and Chochmah remained in the Head of Arich Anpin, and its Binah, Tiferet, and Malchut fell to the Body, and so it was in every [level]. Thus, all the levels diminished to be Six Corners [Sefirot] with no Head, and this reality is called the vowel of Cholam (˙).

Afterwards, at the time of Gadlut (Maturity), through the Illumination of AV (ע"ב) and SaG (ס"ג) of Adam Kadmon, Malchut descends and returns from the place of Binah to its own place, and all the half levels that fell from their grade return to their grade, thus completing the levels again with the Upper Three. This reality is called the vowel of Shuruk (ּ), where those Binah, Tiferet, and Malchut that returned to their grade take up with them also the lower [grade] they were in at the time of their falling, and thus the Lower one receives the Mochin of the Higher one because of this.

It is found that during Katnut (Immaturity), Binah, Tiferet, and Malchut of Israel-Saba and Tevunah—which are Ima—fell to Zeir Anpin and Nukva. And during Gadlut, when Binah, Tiferet, and Malchut return to their grade, to Binah, they also take Zeir Anpin and Nukva with them to the place of Binah. Then Zeir Anpin and Nukva receive the Mochin of Binah via the Vessels of Binah, Tiferet, and Malchut of Binah that were with them at the time of Katnut. It is found now that Zeir Anpin and Nukva are fit to receive the Supernal Light of Binah, as well as all the Worlds, Briyah, Yetzirah, and Asiyah that are drawn from them. Then the world [is sustained and] can exist. If not for the elevation of Malchut to Binah there would be no reality where the world can exist.

This is [in verse 134]: **"When the world was created, this verse was said."** Namely, when He paired Malchut with the attribute of Mercy so that the world could exist. "**When Chochmah started to emerge from the unknown and unseen place,"** namely when Malchut ascended to the place of the Binah of the Head of Arich Anpin—thus leaving Arich Anpin with Keter and Chochmah, while its Binah, Tiferet and Malchut fell to the aspect of its Body—this Binah that went out of the Head split in two: its Upper Three were set in Supernal Aba and Ima and are called Chochmah, and its Lower Seven were set in Yisrael-Saba and Tevunah and are called Binah.

This is [in verse 135]: **"then a curtain emerged..."** namely the Masach of Malchut that ascended to the Head of Arich Anpin, **"...and struck,"** namely it took Binah of Arich Anpin out of the Head. **"That Supernal Chochmah..."** which is the Upper Three of Binah that were set to be Supernal Aba and Ima, **"...sparkled..."** in the aspect of Katnut, when its Binah, Tiferet, and Malchut fell down to Binah, **"...and spread in all directions in the secret of the Supernal Tabernacle,"** namely during Gadlut when its Binah, Tiferet, and Malchut returned the Supernal Tabernacle, Binah, also ascended to it and received Mochin from it.

In the same way, **"That Supernal Tabernacle brought forth Six Corners,"** as also Binah returned its Binah-Tiferet-Malchut that fell to Zeir Anpin and Nukva, and with that Zeir Anpin and Nukva received the Mochin of Binah, and Binah brought forth six sides—which are Zeir Anpin and Nukva. **"...and then the sparkling of the curtain..."** namely the secret of the Illumination of the Masach and the diminishment that was made by Malchut elevating to Binah, **"...illuminated everything..."** Illuminated the Mochin of Binah to all, meaning to Zeir Anpin and

Nukva, **"...and said..."** to the Mochin, which are Chesed-Gevurah-Tiferet and Netzach-Hod-Yesod of Binah, **"...You shall dwell in booths (*sukkot*) seven days..." (Leviticus 23:42),** namely that they should spread to Malchut called *Sukkot* without a Vav. It is considered that it **"said"** that if not for the shade, meaning the diminishment of Light, of the sparkling of the curtain that is made in Binah, the secret of the *Schach,* the seven days— Chesed-Gevurah-Tiferet and Netzach-Hod-Yesod of Binah—would never be drawn to *Sukkot,* which is Malchut below.

Indeed, also in [Malchut] there is the shade of the sparkling of the Curtain, which is the secret of *Schach* because it too has Ten Sefirot and its own Malchut ascended to its Binah, and [Malchut's] Binah-Tiferet-Malchut fell to Briyah-Yetzirah-Asiyah. Because of this, during Gadlut, when its Binah-Tiferet-Malchut return to Atzilut, also Briyah-Yetzirah-Asiyah ascend with them in the way of the grade to Atzilut and receive from it the Mochin of the seven days. So the root of the *Schach* is in Binah, and from there it says "You shall dwell in booths (*sukkot*) seven days...." (Leviticus 23:42) This is [in verse 134]: **"This verse refers to the Supernal World."** Indeed, that shade and *schach* also exists in Malchut, and therefore it is called Sukkah (סכה) without a Vav (ו), indicating the *Schach* of Binah that exists in Malchut.

Connecting to Binah by sitting under the shade of the Sukkah.

137. וְעַ"ד כֻּלְּהוּ בַּסֻּכֹּת בְּסֻכֹּת וְחַד בְּסוּכּוֹת שְׁלִים, חַד שְׁלִים, לְאַחֲזָאָה דְּמַאן דְּיָתִיב בְּצִלָּא דָא, יָתִיב בְּאִינּוּן יוֹמִין עִלָּאִין לְעֵילָּא, דְּקַיְימִין עַל הַאי תַּתָּאָה, לְאַנְהָרָא לֵיהּ, לְחַפְּיָא עֲלֵיהּ, וּלְאַגָּנָא לֵיהּ, בְּשַׁעְתָּא דְּאִצְטְרִיךְ.

137. Therefore, *Sukkot* is always spelled without a Vav (סכת), which alludes to Malchut, as mentioned. But in **one** place, **it is fully spelled *Sukkot* (סוכות). The one fully spelled indicates that whoever sits in the shade** of the mentioned glittering of the Curtain **sits among these Supernal Days that are Above,** namely Chesed, Gevurah, Tiferet,

Netzach, Hod, Yesod, and Malchut of Binah, **which are over the Lower,** Malchut, **to Illuminate Her, cover Her and protect Her when necessary,** as that *Schach* of Binah is also drawn to [Malchut], as it will say shortly.

Malchut nourishes the Ministers of the nations during Sukkot.

138. וְתוּ, כֻּלְּהוּ אִקְרוּן סֻכּוֹת בִּשְׁלִימוּ, וּכְתִיב סֻכַּת חָסֵר, דָּא עָלְמָא תַּתָּאָה, דְּבָעָא בְּהָנֵי ז' יוֹמִין קַדִּישִׁין, לְמֵיזַן לִשְׁאַר מְמַנָּן רַבְרְבָן דְּעַמִּין, בְּעוֹד דְּאִיהִי נַטְלָא חֶדְוָה בְּבַעְלָהּ, וְלָא יְקַטְרְגוּן חֶדְוָותָא, בְּגִין דְּיִתְעַדְּנוּן בְּהַהוּא מְזוֹנָא, קָרְבָּנִין דִּלְהוֹן סַגִּיאִין יַתִּיר מִשְּׁאָר יוֹמִין, בְּגִין דְּיִתְעַסְּקוּן בְּהוּ, וְלָא יִתְעָרְבוּן לְבָתַר בְּחֶדְוָה דְּיִשְׂרָאֵל. וּמַאן חֶדְוָה דְּיִשְׂרָאֵל, דָּא יוֹמָא תְּמִינָאָה דַּעֲצֶרֶת.

138. It can **also** be said **that they are all read *Sukkot* in full,** namely the *Schach* of Binah and the *Schach* of Zeir Anpin, **and that which is written *Sukkot* without the Vav refers to the Lower World,** which is Malchut, **that needs to nourish the other appointed Ministers of the world,** which is the secret of the seventy oxen that are offered during the seven days of Sukkot, as [Malchut] needs to be diminished of Light and awaken the Mochin of the Left, which are Her Achorayim, from which the seventy Ministers nourish, **while She still receives joy from Her husband,** with the Mochin of the Face. She needs this **so that they do not incite during the joy,** and She allows them **to delight themselves with that food. Their offerings are more plentiful than usual so that they are occupied with them and do not mingle in the joy of the children of Israel,** in the same way we give them a portion in the goat of Rosh Chodesh and the goat to Azazel. Because of this diminishment for the sake of nourishing the Ministers of the world She is called *Sukkot* (**סכת**) without a Vav. **What is the joy of Israel? This is the day of Shmini Atzeret.**

Giving Light to the nations enable Israel to do the work of Sukkot to correct Malchut.

139. וְת"ח, בְּעוֹד דְּאִינּוּן שְׁאַר מְמַנָּן חַדָּאן, וְאַכְלִין בְּהַהוּא מְזוֹנָא דִּמְתַקְּנֵי לוֹן יִשְׂרָאֵל. אִינּוּן מְתַקְּנֵי כּוּרְסַיָּיא לְקוּדְשָׁא בְּרִיךְ הוּא מִתַּתָּא, וּלְסַלְּקָא לֵיהּ לְעֵילָּא, בְּאִינּוּן זִינִין, וּבְחֶדְוָה, וּבְהִלּוּלָא, וּלְאַקָּפָא מַדְבְּחָא. כְּדֵין אִיהִי סַלְקָא, וְנַטְלָא בִּרְכָאן וְחֶדְוָה בְּבַעְלָהּ.

139. Come and see, while the other appointed Princes are rejoicing and eating that food that Israel prepare for them, namely the seventy oxen, at that time **they prepare a Throne for the Holy One, blessed be He, below,** meaning that they prepare Malchut to be a Throne for the Holy One, blessed be He, **to elevate Her up with these** four **species, with the joy** of the Holiday, the recitation of **Halel, and by circling the altar. Then She,** Malchut, **ascends and receives blessings and joy in Her husband,** Zeir Anpin.

The seven days of Sukkot are a preparation for Shmini Atzeret.

140. וּשְׁאַר חֵיוָון רַבְרְבָן מְמַנָּן דְּעַמִּין, אָכְלָן וּמַדְקָן וְרַפְסָן וְאִתְּזָנוּ. וְאִיהִי נַקְטָא נַפְשָׁאן בְּעִנּוּגִין לְעֵילָּא, כְּמָה דְּאִתְּמַר. כֵּיוָן דְּנַחְתָּא, וְהָא נַקְטָא כָּל בִּרְכָאן וְכָל קִדּוּשִׁין וְכָל עִנּוּגִין, וְיִשְׂרָאֵל כָּל הָנֵי שִׁבְעָה יוֹמִין הֲווֹ מַשְׁכִין לָהּ בְּאִינּוּן עוֹבָדִין דְּקָא עָבְדִין וּמְקָרְבִין בַּהֲדָהּ, כְּדֵין נַחְתָּא לְקָרְבָא בִּבְנָהָא, וּלְמֶחֱדֵי לוֹן יוֹמָא חַד, וְהַהוּא יוֹמָא אִיהוּ יוֹמָא תְּמִינָאָה, בְּגִין דְּכָל ז' יוֹמִין אַחֲרָנִין בַּהֲדָהּ. וְע"ד אִיהוּ תְּמִינָאָה, וּתְמַנְיָא יוֹמִין כַּחֲדָא. וּבְגִין כַּךְ אִקְרֵי עֲצֶרֶת: כְּנִישִׁין. כְּנִישִׁין כֻּלְּהוּ בְּהַאי יוֹמָא. וְאִקְרֵי שְׁמִינִי, וְלֵית שְׁמִינִי אֶלָּא מִגּוֹ שִׁבְעָה.

140. The other Living Creatures, which are the seventy **appointed Ministers of the nations, devour, crush, stamp** the remains of their food **with their feet and are sustained,** namely by the seventy oxen, as mentioned. **She,** Malchut, **takes the souls and elevates them to the Supernal Delight,** to Zeir Anpin, **as we have said. Once She descends and holds all the blessings, Holiness, and delights that Israel drew to**

Her during all these seven days, through these actions they did and offered to Her, She then descends to be close to Her children and to make them happy for one day. That day is the eighth day because all the other seven days are with Her, as explained. Therefore, it is the eighth, and it is eight days united. Therefore, it is called *Atzeret,* meaning **gathering because all** the seven days **gather together on that** eighth **day, and it is called "eighth,"** namely Shmini Atzeret (Eighth Day of Convocation). **And the eighth only comes about because of the seven.** Therefore, it is called by two names: it is called "Eighth" because it is eighth of the seven days, and it is called "Convocation" (*Atzeret*) because it includes within itself all the seven days together.

Emor

35. "The fifteenth day"

A Synopsis

Rav Aba tells Rav Yosi the meaning of the fifteen days in the verse, "The fifteenth day of this seventh month," saying that the first ten belong to the Matron and the next five to the King. On the fifteenth day the moon is full, and the full moon is the secret of Malchut.

The tenth day is Malchut, and the following five are Zeir Anpin.

257. וּבַחֲמִשָּׁה עָשָׂר יוֹם לַחֹדֶשׁ הַשְּׁבִיעִי וְגוֹ'. ר' יוֹסֵי שָׁאַל לְרִבִּי אַבָּא, א"ל, הָנֵי חֲמִשָּׁה עָשָׂר יוֹם, מַאי קָא מַיְירֵי. א"ל, וַדַּאי רָזָא יַקִּירָא הוּא. ת"ח, בֵּין לְעֵילָּא בֵּין לְתַתָּא, כָּל חַד וְחַד, בְּאָרְחֵיהּ נַטְלָא. וּבְאָרְחֵיהּ יָתְבָא, וּבְאָרְחֵיהּ אִתְּעַר וְעָבֵיד מַאי דְּעָבֵיד. הַאי עָשׂוֹר מִכְּנֶסֶת יִשְׂרָאֵל אִינּוּן. וְיוֹמָא עֲשִׂירָאָה, בַּעֲשִׂירָאָה קַיְּימָא. וְעַל דָּא בֶּעָשׂוֹר לַחֹדֶשׁ הַזֶּה וְיִקְחוּ לָהֶם אִישׁ שֶׂה לְבֵית וְגוֹ'. וְהַאי יוֹמָא, הוּא דִּילָהּ. וַחֲמִשָּׁה יוֹמִין אָחֳרָנִין, דְּמַלְכָּא הוּא. הַהוּא יוֹמָא דְּאָתֵי עָלָהּ. דְּהָא וַחֲמִשָּׁאָה, בֵּיהּ יָתִיב מַלְכָּא, בְּכוּרְסְיָיא.

257. "On the fifteenth day of the seventh month...." (Numbers 29:12) Rav Yosi asked Rav Aba and said, "What is the meaning of those fifteen days?" He said to him, "Certainly they are a precious secret. Come and see, whether Above or Below, everything journeys in its own way, sits in its own way, and awakens in its own way to do whatever it does. That is, there is not one thing that is similar to the other, whether Above or Below. **The tenth is from the Congregation of Israel,** that is, it alludes to Malchut, **since the tenth day is based on the tenth** Sefirah, Malchut. **Hence** it is said, **'...On the tenth day of this month they shall take to them every man a lamb, according to the house of their fathers.' (Exodus 12:3)** For the tenth is Malchut, and since the Ten Sefirot reached completion on the tenth day, 'they shall take...' (Ibid.) **That day,** the tenth day of the month, **is hers, while**

the other five days are the King's, Zeir Anpin's. **That day comes upon her** and fills her with her Lights. Hence, on the fifteenth day the moon is full, **for on the fifth day,** when the five Sefirot of Zeir Anpin reach completion, **the King sits on the Throne,** which is Malchut, the secret of the full moon.

Explanation: The ten days allude to the Ten Sefirot in Malchut, which clothes Zeir Anpin from the Chest down. Until then, She has nothing from the five Sefirot Above the Chest of Zeir Anpin, which are Chochmah, Binah, Da'at, Chesed and Gevurah. Da'at and the Tiferet above the Chest are considered one Sefirah, because the Tiferet that ascends to Binah becomes Da'at. And together with Chesed and Gevurah they are three, and with Chochmah and Binah they are five. Once five more days of the month pass, She receives from the five Sefirot above the Chest of Zeir Anpin, and She is unified with Him. This is why on the fifteenth of the month Malchut is found in completion.

This is: **"The tenth is from the Congregation of Israel,"** as the tenth of the month is the Ten Sefirot of Malchut, which reaches up to the Chest of Zeir Anpin, **"while the other five days are the King's,"** namely the five days after the tenth of the month, which are the five Sefirot above the Chest of Zeir Anpin—Chochmah, Binah, Da'at, Chesed and Gevurah. **"That day comes upon her,"** as once fifteen days are complete, Zeir Anpin unites with Her and gives Her of the five Sefirot above His Chest. **"for on the fifth day the King sits on the Throne,"** meaning that on the fifth day, which is Zeir Anpin, the King bestows to His Throne, which is Malchut, from the Upper Five Sefirot.

Five and seven both allude to Zeir Anpin.

258. וּבְכָל אֲתַר בְּעָשׂוֹר, דְּמַטְרוֹנִיתָא הוּא. וַחֲמִשָּׁה עָלַיְיהוּ, דְּמַלְכָּא הוּא. הַהוּא יוֹמָא דְּאָתֵי עָלָהּ. בְּגַ"כ וַחֲמִשָּׁה יוֹמִין מִיַּרְחָא, לְאוֹרַיְיתָא. וְאִי תֵּימָא

שְׁבִיעָאָה, בְּזִמְנָא דִתְרֵין אֲבָהָן מִשְׁתַּכְּחֵי בֵּיהּ, דְּהָא מַלְכָּא בְּהוּ, וּכְדֵין מִתְעַטֵּר בְּכֹלָּא. וְחַד מִלָּה, שְׁבִיעָאָה וַחֲמִשָׁאָה.

258. Any place it says "on the tenth" it refers to the Matron, namely Malchut. **Five above them,** namely the upper five Sefirot of Zeir Anpin, **are the King's**, Zeir Anpin, **who is the day that comes upon Her. For that reason, after the five days of the month** of Sivan**, the Torah** is given, which indicates the first five Sefirot of Zeir Anpin that bestowed abundance at the Giving of the Torah. **You may argue that** the Torah should have been given **on the seventh day,** namely **when the two parents,** Aba and Ima, **are** clothed **in Him,** in Zeir Anpin. **For the King,** when He is **in them, is then adorned with everything** and is then worthy to give the Torah. He answers, **"The fifth and the seventh are the same issue.**

Five are the five Sefirot of Zeir Anpin and seven includes Aba and Ima that adorn Him.

259. ת"ח, וַחֲמִשָׁאָה דִּילֵיהּ הוּא וַדַּאי, כְּמָה דְּאִתְּמַר, וּכְדֵין נָהִיר אַבָּא לְאִימָּא, וְאִתְנְהִירוּ מִנָּהּ חַמְשִׁין תַּרְעִין לְאַנְהָרָא לַחֲמִשָׁאָה. וְאִי תֵּימָא שְׁבִיעָאָה, בְּגִין דְּמַלְכָּא בִּשְׁלִימוּ דַּאֲבָהָן, וַעֲטָרָה יָרִית מִשְּׁבִיעָאָה, כְּמָה דִּכְתִיב צְאֶינָה וּרְאֶינָה בְּנוֹת צִיּוֹן. וְעַ"ד בִּשְׁבִיעָאָה הוּא יוֹמָא דְּמִעַטְּרָא מַלְכָּא בְּעִטְרוֹי, וּכְדֵין יָרִית מַלְכָּא לְאַבָּא וְאִימָּא, דְּמִזְדַּוְּוגִין כַּחֲדָא. וְעַ"ד כֹּלָּא בְּחַד תַּלְיָיא.

259. "Come and see, the fifth is surely His, as we said it refers to His five Sefirot, Chochmah, Binah, Da'at, Chesed, and Gevurah. **Aba then shines upon Ima, and from Her the Fifty Gates shine upon the fifth.** The Fifty Gates of Binah shine to the Upper Five Sefirot of Zeir Anpin. And even though Aba and Ima shine in Him, we are only discussing His five Sefirot, Chochmah, Binah, Da'at, Chesed, and Gevurah. Therefore He is complete in the fifth. **We may argue that it is the seventh. This is because the King abides in the wholeness of the Patriarchs that shine** on Him, as His five together with Aba and Ima amount to seven.

Moreover, **He receives a crown from** Binah that is called **the seventh.** If you count from Yesod, Binah is the seventh Sefirah. **As it is written: "Go forth, daughters of Zion, and behold** King Solomon with the crown with which his mother crowned him…." **(Song of Songs 3:11) Hence, the seventh day is the day when** Binah **crowns the King,** Zeir Anpin, with His crowns. **The King** also **inherits then Aba and Ima that unite** and shine into Him **together** as with his own five they are seven. **Thus it all depends on the same thing.** In other words, everything alludes to the completion of Zeir Anpin, meaning when He clothes Aba and Ima. When we consider only his Sefirot then for sure he is complete on the fifth, but when we consider Aba and Ima that are clothed in Him we can say that He is complete on the seventh. And they both refer to the same thing.

36. Manna, the Well, and the Clouds of Glory

A Synopsis

Rav Yehuda tells us that Moses, Aaron, and Miriam, through their merit, gave Israel the Manna, the Clouds of Glory and the Well, and that all of these Celestial gifts are attached Above. He emphasizes that there were seven Clouds of Glory, and that after Aaron died the Clouds were gone and they no longer protected Israel. Rav Aba says that whoever excludes himself from the Shadow of Faith as represented by those Clouds is worthy only of being a servant to servants of servants, yet whoever dwells under the Shadow of Faith bequeaths freedom to all his descendants forever.

The Israelites received three gifts in the desert.

260(1). וּבַחֲמִשָּׁה עָשָׂר יוֹם, ר׳ יְהוּדָה פָּתַח, וַיִּשְׁמַע הַכְּנַעֲנִי מֶלֶךְ עֲרָד. תָּנִינָן, ג׳ מַתְּנָן עִלָּאִין, אִזְדַּמְּנוּ לְהוּ לְיִשְׂרָאֵל, ע״י תְּלָתָא אַחִין: מֹשֶׁה, אַהֲרֹן, וּמִרְיָם. מָן, בִּזְכוּת מֹשֶׁה. עֲנָנֵי כָּבוֹד, בִּזְכוּת אַהֲרֹן. בְּאֵר, בִּזְכוּת מִרְיָם. וְכֻלְּהוּ אֲחִידָן לְעֵילָּא. מָן בִּזְכוּת מֹשֶׁה, דִּכְתִיב הִנְנִי מַמְטִיר לָכֶם לֶחֶם מִן הַשָּׁמַיִם, דָּא מֹשֶׁה.

260(1). "And on the fifteenth day...." (Numbers 29:12) Rav Yehuda opened the discussion with, "'And when the Canaanite, the king of Arad....' (Numbers 21:1) We learned that three Supernal gifts were given to Israel by the three siblings: Moses, Aaron, and Miriam. The Manna through the merit of Moses, the Clouds of Glory through the merit of Aaron, and the Well through the merit of Miriam. They are all attached Above. The Manna is by the merit of Moses, as it is written, 'Behold, I will rain bread from Heaven for you...' (Exodus 16:4) 'from Heaven' (Ibid.) refers to Moses, namely the Chariot to Zeir Anpin called Moses and also called Heaven.

The Clouds of Glory were in the merit of Aaron.

260(2). עֲנָנֵי כָּבוֹד בִּזְכוּת אַהֲרֹן, דִּכְתִּיב אֲשֶׁר עַיִן בְּעַיִן נִרְאָה אַתָּה יְיָ' וְגוֹ', וּכְתִיב וְכִסָּה עֲנַן הַקְּטֹרֶת. מַה לְּהַלָּן, שִׁבְעָה. אַף כָּאן נָמֵי שִׁבְעָה. דְּהָא בִּקְטֹרֶת שִׁבְעָה עֲנָנִין מִתְקַשְּׁרָן כַּחֲדָא. וְאַהֲרֹן רֵישָׁא לְכָל שִׁבְעָה עֲנָנִין הוּא וְהוּא קָשִׁיר לְשִׁית אָחֳרָנִין בֵּיהּ בְּכָל יוֹמָא.

260(2). "The Clouds of Glory are by merit of Aaron, a Chariot to Chesed, **as it is written, '...that face to face You, the Lord, appear to them, and that Your cloud stands over them...' (Numbers 14:14), and '...the cloud of the incense may cover....' (Leviticus 16:13) Just as in the latter verse,** in relation to incense, **there are seven** clouds, **so in the former,** in '...Your cloud stands over them...' (Numbers 14:14), **there are also seven** clouds. **With the incence, there were seven clouds joined together, and Aaron is the head of the seven clouds.** The seven clouds are the secret of Chesed, Gevurah, Tiferet, Netzach, Hod, Yesod, and Malchut. Aaron, who is a Chariot to Chesed, is the first Sefirah, **and he is connected through it to the six other clouds,** Gevurah, Tiferet, Netzach, Hod, Yesod, and Malchut, **every day.** Therefore the clouds are considered to come by the merit of Aaron, as he is the aspect of Chesed, the head of the clouds, which includes them.

The Well was in the merit of Miriam.

261. בְּאֵר בִּזְכוּת מִרְיָם, דְּהָא הִיא וַדַּאי בְּאֵר אִתְקְרֵי. וּבְסִפְרָא דְאַגַּדְתָּא, וַתֵּתַצַּב אֲחוֹתוֹ מֵרָחוֹק לְדֵעָה וְגוֹ'. דָּא הוּא בְּאֵר מַיִם חַיִּים, וְכֹלָּא קְשׁוּרָא חָד. מֵתָה מִרְיָם, אִסְתַּלַּק בְּאֵר. דִּכְתִיב, וְלֹא הָיָה מַיִם לָעֵדָה. וּבְהַהִיא שַׁעֲתָא בָּעָאת בְּאֵר אָחֳרָא לְאִסְתַּלְּקָא, דַּהֲוָה שְׁכִיחַ עִמְּהוֹן דְּיִשְׂרָאֵל. כַּד חָמָאת שִׁיתָּא עֲנָנִין דַּהֲווֹ קְשִׁירִין עָלָהּ, אִתְקַשְּׁרַת הִיא בְּהוּ.

261. "The Well comes by merit of Miriam, who was a Chariot to Malchut, **since she is surely called a Well. In the Book of Agadah,** we learned, **'And his sister stood afar off, to know....' (Exodus 2:4) This is a Well of Living Water,** namely Malchut, **and it was all bound as one,** since Miriam was connected to Malchut. **When Miriam died, the well was gone, as written, 'And there was no water for the congregation....' (Numbers 20:2) At that time, another Well,** Malchut, **that was with Israel wished to depart,** but **when it saw the six Clouds,** Chesed, Gevurah, Tiferet, Netzach, Hod and Yesod, **that were connected to it,** to the Cloud of Malchut, which is Her aspect, Malchut **became connected to them.**

The Well and the Clouds returned in the merit of Moses.

262. מִית אַהֲרֹן, אִסְתַּלְּקוּ אִינּוּן עֲנָנִין, וְאִסְתַּלַּק עֲנָנָא דְבֵירָא עִמְּהוֹן. אָתָא מֹשֶׁה, אַהְדַּר לְהוּ. הה"ד, עָלִיתָ לַמָּרוֹם שָׁבִיתָ שֶּׁבִי לָקַחְתָּ מַתָּנוֹת בָּאָדָם. לָקַחְתָּ מַתָּנוֹת וַדַּאי, אִינּוּן מַתָּנוֹת דַּהֲווֹ בְּקַדְמֵיתָא בְּאֵר וַעֲנָנִין.

262. "When Aaron died, the Clouds of Glory were gone, and with them the seventh **cloud,** to which **the Well,** Malchut, was attached**, was gone. Moses came and returned them to them, as it is written, 'You have ascended on high, you have taken captives. You have received gifts from men....' (Psalms 68:19) Surely, '...you have received gifts from men...' (Ibid.) are the presents that were there before,** namely, **the Well and the Clouds.**

Aaron had affinity with the Clouds due to his loving-kindness.

263. בְּאֵר, דָּא בְּאֵר דְּיִצְחָק. עֲנָנִים, אִלֵּין עֲנָנִים דְּאַהֲרֹן. א"ר יִצְחָק, מִפְּנֵי מַה זָּכָה אַהֲרֹן לְדָא, בְּגִין דְּאִיהוּ קָשִׁיר בַּעֲנָנִים. וְהוּא אַקְשִׁיר כָּל יוֹמָא וְיוֹמָא לְכֻלְּהוּ כַּחֲדָא, דְּמִתְבָּרְכָאן כֻּלְּהוּ עַל יְדוֹי.

263. "A Well refers to Isaac's Well, meaning that Malchut is called 'Well' when receiving the Illumination of Chochmah from the Left called Isaac. **These Clouds are the Clouds of Aaron,"** meaning that Clouds are Chasadim because they are of the aspect of Aaron who is Chesed. This explains what it states in verse 261, that the Malchut of the Well connected to the Malchut of the Clouds, as they are different from each other. One of Chesed of Malchut and the other is Gevurah of Malchut. **Rav Yitzchak said, "What is the reason Aaron was worthy** that the Clouds of Glory will come over Israel by his merit?" He answers: **"This is because he is connected to the Clouds,** meaning that he is the attribute of Chesed like them. **And he,** being a Chariot to Chesed of Zeir Anpin, the top Cloud, **used to connect** and unite **them all daily into one so they will all be blessed by him.**

The seven days of Sukkot correspond to the Seven Clouds of Glory.

264. תָּא חֲזֵי, עַל כָּל חֶסֶד דְּעָבֵד קוּדְשָׁא בְּרִיךְ הוּא בְּיִשְׂרָאֵל. קָשִׁיר עִמְּהוֹן ז' עֲנָנֵי יְקָרָן, וְקָשִׁיר לְהוּ בִּכְנֶסֶת יִשְׂרָאֵל, דְּהָא עֲנָנָא דִּילָהּ אִתְקַשַּׁר בְּשִׁיתָא אָחֳרָנִין. וּבְכֻלְּהוּ שִׁבְעָה, אַזְלוּ יִשְׂרָאֵל בְּמַדְבְּרָא. מַאי טַעֲמָא, בְּגִין דְּכֻלְּהוּ קִשְׁרָא דִּמְהֵימְנוּתָא נִינְהוּ וְעַל דָּא בַּסֻּכּוֹת תֵּשְׁבוּ שִׁבְעַת יָמִים. מַאי קָא מַיְירֵי. בְּגִין דִּכְתִיב, בְּצִלּוֹ חִמַּדְתִּי וְיָשַׁבְתִּי וּפִרְיוֹ מָתוֹק לְחִכִּי. וּבָעֵי בַּר נָשׁ לְאַחֲזָאָה גַּרְמֵיהּ, דְּיָתִיב תְּחוֹת צִלָּא דִּמְהֵימְנוּתָא.

264. "Come and see, for each kindness (Chesed) the Holy One, blessed be He, did to Israel, He attached Seven Clouds of Glory to it, which correspond to Chesed, Gevurah, Tiferet, Netzach, Hod, Yesod, and Malchut **and He tied them to the Congregation of Israel,**

which is Malchut, **since her Cloud was connected to the other six,** Chesed, Gevurah, Tiferet, Netzach, Hod, and Yesod. **Thus Israel walked in the desert with all Seven Clouds. The reason is that they were all the bonds of Faith,** as they were attached to Malchut called 'Faith.' **About this** scripture says, **'You shall dwell in booths seven days...' (Leviticus 23:42),** which is the secret of the Seven Clouds of Glory that went with Israel in the desert." He asks: **"What does that teach us?"** He answers, **"It is written, '...For His shade did I long for and dwelled, and his fruit was sweet to my taste' (Song of Songs 2:3),** which is the secret of the shadow of the Clouds of Glory and the secret of the shadow of the Sukkah. **Man should display himself sitting under the shadow of Faith.**

The Israelites were protected by the Clouds of Aaron.

265. ת"ח, כָּל אִינּוּן שְׁנִין דְּקָאֵים אַהֲרֹן, הֲווֹ יִשְׂרָאֵל בְּצִלָּא דִּמְהֵימְנוּתָא, תְּחוֹת אִלֵּין עֲנָנִין. בָּתַר דְּמִית אַהֲרֹן, אִסְתַּלַּק עֲנָנָא חַד, דְּהוּא יְמִינָא דְּכֹלָּא. וְכַד הַאי אִסְתַּלַּק, אִסְתַּלָּקוּ כָּל שְׁאָר עִמֵּיהּ וְאִתְחֲזִיאוּ כֻּלְּהוּ בִּגְרִיעוּתָא. וְהָא אוּקְמוּהָ, דִּכְתִּיב וַיִּרְאוּ כָּל הָעֵדָה כִּי גָוַע אַהֲרֹן. אַל תִּקְרֵי וַיִּרְאוּ, אֶלָּא וַיֵּירָאוּ. מִיַּד וַיִּשְׁמַע הַכְּנַעֲנִי מֶלֶךְ עֲרָד יוֹשֵׁב הַנֶּגֶב כִּי בָא יִשְׂרָאֵל דֶּרֶךְ הָאֲתָרִים. שְׁמַע דְּאִסְתַּלָּקוּ אִינּוּן עֲנָנִים, וּמִית תַּיָּירָא רַבְרְבָא דְּכָל אִינּוּן עֲנָנִים אִתְקַשָּׁרוּ בֵּיהּ.

265. "Come and see, all the years Aaron was present, Israel were under the shadow of Faith, under these Seven **Clouds. After Aaron died, one Cloud was gone,** which is Chesed of the Clouds, his own attribute, **which was the Right of all.** All the Clouds were aspects of Chasadim, which are included in the Right, and the Chesed of them is more Right than the rest, as they are all included in it. They are the aspect of the seven Sefirot that are included in the Sefirah of Chesed. Therefore, **when that was gone,** namely the Chesed of the Clouds, **the other Clouds were gone with it,** the six Sefirot included in it. **Everyone** of Israel **were left in lack. We explained the verse, 'And when all the congregation saw that Aaron was dead....' (Numbers 20:29) Do not**

pronounce it as *vayir'u* (saw) but *vayera'u* (were seen), which means that the shadow of the Clouds disappeared from them and they were exposed. **Immediately, 'And when the Canaanite, the king of Arad, who dwelt in the Negev, heard that Israel came by the way of Atarim... (Numbers 21:1), he heard that the Clouds of Glory were gone and the great guide died, to whom all the Clouds were attached."**

The Negev alludes to Amalek.

266. א"ר יִצְחָק, הַכְּנַעֲנִי מֶלֶךְ עֲרָד יוֹשֵׁב הַנֶּגֶב וַדַּאי. וְכַד אָתוּ אִינּוּן מְאַלְּלִין דְּשַׁדַּר מֹשֶׁה, אַמְרוּ עֲמָלֵק יוֹשֵׁב בְּאֶרֶץ הַנֶּגֶב, בְּגִין לְתַבְרָא לִבַּיְיהוּ. דְּהָא בַּעֲמָלֵק אִתְּבַר חֵילֵיהוֹן בְּקַדְמֵיתָא.

266. Rav Yitzchak said, "'...the Canaanite, the king of Arad, who dwelt in the Negev...' (Numbers 21:1) specifically. When the spies Moses sent returned, they said, 'Amalek dwells in the land of the Negev...' (Numbers 13:29), so as to break their heart, since their strength was first broken by Amalek."

Whoever excludes themselves from the shadow of Faith ends up being a slave.

267. א"ר אַבָּא, וַיִּשְׁמַע הַכְּנַעֲנִי, מַאי קָא מַיְירֵי הָכָא. בָּתַר דְּאִסְתַּלָּקוּ אִינּוּן עֲנָנִים. אֶלָּא כְּנַעַן כְּתִיב בֵּיהּ, וַיֹּאמֶר אָרוּר כְּנָעַן עֶבֶד עֲבָדִים יִהְיֶה לְאֶחָיו. הָכָא אוֹלִיפְנָא, מַאן דְּאַפִּיק גַּרְמֵיהּ מִצִּלָּא דִּמְהֵימְנוּתָא, אִתְחֲזֵי לְמֶהֱוֵי עֶבֶד לְעַבְדֵי עַבְדִין, הה"ד וַיִּלָּחֶם בְּיִשְׂרָאֵל וַיִּשְׁבְּ מִמֶּנּוּ שֶׁבִי. הוּא נָטַל עַבְדִין מִיִּשְׂרָאֵל לְגַרְמֵיהּ.

267. Rav Aba said, "'...the Canaanite... heard....' (Numbers 21:1) Why is the Canaanite mentioned **here, after** stating **the Clouds were gone?"** He answers, **"It is written of Canaan, '..."Cursed be Canaan; a servant of servants shall he be to his brethren.' (Genesis 9:25) We learned here** from the verse, '...the Canaanite... heard,' **that**

whoever excludes himself from the shadow of Faith is worthy of being a servant to servants of servants, namely to the Canaanites. **This is the meaning of, '...he fought against Israel, and took some of them prisoner' (Numbers 21:1), taking slaves for himself from among Israel.**

Every Israelite must sit under the shadow of Faith.

268. וְעַל דָּא כְּתִיב, כָּל הָאֶזְרָח בְּיִשְׂרָאֵל יֵשְׁבוּ בַּסּוּכּוֹת. כָּל מַאן דְּאִיהוּ מִשָּׁרְשָׁא וְגִזְעָא קַדִּישָׁא דְּיִשְׂרָאֵל, יֵשְׁבוּ בַּסֻּכּוֹת, תְּחוֹת צִלָּא דִּמְהֵימְנוּתָא. וּמַאן דְּלֵיתֵיהּ מִגִּזְעָא וְשׁוֹרְשָׁא קַדִּישָׁא דְּיִשְׂרָאֵל, לָא יָתִיב בְּהוּ, וְיִפּוֹק גַּרְמֵיהּ מִתְּחוֹת צִלָּא דִּמְהֵימְנוּתָא.

268. "It is therefore written, '...all that are home born in Israel shall dwell in booths" (Leviticus 23:42), for whoever is from the root and holy stock of Israel shall dwell in booths under the shadow of Faith. Whoever is not from the holy stock and root of Israel shall not dwell in them, but excludes himself from under the shadow of Faith.

Eliezer sat under the shadow of Faith and escaped his curse.

269. כְּתִיב כְּנַעַן בְּיָדוֹ מֹאזְנֵי מִרְמָה, דָּא אֱלִיעֶזֶר עֶבֶד אַבְרָהָם. ות"ח, כְּתִיב אָרוּר כְּנַעַן וּבְגִין דְּזָכָה כְּנַעַן דָּא, לְשַׁמְּשָׁא לְאַבְרָהָם, כֵּיוָן דְּשַׁמֵּשׁ לְאַבְרָהָם, יָתִיב תְּחוֹת צִלָּא דִּמְהֵימְנוּתָא, זָכָה לְמֵיפַּק מֵהַהוּא לָטְיָיא דְּאִתְלַטְיָיא, וְלֹא עוֹד אֶלָּא דִּכְתִּיב בֵּיהּ בְּרָכָה. דִּכְתִּיב, וַיֹּאמֶר בֹּא בְּרוּךְ יְיָ'. מַאי קָא מַיְירֵי. דְּכָל מַאן דְּיָתִיב תְּחוֹת צִלָּא דִּמְהֵימְנוּתָא, אַחֲסִין חֵירוּ לֵיהּ וְלִבְנוֹי לְעָלְמִין, וְאִתְבָּרַךְ בִּרְכָתָא עִלָּאָה, וּמַאן דְּאַפִּיק גַּרְמֵיהּ מִצִּלָּא דִּמְהֵימְנוּתָא, אַחֲסִין גָּלוּתָא לֵיהּ וְלִבְנוֹי, דִּכְתִּיב וַיִּלָּחֶם בְּיִשְׂרָאֵל וַיִּשְׁבְּ מִמֶּנּוּ שֶׁבִי.

269. "It is written, 'As for the merchant (also 'the Canaanite'), the balances of deceit are in his hand.' (Hosea 12:8) This refers to Eliezer, Abraham's servant. Come and see, it is written, 'Cursed be Canaan,' (Genesis 9:25) since this Canaan, Eliezer, **merited to serve**

Abraham, once he served Abraham and dwelt under the shadow of Faith, he merited to leave the curse he was cursed with. Not only that, but 'blessing' is written regarding him, as it is written, 'And he said, "Come, blessed of the Lord...."' (Genesis 24:31) This teaches us that whoever dwells under the shadow of Faith bequeaths freedom for himself and for his descendants forever, and is blessed with a Celestial blessing. Whoever excludes himself from the shadow of Faith bequeaths exile for himself and for his descendants, as it is written, '...he fought against Israel, and took some of them prisoner.' (Numbers 21:1)

The first Cloud guided the other Clouds.

270. בַּסֻּכֹּת תֵּשְׁבוּ חָסֵר, וְדָא עֲנָנָא חַד, דְּכֻלְּהוּ קְשִׁירִין בֵּיהּ. דִּכְתִּיב, כִּי עֲנַן יְיָ' עֲלֵיהֶם יוֹמָם. וּכְתִיב, וּבְעַמּוּד עָנָן אַתָּה הוֹלֵךְ לִפְנֵיהֶם יוֹמָם. דָּא הוּא עֲנָנָא דְּאַהֲרֹן, דְּאִקְרֵי יוֹמָם, דִּכְתִּיב יוֹמָם יְצַוֶּה יְיָ' חַסְדּוֹ. עֲנָנָא חַד, נָטִיל עִמֵּיהּ חָמֵשׁ אָחֳרָנִין, וְאִינּוּן שִׁית. וַעֲנָנָא אָחֳרָא, דִּכְתִּיב וּבְעַמּוּד אֵשׁ לָיְלָה, דָּא נָהֲרָא לְהוּ לְיִשְׂרָאֵל, מִנְּהִירוּ דְּאִינּוּן שִׁית.

270. "'You shall dwell in booths (*basukkot*; בַּסֻּכֹּת)...' (Leviticus 23:42) Sukkot is spelled without Vav (ו) **because** this Sukkot alludes **to only one Cloud,** which is Chesed, **to which all** six Clouds **are attached.** Hence there are seven days, **as it is written, 'And the cloud of the Lord was upon them by day (yomam)...' (Numbers 10:34) and 'and that You go before them by day time (*yomam*) in a pillar of cloud' (Numbers 14:14), which is Aaron's cloud,** which is Chesed **that is called 'by day' (*yomam*) as it is written, 'Yet the Lord will command His Chesed in the daytime (*yomam*)' (Psalms 42:9) One Cloud,** which is Chesed, **receives with it five other Clouds,** which are Gevurah, Tiferet, Netzach, Hod, and Yesod, **so they are six. Another Cloud, of which it is written, 'and in a pillar of fire by night' (Numbers 14:14),** which is Malchut, **shines on Israel from the Illumination of the six** Clouds."

37. The holiday of Sukkot

A Synopsis

We learn that whoever is in the secret of Faith dwells in a Sukkah (Booth), and that one must offer a daily sacrifice on the seven days of Sukkot. Offerings are made to the other nations because God wants them to be friends with Israel.

Sitting securely under the shade of the Sukkah,
without fear of the prosecutors.

רעיא מהימנא

271. בַּסֻּכּוֹת תֵּשְׁבוּ שִׁבְעַת יָמִים וְגוֹ', פִּקּוּדָא דָא, לֵישֵׁב בַּסּוּכָּה. וְהָא אוֹקִימְנָא, בְּגִין לְאִתְחֲזָאָה דְּיִשְׂרָאֵל יַתְבֵי בְּרָזָא דִּמְהֵימְנוּתָא, בְּלָא דְּחִילוּ כְּלָל, דְּהָא מְקַטְרְגָא אִתְפְּרַשׁ מִנַּיְיהוּ. וְכָל מַאן דְּאִיהוּ בְּרָזָא דִּמְהֵימְנוּתָא, יָתִיב בַּסּוּכָּה. כְּמָה דְּאוֹקִימְנָא, דִּכְתִּיב, כָּל הָאֶזְרָח בְּיִשְׂרָאֵל יֵשְׁבוּ בַּסֻּכּוֹת. מַאן דְּאִיהוּ בְּרָזָא דִּמְהֵימְנוּתָא, וּמִזַּרְעָא וְשָׁרְשָׁא דְּיִשְׂרָאֵל, יֵשְׁבוּ בַּסֻּכּוֹת. וְרָזָא דָא אִתְּמַר בְּכַמָּה דּוּכְתֵּי.

Ra'aya Meheimna (Faithful Shepherd)

271. "You shall dwell in Booths (Sukkot) seven days…." (Leviticus 23:42) This Precept is to dwell in a Sukkah. We explained that its purpose is to show that Israel dwell in the secret of Faith, the secret of the shade of the Sukkah **entirely without fear** of denouncing, **since the prosecutor has already separated from them** on Yom Kippur through the goat to Azazel. **Whoever is in the secret of Faith dwells in a Sukkah, as we explained from the words, "…all that are born in Israel shall dwell in booths" (Ibid.)** namely **whoever is in the secret of Faith of the seed and root of Israel shall dwell in Sukkot. This secret was brought in several places.**

We bring 70 sacrifices during Sukkot so that everyone can have a part in the joy of Israel.

272. פִּקּוּדָא בָּתַר דָּא, לְקָרְבָא קָרְבְּנָא בְּכָל יוֹמָא, וְקָרְבְּנָא דָּא, לְמֶהֱוֵי חוּלָקָא בְּכֹלָּא, בְּחֶדְוָותָא דִּבְנוֹי. בְּגִין דְּכֻלְּהוּ אֲחִידָן בְּאִילָנָא. עַנְפִּין דִּלְתַתָּא דִּלְגַּבֵּי שָׁרְשָׁא דְּאִילָנָא, כֹּלָּא אִתְבָּרְכָן בְּגִין אִילָנָא. אַף עַל גַּב דְּלֵית בְּהוּ תּוֹעַלְתָּא, כֹּלָּא אִתְבָּרְכָאן. וְחֶדְוָותָא דְּיִשְׂרָאֵל בַּאֲבוּהוֹן דִּלְעֵילָּא, יַהֲבֵי חוּלָקָא דְּבִרְכָאן, לְכָל אִינּוּן שְׁאָר עַמִּין, דְּאִית לוֹן אֲחִידוּ, וְאִתְאַחֲדוּ בְּהוּ בְּיִשְׂרָאֵל.

272. The following Precept is to offer a daily sacrifice on the seven days of Sukkot. **Everyone should have a part in that sacrifice, in His children's joy,** since the seventy bullocks correspond to the seventy Ministers of the nations. **They are all attached to the Tree,** Zeir Anpin, **since the branches below that come from the root of the Tree are all blessed because of the Tree. Even though they are useless,** they **are all** also **blessed. Israel rejoice in their Supernal Father,** namely in the root of the Tree, **and they give a portion of the blessings to the rest of the nations, who can hold and do hold to Israel.**

The sacrifices of Sukkot turn all the enemies into loving friends.

273. וְכָל אִלֵּין קָרְבְּנִין, לְמֵיהַב מְזוֹנָא, לְאִינּוּן מְמָנָן דִּשְׁאָר עַמִּין, דְּהָא מִגּוֹ רְחִימוּ דְּקָא רָחִים קוּדְשָׁא בְּרִיךְ הוּא לִבְנוֹי, בָּעֵי דְּכֹלָּא יְהוֹן רְחִימִין דִּלְהוֹן. וְרָזָא דָּא, בִּרְצוֹת יְיָ' דַּרְכֵי אִישׁ גַּם אוֹיְבָיו יַשְׁלִים אִתּוֹ. אֲפִילּוּ כָּל אִינּוּן מְקַטְרְגֵי עִלָּאֵי כֻּלְּהוּ אֲהַדְרָן רְחִימִין לְיִשְׂרָאֵל וְכַד חַיָּילִין דִּלְעֵילָּא אֲהַדְרוּ רְחִימִין לְיִשְׂרָאֵל, כָּל אִינּוּן דִּלְתַתָּא, עַל אַחַת כַּמָּה וְכַמָּה.

273. All those offerings, the seventy bullocks, **were made to give nourishment to all the Ministers appointed over the other nations, since for the love the Holy One, blessed be He, has for His children, He wants all** the Ministers **to be their friends. This is the secret of, "When a man's ways please the Lord, He makes even his enemies to be at peace with him." (Proverbs 16:7)** Namely **even the highest**

prosecutors become friendly again with Israel. When the forces Above return to love Israel, then all the more so will those Below.

The sacrifices are for the Creator, and He distributes the blessings to the nations.

274. וְאִי תֵּימָא לְהוֹן הֲווּ מְקָרְבֵי קָרְבְּנָא, לָאו הָכִי, אֶלָּא כֹּלָּא לְקוּדְשָׁא בְּרִיךְ הוּא סָלִיק וּמִתְקָרֵב. וְאִיהוּ פָּרִישׁ מְזוֹנָא לְכָלְהוּ אוּכְלוּסִין דְּסִטְרִין אָחֳרָנִין, דְּיִתְהֲנוּן בְּהַהוּא דּוֹרוֹנָא דִּבְנוֹי, וְיִתְהַדְרוּן רְחִימִין דִּלְהוֹן, דְּיִנְדְּעוּן עֵילָּא וְתַתָּא, דְּהָא לֵית עַמָּא כְּעַמָּא דְּיִשְׂרָאֵל, דְּאִינּוּן חוּלָקֵיהּ וְעַדְבֵיהּ דְּקוּדְשָׁא בְּרִיךְ הוּא, וְאִסְתַּלָּק יְקָרָא דְּקוּדְשָׁא בְּרִיךְ הוּא עֵילָּא וְתַתָּא כַּדְקָא יָאוּת. וְכָל אוּכְלוּסִין עִלָּאִין פַּתְחֵי וְאַמְרֵי, וּמִי כְעַמְּךָ כְּיִשְׂרָאֵל גּוֹי אֶחָד בָּאָרֶץ.
ע"כ רעיא מהימנא

274. If you say that the sacrifices were offered to them, to the seventy Ministers, **it is not so. Rather, everything was offered and sacrificed to the Holy One, blessed be He, and He divides the nourishment among the multitudes of the other sides,** namely the Ministers of the seventy nations, **so they will enjoy His children's gift and return to be their friends. Thus it shall be known Above and Below that there is no nation like Israel, who are the portion and lot of the Holy One, blessed be He. And the glory of the Holy One, blessed be He, rises Above and Below as it should and all the Celestial multitude open and say, "And who is like Your people Israel, a unique nation on earth…." (II Samuel 7:23)**

End of Ra'aya Meheimna (Faithful Shepherd)

A Synopsis

Rav Elazar talks about the clouds that went with Israel through the wilderness. We hear about the invitation for the guests of Faith to enter the Sukkah, and how important it is to give a portion of the meal to the poor.

When Israel were in the wilderness they were protected by the clouds.

275. רִבִּי אֶלְעָזָר פָּתַח, כֹּה אָמַר יְיָ' זָכַרְתִּי לָךְ חֶסֶד נְעוּרַיִךְ וְגוֹ'. הַאי קְרָא עַל כ"י אִתְּמַר, בְּשַׁעֲתָא דַּהֲוַת אַזְלָא בְּמַדְבְּרָא עִמְּהוֹן דְּיִשְׂרָאֵל. זָכַרְתִּי לָךְ חֶסֶד: דָּא עֲנָנָא דְּאַהֲרֹן, דְּנַטְלָא בְּחָמֵשׁ אָחֳרָנִין, דְּאִתְקְשָׁרוּ עֲלָךְ, וּנְהִירוּ עֲלָךְ. אַהֲבַת כְּלוּלוֹתָיִךְ, דְּאִשְׁתַּכְלְלוּ לָךְ, וְאַעֲטָרוּ לָךְ, וְאַתְקִינוּ לָךְ כְּכַלָּה דְּתַעֲדֵי תַּכְשִׁיטָהָא. וְכָל כַּךְ לָמָּה. בְּגִין לֶכְתֵּךְ אַחֲרַי בַּמִּדְבָּר בְּאֶרֶץ לֹא זְרוּעָה.

275. Rav Elazar opened with, “Thus says the Lord: ‘I remember to you the lovingkindness of your youth....’” (Jeremiah 2:2) This verse was said about the Congregation of Israel, which is Malchut, **when she was walking with Israel in the wilderness. ‘I remember to you the lovingkindness (*chesed*) of your youth...’” (Ibid.) refers to Aaron’s cloud,** which is Chesed **that traveled with five other** clouds, Gevurah, Tiferet, Netzach, Hod, and Yesod **that joined over you and shone upon you. “‘...Your love as a bride (*klulotayich*)...” (Ibid.)** as those clouds **that incorporated (*kalelu*) you, adorned you and bedecked you as a bride wearing her jewelry.”** [He asks:] **“Why all that?”** [He answers:] **“Because, ‘...you did go after Me in the wilderness, in a land not sown’ (Ibid.)** since she walked with Israel in the wilderness.

Every day of Sukkot represents a Sefirah.

276. תָּא חֲזֵי, בְּשַׁעֲתָא דְּבַר נָשׁ יָתִיב בְּמָדוֹרָא דָּא, שְׁכִינְתָּא פַּרְסָא גַּדְפָּהָא עָלֵיהּ מִלְּעֵילָּא, וְאַבְרָהָם וַחֲמִשָּׁה צַדִּיקַיָּיא אָחֳרָנִין שַׁוְיָין מָדוֹרֵיהוֹן עִמֵּיהּ. אָמַר רִבִּי אַבָּא, אַבְרָהָם וַחֲמִשָּׁה צַדִּיקַיָּיא, וְדָוִד מַלְכָּא, שַׁוְיָין מָדוֹרֵיהוֹן עִמֵּיהּ. הֲדָא הוּא דִּכְתִּיב, בַּסֻּכּוֹת תֵּשְׁבוּ שִׁבְעַת יָמִים. שִׁבְעַת יָמִים כְּתִיב, וְלָא בְּשִׁבְעַת יָמִים. כְּגַוְונָא דָּא כְּתִיב כִּי שֵׁשֶׁת יָמִים עָשָׂה יְיָ' אֶת הַשָּׁמַיִם וְגוֹ'. וּבָעֵי בַּר נָשׁ לְמֶחֱדֵי בְּכָל יוֹמָא וְיוֹמָא, בְּאַנְפִּין נְהִירִין, בְּאוּשְׁפִּיזִין אִלֵּין דְּשַׁרְיָין עִמֵּיהּ.

276. “Come and see, when man sits in this abode, in the Sukkah, **which is the shade of Faith, the Shechinah spreads her wings over him from Above, and Abraham,** Chesed, **and five other Righteous,**

the secret of Gevurah, Tiferet, Netzach, Hod, and Yesod, **fix their dwelling with him." Rav Aba said: "Abraham, five Tzadikim, and King David,** Malchut, **fix their dwelling with him. As it is written: 'You shall dwell in booths (*Sukkot*) seven days….' (Leviticus 23:42) It is written, 'seven days,'** which alludes to Chesed, Gevurah, Tiferet, Netzach, Hod, Yesod, and Malchut, **instead of, 'in seven days.' Similarly it is written, '…for six days the Lord made Heaven and Earth…' (Exodus 31:17)** instead of 'in six days.' They too indicate the Supernal Six Days, Chesed, Gevurah, Tiferet, Netzach, Hod, and Yesod that made Heaven and Earth. **One should rejoice every day with a joyful countenance in those guests,** Chesed, Gevurah, Tiferet, Netzach, Hod, Yesod, and Malchut **that dwell with him."**

Rav Hamnuna Saba would invite the Seven Guests before entering the Sukkah.

277. וְאָמַר רִבִּי אַבָּא, כְּתִיב בַּסֻּכּוֹת תֵּשְׁבוּ שִׁבְעַת יָמִים, וּלְבָתַר יֵשְׁבוּ בַּסֻּכּוֹת. בְּקַדְמֵיתָא תֵּשְׁבוּ, וּלְבָתַר יֵשְׁבוּ. אֶלָּא, קַדְמָאָה לְאוּשְׁפִּיזֵי. תִּנְיָינָא, לִבְנֵי עָלְמָא. קַדְמָאָה לְאוּשְׁפִּיזֵי, כִּי הָא דְּרַב הַמְנוּנָא סָבָא, כַּד הֲוָה עָיֵיל לַסּוּכָּה הֲוָה חַדֵּי, וְקָאִים עַל פִּתְחָא לַסּוּכָּה מִלְּגָאו, וְאָמַר נְזַמֵּן לְאוּשְׁפִּיזִין. מְסַדֵּר פָּתוֹרָא, וְקָאֵים עַל רַגְלוֹהִי, וּמְבָרֵךְ, וְאוֹמֵר בַּסֻּכּוֹת תֵּשְׁבוּ שִׁבְעַת יָמִים. תִּיבוּ אוּשְׁפִּיזִין עִלָּאִין, תִּיבוּ. תִּיבוּ אוּשְׁפִּיזֵי מְהֵימְנוּתָא, תִּיבוּ. אָרִים יְדוֹי, וְחַדֵּי, וְאָמַר זַכָּאָה חוּלָקָנָא, זַכָּאָה חוּלָקֵיהוֹן דְּיִשְׂרָאֵל, דִּכְתִיב, כִּי חֵלֶק יְיָ' עַמּוֹ וְגוֹ', וַהֲוָה יָתִיב.

277. Rav Aba said: "It is written, 'You shall dwell in Booths (Sukkot) **seven days…' and then, '…[all that are born in Israel] shall dwell in booths….' (Leviticus 23:42)** It **first** says, **'You shall dwell' and then, they 'shall dwell.'"** He answers, **"The first one is for the guests,** Chesed, Gevurah, Tiferet, Netzach, Hod, Yesod, and Malchut, and therefore the text speaks in the second person. **The second is for the people of the world,** therefore the text speaks in the third person, 'all… shall dwell.' **The first is for the guests. Rav Hamnuna Saba, for example, when he entered the Sukkah, used to stay happily on the**

inner threshold of the Sukkah, and say, 'Let us invite the guest.' He set the table, stood up and blessed, 'to dwell in the Sukkah,' **then said: "You shall dwell in booths seven days...." (Ibid.) 'Sit down, lofty guests, sit you down. Sit down, guests of Faith, sit you down.' He joyfully raised his hands and said: 'Happy is our lot, happy is the lot of Israel, as it is written: "For the Lord's portion is His people...." (Deuteronomy 32:9)' Then he would sit down.**

For the Ushpizin to enter, one needs to bring in guests to the Sukkah.

278. תִּנְיָינָא, לִבְנֵי עָלְמָא, דְּמַאן דְּאִית לֵיהּ חוּלָקָא בְּעַמָּא וּבְאַרְעָא קַדִּישָׁא, יָתִיב בְּצִלָּא דִּמְהֵימְנוּתָא, לְקַבְּלָא אוּשְׁפִּיזִין, לְמֶחֱדֵי בְּהַאי עָלְמָא וּבְעָלְמָא דְּאָתֵי וּבָעֵי לְמֶחֱדֵי לְמִסְכְּנֵי. מַאי טַעֲמָא. בְּגִין דְּחוּלָקָא דְּאִינּוּן אוּשְׁפִּיזִין דְּזַמִּין דְּמִסְכְּנֵי הוּא. וְהַהוּא דְּיָתִיב בְּצִלָּא דָּא דִּמְהֵימְנוּתָא, וְזַמִּין אוּשְׁפִּיזִין אִלֵּין עִלָּאִין, אוּשְׁפִּיזֵי מְהֵימְנוּתָא, וְלָא יָהִיב לוֹן חוּלָקֵיהוֹן, כֻּלְּהוּ קַיְימֵי מִנֵּיהּ, וְאַמְרֵי אַל תִּלְחַם אֶת לֶחֶם רַע עָיִן וְגוֹ', אִשְׁתְּכַח דְּהַהוּא פָּתוֹרָא דְּתַקִּין, דִּילֵיהּ הוּא, וְלָאו דְּקוּדְשָׁא בְּרִיךְ הוּא, עָלֵיהּ כְּתִיב וְזֵרִיתִי פֶרֶשׁ עַל פְּנֵיכֶם וְגוֹ', פֶּרֶשׁ חַגֵּיכֶם, וְלָא חַגַּי. וַוי לֵיהּ לְהַהוּא בַּר נָשׁ, בְּשַׁעֲתָא דְּאִלֵּין אוּשְׁפִּיזֵי מְהֵימְנוּתָא קַיְימֵי מִפָּתוֹרֵיהּ.

278. "The second mention of "shall dwell" in the verse, in the third person, **is for the people of the world. For whoever has a share in the nation and the Holy land, dwells in the secret of Faith to receive guests and rejoice in this world and in the World to Come. It behooves us to gladden the poor."** [He asks:] **"What is the reason?"** [He answers:] **"It is because the portion of the guests he invited** to his meal **belongs to the poor. He that sits in the shade of Faith and invites these lofty guests, the guests of Faith, yet does not give them,** namely the poor, **their share** of the meal, **all** the guests **stand back from him and say, 'Do not eat the bread of him who has an evil eye....' (Proverbs 23:6) Thus the table he set belongs to** the one who has an evil eye, **and not to the Holy One, blessed be He. Of him it is written, '...and I will strew dung upon your faces, the dung of your festal**

sacrifices...' (Malachi 2:3) and not 'My festal sacrifices.' Woe to that man when those guests of Faith stand back from his table."

The Ushpizin exit the Sukkah of one who does not bring in guests.

279. וְאָמַר ר' אַבָּא, אַבְרָהָם, כָּל יוֹמוֹי הֲוָה קָאֵים בְּפָרָשַׁת אוֹרְחִין, לְזַמְּנָא אוּשְׁפִּיזִין, וּלְתַקְּנָא לוֹן פָּתוֹרֵי, הַשְׁתָּא, דִּמְזַמְּנִין לֵיהּ, וּלְכֻלְּהוּ צַדִּיקַיָּיא, וּלְדָוִד מַלְכָּא, וְלָא יָהֲבִין לוֹן חוּלָקֵיהוֹן, אַבְרָהָם קָאֵים מִפָּתוֹרָא, וְקָרֵי, סוּרוּ נָא מֵעַל אָהֳלֵי הָאֲנָשִׁים הָרְשָׁעִים הָאֵלֶּה. וְכֻלְּהוּ סַלְּקִין אֲבַתְרֵיהּ. יִצְחָק אָמַר, וּבֶטֶן רְשָׁעִים תֶּחְסָר. יַעֲקֹב אָמַר, פִּתְּךָ אָכַלְתָּ תְקִיאֶנָּה. וּשְׁאָר כָּל צַדִּיקַיָּיא אַמְרֵי, כִּי כָּל שֻׁלְחָנוֹת מָלְאוּ קִיא צוֹאָה בְּלִי מָקוֹם.

279. Rav Aba said: "Throughout his life, Abraham used to stand at the crossroad to invite guests and set the table for them. Now, on Sukkot, **if one invites him, and all the other Righteous and King David, but does not give them their share, Abraham stands up from the table and cries, 'Move away from the tents of these wicked men...' (Numbers 16:26) and everyone walks away after him. Isaac says, '...but the belly of the wicked is empty' (Proverbs 13:25) and Jacob says, 'The morsel which you have eaten shall you vomit up....' (Proverbs 23:8) The rest of the Righteous,** namely Moses and Aaron, **say, 'For all tables are full of vomit and filth, so that no space is left.' (Isaiah 28:8)**

During the Ten Days of Repentance,
those who do not bring in guests are punished.

280. דָּוִד מַלְכָּא אָמַר, וְאַשְׁלִים דִּינוֹי, דִּכְתִּיב וַיְהִי כַּעֲשֶׂרֶת הַיָּמִים וַיִּגֹּף יְיָ' אֶת נָבָל וַיָּמֹת. מַאי קָא מַיְירֵי. בְּגִין דְּדָוִד שָׁאַל לְנָבָל, וְאִתְעֲבֵיד לֵיהּ אוּשְׁפִּיזָא, וְלָא בָּעָא. וְדָא זַמִּין לֵיהּ, וְלָא יָהַב לֵיהּ חוּלָקָא, וּבְאִינּוּן עֲשָׂרָה יוֹמִין דְּדָוִד מַלְכָּא דְּאִין עָלְמָא, אַתְדָּן עָלֵיהּ הַהוּא בַּר נָשׁ דְּאַשְׁלִים לֵיהּ בִּישׁ יַתִּיר מִנָּבָל.

280. "King David said: 'And He completes the execution of His punishments, as written: "And it came to pass about ten days after, that the Lord smote Nabal, and he died." (I Samuel 25:38)" He asks: **"What does this mean?"** He answers: **"This is because David asked Nabal to accept him as a guest, but he declined. Also he** who sits at the Sukkah **invited him,** King David, **yet did not give him his share.** Therefore King David recited this verse about Nabal over him. **During the ten days,** the Ten Days of Repentance, **when King David,** Malchut, **judges the world, that man is punished for it, for doing evil to him worse than Nabal,** by inviting him yet not giving him his share. Nabal at least did not invite him."

The Torah does not trouble man to give more than what he can afford.

281. אָמַר רִבִּי אֶלְעָזָר אוֹרַיְיתָא לָא אַטְרַח עָלֵיהּ דְּבַר נָשׁ יַתִּיר, אֶלָּא כְּמָה דְּיָכִיל, דִּכְתִּיב אִישׁ כְּמַתְּנַת יָדוֹ וְגוֹ'. וְלָא לֵימָא אִינִישׁ אֱכוֹל וְאֶשְׂבַּע וְאַרְוֵי בְּקַדְמֵיתָא, וּמַה דְּיִשְׁתְּאַר אֶתֵּן לְמִסְכְּנֵי, אֶלָּא רֵישָׁא דְּכֹלָּא דְּאוּשְׁפִּיזִין הוּא, וְאִי חַדֵּי לְאוּשְׁפִּיזִין וְרַוֵּי לוֹן, קוּדְשָׁא בְּרִיךְ הוּא חַדֵּי עִמֵּיהּ, וְאַבְרָהָם קָרֵי עָלֵיהּ, אָז תִּתְעַנַּג עַל יְיָ' וְגוֹ'. וְיִצְחָק קָאָרֵי עָלֵיהּ, כָּל כְּלִי יוּצַר עָלַיִךְ לֹא יִצְלָח. אָמַר רִבִּי שִׁמְעוֹן, הַאי, דָּוִד מַלְכָּא אָ"ל, בְּגִין דְּכָל זַיְינִין דְּמַלְכָּא, וְקָרְבִין דְּמַלְכָּא, בִּידוֹי דְּדָוִד אִתְפְּקָדוּ, אֲבָל יִצְחָק קָאָמַר, גִּבּוֹר בָּאָרֶץ יִהְיֶה זַרְעוֹ וְגוֹ', הוֹן וָעוֹשֶׁר וְגוֹ'.

281. Rav Elazar said: "The Torah did not trouble man to give **more than what he can afford, as it is written, 'Each man shall give as he is able....' (Deuteronomy 16:17) One must not say, 'Let me eat and be full and slake my thirst first, and give the rest to the poor.' Rather, the first part belongs to the guests. He who gladdens the guests and gives them to drink, the Holy One, blessed be He, is happy with him and Abraham says about him: 'Then shall you delight yourself in the Lord...' (Isaiah 58:14) and Isaac proclaims, 'No weapon that is formed against you shall succeed....' (Isaiah 54:17)" Rav Shimon said: "King David,** Malchut, **recited this** verse **to him because all the**

weapons of the King and the King's wars were delivered to David's hands. But Isaac says: 'His seed shall be mighty upon earth... Wealth and riches shall be in his house....' (Psalms 112:2-3)

Joyous is the portion of the one who brings in guests.

282(1). יַעֲקֹב אָמַר, אָז יִבָּקַע כַּשַּׁחַר אוֹרֶךָ וְגוֹ', שְׁאָר צַדִּיקַיָּיא אַמְרֵי, וְנָחֲךָ יְיָ' תָּמִיד וְהִשְׂבִּיעַ וְגוֹ', דָּוִד מַלְכָּא אָמַר, כָּל כְּלִי יוּצַר עָלַיִךְ לֹא יִצְלָח, דְּהָא הוּא עַל כָּל זַיְינֵי עָלְמָא אִתְפַּקַּד. זַכָּאָה חוּלָקֵיהּ דְּבַר נָשׁ, דְּזָכֵי לְכָל הַאי. זַכָּאָה חוּלָקֵיהוֹן דְּצַדִּיקַיָּיא, בְּעָלְמָא דֵין, וּבְעָלְמָא דְּאָתֵי, עֲלַיְיהוּ כְּתִיב וְעַמֵּךְ כֻּלָּם צַדִּיקִים וְגוֹ'.

282(1). "Jacob said: 'Then shall your light break forth (*yibaka*; יִבָּקַע) like the dawn...' (Isaiah 58:8) because *yibaka* is spelled with the same letters as Jacob (יַעֲקֹב). **The other Righteous say, 'And the Lord shall guide you continually, and satisfy....' (Isaiah 58:11) King David said: 'No weapon that is formed against you shall succeed,' (Isaiah 54:17) because he was appointed over all the weapons in the world. Happy is the lot of the man who merited all this. Happy is the lot of the Righteous in this world and in the World to Come. Of them it is written, 'And your people, all of them righteous....' (Isaiah 60:21)"**

A Synopsis

We are told that it is a Precept to take a *Lulav* on the day of Sukkot.

The four species are the secret of the shape of man.

רעיא מהימנא

282(2). פִּקּוּדָא דָּא לִיטּוֹל לוּלָב בְּהַהוּא יוֹמָא בְּאִינּוּן זִינִין דִּילֵיהּ וְהַאי רָזָא אוּקִימְנָא וְאוּקְמוּהָ חַבְרַיָּיא כְּמָה דְּקוּדְשָׁא בְּרִיךְ הוּא נָטִיל לוֹן לְיִשְׂרָאֵל בְּהָנֵי יוֹמִין וְחַדֵּי בְּהוֹן. אוּף הָכִי יִשְׂרָאֵל נַטְלֵי לֵיהּ לְקוּדְשָׁא בְּרִיךְ הוּא לְחוּלָקֵיהוֹן

וְחַדָּאן בֵּיהּ. וְדָא הוּא רָזָא דְּלוּלָב. וּמִינִין דְּבֵיהּ דְּאִיהוּ רָזָא דְיוּקְנָא דְאָדָם וְהָא אִתְּמַר.
ע"כ רעיא מהימנא

Ra'aya Meheimna (Faithful Shepherd)

282(2). This Precept is to take a *Lulav* with its species on that day. We explained this secret, as did the friends. Just as the Holy One, blessed be He, takes Israel during those days and rejoices in them, so do Israel take the Holy One, blessed be He, as their portion and rejoice in Him. This is the secret of the *Lulav* and its species, as it is the secret of the form of man, namely the secret of the Seven Sefirot: Chesed, Gevurah, Tiferet, Netzach, Hod, Yesod, and Malchut. The three Myrtle branches correspond to Chesed-Gevurah-Tiferet, the two Willow branches to Netzach and Hod, the *Lulav* to Yesod and the *Etrog* to Malchut. **We already learned this.**

End of Ra'aya Meheimna (Faithful Shepherd)

Pinchas

121. The Holiday of Sukkot

A Synopsis

We are reminded of the origin of this Festival dating from the time when Israel were led out of Egypt. The size and construction of the Tabernacle is described, and the point is made that the shadow cast by the roof is not an ordinary shadow but is really the protection cast over the soul. There are seven letters that incorporate the shape of a shelter or Tabernacle: Bet, Gimel, Dalet, Caf, Pei, Resh, and Tav. The seven planets are said to correspond to these letters, and many other analogies are drawn by means of the number seven. We hear about the meaning, composition, and purpose of the *Lulav*, and why the *Lulav* is taken in the right hand and the *Etrog* in the Left. Next we hear that the Patriarchs, together with Moses, Aaron, David, and Solomon, all come to Rav Shimon and bless him and praise his Light. Rav Shimon begins talking about the seventy bullocks that Israel used to sacrifice during the seven days of Sukkot—one less bullock every day. He says that the clue to this decrease is found in the fact that the Ark came to rest in the seventh month, when the waters were continually receding. In the same way, the sins of Israel decrease and so too do the number of Accusers. The purpose of Noah's Ark and the purpose of the Sukkah are the same—to give protection. The Shechinah protects all those who keep the Sign of the Covenant.

The Sukkah is the Supernal Mother that provides protection for Her children.

814. בַּחֲמִשָּׁה עָשָׂר יוֹם לַחֹדֶשׁ הַשְּׁבִיעִי וְגוֹ׳, דְּאִיהִי תִּשְׁרֵי, מִקְרָא קֹדֶשׁ יִהְיֶה לָכֶם כָּל מְלֶאכֶת עֲבוֹדָה לֹא תַעֲשׂוּ וְחַגּוֹתֶם אוֹתוֹ חַג לַיְיָ׳ שִׁבְעַת יָמִים וְגוֹ׳. בַּחֲמִשָּׁה עָשָׂר, מִסִּטְרָא דְּיָ״הּ. וְחַגּוֹתֶם אוֹתוֹ, דָּא אוֹת ו׳, עַמּוּדָא דְּאֶמְצָעִיתָא. שִׁבְעַת יָמִים, מִסִּטְרָא דְּבַת שֶׁבַע, דְּאִיהִי מַלְכוּת. אֲבָהָן, וְרַעְיָא מְהֵימְנָא,

וְאַהֲרֹן, דָּוִד וּשְׁלֹמֹה, הָא אִינּוּן שֶׁבַע, לָקֳבֵל שֶׁבַע סְפִירָאן. אֲנָא בָּעֵינָא לְתַקְּנָא לְכוֹן סֻכָּה, דְּאִיהִי אִימָּא עִלָּאָה, לְסַכְכָא עֲלַיְיהוּ, כְּאִמָּא עַל בְּנִין.

814. "On the fifteenth day of the seventh month..." which is Tishrei, "...you shall observe a sacred occasion: you shall not work at your occupations. And you shall observe it as a festival of the Lord for seven days." (Numbers 29:12) "On the fifteenth day" means from the side of Yud-Hei, namely Chochmah and Binah. **"...you shall observe it (*oto;* אותו)"** is the letters of **"the letter Vav" (אות ו), which is the Central Column,** Zeir Anpin. **"...seven days" is from the side of Bat Sheva (Daughter of Seven), which is Malchut,** the last Hei. **The Patriarchs,** Chesed-Gevurah-Tiferet, **the Faithful Shepherd [Moses],** who is Netzach, **Aaron,** who is Hod, **David,** who is Malchut, **and Solomon (*Shlomo*),** who is Yesod that is called Peace (*Shalom*), **total seven, corresponding to Seven Sefirot. I want to construct for you a Sukkah, which is Supernal Ima, who will provide a shelter over them,** over the Seven Sefirot, **as the mother over the children.**

The numerical value of Sukkah is 91,
like Yud-Hei-Vav-Hei plus Alef-Dalet-Nun-Yud.

815. וּבְגִין ז' סְפִירָאן אָמַר קְרָא, כִּי בַסֻּכּוֹת הוֹשַׁבְתִּי אֶת בְּנֵי יִשְׂרָאֵל, בְּמִפְקָנוּתְהוֹן מֵאַרְעָא דְּמִצְרַיִם, בְּז' עֲנָנֵי כָּבוֹד. סוּכָּה בְּאָת ו', אִיהוּ בְּרָזָא דִּתְרֵין בְּנִין, יְדֹוָד אֲדֹנָי. וְהָכִי סָלִיק סוּכָּ"ה בְּחוּשְׁבַּן יְאֲהדֹוָנָהי. תְּרֵין כְּרוּבִים, דְּהֵם סוֹכְכִים בְּכַנְפֵיהֶם עַל הַכַּפּוֹרֶת וּפְנֵיהֶם אִישׁ אֶל אָחִיו.

815. And on account of the Seven Sefirot, scripture said: "...in booths (Sukkot) did I settle the children of Israel when I brought them out of the land of Egypt..." (Leviticus 23:43) namely with seven clouds of glory, which are the secret of Seven Sefirot. **Sukkah** when spelled **with a letter Vav is in the secret of the two children,** over whom Binah provides a shelter, namely **Yud-Hei-Vav-Hei (יהוה) and Alef-Dalet-Nun-Yud (אדני),** Zeir Anpin and Malchut, **for the**

numerical value of Sukkah amounts to Yud-Alef-Hei-Dalet-Vav-Nun-Hei-Yud (יאהדונהי), for Sukkah (סוכה) consists of the letters Caf-Vav (כו; 26), which have the same numerical value as the letters of Yud-Hei-Vav-Hei, and the letters Samech-Hei (סה; 65), which have the same numerical value as Alef-Dalet-Nun-Yud. They are the secret of **the two Cherubs,** the secret of Zeir Anpin and Malchut, **who are "… spreading their wings over the covering, and their faces shall look one to another…." (Exodus 25:20)**

The secret of the height of the Sukkah.

816. וְאִית עֲשָׂרָה טְפָחִים בִּכְרוּבִים מִתַּתָּא לְעֵילָּא, מֵרַגְלֵיהוֹן עַד רֵישַׁיְיהוֹן, וּמֵרֵישַׁיְיהוֹן וְעַד רַגְלֵיהוֹן, וְשַׁרְיָין עַל טֶפַח דְּאִיהוּ י'. וַעֲשָׂרָה מֵעֵילָּא לְתַתָּא, וּמִתַּתָּא לְעֵילָּא, הַיְינוּ יו"ד. וּבג"כ, שִׁיעוּרָא דְּסֻכָּה אָמְרוּ רַבָּנָן, לֹא פָּחוֹת מֵעֲשָׂרָה, וְלֹא לְמַעְלָה מֵעֶשְׂרִים. סֻכָּה הָעֲשׂוּיָה כְּכִבְשָׁן מִסִּטְרָא דְּאִימָּא, עָלָהּ אִתְּמַר, וְהַר סִינַי עָשַׁן כֻּלּוֹ מִפְּנֵי אֲשֶׁר יָרַד עָלָיו יְיָ' בָּאֵשׁ וַיַּעַל עֲשָׁנוֹ כְּעֶשֶׁן הַכִּבְשָׁן. וְכֹלָּא חַד.

816. And the Cherubs, who are Zeir Anpin and Nukva, **are ten handbreadths from bottom to top,** namely Ten Sefirot of Returning Light, **from their feet to their heads**, and Ten Sefirot of Direct Light **from their heads to their feet, and they rest on a handbreadth, which is** the secret of **Yud (י; 10).** They therefore contain **ten from top to bottom and ten from bottom to top,** namely the Ten Sefirot of Direct Light and the Ten Sefirot of Returning Light, **and this is Yud-Vav-Dalet (יוד),** whose numerical value is twenty. **And this is why the sages ruled that the size of a Sukkah should be not less than ten and not more than twenty. A Sukkah that is built in the shape of a furnace is from the side of Ima,** which is Judgment, **about which it is said: "And Mount Sinai smoked in every part, because the Lord descended on it in fire: and the smoke of it ascended like the smoke of a furnace…" (Exodus 19:18) and it is all one.**

The Sukkah produces a protective shade over the soul.

817. וְסֻכָּה תִּהְיֶה לְצֵל יוֹמָם, דִּסְכָךְ בָּעֵינָן. וּסְכָךְ אִתְעֲבֵיד לַצֵּל. דְּאִתְּמַר בֵּיהּ, בְּצֵל שַׁדַּי יִתְלוֹנָן. וְלֹא בְּצֵל סֻכַּת הֶדְיוֹט, דְּאָגִין עַל גּוּפָא מִשִּׁמְשָׁא. אֶלָּא צֵל לְאַגָּנָא עַל נִשְׁמְתָא. בְּצִלּוֹ חִמַּדְתִּי וְיָשַׁבְתִּי. אֲשֶׁר אָמַרְנוּ בְּצִלּוֹ נִחְיֶה בַגּוֹיִם. צֵל עִם ם׳, אִיהִי צֶלֶם. דְּאִתְּמַר בֵּיהּ, אַךְ בְּצֶלֶם יִתְהַלֶּךְ אִישׁ. ם׳ סְתוּמָה אִית לָהּ אַרְבָּעָה דְּפָנוֹת.

817. “And there shall be a Sukkah for shade in the daytime….” (Isaiah 4:6) This is because a roof is required, and this casts a shade (*tzel*), about which it is said: “…shall dwell under the shadow (*tzel*) of Shadai….” (Psalms 91:1) And not a shade of an ordinary Sukkah that protects the body from the sun, but a shade that casts a protection over the Soul, in the secret of: **“…in his shade I delighted and dwelled…” (Song of Songs 2:3) and “…of Whom we said: ‘Under His shade we shall live among the nations.’” (Lamentations 4:20) *Tzel* (shade; צל) with Mem (ם) is *tzelem* (image; צלם),** where *tzel* is the secret of the roofing material (*Schach*) and the Mem (ם) is the secret of the four walls of the Sukkah, **and it is said: “Man walks about as a mere shadow (*tzelem*)….” (Psalms 39:7) Closed Mem (ם) has four sides to it,** which are the secret of the four walls of the Sukkah.

No less than ten, representing Malchut,
and no more than twenty, representing Keter.

818. וּמַה דְּאוּקְמוּהָ שְׁתַּיִם כְּהִלְכָתָן וּשְׁלִישִׁית אֲפִילּוּ טֶפַח. וּלְמ״ד שְׁלֹשָׁה כְּהִלְכָתָן וּרְבִיעִית אֲפִילּוּ טֶפַח. וְאִינּוּן בְּגִין דָּא, תְּרֵין, תְּלַת, אַרְבַּע, הָא תֵּשַׁע, טֶפַח אִיהִי עֲשִׂירָאָה, לְאַשְׁלְמָא כָּל חֶסְרוֹן. וּבְגִין דָּא, שִׁיעוּר סֻכָּה לֹא פָּחוֹת מֵעֶשֶׂר, דְּאִיהִי מַלְכוּת, עֲשִׂירָאָה דְּכָל דַּרְגִּין. וְלָא לְמַעְלָה מֵעֶשְׂרִין, דְּאִיהִי כ׳, כֶּתֶר עֶלְיוֹן, דְּלָא שָׁלְטָא בֵּיהּ עֵינָא. כְּבוֹד עִלָּאָה, עָלֵיהּ אָמַר מֹשֶׁה, הַרְאֵנִי נָא אֶת כְּבוֹדֶךָ. וְאָתִיב לֵיהּ קוּדְשָׁא בְּרִיךְ הוּא, לֹא תוּכַל לִרְאוֹת אֶת פָּנָי. וְלֵית כָּבוֹד, בְּלָא כ׳.

818. And with regard to the teaching: Two according to the regulations, and a third of even a handbreadth; and of him who says three according to the regulations, and a fourth of even a handbreadth; this is because of the three measurements, **two, three, four, which** together make **nine,** where two are Chochmah and Binah, three are Chesed-Gevurah-Tiferet, and four are Netzach, Hod, Yesod and Malchut. **And the handbreadth** mentioned with the two or with the three **is the tenth,** namely Malchut **that makes up every shortage. And this is why the size of a Sukkah is not less than ten, referring to Malchut, which is the tenth of all the Sefirot, and not more than twenty, which is Caf (כ; 20),** which alludes to **Upper Keter (כתר), which no eye can control,** as it is unattainable. **About the Supernal Glory, Moses said: "...'I pray You, show me Your glory'" (Exodus 33:18), to which the Holy One, blessed be He, responded: "...'you can not see My face...'" (Exodus 33:20), and there is no glory (*kavod;* כבוד) without Caf.**

Seven types of Sukkahs that are invalid.

819. וּבְגִּין דָּא שַׁוִּירוּ מָארֵי מַתְנִיתִין לָקֳבְלַיְיהוּ, סֻכָּה הָעֲשׂוּיָה כְּמָבוֹי, מִסִּטְרָא דְּאָת ב', כְּמִין גא"ם, מִסִּטְרָא דְּאָת ג'. כְּמִין צְרִיף, מִסִּטְרָא דְּאָת ד'. וְשֶׁבַע אַתְוָון אִינּוּן, בג"ד כפר"ת. כ', כִּבְשָׁן. ב', בּוּרְגָּנִין. וּשְׁאַר סֻכּוֹת. וְכֻלְּהוּ רְמִיזֵי לְגַבֵּי מָארֵי מַתְנִיתִין. וְלֵית לְאַרְכָא בְּהוֹן.

819. And for this reason the sages of the Mishnah viewed as corresponding to them, a Sukkah made like an alleyway, which is from the side of the letter Bet (ב), and in the shape of a right angle, which is from the side of the letter Gimel (ג), and like a hut, which is from the side of the letter Dalet (ד). And these seven letters Bet-Gimel-Dalet-Caf-Pei-Resh-Tav (בג"ד כפר"ת), which are doubled by the addition of a *dagesh* (a dot) in them, allude to the Seven Sefirot Chesed, Gevurah, Tiferet, Netzach, Hod, Yesod and Malchut, due to the aspect of Judgment that is in them. And they are the initial letters that allude to the seven Sukkahs made invalid, because of the Judgment that is in them. **Caf (כ)** alludes to a Sukkah made **like a furnace (*kivshan;* כבשן)**, and **Bet (ב)** to a Sukkah **that is a wayside station (*burganin;* בורגנין), and** the other letters **to the remaining** invalid **Sukahs, all of which are referred to by the sages of the Mishnah,** such as the Sukkah of fruit (*perot;* פירות) watchmen, the Sukkah of shepherds (*ro'im;* רועים), or the Sukkah of Samaritans (*kutim;* כותים) (Tractate Sukkah 8b), **and there is no need to prolong the discussion on them.**

Seven Sefirot of Judgment and Seven Sefirot of Mercy.

820. וְאִינּוּן לָקֳבְלַיְיהוּ שִׁבְעָה כֹּכְבֵי לֶכֶת, וְאִינּוּן דְּכַר וְנוּקְבָא. וּבְגִין דָּא אִתְקְרִיאוּ ז' כְּפוּלוֹת. כְּגוֹן שִׁבְעָה שְׁרָגִין דִּמְנַרְתָּא, דְּאִתְּמַר בָּהּ שֶׁבַע בַּיּוֹם הִלַּלְתִּיךָ. הָכִי שִׁבְעָה וְשִׁבְעָה מוּצָקוֹת. הָכִי שִׁבְעָה סְפִירָאן כְּפוּלוֹת. וְשִׁבְעָה יוֹמֵי בְּרֵאשִׁית לְתַתָּא, שִׁבְעָה לְעֵילָּא, אֵין כָּל חָדָשׁ תַּחַת הַשָּׁמֶשׁ.

820. And corresponding to them, to the seven letters Bet-Gimel-Dalet-Caf-Pei-Resh-Tav (**בג"ד כפר"ת), are the seven planets, and they are Male and Female,** for when these seven letters are weak (*rafeh,* without a dot in them) they are of the Male and when they are strong (with a dot—*dagesh*—in them) they are of the Female. **And they are therefore called the Seven Double Letters and are like the seven candles of the candelabrum,** which are the secret of the Seven Sefirot: Chesed, Gevurah, Tiferet, Netzach, Hod, Yesod, and Malchut, **about which is said: "Seven times a day I praise You…." (Psalms 119:164) And so** it is said: **"…and seven pipes to the seven lamps, which were upon the top of it" (Zechariah 4:2)** which are the secret of the Seven Double Letters, namely the seven letters in their weak form and the seven letters in their strong form, **and likewise, the Seven Sefirot are double,** containing seven of Judgment and seven of Mercy. **And so too, are the Seven Days of Creation Below,** namely the Seven Sefirot of Malchut, which have a dot (*dagesh*) with Judgments, **and the seven Above,** namely the seven Sefirot of Zeir Anpin, which are weak (*rafeh*) in Judgments.

Since about the Seven Sefirot that are Below it is said: **"...and there is nothing new under the sun" (Ecclesiastes 1:9)** for all innovations come from the sun, namely the Seven Sefirot of Zeir Anpin and not from under the sun, which are the Seven Sefirot of Malchut.

The Lulav and its eighteen shakings represent
the eighteen vertabrae of the spine.

821. לוּלָב דָּא צַדִּיק. דְּדָמֵי לְחוּט הַשִּׁדְרָה, דְּבֵיהּ ח"י חוּלְיָין, לְקָבֵל ח"י נִעְנוּעִין דְּלוּלָב. וְאִינּוּן לָקֳבֵל ח"י בִּרְכָאן דִּצְלוֹתָא. לָקֳבֵל שְׁמֹנָה עָשָׂר אַזְכָּרוֹת, דְּהָבוּ לַיְיָ' בְּנֵי אֵלִים. לָקֳבֵל שְׁמֹנָה עָשָׂר אַזְכָּרוֹת דק"ש. וְנִעְנוּעַ לְשִׁית סִטְרִין, בְּחוּשְׁבַּן ו'. תְּלַת נִעְנוּעִין בְּכָל סִטְרָא, אִינּוּן ח"י.

821. *Lulav* is the Righteous, Yesod, **for the *Lulav* is likened to the spinal cord that contains eighteen vertebrae, corresponding to the eighteen shakings of the *Lulav*. And they correspond to the eighteen blessings of the Amidah Prayer, and they correspond to the eighteen mentions** of Yud-Hei-Vav-Hei **in "...ascribe to Lord, you mighty (*havu le'Adonai bnei elim*)..." (Psalms 29:1), and the eighteen mentions of the Shema Reading. The** Shaking of the ***Lulav* is to six directions:** south, north, east, up, down, and west, **which makes six, and it is shaken three times in each direction, thus** totaling **eighteen.**

Seven Sefirot are alluded in the Lulav and Etrog.

822. לוּלָב בְּיָמִין, כָּלִיל שִׁשָּׁה דְּאִינּוּן ג' הֲדַסִּין, גְּדוּלָּה גְּבוּרָה תִּפְאֶרֶת. וְדַמְיָין לִתְלַת גַּוְונֵי עֵינָא. ב' בַּדֵּי עֲרָבוֹת, נֶצַח וְהוֹד. וְדַמְיָין לִתְרֵין שִׂפְוָון. לוּלָב, יְסוֹד, דּוֹמֶה לַשִּׁדְרָה. דְּבֵיהּ קִיּוּם דְּכָל גַּרְמִין. וְעָלֵיהּ אָמַר דָּוִד, כָּל עַצְמוֹתַי תֹּאמַרְנָה יְיָ' מִי כָמוֹךָ. אֶתְרוֹג, מַלְכוּת. דּוֹמֶה לְלִבָּא. דְּבֵיהּ הִרְהוּרִין.

822. The *Lulav* is taken **in the right** hand, **and is comprised of six, which are: three Myrtle branches,** corresponding to **Gedulah (Greatness), Gevurah (Judgment), and Tiferet (Beauty), and they**

are like the three colors in the eye, which are white, red, and green. **And the two Willow twigs are Netzach and Hod, and they are similar to the two lips. The *Lulav*** is **Yesod and is like the spine that supports all the bones and about which David said: "All my bones shall say, 'Lord, who is like You?'...." (Psalms 35:10) And the *Etrog* is Malchut and is likened to the heart, in which are thoughts.**

Seventy-Two shakings of the Lulav, like the numerical value of Chesed (Kindness).

823. וְנִעֲנוּעִין דְּהַלֵּל, אִינּוּן מִשׁוּתָּפִין בְּנִעֲנוּעִין דִּנְטִילַת לוּלָב, וְאִינּוּן ח"י בְּאָנָּא. ח"י ח"י, בְּהוֹדוּ תְּחִלָּה וָסוֹף. ח"י דִּנְטִילַת לוּלָב, הֲרֵי ע"ב. וּבְגִין דָּא לוּלָב בְּחוּשְׁבַּן ח"ס, וְד' מִינִין דְּלוּלָב, הָא חֶסֶד, דְּרוֹעָא יְמִינָא. וּבְגִין דָּא תַּקִּינוּ לוּלָב בַּיָּמִין, לְסִטְרָא דְּחֶסֶד. אֶתְרוֹג לְסִטְרָא דִּגְבוּרָה, לִשְׂמָאלָא לִבָּא. וּבְגִין דָּא אֶתְרוֹג הַדּוֹמֶה לַלֵּב, תַּקִּינוּ לְמֶהֱוֵי בְּיַד שְׂמֹאל. כְּמָה דְּאוּקְמוּהָ, לוּלָב בַּיָּמִין, וְאֶתְרוֹג בִּשְׂמֹאלוֹ. אִינּוּן לְקַבֵּל זָכוֹר וְשָׁמוֹר. וּמַאן נָטִיל תַּרְוַויְיהוּ. עַמּוּדָא דְּאֶמְצָעִיתָא. לוּלָב בִּימִינֵיהּ, וְאֶתְרוֹג בִּשְׂמָאלֵיהּ.

823. The shakings of the Halel are joined with the shakings of the Taking of the *Lulav*. There are eighteen shakings **at "Save us, Lord, we pray You (*Ana Adonai hoshia Na*)..." (Psalms 118:25), eighteen each at the first and last "Give thanks (hodu Adonai)..." (Psalms 118:1 and 29), and eighteen at the Taking of the *Lulav*, making a total of 72** shakings. **And this is why the numerical value of *Lulav* (לולב) is 68, and together with the four species of the *Lulav*** it is 72, **and it is the same as the numerical value of Chesed, which is the right arm. And this is why it was decreed that the *Lulav* be taken in the right hand, which is the side of Chesed, and the *Etrog* in the side of Gevurah, in the left,** corresponding to **the heart. And this is why it was decreed that the *Etrog*, which is like the heart, be held in the left hand, as it has been taught: *Lulav* in the right hand and *Etrog* in the left, corresponding to "Remember..." (Exodus 20:8) and "Guard...." (Deuteronomy 5:12) Who is the one taking both**

Lulav and *Etrog*? **It is the Central Column,** Zeir Anpin. **The *Lulav* is His right, the *Etrog* is His left.**

Rav Shimon and his six students are like the seven lamps of the Candelabra.

824. אָתוּ אֲבָהָן, וְרַעְיָא מְהֵימְנָא, וְאַהֲרֹן וְדָוִד וּשְׁלֹמֹה, וּבָרִיכוּ לֵיהּ, וְאָמְרוּ לֵיהּ, אַנְתְּ בּוּצִינָא קַדִּישָׁא, וְחַבְרַיָּיא דִּילָךְ דְּאִינּוּן שִׁית, לָקֳבֵל אִינּוּן ז'. וְאַנְתְּ בּוּצִינָא קַדִּישָׁא נֵר מַעֲרָבִי בְּאֶמְצַע, דְּכָל שִׁית נֵרוֹת נְהִרִין מִנָּךְ. בְּכָל חַד אִתְּמַר בֵּיהּ, נֵר יְיָ' נִשְׁמַת אָדָם. וְרַעְיָא מְהֵימְנָא נָהִיר בָּךְ, וְאַנְתְּ בְּחַבְרַיָּיא דִּילָךְ, וְכֻלָּא חַד, בְּלָא פֵּרוּדָא כְּלָל. וּמִתַּמָּן וְאֵילָךְ מִתְפַּשְּׁטִין עַנְפִּין לְכָל מָארֵי חָכְמְתָא, אַשְׁלִים מִלִּין דְּחִבּוּרָא קַדְמָאָה דִּילָךְ לְאַעְטְרָא לוֹן.

824. The Patriarchs, along with the Faithful Shepherd (Moses), Aaron, David and Solomon came and blessed him, Rav Shimon, **saying to him: "You, Holy Luminary, and your friends, who are six in number, correspond to these seven** Sefirot, **and you, the Holy Luminary, are the western Light in the middle of the six Lights that shine from you. And about each one it is said: 'The soul of man is the candle of the Lord....'** (Proverbs 20:27) **And the Faithful Shepherd (Moses) shines in you, and you in your friends and all of you are one, without any separation whatsoever. And from there and onward, the branches,** namely, the Illuminations, **spread out, to all masters of wisdom. Complete the matters of your first compilation, to crown them."**

The water libation occurs on the second, sixth, and seventh day.

825. פָּתַח בּוּצִינָא קַדִּישָׁא וְאָמַר, מַיִם רַבִּים לֹא יוּכְלוּ לְכַבּוֹת אֶת הָאַהֲבָה וְגוֹ'. מַאי בּוֹז. יוֹמָא תִּנְיָינָא, וְיוֹמָא שְׁתִיתָאָה, וְיוֹמָא שְׁבִיעָאָה דְּסוּכּוֹת. דִּבְהוֹן הֲווֹ מְנַסְּכִים מַיִם וְיַיִן.

825. The Holy Luminary opened and said: "Many waters cannot quench love... it would be utterly scorned." **(Song of Songs 8:7)** [He asks:] **"What is the meaning of** 'it would be utterly **scorned (*boz*; בוז)'?"** [He answers:] **"This refers to the second day (ב), the sixth day (ו), and the seventh day (ז) of Sukkot on which libations of water and wine were poured out.**

Sevent bullocks were offered to atone for the seventy nations.

826. דְּשֶׁבַע יוֹמִין דְּסוּכּוֹת, בְּהוֹן הֲווֹ מַקְרִיבִין יִשְׂרָאֵל שִׁבְעִים פָּרִים, לְכַפָּרָא עַל שַׁבְעִין מְמַנָּן, בְּגִין דְּלָא יִשְׁתְּאַר עָלְמָא חָרוּב מִנַּיְיהוּ. הה"ד, וּבַחֲמִשָּׁה עָשָׂר יוֹם וְהִקְרַבְתֶּם עוֹלָה אִשֵּׁה רֵיחַ נִיחוֹחַ לַיְיָ' פָּרִים בְּנֵי בָקָר שְׁלֹשָׁה עָשָׂר תְּמִימִים. וּבַיּוֹם הַשֵּׁנִי פָּרִים י"ב. וּבַיּוֹם הַשְּׁלִישִׁי י"א. וּבַיּוֹם הָרְבִיעִי עֲשָׂרָה. וּבַיּוֹם הַחֲמִישִׁי פָּרִים תִּשְׁעָה. וּבַיּוֹם הַשִּׁשִּׁי פָּרִים שְׁמֹנָה. וּבַיּוֹם הַשְּׁבִיעִי שִׁבְעָה. וְכֻלְּהוּ שַׁבְעִין. וּבְכָל יוֹמָא הֲווּ חָסֵרִים. אַמַּאי חָסֵרִים.

826. "During the seven days of Sukkot, Israel used to sacrifice seventy bullocks to make atonement for the seventy Ministers of the seventy nations, **so that the world would not remain destroyed because of them. And this is what the verse says: 'And on the fifteenth day... you shall offer a burnt offering, a sacrifice made by fire, of a sweet savor to the Lord; thirteen young bullocks... without blemish.' (Numbers 29:12-13) And on the second day—twelve, and on the third day—eleven bullocks, and on the fourth day—ten, and on the fifth day—nine bullocks, and on the sixth day—eight bullocks, and on the seventh day—seven. And all of them** together are **seventy bullocks, and each day they would be reduced."** He asks: **"Why was there a reduction?"**

The reduction of the bullocks represent
a reduction of the angels of destruction.

827. אֶלָּא הָכָא קָא רָמִיז, וַתָּנַח הַתֵּיבָה בַּחֹדֶשׁ הַשְּׁבִיעִי. וּמַה הָתָם בִּימֵי טוֹפָנָא, וְהַמַּיִם הָלְכוּ הָלוֹךְ וְחָסוֹר. אוּף הָכִי בְּתִשְׁרֵי, דְּאִיהוּ יַרְחָא שְׁבִיעָאָה, דְּבֵיהּ כַּמָּה פְּקוּדִין, רֹאשׁ הַשָּׁנָה וְיוֹם הַכִּפּוּרִים, סֻכָּה וְלוּלָב אֶתְרוֹג, מִינִין דְּלוּלָב

שׁוֹפָר. שְׁכִינְתָּא עִלָּאָה שַׁרְיָיא עַל יִשְׂרָאֵל, דְּאִיהִי תְּשׁוּבָה, סוּכָּה. אֶתְרוֹג, וְקוּדְשָׁא בְּרִיךְ הוּא דְּאִיהוּ לוּלָב. מִיַּד וְהַמַּיִם הָיוּ הָלוֹךְ וְחָסוֹר, מִתְמַעֲטִין חוֹבִין דְּיִשְׂרָאֵל, אוּף הָכִי מִתְמַעֲטִין מְמָנָן דְּאִינּוּן מַלְאֲכֵי חַבָּלָה, דִּמְמָנָן עֲלַיְיהוּ, דְּדַמְיָין לְמֵי טוֹפָנָא. כְּמָה דְּאוּקְמוּהָ, עָשָׂה עֲבֵרָה אַחַת קָנָה לוֹ קַטֵּיגוֹר אֶחָד. בְּהַהוּא זִמְנָא דְּמִתְמָעֲטִין חוֹבִין, מִתְמַעֲטִין פָּרִים דִּלְהוֹן, מִתְמַעֲטִין מְמָנָן דְּע' אוּמִין, מִתְמַעֲטִין ע' אוּמִין, מִתְמַעֵט טוּבָא דִּלְהוֹן.

827. He answers: **"Rather here** the verse **gives us a hint: '...and the ark rested in the seventh month...' (Genesis 8:4)** which is Tishrei. **And just as then in the days of the Flood, when the waters decreased continually, so too here, in Tishrei, which is the seventh month, in which there are a number of precepts, Rosh Hashanah and Yom Kippur, Sukkah, *Lulav* and *Etrog*, the species of the *Lulav* and Shofar.** For then **the Upper Shechinah rests on Israel, which is Repentance,** namely Binah called 'Repentance,' and is the secret of **Sukkah, *Etrog*,** which is Malchut, **and *Lulav*, which is the Holy One, blessed be He,** namely Zeir Anpin. **Immediately '...and the waters decreased continually...' (Genesis 8:5) since the sins of Israel become less. So too, the angels of destruction who are appointed over them,** over the iniquities, **become less,** since the iniquities **are similar to the waters of the Flood, as has been taught: He that commits one transgression, gets for himself one Accuser (Pirkei Avot 4:11). And at the time that the iniquities become less, their bullocks are reduced in number, the appointees over the seventy nations are reduced, the seventy nations diminish, and their goodness becomes less."**

Eighteen Holidays corresponding to the eighteen sacrifices of Noah.

828. תֵּיבַת נֹחַ, מָנֵי קוּדְשָׁא בְּרִיךְ הוּא, לְאַעֲלָא עִמֵּיהּ שְׁנַיִם שְׁנַיִם שִׁבְעָה שִׁבְעָה זָכָר וּנְקֵבָה, לְקָרְבָּנָא, לְאַגָּנָא עַל נֹחַ, וְעַל כָּל אִינּוּן דְּעָאלִין עִמֵּיהּ לְתֵיבָה. אוּף הָכִי אִלֵּין דְּמִנַּטְרִין חַגִּין וּזְמַנִּין, דְּאִינּוּן יָמִים טוֹבִים, שְׁנַיִם שְׁנַיִם שִׁבְעָה שִׁבְעָה, שְׁנַיִם שְׁנַיִם תְּרֵין יוֹמִין דר"ה, וּתְרֵין יוֹמִין דְּשָׁבוּעוֹת, וּבְגִין דְּאִינּוּן תְּרֵין מִנַּיְיהוּ

בְּסָפֵק, הָא אִית שְׁנֵי יְמֵי הַפּוּרִים בְּאַתְרַיְיהוּ. שִׁבְעָה שִׁבְעָה, ז' יוֹמִין דְּפֶסַח, ז' יוֹמִין דְּסוּכּוֹת. נֹחַ לָקֳבֵל יוֹם הַשַּׁבָּת, וְהַאי אִיהוּ מִכָּל הַחַי.

828. And the Holy One, blessed be He, commanded Noah to take into the Ark two and two, seven and seven, male and female, to be a sacrifice to protect Noah and all those who went into the Ark with him. So too, those who observe Holidays and times, which are Good Days, are two and two, seven and seven. Two and two refers to the two days of Rosh Hashanah and the two days of Shavuot, and because there are two of Shavuot **because of doubt, therefore, there are two days of Purim in their stead. Seven and seven refer to the seven days of Pesach, and the seven days of Sukkot. Noah corresponds to the Shabbat day, and this is: "Of every living (*chai*; חי; 18) thing..." (Genesis 6:19),** because two + two + seven + seven = eighteen, which is *Chai* (Life).

The Sukkah protects like Noah's ark.

829. סֻכָּה קָא אֲגִינַת עֲלַיְיהוּ דְּיִשְׂרָאֵל, הה"ד וְסֻכָּה תִּהְיֶה לְצֵל יוֹמָם מֵחֹרֶב. סֻכָּה קָא אֲגִינַת. מַה תֵּיבַת נֹחַ לְאַגָּנָא, אוּף הָכִי סֻכָּה לְאַגָּנָא. וְעוֹד מִכָּל הַחַי, חי"ו בִּרְכָאן דִּצְלוֹתָא, מֵאִינּוּן ט' ט', בִּרְכָתָא דְּמִינִין בָּהּ אִשְׁתְּלִימוּ י' סְפִירָאן מֵעֵילָּא לְתַתָּא, וּמִתַּתָּא לְעֵילָּא. וְאִיהוּ לָקֳבֵל נֹחַ.

829. The Sukkah protects Israel, as it is written: "And there shall be a Sukkah (Tabernacle) for shade in the daytime...." (Isaiah 4:6) Thus **the Sukkah gives protection. Just as the purpose of Noah's Ark was to give protection, so is the Sukkah to give protection. Furthermore: "Of every living (*chai*; 18) thing..." (Genesis 6:19) refers to the eighteen blessings of the prayer, which** sub-divide into **two groups of nine each.** And with **the blessing concerning the heretics, the Ten Sefirot are completed,** for this makes ten together with the first nine, and again together with the last nine. **And they correspond to the Ten Sefirot** of Direct Light **that is from above**

downward, and the Ten Sefirot of Returning Light **that is from below upward. And this corresponds to Noah,** in other words, the eighteen blessings of the prayer correspond to the eighteen of Noah, namely, two and two, seven and seven, which add up to eighteen.

Allusions of the word chai (living; 18).

830. וְעוֹד מִכָּל הַחַי, שְׁכִינְתָּא אֲגִינַת עַל אִלֵּין דְּנַטְרִין י׳, אוֹת שַׁבָּת בִּתְחוּמָא דִּילֵיהּ, דְּאִיהוּ ח׳ אֲלָפִים, תְּרֵין אַלְפִּין לְכָל צַד. וְעוֹד, מִכָּל הַחַי, אִלֵּין דְּנַטְרִין י׳ אוֹת בְּרִית, דְּאִיהוּ בְּח׳ יוֹמִין, דְּאִתְּמַר עֲלַיְיהוּ, וּבַיּוֹם הַשְּׁמִינִי יִמּוֹל בְּשַׂר עָרְלָתוֹ. וְעוֹד, מִכָּל הַחַי, אִלֵּין דְּנַטְרִין אוֹת י׳, תְּפִלִּין בִּתְמַנְיָא פָּרְשִׁיָּין.

830. Furthermore, "Of every living thing…" (Genesis 6:19) means that the Shechinah protects all those who keep the Yud (כ; 10), which is the Sign of the Shabbat, in its limits, namely, eight thousand cubits, **two thousand in each direction.** The Yud of the Sign of the Shabbat and the Chet (ח; 8) of the limits are Chet-Yud (*Chai*; Living; חי). **Furthermore, "Of every living thing…" (Ibid.) means those who keep the Sign of the Covenant, which is Yud (י) that is at the eighth day, about which it is said: "And on the eighth day the flesh of his foreskin shall be circumcised." (Leviticus 12:3)** And the Yud of the Sign of the Covenant and the Chet of the eight days form *chai* (חי). **Furthermore, "Of every living thing…" (Ibid.) refers to those who observe the Sign of the Tefilin, which is Yud,** and in which are **eight passages,** thus: Chet-Yud (*chai*; חי).

In Tishrei, no external force can extinguish the love of Israel for the Creator.

831. שְׁכִינְתָּא דְּאִיהִי סוּכָּה, אֲגִינַת עֲלַיְיהוּ, וּפְרִישַׂת גַּדְפָּאָה עֲלַיְיהוּ, כְּאִמָּא עַל בְּנִין, וּבְגִין דָּא תַּקִּינוּ לְבָרְכָא, הַפּוֹרֵס סוּכַּת שָׁלוֹם עָלֵינוּ. וּבְגִין דָּא בְּיַרְחָא שְׁבִיעָאָה, דְּבֵיהּ כָּל פִּקּוּדִין אִלֵּין, מַיִם רַבִּים לֹא יוּכְלוּ לְכַבּוֹת אֶת הָאַהֲבָה. עַם יִשְׂרָאֵל בַּאֲבוּהוֹן שֶׁבַּשָּׁמַיִם. וְלֵית מַיִם רַבִּים, אֶלָּא כָּל אוּמִין וּמְמַנָּן דִּלְהוֹן.

אִם יִתֵּן אִישׁ, דְּאִיהוּ סָמָאֵל, כָּל מַה דְּאִית לֵיהּ בְּעָלְמָא דֵּין, בְּגִין דְּיִשְׁתַּתַּף בְּאִלֵּין פִּקּוּדִין עִם יִשְׂרָאֵל, בּוֹז יָבוּזוּ לוֹ.

831. The Shechinah, which is the Sukkah, protects them and spreads Her wings over them, as does the mother bird over the young. And this is why the text of the prayer (on Friday Night) was worded: "who spreads Sukkat Shalom (the Shelter of Peace) over us." And for this reason, in the seventh month, which contains all these Precepts, "Many waters cannot quench love..." (Song of Songs 8:7) of Israel for their Father Who is in Heaven. And there is no meaning to "many waters" except all the nations and their ministers. "...if a man..." (Ibid.) this being Sama"el, gives all that he possesses in this world to join in partnership with Israel in these precepts, "...it would be utterly scorned." (Ibid.)

129. Sukkot

A Synopsis

Rav Aba and Rav Elazar talk about the third day of Sukkot, employing the analogy of Noah's Ark landing on Mount Ararat and the waters receding.

From Yom Kippur to Sukkot the Shechinah protects Israel from the Other Side.

884. וּבַחֲמִשָּׁה עָשָׂר יוֹם וְגוֹ'. ר' אַבָּא פָּתַח, וַתָּנַח הַתֵּיבָה בַּחֹדֶשׁ הַשְּׁבִיעִי וְגוֹ', ת"ח, כָּל הָנֵי יוֹמִין, אַזְלַת אִימָּא עַל בְּנַיָּיא, בְּגִין דְּלָא יִשְׁלוֹט סִטְרָא אַחֲרָא עֲלַיְיהוּ, וּבְגִין לְשֵׁיזָבָא לוֹן. כֵּיוָן דְּאִשְׁתְּזִיבוּ בְּהָא, וְהָא יַתְבִין בַּסֻּכּוֹת, מִתְנַטְּרִין בְּנְטוּרָא. יוֹמָא קַדְמָאָה, וְיוֹמָא תִּנְיָנָא, פַּקְדַת לוֹן לְיִשְׂרָאֵל, לְמֶעְבַּד סְעוּדָתָא לִמְמָנָן דְּשְׁאַר עַמִּין, וְאִיהִי לָא שַׁרְיָא תַּמָּן. בְּיוֹמָא תְּלִיתָאָה, דְּאִיהוּ י"ז לַחֹדֶשׁ, שָׁרִיאַת לְמִשְׁרֵי עֲלַיְיהוּ. הה"ד, וַתָּנַח הַתֵּיבָה בַּחֹדֶשׁ הַשְּׁבִיעִי בְּשִׁבְעָה עָשָׂר יוֹם לַחֹדֶשׁ עַל הָרֵי אֲרָרָט, טוּרִין דְּכָל לְוָוטִין וּמְרָדִין שָׁרָאן בְּגַוַּייהוּ.

884. "And on the fifteenth day of the seventh month…." (Numbers 29:12) Rabbi Aba began by quoting: "'And the ark rested in the seventh month….' (Genesis 8:4) Come and see, throughout these days, from Yom Kippur to Sukkot, **the Mother,** which is the Shechinah, **hovers over the children,** who are Israel, **so that the Other Side should not have control** over Israel, **and in order to save them. After the children have been saved and are sitting in their booths (sukkot), they are guarded with the protection** of the Mother, which is the Shechinah. **On the first and second days** of the holiday of Sukkot, **She commanded Israel to make a feast for the ministering angels of the other nations,** namely the seventy bullocks for the seventy ministers, **and She does not dwell there** with them. **On the third day, which is the seventeenth day of the month,** the Shechinah **begins to rest on them, which is the meaning of the verse, 'And the ark rested in the seventh month, on the seventeenth day of the month, upon the mountains of Ararat.' (Genesis 8:4)** The Ark is the secret of the Shechinah, and the mountains of Ararat are **the mountains in the midst of which rest all the curses and all the punishments,** which are the appointees of the nations."

On the third day there is an increase in letter and a decrease in sacrifices.

885. אָמַר רִבִּי אֶלְעָזָר, יוֹמָא קַדְמָאָה דְּחַג, לָא שַׁרְיָא עָלַיְיהוּ, וְלָא יוֹמָא תִּנְיָינָא, אֶלָּא יוֹמָא תְּלִיתָאָה, דְּאוֹסִיף וְגָרַע שַׁרְיָא עָלַיְיהוּ, אוֹסִיף אַתְוָון, וְגָרַע קָרְבְּנִין. דִּכְתִּיב עַשְׁתֵּי עָשָׂר וְגוֹ'. וְהָכִי אִתְחֲזֵי לְרַע עַיִן, בְּגִין דְּיוֹמָא קַדְמָאָה וְיוֹמָא תִּנְיָינָא חֶדְוָה דִּבְנָהָא, וְאִינּוּן מְפַלְּגֵי עַדָאן לוֹן. מִיּוֹמָא תְּלִיתָאָה וּלְהָלְאָה, דְּאִיהִי שַׁרְיָא עָלַיְיהוּ, מַה כְּתִיב. וְהַמַּיִם הָיוּ הָלוֹךְ וְחָסוֹר עַד הַחֹדֶשׁ הָעֲשִׂירִי בָּעֲשִׂירִי בְּאֶחָד לַחֹדֶשׁ נִרְאוּ רָאשֵׁי הֶהָרִים וְהַמַּיִם הָיוּ הָלוֹךְ וְחָסוֹר, אִלֵּין קָרְבְּנִין, דְּאַזְלִין וּמִתְמַעֲטִין. וּכְמָה דְּאִינּוּן מִתְמַעֲטִין, הָכִי נָמֵי אִתְמְעַט טוּבָא דִּלְהוֹן.

885. Rav Elazar said, "On the first day of Sukkot, Malchut **does not rest on them,** on the ministers of the seventy nations, **nor on the**

second day, but only on the third day does She rest on them, which decreases by addition—adding letters and decreasing in sacrifices—as it is written, '...Eleven (ashtei asar) bullocks...' (Numbers 29:20), which is appropriate for the evil eye. For on the first day and the second day there is rejoicing of the children, and Israel distributes spoils to them, to the appointees of the nations. **From the third day and onwards, when** Malchut **rests upon them, what is written? 'And the waters decreased continually until the tenth month; in the tenth month, on the first day of the month, were the tops of the mountains seen.' (Genesis 8:5) 'And the waters decreased continually'—these are the sacrifices that are continually reduced, and as they become fewer in number so does their goodness become less."**

Explanation: The main construction of Malchut is from the Left Column, namely the Illumination of Chochmah of the Left. However when She dwells on Israel She is in unification with Zeir Anpin, the Central Column. At that point, the Chochmah of Malchut only shines from below upward, and Her main Illumination is from the aspect of the Chasadim She receives from Zeir Anpin. But when Malchut dwells on the nations of the world and the Other Side, the opposite occurs, where she only dwells on them when She is separated from Zeir Anpin since the nations of the world and the Other Side do not wish to receive from the Central Column, Zeir Anpin, but only from the aspect of the Left in Malchut alone.

This is: **"throughout these days, the Mother hovers over the children,"** namely Malchut when She is in union with Zeir Anpin, the Central Column, **"so that the Other Side should not have control on them,"** namely so that the Other Side would not awaken them to draw Chochmah from above downward from Malchut, as is the way of the Other Side. **"After the children have been saved and are sitting in their booths (sukkot), they are guarded,"** as once they merit the Sukkah they are divinely protected so that the Other Side can no longer have dominion over them to entice them to draw the Left from above downward. Therefore **"She commanded Israel to make a feast for the ministering angels of the other nations,"** to sacrifice seventy bullocks, which is the secret of drawing the Illumination of the Left to the ministers of the nations and the Other Side only to a degree that sustains them, as the only life and existence of the nations and the Other Side is from the Illumination of the Left alone.

"and She does not dwell there," since Malchut does not dwell on them unless She is separated from Zeir Anpin, for then She increases the lifeforce of the Other Side. Therefore instead of dwelling on them, which would increase their vitality, Israel draw to them their portion from the sacrifices, as Israel only draw Illumination from below upward, like the correction of the Central Column. This Illumination comes by way of Three Columns that shine to Malchut, which is the secret of Chesed, Gevurah, Tiferet, and Malchut. After they are incorporated with each other, Three Columns exist in each of the Chesed, Gevurah, Tiferet, and Malchut, which adds up to twelve, thus the twelve bulls. And one for the collective, equals thirteen bulls. This is the secret of the thirteen bulls they sacrificed on the first day, and the twelve bulls they sacrificed on the second day. They are in the aspect of the drawing of Chochmah in the secret of the Three Columns and Malchut that receives them, where once they are incorporated with each other they are the secret of twelve, and with the collective they are thirteen.

This is: **"For on the first day and the second day there is rejoicing of the children, and Israel distributes spoils to them,"** for Israel are the ones who distribute the Illumination of the Left to the ministers of the nations, and therefore they distribute to them in the secret of the number thirteen on the first day and twelve on the second, which is the secret of the incorporation of the Three Columns and Malchut with each other, as is the way of the Illumination of the Central Column.

This is: **"On the third day...** the Shechinah **begins to rest on them,"** since after they have already received from Israel everything they could shine to them, which is the secret of the twelve bulls, then Malchut begins to rest on the ministers of the nations. In other words, from the power of the Illumination they received from the twelve bulls of Holiness, which was from the Central Column, they proceed to draw from Malchut alone, namely from Her own aspect that is Left without Right, so that they can draw from above downward as is their desire. This is the secret of why Israel was commanded then to sacrifice eleven bulls.

This is: **"but only on the third day does She rest on them, which decreases by addition—adding letters and decreasing in sacrifices—as it is written, '...Eleven (*ashtei asar;* עַשְׁתֵּי עָשָׂר) bullocks....'" (Numbers 29:20)** On the first and second day Israel bestowed upon them from Holiness, in the secret of twelve (*shtei asar;* שְׁתֵּי עָשָׂר), which is the secret of the incorporation of the Three Colums, as mentioned. But when they proceeded to draw from the aspect of the Left without Right, namely from Malchut separated [from Zeir Anpin], they added evil eye (*ayin;* עַיִן) to the twelve (*shtei asar;* שְׁתֵּי עָשָׂר) bulls they received on the first and second day, and it became eleven (*ashtei asar;* עַשְׁתֵּי עָשָׂר), for when you add an ayin (ע) to *shtei asar* (שְׁתֵּי עָשָׂר) it becomes *ashtei asar* (עַשְׁתֵּי עָשָׂר). It is found that it increased in letters, the letter Ayin, and decreased in sacrifice, since there are no longer twelve bulls but eleven bulls. Thus it continued to decrease until they completely stopped. This is: **"what is written? 'And the waters decreased continually'—these are the sacrifices that are continually reduced."**

SUKKOT: THE FOUR SPECIES

Vayechi

26. The four species

A Synopsis

This further describes the importance of the root connection between aspects of the Upper and Lower Worlds. There are four things to cleave to: the *Lulav, Etrog* (citron), Hadas (Myrtle), and (Aravah) Willow. We learn of the significance of "the fifteenth day," the first of the three travelling Columns. Next, we are told that Yom Kippur is the secret of Ima, the day in which Binah sets the prisoners free, who name that day "the first day," and ask Binah for water. It is either the beginning of "Clouds of Glory" or of "Living Water."

The relevance of this Passage

Here we connect ourselves to the internal spiritual forces associated with the *Lulav, Etrog,* Myrtle branch, and Willow. These physical items work like an antenna. They have powerful spiritual counterparts in the Upper World, which help us draw the Light of protection to our lives. We also destroy any judgments that might be pending in the Upper Courts, provided our hearts are filled with repentance.

Every action Below has a Root Above.

210. תָּא וַחֲזֵי כָּל הַנִּקְרָא בִשְׁמִי, כַּמָּה עִלָּאִין עוֹבָדֵי מַלְכָּא קַדִּישָׁא, דְּהָא בְּאִינּוּן עוֹבָדֵי דְּאִיהוּ עָבֵיד לְתַתָּא, קָטֵיר לוֹן בְּמִלִּין עִלָּאִין דִּלְעֵילָּא, וְכַד נָטְלִין לוֹן לְתַתָּא, וְעָבְדֵי בְּהוֹ עוֹבָדָא, אִתְעַר הַהוּא עוֹבָדָא דִּלְעֵילָּא דְּקָטֵיר בָּהּ, כְּגוֹן אֵזוֹבָא, עֵץ אֶרֶז, וְהָא אוּקְימְנָא מִלֵּי.

210. Come and see, "All who are called by My Name...." (Isaiah 43:7) How exalted are the servants of the Holy King, for their actions Below connect them to the higher things Above, namely to their

Roots. For each thing Below in this world has a root Above in the Upper Worlds. **When they take them Below and do an action with them, the action Above,** their root in Upper Worlds, awakens **in accordance with it. This is like the hyssop and the cedar wood** the Torah commands to take for the one being purified, **as we already explained.**

We shake the four species Below to rouse joy Above.

211. וְאִית מִנַּיְיהוּ דְּאֲחִידָן בִּשְׁמָא קַדִּישָׁא, כְּגוֹן לוּלָב, וְאֶתְרוֹג, הֲדַס, וַעֲרָבָה, דְּכֻלְּהוּ אֲחִידָן בִּשְׁמָא קַדִּישָׁא, לְעֵילָא. וְעַל דָּא תָּנִינָן, לְאַחֲדָא לוֹן, וּלְמֶעְבַּד בְּהוֹ עוֹבָדָא, בְּגִין לְאִתְעָרָא חֶדְוָה הַהוּא דְּאָחִיד בֵּיהּ. וְעַל דָּא תָּנִינָן, בְּמִלִּין וְעוֹבָדָא בָּעְיָין לְאַחֲזָאָה מִלָּה, בְּגִין לְאִתְעָרָא מִלָּה אָחֳרָא.

211. Some of them cleave to the Holy Name Above, like the *Lulav*, *Etrog* (Citron), Hadas (Myrtle), and Aravah (Willow). In relation to them, we learned that we should unite them, namely to bind them together, **and perform an action with them,** namely to shake them, **to arouse joy in the root to which it cleaves Above. We have learned that with speech,** the blessing of the Precepts, **and with deed,** the precept, **we should exhibit it** Below **so as to awaken another matter** Above, namely its Supernal Root.

Everything was created so we can use it to reveal Light.

212. הה"ד כָּל הַנִּקְרָא בִשְׁמִי וְלִכְבוֹדִי: לְאַתְעָרָא יְקָרִי, בְּרָאתִיו: לְיַיחֲדָא לִי. יְצַרְתִּיו: לְמֶעְבַּד בֵּיהּ עוֹבָדָא. אַף עֲשִׂיתִיו: לְאַתְעָרָא בֵּיהּ חֵילָא דִּלְעֵילָא.

212. This is as is written: "Every one that is called by My Name, and for My Glory" (Isaiah 43:7) namely, **so it would glorify Me; "I have created him" so he would declare My unity; "I have formed him" so he would perform good deeds for My sake; "I have made him" so that through him the Supernal Force will awaken.**

The Four Species correspond to the Four Worlds.

213. ד"א, כָּל הַנִּקְרָא בִשְׁמִי: הַיְינוּ דִּכְתִיב פְּרִי עֵץ הָדָר. וְלִכְבוֹדִי בְּרָאתִיו: הַיְינוּ כַּפּוֹת תְּמָרִים. יְצַרְתִּיו: הַיְינוּ וַעֲנַף עֵץ עָבוֹת. אַף עֲשִׂיתִיו: הַיְינוּ וְעַרְבֵי נָחַל.

213. Another explanation, "Every one that is called by My Name..." (Isaiah 43:7) namely what is written: "...the fruit of the Hadar (citrus) tree..." (Leviticus 23:40); "For My glory I have created him" namely the "...branches of palm trees..."; "I have formed him," [namely] "...the boughs of thick leaved trees..."; "I have made him," the "...Willow of the brook." (Ibid.)

Explanation: Here the Zohar explains that the roots of the Four Species are the Four Worlds: Atzilut, Briyah, Yetzirah and Asiyah. The *Etrog* corresponds to the World of Atzilut, of which is written: "Every one that is called by My Name..." (Isaiah 43:7) as the Nukva of Aztilut is called "Name." **"...branches of palm trees..." (Leviticus 23:40)** corresponds to the World of Briyah, of which is written: **"For My glory I have created him." "...the boughs of thick leaved trees..."** corresponds to the World of Yetzirah, of which is written **"I have formed him." "...Willows of the brook..." (Ibid.)** corresponds to the World of Asiyah, of which is written **"I have made him."**

Why Sukkot is on the fifteenth day.

214. וְתִקּוּנָא דְּהַאי דְּאָמַר קְרָא, וּלְקַחְתֶּם לָכֶם בַּיּוֹם הָרִאשׁוֹן, דַּיְיקָא דְּהוּא חֲמִישָּׁאָה עַל עָשׂוֹר.

214. Their correction is that when the verse says: "And you shall take for yourselves on the first day..." (Leviticus 23:40) it is precise, as it is five on ten (15).

Explanation: The fifteenth of the month indicates that Nukva, which is the tenth Sefirah and is alluded to in the number ten, elevated and became included in Ima, categorized by the number five, as it includes within it five Sefirot: Chesed, Gevurah, Tiferet, Netzach, and Hod, and each one comprises ten as is known. When these five Sefirot shine in Nukva, She is called "the fifteenth of the month," as then the moon, who is Nukva, is in her utmost fulfilment.

Sukkot is the time to draw Chasadim.

215. אֲבָל בַּיּוֹם הָרִאשׁוֹן, הַהוּא יוֹם רִאשׁוֹן מַאן הוּא. אֶלָּא יוֹם דְּנָפִיק רִאשׁוֹן, לְנַטְלָא בְּמַבּוּעֵי דְּמַיִין נְבִיעִין, וַאֲנַן בָּעֵינָן לְאַמְשָׁכָא לֵיהּ לְעָלְמָא.

215. [He asks:] "**But** when scripture says: **'...the first day...' (Leviticus 23:40) what is this first day?"** What does it allude to? He replies: **"It is the day that was first to emerge to travel in the sources of Living Water,** namely the first Column of the three traveling Columns. From their travel emerge Chasadim revealed in Chochmah called 'Living Water.' It is the Right Column, Chesed, which travels first. **And we need to draw it into the world.** For Sukkot is a time for drawing Chasidim, in the secret of "...His right hand embraces me." (Song of Songs 8:3)

Freedom is not enough. We still need food and drink.

216. מָתָל לְמַלְכָּא דְּקָטַר בְּנֵי נָשָׁא בְּקִטְרוֹי, אִמֵּיהּ מַטְרוֹנִיתָא אָתַת, וְאַפִּיקַת לוֹן לְחֵירוּת, וּמַלְכָּא אַשְׁגַּח לִיקָרָא דִּילָהּ, וְיָהַב לוֹן בִּידָהָא. אַשְׁכַּחַת לוֹן כַּפְיָין וְצָחִין, אָמְרַת, הָא אַפִּיקַת לוֹן לְחֵירוּ, אַיְיתֵי לוֹן מֵיכְלָא וּמִשְׁתְּיָיא.

216. "This is compared to a king who put people into his prison. The lady, his mother, came and set them free. The king, mindful of her honor, put them under her authority. She found them hungry and thirsty and said to her son the king, **'Now that I set them free, give them food and drink.'**

Yom Kippur set us free, and Sukkot nourishes us with everything we need.

217. כָּךְ, הָא יוה"כ אַפִּיק לְכֹלָּא לְחֵירוּ, וַאֲנַן כַּפְנֵי מְזוֹנָא קָאִיבְנָא, וְצַחִיָּין לְמִשְׁתַּיָּא, הִיא אַעֲטָרַת לְמַלְכָּא בְּעִטְרוֹי. בְּהַאי יוֹמָא יָדַעְנָא, דְּהָא מַיִין נָבִיעִין עִמָּהּ שַׁרְיָין, שָׁאֵילְנָא לְמִשְׁתַּיָּיא, לְמַאן דְּאַפִּיק לוֹן לְחֵירוּ, וְעַל דָּא קָרִינָן לֵיהּ יוֹם רִאשׁוֹן.

217. "Thus Yom Kippur, which is the secret of Ima, Binah, **sets them free. We are hungry for nourishment and thirsty for a drink,** since no physical food and drink is drawn from Binah, for which reason we fast and afflict our souls on Yom Kippur. **She therefore adorns** the King, Zeir Anpin, the Son of Binah, **with His Crown,** Mochin of Chasadim. **On this day,** the first day of Sukkot, **we know that there is Living Water with Her, and we ask for water from the One Who set us free,** namely for her to give Chasadim to Zeir Anpin for us, after we attained Mochin of Chochmah, the secret of freedom, from her on Yom Kippur. **We therefore name this day the first day.**

The first day corresponds to Abraham.

218. דָּא בְּסִפְרָא דְּאַגַּדְתָּא וְשַׁפִּיר הוּא. אֲבָל בְּהַאי יוֹמָא, לְאַבְרָהָם שֵׁירוּתָא דְּכֹלָּא, אִי בַּעֲנָנֵי יְקָר הוּא שֵׁירוּתָא, אִי בְּמַיָּא הוּא שֵׁירוּתָא, דְּאַבְרָהָם שָׁארֵי לְמֶחְפְּרֵי בֵּירֵי דְּמַיָּא.

218. "All this is written in the Book of Agadah, and is correct. But besides what was said: **"this day"** that alludes to **Abraham,** the secret of the Sefirah of Chesed, **is the starting point of everything—whether it is the beginning of the Clouds of Glory,** which are the secret of the Surrounding Lights, as the first Surrounding Light is Chesed, **or the beginning of water,** the secret of Inner Light, as the first Inner Light is Chesed, **which** is why **Abraham started to dig wells of water."**

Uniting the Etrog-Nukva with the Lulav-Zeir Anpin.

219. פְּרִי עֵץ הָדָר: דָּא בֵּירָא דְּיִצְחָק, דְּיִצְחָק אַהֲדַר לֵיהּ לְקוּדְשָׁא בְּרִיךְ הוּא וְקָרָא לֵיהּ עֵץ הָדָר, פְּרִי דְּהַאי עֵץ הָדָר יְדִיעָא. כַּפּוֹת תְּמָרִים: דִּכְתִיב, צַדִּיק כַּתָּמָר יִפְרָח, וְלָא אִשְׁתַּכַּח בֵּינַיְיהוּ פֵּרוּדָא, וְע"ד לָא כְתִיב וְכַפּוֹת, אֶלָּא כַּפּוֹת, בְּגִין דְּלָא סָלֵיק דָּא בְּלָא דָא, וּבְהַאי אִתְמַלְיָא הַאי בְּאֵר, מִבְּאֵר מַיִם עִלָּאִין נְבִיעִין, הַהוּא אִתְמַלֵּי בְּקַדְמֵיתָא, וּמִנֵּיהּ אִתְמַלְיָיא בֵּירָא, עַד דְּאִיהוּ נְבִיעוּ לְכֹלָּא.

219. "...the fruit of the Hadar tree..." (Leviticus 23:40) is the Well of Isaac, namely the Nukva called "Well" when receiving Chochmah from the Left Column of Zeir Anpin called Isaac. **For Isaac glorified (*hider*) the Holy One, blessed be He, and called Him "the Hadar tree"** and the Nukva is **the fruit of this Hadar tree that is known. "...branches of palm trees..." are as it is written: "The righteous flourish like the palm tree..." (Psalms 92:13)** namely the Righteous Yesod. **There is no dividing between** Yesod and the Nukva **and therefore it does not say "and branches" but just "branches (*kapot*),"** which is an indication of binding and unity, **since they cannot exist without each other** but are always bound (*kfutim*) together. **Through this, the well,** the Nukva, **is filled from the Well of the Supernal Living Water,** Binah, **for** Yesod **is filled first** from Tiferet, and Tiferet from Binah, **and from it, the Well is filled until it** becomes **a gushing spring for everyone.**

The Myrtles represent the Tree that holds onto the Patriarchs.

220. וַעֲנַף עֵץ עָבוֹת: דָּא עֲנָפָא דְּאִילָנָא רַבְרְבָא, דְּאִתְתַּקִּיף וְאִשְׁתַּרְשָׁא בְּשָׁרְשׁוֹי, אִתְעֲבֵיד אִילָנָא עִלָּאָה עַל כֹּלָּא, דְּאָחִיד בְּכָל סִטְרֵיהּ, עֲנַף דְּאִיהוּ עֵץ עָבוֹת, עֵץ דְּאָחִיד לַעֲבוֹת, דְּהָא מֵהַאי נָטֵל יְסוֹדָא דְּעָלְמָא, וְאִתְמַלְיָא לְאַרְקָא בְּבֵירָא, הַאי הוּא עָלְמָא אַרְקָא דְּשַׁקְיוּתָא.

220. "...the bough of thick leaved tree...." (Leviticus 23:40) This is the bough of the Great Tree, Tiferet, **which was strengthened,**

struck root and became the highest Tree, connected on every side, namely Tiferet that includes the six Sefirot—Chesed, Gevurah, Tiferet, Netzach, Hod, and Yesod and are attached to it on every side. **This bough is a thick (*avot*; עֲבוֹת) tree, namely a Tree that holds onto the Patriarchs (*avot*; אָבוֹת).** For it is the Central Column that comprises Right and Left, Chesed and Gevurah, called Abraham and Isaac. He interprets *avot* (thick) like *avot* (patriarchs), as Ayin (ע) and Alef (א) are interchangeable. **For from here,** Tiferet, **the Foundation (Yesod) of the World receives and is filled to pour unto the well,** the Nukva, **which is a land that is all watered.** When Nukva receives from Yesod She is called a "land that is all watered."

The Willows represent the Left Column, Judgment.

221. וְעַרְבֵי נַחַל: תְּרֵי אִינּוּן, תְּרֵין נַחֲלִין דְּמַיָּיא אִתְכַּנִּישׁ בְּהוֹ, לְאַרְקָא לְצַדִּיק. ד"א, וְעַרְבֵי נַחַל: אִלֵּין אִינּוּן גְּבוּרָן, דַּאֲחִידָן בֵּיהּ בְּיִצְחָק, דְּאַתְיָין מִסִּטְרָא דְּהַהוּא נַחַל עִלָּאָה, וְלָא מִסִּטְרָא דְּאַבָּא. בְּגִ"כ, כֻּלָּא יָאֵי, וְלָא בְּסִימָא לְפֵירִין, וְלָא עָבֵיד פֵּירִין.

221. There are two "...Willows of the brook..." (Leviticus 23:40) alluding to **the two brooks of water,** the two Sefirot, Netzach and Hod, **where the water gathers to pour upon the Righteous,** Yesod, which receives from Netzach and Hod. **Another explanation [is that] the "...Willows of the brook..." are the Gevurot that are attached to Isaac,** the Left Column, **which come from the Supernal Brook,** Ima, **and not from the side of Aba,** the Right Column. **This is why the Willows are all beautiful but are not sweet like fruit, and they do not produce fruit.**

Explanation: The Judgments in the Left are many. Although they are beautiful, they do not produce fruit, meaning they contain Chochmah, as beauty alludes to Chochmah. Therefore it is represented by the Willows of the brook, as they are beautiful but do not produce fruit.

The Willows are Netzach and Hod.

222. וְעַרְבֵי נַחַל: תְּרֵין קָיְימִין, דְּגוּפָא קָיְימָא עֲלַיְיהוּ, אֲבָל וְעַרְבֵי נַחַל וַדַּאי, כְּמָה דְאִתְּמַר, וְאִלֵּין אִינוּן כֻּלְּהוּ לְאַרְקָא מַיָּא לְבֵירָא.

222. The "…Willows of the brook…" (Leviticus 23:40) **are the two pillars,** Netzach and Hod, **which support the body. Yet the "… Willows of the brook" is certainly as was explained,** namely that these Gevurot that are drawn from the Left Column continue to Netzach and Hod. **They all pour water to the Well,** meaning to give to the Nukva.

Another interpretation of the Four Species.

223. ד"א, וּלְקַחְתֶּם לָכֶם בַּיּוֹם הָרִאשׁוֹן פְּרִי עֵץ הָדָר: דָּא אַבְרָהָם. כַּפֹּת תְּמָרִים: דָּא יִצְחָק. וַעֲנַף עֵץ עָבוֹת: דָּא יַעֲקֹב. וְעַרְבֵי נַחַל: אִלֵּין אִינוּן תְּרֵין דַּרְגִּין דַּאֲמָרָן.

223. Another explanation for, "And you shall take for yourselves on the first day the fruit of the tree Hadar" is that it is Abraham; namely Chesed. **"Branches of palm tree" is Isaac,** namely Gevurah; **"the bough of thick leaved trees" is Jacob,** namely Tiferet; **and the "Willows of the brook" are the two grades we mentioned,** Netzach and Hod.

The Myrtles allude to Jacob, the Central Column.

224. וּמַאן דְּמַתְנֵי הַאי, בְּגִין דְּעֵץ עָבוֹת דָּא יַעֲקֹב, דְּאָמֵיד לְכֻלְּהוּ לַחֲלָקִין, וַדַּאי דָּא יַעֲקֹב. אֲבָל הָא אוֹקִימְנָא, פְּרִי עֵץ הָדָר, דָּא בֵּירָא דְיִצְחָק, דָּא גְּבוּרָה תַּתָּאָה. כַּפֹּת תְּמָרִים. כַּפֹּת חָסֵר, קְשׁוּרָא דְּאִתְקְשַׁר בְּבֵירָא, כְּד"א כְּפִיתוּ בְּסַרְבָּלֵיהוֹן, בְּגִין דְּאִלֵּין לָא סָלְקִין דָּא בְּלָא דָא. וַעֲנַף עֵץ עָבוֹת, עֲנָפָא הוּא עִלָּאָה, דְּאִתְעֲבֵיד עֵץ עָבוֹת, וְאָמֵיד לְכָל סִטְרָא, כְּמָה דְאִתְּמַר. עַרְבֵי נַחַל דָּא יִצְחָק, בְּכָל סִטְרֵי, דַּאֲחִידָן בְּסִטְרָא דְנוּקְבָא, וְלָא בְּסִטְרָא דְאַבָּא. דְּתָנֵינָן, אע"ג דִּבְהַאי נַחַל נַחֲלָא לָא אִשְׁתְּכַח בֵּיהּ, דִּינִין מִתְעָרִין מִנֵּיהּ.

224. He who learns this, that the fruit of the Hadar tree is Abraham and the branches of palm trees are Isaac, it is **because the thick tree is Jacob, who holds all the parts,** namely that the Six Corners: Chesed, Gevurah, Tiferet, Netzach, Hod, and Yesod, are included in him, and thus he is called a "thick tree." Therefore, he says that the fruit of the Hadar tree is Abraham. **Assuredly it is Jacob**, but it is not because of this that we are forced to say that the fruit of the Hadar tree is Abraham. **Rather, we have already explained that "the fruit of the Hadar tree" is the well of Isaac, the Lower Gevurah,** namely the Nukva. **In "... branches (*kapot*) of palm trees..." (Leviticus 23:40) *kapot* is spelled without** Vav (ו), which means it is tied; namely **a tie upon the well, as it is written "...bound (*kephitu*) in their mantles..." (Daniel 3:21),** namely Yesod and Nukva, **which do not exist without one another,** as if they are bound. **"...the bough of thick leaved tree" (Leviticus 23:40) is the Supernal Bough turned into a thick Tree cleaving to every side,** namely Chesed, Gevurah, Tiferet, Netzach, Hod, and Yesod, since Tiferet is the torso, Chesed and Gevurah the arms, Netzach and Hod the legs, and Yesod the Holy Covenant, **as we explained. The "... Willows of the brook..." (Leviticus 23:40) is Isaac, since on all sides they hold to the side of the brook,** Ima, **instead of the side of Aba. As we learned, even though there are no Judgments in this brook,** Binah, **all Judgments are yet awakened thence.**

The Willows are Netzach and Hod when they receive Gevurot from the Left Side.

225. וְרַב הַמְנוּנָא סָבָא פָּרִישׁ, וְעַרְבֵי נַחַל, אִינּוּן תְּרֵין קַיְימִין דְּקָאֲמָרָן, דְּבַיְיא נָפְקֵי מִנַּיְיהוּ, וְשַׁפִּיר. אֲבָל תָּא וְחֲזֵי, הָא וְחָזִינָן דִּתְרֵין דַּרְגִּין אִלֵּין דְּקַיְימֵי עַל דַּרְגָּא דְּצַדִּיק, אִיבָּא וּכְנִישׁוּ דְּבִרְכָאן נָפְקֵי מִנַּיְיהוּ, וְעַרְבֵי נַחַל לָא נָפְקֵי מִנַּיְיהוּ, אִיבָּא, וְלָא טַעְמָא, וְלָא רֵיחָא, וְהָא אוֹקִימְנָא וְכֹלָּא שַׁפִּיר.

225. Rav Hamnuna Saba explained that "Willows of the brook" are the two pillars we mentioned, Netzach and Hod, **from which**

water comes out. The explanation **is good, yet come and see, we see that these two grades,** Netzach and Hod, **stand on the grade of the Righteous,** Yesod. **Fruits and gathered blessings are issued from them; but from the Willows of the brook,** which also allude to Netzach and Hod, **no fruits are produced, nor taste nor smell, as we already explained. And all is correct.** Namely, [as said in verse 221] "...the Willows of the brook..." (Leviticus 23:40) allude to Netzach and Hod only when they receive the Gevurot of Isaac from the Left Side, and therefore they do not produce fruits because Judgments hover over them. But when they receive Chasadim as well, all the blessings in the world issue from them.

The Lulav is held in the right hand, and the Etrog in the left hand.

226. וְעַל דָּא אֶתְרוֹג בִּשְׂמָאלָא, לָקֳבֵיל לִבָּא, לוּלָב בִּימִינָא, כַּפּוֹת בְּכֹלָּא, וְקָטִיר בְּכֹלָּא, דְּהָא צַדִּיק כַּפּוֹת הוּא בְּכָל סִטְרִין, וְקָטִיר בְּכֹלָּא. וְדָא הוּא קִשּׁוּרָא דִּמְהֵימְנוּתָא.

226. Therefore we hold **the *Etrog* with the left hand against the heart. The *Lulav* is held by the right bundled together with all the species all tied up, as the Righteous,** Yesod, **is united with all** the Sefirot, **and bound to them all. This is the bond of Faith,** shining upon the Nukva called Faith.

We connect to the Seven Guests through the Four Species.

227. וּבְסִפְרָא דְּאַגַּדְתָּא שַׁפִּיר קָאָמַר, דְּכָל אִלֵּין אִינּוּן אוּשְׁפִּיזִין, דְּזַמִּינִין עַמָּא קַדִּישָׁא בְּהַאי יוֹמָא, דְּבַעְיָין לְאַשְׁכָּחָא לְהוֹ, כֵּיוָן דְּזַמִּין לוֹן, וּבְהוֹ בָּעֵי ב"נ לְמַלְכָּא בְּעוּתֵיהּ, זַכָּאִין אִינּוּן יִשְׂרָאֵל דְּיָדְעִין אָרְחוֹי דְּמַלְכָּא קַדִּישָׁא, וְיָדְעִין אָרְחוֹי דְּאוֹרַיְיתָא, לְמֵהַךְ בְּאוֹרַח קְשׁוֹט, לְמִזְכֵּי בְּהוֹ בְּעַלְמָא דֵּין וּבְעַלְמָא דְּאָתֵי.

227. In the Book of Agada it is beautifully said that all the four species **are the guests,** the secret of the Seven Sefirot: Chesed, Gevurah, Tiferet, Netzach, Hod, Yesod, and Malchut, **who were invited by the Holy Nation on this day,** namely in the way that we pray on the days of Sukkot before the meal and say "Come Supernal Guests…." **They should be found there once they are invited, and in them man needs to plead his request to the King.** Through the four species, which allude to these Sefirot, one attains them. **Happy are Israel who know the ways of the Holy King, and know the ways of the Torah, with which to walk the path of Truth and merit this world and the World to Come.**

The Four Species are the signs that Israel won over the Judgment.

228. בְּיוֹמָא דָא נָפְקֵי יִשְׂרָאֵל, בְּסִימָנִין רְשִׁימִין מִגּוֹ מַלְכָּא, בְּגִין דְּאִינּוּן נָצְחִין דִּינָא, וּמַאי סִימָנִין אִינּוּן, סִימָנֵי מְהֵימְנוּתָא, חוֹתָמָא דְּמַלְכָּא עִלָּאָה. לִתְרֵי בְּנֵי נָשָׁא, דְּעָאלוּ קֳדָם מַלְכָּא לְדִינָא וְלָא יָדְעֵי עַלְמָא מַאן מִנַּיְיהוּ נָצַח, נָפַק חַד לְגָיוֹן מִבֵּי מַלְכָּא, שְׁאִילוּ לוֹ, אֲמַר לוֹן, מַאן דְּיִפּוֹק וּבִידוֹי סִימָנִין דְּמַלְכָּא, הוּא נָצַח.

228. On this day, Israel come out from before the King with certain signs, namely the four species, **for they won over the Judgment. What are these signs? The Signs of the Faith,** the Shechinah, **the Seal of the most high King,** Zeir Anpin. **It is like two men come before the king to be judged. The people in the world did not know who won. A minister came from the king's house and they asked him. He said to them, "Whoever leaves** the king's house **with the king's signs in his hands, he is the winner."**

The Angels see Israel with the signs of the King.

229. כָּךְ, כּוּלֵּי עַלְמָא עָאלִין לְדִינָא, קֳדָם מַלְכָּא עִלָּאָה, וְדָאִין לוֹן מִיּוֹמָא דְּר"ה וְיוֹם הַכִּפּוּרִים, עַד חֲמֵשׁ סְרֵי יוֹמִין לְיַרְחָא, וּבֵין כָּךְ אִשְׁתַּכָּחוּ יִשְׂרָאֵל

זַכָּאִין כֻּלְּהוּ בִּתְיוּבְתָּא, טָרְחִין בְּסֻכָּה וְלוּלָב וְאֶתְרוֹג, וְלָא יָדְעֵי מַאן נָצַח דִּינָא, מַלְאֲכֵי עִלָּאֵי שָׁאֲלוּ מַאן נָצַח דִּינָא. קוּדְשָׁא בְּרִיךְ הוּא א"ל, אִינּוּן דְּמַפְקֵי בִּידַיְיהוּ סִימָנִין דִּילִי, אִינּוּן נָצְחִין דִּינָא.

229. So too, all the people in the world come to be judged before the most high King and He judges them on Rosh Hashanah and on Yom Kippur until the fifteenth day of the month. Among this, Israel are found to have merited to do Teshuvah and toil in building the Sukkah and acquiring a *Lulav* and *Etrog*. It is not known who won the Judgment. The Supernal Angels ask: "Who has won?" and the Holy One, blessed be He, says: "They who hold My Signs in their hands, the four species, **have won over judgment."**

The Angels praise Israel when they see them with the mark of the King.

230. בְּהַאי יוֹמָא, נָפְקֵי יִשְׂרָאֵל בִּרְשִׁימוּ דְּמַלְכָּא, בְּתוּשְׁבַּחְתָּא דְּהִלֵּילָא, עָאלִין בְּסֻכָּה, אֶתְרוֹג בִּשְׂמָאלָא, לוּלָב בִּימִינָא, וְחָמָאן כֻּלְּהוּ, דְּיִשְׂרָאֵל רְשִׁימִין בִּרְשִׁימִין דְּמַלְכָּא קַדִּישָׁא, פָּתְחֵי וְאָמְרֵי, אַשְׁרֵי הָעָם שֶׁכָּכָה לּוֹ אַשְׁרֵי הָעָם שֶׁה' אֱלֹהָיו.

230. On this day, Israel leave with a mark from the King with a song of glory and enter the Sukkah, *Etrog* in their left hand, a *Lulav* in their right. Everyone sees that Israel are written in the King's list, and open and say, "Happy are the people who have it so; happy are the people whose God is the Lord." (Psalms 144:15)

Even the nations benefit from Sukkot but on Shmini Atzeret, it is for Israel alone.

231. עַד כָּאן חֶדְוְותָא דְּכֹלָּא, חֶדְוְותָא דְּאוּשְׁפִּיזִין, וַאֲפִילוּ אוּמּוֹת הָעוֹלָם חָדָאן בְּחֶדְוְותָא, וּמִתְבָּרְכִין מִנֵּהּ, וְעַל דָּא קָרְבָּנִין בְּכָל יוֹמָא עֲלַיְיהוּ, לְאַטָּלָא עֲלַיְיהוּ שְׁלָם, וְיִתְבָּרְכוּן מִינָן. מִכָּאן וּלְהָלְאָה, יוֹמָא חַד, דְּמַלְכָּא עִלָּאָה, דְּחָדֵי בְּהוּ

בְּיִשְׂרָאֵל, דִּכְתִיב בַּיּוֹם הַשְּׁמִינִי עֲצֶרֶת תִּהְיֶה לָכֶם, דְּהָא יוֹמָא דָא מִן מַלְכָּא בִּלְחוֹדוֹי, וְחֶדְוָותָא דִּילֵיהּ בְּיִשְׂרָאֵל, לְמַלְכָּא דְּזַמִּין אוּשְׁפִּיזִין וכו'.

231. Now all rejoice, and the guests rejoice. Even the nations of the world participate in that joy and are blessed by it. Hence sacrifices are offered for them every day, so there will be peace upon them, and they will be blessed by it. From now on, there is one day in which the highest King rejoices with the people of Israel, as it is written: "On the eighth day you shall have a solemn assembly…." (Numbers 29:35) This day comes solely from the King, who delights in Israel as a king who has invited guests. The end of the article is found in [Zohar,] Emor 288.

Tetzave

15. Four kinds

A Synopsis

Rav Shimon and the Old Sage discuss the verse, "And you shall take for yourselves on the first day the fruit of the hadar tree," saying that "hadar" is the Righteous, namely Yesod, and that Malchut is the "fruit of the tree hadar." They speak about the palm trees, the boughs of thick leaved trees, and the two willows of the brook. They conclude that we are commanded to take these four kinds since we need to awaken Below in the likeness of Above. There is nothing in the world that has no counterpart above, and the reverse is also true.

The Creator spreads His wings over Israel on Sukkot.

130. וְכַד יִשְׂרָאֵל אִינּוּן בַּחֲמֵיסַר יוֹמִין, כְּדֵין נָטִיל לִבְנוֹי, לְפָרְשָׂא גַּדְפּוֹי עֲלַיְיהוּ, וּלְמֶחֱדֵי עִמְּהוֹן. וְע"ד כְּתִיב וּלְקַחְתֶּם לָכֶם בַּיּוֹם הָרִאשׁוֹן, פְּרִי דָא אִיהוּ אִילָנָא דְּאִקְרֵי עֵץ פְּרִי, וְאִשְׁתְּכַח בֵּיהּ פְּרִי. עֵץ הָדָר: כד"א הוֹד וְהָדָר לְפָנָיו. מ"ט אִקְרֵי הָדָר, וּמַאן אִיהוּ הָדָר. אֶלָּא דָא צַדִּיק.

130. When Israel are in the fifteenth day of the seventh month, **the Holy One, blessed be He, takes His children and spreads His wings over them to rejoice with them. Therefore, it is written: "And you shall take for yourselves on the first day** the fruit of the hadar tree…." **(Leviticus 23:40) This fruit is the tree that is called 'fruit tree,'** namely Malchut, **and bears fruit. "Hadar tree," as it is written: "Honor and majesty (hadar) are before Him…." (Psalms 96:6)** He asks: **"Why is it called hadar and who is hadar?"** He answers: **"It is the Righteous,** namely Yesod. And Malchut is called "the fruit of the hadar tree," meaning Malchut that receives from Yesod that is called hadar."

All majesty comes from Yesod.

131. אֲמַאי אִקְרֵי הָדָר, וְהָא אֲתָר טְמִירָא אִיהוּ דְּלֵית לֵיהּ גְּלוּיָא, וּצְרִיכָא לְאִתְכַּסְיָיא תָּדִיר, וְלֵית הָדָר אֶלָּא מַאן דְּאִתְגַּלְיָיא וְאִתְחֲזֵי. אֶלָּא, אע״ג דְּאִיהוּ דַּרְגָּא טְמִירָא, הַדּוּרָא אִיהוּ דְּכָל גּוּפָא, וְלָא אִשְׁתְּכַח הַדּוּרָא לְגוּפָא, אֶלָּא בֵּיהּ. מַאי טַעְמָא. מַאן דְּלֵית עִמֵּיהּ הַאי דַּרְגָּא, לֵית בֵּיהּ הַדּוּרָא, לְמֵיעַל בִּבְנֵי נָשָׁא. קָלָא לָאו עִמֵּיהּ בְּדִבּוּרָא, וְהַדּוּרָא דְּקָלָא אִתְפְּסַק מִנֵּיהּ. דִּיקְנָא, וְהַדּוּרָא דְּדִיקְנָא לָאו עִמֵּיהּ, וְאע״ג דְּאִתְכַּסְיָיא הַהוּא דַּרְגָּא, כָּל הַדּוּרָא דְּגוּפָא בֵּיהּ תַּלְיָא. וְאִתְכַּסֵּי וְאִתְגַּלְיָיא. וּבְג״כ עֵץ הָדָר אִיהוּ, עֵץ דְּכָל הַדּוּרָא דְּגוּפָא בֵּיהּ תַּלְיָא, וְדָא אִיהוּ עֵץ עוֹשֶׂה פְּרִי.

131. He asks: **"Why is** Yesod **called hadar? It is a covered place, which is not revealed but should always be covered, yet majesty is only upon someone that is revealed and seen."** He answers: **"Even though it is a covered level, it is the majesty of the whole body, and there is no majesty to the body but in it."** He asks: **"What is the reason?"** He answers: "It is **because one who does not have that grade has no majesty to come among people; he has no voice when he speaks because the majesty of the voice is cut from him. He has no beard or the majesty of a beard.** So **even though that grade is covered,** nevertheless **all the majesty of the body originates in it, and is covered and revealed** through the majesty of the body. **Therefore, it is the hadar (majesty) tree,** meaning **a tree from which all the majesty of the body comes. This is a fruit tree yielding fruit.** But Malchut is called 'fruit tree.'"

The Lulav, Myrtles, and Willows.

132. כַּפֹּת תְּמָרִים, הָכָא אִתְכְּלִילַת אִתְּתָא בְּבַעְלָהּ בְּלָא פֵּרוּדָא, כַּפּוֹת תְּמָרִים כַּחֲדָא. וַעֲנַף עֵץ עָבוֹת, תְּלָתָא. וְעָלַיְין דִּילֵיהּ, דָּא בְּסִטְרָא דָּא, וְדָא בְּסִטְרָא דָּא, וְחַד דְּשַׁלִּיט עֲלַיְיהוּ. וְעַרְבֵי נַחַל, תְּרֵין. דְּלֵית לְהוּ רֵיחָא וְטַעְמָא, כְּשׁוֹקִין בִּבְנֵי נָשָׁא. לוּלָב נָטִיל כֻּלְּהוּ, כְּחוּטָא דְּשִׁדְרָה קַיְּימָא דְּגוּפָא. וּמַה דְּנָפִיק לְבַר טֶפַח, הָכִי הוּא, בְּגִין לְאַשְׁלְמָא וּלְאַפָּקָא כֹּלָּא, וּלְשַׁמְּשָׁא כַּדְקָא חֲזֵי.

132. "...branches of palm trees..." (Leviticus 23:40) is Yesod, the Righteous, as it is written: "The righteous man flourishes like the palm tree...." (Psalms 92:13) **Here, the woman is included in her husband without separation,** because it is written: **"...branches of palm trees..." (Ibid.)** instead of "And branches of palm trees." For the Vav (and) would divide between fruit of the Hadar tree and the branches of palm trees. This shows that they are tied **together,** for Yesod and Malchut are together. **"...and the boughs of thick leaved trees..." (Leviticus 23:40), they are three,** meaning the three Columns—Chesed, Gevurah and Tiferet—**because it has** three **leaves, one on** the right **side, one on the** left **side and the one** in the center **that controls them,** because the Central Column unites the Right and Left into one. **"...there are willows of the brook..." (Ibid.),** namely Netzach and Hod, **which have neither scent nor taste,** being **the aspect of legs in people. *Lulav* (palm leaf),** which is Yesod, **receives** and combines **them all, like the spinal cord that is in the body. It protrudes outside** the other kinds **by a hand's breadth** upwards, **and so it needs to be to perfect and bring forth all** the levels **for proper union.**

Explanation: Yesod ascends through the spinal cord and releases the drop of semen from the Brain of Da'at in the Head. This is what the ***Lulav*** alludes to when it protrudes a hand's breadth above the Myrtles and the Willows, which are Chesed, Gevurah, Tiferet, Netzach and Hod, as this hand's breath indicates the Da'at of the head, where the ***Lulav***—Yesod—reaches up to.

Through the species Below we awaken their counterpart Above.

133. בְּהָנֵי זִינִין, בָּעֵי בַּר נָשׁ לְאִתְחֲזָאָה קָמֵי קוּדְשָׁא בְּרִיךְ הוּא. עָלִין וְטַרְפִּין דְּהָנֵי לְתַתָּא כְּגַוְונָא דִּלְעֵילָּא, דְּלֵית לָךְ מִלָּה בְּעָלְמָא, דְּלָא אִית לָהּ דּוּגְמָא לְעֵילָּא, כְּגַוְונָא דִּלְעֵילָּא הָכִי אִית לְתַתָּא, וּבְעוּ יִשְׂרָאֵל לְאִתְאַחֲדָא בְּרָזָא דָּא דִּמְהֵימְנוּתָא, קָמֵי קוּדְשָׁא בְּרִיךְ הוּא.

133. With these kinds one must show himself before the Holy One, blessed be He, for they correspond to Chesed, Gevurah, Tiferet, Netzach, Hod, Yesod, and Malchut. **The leaves of these palm trees allude to all the other hosts that join together in these Names that the Holy One, blessed be He, is called.** Therefore, we are commanded to take these four kinds **since we need** to awaken **Below in the likeness of Above, for there is nothing in the world that does not have a counterpart Above.** And vice versa, **as it is Above, so is it Below,** because the worlds are imprinted by one another, and the roots are Above, for there is nothing in the Lower Worlds whose root cannot be found in the Upper Worlds. Therefore, the roots of the four kinds are Chesed, Gevurah, Tiferet, Netzach, Hod, Yesod, and Malchut that are in Atzilut. **And Israel must unite by means of this secret of Faith before the Holy One, blessed be He.**

17. "May the Name of the Lord be blessed"

A Synopsis

We learn that the secret of the title verse was revealed to Rabbi Yitzchak Kaftora in a dream. It means that the word "blessed" (*mevorach*) begins hard but ends soft; this is like on Rosh Hashanah where it is hard with Harsh Judgment, and on Shmini Atzeret where it is soft with joy. We read of the difference between the Upper Judgment that is Male, and the Lower Judgment that is Female; the latter begins hard but softens until it is joyful on Shmini Atzeret.

Rosh Hashanah is tough and Atzeret is soft.

141. כְּתִיב יְהִי שֵׁם יְיָ' מְבוֹרָךְ. מַאי מְבוֹרָךְ. אֲבָל רָזָא וְחָדָא יָדַע חַד מֵחַבְרָנָא, בְּמַדְבְּרָא אַחְזִיאוּ לֵיהּ בְּחֶלְמָא, וְרַבִּי יִצְחָק כַּפְתּוֹרָא שְׁמֵיהּ. מַאי מְבוֹרָךְ. שֵׁירוּתָא קָשֶׁה, וְסוֹפֵיהּ רַךְ. מ"ב קָשֶׁה, וְדִינָא אִיהוּ וַדַּאי. כְּגַוְונָא דָא, יוֹמָא דְּר"ה מ"ב, דְּהָא בְּמ"ב אַתְוָון אִתְבְּרֵי עָלְמָא, וְע"ד אִתְבְּרֵי בְּדִינָא. לְבָתַר

רַךְ, וְעַל דָּא תָּנֵינָן, כָּל שֵׁירוּתִין קָשִׁין, וְסוֹפָא דִּלְהוֹן רַכִּין. בְּיוֹמָא דְּרֹאשׁ הַשָּׁנָה מ"ב קָשֶׁה בְּדִינָא. בְּיוֹמָא דַּעֲצֶרֶת רַךְ בְּחֶדְוָה.

141. It is written: "...blessed be the Name of the Lord." (Job 1:21) He asks: **"What is meant by 'blessed'?"** He answers: **"There is one secret that one of our friends knew that was shown to him in a dream, and his name is Rabbi Yitzchak Kaftora."** He said: **"What is meant by 'blessed (mevorach)'?"** It means **that its beginning is hard and its end soft,** because *mevorach* (מבורך) is spelled with the letters *Mem-Bet-Vav-Resh-Caf.* **Mem-Bet (מ"ב) is hard and is definitely Judgement, like the day of Rosh Hashanah is Mem Bet, because the world was created with Mem-Bet (42) letters,** namely 32 times Elohim and the ten sayings, which equal 42. Similarly, there are 42 letters from the Bet of *beresheet* (In the beginning), until the Bet of the word *vohu* (void). **Therefore, it was created with Judgment; but afterwards it is Rach (Resh-Caf; soft; רך). Therefore, we have learned that all beginnings are hard but their endings are easy because on the day of Rosh Hashanah, it is Mem-Bet with Harsh Judgment, and on Shmini Atzeret, it is soft with joy.**

Vayikra

64. The four species

A Synopsis

Rav Yehuda says that man is called a tree, and that the woman that was taken from his side refers to the fruit of the Hadar tree. He speaks as well about the palm tree that grows for seventy years. Rav Yosi says that the fruit of the Hadar tree is an altar (Malchut) because all of the seventy years give Malchut a portion and she is blessed by them all. From this he deduces that whoever sins and renders the altar (Malchut) defective, sins against and renders all the Seven Sefirot of Zeir Anpin defective. We read about *zot,* the altar anointed by Aaron; the children of Israel circle the altar during the Feast of Sukkot, thus bringing offerings for all the nations of the world. The altar is circled so as to supply it with blessings from the source of the Spring, Binah. The numbers seven and seventy are heavily emphasized in this section for our consideration.

The Etrog-Malchut is the fuit of the Hadar Tree-Zeir Anpin.

412. רִבִּי יְהוּדָה פָּתַח, כְּתִיב פְּרִי עֵץ הָדָר כַּפֹּת תְּמָרִים. פְּרִי עֵץ הָדָר, מַאן הוּא. דָּא אֶתְרוֹג. וְכִי אֶתְרוֹג מֵעֵץ הָדָר הוּא, וְהָא כַּמָּה קוֹצִין אִית סַחֲרָנֵיהּ, מִכָּאן וּמִכָּאן, וְאַתְּ אַמְרַת פְּרִי עֵץ הָדָר. אֶלָּא רָזָא דְּמִלָּה, דִּכְתִיב וַיִּבֶן יְיָ' אֱלֹהִים אֶת הַצֵּלָע אֲשֶׁר לָקַח מִן הָאָדָם לְאִשָּׁה וַיְבִאֶהָ אֶל הָאָדָם. וּכְתִיב עֶצֶם מֵעֲצָמַי וּבָשָׂר מִבְּשָׂרִי, וְדָא הוּא פְּרִי עֵץ הָדָר. מְנָלָן דְּאָדָם עֵץ אִקְרֵי. דִּכְתִיב כִּי הָאָדָם עֵץ הַשָּׂדֶה.

412. Rav Yehuda opened: "It says, '...the fruit of the Hadar tree, branches of palm trees....' (Leviticus 23:40) [He asks:] **"What is the fruit of the Hadar tree?"** [He answers]: **"It is the *Etrog.*"** He asks: **"Does the *Etrog* grow on a Hadar (lit. elegant) tree? There are many thorns to the tree of the *Etrog,* around it in every direction, and you say, 'the fruit of the Hadar tree'?"** He answers: **"The secret of**

these words is that it is written, 'And the Lord God fashioned the side that had been taken from the man into a woman, bringing her to the man.' (Genesis 2:22) It is also written, '...bone of my bones and flesh of my flesh....' (Ibid. 23) This refers to the fruit of the Hadar tree. Whence do we know this? Because man is called a tree? Because it is written, '...for a man is the tree of the field....' (Deuteronomy 20:19)"

Explanation: The inner meaning of the verse: **"And the Lord God fashioned the side..." (Genesis 2:22)** relates to Zeir Anpin and Malchut that emanated as two faces (Siamese twins) and afterward the Emanator sawed them from each other. It is found that Malchut is the side from Zeir Anpin, and Zeir Anpin is called the Tree of Life, and Malchut is the fruit of this Tree. He says that this is the secret of the *Etrog,* which alludes to Malchut. This is why the Torah called it a fruit of a Hadar tree, since it is the tree of an elegant (Hadar) tree, which is Zeir Anpin.

The Lulav is Yesod that is attached Above and Below.

413. כַּפֹּת תְּמָרִים, דְּסָלִיק לְשַׁבְעִין שְׁנִין, וּבֵיהּ אִשְׁתַּכְלְלוּ שַׁבְעִין שְׁנִין עִלָּאִין. וְדָא אַכְפָּת וְאִתְקְשַׁר לְעֵילָּא וְתַתָּא. וְעַ"ד אִקְרֵי כַּפּוֹת, כד"א כְּפִיתוּ, דְּסָלִיק לְהָכָא וּלְהָכָא. הה"ד כִּי כֹל בַּשָּׁמַיִם וּבָאָרֶץ דַּיְיקָא.

413. "...branches of palm trees...." The palm tree **grows for seventy years,** an allusion to the Yesod of Zeir Anpin, **in which are constructed the Seventy Supernal Years,** the secret of the Seven Sefirot: Chesed, Gevurah, Tiferet, Netzach, Hod, Yesod, and Malchut, each including ten, and altogether seventy. **It is tied (*nichpat*),** namely **attached Above** to Zeir Anpin **and Below** to Malchut. **It is therefore called branches (*kapot*), as it says "...bound (*kephitu*)..." (Daniel 3:21)** since Yesod **rises to here and to there,** to Zeir Anpin and Malchut. **As it says, "... for all that is in Heaven and on Earth..." (I Chronicles 29:11) which**

is precise, meaning that Yesod called "all" is attached to Heaven (Zeir Anpin) and Earth (Malchut).

One who sins against Malchut, sins against all Seven Sefirot.

414. ר' יוֹסֵי אָמַר, פְּרִי עֵץ הָדָר דָּא מִזְבֵּחַ, דְּעָבֵיד פֵּירִין, וְסָלִיק אֵבִּין לְכָל סִטְרִין. מַאי טַעֲמָא. בְּגִין דְּכָל ע' שְׁנִין, יָהֲבִין לָהּ חוּלָקָא, וְאִתְבָּרְכָא מִכֻּלְּהוּ. מַאי קָא מַיְירֵי. בְּגִין דְּמַאן דְּחָטֵי לְגַבֵּי מִזְבֵּחַ, בְּכֹלָּא חָטֵי, דְּהָא כְּפִית לְקִבְלֵי הַהוּא דִּכְפִית לְעֵילָּא, וְעַל דָּא אִתְקְשַׁר דָּא בְּדָא, פְּרִי עֵץ הָדָר כַּפֹּת תְּמָרִים וְלָא כְּתִיב וְכַפֹּת תְּמָרִים.

414. Rav Yosi said: "The 'fruit of the Hadar tree' is an altar, Malchut, **which produces fruit and buds in every direction."** [He asks:] **"Why** is it called the fruit of a Hadar tree?" [He answers:] **"Because all of the seventy years,** the Seven Sefirot: Chesed, Gevurah, Tiferet, Netzach, Hod, Yesod, and Malchut of Zeir Anpin, each including ten, which makes them seventy, **give** Malchut **a portion and she is blessed by them all,** and Zeir Anpin is called a Hadar tree." [He asks:] **"What does that teach us?"** [He answers:] **"That whoever sins and damages the altar,** Malchut, **sins against and damages all** the Seven Sefirot of Zeir Anpin, **for** Malchut **is attached to that which is bound** and connected **Above,** which is Yesod of Zeir Anpin. **They are therefore mutually attached,** Malchut and the Seven Sefirot of Zeir Anpin, **and it is written, 'The fruit of the Hadar tree, branches (*kapot;* כפת) of palm trees,'** to show that they are tied (*kefutim*) to each other, **instead of 'and branches (*vekapot;* וכפת),'** where the Vav (ו) would have interjected between the fruit of the Hadar tree, Malchut, and the dates, which are Yesod." Rav Yosi and Rav Yehuda are not in disagreement except for the order of the verses.

The alter is anointed and blessed by the Seven Sefirot of Zeir Anpin.

415. כְּתִיב זֹאת מִשְׁחַת אַהֲרֹן וּמִשְׁחַת בָּנָיו. מַאי קָא מַיְירֵי. אֶלָּא, זֹאת: דָּא מִזְבֵּחַ, דְּאִתְמְשַׁח עַל יְדָא דְּאַהֲרֹן, דִּכְתִיב וּמָשַׁחְתָּ אֶת מִזְבַּח הָעֹלָה וְאֶת כָּל כֵּלָיו. וּמִשְׁחַת בָּנָיו, דְּהָא מִכֻּלְּהוּ אִתְמְשַׁח, וְאִתְרַבֵּי, וְאִתְבָּרְכָא, וְאִתְדַּכָּא.

415. It is written: "This (*zot*) is the portion of the anointing of Aaron, and of the anointing of his sons…." (Leviticus 7:35) [He asks:] **"What does this teach us?"** [He answers:] **"That *zot* is the altar,** Malchut, **anointed by Aaron,** who is Chesed of Zeir Anpin, **as it is written, 'And you shall anoint the altar of the burnt offering, and all its vessels…. (Exodus 40:10) '…and of the anointing of his sons…' (Leviticus 7:35)** are the rest of the Sefirot of Zeir Anpin that descend from Chesed, **since** the altar, Malchut, **is anointed by all of them, magnified, blessed, and purified.**

We surround the altar once per day, and seven times on the seventh day.

416. ת"ח, בְּחַג סוֹבְבִים אֶת הַמִּזְבֵּחַ זִמְנָא וְחָדָא בְּכָל יוֹמָא, וְשִׁבְעָה זִמְנִין לְבָתַר. מַאי קָא מַיְירֵי. אֶלָּא, לְמַלְכָּא דְּזַמִּין אוּשְׁפִּיזִין, וְאִתְעֲסַק בְּהוּ, וַהֲוָה לֵיהּ לְמַלְכָּא בַּת יְחִידָאָה, אָמְרָה לֵיהּ, מָארִי מַלְכָּא, בְּגִין אוּשְׁפִּיזִין לָא אִשְׁגַּחְתְּ עָלַי. א"ל, וְחַיֶּיךָ בְּרַתִּי פַּרְקְטָא וְחָדָא אַסְלִיק לָךְ בְּכָל יוֹמָא, דְּשַׁוֵּי כְּכֻלְּהוּ.

416. "Come and see, on the Holiday of Sukkot, **the altar is circled once every day and seven times in the end."** [He asks:] **"What does that teach us?"** [He answers:] **"A king invited guests and was occupied with them. The king had an only daughter. She said to him: 'My Master the king, you do not care for me because of the guests.' He said to her: 'I promise you daughter, each day I will give you a gift that is worth the like of them all.'**

Encircling the altar draws blessings from the Supernal Days to Malchut.

417. כַּךְ, בְּכָל יוֹמָא וְיוֹמָא דְּוָזג, מַקְרִיבִין יִשְׂרָאֵל לָקֳבֵל אוּמִין דְּעָלְמָא. אָמַר מִזְבֵּחַ לְמַלְכָּא קַדִּישָׁא, לְכֻלְּהוּ מִשְׁתַּכְחֵי מָאנִין וְחוּלָקִין, וְלִי מַה אַנְתְּ יָהִיב. אָמַר לָהּ, בְּכָל יוֹמָא וְיוֹמָא יְסוֹבְבוֹן לֵיךְ שִׁבְעָה יוֹמִין עִלָּאִין, לְבָרְכָא לָךְ, וְיָהֲבִין לָךְ שִׁבְעִין חוּלָקִין בְּכָל יוֹמָא, לָקֳבֵל שִׁבְעִין פָּרִים דְּמִתְקָרְבִין בְּחָג.

417. "Similarly did Israel bring an offering every day during the Holiday for the nations of the world, seventy bulls corresponding to the seventy nations. **The altar,** Malchut, **said to the Holy King,** Zeir Anpin, **'Why is everyone,** namely the nations, **given parts and portions, and to me what do You give?' He said to it: 'You shall be circled every day by the Seven Supernal Days,** the secret of the Seven Sefirot of Zeir Anpin as each includes all of them, **to bless you. They shall give you seventy parts daily,** as each includes ten, **against the seventy bulls offered during the Holiday** for the seventy nations.' Thus every day, Israel bring offerings for the nations of the world."

Seven days of encircling enable Malchut to be blessed by Binah.

418. רִבִּי יְהוּדָה אָמַר, שִׁבְעָה בְּכָל יוֹמָא, בְּגִין דְּהָא אִתְבָּרְכָא מִכֻּלְּהוּ, וּלְסוֹף, שִׁבְעָה יוֹמִין, מִתְבָּרְכָא מֵאֲתָר דִּמְשַׁח רְבוּתָא אִשְׁתְּכַח. שִׁבְעָה זִמְנִין, לָקֳבֵל כָּל אִינּוּן שִׁבְעָה יוֹמִין, בְּגִין לְקַיְּימָא לָהּ בִּרְכָאן מִן מַבּוּעָא דְּנַחֲלָא, דְּנָגִיד תָּדִיר וְלָא פָּסִיק, אִשְׁתְּכַח דְּאִתְבָּרְכָא בְּכָל יוֹמָא וְיוֹמָא, עַד שִׁבְעָה דְּאִתְבָּרְכָא מִמַּבּוּעָא דְּנַחֲלָא. וְכֵן זִמְנָא אַחֲרָא שִׁבְעָה זִמְנִין כַּחֲדָא וְאִתְקַיְּימוּ בִּרְכָאן לְבָתַר מֵאֲתָר עִלָּאָה דְּמַבּוּעָא נָפִיק וְלָא פָּסִיק, כְּדְקָאמְרָן.

418. Rav Yehuda said: "There are seven parts **every day** and only one circling, **which is because** Malchut **is blessed** daily **by them all,** as the Seven Sefirot are composed of each other, and the particular Sefirah of each day includes all seven and they are seventy, corresponding to the seventy nations. **By the end of the seven days,** namely on Hoshana Raba, Malchut **is blessed by the place from where the anointing oil**

comes, namely from Binah, where abundance of Chochmah called "oil" is found. It is therefore circled **seven times corresponding with these seven days,** the Seven Sefirot of Zeir Anpin, **so as to** draw and **supply it with blessings from the source of the Spring,** Binah, **which always flows and never stops. Thus it is blessed daily from the source of the river,** Yesod of Zeir Anpin, on the seven days of the Holiday of Sukkot **until the seventh day.** It does not always flow but stops, for it does not shine fully except during prayers, Shabbats, and Holidays. **And also one other time,** on Hoshana Raba, when the altar is circled seven times, it is blessed **seven times together and all the blessings are then established in it from the Supernal Place, where the Source,** which is Binah **comes and never stops, as we have said."**

The altar atones for Israel's sins.

419. בְּכָל יוֹמָא, מַכְרִיזִין עָלָהּ וְאָמְרִין, עַד עֲקָרָה יָלְדָה שִׁבְעָה וְרַבַּת בָּנִים אֻמְלָלָה. עַד עֲקָרָה יָלְדָה שִׁבְעָה: דָּא כְּנֶסֶת יִשְׂרָאֵל, דְּאִתְבָּרְכָא מִשִּׁבְעָה בְּכָל יוֹמָא, וְסָלִיק לְחוּשְׁבָּן עִלָּאָה. וְרַבַּת בָּנִים אֻמְלָלָה, אִלֵּין אוּמִין עע"ז, דְּסַלְקִין בְּיוֹמָא קַדְמָאָה לְחוּשְׁבָּן רַב, וּלְבָתַר מִתְמַעֲטִין וְאַזְלִין בְּכָל יוֹמָא וְיוֹמָא. וְעַ"ד, מִזְבֵּחַ מְכַפֵּר עַל חוֹבֵיהוֹן דְּיִשְׂרָאֵל מִזְבֵּחַ מַדְכֵּי לְהוֹן, וְאָרִיק לְהוֹן בִּרְכָאן מֵעֵילָּא לְתַתָּא.

419. On every day of the Holiday, **a proclamation sounds regarding her, saying, "...While the barren woman bears seven, the mother of many is forlorn." (I Samuel 2:5) "...While the barren woman bears seven...." this is the Congregation of Israel, which is blessed daily** by the Seven Sefirot of Zeir Anpin **and** eventually **rises to be part of the Supernal count,** namely Binah, as was explained before. **"...the mother of many is forlorn" (Ibid.); these are the heathen nations that receive a big number on the first day,** namely thirteen bullocks, **which gradually diminishes every day** until there are only seven bullocks. **The altar therefore atones for the sins of Israel, purifies them, and causes blessings to flow on them from above downward.**

Everything that manifests in the world comes from the Four Species.

420. וַעֲנַף עֵץ עָבוֹת: דָּא מַלְכָּא קַדִּישָׁא, דְּאָחִיד לִתְרֵין סִטְרִין. ובג"כ הֲדַס תְּלַת עֲנָף, דְּיִתְעֲבֵד עֲנַף עֵץ עָבוֹת, דְּאָחִיד לְכָל סִטְרָא. וְעַרְבֵי נַחַל: אִלֵּין תְּרֵין קַיְימִין, דְּמֵהָכָא נָפִיק, לְכַפּוֹת תְּמָרִים. כַּפּוֹת תְּמָרִים, אָחִיד לְעֵילָא וְאָחִיד לְתַתָּא, וְהָא אִתְּמַר. אֶתְרוֹג נָפְקָא מִגּוֹ כּוּבִין דְּאִילָנָא וְהָכִי הוּא. כַּפּוֹת תְּמָרִים הָכִי נָמֵי אָחִיד בְּהוּ וַדַּאי, כָּל מַה דְּנָפִיק לְעָלְמָא מֵהָכָא נָפְקָא וּמֵהָכָא אַתְיָין.

420. "...and the boughs of a thick leaved tree...." (Leviticus 23:40) This is the Holy King, Tiferet, **attached to both sides,** Chesed and Gevurah, as Tiferet is the Central Column that includes the two Columns in it. **Of the Myrtle, therefore, three** branches are taken. **"...a thick leaved tree..." (Ibid.)** means **a bough that would become a bough of a thick leaved tree,** namely **that it will be attached on every side,** to the right and to the left. **"...and Willows of the brook..." (Ibid.) are two pillars,** namely Netzach and Hod, **from where abundance flows on the branches of the palm,** namely Yesod. **The palm trees are attached Above** to Zeir Anpin **and Below** to Malchut, **as we have already said. The *Etrog,*** Malchut, **comes from the tree thorns,** namely the Judgments called "thorns of Zeir Anpin" called "Tree," for She is built from the Judgments of Zeir Anpin. **Similarly, the branches of the palm trees,** which are Yesod, **are always attached to** the thorns of the Tree, which are the Judgments of Zeir Anpin, since Yesod tends towards the Left of Zeir Anpin, where Judgments are. **Surely whatever emerges into the world emerges from here, and come from here,** namely from the four mentioned species.

Tzav

16. The four species and Hoshana Raba

A Synopsis

This essay tells about the three boughs of Hadas (Myrtle), the two *Aravot* (Willows), the *Lulav,* and the *Etrog;* these are waved to observe the Precept and then the Seven Sefirot Above are stirred. We read of the infinite flow of abundance down through the Sefirot from Binah to Malchut, the Congregation of Israel. Waving the fresh branches draws blessings to this world. Rav Yosi says that on the seven days of Sukkot, actions are needed, not just words, and he emphasizes the number seven in regard to voices, Sefirot, days, and times that the altar must be circled. Rav Chiya explains that the Illumination of Chochmah comes down and is revealed only with Judgment. Through the deed and sacrifice of the Priest Below, both the Upper and Lower are corrected. On the day that God orders the verdicts, Judgments are brought to an end and the evil tongue is ended in the world. God pronounces a decree and then it is referred to as though the punishment has already happened, although it is still to come. He tells of the necessity for the Priests, the Levites, and the children of Israel to participate in the sacrifice so that their transgressions will be atoned for.

Four Species that include a total of seven aspects.

108. ד' מִינִין בְּלוּלָב, וְאִינּוּן שִׁבְעָה. וְאִי תֵּימָא דְּז' מִינִין אִינּוּן. לָאו הָכֵי, אֶלָּא אַרְבְּעָה נִינְהוּ וְאִינּוּן מִתְפָּרְשִׁין לִתְלָתָא אוֹחֲרָנִין. וּבְעוֹבָדָא דִּלְהוֹן אִתְּעָרוּ שִׁבְעָה אָחֳרָנִין לְעֵילָא, לְאוֹטָבָא עָלְמָא בְּכַמָּה סִטְרִין.

108. There are four species in the *Lulav,* which are seven; namely, three boughs of Hadas (Myrtle), and two boughs of *Aravot* (Willow), *Lulav,* and *Etrog.* **It may be argued that there are seven species but it is not so, for there are four divided into three more,** the Myrtle into three and the Willows into two. Thus two were added to the Myrtle and one to the Willow; hence there are seven. **Through the action of** waving them to observe the Precept, **seven other ones are awakened Above,** which are the Seven Sefirot: Chesed, Gevurah, Tiferet, Netzach, Hod, Yesod, and Malchut; the three boughs of Myrtle correspond to Chesed-Gevurah-Tiferet, the two boughs of Willow to Netzach and Hod, the *Lulav* to Yesod, and the *Etrog* to Malchut, **to bestow goodness to the world in many aspects,** from the above mentioned Seven Sefirot.

When Malchut receives abundance from the Seven Sefirot,
the entire world is blessed.

109. כ"י, אע"ג דְּאִיהִי בִּכְלָלָא, מִתְבָּרְכָא מִכֻּלְּהוּ שִׁית, וּמִנַּחֲלָא דְּעַמִּיקָא דְּמַבּוּעָא, דְּנָגִיד וְלָא פָּסִיק לְעָלְמִין מֵימוֹי מִלְּנַגְּדָא עֲלַיְיהוּ, וְיַנְקָא לְבַת. דְּהָא בְּגִין דְּאִיהִי בַּת לָהּ לְעָלְמָא עִלָּאָה וְתַתָּאָה, אִתְבָּרְכָא מִנַּיְיהוּ בְּאִתְעָרוּתָא דָא. דְּהָא בְּשַׁעֲתָא דִּכְנֶסֶת יִשְׂרָאֵל אִתְבָּרְכָא מִנַּיְיהוּ, כֻּלְּהוּ עָלְמִין אִתְבָּרְכָן. עַ"ד סוֹבְבִים אֶת הַמִּזְבֵּחַ כְּמָה דְּאִתְּמַר.

109. Although She is included in the Seven Sefirot, **the Congregation of Israel,** Malchut, **is blessed from all six** Sefirot above Her, which are Chesed, Gevurah, Tiferet, Netzach, Hod, and Yesod, **and from the deep River that gushes out, whose waters never stop flowing to** the six Sefirot: Chesed, Gevurah, Tiferet, Netzach, Hod, and Yesod. **It nourishes the Daughter,** Malchut, **for She is a Daughter to it, to the Supernal World,** Binah, **and to the Lower World,** Zeir Anpin, **and receives blessings from them by this awakening. When the Congregation of Israel is blessed by them, all the Worlds are blessed,** for they receive from Her. **Therefore we encircle the altar, as we learned,** on the seven days of the Holiday of Sukkot since the altar corresponds to Malchut, Who receives from Binah and Zeir Anpin. Through the seven encirclings, She is filled with the Seven Sefirot.

The Four Species need to be fresh, alluding to abundance.

110. וְעוֹד בְּאִתְעֲרוּתָא דָא, שִׁיתָא כֻּלְּהוּ מִתְבָּרְכָא בְּמַיָּא, לְאִסְתַּפְּקָא בֵּיהּ, וְאִשְׁתַּאֲבִין כֻּלְּהוּ מִמַּבּוּעָא דְּנַחֲלָא עֲמִיקָא דְּכֹלָּא, לְנַחֲתָא לְעָלְמָא. וּבְגִ"כ, בָּעְיָין כֻּלְּהוּ לַחִין וְלָא יַבְשִׁין, לְאַמְשָׁכָא בִּרְכָאן לְעָלְמָא, בְּגִין דְּאִילָנֵי אִלֵּין, כֻּלְּהוּ לַחִין תְּדִירָא, וְטַרְפִּין דִּלְהוֹן מִשְׁתַּכְּחִין תְּדִירָא, וְזִמְן חֶדְוָותָא דִּלְהוֹן בְּהַאי זִמְנָא.

110. Moreover, with this awakening, by waving the four species, **all six** Sefirot—Chesed, Gevurah, Tiferet, Netzach, Hod, and Yesod—**are blessed with water,** namely abundance, **to be quenched by it. They all draw from the Stream of the deepest River,** Binah, **to bring down to the world. This is why all** the four species **need to be fresh, not dry,** since "fresh" indicates that they are full of abundance, **to draw blessings to the world. Those trees,** Myrtle, Willow, and *Lulav,* **are always fresh and their leaves are ever present** in the tree, whether summer or winter, **and the time of their joy is at that time** of the seven days of Sukkot.

The trees that produce the Four Species receive their energy on Sukkot.

111. וְתָנֵינָן בְּסִפְרָא דְּרַב הַמְנוּנָא סָבָא, דְּהָא הַהוּא חֵילָא דְּאִתְפְּקָדָא עַל אִילָנִין אִלֵּין, כָּל חַד וְחַד מֵאִלֵּין, לָא נָטִיל בִּרְכָאן דְּחֶדְוָותָא לְעֵילָּא, אֶלָּא בְּזִמְנָא דָא. וְחֶדְוָותָא דִּלְהוֹן כֻּלְּהוּ לְעֵילָּא, וְחֶדְוָותָא דְּאִילָנִין אִלֵּין לְתַתָּא, כֻּלְּהוּ בְּזִמְנָא דָא הוּא. וְאִתְעֲרוּתָא דִּלְהוֹן בְּאִינּוּן קַדִּישֵׁי מַלְכָּא תַּלְיָין. וְכַד יִשְׂרָאֵל נַטְלֵי לוֹן, כֹּלָּא אִתְּעַר בְּזִמְנָא דָא, וְעָלְמָא מִתְבָּרְכָא, לְאַרְקָא בִּרְכָאן לְעָלְמָא.

111. We learned in the Book of Rav Hamnuna Saba that the Force appointed over those trees, of the four species, **bestows joyful blessings to each of them from Above only at that time. They all rejoice Above, and the rejoicing of those trees is Below at the time** of the days of Sukkot. **Their awakening depends upon the Holy Ones of the King,** namely upon Israel taking the *Lulav.* **When Israel take**

them, everything is awakened at that time, and the world, Malchut, **is blessed and pours blessings upon** this **world.**

The Seven Sefirot of Zeir Anpin receive their abundance from Binah.

112. כְּתִיב קוֹל יְיָ' עַל הַמָּיִם אֵל הַכָּבוֹד, א"ר יוֹסֵי, דָּא אַבְרָהָם. קוֹל יְיָ' בַּכֹּחַ: דָּא יִצְחָק. קוֹל יְיָ' בֶּהָדָר: דָּא יַעֲקֹב. קוֹל יְיָ' שׁוֹבֵר אֲרָזִים: דָּא נֶצַח. קוֹל יְיָ' חוֹצֵב לַהֲבוֹת אֵשׁ: דָּא הוֹד. קוֹל יְיָ' יָחִיל מִדְבָּר: דָּא צַדִּיק. קוֹל יְיָ' יְחוֹלֵל אַיָּלוֹת: דָּא צֶדֶק. וְכֻלְּהוּ מִתְגַּדְּלֵי עַל יַמָּא וְאִתְשַׁקְיָין בְּמַיָּא, לְגַדְּלָא. הה"ד, וְנָהָר יוֹצֵא מֵעֵדֶן לְהַשְׁקוֹת אֶת הַגָּן. וְכֻלְּהוּ הָנֵי מִתְעָרֵי בִּרְכָאן לְעָלְמָא, מֵהַהוּא שַׁקְיוּ, דְּאִתְשַׁקְיָין כֻּלְּהוּ.

112. It is written: "The Voice of the Lord is upon the waters; the God of Glory…." (Psalms 29:3) Rav Yosi said: "This is Abraham, namely the attribute of Chesed. **'The Voice of the Lord is powerful…' (Ibid. 4) is Isaac,** namely Gevurah; **'…the Voice of the Lord is full of majesty' (Ibid. 4) is Jacob,** namely Tiferet; **'the Voice of the Lord breaks the cedars…' (Ibid. 5) is Netzach; 'The Voice of the Lord hews flames of fire' (Ibid. 7) is Hod; '…the Voice of the Lord shakes the wilderness…' (Ibid. 8) is the Righteous,** Yesod; **and "the Voice of the Lord makes the hinds to calve…' (Ibid. 9) is Righteousness,** namely Malchut. **They all grow through the sea,** Binah, **and are given water,** namely the abundance of Binah, **so as to grow. Therefore it says: 'And a river went out of Eden to water the garden….' (Genesis 2:10) They all arouse blessings to the world by the drink they give to all.**

On Sukkot we need to awaken actions, not speech.

113. ת"ח, הָנֵי שֶׁבַע קָלִין, תַּלְיָין בְּמִלָּה דְּפוּמָא בִּשְׁאָר יוֹמֵי שַׁתָּא, וְהַשְׁתָּא, לָא תַּלְיָין אֶלָּא בְּעוֹבָדָא, וַאֲנָן עוֹבָדָא קָא בָּעֵינָן, וְלָא מִלָּה. בְּגִין דְּבִזְמְנָא דָּא, מְבָרֵךְ לְכָל שַׁתָּא.

113. "Come and see, these seven Voices—Chesed, Gevurah, Tiferet, Netzach, Hod, Yesod, and Malchut—**depend upon the words of the mouth throughout the year but now,** on the seven days of Sukkot **they depend only upon deed. We then need an action, not speech, since during this time,** of the seven days of Sukkot **the whole year is blessed."**

Explanation: Precepts that depend on speech draw the Internal, which is the secret of Chasadim. They do not draw the Illumination of Chochmah from the Left Column, as it is External. Precepts that depend on action draw the External, namely, the Illumination of Chochmah from the Left Column, which are Mochin of the Six Corners and External. In the seven days of Sukkot we need to correct the External, which is the secret of drawing Chochmah from the Left, and therefore we need action-based Precepts that are capable of awakening this.

This is: **"but now they depend only upon deed. We need then an action"** to draw the External, which is the secret of the Illumination of Chochmah of the Left, **"not speech,"** as speech only draws the Internal, which is the secret of Chasadim that we draw throughout the year, which is **"these seven voices depend upon the words of the mouth throughout the year"** and do not need action. The reason is **"since during this time** of the seven days of Sukkot **the whole year is blessed."** For after we drew the Illumination of Chochmah of the Left in the seven days of Sukkot to Chesed, Gevurah, Tiferet, Netzach, Hod, Yesod, and Malchut, this suffices for the whole year. It happens in a way that the Chasadim we draw through the speech-based Precepts throughout the year are blessed with the Illumination of Chochmah through the seven days of Sukkot thus becoming revealed Chasadim. Then we no longer need action-based Precepts for this matter but rather for other things, as it will be explained in its place.

On Hoshana Raba the verdicts are sent out
and Gevurot awaken and cease.

114. בְּיוֹמָא שְׁבִיעָאָה דְּחַג, הוּא סִיּוּמָא דְּדִינָא דְּעָלְמָא, וּפִתְקִין נָפְקִין מִבֵּי מַלְכָּא, וּגְבוּרָן מִתְעָרֵי וּמִסְתַּיְּימָן בְּהַאי יוֹמָא, וְעַרְבֵי נַחַל תַּלְיָין בְּהוּ. וּבָעֵינָן לְאִתְעָרָא גְּבוּרָן לְמַיָּא. וּלְסַחֲרָא ז' זִמְנִין, לְרַוָּואָה לְהַאי מַדְבְּחָא, מִמַּיָּא דְּיִצְחָק, בְּגִין דְּאִתְמַלְיָא מַיָּא הַאי בֵּירָא דְּיִצְחָק, וְכַד הוּא אִתְמַלְיָא, כָּל עָלְמָא אִתְבָּרְכָא בְּמַיָּא.

114. On the seventh day of the Holiday, namely Hoshana Raba, **it is the end of Judgment of the world. Sentences are sent from the King's House and the Gevurot are aroused and ended on that day. The Willows of the Brook depend upon them,** these Gevurot. **One needs to arouse the Gevurot toward the water and to circle the altar,** which corresponds to Malchut, **seven times,** corresponding to Chesed, Gevurah, Tiferet, Netzach, Hod, Yesod, and Malchut, **to water the altar with Isaac's water,** namely with the Illumination of Chochmah of the Left Column called Isaac, **so that the water will fill Isaac's well,** namely Malchut that is called so when She receives from the left. **When she is filled, the whole world is blessed with water.**

Explanation: On Rosh Hashanah three Books are open: that of the Completely Righteous, that of the Completely Wicked and that of the In-Betweeners. The Completely Righteous are written immediately for life, the Completely Wicked are written immediately for death and the In-Betweeners are suspended and stand until Yom Kippur. (Tractate Rosh Hashanah 16b) It does not discuss the Completely Righteous and Completely Wicked, as their Judgment was set on the first day of Rosh Hashanah. Everything mentioned only refers to the In-Betweeners who are suspended and stand until Yom Kippur; if they do Teshuvah they are sealed for life, and the Wicked who do not do Teshuvah are sealed for death.

The secret of the atonement of sins on Yom Kippur is the secret of drawing the Illumination of Chochmah through Malchut ascending to Binah, as no atonement of sins happen unless there is the revelation of the Light of Chochmah, which is the secret of the Light of Life. This is why the In-Betweeners who did Teshuvah merit then the atonement of sins and a sealing for life. However it is not yet complete because the Light of Chochmah does not shine without Chasadim, and the time to draw Chasadim to clothe Chochmah is in the seven days of Sukkot.

It turns out that on the seventh day, Hoshana Raba, the clothing of Chochmah with Chasadim finishes, and then the Seal for Life that was made on Yom Kippur is completed. Similarly, regarding those who did not do Teshuvah and were sealed for death on Yom Kippur, the seal is not yet complete since they still have time to repent until the seventh day of Sukkot because Chochmah is still drawn until that time, and if they repent, their sins will be atoned through it and they will merit the Light of Life. Therefore the day of Hoshana Raba is considered the day the sentences of Judgment are given to the angels, whether to life or death. After the sentences of Judgment are given to those who carry them out they are not returned because after Hoshana Raba,`` there is no more drawing of Chochmah, as mentioned in verse 113.

Thus **"On the seventh day of the Holiday it is the end of Judgment,"** as there is no more drawing of Chochmah after that, and therefore **"sentences are sent from the King's House,"** as they are given over to those who carry them out and do not return again. **"...and the Gevurot are aroused and ended on that day"** because the Gevurot, which are the secret of the drawing of Chochmah, are ended on this day and we do not draw Chochmah after this. The rest is clear.

The striking of the Willows on the ground.

115. וּבְהַאי יוֹמָא גְּבוּרוֹת בָּעְיָין לְמַיָּא, וּלְסַיְּימָא לוֹן לְבָתַר, דְּהָא בְּהַאי יוֹמָא מִסְתַּיְּימֵי דִּינָא. וּבג״כ בָּעְיָין לְבַטְּשָׁא לוֹן בְּאַרְעָא, וּלְסַיְּימָא לוֹן דְּלָא מִשְׁתַּכְחוּ, דְּהַאי יוֹמָא אִתְעָרוּתָא וְסִיּוּמָא הוּא. וְעַ״ד אִתְעָרוּתָא וְסִיּוּמָא הוּא דְּעַבְדִּינָן בְּעַרְבֵי נַחַל.

115. On that day, Hoshana Raba, **there is need of Gevurot** in order to draw **water,** the secret of the mentioned Illumination of Chochmah, which is drawn only together with Gevurot and Judgments, **and to conclude them later. On that day, Judgment is concluded,** as there is no further need to draw the Illumination of Chochmah drawn through Judgment. **Therefore we need to beat** the Willow boughs **on the ground and end them,** namely their Illumination, **so that they will not be found. On that day, there is an awakening** of Chochmah **and conclusion** of Chochmah, **and therefore with Willows of the Brook,** which alludes to Netzach and Hod through which Chochmah is revealed by means of Judgments, **we cause an awakening and conclusion.**

Explanation: The ground is the final aspect of Malchut, and when we beat the Willows on the ground the Illumination of Chochmah is drawn with the Judgments to the final aspect of Malchut, where the Illumination concludes. The reason why the Chochmah is only revealed in the secret of the Willows, which are Netzach and Hod, is because from the Chest up is the secret of the Upper Three of the Body, and Netzach and Hod that are below the Chest are the Six Corners of the Body. And because the Upper Three of Chochmah were stored away and only the Six Corners of Chochmah are revealed, therefore their place is in the Six Corners of the Body, which are Netzach and Hod, which are the secret of the Willows of the Brook.

On Hoshana Raba. there is a final reawakening of Judgment.

116. א"ר חִיָּיא וַדַּאי הָכִי הוּא, וְשַׁפִּיר. וְעַרְבֵי נַחַל, מִסִּטְרָא דְּנַחַל, נַפְקֵי גְּבוּרָאן. וּבְהַאי יוֹמָא מִתְעָרֵי וּמִסְתַּיְּימֵי. בְּהַאי יוֹמָא כְּתִיב, וַיָּשָׁב יִצְחָק וַיַּחְפּוֹר אֶת בְּאֵרֹת הַמַּיִם. בְּאֵרֹת כְּתִיב חָסֵר. וַיָּשָׁב, מַהוּ וַיָּשָׁב. אֶלָּא יוֹמָא קַדְמָאָה דְּיַרְחָא, שֵׁירוּתָא דְּדִינָא הֲוָה בְּכָל עָלְמָא, וְיִצְחָק קַיְּימָא לְכוּרְסְיָּיא לְמֵידַן עָלְמָא. בְּהַאי יוֹמָא, וַיָּשָׁב יִצְחָק לְאִתְעָרָא דִּינִין וּלְסַיְּימָא דִּינִין. וַיַּחְפּוֹר אֶת בְּאֵרֹת הַמַּיִם, לְאַרְקָא גְּבוּרָן לִכְנֶסֶת יִשְׂרָאֵל, לְאִתְעָרָא לְמַיָּא, דְּהָא מַיָּא בִּגְבוּרָן נַחְתָּן לְעָלְמָא.

116. Rav Chiya said: "This is surely so, and it is well spoken. The Willows of the Brook are so called **because from the side of the Brook,** namely Binah, **Gevurot come out,** namely the Illumination of Chochmah with their Judgments. **On that day, they are aroused and ended. Of that day, it is written: 'And Isaac returned and dug the wells of water....' (Genesis 26:18) The word wells (*be'erot;* בארת) is written without the Vav (ו),** since it alludes to Malchut called 'Well' (*be'er;* באר). [He asks:] **"What is 'returned'?"** [He answers:] **"Rather, the first day of the month,** namely on Rosh Hashanah, **is the day of the beginning of Judgments throughout the world, and Isaac,** the secret of the Left Column, **rose to the Throne of Judgment to sentence the world. On that day** of Hoshana Raba, **'Isaac returned' to awaken Judgments and bring verdicts to an end, '...and dug the wells of water,'** namely **to pour Gevurot upon the Congregation of Israel,** which is Malchut called 'Well,' **to arouse the water,** the secret of the Illumination of Chochmah. This is **because water descends upon the world through Gevurot;** in other words, the Illumination of Chochmah comes down only together with Judgment."

Explanation: On Rosh Hashanah, the Judgments of the Left Column started to be revealed, as then Malchut was in the secret of the two Great Luminaries and clothed the Left Column of Binah. With the Blowing of the Shofar, the Left Column became diminished through the Central

Column by virtue of two actions. First in the secret of the Man'ula (Lock) that diminishes it completely, and then with the Maftecha (Key) that makes it viable to receive the Six Corners of Chochmah. On Yom Kippur, through the ascension of Malchut to Binah the Six Corners of Chochmah are revealed in Her, in the secret of the five afflictions She received from the Left Column of Binah. After Yom Kippur, the Chasadim begin to be revealed to clothe the Chochmah, without which the Chochmah cannot shine.

The correction of Chochmah with Chasadim continue through the circling of the altar until Hoshana Raba, which is the aspect of Malchut since the seven days of Sukkot represent Chesed, Gevurah, Tiferet, Netzach, Hod, Yesod, and Malchut. Therefore, we again need to awaken the Chochmah with the correction of Chasadim in the secret of circling the altar, by which we correct the seventh day and collectively end the drawing of Chochmah because it does not need to be drawn once it reaches Malchut. **"On that day 'Isaac returned' to awaken Judgments and bring verdicts to an end"** because there is no more need to draw it.

Judgments are always revealed together with the Illumination of Chochmah so that the wicked have no access to it.

117. וּבְגִין דְּאִלֵּין גְּבוּרָן, לָא נַחְתִּין אֶלָּא בְּעִיבָא, וְיוֹמָא דְּעִיבָא לָא נַיְיחָא רוּחֵיהוֹן דְּקַיְימֵי עָלְמָא, אֶלָּא בְּגִין דְּעָלְמָא אִצְטְרִיךְ לְהוּ. מַאי טַעֲמָא. בְּגִין דְּעָלְמָא בְּדִינָא אִתְבְּרֵי, וְכֹלָּא בַּעְיָא הָכִי. בְּגַ"כ כֹּלָּא בְּעוֹבָדָא תַּלְיָא מִלְּתָא. וְעַ"ד, כַּהֲנָא בְּעוֹבָדָא וְתִקּוּנָא דְּאִיהוּ עָבֵיד לְתַתָּא, אִתְעֲרוּ עִלָּאִין וְתַתָּאִין לְתַקְּנָא לוֹן, וּמִתְתַּקְּנֵי עַל יְדוֹי.

117. Since these Gevurot descend only by means of clouds, which are Judgments, **and on a cloudy day the wind of the Pillars of the world rests upon them only** since it must be so **since the world needs them.** [He asks:] **"Why is it so?"** [He answers:] **"Because the world was created through Judgment,** namely on Rosh Hashanah. Therefore Judgments are always revealed together with water, the secret of the Illumination of Chochmah, so that the wicked will not grasp the Left Column and bring back the Judgments of Rosh Hashanah. **Everything must be this way, and this is why it all depends upon actions. Therefore through the action and correction that the Priest does Below,** namely the action of the sacrifice, **the Upper and Lower are aroused to be corrected, and are corrected by him.** In the same manner, through the action of the four species and the Willow of Hoshana Raba, Chochmah is corrected by means of the Judgments that are revealed together with it so that the wicked will not be able to take hold of it.

On Hoshana Raba everything depends on the lips.

118. א"ר יוֹסֵי הָא תָּנִינָן, הָעֲרָבָה דְּדַמְיָא לְשִׂפְוָון בְּהַאי יוֹמָא, וּמַאי הִיא. אָמַר ר' חִיָּיא, אע"ג דִּלְדְרָשָׁא הוּא דְּאָתֵי, הָכִי הוּא וַדַּאי. דְּהָא בְּהַאי יוֹמָא בְּשִׂפְוָון תַּלְיָא, בְּהַאי יוֹמָא פָּקִיד מַלְכָּא לְמֵיהַב פִּתְקִין לְסַנְטִירָא, וּמִסְתַּיְּימֵי דִּינִין, וְאַסְתִּים לִישָּׁנָא בִּישָׁא מֵעָלְמָא. בְּיוֹמָא קַדְמָאָה דְּיַרְחָא שֵׁירוּתָא דְּדִינָא הוּא, וְסִיּוּמָא הוּא בְּהַאי יוֹמָא. וְהָא אִתְּמַר.

118. Rav Yosi said: "We learned that the Willow resembles lips on this day. What is the meaning of this?" Rav Chiya said: "This is only according to homiletic interpretation, yet it is surely so. On this day, it depends upon lips. On this day, the King orders to give the verdicts to the minister, Judgments are brought to an end and evil speech is blocked from the world. On the first day of the month it is the beginning of Judgment, and the conclusion is on this day [Hoshana Raba], as has been explained.

Explanation: On the first day of the month Malchut takes hold of the Left Column of Binah, the secret of Isaac, **"and Isaac rose to the Throne of Judgment to sentence the world."** (Verse 116) Through the Blowing of the Shofar, the Central Column awakened a Zivug (Unification) on the Masach (Curtain) of Chirik to diminish the Left Column, first with Man'ula (Lock) and then with Maftecha (Key), which means that Malchut ascended to Binah and Binah returned to become the aspect of Six Corners [Sefirot] with no Head. On one hand, a correction is made by this to subdue the Judgments of the Left Column and prepare it to unite with the Right. However on the other hand, the Judgments of Katnut (Immaturity) grasped onto Binah due to Malchut ascending there and because of this the Externals emerged with evil speech about Binah saying it has a lack, so that they can grasp onto the place of lack, as is their way. Therefore there was a need to shut the mouths of the Externals to not speak evil speech about Binah. This happens on Yom Kippur and on the seven days of Sukkot, when Malchut descends and returns from Binah and Binah again receives its Upper Three from the aspect of the Six Corners of Chochmah.

This is [in verse 118]: **"and evil speech is blocked from the world,"** since on the day of Hoshana Raba the Six Corners of Chochmah finish returning to Binah like before, and the mouths of the Externals are shut from speaking evil speech about Binah. After the evil speech ends, there is no more need to draw Chochmah, which brings with it Judgments. Thus **"On this day, the King orders to give the verdicts to the minister, and Judgments are brought to an end"** because after the evil speech is blocked there is no more need to reveal Chochmah. And it was explained earlier that through the action-based Precepts, which are the Taking of the *Lulav* and the Willows, Chochmah is drawn, through the speech-based Precepts, which are the lips, Chasadim are drawn (as mentioned in verse 111). This is: **"the Willow resembles lips... on this day it depends upon lips"** because through the Willow we awaken Chochmah with the Gevurot and end it, since from here on we will only draw Chasadim through the Precepts that depend on the lips, as mentioned earlier, and therefore the allusion to this is that the leaves of the Willows are likened to lips.

On Hoshana Raba, the blessing of the nations cease and the blessings of Israel begin.

119. ת"ח, בְּיוֹמָא דָא שְׁלִמִין וּמְסַיְּימֵי עַמִּין עע"ז בִּרְכָאן דִלְהוֹן, וְשָׁרָאן בְּדִינָא. וְיִשְׂרָאֵל בְּיוֹמָא דָא מְסַיְּימֵי דִינִין דִלְהוֹן וְשָׁרָאן בְּבִרְכָתָא. דְהָא לְיוֹמָא אָחֳרָא זְמִינִין לְאִשְׁתַּעְשְׁעָא בְּמַלְכָּא, לְנַטְלָא מִינֵּיהּ בִּרְכָאן לְכָל שַׁתָּא, וּבְהַהוּא חֶדְוְותָא לָא מִשְׁתַּכְּחֵי בְּמַלְכָּא אֶלָּא יִשְׂרָאֵל בִּלְחוֹדַיְיהוּ. וּמַאן דְיָתִיב עִם מַלְכָּא, וְנָטַל לֵיהּ בִּלְחוֹדֵיהּ, כָּל מַה דְבָעֵי שָׁאִיל, וְיָהִיב לֵיהּ. וְעַ"ד יִשְׂרָאֵל שָׁרָאן, וְעַמִּין עע"ז מְסַיְּימֵי. וְעַ"ד כְּתִיב, אָהַבְתִּי אֶתְכֶם אָמַר יְיָ' וְגוֹ'.

119. Come and see, on this day, the heathen nations complete and end their blessings and abide in Judgment. On this day, the children of Israel end their Judgments and abide in blessings, since on another day, namely Shmini Atzeret, **they will take delight with the King and take blessings from Him for the whole year. In that joy no one is found with the King except Israel alone. He who sits with the King and takes Him alone, whatever he wishes he asks, and** the King **gives him. Israel therefore begin** to receive blessings **and the heathen nations end** their blessings. **It is therefore written: "'I have loved you,' says the Lord...." (Malachi 1:2)**

Explanation: The nations of the world are latched to the Left Column, where the Illumination of Chochnah comes from, and they cannot receive from the Right Column, which is Chasadim, since their root is only in the Left. Therefore in the seven days of Sukkot—when Chochmah is drawn from the Left Column by virtue of the Precepts, as mentioned earlier—the nations of the world receive their blessings. This is the secret of the 70 bulls we sacrifice in the seven days of the Holiday, corresponding to the 70 nations, as their nourishment is from there. It turns out that on the seventh day after the Beating of the Willows, when the drawing of Chochmah has already stopped, the blessings of the nations stop, as they have nothing from which to nourish.

This is: **"On this day, the heathen nations complete and end their blessings..."** as the drawing of Chochmah had already ended on this day, which is their entire blessings, **"...and abide in Judgment"** as they cannot suckle Chasadim from the Right, as mentioned earlier, and they are in emptiness. But Israel cleave to the Central Column, where Chasadim are from, and their entire root is there. And since the Chochmah drawn during the seven days of the Holiday from the Left Column is only drawn with Judgments, it is found that after the Illumination of Chochmah stopped, the Judgments in it also stopped. This is: **"On this day, the children of Israel end their Judgments"** because we no longer draw the Illumination of Chochmah, **"and abide in blessings,"** namely in Chasadim that are drawn from the Central Column, which is their root, **"since on another day... blessings for the whole year."** From the Unification (Zivug) of Zeir Anpin and Malchut on Shmini Atzeret blessings, namely Chasadim, are drawn to the Israelites for the whole year. This is: **"In that joy no one is found with the King except Israel alone"** because since the joy is from the bestowal of Chasadim, which no nation except Israel alone can receive, it is found that no one is with the King then except Israel alone. **"Israel therefore begin and the heathen nations end"** because the Illumination of the Left stopped, which is of the root of the nations, and they have nothing else from which to nourish. And the Illumination of the Central Column, which is of the root of Israel, begins on Shmini Atzeret and continues throughout the year, which is the Illumination of Chasadim.

Tikunei HaZohar: Prologue

3. "Do not take the mother with the young; but be sure to let the mother go."

The Sukkah covers and shelters like a mother bird to her young.

35. וְעַל קַן דְּצִפּוֹרָא דָא, אִתְּמַר וְסֻכָּה תִּהְיֶה לְצֵל יוֹמָם וגו'. וְאִיהוּ לָשׁוֹן סְכָךְ, שֶׁמְּסַכֶּכֶת בָּהּ אִימָא עַל בָּנֶיהָ, אֶפְרוֹחִים דִּילָהּ, תְּלַת הֲדַסִּים, וּתְרֵי בַּדֵּי עֲרָבוֹת, וְלוּלָב. אוֹ בֵּיצִים, דָּא אִינּוּן אֶתְרוֹגֵי דְּכָל חַד שִׁיעוּרֵיהּ בִּכְבֵיצָה. וְאִלֵּין דִּרְשִׁימִין בְּהוֹן, כְּתִיב עֲלַיְיהוּ לֹא תִקַּח הָאֵם עַל הַבָּנִים.

35. And about this bird's nest, regarding which it says: "If you come across a bird's nest...," **it says, "...there will be a booth (*sukkah*) for shade by day...."** (Isaiah 4:6) **The word** *sukkah* **is a derivative of *s'chach* (cover), whereby the mother covers and shelters her young. "...the young..."** are **the three myrtle branches (*hadas'im*), and the two willow branches (*aravot*), and the date palm branch (*lulav*). "... or the eggs..." are those citron fruits (*etrog*) whose minimum size is the measurement of an egg. And those who are imprinted by them,** by the four species, **about them is written: "Do not take the mother with the young."**

The Four Species plus the Sukkah contain eight Sefirot.

36. דִּתְלַת הֲדַסִּים רְמִיזִין לִתְלַת אֲבָהָן. תְּרֵי בַּדֵּי עֲרָבוֹת לִתְרֵי נְבִיאֵי קְשׁוֹט לוּלָב, צַדִּיק כַּתָּמָר יִפְרָח אֶתְרוֹג, רָמִיז לִשְׁכִינְתָּא סוּכָּה רְמִיזָא לְאִימָא, דִּמְסַכֶּכֶת עֲלַיְיהוּ. הָא אִינּוּן תְּמַנְיָא לְקַבֵּל יאקדונק"י, דְּאִיהוּ חוּשְׁבַּן סוּכָּ"ה, כ"ו ה"ס.

36. He explains: **the three myrtle branches (hadas'im) represent the three Patriarchs,** Chesed, Gevurah, and Tiferet. **The two willow branches (*aravot*)** allude **to the two true prophets,** Netzach and Hod.

The *lulav* (date palm branch) alludes to the "righteous shall flourish like a date palm," (Psalms 92:12) namely Yesod. **The citron fruit (*etrog*) alludes to the Shechinah,** which is Malchut. **Sukkah (booth) alludes to the mother,** namely Binah that **covers them. We have a total of eight** Sefirot **corresponding to** the eight letters in the two interwoven Names: **Yud-Alef-Hei-Dalet-Vav-Nun-Hei-Yud, which equal the numerical value of the word sukkah, the letters Samech-Vav-Kaf-Hei, of which Kaf-Vav** (26) is the numerical value of **Yud-Hei-Vav-Hei, and Hei-Samech** (65) is the numerical value of Adonai.

Those who do not take the Species in their hands
lose the protection of the Mother.

37. וְאִלֵּין דְּלָא נָטְלִין אִלֵּין סִימָנִין בִּידַיְיהוֹן כְּתִיב בְּהוֹן שַׁלֵּחַ תְּשַׁלַּח, כֶּתֶ"ר וְחָכְמָ"ה. דְּלָא שַׁרְיָין אִלֵּין, בְּאִלֵּין תְּמַנְיָא. לְמֶהֱוֵי כֻּלְּהוּ עֶשֶׂר סְפִירָן בְּכָל נִעֲנוּעַ וְנִעֲנוּעַ דְּנִעֲנוּעֵי דְּלוּלָב וּמִינָיו בְּכָל פִּקּוּדָא וּפִקּוּדָא.

37. Those who do not take these signs in their hands, it says about them. "...but be sure to let the mother go," Keter and Chochmah, for these two, meaning Keter and Chochmah, **do not dwell with these eight,** namely Binah and Zeir Anpin (which includes Chesed, Gevurah, Tiferet, Netzach, Hod, Yesod) and Malchut, **to have all Ten Sefirot in each and every shaking of the shakings of the *Lulav* and its species, in each and every Precept.**

Tikunei HaZohar: Sixth Tikkun

1. A bird's nest

The seventy-two shakings nourish the seventy nations and their root.

50. וּתְלַת נִעֲנוּעִין לְכָל סִטְרָא, סָלְקִין ח״י. וְצָרִיךְ אַרְבַּע זִמְנִין ח״י, חַד בִּנְטִילַת לוּלָב וְחַד בְּאָנָּא יְיָ, תְּרֵין אָחֳרָנִין בְּהוֹדוּ לַיְיָ תְּחִלָּה וָסוֹף. וּבְאִלֵּין נִעֲנוּעִין, אִינּוּן מַשְׁפִּילִין מֵעֵילָא לְתַתָּא לְשַׁבְעִין וּתְרֵין. אוּמִין פָּלְחֵי כּוֹכְבַיָּא.

50. One needs **to shake three times to each side, and three times six equals eighteen. And four sets of eighteen are required,** which all together equals 72. And they are: **One when first taking the *Lulav,* one when saying "*Ana* (please) *haShem;*" and the latter two, at the reading of the first and last "*Hodu* (praise) *laHashem.*" And during these shakings, one bestows to the 72 idol worshipping nations from above downward.** These are the seventy nations of the world and their root, Edom and Ishmael.

The secret of Ani Vahu Hoshia Na.

51. וּלְבָתַר דְּנָצְחֵי לוֹן אָמְרֵי אֲנִ״י וָהֹ״וּ הוֹשִׁיעָה נָּא תְּרֵין זִמְנִין, דְּאִינּוּן וָא״ו מִן וה״ו. אֲנִ״י וה״ו מִן וַיִּסַּע וַיָּבֹא וַיֵּט, וּבְהַהוּא זִמְנָא, לֹא תִקַּח הָאֵם עַל הַבָּנִים.

51. And after we conquer them, we say: *Ani Vahu Hoshia Na* "We beseech You, help us" twice. These are Vav-Alef-Vav from Vav-Hei-Vav, Alef-Nun-Yud, Vav-Hei-Vav (vahu, ani, vahu). Since besides the first *Ani* that is Malchut, there is Vav-Alef-Vav, from the acronym of Vav-Hei-Vav, Alef-Nun-Yud, Vav-Hei-Vav that is Zeir Anpin, **from** the verses: **"And the angel… removed… And it came… And Moses stretched out…"** (Exodus 14:19-21) from which the 72 Names are comprised, since the first of the 72 Names is the Name Vav-Hei-Vav. And in the middle, the 37 Name is Alef-Nun-Yud. And towards the end, meaning the 49 Name, is the second Vav-Hei-Vav. **And during that time: "...you shall not take the mother bird together with the young...."**

Tikunei HaZohar: Thirteenth Tikkun

2. "And you shall take for yourselves on the first day the fruit of the Hadar Tree"

The fifteenth of Tishrei is called the first day to allude to the Right Column.

51. קָם רַבִּי אֶלְעָזָר וְאָמַר, אַבָּא אַבָּא אַמַּאי אִתְּמַר בְּיוֹמָא קַדְמָאָה דְסֻכּוֹת, וּלְקַחְתֶּם לָכֶם בַּיּוֹם הָרִאשׁוֹן פְּרִי עֵץ הָדָר. אָמַר לֵיהּ, בְּרִי, מָאנֵי קְרָבָא בִּימִינָא נָטְלִין לוֹן.

51. Rav Elazar got up and said to Rav Shimon, **"Father, father, why does it say about the first day of Sukkot,** which takes place exactly on the fifteenth of the month, as mentioned, **'And you shall take for yourselves on the first day the fruit of the Hadar tree....'** (Leviticus 23:40), meaning what is the verse alluding to with the words 'on the first day.'?" **He,** Rav Shimon, **said** to Rav Elazar, **"My son,** the verse alludes to **the weapons of war,** which are the four species that represent the four letters Yud-Hei-Vav-Hei. **We take them with the right hand,** and the first day is the secret of the Right Column, Chesed—the first day that accompanies all days.

The Four Species are the sign that Israel won the trial and the war.

52. וּבְאִלֵּין מָאנֵי קְרָבָא, אִינּוּן יִשְׂרָאֵל רְשִׁימִין, דְּנָצְחִין דִּינָא מִתַּל לְמַלְכָּא, דַּהֲוָה לֵיהּ דִּינָא וּקְרָבָא בְּשַׁבְעִין אוּמִין, וְלָא הֲווֹ יָדְעִין מָאן נָצַח דִּינָא, וְשָׁאֲלִין לֵיהּ מָאן נָצַח דִּינָא. אָמַר, תִּסְתַּכְּלוּן בְּאִלֵּין דִּרְשִׁימִין בְּמָאנֵי קְרָבָא בִּידַיְיהוּ, וְתִנְדְּעוּן מָאן נָצַח דִּינָא.

52. "And by these weapons, namely the four species, **are Israel marked to have won the trial. This is likened to a king who had a trial and war against seventy nations, but it was not known who won the trial.**

And they asked him who won the trial. The king **said, 'Look at who has weapons in their hands and you will know who won the trial.'**

The Etrog alludes to the heart, the main organ of the body.

53. וּלְקַחְתֶּם לָכֶם בַּיּוֹם הָרִאשׁוֹן פְּרִי עֵץ הָדָר: דָּא אֶתְרוֹג, דְּאִיהִי שְׁכִינְתָּא, לִבָּא. דְּאִיהִי עִקָּרָא דְּכָל אֵבָרִין דְּגוּפָא, דְּאִינּוּן תְּלַת הֲדַסִּים, וְלוּלָב, וּתְרֵי בַּדֵּי עֲרָבָה. לִבָּא בְּאֶמְצָעִיתָא, וְאֵבָרִין סְחוֹר סְחוֹר לֵיהּ.

53. "'And you shall take for yourselves on the first day the fruit of the Hadar tree....' This is the *Etrog*, which is the Shechinah, namely Malchut, which is the fruit of Zeir Anpin that is called 'hadar tree.' And it corresponds to **the heart, which is the main [organ] among all the organs in the body, which are three myrtles,** Chesed, Gevurah, and Tiferet, **the *Lulav*,** Yesod, **and two willow branches,** Netzach and Hod. **The heart**, which is the *Etrog*, Malchut, **is in the center, and the organs are all around it.**

The Etrog must be unblemished since it alludes to the Shechinah.

54. וּבְגִין דָּא, אֶתְרוֹג דָּא שְׁכִינְתָּא. וְהָכִי אוֹקְמוּהָ מָארֵי מַתְנִיתִין, אִי נִטְּלָה בוֹכְנָתוֹ וְאִי עָלָה חֲזָזִית עַל רֻבּוֹ פָּסוּל. בְּגִין דְּאִיהוּ דָּמֵי לִשְׁכִינְתָּא, דְּאִתְּמַר בָּהּ, כֻּלָּךְ יָפָה רַעְיָתִי וּמוּם אֵין בָּךְ.

54. "Therefore, the *Etrog* that corresponds to the heart **is the Shechinah. And this is** the meaning of **what the masters of the Mishnah established; that if its upper stem was removed or if lichen grew over most of it, it would be unfit to use, because it is compared to the Shechinah, about whom is said: 'You are all fair, my love, and there is no blemish in you.'** (Song of Songs 4:7)

The Lulav must not be severed since it ties everything together.

55. כַּפֹּת תְּמָרִים, דָּא לוּלָב. וַעֲלֵיהּ אִתְּמַר נִפְרְצוּ עָלָיו פָּסוּל בְּגִין דְּדָא אִיהוּ מְקַצֵּץ בִּנְטִיעוֹת מָאן דִּמְבָרֵךְ עָלָהּ בְּיוֹמָא קַדְמָאָה דְּסֻכּוֹת, בְּגִין דְּאִיהוּ קִשּׁוּרָא וְיִחוּדָא דְּכֹלָּא, חַ"י עָלְמִין, דְּאִיהוּ לְקָבֵל חַ"י חוּלְיָין דְּשִׁדְרָה.

55. "'...branches of palm trees...' (Leviticus 23:40) **refers to the *Lulav*, of which we learned that, 'if its leaves are severed it is unfit** to recite a blessing over it.' **Therefore, whoever makes a blessing over** a *Lulav* whose leaves are severed **on the first day of Sukkot,** he **cuts down the young trees,** which are the Sefirot, since his actions below awaken corresponding actions above, **because it,** meaning the *Lulav,* which is Yesod, **is the bond and unity of all** the Sefirot. And it is called **the Life (chai; 18) of the Worlds,** since it includes nine Sefirot of Returning Light from below upward, and 18 in the two worlds, which are Zeir Anpin and Malchut, **which correspond to the eighteen vertebrae of the spinal column.**

The Lulav is Yesod that is attached Above and Below.

56. וּבְגִין דָּא אוּקְמוּהוּ מָארֵי מַתְנִיתִין, לוּלָב דּוֹמֶה לְשִׁדְרָה, וְרָזָא דְּלוּלָב, צַדִּיק כַּתָּמָר יִפְרָח. וְדָא אִיהוּ כִּי כֹל בַּשָּׁמַיִם וּבָאָרֶץ, וְתַרְגֵּם אֻנְקְלוֹס, דַּאֲחִיד בִּשְׁמַיָּא וּבְאַרְעָא.

56. "Therefore, the masters of the Mishnah established that the *Lulav* is compared to the spine, which is the foundation of all the bones. [See Zohar, Pinchas 422] **The secret of the *Lulav*** is **'The righteous shall flourish like the palm tree...'** (Psalms 92:13) because 'the righteous' is Yesod, and the 'palm tree' is the *Lulav,* [as it says] '... branches of palm trees....' **This is** the meaning of what is said: **'for all that is in Heaven and on Earth'** (I Chronicles 29:11) and 'all' alludes to Yesod. **And Onkelos translates: 'That is attached to Heaven and**

Earth,' namely Yesod that is attached to Heaven and Earth, which are Zeir Anpin and Malchut.

Shaking eighteen times in each of the six directions.

57. וְצָרִיךְ לְנַעְנְעָא חַ"י נִעְנוּעִין, בְּשִׁית סִטְרִין. דְּאִינּוּן חוֹתָם מִזְרָח בְּיה"ו וכו'. שִׁית הֲוַיּוֹ"ת דְּאִית בְּהוֹן תַּמְנֵי סְרֵי אַתְוָון. וְכֻלְּהוּ רְמִיזִין בְּסֵפֶר יְצִירָה.

57. "We must shake eighteen times in six directions, three in every direction, **which are the seal of the east with Yud-Hei-Vav** because by the precept of the Taking of the *Lulav* while facing east we awaken the unification of Chochmah and Binah above, in the Chochmah and Binah of Yisrael-Saba and Tevunah, which are Yud and Hei, and Zeir Anpin that elevates and regulated between Chochmah and Binah is the secret of Vav, which is Da'at. In this way, the east, which is the secret of Zeir Anpin, sealed the Mochin, which are Yud-Hei-Vav that are Chochmah, Binah, and Da'at, up in Yisrael-Saba and Tevunah, in the secret of 'three come out of one.' Afterwards, with the shaking of each direction, the Mochin get revealed and sealed below in Zeir Anpin and Nukva, in the secret of 'one is sustained by three,' in the six combinations of Yud-Hei-Vav, each side according to its governing attribute. For example, Yud-Hei-Vav in the south, Hei-Vav-Yud in the north, etc. [as is explained in the Ari's Gate of Meditations, Volume II regarding Sukkot, discourse five]. **There are six** permutations of **Yud-Hei-Vav, which contain eighteen letters, and they are all alluded to in the Book of Formation (*Sefer Yetzirah*).**

Everything belongs to the Creator.

58. וְהָכִי אוּקְמוּהוּ מָארֵי מַתְנִיתִין, מוֹלִיךְ וּמֵבִיא לְמָאן דְּאַרְבַּע רוּחוֹת הָעוֹלָם דִּילֵיהּ, מַעֲלֶה וּמוֹרִיד, לְמָאן דִּשְׁמַיָּא וְאַרְעָא דִּילֵיהּ.

58. "And so have the masters of the Mishnah established (Tractate Sukkah 37b) that it is necessary to shake to the six directions. **One extends and returns** the *Lulav* and its species **to He to Whom the four directions of the world belong, and he raises and lowers to He to Whom Heaven and Earth belong.**

The Myrtles and the Willows.

59. תְּלַת הֲדַסִּין: גּוּף וּתְרֵין דְּרוֹעִין. וְאִינּוּן לָקֳבֵל עֵינָא, וְכַנְפֵי עֵינָא. תְּרֵי בַּדֵּי עֲרָבוֹת, לָקֳבֵל תְּרֵין שׁוֹקִין, וְלָקֳבֵל תְּרֵין שִׂפְוָון.

59. "The three branches of **myrtle** are Chesed, Gevurah, and Tiferet, which are **the body,** Tiferet, **and two arms,** which are Chesed and Gevurah; **they correspond to the eye and the two eyelids. Two boughs of willow,** which are Netzach and Hod**, correspond to the two legs,** which are Netzach and Hod of the body, **and to the two lips,** which are Netzach and Hod of the head.

The Yud-Hei-Vav-Hei rides upon the Four Species.

60. וְכַד אִינּוּן כֻּלְּהוּ אֲגוּדָה חֲדָא בְּלוּלָב דְּאִיהוּ שִׁדְרָה, מַה כְּתִיב אָמַרְתִּי אֶעֱלֶה בְתָמָר: א' אֶתְרוֹג. ע' עֲרָבָה. ל' לוּלָב. ה' הֲדַס. כֻּלְּהוּ אִתְעֲבִידוּ לָקֳבֵל אַרְבַּע מִינִין. דְּמֶרְכַּבְתָּא, הָרוֹכֵב בְּהוֹן אִיהוּ יהו"ה. וְצָרִיךְ לְסַדְרָא בְּהוֹן בְּהַקָּפָה, כְּגַוְונָא דְמִזְבֵּחַ.

60. "And when all the species are in a bundle with the *Lulav*, namely Yesod, **which is the spine** that rises up to the brain, **it is written: 'I said, I will climb up** (*e'eleh,* Alef-Ayin-Lamed-Hei) **into the palm tree....'** (Song of Songs 7:9) The initials of *e'eleh* are **Alef–*Etrog*, Ayin–Arava (willow), Lamed–*Lulav*, Hei–Hadas (myrtle). All of them,** all the hosts of Heaven, **are formed** in lines and are organized under the Three Columns and Malchut, **corresponding to the four species of the chariot** of the *Lulav*. See Zohar, Va'etchanan verse 62, where it says 'When man is about to unite the Name of the Holy One blessed be He, all the hosts of Heaven stand in rows so as to be established and reach perfection by means of that unification.' **The one who rides them,** meaning the four species, **is Yud-Hei-Vav-Hei** because the myrtle is the secret of Yud, the willows are the first Hei, the *Lulav* is Vav, and the *Etrog* is the last Hei. **And they,** the *Lulav* and its species, **must be set in a circle** around the table or the platform in the synagogue, which are **like the altar** of the Temple." [The concept of the shakings and encircling are found in the Gate of Meditations II of the Ari, in the aforementioned discourse.]

Tikunei HaZohar: Twenty-First Tikkun

On Simchat Torah a Crown is given to every Tzadik.

374. בְּהַהוּא זִמְנָא דְשִׂמְחַת תּוֹרָה, שַׁוְיָין עֲטָרָה בְּרֵישׁ כָּל צַדִּיק לְעֵילָא, כְּמָה דְאַתְּ אָמַר בַּעֲטָרָה שֶׁעִטְּרָה לוֹ אִמּוֹ בְּיוֹם חֲתוּנָּתוֹ וּבְיוֹם שִׂמְחַת לִבּוֹ. בְּיוֹם חֲתוּנָּתוֹ: דָּא שְׁכִינְתָּא תַּתָּאָה. וּבְיוֹם שִׂמְחַת לִבּוֹ: דָּא שְׁכִינְתָּא עִלָּאָה. וְהָכִי צְרִיכִין יִשְׂרָאֵל לְאִתְעַטְּרָא בְּכֹלָּא, בַּעֲטָרָה עַל רֵישַׁיְיהוּ בְּיוֹמָא דְשִׂמְחַת תּוֹרָה.

374. At the time of Simchat Torah, they put above in the Upper Worlds **a crown upon the head of every righteous, as you say: "... with the crown that his mother crowned him, in the day of his marriage and in the day of the joy of his heart." (Song of Songs 3:11)** "...in the day of his marriage..." **this is the Lower Shechinah,** which his Malchut, **"...and in the day of the joy of his heart" this is the Upper Shechinah,** which is Binah because Malchut has ascended to Binah and both have become crowns for Zeir Anpin and Nukva. **So too, all Israel** Below **have to crown themselves with a crown on their heads in the day of Simchat Torah,** meaning to include themselves in the unification of face-to-face of Zeir Anpin and Nukva, and to crown themselves with the crowns of Zeir Anpin and Nukva.

Why the Etrog is held in the left hand.

375. וּלְקַחְתֶּם לָכֶם בַּיּוֹם הָרִאשׁוֹן פְּרִי עֵץ הָדָר כַּפּוֹת תְּמָרִים וכו'. אֶתְרוֹג אִיהִי שְׁכִינְתָּא תַּתָּאָה, וְדַמְיָא לְלִבָּא דְאִיהוּ לִשְׂמָאלָא, דְאִיהוּ גְּבוּרָה, וּבְגִין כַּךְ צָרִיךְ בַּר נַשׁ לְנַטְלָא אֶתְרוֹג בִּידָא שְׂמָאלָא.

375. "And you shall take for yourselves on the first day, the fruit of a citrus tree, and branches of palm trees...." (Leviticus 23:40) The fruit of a citrus tree is **the *Etrog*** that alludes to **the Lower Shechinah,** which is Malchut, **and it is like a heart** of a person **that is on his left,**

which is Gevurah, and therefore one needs to take the *Etrog* during the blessing and recting of Halel **in his left hand.**

The Etrog needs to be whole and unblemished.

376. וּצְרִיכָא לְמֶהֱוֵי אֶתְרוֹג דְּדַמְיָא לְלִבָּא, שְׁלִימָא בִּתְיוֹמֶת דִּילָהּ, בְּגִין הַהוּא דְּאִתְּמַר בֵּיהּ וְיַעֲקֹב אִישׁ תָּם, לְמֶהֱוֵי שְׁלִימָא עִמֵּיהּ. וּכְמָה דְּלֵית פְּסוּל בְּיַעֲקֹב דִּלְעֵילָּא, כֵּן צָרִיךְ דְּלָא יְהֵא פְּסוּל בְּאֶתְרוֹג, לְקַיְּימָא קְרָא כֻּלָּךְ יָפָה רַעְיָתִי וּמוּם אֵין בָּךְ.

376. And the *Etrog*, which is similar to the heart, must be whole, with its twinning (teyomet), which is the the tip of the *Etrog* (*pitam*) **because of he of whom is said: "…and Jacob was a whole (tam) person…" (Genesis 25:27) to be whole with him. And just as there is no imperfection in the Jacob Above,** who is Zeir Anpin, **so must there not be imperfection in the *Etrog*,** which is Malchut, **to fulfill the verse: "You are entirely beautiful my love and there is no blemish in you." (Song of Songs 4:7)**

An Etrog green as gold is preferable.

377. וְאִם הִיא יְרוֹקָא, הִיא מְשׁוּבַּחַת יַתִּיר, כְּדִיוֹקְנָא דַּהֲוַת אֶסְתֵּר יְרַקְרֹקֶת. דְּאִתְּמַר בָּהּ וַתִּלְבַּשׁ אֶסְתֵּר מַלְכוּת.

377. And if it, Malchut, which is the *Etrog*, **is green** like gold**, it is even more preferable, similar to Esther who was greenish, as it is said of her: "…and Esther donned majesty (*malchut*)…." (Esther 5:1)**

Esther was called Hadasah.

378. וְאִתְקְרִיאַת הֲדַסָּה, עַל שֵׁם הֲדַס, וַהֲדַס אִית לֵיהּ תְּלַת הֲדַסִּין, לְאִשְׁתַּכְלְלָא בִּתְלַת אֲבָהָן.

378. And Malchut that is Esther, **is called Hadasah, named after myrtle (hadas),** which is Zeir Anpin, **and the myrtle has three leaves,** which is the secret of the Three Column: Right, Left, and Central, **to be integrated with the three Patriarchs,** which are Chesed, Gevurah, and Tiferet.

Malchut is called Willows from the side of Netzach Hod,
and Lulav from the side of Yesod.

379. וְאִתְקְרִיאַת עֲרָבָה מִסִּטְרָא דִּתְרֵין שִׂפְוָון דְּאִינּוּן לִמּוּדֵי יְיָ׳, וְאִתְקְרִיאַת לוּלָב, מִסִּטְרָא דְּחַ״י עָלְמִין, דְּאִיהוּ כְלִיל חַ״י בִּרְכָאָן דִּצְלוֹתָא, וּלְקִבְלַיְיהוּ עָבְדִין חַ״י נִעְנוּעִין בְּלוּלָב בְּשִׁית סִטְרִין. תְּלַת לְכָל סִטְרָא וְסִטְרָא.

379. And Malchut **is called "willow" (*aravah*) because** it is composed **of two lips,** which are Netzach and Hod, **for they are called: "...the teachings of the Lord...." (Isaiah 54:13) and she is called *Lulav* from the side of Life (*chai;* 18) of the Worlds,** which is Yesod; and it lives in two worlds, which are Zeir Anpin and Malchut, **since He includes the Eighteen Blessings of the prayer,** which are the secret of the Nine Sefirot of Direct Light from above downward and the Nine Sefirot of Returning Light from below upward. **Corresponding to them, we do eighteen shakings with the *Lulav* in six directions,** South, North, East, Up, Down and West, which is the secret of the correction of the Three Columns: Right, Left, and Central in every side.

The shakings are during the Halel.

380. שִׁית סִטְרִין דִּכְלִילָן בְּגוּפָא דְּאִיהוּ עַמּוּדָא דְּאֶמְצָעִיתָא. דְּלוּלָב עַל שְׁמֵיהּ אִתְקְרֵי ל״ו ל״ב. וְאִינּוּן נִעְנוּעִין חַ״י אַרְבַּע זִמְנִין. דְּסָלְקִין ע״ב. וְאִינּוּן חַ״י נִעְנוּעִין בִּנְטִילַת לוּלָב, חַ״י וְחַ״י תְּרֵין זִמְנִין בְּהוֹדוּ לַיְיָ׳ תְּחִלָּה וָסוֹף, חַ״י בְּאָנָּא יְיָ׳ הוֹשִׁיעָה נָא, הָא ע״ב.

380. The six sides that are included in the body, which is Tiferet, where Chesed and Gevurah are the secret of His arms, and Netzach and Hod His legs, and Yesod the Holy Covenant, **which is the Central Column,** to which they all are attached, **which the *Lulav* is named after** Tiferet **and is called "to Him" (*Lu;* Lamed-Vav) "a heart" (*Lev;* Lamed-Bet)**—Lamed-Bet (32) is the secret of the Thirty-Two Paths of Wisdom (Chochmah) that are bestowed from Zeir Anpin to Malchut because in the place of Malchut there is the revelation of Chochmah, and the beginning of the stature of Malchut is opposite the chest, where the heart is. **And the shakings are four times eighteen, which equals 72,** which is the numerical value of Chesed. *Lulav* equals 68, which is the numerical value of life (*chaim*), meaning Chochmah and Chasadim because the Light of Life is the secret of Chochmah. **And there are eighteen shakings when taking the *Lulav*** during the reciting of the blessing: **eighteen, eighteen, two times in *Hodu LaHashem* in the beginning and the end; eighteen in *Ana HaShem Hoshia Na,* thus it all equals 72.** And the Name of 72 (Ayin-Bet) is the source of the correction of the Three Columns, which is the secret of: "And He traveled... and came... and stretched...." (Exodus 14:19-21)

Four sets of eighteen corresponding to Chesed,
Gevurah, Tiferet, and Malchut.

381. וְאִינּוּן תַּלְיָין מִן דַּלֵת, דְּאִיהִי שְׁכִינְתָּא. וְצַדִּיק בָּהּ אִתְקְרֵי אַרְבַּע זִמְנִין חַ"י חַ"י חַ"י חַ"י דְּסָלִיק ע"ב, מִסִּטְרָא דִּתְלַת אֲבָהָן, וּשְׁכִינְתָּא דְּאִשְׁתַּתְּפַת עִמְּהוֹן. דְּאִינּוּן חַ"י פִּרְקִין בִּדְרוֹעָא יְמִינָא, וְחַ"י בִּשְׂמָאלָא, וְחַ"י בְּגוּפָא לְגַבֵּי שִׁדְרָה. וְחַ"י בִּבְרִית מִילָה.

381. And those four times eighteen of the shakings in the Halel **are suspended from Dalet, which is the** stature of the **Shechinah,** namely Malchut, whose stature is Chesed, Gevurah, Tiferet, and Malchut **and the Righteous,** which is Yesod—whence the sustenance comes—to Malchut, **with it,** with the structure of Malchut, in the secret of: "Your stature is like a palm tree..." (Song of Songs 7:8) **is called four times eighteen, eighteen, eighteen, eighteen, which equals 72 because** it is composed **of the three Patriarchs,** which are Chesed, Gevurah, and Tiferet, **and the Shechinah,** which is Malchut that includes Netzach, Hod, and Yesod, **that joins with them,** with Chesed, Gevurah, and Tiferet, since She ascended to Tiferet and occupies all the space from the chest below into Her domain. **They are eighteen in the right arm,** which is Chesed that is composed of all the Lower Six [Sefirot], each one containing the correction of the Three Columns, thus eighteen; **eighteen in the left arm,** which is Gevurah; **eighteen in the body,** which is Tiferet, **in the spine,** which has eighteen vertebrae; **and eighteen in the Covenant of Circumcision,** which is Yesod that also includes Netzach and Hod.

The eighteen shakings correspond to the eighteen vertabrae of the spine.

382. וְאִינּוּן שִׁית סִטְרִין תְּרֵין דְּרוֹעִין דְּמַלְכָּא. וּתְרֵין שׁוֹקִין דְּמַלְכָּא דְּאִינּוּן תְּרֵי נְבִיאֵי קְשׁוֹט, וְגוּפָא וּבְרִית הָא שִׁית. י"ח נִעְנוּעִין לְקָבֵל חַ"י חוּלְיָין דְּשִׁדְרָה מִסִּטְרָא דְּגוּפָא.

382. And they are the six corners, Chesed, Gevurah, Tiferet, Netzach, Hod and Yesod. **Two arms of the king,** which are Chesed and Gevurah of Zeir Anpin, **two legs, which are two true prophets,** meaning Netzach and Hod of Zeir Anpin, **the body,** meaning Tiferet, **and the Covenant,** which is Yesod, **thus six. Eighteen shakings correspond to the eighteen vertebrae of the spine, from the side of the body,** from which all the Lower Six emerge.

HOSHANA RABA: SHADOW CHECKING AND THE WATER OF LIBATION

Vayechi

25. The Image

A Synopsis

This section begins by describing the difference between what happens when a person dies to the body of a man of Israel, and to the body of an idolatrous heathen. Unlike Israel, a heathen's impurities cannot be defiled. Each Israelite contains two Images (*Tzelamim*): the Ordinary and the Holy Shadow. As he approaches death, both shadows depart, since they are joined together. He must write letters and put them in a bag, and then on Yom Kippur (Day of Atonement), he must repent. If he attains repentance, the letters are torn; if not, they are read in consideration for Judgment. Then, there follows a description of the significance of various parts of a man's image and what it means if one or many of them are missing. Everything in the Lower World has its root in Upper Worlds. When one stirs, so does the other.

The Relevence of this Passage

The Light to cleanse ourselves from sin and wrongdoing is bestowed upon readers of this passage. The importance of repentance is awakened within us and we remove Judgments decreed against us in the Upper Worlds. Our image is the link between the body and soul, and when a person is about to leave this world, the image becomes dimmer. This section helps strengthen our shadow, removing the force of death from life.

Not mixing your Tzelem with the Tzelem of a heathen.

195. וַיְחִי יַעֲקֹב בְּגַוְויְהוּ. ע״ד לְבָעֵי לֵיהּ לְבַר נָשׁ דְּלָא לְאִתְעַרְבָא צוּלְמָא דִילֵיהּ בְּצוּלְמָא דְעַכּו״ם, בְּגִין דְּהַאי קַדִּישָׁא, וְהַאי מְסָאֳבָא.

195. "And Jacob lived..." (Genesis 47:28) among them. Therefore, man should not mingle his Image (Tzelem) with that of the idolatrous nations, for the one is Holy and the other defiled.

The difference between a heathen corpse and an Israelite corpse.

196. תָּא וַחֲזֵי, מַה בֵּין יִשְׂרָאֵל לְעַמִּין עכו"ם, דְּיִשְׂרָאֵל כַּד אִשְׁתַּכַּח ב"נ מִית הוּא מְסָאֵב לְכָל גּוּפָא, וּבֵיתָא מְסָאֲבָא, וְגוּפָא דְּעכו"ם, לָא מְסָאִיב לְאָחֳרָא, וְגוּפֵיהּ לָא מְסָאֲבָא כַּד אִיהוּ מִית, מ"ט.

196. Come and see, the difference between Israel and the idolatrous nations. When a man of Israel dies, he defiles the body and the house. But the body of a heathen man does not defile and his body is not defiled in his death. [He asks:] **"Why is it so?"**

When an Israelite dies, his Holiness departs and leaves a void.

197. יִשְׂרָאֵל בְּשַׁעְתָּא דְּאִיהוּ מִית כָּל קְדוּשֵׁי דְּמָארֵיהּ מִתְעַבְּרָן מִנֵּיהּ, אִתְעֲבַר מִנֵּיהּ הַאי צוּלְמָא קַדִּישָׁא, וְאִתְעֲבַר מִנֵּיהּ הַאי רוּחַ קוּדְשָׁא, אִשְׁתְּאַר גּוּפָא מְסָאֲבָא.

197. He answers: **"When a man from Israel dies, all the Holiness of his Master is removed from him, the Holy Image and the Holy Spirit is gone from him and leave his body defiled.**

The heathen has no holiness, so he does not leave a void when he dies.

198. אֲבָל עכו"ם עוֹבֵד ע"ז, לֵית הָכֵי, דְּבְחַיֵּי מְסָאֵב בְּכָל סִטְרִין, צוּלְמָא דִּילֵיהּ מְסָאֲבָא, וְרוּחָא דִּילֵיהּ מְסָאֲבָא, וּבְגִין דְּסוֹאֲבוּתֵי אִלֵּין שַׁרְיָין בְּגַוֵּיהּ, אָסִיר לְמִקְרַב לְגַבֵּיהּ, כֵּיוָן דְּמִית, נָפְקֵי כָּל אִלֵּין מְסָאֲבוּתָא וְאִשְׁתְּאַר גּוּפָא בְּלָא מְסָאֲבוּתָא לְסוֹאֲבָא.

198. "But this is not so for an idolatrous heathen. For during his lifetime he is impure on all sides, his image is impure and his spirit is impure. Since impurities lie within him, it is forbidden to come near him. Once he dies, all the impurities depart from him and the body is left without defiling impurity.

The heathen can impurify others while he is alive.

199. וְאע"ג דְּגוּפָא דִּלְהוֹן מְסָאַב, בֵּין בְּחַיֵּיהוֹן וּבֵין בְּמִיתַתְהוֹן, אֲבָל בְּחַיֵּיהוֹן דְּכָל אִינּוּן מְסָאֲבִין אִשְׁתַּכְּחֵי לְגַבַּיְיהוּ, אִית לוֹן חֵילָא לְסוֹאֲבָא לְאַחֲרִינֵי, בְּמִיתַתְהוֹן דְּנָפְקֵי כָּל אִינּוּן מְסָאֲבִין מִנַּיְיהוּ, לָא יָכְלִין לְסָאֲבָא. וּדְיִשְׂרָאֵל, יָכִיל לְסָאֲבָא לְאַחֲרִינֵי, בְּגִין דְּכָל קַדִּישִׁין נָפְקִין מִנֵּיהּ וְשָׁרָא עֲלֵיהּ סִטְרָא אָחֳרָא.

199. "Though their bodies are defiled, both during their life and in their deaths, when they are alive all the impurities within them have the power to defile others. In their deaths, when impurities leave them, they cannot defile. A body of **an Israelite** after death **can defile others, since all that is Holy has left him and the Other Side dwells upon him.**

Two Images (Tzelemim).

200. תָּא חֲזֵי, הַאי צֶלֶם קַדִּישָׁא, כַּד אָזִיל ב"נ וְאִתְרַבֵּי, וְאִתְעֲבֵיד מֵהַאי פַּרְצוּפָא דְּיוֹקְנָה דִּילֵיהּ, אִתְעֲבֵיד צוּלְמָא אָחֳרָא, וּמִתְחַבְּרָן כַּחֲדָא, וְדָא נָטִיל לְדָא, בְּשַׁעְתָּא דְּאִשְׁתַּכְּחוּ תְּרֵין צוּלְמִין, נָטִיר הוּא ב"נ, וְגוּפָא דִּילֵיהּ בְּקִיּוּמָא, וְרוּחֵיהּ שַׁרְיָא בְּגַוֵּיהּ.

200. "Come and see, [concerning] this Holy Image, when a man grows and his shape is made and completed **with a face, another image is made and joins** the first one, **each embracing the other. When a man has two images, he is protected and his body lives with a Spirit abiding within it.**

The Tzelem leaves an individual before they die.

201. בְּשַׁעְתָּא דְקָרִיבוּ יוֹמוֹי, מִתְעַבְרָן מִנֵּיהּ, וְדָא סָלֵיק לְדָא, וְאִשְׁתָּאַר בַּר נָשׁ בְּלָא נְטִירוּ, כְּדֵין עַד שֶׁיָּפוּחַ הַיּוֹם וְנָסוּ הַצְּלָלִים: תְּרֵי.

201. "When his time draws near for him to die, the images (*tzelamim*) depart from him; the one causes the other to depart since they are joined together. **The man remains without protection, in accordance with the verse, 'Before the day cools, and the shadows (*tzelalim*) flee away...' (Song of Songs 2:17)** not saying 'shadow' but 'shadows,' namely **two** as we said.

Explanation of the matter: The *Tzelamim* (Images) are the secret of the clothing of the Mochin, where the Lower receives from the Upper. Zeir Anpin and Nukva from their own side are not worthy of receiving Mochin because their Vessels are from the aspect of Malchut, on which was the first Tzimtzum (Contraction) to not receive the Supernal Light. But during the Katnut (Immaturity) of Aba and Ima, Binah-Tiferet-Malchut of Aba and Ima descend to the Vessels of Zeir Anpin and Nukva, and Zeir Anpin and Nukva ascend to Aba and Ima with those [unfit] Vessels during their Gadlut (Maturity), when their Binah-Tiferet-Malchut return to their grade. That is when Zeir Anpin and Nukva receive the Mochin of Aba and Ima. Know that just like they receive Mochin from Aba and Ima, they also of necessity receive their Vessels to clothe the Mochin because their own vessels are unworthy of receiving Light. Therefore, from those Binah-Tiferet-Malchut of Aba and Ima that descended in Them They receive Vessels called *Tzelamim* (Images) that clothe the Mochin. They are two: one from Binah-Tiferet-Malchut of Aba, and one from Binah-Tiferet-Malchut of Ima.

Just like we explained that the two *Tzelamim* of Zeir Anpin and Nukva receive from Aba and Ima, so too this applies in the very same way to the souls of people that are birthed by Zeir Anpin and Nukva to be clothed in people. Zeir Anpin and Nukva do not birth souls before they ascend and clothe Supernal Aba and Ima, and because the Lower that ascends to the Upper becomes like it, then they are considered completely like Aba and Ima themselves. The Male and Female souls that are born from Zeir Anpin and Nukva have the same relation as Zeir Anpin and Nukva to Aba and Ima. And the souls also receive the clothing of the Mochin from Zeir Anpin and Nukva, from their Binah-Tiferet-Malchut, and they are called *Tzelamim* (images), one from Nukva and one from Zeir Anpin. First one receives the *tzelem* from Nukva and then from Zeir Anpin.

This is [in verse 200]: **"Come and see, this Holy image. When a man grows..."** because first he receives the *Tzelem* from Nukva, and after this *Tzelem* grows and its shape finishes he receives then the second *Tzelem* from Zeir Anpin. This is: **"another image is made"** namely from Zeir Anpin, **"and joins** the first one, **each embracing the other"** because they need each other, since the *Tzelem* of Nukva draws Chochmah that cannot shine without Chasadim, and the *Tzelem* of Zeir Anpin draws the Chasadim to clothe Chochmah. Then they join together and shine together, **"each embracing the other"** because one without the other cannot shine. This is [in verse 201]: **"when his time draws near for him to die, they depart from him"** in other words, the departure of the *Tzelamim* cause him to die because they are the Vessels and clothing of the Mochin, which are the Light of Life. Once the Vessels leave, the Light of Life leaves, for there is no Light without Vessel, and therefore he dies. **"The one causes the other to depart"** because they need each other, as Chochmah—the Light of Life—cannot shine without Chasadim, as mentioned earlier. **"The man remains without protection"** namely without Vessels to protect the Mochin, and therefore the Mochin—the Light of Life—depart.

On Rosh Hashanah, letters are written and put in a bag.

202. תָּא חֲזֵי, כַּד אִתְעַר דִּינָא בְּעָלְמָא, דְּקוּדְשָׁא בְּרִיךְ הוּא יָתִיב עַל כֻּרְסֵי דְּדִינָא לְמֵידַן עָלְמָא, בָּעֵי ב"נ לְאַתְעָרָא תְּשׁוּבָה, דְּיֵיתוּב מֵחוֹבָא, דְּהָא הַהוּא יוֹמָא, פִּתְקִין כְּתִיבוּ, וּמִשְׁתַּכְּחֵי כֻּלְּהוּ בְּאַחְמָתָא הָא כְּתִיבִין, אִי זָכֵי ב"נ דְּיֵיתוּב קַמֵּי מָארֵיהּ, קָרְעִין פִּתְקִין דַּעֲלֵיהּ.

202. "Come and see, when Judgment awakens in the world and the Holy One, blessed be He, sits on His throne of Judgment to sentence the world on Rosh Hashanah, **one should be awakened with Teshuvah to repent his sins. For on that day, letters are written and put in a bag all written down. If one succeeded and returned** in repentance **before his Master, the letters concerning him are torn.**

Yom Kippur is our opportunity to transform before the letters are sealed.

203. לְבָתַר קוּדְשָׁא בְּרִיךְ הוּא זַמִּין קַמֵּיהּ דְּב"נ, יוֹמָא דְּכִפּוּרֵי יוֹמָא דִּתְשׁוּבָה, אִי תָּב מֵחֲטָאוֹי טַב. וְאִי לָא, פַּקֵּיד מַלְכָּא לְמֶחְתַּם פִּתְקִין, וַוי דְּהָא תְּשׁוּבָה בַּעְיָא לְאִסְתַּלְּקָא מִנֵּיהּ.

203. "After that, the Holy One, blessed be He, prepared Yom Kippur for man. If he repents his sins, it is well. If not, the King commands to seal the letters. Woe to him, for repentance wants to depart from him.

On Hoshana Raba, the sealed letters are given to be executed.

204. אִי זָכֵי בִּתְשׁוּבָה, וְלָא שְׁלֵימָתָא כִּדְקָא יָאוֹת, תַּלְיָין לֵיהּ עַד הַהוּא יוֹמָא בַּתְרָאָה דַּעֲצֶרֶת, דְּהוּא תְּמִינָאָה לְחָג, וְאִי עָבַד תְּשׁוּבָה שְׁלֵימָתָא לְקַמֵּי מָארֵיהּ, אִתְקְרָעוּ. וְאִי לָא זָכֵי, אִינּוּן פִּתְקִין נָפְקִין מִבֵּי מַלְכָּא, וְאִתְמַסְרָן בִּידוֹי דְּסַנְטִירָא, וְדִינָא מִתְעֲבִיד, וּפִתְקִין לָא מִהַדְרָן תּוּ לְבֵי מַלְכָּא.

204. "If he merits to do repentance, yet it is not complete as is needed, they suspend for him until the last day called Atzeret, which is the eighth day of the Holiday of Sukkot. If he wholly repented before his Master, the letters are torn; if he has not, the letters are sent from the King's House and given to the Punishing Angel for the Judgment to be executed. After the letters are handed out, they return no more to the King's House, and the Judgment written in them must be executed.

On Shmini Atzeret, punishments are ready for one who is found without a Tzelem.

205. כְּדֵין צוּלְמִין אִתְעֲבָרוּ מִנֵּיהּ, וְלָא מִשְׁתַּכְּחִין עִמֵּיהּ, כֵּיוָן דְּמִתְעַבְּרָן מִנֵּיהּ, הָא וַדַּאי טוּפְסְקָא דְּמַלְכָּא יַעֲבֹר עֲלֵיהּ, וְיִטְעוֹם כַּסָּא דְּמוֹתָא. וּבְהַהוּא לֵילְיָא דְּחַגָּא בַּתְרָאָה, סַנְטִירִין זְמִינִין, וּפַתְקִין נָטְלִין, בָּתַר דְּנַטְלֵי לוֹן, צוּלְמִין מִתְעַבְּרָן, וְלָא מִשְׁתַּכְּחִין בְּהוֹ יָדֵי, וְאִי מִשְׁתַּכְּחִין בְּהוֹ יָדֵי, דִּינָא גְּרִיעָא, אוֹ יַעֲבֹר עֲלוֹי דִּינָא מַרְעִין בִּישִׁין, בִּגְרִיעוּתָא דִּלְהוֹן, וְהָא אוֹקִימְנָא לְהָא.

205. "Then, the Images are gone and do not abide with him. Once they are gone from him, the King's punishment comes upon him, and he tastes the Cup of Death. On the night of the last Festival, the night of Shmini Atzeret, **the executioners are ready and receive the letters. After they do, the Images depart and are not found in them. If** the images **are with him, no Judgment comes upon him, nor evil illnesses** that come **when the images are flawed, as we already explained elsewhere.**

If the head of the Tzelem is missing.

206. וּבְסִפְרֵי קַדְמָאֵי אַמְרֵי יַתִּיר, כַּד רֵישָׁא אִגָּרַע, וְיִשְׁתַּכַּח גּוּפָא, בְּרֵיהּ, אוֹ אִנְתְּתֵיהּ, יִשְׁתַּכָּחוּ, וְהוּא יִסְתַּלֵּק. וְה"מ, כַּד לָא אַהֲדַר כָּל הַהוּא זִמְנָא בִּתְיוּבְתָּא, אֲבָל אִי אַהֲדַר, טַעֲמָא דְּמוֹתָא יִטְעַם, וְיִתַּסֵּי.

206. "In ancient books, this is explained further. When the head of his shadow is missing but the body is not, it indicates that his child or wife will survive but he will pass away. This is true as long as he does not repent. If he does, he will only taste death and recover from his illness.

If the body of the Tzelem is missing.

207. וְאִי גּוּפָא לָא אִתְחֲזֵי, וְיִשְׁתַּכַּח רֵישָׁא, אִינּוּן סָלְקִין, וְהוּא אִתְקַיֵּים. וְה"מ, כַּד בְּרֵיהּ זְעִירָא בִּרְשׁוּתֵיהּ.

207. "If the body of his shadow **will not be seen but only the head,** his family will die **and he will stay alive. This applies only when his youngest child is still in his care.**

If the hands or legs of the Tzelem are missing.

208. וְאִי יְדוֹי פְּגִימוּ, עֲבִידְתָּא דִּידוֹי פְּגִימִין. רַגְלוֹי, מַרְעִין רָדְפִין עֲלֵיהּ. עָרַק צוּלְמָא וְאַהֲדַר, עָרַק וְאַהֲדַר, עֲלֵיהּ כְּתִיב, בַּבֹּקֶר תֹּאמַר מִי יִתֵּן עֶרֶב, וְהַאי כַּד נְהָרָא סִיהֲרָא, וְלֵילְיָא אִתְתַּקַּן בִּנְהוֹרָא.

208. "If the hands of the shadow **are flawed,** it is an indication that **the works of his hands will deteriorate, and if his legs** are flawed, it is an indication that **illnesses pursue him. If the shadow flees and returns, then flees and returns again, it is said of him, 'In the morning you shall say, "If only it were evening!"...' (Deuteronomy 28:67) This is true only when the moon shines and the night is corrected by her light,** when he checks his shadow.

The righteous live every day as if it is their last.

209. אֲבָל זַכָּאֵי וַחֲסִידֵי, בְּכָל יוֹמָא וְיוֹמָא מִסְתַּכְּלֵי בְּלִבַּיְיהוּ, כְּאִלּוּ הַהוּא יוֹמָא מִסְתַּלְּקֵי מֵעָלְמָא, וְעָבְדִין תְּיוּבְתָּא שְׁלֵימָתָא קַמֵּי מָארֵיהוֹן, וְלָא יִצְטָרְכוּן לְמִלָּה אָחֳרָא, זַכָּאָה חוּלָקֵהוֹן, בְּעָלְמָא דֵין, וּבְעָלְמָא דְאָתֵי.

209. "But the Righteous and the pious see in their hearts every day as if on that very day they are to pass away from the world, and they repent wholly before their Master. They have need of nothing else, namely checking their shadow or the like of it. **Happy is their portion in this world and in the World to Come."**

Terumah

29. Nefesh, Ruach, Neshamah

On Hoshana Raba, those who are sentenced to death lose their shadow.

296. בְּלֵילְיָא בַּתְרָאָה דְּחַגָּא, דְּקָא נַפְקָן פִּתְקִין מִבֵּי מַלְכָּא, וְהַהוּא צֵל אַעְדִּיאוּ מִבְּנֵי גְּרִיעוּ דְּהַאי עָלְמָא, הַהוּא נֶפֶשׁ דְּקָאמָרָן, אַזְלָא וּמְשַׁטְּטָא, וְחַד מְמָנָא סָרְכָא, בְּרָזָא גְּלִיפָא בְּעִזְקָא בִּכְתַב מְפֹרָשׁ, יְדוּמִיעָ"ם, דְּפָקִיד בִּכְתַב דְּזִיוָא גְּלִיפָא, וּבְגוֹ חֶזְוָון עִלָּאִין. בְּהַהוּא לֵילְיָא נָחִית, וְכַמָּה אֶלֶף אַלְפִין וְרִבּוֹא רִבְוָון עִמֵּיהּ, וְנַטְלִין לְהַהוּא צֵל מִכָּל חַד וְחַד, וְסַלְּקִין, לֵיהּ לְעֵילָּא.

296. On the last night of the Holiday, when the sentences emerge from the house of the King, and that shadow is removed from the people who are to be removed from this world, then **that Nefesh that we mentioned goes and floats** above. **An appointed angel, who supervises the secret of the engraving on the seal in clear writing,** meaning over the writing in the aforementioned verdicts, **whose name is Yedomi"am, authorizes the writing of the engraved Light and within Supernal Visions descends during that night. Many thousands upon thousands and ten thousands upon ten thousands go with him. They take that shadow from each one** who was sentenced to death, **and bring it up Above.**

The shadow is given to Metatro"n to be elevated to its place.

297. וְהַהִיא נֶפֶשׁ דְּקָאמָרָן, אַזְלָא וּמְשַׁטְּטָא וְחָמָאת לְהַהוּא צֵל, וְתָב לְאַתְרֵיהּ גּוֹ קִבְרָא, וְקָא מַכְרֶזֶת לִשְׁאַר מֵתַיָּיא, פְּלוֹנִי אָתֵי לְגַבָּן, פְּלוֹנִי אָתֵי לְגַבָּן. אִי זַכָּאָה טָבָא אִיהוּ, כֻּלְּהוּ חַדָּאן, וְאִי לָאו, כֻּלְּהוּ אַמְרֵי וַוי. כַּד סַלְּקִין הַהוּא צֵל, סַלְּקִין לֵיהּ לְגַבֵּי הַהוּא עֶבֶד מְהֵימָן, דִּשְׁמֵיהּ מְטַטְרוֹ"ן, וְנָטִיל הַהוּא צֵל לְגַבֵּיהּ, וְסַלִּיק לֵיהּ לְאַתְרֵיהּ, כד"א, כְּעֶבֶד יִשְׁאַף צֵל, יִשְׁאַף צֵל וַדַּאי.

297. The Nefesh that we mentioned goes and floats and sees that shadow, and knows who is going to die, **and returns to Her place at the grave. It proclaims to the other dead, "So-and-so is coming to us, so-and-so is coming to us." If he is righteous and good, they all rejoice and if not they all say, "Woe." When they elevate that shadow, they elevate it to the faithful servant whose name is Metatro"n, who takes that shadow near him and elevates it to its place, as it is written: "As a servant earnestly desires the shadow...." (Job 7:2) he certainly desires the shadow earnestly.**

Explanation: The souls are born from Zeir Anpin and Nukva, and as each soul is born it is given a shadow (*tzel*) from Zeir Anpin, in the secret of the verse: "For His shade did I long for and dwelled...." (Song of Songs 2:3) Zeir Anpin is the secret of the Tree of Life, and therefore all life depends on this shadow that is drawn from Him. Therefore, when an individual is sentenced to die they take from him that Shadow and Metatro"n the Angel returns it to its place, namely Zeir Anpin.

Emor

38. An image and a likeness

A Synopsis

Rav Shimon talks about how Elohim created man in His own Image and gave him His Name when he produced truth and law in the world, since the word for "judges" is Elohim. He says that man was created both Male and Female, an Image and a Likeness. When people copulate Below, God sends a certain image as the countenance of man that hovers over the union, and with that Image man is created. When the man grows in the world, he grows through that Image that came from Above and walks by that Image. For Holy Israel that Image comes from the side of Holiness but for the heathen nations the image comes from the Other Side; this is why one must not mix his image with that of the heathen.

Adam was created in God's Image.

283. וּלְקַחְתֶּם לָכֶם בַּיּוֹם הָרִאשׁוֹן וְגוֹ', רִבִּי שִׁמְעוֹן פָּתַח, כֹּל הַנִּקְרָא בִשְׁמִי וְלִכְבוֹדִי בְּרָאתִיו יְצַרְתִּיו אַף עֲשִׂיתִיו. כֹּל הַנִּקְרָא בִשְׁמִי, דָא אָדָם, דְּקוּדְשָׁא בְּרִיךְ הוּא בָּרָא לֵיהּ בִּשְׁמֵיהּ, דִּכְתִּיב וַיִּבְרָא אֱלֹהִים אֶת הָאָדָם בְּצַלְמוֹ. וְקָרָא לֵיהּ בִּשְׁמֵיהּ, בְּשַׁעֲתָא דְּאַפִּיק קְשׁוֹט וְדִינָא בְּעָלְמָא, וְאִקְרֵי אֱלֹהִים, דִּכְתִּיב אֱלֹהִים לֹא תְקַלֵּל.

283. "And you shall take for yourselves on the first day…." (Leviticus 23:40) Rav Shimon opened: "Everyone that is called by My Name, and whom I have created for My Glory, I have formed him, yea, I have made him' (Isaiah 43:7) 'every one that is called by My Name' refers to man, whom the Holy One, blessed be He, created by His Name, as written: 'So God created man in His own Image…' (Genesis 1:27) and called him after His Name, when he produced Truth and Law in the world and is called Elohim, as written: 'You shall not revile God (Elohim)….' (Exodus 22:27)

Image and Likeness.

284. קָרָא לֵיהּ בִּשְׁמֵיהּ, דִּכְתִיב וַיִּבְרָא אֱלֹהִים אֶת הָאָדָם בְּצַלְמוֹ וְשַׁפִּיר. הָא אוֹקִימְנָא, דִּכְתִיב נַעֲשֶׂה אָדָם בְּצַלְמֵנוּ כִּדְמוּתֵנוּ, בְּשַׁעֲתָא דְּזִוּוּגָא אִתְּמַר. וְכַךְ הוּא בְּזִוּוּגָא דְּתַרְוַויְיהוּ, בְּצֶלֶם וּדְמוּת. וְאָדָם מִדְּכַר וְנוּקְבָּא נָפַק.

284. "He called him by His name, as written, 'So God created man in His own Image….' (Genesis 1:27) This is well. We explained that the words, 'Let Us make man in Our Image, after Our Likeness…' (Ibid. 26) were uttered during the union of Zeir Anpin and Malchut. And so, when the two have intercourse there is an Image and a Likeness, since the Image (*Tzelem*) is from Zeir Anpin and the Likeness (*Dmut*) from Malchut, and man emerged from Male and Female, namely Zeir Anpin and Malchut.

The Tzelem hovers over the conception of an individual.

285. וַיִּבְרָא אֱלֹהִים אֶת הָאָדָם בְּצַלְמוֹ, בְּסִפְרָא דִּשְׁלֹמֹה מַלְכָּא אַשְׁכַּחְנָא, דְּבְשַׁעֲתָא דְּזִוּוּגָא אִשְׁתְּכַח לְתַתָּא, שָׁדַר קוּדְשָׁא בְּרִיךְ הוּא חַד דִּיּוּקְנָא כְּפַרְצוּפָא דְּב״נ, רְשִׁימָא וַחֲקִיקָא בְּצוּלְמָא, וְקַיְּימָא עַל הַהוּא זִוּוּגָא. וְאִלְמָלֵא אִתְיְיהִיב רְשׁוּ לְעֵינָא לְמֵחֱמֵי, חָמֵי ב״נ עַל רֵישֵׁיהּ חַד צוּלְמָא, רְשִׁימָא כְּפַרְצוּפָא דְּב״נ, וּבְהַהוּא צוּלְמָא אִתְבְּרֵי ב״נ, וְעַד לָא קַיְּימָא הַהוּא צוּלְמָא דְּשָׁדַר לֵיהּ מָארֵיהּ עַל רֵישֵׁיהּ, וְיִשְׁתְּכַח תַּמָּן, לָא אִתְבְּרֵי ב״נ, הֲדָא הוּא דִכְתִיב, וַיִּבְרָא אֱלֹהִים אֶת הָאָדָם בְּצַלְמוֹ.

285. "'So God created man in His own Image…' (Genesis 1:27) I found in the Book of King Solomon that when intercourse happens Below, the Holy One, blessed be He, sends a certain shape as the countenance of man, imprinted and engraved with an Image (Tzelem). It hovers over that union. If the eye had permission to behold, man would see over his head an Image inscribed as a man's face. With this Image man is created. Until this image, which his Master sent him, is stationed over his head, man is not created.

This is the meaning of, 'So God created man in His own Image…' (Genesis 1:27)

The Tzelem fuels and enables growth.

286. הַהוּא צֶלֶם אִזְדַּמַּן לְקַבְלֵיהּ, עַד דְּנָפִיק לְעָלְמָא. כַּד נָפַק, בְּהַהוּא צֶלֶם אִתְרַבֵּי, בְּהַהוּא צֶלֶם אָזִיל, הה״ד אַךְ בְּצֶלֶם יִתְהַלֶּךְ אִישׁ. וְהַאי צֶלֶם אִיהוּ מִלְּעֵילָּא.

286. "This Image comes to him before he goes into the world. When he goes out into the world, **he grows through the Image and walks by that Image. This is the meaning of, 'Man walks about as a mere shadow (*tzelem*)…' (Psalms 39:7). That Image comes from Above.**

The Tzelem of an Israelite and the Tzelem of a heathen.

287. בְּשַׁעֲתָא דְּאִינּוּן רוּחִין נָפְקָן מֵאַתְרַיְיהוּ, כָּל רוּחָא וְרוּחָא אִתְתַּקַּן קַמֵּי מַלְכָּא קַדִּישָׁא בְּתִקּוּנֵי יְקָר, בְּפַרְצוּפָא דְּקָאֵים בְּהַאי עָלְמָא. וּמֵהַהוּא דְּיוּקְנָא תִּקּוּנָא יְקָר, נָפִיק הַאי צֶלֶם. וְדָא תְּלִיתָאָה לְרוּחָא, וְאַקְדִּימַת בְּהַאי עָלְמָא, בְּשַׁעֲתָא דְּזִוּוּגָא אִשְׁתְּכַח. וְלֵית לָךְ זִוּוּגָא בְּעָלְמָא, דְּלָא אִשְׁתְּכַח צֶלֶם בְּגַוַויְיהוּ. אֲבָל יִשְׂרָאֵל קַדִּישִׁין, הַאי צֶלֶם קַדִּישָׁא, וּמֵאֲתַר קַדִּישָׁא אִשְׁתְּכַח בְּגַוַויְיהוּ. ולעכו״ם, צֶלֶם מֵאִינּוּן זִינִין בִּישִׁין. מִסִּטְרָא דִּמְסָאֲבוּתָא אִשְׁתְּכַח בְּגַוַויְיהוּ. וְעַ״ד, לָא לִיבְעֵי לֵיהּ לְאִינִישׁ, לְאִתְעָרְבָא צוּלְמָא דִּילֵיהּ, בְּצוּלְמָא דְּעוֹבְדֵי עֲבוֹדָה זָרָה, בְּגִין דְּהַאי קַדִּישָׁא, וְהַאי מִסְאֲבָא. ת״ח מַה בֵּין יִשְׂרָאֵל לְעכו״ם וְכו'.

287. "When those spirits leave their place, each spirit is fixed before the Holy King with a precious correction, in that Countenance that is found in this world. This Image comes from that shape and precious correction, for the image is clothing for the spirit of that man and comes down together with it, as they are like Light and Vessel. **It is the third to the Spirit (*Ruach*),** namely a third category. The Ruach is the first, Nefesh is the second and the Image (*Tzelem*) is the third. **It is the first to come into the world during intercourse, and no**

intercourse takes place in the world without an Image in it. But for Holy Israel, that Holy Image comes to them from a Holy Place, while the image of the idolatrous comes to them from those evil species on the side of Impurity. For that reason, one must not mix his Image with that of the heathen because the one is Pure while the other is Impure. Come and see the difference between Israel and the heathen nations." The end was printed in [Zohar,] Vayechi, 196-232.

Pinchas

130. The Water Libation

A Synopsis

Rav Shimon explains about the contraction as the waters receded and the relevance to the Water Libation during the second, sixth, and seventh days of Sukkot. He compares the mountains of Ararat to the mountains of darkness and the curses of the Other Side, which gradually become visible as the waters recede. We hear about the sacrifices of the rams, lambs, and bullocks and their effect on the seventy heathen nations for whom they are offered. Lastly we are reminded how Israel break through all the Klipot to find joy on the Eighth Day of Assembly (Shmini Atzeret). In this the Other Side has no part.

Where the Water libation is alluded to in the Torah.

886. אר"ש, אֶלְעָזָר, ת"ח, מִיּוֹמָא תִּנְיָינָא שָׁרִיאוּ מַיָּיא לְאִתְחֲזָאָה, כֵּיוָן דְּשָׁרִיאוּ מַיִם, מִיּוֹמָא תְּלִיתָאָה אִיהִי שָׁרַת עֲלַיְיהוּ, וְאִינּוּן מַיִם לָא הֲווּ יַדְעֵי בַּבְלָאֵי, אֲמַאי רְשִׁימִין הָכָא, דְּהָא טוּבָא דְּיִשְׂרָאֵל לָא הֱוֵי בַּאֲתָר דְּמִעוּטָא, אֶלָּא בַּאֲתָר דְּרִבּוּיָא. וּבְגִין דְּאִלֵּין מַיִין דִּרְשִׁימִין הָכָא אִתְמַעֲטָן, אָתֵי קְרָא לְאַשְׁמוּעִינָן דִּכְתִיב, וְהַמַּיִם אִינּוּן דְּיָדִיעָן בְּיוֹמֵי דְּחַג, אִינּוּן דִּרְשִׁימִין גּוֹ קָרְבְּנִין, דְּאִינּוּן טוּרֵי לְוָוטִין, הָיוּ הָלוֹךְ וְחָסוֹר טוּבָא דִּלְהוֹן, וּנְגִידוּ דְּאַנְגִּיד עֲלַיְיהוּ, הָיוּ הָלוֹךְ וְחָסוֹר, וּבְגִין דְּאִינּוּן מַיִם דִּלְהוֹן הוּא, לָא אִתְחַבְּרָן אִתָּוָן, דְּלָא יִתְחַבָּר טוּבָא דִּלְהוֹן, אֶלָּא זְעֵיר זְעֵיר.

886. Rav Shimon said: "Elazar, come and see, from the second day, the waters began to appear, namely, the Libation of Water on the altar began. For its purpose was also to draw vitality and existence for the Other Side, as mentioned later in verse 890: '...if he be thirsty, give him water to drink' (Proverbs 25:21) [where] 'water' refers to that water that is marked on the days of Sukkot. **And after the water had begun,** and the Other Side and the seventy nations had received plenty, they then grew in strength, and **from the third day** Malchut **rested on them**, as they drew Her separated from Zeir Anpin. **And the Babylonians did not know why these waters are mentioned here** in connection with Sukkot. In other words, they did not know that their purpose was to provide existence to the nations of the world. **For the goodness of Israel does not lie where there is contraction,** namely in the bullocks of Sukkot that are reduced in number **but in a place of expansion. And since these waters that are mentioned here decrease,** together with the bullocks of Sukkot, **scripture comes to inform us that it is written: 'And the waters...' (Genesis 8:5) namely the waters that are known from the days of Sukkot are the ones that are mentioned among the sacrifices.** For on the second day, about the sacrifices it is said that is '...their drink offerings (*veniskeihem*; וְנִסְכֵּיהֶם)...' (Numbers 29:18) the last letter of which is Mem (ם). And on the sixth day, it is said: '... and its drink offerings' (*unsacheiyah*; וּנְסָכֶיהָ)" (Ibid. 31), with Yud (י). And on the seventh day 'after the ordinance (*kemishpatam*; כְּמִשְׁפָּטָם)' (Ibid. 33), the last letter of which is Mem (ם). And these three letters together spell *mayim* (waters; מים; Mem-Yud-Mem), thus it follows that there is an allusion to the Water Libation in the Torah. **For they,** the sacrifices, **are mountains of curses that continually decrease, and their goodness, and the abundance that is drawn down on them '... decreased continually....' (Genesis 8:5) And because these waters belong to them,** to the nations and to the Other Side, **the letters** Mem-Yud-Mem (מים) **were not joined together** and the word did not appear explicitly written in the Torah. But the letters are scattered, with Mem being in *veniskeihem* (וְנִסְכֵּיהֶם), the Yud in *unsacheiyah* (וּנְסָכֶיהָ), and the final Mem in *kemishpatam* (כְּמִשְׁפָּטָם) as mentioned earlier. **This is so that their goodness should not be joined but** be **little by little."**

The months of Tevet and Shvat are days of Judgment.

887. אֲבָל לְיִשְׂרָאֵל, דְּאִינּוּן מְקוּדְשָׁא בְּרִיךְ הוּא, מַה כְּתִיב. וְדוֹרְשֵׁי יְיָ' לֹא יַחְסְרוּ כָל טוֹב. רֵישֵׁיהּ דִּקְרָא, כְּפִירִים רָשׁוּ וְרָעֵבוּ, אִלֵּין מִמְּנָן דִּשְׁאָר עַמִּין.

וְדוֹרְשֵׁי יְיָ', אִלֵּין יִשְׂרָאֵל, לֹא יַחְסְרוּ כָל טוֹב, אִלֵּין אַזְלִין וְאִסְתַּלְּקוּ לְעֵילָּא לְעֵילָּא. וּבג"כ, טוּבָא דִלְהוֹן דְּאִינּוּן מַיִם, הָיוּ הָלוֹךְ וְחָסוֹר. עַד הַחֹדֶשׁ הָעֲשִׂירִי. דָא טֵבֵת, דְּהָא כְּדֵין יְמֵי הָרָעָה הֲווֹ, וְאִתְעֲרַת הַהִיא רָעָה וְאִתְתַּקְפַת, וְכַלָּה קַדִּישָׁא לָא אַנְהִירַת מִגּוֹ שִׁמְשָׁא, כְּדֵין נִרְאוּ רָאשֵׁי הֶהָרִים, אִלֵּין אִינּוּן הָרֵי חֲשׁוֹכָא, טוּרִין דִלְוָוטִין אִתְחָזוּן וְאִתְתַּקָּפוּ, וְעַבְדִין בִּישִׁין בְּעָלְמָא.

887. [He asks:] **"But regarding Israel, who are from the Holy One, blessed be He,** who is the Central Column, **what is written?"** [He answers:] **"'…but those who turn to the Lord shall not lack any good.' (Psalms 34:11) The first half of this verse is: 'The young lions lack, and suffer hunger….'' (Ibid.) The 'young lions' are the appointees of the other nations. They that seek the Lord are Israel, who will not lack all good things because they continually ascend higher and higher,** for one may promote to a higher degree of sanctity but not demote. **For this reason, their good,** that of the nations and of the Other Side, **which are waters, '…decreased continually until the tenth month…' (Genesis 8:5) which is the month of Tevet, for then are the days of evil,** for the months of Tevet and Shevat are the period of Judgment and are called 'the days of evil.' **And this evil awakens and grows stronger, and the Holy Bride,** which is Malchut, **does not illuminate from the midst of the sun,** namely is separated from the sun, which is Zeir Anpin. **And then the tops of these mountains became visible,** that is the Judgments of the Left Side that are drawn down with the bullocks of Sukkot, **namely those mountains of darkness and mountains of curses that appear and grow stronger and do evil things in the world."**

Seventy bullocks, fourteen rams, ninety-eight lambs.

888. בְּיוֹמִין אִלֵּין, אִשֶּׁה בְּהַאי עוֹלָה, דְּהָא כְּדֵין הָנֵי אִשִּׁים אָכְלֵי חוּלָקֵהוֹן. שִׁבְעִים פָּרִים אִלֵּין, אִינּוּן לְקָבֵל שִׁבְעִים מְמָנָן, דְּשַׁלְטוּ עַל שַׁבְעִין עַמִּין. וְסַלְּקִין בְּיוֹמָא קַדְמָאָה, וְנַחְתֵּי בְּכָל יוֹמָא וְיוֹמָא, וְאִקְרוּן פָּרִים מִנַּגְּחִין בְּיוֹמִין דִּלְהוֹן.

אֵילִם, אַרְבֵּיסַר, תְּרֵין בְּכָל יוֹמָא אִינּוּן יַ"ד יְהֹוָ"ה. יְדָא דְּשַׁלִּיטָא עֲלַיְיהוּ תָּדִיר, בְּכָל יוֹמָא וְיוֹמָא. אִמְּרִין בְּנֵי שָׁנָה, מִנְיָינָא דִּלְהוֹן צַ"ח.

888. About these days of the Holiday of Sukkot it is written: **"...a sacrifice made by fire..." (Numbers 29:13) regarding** their **burnt offering,** namely the words, "And you shall offer a burnt offering for a sacrifice made by fire...." (Ibid.) **For then these offerings made by fire devour their portions, namely those seventy bullocks corresponding to the seventy appointees who rule over the seventy nations.** And their number **is greatest on the first day and decreases with each passing day. And they are called "goring bullocks" on their days. Fourteen rams.** [The text here is missing but should read as follows: "...two rams, and fourteen lambs of the first year...." (Numbers 29:13)] **The two** rams **on each day are the Hand of God (*Yad* Yud-Hei-Vav-Hei),** as seven times two is fourteen [the numerical value of *yad*]. **And this refers to the hand (*yad*; 14) that controls them continually, every day. And the total number of the lambs of the first year is 98,** since seven times fourteen equals 98.

Giving the offerings to the nations out of joy and not with an evil eye.

889. וְאִי תֵּימָא אִי הָכִי, רַע עַיִן הֲוֵינָן לְגַבַּיְיהוּ. אִין, דְּהָא כְּתִיב, כִּי גֶחָלִים אַתָּה חוֹתֶה עַל רֹאשׁוֹ. אֲבָל אֲנָן לָא יַהֲבִינָן אֶלָּא בְּחֶדְוָותָא, דְּלֵית בְּיוֹמֵי שַׁתָּא, חֶדְוָותָא, כְּאִלֵּין יוֹמִין. וּבְגִין דַּאֲנָן יָהֲבִין בְּטוּב לִבָּא, וּבְחֶדְוָותָא דִּרְעוּתָא, אִתְהַפַּךְ עֲלַיְיהוּ גֶחָלִים עַל רֵישַׁיְיהוּ, גּוֹמְרִין מְלַהֲטָן, דְּחֶדְוָותָא דִּילָן, עַבְדֵּי לוֹן בִּישׁ. י"ד, ע', ווזץ. כַּךְ סַלְקִין בְּחוּשְׁבְּנָא דִּילְהוֹן.

889. And you might ask: "If so, if we offer fourteen rams so that the Hand (*yad*; 14) of Yud-Hei-Vav-Hei will rule; and if we offer 98 lambs, which is a bad omen, for it corresponds to the 98 curses in the admonition and also it is said that 'Until a dart (*chetz*; 98) strikes through his liver...' (Proverbs 7:23) **then are we not being evil-eyed toward them?** For he says to him: 'Eat and drink,' but '...he does not really mean it.'

(Proverbs 23:7)" He answers: **"Yes, for it is written:** 'If your enemy be hungry, give him bread to eat, and if he be thirsty, give him water to drink. **For you shall heap coals of fire upon his head....' (Proverbs 25:21-22) But we give only out of rejoicing, for throughout the whole year, there is no rejoicing like that on these days** of Sukkot. **And since we give out of the goodness of our hearts, gladly and willingly,** our gifts **to them turn into coals of fire on their head, burning coals, for our rejoicing affects them badly, namely, the fourteen** rams, **seventy** bullocks, **and 98** lambs, **which is their sum total** of sacrifices, where the fourteen rams indicate the hand (*yad;* 14) of Yud-Hei-Vav-Hei that controls them, and the seventy bullocks in their decreasing progression teach that their goodness will continually decrease, while the 98 lambs teach about the 98 curses that rest on them: '...a dart (*chetz;* 98) strike through their liver....' (Proverbs 7:23)"

There is no joy for the minister of the nations like the joy of Sukkot.

890. וְכָל דָּא אִיתֵּימָא מַאן יָהִיב לָן לְאַקְרְבָא עֲלַיְיהוּ, דִּלְמָא אִינּוּן לָא בָּעָאן כָּל דָּא. אֶלָּא לֵית חֶדְוָוה לְכָל אִינּוּן מְמָנָן, בְּכָל אִינּוּן תּוֹרִים אֵילִים וְאִמְרִין כְּהָנֵי, בְּשַׁעֲתָא דְּיִשְׂרָאֵל יַהֲבֵי לוֹן סְעוּדָתִין אִלֵּין. וְעִם כָּל דָּא לָא מִתְקַרְבוּ כֹּלָּא, אֶלָּא לְקוּדְשָׁא בְּרִיךְ הוּא בִּלְחוֹדוֹי, וְאִינּוּן מִתְקָרְבֵי תַּמָּן, וְאִיהוּ פָּלִיג לוֹן. וְעַל דָּא כְּתִיב, אִם רָעֵב שׂוֹנַאֲךָ הַאֲכִילֵהוּ לָחֶם, אִלֵּין אִינּוּן קָרְבְּנִין דְּחָג. וְאִם צָמֵא הַשְׁקֵהוּ מָיִם, אִלֵּין מַיִם דְּרַשִׁימִין הָכָא בְּיוֹמֵי דְּחָג. וּבְיוֹמָא תִּנְיָינָא, וּבְיוֹמָא שְׁתִיתָאָה וּשְׁבִיעָאָה, וְסִימָן בּו"ז יָבוּזוּ לוֹ.

890. And regarding all this, but you might ask: "Who asked us to sacrifice for them, for the appointees of the seventy nations? **Perhaps they are not interested in our doing so?"** [He answers:] **"But all of these appointees have no such rejoicing at that time as they have with all these bullocks and rams and lambs that Israel offer to them at these banquets. Nevertheless, nothing is offered except to the Holy One, blessed be He alone, while they,** the appointees, **come close and the Holy One, blessed be He, distributes to them. And**

about this it is written: 'If your enemy be hungry, give him bread to eat…' (Proverbs 25:21) where 'bread' refers to the festival offerings; and in "and if he be thirsty, give him water to drink…' (Ibid.); 'water' refers to that water that is marked to be poured out in a Libation **on the days of Sukkot, on the second, sixth, and seventh days. And this is derived from, '…he would be utterly scorned (*boz*; בּוֹז; Bet-Vav-Zayin)" (Song of Songs 8:7)** where the numerical values of the letters Bet (ב), Vav (ו), and Zayin (ז) are two, six and seven, respectively.

The Water Libation evokes love towards the Creator.

891. מַיִם רַבִּים לֹא יוּכְלוּ לְכַבּוֹת אֶת הָאַהֲבָה, אִלֵּין אִינּוּן מַיִם, דִּי מְנַסְּכֵי יִשְׂרָאֵל, בְּחֶדְוָה וּבִרְחִימוּ דְקוּדְשָׁא בְּרִיךְ הוּא, דִּכְתִּיב וּשְׁאַבְתֶּם מַיִם בְּשָׂשׂוֹן. וּנְהָרוֹת לֹא יִשְׁטְפוּהָ, אִלֵּין אִינּוּן נַהֲרֵי דְּאֲפַרְסְמוֹנָא דַּכְיָא, דְּכֻלְּהוּ דַּבְקֵי וּמִתְקַשְּׁרֵי בִּרְחִימוּ דָּא. אִם יִתֵּן אִישׁ אֶת כָּל הוֹן בֵּיתוֹ בְּאַהֲבָה בּוֹז יָבוּזוּ, דָּא סַמָּאֵל, בְּאַהֲבָה דְּיִשְׂרָאֵל, לְמֶהֱוֵי לֵיהּ חוּלָקָא בַּהֲדַיְיהוּ, בְּאִינּוּן מַיִם דִּרְשִׁימִין הָכָא בְּפַרְשְׁתָּא, דִּכְתִּיב אִם יִתֵּן אִישׁ אֶת כָּל הוֹן בֵּיתוֹ בְּאַהֲבָה בּוֹז יָבוּזוּ, סִימָנָא דְּאִינּוּן מַיִם בּו"ז, יָבוּזוּ לוֹ וַדַּאי, דְּהָא כֻּלְּהוּ אִתְחֲשִׁיבוּ לְגַבָּן, חֶרֶשׂ נִשְׁבָּר, דְּלֵית לֵיהּ תַּקָּנָה לְעָלְמִין.

891. "'Many waters cannot quench love….' (Song of Songs 8:7) refers to the 'waters' that Israel pour out in Libation by way of rejoicing and love for the Holy One, blessed be He, as it is written: 'Joyfully shall you draw water…'(Isaiah 12:3) [and] '…nor can the floods drown it….' (Song of Songs 8:7) These are the floods of the pure balsam, namely the eighteen rivers of plenty that are drawn down from Yesod of Binah. **For all of them cleave to, and form a bond with, this love. '…If a man offered all his wealth for love…' (Ibid.). This refers to Sama"el; and he gives '…for love…' (Ibid.) of Israel, namely so that he should have a portion with them in these waters about which it is written: '…If a man offered all his wealth for love, it would be utterly scorned (*boz*; בּוֹז),' (Ibid.) which is a mnemonic for these waters** that are poured out on the second (ב), sixth (ו), and seventh (ז) days.

'...it would certainly be scorned,' for all the substance of Sama"el is considered for us as a broken potsherd (cheres; חֶרֶשׂ) that can never be repaired."

The Water Libation that the Other Side has a hold on.

892. מַיִם דִּלְהוֹן אִתְפַּלִּיגוּ בְּיוֹמִין בּוֹ"ז, אִשְׁתָּאֲרוּ שְׁאַר יוֹמִין, דְּאִינּוּן חֲמִישִׁי רְבִיעִי שְׁלִישִׁי, וְסִימָן, חֶ"רֶ"שׂ אֶת חַרְשֵׁי הָאֲדָמָה, וְלֵית לוֹן תִּקּוּנָא בַּהֲדָן, וְלָא לְעָלְמִין. וְאִי תֵּימָא בּוֹז יָבוּזוּ לוֹ כְּתִיב. הָתָם כִּי לֹא בָזָה וְלֹא שִׁקַּץ עֱנוּת.

892. He explains his words: **"The water** of Sama"el, the Other Side and the nations, **is distributed on the days of** *boz* **(Bet-Vav-Zayin). This leaves the other days, namely, the fifth, fourth, and third days of Sukkot,** on which there is no Water Libation. **The mnemonic for this:** 'Let the potsherd (cheres; חֶרֶשׂ) strive with the potsherds of the earth' (Isaiah 45:9)**,** where the letters of *cheres* (חֶרֶשׂ) stand for *chamishi* (חֲמִישִׁי; fifth), *revi'i* (רְבִיעִי; fourth) and *shlishi* (שְׁלִישִׁי; third), on which days there is no Libation of Water, **and they have no correction through us, nor indeed forever.** For just as they have no correction on the fifth, fourth, and third days, so they never will have any correction. **And should you wish to point that it is written '...he would be utterly scorned,' (Song of Songs 8:7)** whereas, according to the above, it should have been written: 'it would not be utterly scorned (boz; בּוֹז)' namely that they do not want the scorn (second, sixth, and seventh), which is the substance of Sama"el." He then responds: **"Elsewhere it is written: 'For He has not scorned nor abhorred the affliction....' (Psalms 22:25)"**

Explanation: This alludes to the fact that Israel do not want to give up on love for the sake of the Illumination of the Libation of Water that is in scorn (boz; second, sixth, and seventh), which is the wealth of the Other Side, meaning that the Other Side has a hold on it. "...it would be utterly scorned" (Song of Songs 8:7) is not referring to the Light in boz, but rather simply that they scorn it. The explanation of the verse is as follows: **"Many waters cannot quench love..." (Song of Songs 8:7)** namely the waters of Chochmah, of which is written **"Joyfully shall you draw water from the fountains of salvation." (Isaiah 12:3)** Even though they are Chochmah, they do not extinguish the Chasadim called "love." Similarly, "...nor rivers drown it..." (Song of Songs 8:7) namely the streams of balsam, even though they contain the Illumination of Chochmah they nevertheless do not drown the love, meaning that they do not diminish the Chasadim.

However concerning, **"...if a man**, which is Sama"el, **offered all his wealth..." (Ibid.)** namely all the Lights he has **"...for love" (Ibid.)** [we see] that in exchange for nullifying the love he will give us the Lights of the Water Libation that are in the days of *boz* (second, sixth, and seventh), since the Illumination of the water of boz decrease as they go, which implies that it diminishes the love, Chasadim because Chochmah that has a part in the Other Side constantly diminishes the Chasadim. It is found that his Illumination of Chochmah extinguishes the love, until the Chochmah is left without Chasadim. Then the Illumination of Chochmah is also extinguished because it cannot shine without Chasadim, and therefore: **"it would be utterly scorned."** This is not the case with the Illumination of Chochmah that Israel receive, which do not extinguish the Chasadim, the secret of love.

Why the Water Libation starts on the second day and not the first.

893. יוֹמָא קַדְמָאָה מַאי עָבֵיד לֵיהּ. אֶלָּא לָא אִקְרֵי רִאשׁוֹן, וְלָא אִקְרֵי אֶחָד, אֶלָּא חֲמִשָּׁה עָשָׂר סְתָם, בְּלָא רְשׁוּמָא כְּלַל. אֲבָל שֵׁירוּתָא דִּרְשִׁימוּ דְּמַיִין, מִיּוֹם שֵׁנִי הֲוֵי. וְהָכִי אִתְחֲזֵי, בְּגִין דְּלֵית טוֹב בַּשֵּׁנִי, וּבגַ"כ, לָא רְשִׁים רִאשׁוֹן וְלָא אֶחָד כְּלַל, וַהֲוֵי בִּסְתָם, וְשָׁרֵי רְשִׁימוּ דְּיוֹמִין, בְּיוֹם שֵׁנִי. וְאִתְפַּלְגוּ מַיִם בְּבוֹ"ז, וְאִשְׁתְּאָרוּ בְּיוֹמִין חֲזָ"ש, כְּמָה דְּאִתְּמַר, וְכֹלָּא כַּדְקָא יֵאוֹת.

893. He asks: **"What does he do on the first day** of the holiday? The second, sixth, and seventh (*boz*) days are considered those of the Water

Libation, and the fifth, fourth, and third (*cheres*) days are free of the Libation of Water but he does not mention the first day of the Holiday at all." He answers: "The first day **is not called 'first' nor 'one' but** is called **simply '...the fifteenth day....' (Numbers 29:12) No special mention is made of it** because there is nothing special about it to mention **but the Water Libation is first mentioned on the second day, and this is how it should be.** Since on this day, a portion is given to the Other Side, it is fitting that this should be on the second day, **for about the second day** it was **not** said: 'that it was **good.' This is why he does not mention the first or one day at all but just simply** the fifteenth day, **and the first mention of the days, and the renewal of the days, begins on the second day. And the water is distributed on the second, sixth and seventh days, and there is no Libation of Water on the fifth, fourth, or third days, as we have learned—and it is all as it should be.**

Israel know how to break the Klipot and enter to be close the Creator.

894. זַכָּאָה חוּלָקֵהוֹן דְּיִשְׂרָאֵל, דְּיָדְעֵי לְאַעֲלָאָה לְגוֹ מוֹחָא דֶּאֱגוֹזָא. וּבְגִין לְמֵיעָאל לְגוֹ מוֹחָא, מִתַּבְּרִין קְלִיפִּין אִלֵּין, וְעָאלִין. מַה כְּתִיב לְבָתַר כָּל הַאי. בַּיּוֹם הַשְּׁמִינִי עֲצֶרֶת תִּהְיֶה לָכֶם. לְבָתַר דְּתַבְּרוּ כָּל הָנֵי קְלִיפִּין, וְתַבְּרוּ כַּמָּה גִּזְּיִין, וְכַמָּה נְחָשִׁים קַטְלוּ, וְכַמָּה עַקְרַבִּים דַּהֲווּ לוֹן בְּאִינּוּן טוּרֵי דַּחֲשׁוֹכָא, עַד דְּאַשְׁכָּחוּ אֲתַר דְּיִשׁוּבָא, וְקַרְתָּא קַדִּישָׁא, מַקְפָּא שׁוּרִין סְחוֹר סְחוֹר, כְּדֵין עָאלוּ לְגַבָּהּ, לְמֶעְבַּד נַיְיחָא תַּמָּן, וּלְמֶחֱדֵי בָּהּ. וְהָא אוֹקִימְנָא מִלָּה.

894. Happy is the portion of Israel, who know how to enter the brain of the nut, as Holiness is like the brain of a nut that is surrounded by shells, **and in order to get into the brain, they break off these shells** that surround it, **and enter. What is written subsequently? "On the eighth day you shall have a solemn assembly...." (Numbers 29:35) For after they break through all these Klipot and break down a number of forces and kill a number of Serpents and a number of scorpions, which were there in wait for them in those mountains of darkness, until they managed to find the place of settlement and**

a holy city which is the Holy Malchut, **surrounded by walls on all sides, they then entered it** on the Eighth Day of Assembly (Shmini Atzeret) **to give it satisfaction there, and rejoice in it. And we already explained the matter.**

Malchut is the receptacle for the Light.

895. וְדָא אִיהוּ עֲצֶרֶת, כְּנִישׁוּ. אֲתַר דְּמִתְכַּנַּשׁ כֹּלָּא לְגַבָּהּ. תִּהְיֶה לָכֶם, וְלָא לְאַחֲרָא, לְמֶחֱדֵי אַתּוּן בְּמָארֵיכוֹן, וְאִיהוּ בַּהֲדַייכוּ. וְעַל דָּא כְּתִיב, שִׂמְחוּ בַּיְיָ' וְגִילוּ צַדִּיקִים וְהַרְנִינוּ כָּל יִשְׁרֵי לֵב.

895. And this is "...a solemn assembly (*atzeret*)..." (Numbers 29:35) the meaning of which is **a gathering,** namely Malchut, **for she is a place where everything gathers,** for she is a receptacle for all the higher luminaries. **"...you shall have..." (Ibid.) namely you and nobody else shall have,** for the Other Side has no part of it, **but it is you who rejoice with your Master, and He with you. And about this it is written: "Be glad in the Lord and rejoice, you righteous; and shout for joy, all you who are upright in heart." (Psalms 32:11)**

SIMCHAT TORAH

Emor

27. The Festival of Shavuot

A Synopsis

We hear about the rejoicing of all the trees when Malchut is perfected. The entire bond of faith comes from the Tree, Zeir Anpin. We are told that the Congregation of Yisrael, like a bride, is given portions from each of the grades. Rabbi Shimon tells about the union of Zeir Anpin and Malchut. We hear about the tree that is the torso and about all the limbs that are the Sefirot that are attached to it. The feast days of the branches of the Tree were throughout the days of Sukkot, and after that on Shmini Atzeret is the joy of the Tree itself. The Tree atones for the Evil Inclination in man when the leavened bread is brought. The Torah is called a Tree of Life because its roots are in the deep river of Binah.

Atzeret refers to the place in which everything is connected together.

155. תָּא חֲזֵי, כְּתִיב בַּיּוֹם הַשְּׁמִינִי עֲצֶרֶת. מַאן עֲצֶרֶת. אֶלָּא בְּהַהוּא אֲתָר, דְּכֹלָּא מִתְקַשְּׁרָן כַּחֲדָא, אִקְרֵי עֲצֶרֶת, מַאי עֲצֶרֶת, כְּנִישׁוּ. וְאִי תֵּימָא הָכָא דְּאִקְרֵי עֲצֶרֶת, מַאי טַעֲמָא. אֶלָּא בְּכָל אִינּוּן יוֹמִין, יוֹמֵי סְעוּדָתֵי דְּעַנְפֵי אִילָנָא הֲווֹ. וְעַל דָּא, שִׁבְעִים פָּרִים אִינּוּן. לְבָתַר, חֶדְוְותָא דְּאִילָנָא מַמָּשׁ, וְחֶדְוְותָא דְּאוֹרַיְיתָא. וּבְגִּינֵיהּ הוּא יוֹמָא חַד עֲצֶרֶת. חֶדְוְותָא דְּאוֹרַיְיתָא, חֶדְוְותָא דְּאִילָנָא, דְּהוּא גּוּפָא.

155. Come and see, it is written: "On the eighth day you shall have a solemn assembly (*atzeret*)...." (Numbers 29:35) He asks: **"What is the assembly?"** He answers: **"That the place in which everything is connected together,** which is Malchut that receives from all the Sefirot, **is called an assembly (*atzeret*)."** He asks: **"What does *atzeret* mean?"** He answers: **"A gathering."** He asks: **"One may ask what is the reason that it is called an assembly (*atzeret*) here?"** He answers: **"All these days** of Sukkot **were feast days of the branches of the Tree,** namely the seventy ministers that come from the outer part of Zeir Anpin, **and hence there are seventy bullocks** sacrificed on the seven days of Sukkot. **After that,** on Shmini Atzeret **comes the joy of the Tree itself,** Zeir Anpin Himself, **and for its sake there is an assembly for one day, which is the joy of the Torah, the joy of the Tree, which is the body,** namely Zeir Anpin.

Atzeret is "for you" and no one else.

156. וְעַל דָּא לֵית חוּלָקָא בְּהַאי יוֹמָא, אֶלָּא לְקוּדְשָׁא בְּרִיךְ הוּא וכנ"י. בְּג"כ, עֲצֶרֶת תִּהְיֶה לָכֶם, לָכֶם, וְלָא לְאָחֳרָא. דְּהָא בְּשַׁעְתָּא דְּמַלְכָּא אִשְׁתְּכַח, כֹּלָּא אִשְׁתְּכַח בֵּיהּ. וְעַ"ד תְּנִינָן, בַּעֲצֶרֶת עַל פֵּירוֹת הָאִילָן, וְהָא אוּקְמוּהָ בְּג"כ אֶחָד אִקְרֵי, אֶחָד וַדַּאי, כְּמָה דְּאַמָרָן.

156. "Therefore only the Holy One, blessed be He, and the Congregation of Israel take part in this day, Shmini Atzeret. **For that reason, '...you shall have a solemn assembly...' (Ibid.) you and no other, for when the King is present, everything is there in Him. We therefore learned: "on *atzeret*** the world is judged **concerning the fruits of the tree," (Tractate Rosh Hashanah 16a)** which alludes to Zeir Anpin that is called 'Tree,' whose day it is. **This was already explained. For that reason He is called one,** being **united with Malchut. Certainly one, as we said."**

39. Shmini Atzeret

A Synopsis

We read about the eighth day, the assembly that is Sukkot and that is the day of rejoicing. The Supernal Candles cause the Supernal Anointing Oil to burn, which draws the blessings to Israel. Through the deed of lighting the candles Below the Candles Above are lit because deeds Below cause deeds to awaken Above.

On Shmini Atzeret the Creator rejoices with Israel alone.

288. דִּכְתִיב בַּיּוֹם הַשְּׁמִינִי עֲצֶרֶת תִּהְיֶה לָכֶם, דְּהָא יוֹמָא דָא, מִמַּלְכָּא הוּא בִּלְחוֹדוֹי, חֶדְוָותָא דִילֵיהּ בְּהוּ בְּיִשְׂרָאֵל. מְתַל לְמַלְכָּא דְּזַמִּין אוּשְׁפִּיזִין, אִשְׁתְּדָלוּ בְּהוּ כָּל בְּנֵי הֵיכָלֵיהּ, לְבָתַר אָמַר מַלְכָּא, עַ"כ אֲנָא וְאַתּוּן אִשְׁתַּדַּלְנָא כֻּלְּהוּ בְּאוּשְׁפִּיזִין, וְקָרַבְתּוּן קָרְבְּנִין עַל שְׁאָר עַמִּין בְּכָל יוֹמָא, מִכָּאן וּלְהָלְאָה, אֲנָא וְאַתּוּן נֶחֱדֵי יוֹמָא חַד, הה"ד בַּיּוֹם הַשְּׁמִינִי עֲצֶרֶת תִּהְיֶה לָכֶם. לָכֶם: לְקָרְבָא קָרְבְּנִין עֲלַייכוּ. אֲבָל אוּשְׁפִּיזֵי מְהֵימְנוּתָא, בְּמַלְכָּא מִשְׁתַּכְחֵי תְּדִירָא. וּבְיוֹמָא דְּחֶדְוָותָא דְּמַלְכָּא, כֻּלְּהוּ מִתְכַּנְּשֵׁי עִמֵּיהּ, וּמִשְׁתַּכְחָן. וְעַל דָּא כְּתִיב, עֲצֶרֶת, תַּרְגּוּמוֹ: כְּנִישׁוּ.

288. As it is written: "On the eighth day (*shmini*) you shall have a solemn assembly (*atzeret*)…." (Numbers 29:35) (This is the ending of the article from Vayechi 231) **For this day is from the King solely, His rejoicing in Israel. This is like a king who invited guests. The household people entertained them. At the end the king said** to his household, **"Until now I and you all entertained the guests. You offered sacrifices for the other nations every day,** namely the seventy bullocks. **From now on, for one day, let you and Me rejoice." This is as it says [concerning]: "On the eighth day you shall have a solemn assembly…" (Numbers 29:35) "you"** means **offering sacrifices for you. But the guests of Faith** on the seven days of Sukkot **are always with the King,** on Shmini Atzeret as well. **On the day of the King's joy they all gather to Him, and stay with Him. Hence it is written: "assembly" (*atzeret*) which is translated into Aramaic as *knishu*,** "gathering."

Jacob leads the rejoicing.

289. וְהַאי יוֹמָא, יַעֲקֹב הוּא רֵישָׁא לְחֶדְוָותָא, וְכָל אִינּוּן אוּשְׁפִּיזֵי חַדָּאן עִמֵּיהּ. וְעַ"ד כְּתִיב, אַשְׁרֶיךָ יִשְׂרָאֵל מִי כָמוֹךָ. וּכְתִיב, וַיֹּאמֶר לִי עַבְדִּי אָתָּה יִשְׂרָאֵל אֲשֶׁר בְּךָ אֶתְפָּאָר.

289. On that day, Jacob, who is Tiferet, **is the first to rejoice and all the other guests,** Abraham, Isaac, Moses, Aaron, Joseph, and David **rejoice with him. Hence it is written: "Happy are you, Israel. Who is like you…" (Deuteronomy 33:29) and "… 'You are My servant, Israel, in whom I will be glorified.'" (Isaiah 49:3)**

Through Israel, all the Supernal Candles are kindled.

290. וְיִקְחוּ אֵלֶיךָ שֶׁמֶן זַיִת זָךְ כָּתִית לַמָּאוֹר וְגוֹ', א"ר אֶלְעָזָר, הָא אוּקְמוּהָ. אֲבָל אֲמַאי אַסְמִיךְ קוּדְשָׁא בְּרִיךְ הוּא פָּרָשָׁה דָא, לְפָרָשַׁת מוֹעֲדִים. אֶלָּא, כֻּלְּהוּ בּוּצִינִין עִלָּאִין, כֻּלְּהוּ בּוּצִינִין לְאַדְלָקָא מִשַּׁח רְבוּת עִלָּאָה, וְהָא אִתְּמַר. וְעַל יְדַיְיהוּ דְיִשְׂרָאֵל, מִתְבָּרְכָאן עִלָּאִין וְתַתָּאִין, וְאַדְלִיקוּ בּוּצִינִין, כְּמָה דְאוּקְמוּהָ דִכְתִיב, שֶׁמֶן וּקְטֹרֶת יְשַׂמַּח לֵב, חֶדְוָותָא דְעִלָּאִין וְתַתָּאִין.

290. "that they bring to you pure oil olive pressed for the light…." (Leviticus 24:2) Rav Elazar said: "This was explained. But why would the Holy One, blessed be He, place this passage next to the passage of the holidays?" He answers: **"All the Supernal Candles,** namely the Sefirot, the secret of the holidays, **are all candles that light the Supernal Anointing Oil,** namely to draw the abundance of Chochmah called 'oil.' **We already learned this. Through Israel, the Upper and Lower Beings are blessed and the candles are kindled,** namely they shine upon the world. **We explained it according to the words, 'Oil and incense rejoice the heart…' (Proverbs 27:9)** namely **it gladdens the Upper and Lower Beings."**

On the Holidays we need to be in a state of joy.

291. רִבִּי אַבָּא פָּתַח, שִׂמְחוּ בַּיְיָ' וְגִילוּ צַדִּיקִים, וּכְתִיב, זֶה הַיּוֹם עָשָׂה יְיָ' נָגִילָה וְנִשְׂמְחָה בוֹ. וְאוּקְמוּהָ, דְהָא בְּקוּדְשָׁא בְּרִיךְ הוּא בָּעֵי לְמֶחֱדֵי, וּלְאַנְהָרָא אַנְפִּין, וְיִשְׁתְּכַח ב"נ בְּחֶדְוָה, בְּגִין דְהַהוּא חֶדְוָה דְקוּדְשָׁא בְּרִיךְ הוּא הֲוֵי, דִכְתִיב נָגִילָה וְנִשְׂמְחָה בוֹ בְּיוֹמָא. בּוֹ: בְּקוּדְשָׁא בְּרִיךְ הוּא, וְכֹלָּא וַחַד מִלָּה.

291. Rav Aba opened: "'Be glad in the Lord, and rejoice, you righteous....' (Psalms 32:11) and 'This is the day which the Lord has made; let us rejoice and be glad in it.' (Psalms 118:24) It was explained that one should rejoice with and display a joyous face to the Holy One, blessed be He. Man should be in a state of joy in it because that joy is of the Holy One, blessed be He, as written, '...let us rejoice and be glad in it (or 'Him').' (Ibid.) "In it" namely **on that day; 'in Him'** namely **in the Holy One, blessed be He. It is all the same matter.**

When Judgment is subdued and Mercy is roused,
Yesod and Malchut are ready to bestow abundance to the world.

292. שִׂמְחוּ בַּיְיָ', כַּד דִּינִין אִתְכַּפְיָין, וְרַחֲמֵי אִתְעֲרוּ, וְכַד מִתְעָרֵי רַחֲמֵי, כְּדֵין וְגִילוּ צַדִּיקִים, צַדִּיק וְצֶדֶק מִתְבָּרְכָאן כַּחֲדָא, דְּאִקְרוּן צַדִּיקִים, כְּמָה דְּאִתְּמַר, דְּהָא אִלֵּין מִתְבָּרְכָאן לְעָלְמִין, וְחֶדְוָאן לְעָלְמִין כֻּלְּהוּ. וְהַרְנִינוּ כָּל יִשְׁרֵי לֵב, אִלֵּין בְּנֵי מְהֵימְנוּתָא, לְאִתְקַשְּׁרָא בְּהוּ.

292. "'Be glad in the Lord...' (Psalms 32:11) namely **when Judgments are subdued and Mercy is roused. When it does, "Be glad in the Lord... you righteous." (Ibid.) The Righteous and Righteousness,** which are Yesod and Malchut, **who are called Righteous, are blessed together, as we learned. For they are blessed** to bestow plenty **upon the Worlds and cause all the Worlds to rejoice. "...and shout for joy, all you who are upright in heart" (Psalms 32:11) refers to people of Faith that should connect to them,** to Yesod and Malchut.

Pinchas

122. Shmini Atzeret

A Synopsis

Rav Shimon explains the small banquet on the eighth day, which he says is from the aspect of Malchut. He answers his son's query as to why the banquet for Israel was from the Lower Shechinah but the banquet for all seventy nations was from the Upper Mother, Binah.

Shmini Atzeret is the after-party for the members of the King's household.

832. וּבַיּוֹם הַשְּׁמִינִי עֲצֶרֶת פַּר אֶחָד אַיִל אֶחָד, הָא אוּקְמוּהָ מָארֵי מַתְנִיתִין, לְמַלְכָּא דְּזַמִּין אוּשְׁפִּיזִין, לְבָתַר דְּשָׁלַח לוֹן, אָמַר לְאִלֵּין בְּנֵי בֵּיתָא דִּילֵיהּ, אֲנָא וְאַתּוּן נַעְבִּיד סְעוּדָה קְטַנָּה. וּמַאי עֲצֶרֶת. כמד"א, זֶה יַעְצוֹר בְּעַמִּי, וְלֵית עֶצֶר אֶלָּא מַלְכוּת. מִסִּטְרָא דִּשְׁכִינְתָּא עִלָּאָה, עָבֵיד סְעוּדָתָא רַבְרְבָא, וּמִסִּטְרָא דְּמַלְכוּתָא, סְעוּדָתָא זְעֵירָא. וְנוֹהֲגִין לְמֶעְבַּד יִשְׂרָאֵל עִמָּהּ חֶדְוָה, וְאִתְקְרִיאַת שִׂמְחַת תּוֹרָה. וּמְעַטְּרָן לס"ת בְּכֶתֶר דִּילֵיהּ, רֶמֶז ס"ת לְתִפְאֶרֶת, שְׁכִינְתָּא עֲטֶרֶת תִּפְאֶרֶת.

832. "On the eighth day you shall have a solemn assembly... one bullock, one ram...." (Numbers 29:35-36) The sages of the Mishnah have already taught that the matter is to be likened to the case of a king who invites guests to his house, and after he has sent them on their way, says to the members of his household:" Let us, you and I, make a small banquet." And what is the meaning of "solemn assembly" (*atzeret*)? It is as is written: "...this one shall reign (*ya'atzor*) over My people." (I Samuel 9:17) And there is no reign apart from Malchut. For **from the aspect of the Upper Shechinah,** which is Binah, **he made the large banquet but he made the small banquet from the aspect of Malchut. And Israel are joyful with her, and she is called Simchat Torah (Joy of the Torah). They adorn the scrolls of**

the Torah with their Crowns, as the Torah alludes to Tiferet, while the Shechinah is its Crown, namely **the Crown of Tiferet.**

Why Binah is for all and Malchut is for Israel alone.

833. אָמַר ר׳ אֶלְעָזָר, אַבָּא, אֲמַאי מִסִּטְרָא דְּאִמָּא עִלָּאָה, זַמִּין לְכָל מְמַנָּן דְּכָל אוּמִין, וּמִסִּטְרָא דִּשְׁכִינְתָּא תַּתָּאָה, לָא זַמִּין אֶלָּא לְאוּמָּה יְחִידָה, לָקֳבֵל פַּר יְחִידָה.

833. Rav Elazar said: "Father, why is it that from the side of Supernal Ima, which is Binah, **He invited all the appointees of all the nations,** namely with the seventy bullocks, referred to above, **and from the side of the Lower Shechinah, He invited only a solitary nation, corresponding to the one bullock?"** Should it not have been the other way around, with Israel receiving from supernal Ima, and the ministers of the nations from Malchut?

Binah is the mother and Malchut is the betrothed daughter.

834. אָמַר לֵיהּ בְּרִי, שַׁפִּיר שְׁאִילַת. בְּגִין דְּמַלְכוּת אִיהִי רְמִיזָא לִבְרַתָּא, דְּאִיהִי צְנוּעָה בְּבֵית אָבִיהָ וְאִמָּהּ. וְאִיהִי אֲרוּסָה וְלָא נְשׂוּאָה. לָאו אוֹרַח אַרְעָא, לְמֵיכַל עִם אוּשְׁפִּיזִין. אֲבָל אִימָּא דְּהִיא נְשׂוּאָה, אוֹרַח אַרְעָא אִיהוּ בָּתַר דִּמְזַמִּין בַּעְלָהּ אוּשְׁפִּיזֵי, לְמֵיכַל עַל פָּתוֹרָא עִם בַּעְלָהּ. וְאִי אִינּוּן אוּשְׁפִּיזִין נֻכְרָאִין, לָא אַכְלֵי עִמְּהוֹן, לָא אַבָּא, וְלָא אִמָּא, וְכָל שֶׁכֵּן בְּרַתָּא. וּבְגִין כָּךְ בִּסְעוּדְתָא דְּשַׁבְעִין מְמַנָּן, לָא אִשְׁתַּתַּף לְמֵיכַל עִמְּהוֹן, וַחַד מִן מָארֵי מַלְכָּא, בְּגִין דְּאִינּוּן נוּכְרָאִין. אָמַר לֵיהּ וַדַּאי כְּעַן אִתְיַישְׁבַת מִלָּה בְּלִבָּאִי, עַל בּוּרְיֵיהּ.

834. He replied: "My son, you asked well, and the answer is that because Malchut alludes to a daughter who is hidden in the house of her father and mother, and she is engaged but not married, it is not the way of the world for her to eat with the guests. But as for the mother, who is married, it is the way of the world that when her husband invites guests, she does eat with the guests **at the table with**

her husband. And if they are foreign guests, then no one eats with them, neither father nor mother, and certainly not the daughter, who is Malchut. **This is why at the banquet for the seventy ministers not one of the members of the King's household joins in to eat with them, because they are foreigners." He said: "Surely the matter has now been settled in my heart correctly."**

Explanation: On Sukkot there are two types of guests. There are the Ushpizin (Avraham, Yitzchak, Yaakov, Moshe, Aharon, Yosef and David) of the Sukkah, the secret of the seven attributes of Holiness, and there are the 70 ministers that receive from the 70 bullocks. Both receive from the side of Supernal Ima, Binah, and not Malchut. The reason is that Binah is married to Aba, Chochmah, and is in the utmost completeness, and therefore her way is to eat with the guests, who are the Ushpizin of the Sukkah. However, Malchut is engaged and not married; even though she has unification with Zeir Anpin it is not from Her own aspect but from the aspect of her borrowing Vessels from Ima. From her own aspect She is not married at all until the Final Correction, when Her aspect will be revealed and She will have unification with Zeir Anpin. Therefore, she cannot bestow to the holy guests and definitely not the foreign guests, which are the 70 ministers.

This is: **"Because Malchut alludes to a daughter who is hidden in the house of her father and mother..."** as all her Vessels are from Aba and Ima, and her own aspect is hidden and stored in the internal of the vessels of Aba and Ima, namely in the house of Aba and Ima. **"...She is engaged but not married..."** as she does not have a unification from her own aspect until the Final Correction. **"...it is not the way of the world for her to eat with the guest..."** since she needs to be stored and covered in the Vessels of Ima, and to not be revealed. **"But as for the mother..."** is in the utmost completeness, and all abundance that exists in the Worlds in the 6,000 years come from Her, and therefore She is revealed to the guests. Nevertheless Ima is not revealed to the 70 ministers but gives them their existence in the aspect of them gradually decreasing, as they are foreign and strange to Holiness and want to draw Chochmah from above downward. Therefore, they are rejected after the seven days of Sukkot. Then He makes a small banquet to the members of his house from the aspect of Malchut. And even though She is still hidden in the Vessels of Ima, since the essence of Malchut as well receives its correction from this unification it is therefore named after Her. The matters are understood based on what we explained earlier. (Zohar, Tzav 119)

RACHEL THE MATRIARCH

Vayetze

24. "And it came to pass, when Rachel had born Joseph"

A Synopsis

This is an enigmatic passage in which Rav Elazar comments on the symbolic and mystical importance of Jacob's leaving his father-in-law, Laban, and going into the land of Israel, once Joseph has been born and Benjamin has been conceived. For these commentators, Leah symbolizes the Upper World, or all that is mysterious in life.

The Relevance of this Passage

Jacob's ability to evolve spiritually was limited during his stay with Laban. His going into the Land of Israel is a metaphor for his readiness to ascend to the level of the Upper World. The lesson for the reader is this: our physical location is a mirror of where we are spiritually. This passage awakens us to the importance of constant forward motion, both physically and spiritually, so as to continue the evolution of our souls, which is the very purpose of our life. Moreover, the act of meditating upon these verses helps our soul ascend to higher levels.

Esau's Adversary.

238. וְאָמַר רִבִּי אֶלְעָזָר, כְּתִיב וַיְהִי כַּאֲשֶׁר יָלְדָה רָחֵל אֶת יוֹסֵף וגו', מַה חָמָא יַעֲקֹב לְמֵיהַךְ לְאוֹרְחֵיהּ, כַּךְ אִתְיְלִיד יוֹסֵף, וְעַד לָא אִתְיְלִיד יוֹסֵף, לָא בָעָא לְמֵיהַךְ לְאוֹרְחֵיהּ, הָא אוֹקְמוּהָ, דְּחָמָא דְאִתְיְלִיד שִׂטְנָא דְעֵשָׂו.

238. Rav Elazar quoted: "And it came to pass, when Rachel had born Joseph...." (Genesis 30:25) He asks: **"Why did Jacob ask to leave only after Joseph was born? Before Joseph was born, he did not ask to leave."** He answers: **"As it was explained, he saw that the adversary of Esau was born,** as Joseph would be the adversary of Esau, as it is written, 'And the House of Jacob shall be fire, and the House of Joseph flame, and the house of Esau for stubble….' (Obadiah 1:18)

Joseph is Yesod.

239. וְתָא חֲזֵי, יוֹסֵף אַשְׁלִים דּוּכְתֵּיהּ בַּתְרֵיהּ וְיוֹסֵף זָכֵי לֵיהּ, דְּאִקְרֵי צַדִּיק, וְהָכָא סִיּוּמָא דְּגוּפָא. כֵּיוָן דְּחָמָא יַעֲקֹב, דְּאִשְׁתְּלִים גּוּפָא, בָּעָא גּוּפָא לְמֵיהַךְ לְאוֹרְחֵיהּ, וְסִיּוּמָא דְּגוּפָא הוּא בְּרִית. וְעִם כָּל דָּא בִּנְיָמִן אַשְׁלִים וְחוּשְׁבְּנָא, דְּבֵיהּ אִשְׁתְּלִימוּ תְּרֵיסַר.

239. "Come and see, Joseph completed the place of Jacob **after him,** being the Sefirah of Yesod, the last Sefirah of Jacob. **Also, Joseph deserved to be called Righteous,** namely Yesod, **where the ending of the body is** the last Sefirah. **After Jacob saw that the body was completed** with the birth of Joseph, **the body asked to leave. The final part of the body is the member of the Covenant,** namely Joseph. **Nevertheless, Benjamin completed the count because with him the number twelve was reached.**

Jacob wanted Perfection only in the Holy Land.

240. וְאִי תֵּימָא, וְכִי לָא הֲוָה יָדַע יַעֲקֹב, דְּעַד כְּעַן לָא אִשְׁתַּלִּימוּ שִׁבְטִין, אַף עַל גַּב דְּאִתְיְלִיד יוֹסֵף, מַאי טַעְמָא לָא אוֹרִיךְ עַד דְּיִתְיְלִיד בִּנְיָמִין, וְיִשְׁתַּלִּימוּ שִׁבְטִין. אֶלָּא, יַעֲקֹב בְּחָכְמְתָא עֲבַד, וּמִלָּה יָדַע, אֲמַר, וַדַּאי אִי אִשְׁתַּלִּימוּ הָכָא כֻּלְּהוּ שִׁבְטִין, הָא יְדַעְנָא, דְּתִקּוּנָא דִּלְעֵילָּא שַׁרְיָא עֲלַיְיהוּ כִּדְקָא יָאוֹת, וּבְאַרְעָא דָא, לָא לִיבְעֵי דְּיִשְׁתַּלִּימוּ, אֶלָּא בְּאַרְעָא קַדִּישָׁא.

240. "One may wonder, if Jacob knew that until this time the number of the Tribes was not yet complete, even though Joseph had been born, why then did he not wait for Benjamin to be born and the Tribes to reach completion?" He answers: **"Jacob acted wisely, and he did know** that the Tribes were not yet completed. **He said: 'Surely if the Tribes are completed here, then perfection will be achieved**

here; yet I do not want them to be perfected in this country—only in the Holy Land.'

The Correction of the Lower World.

241. תָּא חֲזֵי, דְּהָכֵי הוּא, דְּכֻלְּהוּ תְּרֵיסַר שִׁבְטִין, תִּקּוּנָא דְּעָלְמָא תַּתָּאָה נִּינְהוּ, וְכֵיוָן דְּאִתְיְלִיד בִּנְיָמִין, מִיתַת רָחֵל, וְנָטְלָא דוּכְתָּא הַאי עָלְמָא תַּתָּאָה, לְאִתְתַּקְּנָא בְּהוּ. וְעַ"ד לָא אִתְיְלִיד בִּנְיָמִין, אֶלָּא בְּאַרְעָא קַדִּישָׁא, הֲדָא הוּא דִּכְתִיב, וַאֲנִי בְּבֹאִי מִפַּדָּן מֵתָה עָלַי רָחֵל בְּאֶרֶץ כְּנַעַן בַּדֶּרֶךְ, וְתַמָּן מִיתַת רָחֵל וְנָטְלָא דוּכְתָּא, הַאי עָלְמָא תַּתָּאָה, לְאִתְיַשְּׁבָא בְּבֵיתָא שְׁלֵימָתָא, וְכָל זִמְנָא דְּרָחֵל קַיְּימָא, עָלְמָא תַּתָּאָה לָא אִתְתַּקְּנָא בְּהוּ, מִיתַת רָחֵל נָטְלָא, בֵּיתָא בִּשְׁלִימוּ.

241. "Come and see, all Twelve Tribes are the correction of the Lower World, the Nukva of Zeir Anpin from the Chest downward. **After Benjamin was born,** and the Twelve Tribes were completed, **Rachel died, and the Lower World,** the Nukva of Zeir Anpin, **assumed its place and was perfected through them. Therefore, Benjamin was born only in the Holy Land. This is the meaning of the verse: 'And as for me, when I came from Paddan, Rachel died by me in the land of Canaan on the way....' (Genesis 48:7) Rachel died there, and was replaced by the Lower World, which received a house in which to dwell. As long as Rachel was alive, the Lower World was not yet perfected** by the twelve tribes. **Rachel died,** became one with the Upper Nukva, **and received a completed house."**

Explanation: Nukva is not corrected by less than twelve. When She is established with Twelve Tribes, the secret of Complete Mochin with the Illumination of Chochmah, then the two Nukvas of Zeir Anpin—Rachel and Leah—become one Partzuf, where Leah is in the Interior and Rachel in the Exterior. Therefore when Benjamin was born and the Twelve Tribes were complete, then the Nukva of Zeir Anpin from the chest up, called Leah, was established in them, since they became one

Partzuf. But before the Twelve Tribes were complete, Nukva of Zeir Anpin divided to two Partzufim, both of which are incomplete. The Upper one, Leah, lacked the Tiferet-Netzach-Hod-Yesod of Zeir Anpin. And the Lower one, Rachel, lacked the Upper Three that are above the chest of Zeir Anpin. This is the secret of why Rachel died then, because the aspect of the Nukva from the chest down was nullified once the two females joined as one, as explained. This is: **"After Benjamin was born,** and the Twelve Tribes were completed, **Rachel died, and the Lower World assumed its place and was perfected through them."** The aspect of the Nukva from below the chest of Zeir Anpin was nullified, since the Lower World is corrected by Twelve Tribes and thus became one Partzuf with the Upper World, as explained.

Vayishlach

18. "If you faint in the day of adversity"

A Synopsis

The rabbis show us that it is incumbent upon man to walk the path of Righteousness and to hold tightly to the Torah. This way, we are told, the Evil Inclination becomes our Advocate rather than our Accuser and rises to vouch for us before God. The sacrifice of the he-goat on Yom Kippur follows this principle. The sacrifice engages the Evil Inclination so that he will ascend and deliver favorable testimony to God. This principle, we learn, is seen in the example of Rachel's death, which was a punishment for Jacob. Because Jacob did not fulfill his vow to God, and because he uttered a "causeless curse" when he said to Laban, "Anyone with whom you find your gods...." (Genesis 31:32) the Evil Inclination accused Rachel during a time of danger, and she perished.

The Relevance of this Passage

Spiritual Light gleams on this page, cleansing us of curses we have uttered in the past. A portion of this Light is given to the Evil Inclination, so that his words of praise replace his condemnation in the Supernal Courts protecting us from Judgments caused by our own negative deeds.

The day of trouble.

190. תָּא חֲזֵי, טוֹב יי׳ לְמָעוֹז בְּיוֹם צָרָה, מַאי בְּיוֹם צָרָה. דָּא יַעֲקֹב כַּד אָתָא עֲלֵיהּ עֵשָׂו, לְקַטְרְגָא לֵיהּ. וְיוֹדֵעַ חוֹסֵי בוֹ, כַּד אָתָא עֲלֵיהּ עָקוּ דְּדִינָא.

190. Come and see, "The Lord is good, a stronghold in the day of trouble...." (Nachum 1:7) He asks: **"What is this 'day of trouble?'"** He answers: **"This is Jacob when Esau came to accuse him. '...He**

knows them that trust in Him' (Ibid.) namely **when the pain of Judgment,** of the death of Rachel, as will be explained, **befell him.**

Jacob's unfulfilled vow caused severe Judgment.

191. וְתָא חֲזֵי, לֵית מְקַטְרְגָא אִשְׁתְּכַח עֲלֵיהּ דְּבַר נָשׁ, אֶלָּא בִּזְמְנָא דְסַכָּנָה, וְתָא חֲזֵי, בְּגִין דְּיַעֲקֹב אַחַר נִדְרֵיהּ, דִּנְדַר קַמֵּי קוּדְשָׁא בְּרִיךְ הוּא, אִתְתַּקַּף דִּינָא עַל יְדָא דִמְקַטְרְגָא, דְּקַטְרִיג עֲלֵיהּ דְּיַעֲקֹב, וּבָעָא דִינָא בְּשַׁעְתָּא דְסַכָּנָה, דַּהֲוַת רָחֵל בָּהּ, אֲמַר קַמֵּיהּ קוּדְשָׁא בְּרִיךְ הוּא, וְהָא יַעֲקֹב נָדַר נִדְרֵיהּ וְלָא שַׁלִּים, וְהָא אִיהוּ תַּקִּיף מִכֹּלָּא, בְּעוּתְרָא, וּבִבְנִין, בְּכָל מַה דְּאִצְטְרִיךְ, וְלָא שַׁלִּים נִדְרֵיהּ דִּנְדַר קַמָּךְ, וְלָא נָסַבְתְּ עוֹנְשָׁא מִנֵּיהּ, מִיָּד וַתֵּלֶד רָחֵל וַתְּקַשׁ בְּלִדְתָּהּ. מַאי וַתְּקַשׁ. דְּאִתְקַשֵּׁי דִינָא לְעֵילָא, גַּבֵּי מַלְאַךְ הַמָּוֶת.

191. Come and see, the Accuser is upon man only at a time of danger. Come and see, because Jacob was late completing **his vow, which he made before the Holy One, blessed be He, the Accuser exacted Judgment from him and demanded justice at the time when Rachel was in danger. He said to the Holy One, blessed be He, Jacob did not fulfill his vow. Although he has wealth and many sons, and lacks nothing, he did not fulfill his vow made before You, and yet You have exacted no punishment. Immediately, "...Rachel travailed and was in hard labor" (Genesis 35:16) because this was the severe Judgment that the Angel of Death above exacted from him.**

Why Rachel died.

192. וְאִתְעֲנַשׁ יַעֲקֹב בְּהַאי, מַאי טַעְמָא. בְּגִין דִּכְתִיב, וְאִם אֵין לְךָ לְשַׁלֵּם לָמָּה יִקַּח מִשְׁכָּבְךָ מִתַּחְתֶּיךָ, וְעַל דָּא מִיתַת רָחֵל, וְאִתְמְסַר דִּינָא, עַל יְדָא דְמַלְאַךְ הַמָּוֶת.

192. He asks: **"Why was Jacob punished in this manner?"** He replies: **"This is in accordance with the verse, 'If you have nothing with which to pay, why should he take away your bed from under you.'**

(Proverbs 22:27) Therefore Rachel died; this was the Judgment exacted by the Angel of Death."

Jacob was afraid for Rachel.

193. וְתָא חֲזֵי, בְּשַׁעְתָּא דַּאֲתָא עֵשָׂו, מָה עֲבַד, וַיָּשֶׂם אֶת הַשְּׁפָחוֹת וְאֶת יַלְדֵיהֶן רִאשֹׁנָה וְאֶת לֵאָה וִילָדֶיהָ אַחֲרֹנִים וְאֶת רָחֵל וְאֶת יוֹסֵף אַחֲרֹנִים, מַאי טַעְמָא, בְּגִין דְּדָחִיל עָלָהּ דְּרָחֵל, דְּלָא יִסְתַּכַּל הַהוּא רָשָׁע, בְּשַׁפִּירוּ דִּילָהּ, וְלָא יְקַטְרֵג לֵיהּ עֲלָהּ.

193. Come and see, what did Jacob **do when Esau came? "And he put the handmaids and their children foremost, and Leah and her children after, and Rachel and Joseph last of all." (Genesis 33:2) What prompted him to do so? He was afraid for Rachel, lest that wicked man should behold her beauty and attack him because of it.**

How Joseph protected Rachel.

194. תוּ, מַה כְּתִיב, וַתִּגַּשְׁןָ הַשְּׁפָחוֹת הֵנָּה וְיַלְדֵיהֶן וַתִּשְׁתַּחֲוֶיןָ. וַתִּגַּשׁ גַּם לֵאָה וִילָדֶיהָ וַיִּשְׁתַּחֲווּ, נָשִׁין מִקַּמֵּי גּוּבְרִין. אֲבָל בְּרָחֵל מַה כְּתִיב, וְאַחַר נִגַּשׁ יוֹסֵף וְרָחֵל, וְיוֹסֵף מִקַּמֵּי אִמֵּיהּ, וְאִיהוּ חָפָא עֲלָהּ, וְעַל דָּא כְּתִיב, בֵּן פֹּרָת יוֹסֵף בֵּן פֹּרָת עֲלֵי עָיִן, דְּאַסְגֵּי גּוּפֵיהּ, וְחָפָא עַל אִמֵּיהּ. עֲלֵי עָיִן: עֲלֵי עֵינָא דְּהַהוּא רָשָׁע.

194. It is also written: "Then the handmaidens came near, they and their children, and they bowed themselves. And Leah also with her children came near, and bowed themselves..." (Genesis 33:6-7), the women before the men. But of Rachel the verse says, "...and after came Joseph near and Rachel." (Ibid.) Joseph stood before his mother, covering, and concealing her. Thus the words, "Joseph is a fruitful bough, a fruitful bough by a well" (Genesis 49:22) whose body grew bigger to protect his mother; "by a well (lit. 'on the eye')" on the eye of that wicked one, so that he would not see her.

Rachel died because of Jacob.

195. וְהָכָא אִתְעֲנָשַׁת עַל יְדָא דְּיֵצֶר הָרָע, דְּקָטְרֵג בְּשַׁעְתָּא דְסַכָּנָה, וְאִתְעֲנַשׁ
יַעֲקֹב, עַל נִדְרָא דְּלָא שְׁלִים, וְדָא קַשְׁיָא לֵיהּ לְיַעֲקֹב, מִכָּל עָקוּ דַּעֲבָרוּ
עֲלֵיהּ. וּמְנָלָן דִּבְגִינֵיהּ דְּיַעֲקֹב הֲוָה, דִּכְתִיב מֵתָה עָלַי רָחֵל: עָלַי וַדַּאי, עַל
דַּאֲחָרִית נִדְרִי.

195. Here, Rachel was punished by the Evil Inclination, which
accused her in a time of danger and punished Jacob for his unfulfilled
vow. This was harder for Jacob than all his previous troubles. We
know that Rachel died because of Jacob from the words, "...Rachel
died by me..." (Genesis 48:7); surely this happened because of me,
because I tarried in fulfilling my vow.

The danger for Righteous Men to curse.

196. רִבִּי יוֹסֵי אָמַר, כְּתִיב קִלְלַת חִנָּם לֹא תָבֹא. וְאוֹקְמוּהָ לוֹ בְּוי"ו, דְּאִי קִלְלַת
צַדִּיקָא הִיא, אֲפִילוּ דְּלָא אִתְכַּוַּון בָּהּ, כֵּיוָן דְּנָפְקָא מִפּוּמֵיהּ, נָטַל לָהּ הַהוּא יֵצֶר
הָרָע, וְקָטְרֵג בָּהּ בְּשַׁעְתָּא דְסַכָּנָה.

196. Rav Yosi said, "It is written, '...so a vain curse shall not come
(*lo tavo*; לֹא תָבֹא).' (Proverbs 26:2) This has been explained as *lo* (to
him, לוֹ) with a Vav (ו), thus it reads: '...so a vain curse shall come to
him.' (Ibid.) This teaches us that once a Righteous Man curses, even
if he did not mean to curse, it is received by the Evil Inclination, who
uses it to accuse in times of danger.

The Satan accuses us if we curse.

197. יַעֲקֹב אָמַר, עִם אֲשֶׁר תִּמְצָא אֶת אֱלֹהֶיךָ לֹא יִחְיֶה. וְאַף עַל גַּב דְּאִיהוּ
לָא הֲוָה יָדַע, נָטִיל לָהּ לְהַהִיא מִלָּה הַהוּא שָׂטָן, דְּאִשְׁתְּכַח גַּבַּיְיהוּ תָּדִיר בִּבְנֵי
נָשָׁא. וְעַל דָּא תָּנֵינָן, לְעוֹלָם לֹא יִפְתַּח בַּר נָשׁ פּוּמֵיהּ לְשִׂטְנָא, בְּגִין דְּנָטִיל הַהִיא

מִלָּה, וְקַטְרַג בָּהּ, לְעֵילָּא וְתַתָּא, כָּל שֶׁכֵּן מִלָּה דְחָכָם, אוֹ מִלָּה דְצַדִּיקָא, וְעַל תְּרֵין אִלֵּין אִתְעֲנָשַׁת רָחֵל.

197. Jacob said, "Anyone with whom you find your gods, let him not live…." (Genesis 31:32) Although he did not know that Rachel had stolen them, **the Satan, who constantly abides among men, heard these words** and used them to accuse in a time of danger. **We therefore learned that a man should never open his mouth for the Satan because he takes that utterance and uses it to accuse Above and Below, especially if the utterance came from the mouth of a Righteous Man or a sage. Rachel was punished for two reasons:** because Jacob was late in fulfilling his vow, and because of the curse he uttered.

19. "And it came to pass, as her soul was departing"

A Synopsis

Although the soul may depart the body and return during one's lifetime, Rachel's soul did not return and she died. Before she died, she named her last-born child Ben-oni, because of the severe Judgment against her. Jacob then renamed his youngest son Benjamin, also to bind him to the Right Side, just as he attached Rachel to Mercy.

The Relevance of this Passage

This section helps deepen our understanding of the importance of names, and of their influence on our destiny through the attraction or deflection of the Light. We achieve a greater connection to our own name and the particular influences that it radiates.

The soul of Rachel departed and did not return.

198. וַיְהִי בְּצֵאת נַפְשָׁהּ כִּי מֵתָה. אָמַר רִבִּי אַבָּא, וְכִי כֵּיוָן דְּאָמַר וַיְהִי בְּצֵאת נַפְשָׁהּ, לָא יָדַעְנָא כִּי מֵתָה. אֶלָּא אִצְטְרִיךְ, בְּגִין דְּלָא אַהַדְרַת לְגוּפָא יַתִּיר, וּמִיתַת רָחֵל מִיתַת גּוּפָא, בְּגִין דְּאִית בְּנֵי נָשָׁא, דְּנָפְקֵי נִשְׁמָתַיְיהוּ וְאַהַדְרָן לְאַתְרַיְיהוּ, וּכְד״א, וַתָּשָׁב נַפְשׁוֹ אֵלָיו, וַיֵּצֵא לִבָּם, נַפְשִׁי יָצְאָה בְדַבְּרוֹ, לֹא נוֹתְרָה בּוֹ נְשָׁמָה. אֲבָל הַאי, נָפְקַת נִשְׁמָתָהּ, וְלָא אִתְהַדְּרַת לְאַתְרָהּ, וּמִיתַת רָחֵל.

198. "And it came to pass, as her soul was departing for she died...." (Genesis 35:18) Rav Aba asks: "Once it said, '...as her soul was departing...' do we not know that she died?" Why does the verse continue with the words, "...for she died?" He replies: "The words, '... for she died,' **were necessary** to indicate that the soul **did not return to the body, and she died the death of the body.** The departure of the soul is not an indication of the death of the body, **for there are people whose souls departed and later returned to their places. This is the meaning of the verses, '...and his spirit returned to him...' (I Samuel 30:12); '...And their heart departed...' (Genesis 42:28); '... my soul departed...' (Song of Songs 5:6); and '...until there was no soul left in him.' (I Kings 17:17) But when** Rachel's **soul departed, it did not return, and she died.**

Benjamin is the Son of the Right.

199. וַתִּקְרָא שְׁמוֹ בֶּן אוֹנִי. דְּקַשְׁיוּ דְּדִינָא דְּאִתְגְּזַר עֲלָהּ. וְיַעֲקֹב אַהֲדַר לֵיהּ, וְקָשִׁיר לֵיהּ בִּימִינָא, בְּגִין דְּמַעֲרָב אִצְטְרִיךְ לְקַשְּׁרָא לֵיהּ לִימִינָא, וְאַף עַל גַּב דְּאִיהוּ בֶּן אוֹנִי, סִטְרָא דְּדִינָא קַשְׁיָא, בֶּן יָמִין אִיהוּ, דְּהָא בִּימִינָא אִתְקַשְּׁרַת.

199. "...that she called his name Ben-oni" (Genesis 35:18) because of the Harsh Judgment decided against her. Jacob, however, went back and tied him to the Right, namely to Chasadim **because one needs to tie the west,** the Nukva, **to the Right. And though he is**

Ben-oni **(lit. 'the Son of sorrow')** of the Nukva **from the aspect of Harsh Judgment,** nevertheless **he is the Son of the Right (*Ben Yamin*) because** the Nukva **became attached to the Right.** He therefore called him Ben-yamin, namely the Son of the Right because he attached Rachel to the Right, to Chasadim.

Rachel was buried in the open and Leah was buried in a concealed place.

200. וְאִתְקְבָרַת בְּאָרְחָא, כְּמָה דְּאִתְּמַר, הָאי אִתְגַּלְיָא מִיתָתָהּ וּקְבוּרָתָהּ, אֲבָל לֵאָה לָא אִתְגַּלְיָא מִיתָתָהּ וּקְבוּרָתָהּ. וְאַף עַל גַּב דְּהַנֵּי אַרְבַּע אִמָּהָן רָזָא אִית לוֹן, וְהָא אוֹקְמוּהָ.

200. She was buried by the road, as was said. Her death and place of burial were revealed, and she was buried by the road in an open place, **but the death and burial place of Leah was not revealed. Although the four mothers share a secret, as has already been explained.**

20. "And Jacob set a pillar"

A Synopsis

This section explains the significance of the phrase, "to this day," which is attached to the title quotation. While Rav Yosi interprets this as a reference to the day when God resurrects the dead, Rav Yehuda explains that it is a reference to the day when the children of Israel return from exile, in accordance with the oath that God swore to the Shechinah. At that time, the children of Israel will weep for Rachel, as she wept for their exile – and Rachel, Israel, and the Shechinah shall rejoice together by the side of the road.

The Relevance of this Passage

A reading of this section accelerates the end of exile for the children of Israel. Moreover, this Light hastens the final Redemption and Resurrection for mankind. On a personal level, this Divine energy helps resurrect areas of our lives that have been disconnected from the Light. We literally gain freedom from the forces of death.

Leah's burial site stays hidden until the Resurrection of the Dead.

201. וַיַּצֵּב יַעֲקֹב מַצֵּבָה עַל קְבוּרָתָהּ, אָמַר רִבִּי יוֹסֵי, מַאי טַעְמָא. בְּגִין דְּלָא אִתְכַּסְיָא אַתְרָהּ, עַד יוֹמָא דְּזַמִּין קוּדְשָׁא בְּרִיךְ הוּא, לְאַחֲיָיא מֵתַיָּיא, כְּמָה דְּאִתְּמַר, עַד הַיּוֹם, עַד הַהוּא יוֹמָא מַמָּשׁ.

201. "And Jacob set a pillar upon her grave." Rav Yosi asks: "Why does the scripture add the words, "to this day?" He replies: **"Because her burial place will remain uncovered until the day when the Holy One, blessed be He, will raise the dead. Thus, it is said, 'to this day,' the very day** of resurrections."

Rachel will rejoice with Israel and the Shechinah.

202. רִבִּי יְהוּדָה אָמַר, עַד יוֹמָא, דְּתֶהֱדַר שְׁכִינְתָּא בְּגָלוּתְהוֹן דְּיִשְׂרָאֵל, בְּהַהוּא אֲתַר, כְּדָבָר אֲחֵר וְיֵשׁ תִּקְוָה לְאַחֲרִיתֵךְ נְאֻם יי' וְשָׁבוּ בָנִים לִגְבוּלָם. וְדָא אוּמָאָה, דְּאוּמֵי לָהּ קוּדְשָׁא בְּרִיךְ הוּא. וּזְמִינִין יִשְׂרָאֵל, כַּד יְתוּבוּן מִן גָּלוּתָא, לְקָיְימָא עַל הַהִיא קְבוּרָה דְּרָחֵל, וּלְמִבְכֵּי תַּמָּן, כְּמָה דְּאִיהִי בָּכַאת עַל גָּלוּתְהוֹן דְּיִשְׂרָאֵל, וְעַל דָּא כְּתִיב, בִּבְכִי יָבֹאוּ וּבְתַחֲנוּנִים אוֹבִילֵם וגו'. וּכְתִיב כִּי יֵשׁ שָׂכָר לִפְעֻלָּתֵךְ. וּבְהַהִיא שַׁעְתָּא, זְמִינַת רָחֵל, דְּאִיהִי בְּאָרְחָא, לְמֶחֱדֵי בְּהוֹ בְּיִשְׂרָאֵל, וְעִם שְׁכִינְתָּא, וְאוּקְמוּהָ חַבְרַיָּיא.

202. Rav Yehuda said that "to this day" refers to the day when the Shechinah shall return Israel from exile to Rachel's burial **place, as it is written: "And there is hope for your future, says The Lord, and your children shall come back again to their own border." (Jeremiah 31:16) This is the oath the Holy One, blessed be He, swore** to the Shechinah. **And Israel, when they return from exile, will stand by Rachel's grave and weep, as she wept for the exile of Israel. The scripture therefore reads, "They shall come with weeping, and**

with supplications will I lead them" (Ibid. 8), and "for your work shall be rewarded." (Ibid. 15) At that time, Rachel will rejoice by the road together with Israel and the Shechinah, as the friends have explained.

Vayechi

11. "Rachel died by me on the way"

A Synopsis

Rav Aba begins by explaining the discrepancy in the verb tense in "they have come back," (Jeremiah 31:16) used in the Creator's promise for the future. Rav Aba then explains how Rav Elazar answers that the Shechinah will think her children have died through Judgement. Only then will She return to Her Husband. "Rachel weeping" refers to the Shechinah being told by Her Husband that Her children have perished. Only then will He tell Her that her children have been redeemed. God then tells Her that those who have died in the war will be resurrected. Rav Shimon tells us that the quotation refers to the Shechinah's children who die in the war but are resurrected and will return to Efrat, the land of Israel. Rav Aba finally explains the meaning of Bread (*Lechem*), derived from [the words] war (*milchamah*) and fought (*lacham*).

The Relevance of this Passage

Two paths to the Final Redemption lie before us, a path of Destruction, war and death, and a path of Mercy that offers us protection, the path of spiritual transformation. We have the free will to choose our fate. In the end, all the souls of humankind will be resurrected and the arrival of the Messiah will bring immortality and endless fulfillment. The Light that radiates from this passage of Zohar awakens the wisdom to walk the path of spiritual transformation. It helps accelerate the arrival of the Resurrection and the Messiah through the path of Mercy for all mankind.

The children have already returned.

81. וַאֲנִי בְּבֹאִי מִפַּדָּן מֵתָה עָלַי רָחֵל בַּדֶּרֶךְ וגו', רִבִּי אַבָּא פָּתַח, כֹּה אָמַר ה' קוֹל בְּרָמָה נִשְׁמָע וגו', מַה כְּתִיב בַּתְרֵיהּ, כֹּה אָמַר ה' מִנְעִי קוֹלֵךְ מִבֶּכִי וְעֵינַיִךְ

מִדִּמְעָה כִּי יֵשׁ שָׂכָר לִפְעוּלָּתֵךְ וגו׳ וְשָׁבוּ בָנִים לִגְבוּלָם לֹא אָמַר וְיָשׁוּבוּ, אֶלָּא וְשָׁבוּ, כְּבָר שָׁבוּ.

81. "And as for me, when I came from Paddan, Rachel died by me…." (Genesis 48:7) Rav Aba opened: "Thus said the Lord: 'A voice was heard in Rama…'" (Jeremiah 31:15) what is written thereafter? "Thus says the Lord: 'Keep your voice from weeping, and your eyes from tears, for your work shall be rewarded,' says the Lord; and they shall (lit. 'they have') come back again to their own border." (Jeremiah 31:16) He asks: **"It does not say 'They shall come back'** in the future tense **but that they have come back.** Yet this is a promise for the future, and it should have been 'and they shall come back.'"

The Shechinah thinks her children died through Judgment, but it is not so.

82. תָּא חֲזֵי אָמַר רִבִּי אֶלְעָזָר, בְּשַׁעְתָּא דִּיהֵא דִּינָא עַל טוּרָא, תִּתְעַטַּר מַטְרוֹנִיתָא עַל טוּרָא, וְהִיא סָבְרַת דִּבְנַיְיהוּ אַבְדִין בְּדִינָא, וְרָזָא רָנִּי עֲקָרָה לֹא יָלָדָה פִּצְחִי רִנָּה וְצַהֲלִי וגו׳, תָּנָא, סַגִּיאִין יְהוֹן בְּנֵי כָּרְסַיָּיא, מִן דִּידָהּ, הה״ד כִּי רַבִּים בְּנֵי שׁוֹמֵמָה מִבְּנֵי בְעוּלָה, תֵּיתוּב מַטְרוֹנִיתָא לְבַעֲלָהּ, בַּיּוֹם הַהוּא יִהְיֶה ה׳ אֶחָד וּשְׁמוֹ אֶחָד.

82. He answers: **"Come and see, Rav Elazar said that when there will be Judgment upon the mountain, and the Shechinah will be adorned on the mountain, She will think Her children perished through Judgment** but it is not so. **The secret is, 'Sing, barren one, you who bore no child; break forth into singing, and cry aloud….' (Isaiah 54:1) We have learned that many children of the Throne will be Her own** children, **as it is written, '…For more are the children of the desolate than the children of the married wife….' (Ibid.) The Shechinah will then return to Her Husband. '…on that day the Lord shall be One, and His Name One.'" (Zechariah 14:9)**

Explanation of the matter. You already know that the Shechinah has two states. The first is when She is fourth to the Patriarchs, when her stature is equal to Zeir Anpin, the secret of Chesed-Gevurah-Tiferet that are called Patriarchs and are called Mountains. This is when they are both Thrones to Binah: He [Zeir Anpin] is the three legs of the Throne, which are Chesed-Gevurah-Tiferet called Mountains, and the Shechinah is the fourth leg of the Throne. Then She too is considered a Mountain like Chesed-Gevurah-Tiferet. In this state She is in the aspect of Back and Judgments. The second state is when She gets rebuilt in the aspect of Front and Mercy. Then her stature gets diminished and she is no longer fit to be a Throne to Binah, but rather she becomes a recipient to Zeir Anpin, meaning that she descends to the aspect of Netzach-Hod-Yesod. They then have a unification in the aspect of Face-to-Face and Mercy. All the Mochin and the birth of the souls of Israel come from this second state because in the first state She is full of Judgment, and all who receive from Her then are obliterated.

This is: **"when there will be Judgment upon the mountain..."** namely when the Shechinah will be in the first state, when she ascends to Chesed-Gevurah-Tiferet that are Mountians, then the Judgments rule over the Mountain, as mentioned earlier, **"the Shechinah will be adorned on the mountain,"** as she receives great Mochin like Zeir Anpin and becomes the aspect of a Throne to Binah like Him, in the secret of the fourth leg, as mentioned earlier, **"She will think her children perished through Judgment,"** namely She considers all who receive from Her in this state as obliterated due to the many Judgments that are bestowed by Her in this first state, as mentioned earlier. Therefore the Shechinah in this state is called "barren," as She has no children, namely recipients, as anyone who receives from Her perishes.

"The secret is, 'Sing, barren one, you who bore no child...'" (Isaiah 54:1) namely in the Final Correction when the essence of Malchut will be completely corrected and she will not need any more sweetening from Binah, then it is said **"Sing, barren one..."** **(Ibid)** And we have learned that it is because **"many children of the Throne will be Her own** children" because all those who received from Her in the first state when She was in the level of a Throne to Binah, who perished from the world due to all the Judgments, as mentioned earlier, now all resurrect. Thus although Shechinah thought of Herself as barren without children in the first state, She will now see that the children from the state of the Throne are more abundant than Her own children, namely children from the second state, which before the correction was the only one who had children, as mentioned earlier.

"As it is written, 'For more are the children of the desolate...'" meaning that the children of the Throne are greater **"'...than the children of the married wife,'"** **(Isaiah 54:1)** namely the children of the second state, who was the only one who was married and had children. This is why it concludes with: **"The Shechinah will then return to Her Husband"** in the secret of **"'...on that day the Lord shall be One, and His Name One'"** **(Zechariah 14:9)** because before the Final Correction it is said only "the Lord is One," because the Shechinah is included in Zeir Anpin called Lord (Yud-Hei-Vav-Hei), but in the Final Correction it is said "... and His Name is One" because she will be corrected in her own right.

The secret of Rachel's weeping.

83. מִן קַדְמַת דְּנָא, תֵּימָא מַטְרוֹנִיתָא לְקוּדְשָׁא בְּרִיךְ הוּא בְּנַיָּיא דִילִי אָן. יֵימָא לָהּ בְּדִינָא. הִיא תִּסְבַּר דְּאָבְדִין בְּדִינָא, וּבְכָה עַל דִּינָא לִבְנַיָּא דִידָהּ, כִּי אֲרֵי סַגִּי אִית לָךְ לְמֵיסַב מִנֵּי בְּדִלְהוֹן, דַּהֲוַת עִמְּהוֹן, וְהָא תָּבוּ מֵאַרְעָא דְשִׂנְאָה.

83. Before that, the Shechinah will say to Her husband, "Where are my children from the first state?" **He will say to Her that they were judged, and She will think they perished by Judgment, and weep for Her children, who perished by justice.** This is the secret of "A voice was heard in Rama... Rachel weeping for her children," and He will say to her, "Keep your voice from weeping... for your work shall be rewarded." **For you are to be greatly rewarded by Me for being with them, and the children have already come back from the hated land,** for they have already been redeemed.

Explanation: This answers the question of why it says "they have come back again to their own border" in past tense, as it asked in verse 81. When the Holy One, blessed be He, answered Her "for your work shall be rewarded" it was already the Final Correction, and the children already returned to their borders, as explained.

The Creator promises the return of all sons, including the deceased.

84. וְכִי לָא הֲוָה יָדַע יוֹסֵף דְּמֵיתָה אִמֵּיהּ, תַּמָּן הֲוָה עִמָּהּ כַּד מֵיתָה. אֶלָּא יֵאמַר יִשְׂרָאֵל עִלָּאָה, כַּד נָּיְיתֵי מִפֻּרְקָנֵיהוֹן דְּיִשְׂרָאֵל, תִּתְעַר מַטְרוֹנִיתָא, וְתִתְעַר כ"י, וְתַגִּיחַ קְרָבָא עִם עַמְמִין, וִימוּתוּן מִנְּהוֹן, וְיִתְקָרְבוּן בְּזְעֵיר לְמֵיתֵי אַרְעָא, יֵימַר לָהּ קוּדְשָׁא בְּרִיךְ הוּא, כַּד הִיא בָּכָה, לָא תִּדְחֲלִי, אַגְרָא לְהוֹן בְּנַיָּיא דְּמִיתָן עַל שְׁמִי, אָחֳרָנִין הָא תָּבוּ, אִינּוּן יְתוּבוּן לְחַיֵּי מֵיתַיָּיא.

84. He asks: **"Did Joseph not know his mother died? Was he not with her when she died?"** Why did Jacob have to tell him that? He answers: **"Supernal Israel said that when he prophesied about the redemption of Israel, the Shechinah will awaken, and the Congregation of Israel will awaken and wage war against the nations. Some** of Israel **will die** in this war. **They will slowly approach the land of Israel. When She weeps** for Her dead sons, **the Holy One, blessed be He, will say to Her, 'Do not be afraid, there is a reward for the sons who died** in the war **for My Name's sake. The others, who did not die, have already returned and those who died will live again through the Resurrection of the Dead.'"**

In the land of Israel, none of the sons shall die.

85. מֵתָה עָלַי רָחֵל, מֵתָה עַל יִיחוּד שְׁמָא דְקוּדְשָׁא בְּרִיךְ הוּא, וְעַ"ד אִתְּמַר בְּעוֹד כִּבְרַת אֶרֶץ לָבֹא, דְּמִיתוּ עַל יִיחוּד שְׁמָא דְקוּדְשָׁא בְּרִיךְ הוּא, לְבַר לְאַרְעָא, בְּאַרְעָא דָא, לָא יָמוּת חַד מִנַּהוֹן.

85. "Rachel died by me." She died for the unity of the Name of the Holy One, blessed be He, namely her sons who were killed for the Sanctification of the Holy Name. **About this it says: "...when still some distance short of** Efrat..." **(Genesis 48:7),** meaning that **they died for the unity of the Name of the Holy One, blessed be He, outside the land of Israel,** at the war to enter Israel. **For in this land,** in the land of Israel, **none of them shall die.** Therefore scripture says, "...when still some distance short of Efrat..." (Ibid.), meaning the land of Israel, since after coming to the land of Israel they will die no more.

A future war on the road of Efrat.

86. תָּנָא, א"ר אַבָּא, עֲתִידִין יִשְׂרָאֵל לְאַגָּחָא קְרָבָא בְּאָרְחָא דְאֶפְרָת, וִימוּתוּן עַמָּא סַגְיָא מִנַּהוֹן, וּבָתַר כֵּן לְזַמְנֵי מֵיתַיָא יְקוּמוּן, וְיַתִּיר שָׁלְטָנָא יְהֵא לְכוֹן דְּמִיתִין בְּאָרְחָא הָדֵין, מִכָּל דְּיֵהָא קָדָמֵיהוֹן בִּירוּשְׁלֵם.

86. We have learned that Rav Aba said: "Israel will be engaged in war on the way to Efrat, and many of them will die. Afterwards they will rise at the Resurrection of the Dead, and will have more power than those who reached Jerusalem before them, who did not die in the war."

The completion of Yud-Hei-Vav-Hei.

87. וְלָמָּה אִתְקְרֵי שְׁמָא דְּאַתְרָא קַדִּישָׁא, דְּאַתְרָא הָדֵין לֶחֶם, בְּגִּ"ל דְּהוּא מִן שְׁמָא דְקוּדְשָׁא בְּרִיךְ הוּא בֵּיהּ, דְּיִמוּתוּן תַּמָּן עַל שְׁמֵיהּ, י"ד: דְּיִמוּתוּן תַּמָּן עַל שְׁמֵיהּ י"ה, לֶחֶם בְּגָלוּתָא, בְּגִּ"ל דְּהוּא מִן שְׁמֵיהּ דְּקוּדְשָׁא בְּרִיךְ הוּא.

87. Why is this Holy Place called Lechem (bread), as it is written "... that is Bet Lechem"? (Genesis 48:7) He answers: **"Since it is one of the Names of the Holy One, blessed be He, they will die there** in war **for sanctifying His Name, "hand** on the Throne of *Yah* (י"ה)... war...." (Exodus 17:16) This means **they will die there** to make complete **the Name *Yah*,** since the Name is not complete in Yud-Hei-Vav-Hei (יהוה) until the memory of Amalek shall be blotted out. Therefore the purpose of this war is to complete the Name of Yud-Hei (יה) with Vav-Hei (וה). Thus the place is called Lechem (לחם) derived from *milchamah* (war; add Hebrew), **for it fought (*lacham;* לחם) in exile to complete the Name of the Holy One, blessed be He.**

Va'era

17. "And the River shall bring forth frogs in swarms"

Rav Shimon questions why only Rachel wept, and not Leah.

146. וְשָׁרַץ הַיְאוֹר צְפַרְדְּעִים וְעָלוּ וּבָאוּ בְּבֵיתֶךָ. ר' שִׁמְעוֹן פָּתַח וְאָמַר, קוֹל בְּרָמָה נִשְׁמָע נְהִי בְּכִי תַמְרוּרִים רָחֵל מְבַכָּה עַל בָּנֶיהָ וְגוֹ'. תָּא חֲזֵי, הַאי קְרָא אוּקְמוּהָ בְּכַמָּה אַתְרֵי. וְהַאי קְרָא קַשְׁיָא, רָחֵל מְבַכָּה עַל בָּנֶיהָ, בְּנָהָא דְּרָחֵל יוֹסֵף וּבִנְיָמִין הֲווֹ וְלָא יַתִּיר, וְלֵאָה שִׁית שִׁבְטִין הֲווֹ דִּילָהּ, אֲמַאי בָּכַת רָחֵל וְלֹא לֵאָה.

146. "And the River shall bring forth frogs in swarms, and these will go up and come into your house...." (Exodus 7:28) Rav Shimon opened and said, "'... "A voice was heard in Ramah, lamentation, and bitter weeping; Rachel weeping for her children..."' (Jeremiah 31:15) Come and see, this passage has been explained in many places. But this passage is difficult, for it says, '...Rachel weeping for her children...' (Jeremiah 31:15) yet only Joseph and Benjamin were the children of Rachel and no more, while Leah had her six tribes, so why did Rachel weep and not Leah?"

Leah feared falling into Esau's fate.

147. אֶלָּא הָכִי אָמְרוּ כְּתִיב, וְעֵינֵי לֵאָה רַכּוֹת. אֲמַאי רַכּוֹת. בְּגִין דְּכָל יוֹמָא נַפְקַת לְפָרָשַׁת אוֹרְחִין, וְשָׁאֲלַת עַל עֵשָׂו, וַהֲווֹ אַמְרִין לָהּ עוֹבָדוֹי דְּהַהוּא רָשָׁע, וְדָחִילַת לְמִנְפַּל בְּגוֹ עַדְבֵיהּ, וַהֲוַת בָּכַת כָּל יוֹמָא, עַד דְּאִתְרְכָכוּ עֵינָהָא.

147. He answers: **"Rather this is what they said. It is written, 'And Leah's eyes were weak....' (Genesis 29:17) Why were they weak? Because every day she would go out to the crossroads and ask about Esau. They would tell her about the actions of that wicked man, and**

she feared she would fall into his lot, so she wept daily until her eyes became weak.

Since Leah cried over Jacob, she was buried next to him.

148. וְקוּדְשָׁא בְּרִיךְ הוּא אָמַר, אַנְתְּ בָּכַת בְּגִין הַהוּא צַדִּיקָא, דְּלָא תֶּהֱוֵי בְּעַדְבֵיהּ דְּהַהוּא רָשָׁע. חַיָּיךְ, אֲחָתָךְ תְּקוּם בְּפָרָשַׁת אָרְחִין, וְתִבְכֵּי עַל גָּלוּתְהוֹן דְּיִשְׂרָאֵל, וְאַתְּ תְּקוּם לְגוֹ וְלָא תִּבְכֵּי עָלַיְיהוּ וְרָחֵל אִיהִי בָּכַת עַל גָּלוּתְהוֹן דְּיִשְׂרָאֵל.

148. "The Holy One, blessed be He, said, 'You are weeping to merit that righteous man, Jacob, and not be the lot of that wicked man? Upon your life, your sister will rise at the crossroads and weep over the exile of Israel. But you will be inside, namely in the Cave of Machpelah, **and will not weep over them. Rachel will be the one to weep over the exile of Israel.'**

Rachel and Leah are two Worlds.

149. אֲבָל הַאי קְרָא, אִיהוּ עַל מַה דְּאַמָרָן. אֲבָל רָזָא דְּמִלָּה, דְּרָחֵל וְלֵאָה תְּרֵי עָלְמִין נִינְהוּ. חַד עָלְמָא דְּאִתְכַּסְיָא, וְחַד עָלְמָא דְּאִתְגַּלְיָא. וע"ד, דָּא אִתְקַבְּרַת וְאִתְחַפִּיאַת לְגוֹ בִּמְעַרְתָּא וְאִתְכַּסִּיאַת. וְדָא קַיְּימָא בְּפָרָשַׁת אָרְחִין בְּאִתְגַּלְיָא. וְכֹלָּא כְּגַוְונָא עִלָּאָה. וּבְגִין כַּךְ לָא אָעִיל לָהּ יַעֲקֹב בִּמְעַרְתָּא, וְלָא בַּאֲתַר אַחֲרָא, דְּהָא כְּתִיב בְּעוֹד כִּבְרַת אֶרֶץ לָבוֹא אֶפְרָתָה, וְלָא אָעִיל לָהּ לְמָתָא. בְּגִין דַּהֲוָה יָדַע דְּאַתְרָהּ הֲוָה בְּאַתְרָא דְּאִתְגַּלְיָא.

149. "However this passage really refers to what we said, meaning that according to the literal meaning it is interpreted this way, **but the secret meaning of the matter is that Rachel and Leah are two Worlds.** The Nukva from the chest up of Zeir Anpin is called Leah, and the Nukva that is from the chest down of Zeir Anpin is called Rachel. **One is the World of Concealment,** namely Leah, **and one is the World of Revelation,** namely Rachel. **Therefore the one,** Leah,

was buried and concealed within the cave and was covered, while the other, Rachel, **remains at the crossroads,** for she was buried on the way to Ephrat, **in the open. And everything is in the likeness of Above. Therefore Jacob did not bring** Rachel **into the cave or to any other place, as it is written, '...yet there was but a little way to come to Ephrat....' (Genesis 48:7) He did not bring her to the city, because he knew that her place was in an open spot.**

Why Rachel becomes mute.

150. תָּא וַחֲזֵי, כְּנֶסֶת יִשְׂרָאֵל הָכִי אִקְרֵי, רָחֵל. כְּמָה דְּאַתְּ אָמֵר, וּכְרָחֵל לִפְנֵי גוֹזְזֶיהָ נֶאֱלָמָה. אֲמַאי נֶאֱלָמָה. דְּכַד שַׁלְטִין שְׁאַר עַמִּין, קָלָא אִתְפְּסָק מִינָהּ, וְהִיא אִתְאַלְּמַת.

150. "Come and see, the Congregation of Israel, which is Malchut, **is called Rachel, as it is written, '...And as a sheep (*rachel*) before her shearers is mute....' (Isaiah 53:7)"** [He asks:] **"Why is she mute?"** [He answers:] "It is **because her voice,** which is Zeir Anpin, **is stopped when other nations rule, and she becomes mute.**

Rachel weeps as long as Israel are in exile.

151. וְדָא הוּא דִּכְתִּיב, קוֹל בְּרָמָה נִשְׁמָע נְהִי בְּכִי תַּמְרוּרִים. קוֹל בְּרָמָה נִשְׁמָע דָּא יְרוּשָׁלַיִם לְעֵילָּא. רָחֵל מְבַכָּה עַל בָּנֶיהָ, כָּל זִמְנָא דְּיִשְׂרָאֵל אִינּוּן בְּגָלוּתָא, אִיהִי מְבַכָּה עֲלַיְיהוּ דְּאִיהִי אִימָּא דִּלְהוֹן. מֵאֲנָה לְהִנָּחֵם עַל בָּנֶיהָ. מ"ט. כִּי אֵינֶנּוּ. כִּי אֵינָם מִבָּעֵי לֵיהּ. אֶלָּא, בְּגִין דְּבַעְלָהּ דְּאִיהוּ קוֹל, אִסְתַּלַּק מִינָהּ, וְלָא אִתְחַבַּר בַּהֲדָהּ.

151. "This is the meaning of, 'A voice was heard in Ramah, lamentation, and bitter weeping...' (Jeremiah 31:15) 'A voice was heard in Ramah...' (Ibid.) refers to Celestial Jerusalem, namely Binah. **'Rachel weeping for her children' (Ibid.): As long as Israel are in exile, she weeps for them because she is their mother. '...she**

refused to be comforted for her children…' (Ibid.)" [He asks:] **"What is the reason?"** [He answers:] **"Because he is not. It should have said, 'Because they are not,'** and answers: **it is because Her Husband,** who is Zeir Anpin **called "voice," is gone from Her** [Machut] **and is not joined to Her.**

The Creator punished the Egyptians.

152. וְתָא חֲזֵי, לָאו שַׁעֲתָא חֲדָא, אִיהִי דְּבָכַת עֲלַיְיהוּ דְּיִשְׂרָאֵל, אֶלָּא בְּכָל זִמְנָא וְזִמְנָא דְּאִינּוּן בְּגָלוּתָא. וּבְגִינֵי כַּךְ, קוּדְשָׁא בְּרִיךְ הוּא גָּרַם לוֹן קָלָא לְמִצְרָאֵי, דִּכְתִיב וְהָיְתָה צְעָקָה גְּדוֹלָה בְּכָל אֶרֶץ מִצְרַיִם אֲשֶׁר כָּמוֹהוּ לֹא נִהְיָתָה וְגוֹ'. וְזָמִין לוֹן קָלִין אַחֲרָנִין, בְּאִינּוּן עוּרְדְּעָנִין, דְּרָמָאן קָלִין בְּמֵעַיְיהוּ, וַהֲווֹ נָפְלֵי בְּשׁוּקֵי כְּמֵתִים.

152. "Come and see, she did not just weep over Israel just once but rather every moment they were in exile. Because of this, that they blemished the voice, which was gone from Rachel, **the Holy One, blessed be He, brought about a voice to the Egyptians** to punish them, **as it is written, 'And there shall be a great cry throughout all the land of Egypt, such as there was none like it….' (Exodus 11:6) He also arranged for them other voices by these frogs that raised their voices in their intestines, so they fell dead in the marketplaces."**

Vayikra

51. "Rachel weeping for her children"

A Synopsis

Rav Yosi says that whenever a prophet begins his words, whichever name is mentioned at first indicates either Judgment or Mercy. He talks about the Shechinah's sorrow when the Temple was destroyed and Israel were sent into exile. He says that Israel would never have gone into exile nor would the Temple have been destroyed if all of Israel had not been found guilty before God and the leaders of the world first. Once the leaders of the people sinned, all the people followed them. After this discussion, Rav Chiya and Rav Yosi miraculously find a cave in which they could hide from robbers who were chasing them.

The significance of a prophet's opening words.

343. רִבִּי יוֹסֵי פָּתַח וְאָמַר, כֹּה אָמַר יְיָ' קוֹל בְּרָמָה נִשְׁמָע נְהִי בְּכִי וְגוֹ'. כֹּה אָמַר יְיָ', הָא אוּקְמוּהָ, בְּכָל אֲתַר דִּנְבִיאָה שָׁרֵי לְמַלְּלָא, הֲווּ מִלּוֹי אִשְׁתְּמוֹדְעָן, וְהָכָא הַאי כֹּה אָמַר יְיָ', קוּדְשָׁא בְּרִיךְ הוּא. וּמַה אָמַר, קוֹל בְּרָמָה נִשְׁמָע.

343. Rav Yosi opened and said: "'Thus says the Lord, "A voice was heard in Rama, lamentation and bitter weeping...."' (Jeremiah 31:15) 'Thus says the Lord....' They have established that whenever a prophet opens his words, they are recognized by the name mentioned at the beginning, whether the name indicates Judgment or Mercy, Zeir Anpin or Malchut, and so on, **'Thus says the Lord': "This is the Holy One, blessed be He,** namely Zeir Anpin." [He asks:] **"What does He say?"** [He answers:] **"'A voice was heard in Ramah...' (Jeremiah 31:15)** of Malchut, as will be explained."

The Shechinah followed Israel into exile.

344. הָכִי תָּנֵינָן, דִּבְהַהוּא יוֹמָא דְּאִתְחֲרַב בֵּי מַקְדְּשָׁא לְתַתָּא, וְיִשְׂרָאֵל אָזְלוּ בְּגָלוּתָא, רֵיחַיָּין עַל צַוְּארֵיהוֹן, וִידֵיהוֹן מְהַדְּקָן לַאֲחוֹרָא. וּכְנֶסֶת יִשְׂרָאֵל, אִתְתָּרְכַת מִבֵּית מַלְכָּא לְמֵיהַךְ בַּתְרֵיהוֹן. בְּשַׁעֲתָא דְּנַחְתַּת, אֲמָרַת אֵיהָךְ בְּקַדְמֵיתָא וְאֶבְכֶּה עַל מָדוֹרָאִי, וְעַל בָּנַי, וְעַל בַּעְלִי. כַּד נַחְתַּת, חָמַת אַתְרָהָא חָרִיב, וְכַמָּה דָּמָא דַּחֲסִידֵי אִתּוֹשַׁד בְּגַוֵּיהּ, וְהֵיכָלָא קַדִּישָׁא וּבֵיתָא אִתּוֹקַד בְּאֶשָּׁא.

344. "We have learned that on the day the Temple was destroyed and Israel went into exile with a millstone around their necks and their hands bound behind them, and the Congregation of Israel, the Shechinah, **was driven from the King's House to follow them** into exile. **When** the Shechinah **descended, She said: 'Let me go first to lament My Abode,** the Temple, **My children,** Israel, **and My Husband** Zeir Anpin,' who separated from Her. **When She came down, She saw her Abode ruined with much blood of the pious flowing in it, and the Temple and Her House consumed by fire.**

Rachel refused to be comforted.

345. כְּדֵין אֲרִימַת קָלָא, וְאִתְרְגִּישׁוּ עִלָּאֵי וְתַתָּאֵי, וּמָטָא קָלָא לְעֵילָּא, עַד אֲתַר דְּמַלְכָּא שָׁרֵי בֵּיהּ. וּבָעָא מַלְכָּא לְאַהְדְּרָא עָלְמָא לְתֹהוּ וָבֹהוּ, עַד דְּנַחְתּוּ כַּמָּה אוּכְלוֹסִין, וְכַמָּה מַשִּׁרְיָין, לְקַבְּלָהּ וְלָא קַבִּלָה תַּנְחוּמִין מִנַּיְיהוּ. הה"ד קוֹל בְּרָמָה נִשְׁמָע נְהִי בְּכִי תַמְרוּרִים רָחֵל מְבַכָּה עַל בָּנֶיהָ מֵאֲנָה לְהִנָּחֵם עַל בָּנֶיהָ, דְּלָא קַבִּלָה מִנַּיְיהוּ תַּנְחוּמִים. כִּי אֵינֶנּוּ: בְּגִין דְּמַלְכָּא קַדִּישָׁא הֲוָה סָלִיק לְעֵילָּא לְעֵילָּא, וְלָא אִשְׁתְּכַח בְּגַוָּהּ, הה"ד כִּי אֵינֶנּוּ, וְלָא כְּתִיב כִּי אֵינָם.

345. "She then raised Her voice in weeping, **and the Upper and Lower Beings were in a tumult. The voice reached up to where the King,** Zeir Anpin, **abides. The King then wanted to bring the world back into chaos. Many legions and hosts** of angels **came down to console Her but She took no consolation, as it is said: '...a voice was**

heard in Rama, lamentation and bitter weeping—Rachel weeping for her children; she refused to be comforted for her children...' (Jeremiah 31:15) because she would not be consoled by them. '... Because he is not' (Ibid.), meaning **the Holy King has ascended Above and is not found in Her. Hence, it says, 'because he is not' and not 'they are not,'** since it alludes to the Holy King."

Rachel is the Shechinah.

346. אָמַר לֵיהּ רִבִּי חִיָּיא, מַאי רָחֵל מְבַכָּה עַל בָּנֶיהָ. אָמַר לֵיהּ אוֹלִיפְנָא, דְּהִיא כְּנֶסֶת יִשְׂרָאֵל. וְדָא אִנְתּוּ דְּיַעֲקֹב וַדַּאי, דִּכְתִיב וַיֶּאֱהַב יַעֲקֹב אֶת רָחֵל. וּכְתִיב, וְרָחֵל עֲקָרָה. וּכְתִיב, הָתָם מוֹשִׁיבִי עֲקֶרֶת הַבַּיִת אֵם הַבָּנִים שְׂמֵחָה.

346. Rav Chiya said to him: "What does '...Rachel weeping for her children...' (Jeremiah 31;15) mean?" It should have said that the Shechinah was weeping for Her children. **He said to him: "We learned that** Rachel **is the Congregation of Israel,** namely the Shechinah. **Surely she is Jacob's wife,** namely the wife of Zeir Anpin called Jacob, **as it is written: 'And Jacob loved Rachel...' (Genesis 29:18) and '...but Rachel was barren.' (Genesis 29:31) It is also written, 'He makes the barren woman to keep house, and be a joyful mother of children....' (Psalms 113:9)"** All these verses speak of the Shechinah.

The Holy One, blessed be He, departed from the Shechinah.

347. דָּבָר אַחֵר כִּי אֵינֶנּוּ, כְּמָה דְּאִתְּמַר, אֵינֶנּוּ גָּדוֹל בַּבַּיִת וְגוֹ', אֵינֶנּוּ: דְּהָא אִסְתָּלִיק לְעֵילָּא וְאִתְרְחִיק מִכֹּלָּא. אֵינֶנּוּ: בְּזִוּוּגָא בָּהּ. אֵינֶנּוּ: לְאִשְׁתַּכְּחָא שְׁמֵיהּ רַבָּא.

347. Another interpretation for: "Because he is not (*einenu*)," is that it resembles the words: "There is none (*einenu*) greater in this house than I...." (Genesis 39:9) Here *einenu* means "is not," meaning that there is no one greater in the house than I. So too "because he is not (*einenu*)" means simply "is not" in general, yet it has many meanings. 1) **"he is not" because** the Holy One, blessed be He, **has ascended Above, away from everything;** 2) **"he is not" united with her,** and 3) **"he is not"** because His Name, the Shechinah, **is no longer His Great Name,** but is in exile.

The Shechinah's journey into exile.

348. א"ר חִיָּיא, מֵאָן אֲתַר שָׁרְיָא לְאִתְגַּלָּאָה. אָמַר לֵיהּ, מִבֵּי מַקְדְּשָׁא. דְּתַמָּן שָׁרְיָא וּלְבָתַר אַסְחָרַת כָּל אַרְעָא דְּיִשְׂרָאֵל. לְבָתַר כַּד נָפְקַת מִן אַרְעָא, קָמַת עַל מַדְבְּרָא וְיָתִיבַת תַּמָּן תְּלַת יוֹמִין. דַּבְּרַת אוּכְלָסָהָא וּמַשִּׁירְיָיהָא וְיַתְבָהָא מִבֵּי מַלְכָּא, וְקָרְאַת עָלָהּ אֵיכָה יָשְׁבָה בָדָד וְגוֹ'. בָּכוּ רִבִּי חִיָּיא וְרִבִּי יוֹסֵי.

348. Rav Chiya said: "Whence is the starting point of the Shechinah's exile?" He said to him: "From the Temple, where She dwelt. She then went around all the land of Israel. When She left the land She stood in the desert and sat there for three days. She led the crowd, the camps, and the inhabitants of the King's House from Jerusalem **and cried to it: 'How (*eicha*) does the city sit solitary....' (Lamentations 1:1)" Rav Chiya and Rav Yosi wept.**

The nation follows wherever its leaders lead.

349. אָמַר רִבִּי יוֹסֵי, לָא גָּלוּ יִשְׂרָאֵל מֵאַרְעָא, וְלָא אִתְחָרַב בֵּי מַקְדְּשָׁא, עַד דְּיִשְׂרָאֵל כֻּלְּהוּ אִשְׁתְּכָחוּ בְּחוֹבָא קָמֵי מַלְכָּא, וְעַד דְּרַבְרְבֵי עָלְמָא אִשְׁתְּכָחוּ בְּחוֹבָא בְּקַדְמֵיתָא. הה"ד עַמִּי מְאַשְּׁרֶיךָ מַתְעִים וְדֶרֶךְ אוֹרְחוֹתֶיךָ בִּלֵּעוּ. דְּכֵיוָן דְּרֵישֵׁי עַמָּא אַזְלִין בְּחוֹבָא, כָּל עַמָּא אִתְמַשְּׁכוּ אֲבַתְרַיְיהוּ. רִבִּי חִיָּיא אָמַר מֵהָכָא, וְאִם כָּל עֲדַת יִשְׂרָאֵל יִשְׁגּוּ, בְּמַאי הֲוֵי. בְּגִין וְנֶעְלַם דָּבָר מֵעֵינֵי הַקָּהָל. דְּעֵינֵי עַמָּא אִינּוּן רֵישַׁיְיהוּ, דְּכָל עַמָּא אִתְמַשְׁכָן אֲבַתְרַיְיהוּ.

349. Rav Yosi said: "Israel would never have been exiled from the land of Israel, nor would the Temple have been destroyed, had not all of Israel been found guilty before the King and until the leaders

of the world been found guilty first, as it is written: '...They that lead you cause you to err, and destroy the way of your paths' (Isaiah 3:12) Once the leaders of the people went the way of evil, the entire nation was drawn after and followed them." Rav Chiya said: "We learn this from the verse: 'And if the whole Congregation of Israel sin through ignorance....' (Leviticus 4:13) In what way? Since '...the thing be hid from the eyes of the assembly...' (Ibid.), for the eyes of the people are their leaders, after whom the entire nation are drawn and follow."

Balak

29. "And he lifted up his eyes, and saw the women and the children"

A Synopsis

We read how and why God protects innocent children during Yom Kippur, so that they are not punished for the sins of Israel. The innocent children are the Torah Scholars, to whom God has told His secrets. No evil eye can have any power over them.

Jacob had to take action due to Esau's wicked deeds.

321. פָּתַח ר"ש וְאָמַר, וַיִּשָּׂא אֶת עֵינָיו וַיַּרְא אֶת הַנָּשִׁים וְאֶת הַיְלָדִים וַיֹּאמֶר מִי אֵלֶּה לָּךְ וַיֹּאמַר הַיְלָדִים אֲשֶׁר חָנַן אֱלֹהִים אֶת עַבְדֶּךָ. ת"ח, הַהוּא רָשָׁע דְּעֵשָׂו, יָהִיב עֵינוֹי לְעַיְּינָא עַל נָשִׁין, וּבְגִינֵיה אַתְקִין תִּיקוּנוֹי. יַעֲקֹב, שַׁוֵּי שִׁפְחוֹת בְּקַדְמֵיתָא, וּבְנֵיהוֹן לְבָתַר, דַּחֲשִׁיבוּ יַתִּיר. לֵאָה אֲבַתְרַיְיהוּ, וּבְנָהָא לְבָתַר. לְבָתַר יוֹסֵף, וּבַתְרָהּ רָחֵל, וְהוּא עָבַר לִפְנֵיהֶם.

321. Rav Shimon opened and said: "'And he lifted up his eyes, and saw the women and the children; and said, "Who are those with you?" And he said, "The children with which God has graciously given Your servant."' (Genesis 33:5) Come and see, that wicked one allowed his eyes to gaze at the women. Due to him, Jacob **had to make some arrangements. Jacob placed the handmaidens in front, and their sons, who were more important, behind them. Leah followed behind them, and her sons were behind her. Behind them was Joseph and behind him Rachel. And he** himself **went in front of all of them.**

Joseph protected his mother.

322. כַּד סָגִידוּ כֻּלְּהוֹן, מַה כְּתִיב. וַתִּגַּשְׁןָ הַשְּׁפָחוֹת הֵנָּה וְיַלְדֵיהֶן וַתִּשְׁתַּחֲוֶיןָ. וּלְבָתַר כְּתִיב, וַתִּגַּשׁ גַּם לֵאָה וִילָדֶיהָ וַיִּשְׁתַּחֲווּ וְאַחַר נִגַּשׁ יוֹסֵף וְרָחֵל וְגוֹ'. וְהָא יוֹסֵף לְבַתְרַיְיתָא הֲוָה, וְרָחֵל לְקַמֵּיהּ. אֶלָּא בְּרָא טָבָא, בְּרָא רְחִימָא, צַדִּיקָא דְּעָלְמָא, יוֹסֵף, כֵּיוָן דְּחָמָא עֵינֵיהּ דְּהַהוּא רָשָׁע מִסְתַּכֵּל בְּנָשִׁין, דָּחִיל עַל אִמֵּיהּ, נָפִיק מֵאֲבַתְרָהּ, וּפָרִישׂ דְּרוֹעוֹי וְגוּפֵיהּ, וְכַסֵּי עָלָהּ, בְּגִין דְּלָא יִתֵּן הַהוּא רָשָׁע עֵינוֹי בְּאִמֵּיהּ. כַּמָּה אִתְסְגֵּי, שִׁית אַמִּין לְכָל סְטַר, וְחָפָא עָלָהּ, וְלָא יָכִיל עֵינֵיהּ דְּהַהוּא רָשָׁע לְשַׁלְטָאָה עָלָהּ.

322. (This is another version, explaining differently). **"After they all bowed down, it is written: 'Then the handmaidens came near, they and their children, and they bowed themselves.' (Genesis 33:6) Afterward, it says, 'And Leah also with her children came near, and bowed themselves: and after came Joseph near and Rachel, and they bowed themselves.' (Ibid. 7)"** He asks: **"But Joseph was last behind Rachel and Rachel was in front of him,"** and not Joseph in front of Rachel. He replies: **"It is just that when this good son, beloved son, the Righteous in the world, Joseph, noticed that the eyes of the wicked were staring at the women, he was fearful for his mother.** Then **he came out from behind her and spread his arms and his body and covered her, so that wicked one would not place his eyes on his mother. How much did he inflate his size? Six cubits in each direction and thus he covered her up so that the eyes of the wicked one shall have no effect over her."** Consequently, at the start, Joseph was indeed behind her, as is written earlier. However, he later came out from behind her and went in front of her.

No evil eye can affect Joseph.

323. כְּגַוְונָא דָּא, וַיִּשָּׂא בִלְעָם אֶת עֵינָיו, עֵינוֹ כְּתִיב, הַהוּא עֵינָא בִּישָׁא דְּבָעָא לְאִסְתַּכְּלָא עֲלַיְיהוּ. וַיַּרְא אֶת יִשְׂרָאֵל שֹׁכֵן לִשְׁבָטָיו. מַהוּ שׁוֹכֵן לִשְׁבָטָיו. אֶלָּא שִׁבְטָא דְּיוֹסֵף הֲוָה תַּמָּן, וְשִׁבְטָא דְּבִנְיָמִין. שִׁבְטָא דְּיוֹסֵף, דְּלָא שַׁלְטָא בְּהוּ

עֵינָא בִּישָׁא, דִּכְתִּיב בֵּן פּוֹרָת יוֹסֵף. מַאן בֵּן פּוֹרָת. דְּאִתְסְגֵּי לְכַסָּאָה עַל אִמֵּיהּ. בֵּן פּוֹרָת עֲלֵי עָיִן, דְּלָא שַׁלְטָא בֵּיהּ עֵינָא בִּישָׁא. שִׁבְטָא דְּבִנְיָמִין, דִּכְתִּיב בֵּיהּ וּבֵין כְּתֵפָיו שָׁכֵן. וּכְתִיב יִשְׁכּוֹן לָבֶטַח. מַאי לָבֶטַח. דְּלָא דָּחִיל מֵעֵינָא בִּישָׁא, וְלָא דָּחִיל מִפְּגָעִין בִּישִׁין.

323. Similar to this, "Bilaam lifted up his eye…." (Numbers 24:2) It is written "eye," which refers to the evil eye that wished to stare at them, meaning that he roused against them that evil Klipah called "evil eye." **"…and he saw Israel abiding according to their tribes" (Ibid.) He asks: "What is the meaning of 'according to their tribes'?** He replies: **"It only refers to the tribes of Joseph and Benjamin that were there. Upon the tribe of Joseph, no evil eye can have any effect, as it is written: 'Joseph is a fruitful bough….' (Genesis 49:22) What does 'a fruitful bough' mean? It means that he increased and spread about to cover his mother** from the evil eye of Esau, as mentioned earlier. **'…a fruitful bough by a well (*alei ayin,* lit. on the eye)…' (Ibid.) means that no evil eye can affect him. It is written about the tribe of Benjamin: '…And he shall dwell between His shoulders…' (Deuteronomy 33:12) and '…He shall dwell in safety….' (Ibid.) What does 'in safety' indicate? It means that he has no fear of the evil eye and is not afraid of any evil plague."**

Rachel spread her wings over her children.

324. אָמַר הַהוּא רָשָׁע, אֲנָא אַעֲבָר שׁוּרָה דָא, דְּלָא אִתְקַיְּימוּ, וַאֲנָא אִסְתַּכַּל כַּדְּקָא יָאוּת. רָחֵל הֲוַת תַּמָּן, וְחָמַאת דְּעֵינָא דְּהַהוּא רָשָׁע מִשְׁנְנָא לְאַבְאָשָׁא, מַה עָבְדַת. נָפְקַת וּפְרִישַׁת גַּדְפָהָא עֲלַיְיהוּ, וְחַפָּאת עַל בְּרָהָא. הה"ד וַיִּשָּׂא בִלְעָם אֶת עֵינָיו וַיַּרְא אֶת יִשְׂרָאֵל. כֵּיוָן דְּחָמָא רוּחָא דְקוּדְשָׁא, עֵינָא מְשַׁנְּנָא, מִיַּד וַתְּהִי עָלָיו רוּחַ אֱלֹהִים. עַל מַאן. עַל יִשְׂרָאֵל. דְּפָרִישׂ גַּדְפוֹי, וְחָפָא עֲלַיְיהוּ. וּמִיַּד תָּב הַהוּא רָשָׁע לַאֲחוֹרָא.

324. The wicked one said, "I will remove and nullify **this line** of the tribes of Joseph and Benjamin **so that they will not last** in the world, **and**

I will gaze at them with my evil eye **as is required." Rachel was present there and noticed that the eye of the wicked one was sharpened to do harm. What did she do? She came out and spread her wings over them, which covered over her children. This is what is said: "And Bilaam lifted up his eye, and he saw Israel…." (Numbers 24:2) Once the Holy Spirit,** which is Malchut called Rachel, **noticed the sharpened eye** of Bilaam, **instantly "…the spirit of God came upon him." (Ibid.) Upon whom? Upon Israel,** meaning that the spirit of God **spread its wings and covered over them. Immediately, the wicked one retreated.**

Rachel and Joseph protect each other.

325. בְּקַדְמֵיתָא בְּרָא חָפָא עַל אִמֵּיהּ. וְהַשְׁתָּא אִימָּא חָפָאת עַל בְּרָא. אָמַר קוּדְשָׁא בְּרִיךְ הוּא, בְּהַהִיא שַׁעֲתָא דְחָפָא אִיהוּ עַל רָחֵל אִמֵּיהּ, דְּלָא יִשְׁלוֹט עֵינָא דְהַהוּא רָשָׁע עָלָהּ, חַיֶּיךָ, בְּשַׁעֲתָא דְיֵיתֵי עֵינָא בִּישָׁא אַחֲרָא לְאִסְתַּכְּלָא עַל בָּנָךְ וְעַל בְּנַי, אִמָּךְ תֵּיחוֹפֵי עֲלַיְיהוּ. אַתְּ חָפִית עַל אִמָּךְ, אִמָּךְ תֵּיחוֹפֵי עֲלַיְיהוּ. אַתְּ חָפִית עַל אִמָּךְ, אִמָּךְ תֵּיחוֹפֵי עֲלָךְ.

325. At first, the son was covering his mother and now the mother covered her son. At that time when Joseph **covered his mother, Rachel, so that the evil eye of the wicked one would not harm her, the Holy One, blessed be He, said** to Joseph, **"Upon your life, when an evil eye approaches to gaze at your children and Mine, your mother will cover over them. You covered over your mother and your mother will cover you."**

MOSHE RABBEINU (MOSES OUR TEACHER)

Shemot

55. "Out of the midst of a bush"

A Synopsis

Rav Yehuda first explains that the burning bush is an allusion to the fire of Gehenom that punishes but does not utterly destroy the wicked. Thus it signifies God's compassion toward the wicked.

We then learn that God appeared to Moses in the flame of fire because Moses was unlike all the other prophets, and only he was able to approach the flame without being burned by it. This was because Moses' soul was drawn from a place from where no other was drawn; his unique connection to Mercy allowed him to confront Judgment without fear. Rav Shimon then establishes that although Bilaam was Moses' counterpart, Bilaam drew strength from the Lower Crowns and he acted according to impurity Below, while Moses drew from the Holy Crown Above and his actions were performed according to Holiness. This follows the duality inherent in all aspects of the universe.

Finally, Rav Yochanan refers to Rav Yitzchak's interpretation of the title verse to explain that the burning bush was a sign to reassure Moses that Israel would not succumb under the burden of their oppression.

The Relevance of the Passage

The Light cast by this narrative painlessly burns away our sins and egocentric qualities from our nature, so that we now merit the World to Come, which really means the arrival of Heaven on Earth. Our fears of Judgment are expunged from our being. When we are born into this world, our dark side and our soul have equal power. Our free will is to choose which voice we will follow.

This good-and-evil duality exists in the world at large. We now stamp out the darkness and tip the scales completely over to the side of good. Evil is banished from all existence. All wicked people of the world are rendered powerless. Their reign of terror is terminated as the Zohar's Light successfully overthrows the powers of darkness.

Through the Holy Names that appear in this Book of Zohar, and upon the merit of Moses, this becomes our ultimate exodus out of evil, our final and complete redemption and lasting freedom from the bondage of darkness.

The Light now shines from one end of the world to the other. And we bathe and bask forevermore in its pleasing and pleasurable radiance.

The Creator has compassion for the wicked.

389. אָמַר ר' יְהוּדָה, מִכָּאן לָמַדְנוּ, רַחֲמָנוּתוֹ שֶׁל מָקוֹם עַל הָרְשָׁעִים, דִּכְתִּיב, וְהִנֵּה הַסְּנֶה בּוֹעֵר בָּאֵשׁ, לַעֲשׂוֹת בָּהֶם דִּין בָּרְשָׁעִים, וְהַסְּנֶה אֵינֶנּוּ אוּכָּל, אֵין לָהֶם כְּלָיָה. בּוֹעֵר בָּאֵשׁ, עכ"פ רֶמֶז, לְאֵשׁ שֶׁל גֵּיהִנָּם. אֲבָל הַסְּנֶה אֵינֶנּוּ אוּכָּל, לִהְיוֹת בָּהֶם כְּלָיָה.

389. Rav Yehuda said: "From here we learn the compassion of the Omnipresent, meaning of the Holy One, blessed be He, **toward the wicked, for it is written: '...and behold, the bush burned with fire...' (Exodus 3:2), to punish the wicked with it,** as mentioned earlier. **'... but the bush was not consumed' (Ibid.) meaning that they were not utterly destroyed. 'Burned with fire' is all the same allusion to the fire of Gehenom,** meaning even though the fire appeared to Moses, who was righteous, it is nonetheless an allusion to the fire of Gehenom, which is for the wicked. **'...but the bush was not consumed' so it does not destroy them utterly."**

Moses was not burnt by the fire.

390. **ד"א וַיֵּרָא מַלְאַךְ יְיָ' אֵלָיו בְּלַבַּת אֵשׁ. מ"ט לְמֹשֶׁה בְּלַבַּת אֵשׁ, וְלִשְׁאַר נְבִיאִים לָא. א"ר יְהוּדָה, לָאו מֹשֶׁה כִּשְׁאַר נְבִיאִים. דְּתָנָן, מַאן דְּקָרִיב לְאֶשָּׁא בֵּיהּ אִתּוֹקַד, וּמֹשֶׁה קָרִיב לְאֶשָּׁא וְלָא אִתּוֹקַד. דִּכְתִּיב, וּמֹשֶׁה נִגַּשׁ אֶל הָעֲרָפֶל אֲשֶׁר שָׁם הָאֱלֹהִים. וּכְתִיב, וַיֵּרָא מַלְאַךְ יְיָ' אֵלָיו בְּלַבַּת אֵשׁ מִתּוֹךְ הַסְּנֶה.**

390. Another explanation of: "And the angel of the Lord appeared to him in a flame of fire…." (Exodus 3:2) He asks: **"Why did He appear to Moses in a flame of fire, and not to the other prophets?" Rav Yehuda said: "Moses is not like the other prophets for we learned that everyone who approaches the fire is burnt by it. Yet Moses approached it and was not burnt, as it is written, 'And Moses drew near to the thick darkness where God was' (Exodus 20:18) and 'And the angel of The Lord appeared to him in a flame of fire out of the midst of a bush.' (Ibid.)"**

Where the soul of Moses was hewn, no other person was hewn.

391. **רִבִּי אַבָּא אָמַר, הַאי דְּמֹשֶׁה, אִית לְאִסְתַּכְּלָא בֵּיהּ בְּחָכְמְתָא עִלָּאָה, עַל מַה כְּתִיב, כִּי מִן הַמַּיִם מְשִׁיתִיהוּ. מַאן דְּאִתְמְשָׁךְ מִן מַיָּא, לָא דָּחִיל מִנּוּרָא. דְּתַנְיָא אָמַר רִבִּי יְהוּדָה, מֵאֲתַר דְּאִתְגְּזַר מֹשֶׁה, לָא אִתְגְּזַר בַּר נָשׁ אָחֳרָא. א"ר יוֹחָנָן, בַּעֲשָׂרָה דַּרְגִּין אִשְׁתַּכְלָל. דִּכְתִּיב, בְּכָל בֵּיתִי נֶאֱמָן הוּא. וְלֹא נֶאֱמָן בֵּיתִי. זַכָּאָה חוּלָקֵיהּ דב"נ, דְּמָרֵיהּ אַסְהִיד כְּדֵין עֲלוֹי.**

391. Rav Aba said: "On **this** subject **of Moses, we should observe it with Supernal Wisdom. Why is it written, '…because I drew him out of the water' (Exodus 2:10)?** This comes to teach us **that one who is drawn from water,** which is Chesed, **does not fear fire,** which is Judgment." **Rav Yehuda said: "Because we have learned the place from where** the soul of **Moses was hewn, no other person was hewn." Rav Yochanan said: "He was composed of the ten levels** of Zeir Anpin **as is written, '…he is the trusted one in all My house'**

(Numbers 12:7) which is the Nukva. **It is not written, 'the trusted of My house,'** which would imply the trusted of the Nukva but rather it is written, 'he is the trusted,' which means the trusted of Zeir Anpin, which is higher than the Nukva. **Blessed is the portion of the person whose Master testifies of him thus."**

It is questioned whether Bilaam is from the same place.

392. אָמַר רַב דִּימִי, וְהָא כְּתִיב וְלֹא קָם נָבִיא עוֹד בְּיִשְׂרָאֵל כְּמֹשֶׁה. וְאָמַר רִיבָ"ל, בְּיִשְׂרָאֵל לֹא קָם, אֲבָל בְּאוּה"ע קָם, וּמַנּוּ בִּלְעָם. א"ל, וַדַּאי שַׁפִּיר קָאַמְרַתְּ, אִשְׁתִּיק. כַּד אָתָא רשב"י, אָתוּ, שָׁאִילוּ קָמֵיהּ הַאי מִלָּה.

392. Rav Dimi said: "Is it not written, 'And there arose not a prophet since, in Israel, like Moses….' (Deuteronomy 34:10)?" And Rav Yehoshua bar Levi said: "In Israel none arose but among the nations of the world there did arise, and who is he? He is Bilaam." So how can you say that no other person was hewn from the place that Moses was hewn? **Rav Elazar said to him: "Certainly, you speak well." He remained silent. When Rav Shimon bar Yochai came, they asked him this matter.**

Moses was from Holiness, Bilaam was from Impurity.

393. פָּתַח וְאָמַר, קוּטִיפָא דְּקַרְנָטֵי, אִתְעָרְבָא בְּאַפַּרְסְמוֹנָא טָבָא ח"ו. אֶלָּא, וַדַּאי כַּךְ הוּא, בְּאוּה"ע קָם, וּמַנּוּ בִּלְעָם. מֹשֶׁה עוֹבָדוֹי לְעֵילָּא, וּבִלְעָם לְתַתָּא. מֹשֶׁה, אִשְׁתַּמַּשׁ בְּכִתְרָא קַדִּישָׁא דְּמַלְכָּא עִלָּאָה לְעֵילָּא. וּבִלְעָם, אִשְׁתַּמַּשׁ בְּכִתְרִין תַּתָּאִין דְּלָא קַדִּישִׁין לְתַתָּא. וּבְהַהוּא גַּוְונָא מַמָּשׁ כְּתִיב, וְאֶת בִּלְעָם בֶּן בְּעוֹר הַקּוֹסֵם הָרְגוּ בְּנֵי יִשְׂרָאֵל בַּחֶרֶב. וְאִי סַלְקָא דַּעְתָּךְ יַתִּיר, זִיל שָׁאִיל לְאַתְנֵיהּ. אָתָא רִבִּי יוֹסֵי, וְנָשַׁק יְדוֹי, אָמַר, הָא חֲמָרָא דְּלִבָּאי נָפַק לְבַר.

393. Rav Shimon **opened the discussion, saying: "Heaven forbid that the fluid flowing from the karnatei** flower, which has a foul odor, **would mix with the good balsam,** meaning are you, Heaven forbid, comparing the wicked Bilaam to our master Moses? **Rather this is certainly** the meaning of, '**...among the nations of the world there did arise, who is Bilaam.' Moses' actions were Above** in Holiness **and Bilaam Below** in impurity. **Moses utilized the Holy Crown of the Supernal King,** which is Zeir Anpin **Above. Bilaam utilized the Lower Crowns, which are unholy Below. And in that exact manner it is written, 'And Bilaam, the son of Beor the sorcerer, the children of Israel slew by the sword.' (Joshua 13:22)** We see that he is called 'the sorcerer' because his actions were in impurity, **and if you cannot conceive that he did more** than this, **look to his mule.** For he became impure with her and copulated with her, as our sages of blessed memory said." **Rav Yosi came and kissed his hands and said: "Behold, the stone that was in my heart has gone,"** meaning that this question weighed upon him like a stone in his heart and now it has left and he is released from it.

Two forces in the world.

394. דְּהָכָא מַשְׁמַע, דְּאִית עִלָּאִין וְתַתָּאִין, יְמִינָא וּשְׂמָאלָא, רַחֲמֵי וְדִינָא, יִשְׂרָאֵל ועכו"ם. יִשְׂרָאֵל, מִשְׁתַּמְּשִׁין בְּכִתְרִין עִלָּאִין קַדִּישִׁין. עכו"ם, בְּכִתְרִין תַּתָּאִין דְּלָא קַדִּישִׁין. אִלֵּין דִּימִינָא, וְאִלֵּין דִּשְׂמָאלָא, ועכ"פ, מִתְפָּרְשִׁין נְבִיאֵי עִלָּאֵי מִנְּבִיאֵי תַּתָּאֵי. נְבִיאֵי דְּקוּדְשָׁא, מִנְּבִיאֵי דְּלָאו דְּקוּדְשָׁא.

394. From this, the words of Rav Shimon, **it appears that there are those Above and those Below, Right and Left, Mercy and Judgment, Israel and the heathen. Israel utilize the Crowns of Above, which are Holy. The heathen utilize the Crowns of Below, which are not holy. Those** of Israel **are of the Right, and those** of the heathen **are of the Left. Nevertheless, the Upper Prophets** of Israel **differ from the Lower Prophets** of the heathen; **the Prophets of Holiness are separate from the prophets that are not from holiness.**

Moses was Above, Bilam was Below

395. אָמַר רַבִּי יְהוּדָה, כְּגַוְונָא דַּהֲוָה מֹשֶׁה, פָּרִישׁ מִכָּל נְבִיאֵי, בִּנְבוּאָה קַדִּישָׁא עִלָּאָה. כַּךְ הֲוָה בִּלְעָם, פָּרִישׁ מִשְּׁאָר נְבִיאֵי וְחָרָשֵׁי, בִּנְבוּאָה דְּלָאו קַדִּישָׁא לְתַתָּא. ועכ"פ מֹשֶׁה הֲוָה לְעֵילָּא, וּבִלְעָם לְתַתָּא, וְכַמָּה דַּרְגִּין וְדַרְגִּין מִתְפָּרְשִׁין בֵּינַיְיהוּ.

395. Rav Yehuda said: "Just as Moses differed from all the prophets in the Holy Supernal Prophecy, Bilaam was similarly separate from the other prophets Below, the magicians of non-holy prophecy. Moses nevertheless was Above and Bilaam Below, and many levels divided them."

The Holy One, blessed by He, separated Israel from all other nations.

396. אָמַר רַבִּי יוֹחָנָן אָמַר רַבִּי יִצְחָק, מֹשֶׁה הֲוָה מְהַרְהֵר וְאוֹמֵר, שֶׁמָּא וח"ו יִשְׂרָאֵל יִכְלוּ בְּהַאי עֲבוֹדָה קָשָׁה, הֲדָא הוּא דִּכְתִּיב, וַיַּרְא בְּסִבְלֹתָם. לְפִיכָךְ, וַיֵּרָא מַלְאַךְ יְיָ' אֵלָיו בְּלַבַּת אֵשׁ וְגוֹ', וַיַּרְא וְהִנֵּה הַסְּנֶה בּוֹעֵר בָּאֵשׁ וְגוֹ'. כְּלוֹמַר, מְשׁוּעֲבָדִים הֵם בַּעֲבוֹדָה קָשָׁה, אֲבָל וְהַסְּנֶה אֵינֶנּוּ אוּכָּל. זַכָּאִין אִינּוּן יִשְׂרָאֵל, דְּקוּדְשָׁא בְּרִיךְ הוּא פָּרִישׁ לוֹן מִכָּל עַמִּין, וְקָרָא לוֹן בְּנִין, דִּכְתִּיב בָּנִים אַתֶּם לַה' אֱלֹהֵיכֶם.

396. Rav Yochanan said in the name of Rav Yitzchak: "Moses thought and said: 'Perhaps, heaven forbid, Israel will expire from this hard labor,' as it is written, '…and looked on their burdens….' (Exodus 2:11) Therefore, 'the angel of the Lord appeared to him in a flame of fire… and he looked, and behold, the bush burned with fire….' (Exodus 3: 2) Namely they are enslaved to hard labor '…but the bush was not consumed' (Ibid.), namely they do not perish in exile, as mentioned earlier. **Happy are Israel that the Holy One, blessed be He, separated them from all nations and called them 'children,' as it is written, 'You are the children of the Lord your God….' (Deuteronomy 14:1)"**

Terumah

52. The center of the world

A Synopsis

Here Rav Yosi discusses, "When you have eaten and are replete, then you shall bless the Lord your God for the good land which He has given you." (Deuteronomy 8:10) He says the Holy Land is the center of the world, and in the center of that is Jerusalem, and in the center of that is the Holy of Holies. Everywhere on Earth is nourished from this one place. In the wilderness where the Other Side dominates, we learn the children of Israel wandered for forty years. If they had been righteous during that time, they would have removed the Other Side from the world but instead they strengthened it. Moses died on Mount Avarim and was buried by the Shechinah. We are next told that Moses dominated the mountain, and that he showed those who die in the wilderness will rise at the Resurrection of the Dead. Rav Yosi then tells us that God sent a goat to a mountain called Azazel, which is the stronghold of the Other Side. Finally, we learn that if one who delights at his table worries about the Holiness of the Holy Land and the Sanctuary of the King that has been destroyed, he will be remembered by God as though he re-built the ruins of the Temple.

The Relevance of this Passage

A reading of this passage joins our souls to the Holy of Holies, the wellspring and fountainhead of all spiritual nourishment. This sacred connection is critical if our prayers are to be answered, if our lives are to be renewed with passion, peace, prosperity, and blessedness.

The Holy Temple is a refuge from death itself, such is the resplendence of this Light. Thus a heartfelt visual embrace of this text rebuilds the Holy Temple, as if by our own hands. The long hidden Light begins to shine and death dies. Evil is laid to waste and goodness fills the land. The dead are readied for Resurrection in a process that will embody sweet mercy and disburden.

All nourishment for every corner of habitation comes from Above.

561. פָּתַח ר׳ יוֹסֵי וְאָמַר, וְאָכַלְתָּ וְשָׂבָעְתָּ וּבֵרַכְתָּ אֶת יְיָ׳ אֱלֹהֶיךָ עַל הָאָרֶץ הַטּוֹבָה אֲשֶׁר נָתַן לָךְ. אִי בְּאַרְעָא דְּיִשְׂרָאֵל מְבָרְכִינָן, לְבַר מֵאַרְעָא מְנָלָן. דְּהָא בְּגַוְונָא דָּא לָא אִצְטְרִיךְ. אֶלָּא, קוּדְשָׁא בְּרִיךְ הוּא כַּד בָּרָא עָלְמָא, פָּלִיג אַרְעָא, יִשּׁוּבָא אִיהוּ לְסִטַר חַד, וְחָרְבָּא אִיהוּ לְסִטַר אָחֳרָא. פָּלִיג יִשּׁוּבָא, וְאַסְחַר עָלְמָא סַחֲרָנֵיהּ דִּנְקוּדָה חֲדָא. וּמַאן אִיהוּ, דָּא אַרְעָא קַדִּישָׁא, אַרְעָא קַדִּישָׁא אֶמְצָעִיתָא דְּעָלְמָא. וּבְאֶמְצָעִיתָא דְּאַרְעָא קַדִּישָׁא, אִיהוּ יְרוּשְׁלֵם. אֶמְצָעִיתָא דִּירוּשְׁלֵם אִיהוּ בֵּית קֹדֶשׁ הַקֳּדָשִׁים, וְכָל טִיבוּ וְכָל מְזוֹנָא דְּכָל יִשּׁוּבָא, תַּמָּן נָחִית מִלְּעֵילָּא. וְלֵית לָךְ אֲתַר בְּכָל יִשּׁוּבָא דְּלָא אִתְּזַן מִתַּמָּן.

561. Rav Yosi opened and said: "'When you have eaten and are replete, then you shall bless the Lord your God for the good land which He has given you.' (Deuteronomy 8:10)" He asks: **"If we bless in the land of Israel, how do we know** that we have to bless **outside of the Land of Israel?** For it seems **that in this circumstance,** outside of the Land of Israel, **it is not necessary to bless."** He answers: **"When the Holy One, blessed be He, created the world, He divided the Earth. The** place of **habitation was on one side and** the place **of desolation was on the other side. And He divided the inhabited** place, **and circled the world around one point. What is it? It is the Holy Land because the Holy Land is the center of the world, and in the center of the Holy Land is Jerusalem, and the center of Jerusalem is the Holy of Holies. Every goodness and all the nourishment of the entire habitation descend there from Above, and in the entire habitation there is not one place that is not nourished from there.**

The children of Israel could have destroyed the Other Side.

562. פָּלִיג וְחָרְבָא. וְלָא אִשְׁתְּכַח חָרְבָא תַּקִּיפָא בְּכָל עָלְמָא, בַּר הַהוּא מַדְבְּרָא, דְּתַבְרוּ חֵילֵיהּ וְתָקְפֵיהּ יִשְׂרָאֵל אַרְבָּעִים שָׁנָה, כְּמָה דְּאַתְּ אָמֵר הַמּוֹלִיכְךָ בַּמִּדְבָּר הַגָּדוֹל וְהַנּוֹרָא. בְּהַהוּא מַדְבְּרָא, שַׁלְטָא סִטְרָא אָחֳרָא, וּבְעַל כָּרְחֵיהּ אָזְלוּ יִשְׂרָאֵל עָלֵיהּ, וְתַבְרוּ חֵילֵיהּ, אַרְבְּעִין שְׁנִין. וְאִי יִשְׂרָאֵל יִשְׁתַּכְחוּ זַכָּאִין בְּאִינּוּן אַרְבְּעִין שְׁנִין, הֲוָה מִתְעַבְּרָא הַהוּא סִטְרָא אָחֳרָא מֵעָלְמָא, וּמִדְּקָא אַרְגִּיזוּ לֵיהּ לְקוּדְשָׁא בְּרִיךְ הוּא כָּל אִינּוּן זִמְנִין, אִתְתַּקַּף הַהוּא סִטְרָא אָחֳרָא, וְנָפְלוּ כֻּלְּהוּ תַּמָּן תְּחוֹת רְשׁוּתֵיהּ.

562. "He divided the desolate place, and there was no greater desolation in the entire world as in that wilderness, that the children of Israel broke its strength and power for forty years, as it is written, 'Who led you through that great and terrible wilderness....' (Deuteronomy 8:15) The Other Side dominates in that wilderness and, against its will, the children of Israel walked on it and smashed its strength forty years. Had they been righteous during the forty years, they would have removed the Other Side from the world but because they angered the Holy One, blessed be He, so many times, the Other Side grow strong. They all fell under its power there."

Moses was not under the jurisdiction of the Other Side.

563. וְאִי תֵּימָא, וְהָא מֹשֶׁה דְּסָלִיק עַל כָּל בְּנֵי עָלְמָא, הֵיךְ מִית תַּמָּן. לָאו הָכִי, דְּהָא מֹשֶׁה מְהֵימְנָא לָא הֲוָה בִּרְשׁוּתֵיהּ, אֶלָּא בְּהַר הָעֲבָרִים. מַאי הָעֲבָרִים. פְּלוּגְתָּא. דְּאִתְפַּלְּגוּ עָלֵיהּ שַׁלִּיטִין עִלָּאִין דִּלְעֵילָּא, וְלָא אִתְמְסַר בִּידָא דִּמְמַנָּא וְשַׁלִּיטָא אָחֳרָא, וְאִשְׁתְּאַר הָכִי, עַד דְּאָתָא מֹשֶׁה עַבְדָּא מְהֵימְנָא, וְשָׁלִיט עָלֵיהּ, וְאִתְקְבַר תַּמָּן, וְלָא אִתְעַסַּק בֵּיהּ בִּקְבוּרְתֵיהּ, בַּר קוּדְשָׁא בְּרִיךְ הוּא בִּלְחוֹדוֹי, דִּכְתִיב וַיִּקְבֹּר אוֹתוֹ בַגַּי.

563. If you ask: "Moses, who was elevated over all the people of the world, how did he die there? "He answers: **"It was not so, for Moses was not under the jurisdiction** of the Other Side **but rather on the**

Mount Avarim. What is Avarim? Quarrels, from the expression wrath (*evra*) and fury. **The Supernal rulers of Above quarreled over it,** for they wanted to dominate the mountain, **but it was not handed to any other ruler and it remained so until Moses, the Faithful Servant, came and dominated it. Moses was buried there, and no one took part in his burial except the Holy One, blessed be He, alone, as it is written, '...and he buried him in the valley....' (Deuteronomy 34:6)"**

Those who died in the wilderness will rise in the Resurrection.

564. וַיִּקְבֹּר אוֹתוֹ, מַאן. הַהוּא דִּכְתִיב בֵּיהּ בְּאֹרַח סְתִים, וְאֶל מֹשֶׁה אָמַר, וְלָא כְּתִיב מַאן אִיהוּ. וַיִּקְרָא אֶל מֹשֶׁה, וְלָא כְּתִיב מַאן אִיהוּ. אוּף הָכָא וַיִּקְבּוֹר אוֹתוֹ, וְלָא כְּתִיב מַאן אִיהוּ, אֶלָּא וַדַּאי הַאי אֲתָר יְדִיעָא אִיהוּ לְגַבֵּי חַבְרַיָּיא. וְעַל דָּא, בְּהַהוּא טוּרָא לָא שַׁלִּיט עָלֵיהּ, בַּר מֹשֶׁה בִּלְחוֹדוֹי, וְאִיהוּ אִתְקְבַר תַּמָּן. וּבְגִין לְמִנְדַּע לְכָל דָּרִין אַחֲרָנִין דְּעָלְמָא, דְּאִינּוּן מֵתֵי מִדְבָּר יְקוּמוּן, הַהוּא רַעְיָא דִּלְהוֹן אַשְׁרֵי לֵיהּ בְּגַוַויְיהוּ, לְמֶהֱוֵי כֻּלְּהוּ בְּאִתְעָרוּתָא דְּקִיּוּמָא לְעָלְמָא דְּאָתֵי.

564. "...and he buried him..." (Deuteronomy 34:6) He asks: **"Who is the one** who buried him?" He answers: **"The one of whom it is written in a non-descriptive way, 'And He (*El*) said to Moses...' (Exodus 24:1) and similarly 'And *El* called to Moses....' (Leviticus 1:1) It did not write who he is. '...and he buried him....' (Deuteronomy 34:6) It is not written who he is. But certainly this place is known to the friends,** that it is the Shechinah called 'place,' for it is the Shechinah wherever it is said just 'he.' **Therefore, no one dominated in this mountain except Moses himself, and he was buried there. So that all the generations of the world would know that those who died in the wilderness will rise** at the Resurrection of the Dead, **the Holy One, blessed be He, placed their shepherd among them, so that they all will be present in the awakening of the reality of the World to Come."**

Why the Holy One commanded to send the goat to Azazel.

565. וְאִי תֵּימָא, אִי הָכִי דְּהַהוּא מַדְבְּרָא אִיהוּ תָּקְפָּא דְּסִטְרָא אָחֳרָא, הֵיךְ פָּקִיד קוּדְשָׁא בְּרִיךְ הוּא, עַל הַהוּא שָׂעִיר, לְשַׁדְּרָא לֵיהּ לְטוּרָא אָחֳרָא, דְּאִקְרֵי עֲזָאזֵל, הֲוָה לוֹן לְשַׁדְּרָא לֵיהּ לְהַהוּא טוּרָא דְּאָזְלֵי יִשְׂרָאֵל בְּמַדְבְּרָא בֵּיהּ. אֶלָּא, כֵּיוָן דְּהָא אָזְלוּ בֵּיהּ יִשְׂרָאֵל אַרְבְּעִין שְׁנִין, הָא אִתְּבַר תָּקְפֵּיהּ. וְתָקְפֵּיהּ אִתְתַּקַּף בְּאֲתַר דְּלָא עָבַר בֵּיהּ גְּבַר תַּמָּן לְעָלְמִין, וּבְהַהוּא טוּרָא, הָא הֲוָה דִּיּוּרֵיהוֹן דְּיִשְׂרָאֵל תַּמָּן אַרְבְּעִין שְׁנִין.

565. If you ask: "If that wilderness is the strength of the Other Side, how could the Holy One, blessed be He, command that this goat shall be sent to a different mountain that is called Azazel? They should have sent it to that mountain that Israel went over in the wilderness, for there is the place of the strength of the Other Side." He answers: **"Rather, since the children of Israel had already gone there forty years, its power was broken. And its power grew strong in a place where nobody ever passed before. Yet that mountain** that is in the wilderness where Israel walked **was the dwelling place of Israel for forty years."**

The Other Side dominates where no man can enter.

566. אֲבָל בְּהַאי שָׂעִיר, הַהוּא אֲתַר אִיהוּ טִנָּרָא תַּקִּיפָא עִלָּאָה, וּתְחוֹת עֻמְקָא דְּהַהוּא טִנָּרָא, דְּבַר נָשׁ לָא יָכִיל לְמֵיעַל תַּמָּן, אִיהוּ שַׁלִּיט יַתִּיר לְמֵיכַל טַרְפֵּיהּ, בְּגִין דְּיִתְעֲבַר מֵעַלַּיְיהוּ דְּיִשְׂרָאֵל, וְלָא יִשְׁתְּכַח בְּהוּ מְקַטְרְגָא עֲלַיְיהוּ בְּיִשּׁוּבָא.

566. But that place, where they send **that goat, is a Supernal strong rock, and under the depths of that rock, where no man can enter,** the Other Side **dominates exceedingly to eat its prey. Then it will be removed from Israel and the Accuser will not be found against them in the inhabited region.**

The entire world's food and sustenance emit from the Holy of Holies.

567. שׁוּלְטָנוּתֵיהּ דְּרָזָא דִּמְהֵימְנוּתָא, גּוֹ אֶמְצָעִיתָא דִּנְקוּדָה דְּכָל אַרְעָא קַדִּישָׁא, בְּבֵי קֹדֶשׁ הַקֳּדָשִׁים. וְאע״ג דְּהַשְׁתָּא לָאו אִיהוּ בְּקִיּוּמָא, בִּזְכוּתֵיהּ כָּל עָלְמָא אִתְּזַן, וּמְזוֹנָא וְסִפּוּקָא מִתַּמָּן נָפְקָא לְכֹלָּא, בְּכָל אֲתַר סִטְרָא דְּיִשּׁוּבָא. וּבְגִין כַּךְ, אע״ג דְּיִשְׂרָאֵל הַשְׁתָּא לְבַר מֵאַרְעָא קַדִּישָׁא, עִם כָּל דָּא מֵחֵילָא וּזְכוּתָא דְּאַרְעָא, אִשְׁתְּכַח מְזוֹנָא וְסִפּוּקָא לְכָל עָלְמָא. וְע״ד כְּתִיב וּבֵרַכְתָּ אֶת יְיָ׳ אֱלֹהֶיךָ עַל הָאָרֶץ הַטּוֹבָה אֲשֶׁר נָתַן לָךְ. עַל הָאָרֶץ הַטּוֹבָה וַדַּאי, דְּהָא בְּגִינָהּ מְזוֹנָא וְסִפּוּקָא אִשְׁתְּכַח בְּעָלְמָא.

567. The reign of the secret of Faith is found in the central point of the entire Holy Land, in the Holy of Holies, and even though it does not exist today, nonetheless, **in its merit the whole world is fed. Food and sustenance emit from there to all, in every place of the inhabited side. Therefore, even though Israel are outside the Holy Land, because of the strength and merit of the Land there is food and sustenance in the world. Therefore, it is written: "And you shall bless the Lord your God for the good land that He has given you," (Deuteronomy 8:10); "the good land" certainly, since food and sustenance are found in the world because of it.**

The importance of remembering the Holiness of the Holy Land.

568. מַאן דְּאִתְעֲדַּן עַל פָּתוֹרֵיהּ וּמִתְעַנַּג בְּאִינּוּן מֵיכְלִין, אִית לֵיהּ לְאַדְכְּרָא וּלְדָאֲגָא עַל קְדוּשָּׁה דְּאַרְעָא קַדִּישָׁא, וְעַל הֵיכָלָא דְּמַלְכָּא דְּקָא אִתְחֲרִיב. וּבְגִין הַהוּא עֲצִיבוּ דְּאִיהוּ קָא מִתְעַצַּב עַל פָּתוֹרֵיהּ, בְּהַהוּא חֶדְוָה וּמִשְׁתְּיָא דְּתַמָּן, קוּדְשָׁא בְּרִיךְ הוּא חָשִׁיב עָלֵיהּ כְּאִלּוּ בָּנָה בֵּיתֵיהּ, וּבָנָה כָּל אִינּוּן חָרְבֵּי דְּבֵי מַקְדְּשָׁא, זַכָּאָה חוּלָקֵיהּ.

568. One who delights at his table and takes pleasure in foods should remember and care for the Holiness of the Holy Land, and the sanctuary of the King that has been destroyed. And due to the pain he feels there at his table, in the midst of joy and feasting, the

Holy One, blessed be He, considers for him as though he built His House and built all these ruins of the Temple. Happy is his portion.

Terumah

90. Moses did not die

A Synopsis

Rav Shimon says here that from our point of view death is called "death" but from the view of those Above, life is increased to one who dies. So Moses did not die, and neither did Jacob, because he had a complete Faith. When Jacob was renamed "Israel," we learn it meant the perfection of everything, which is the lack of death.

The Relevance of this Passage

Death dies. All is perfected and made eternal through Jacob and Moses. Mercy and lovingkindness envelop the entire metamorphose. End of story.

From the view of those Above, Moses's life increased.

888. דְּתַנְיָא אָמַר רַבִּי שִׁמְעוֹן, מֹשֶׁה לָא מִית. וְאִי תֵּימָא הָא כְּתִיב וַיָּמָת שָׁם מֹשֶׁה. כַּךְ בְּכָל אֲתַר לְצַדִּיקַיָּא קָרֵי בְּהוּ מִיתָה. מַאי מִיתָה. מִסִּטְרָא דִּילָן אִקְרֵי הָכִי. דְּתַנְיָא אָמַר רַבִּי שִׁמְעוֹן, וְכֵן תָּנָא, דְּמַאן דְּאִיהוּ בִּשְׁלִימוּתָא דִּמְהֵימְנוּתָא קַדִּישָׁא תַּלְיָיא בֵּיהּ, לָא תַּלְיָיא בֵּיהּ מִיתָה וְלָא מִית. כְּמָה דַּהֲוָה בְּיַעֲקֹב דִּמְהֵימְנוּתָא שְׁלֵימָתָא הֲוָה בֵּיהּ.

888. We have learned that Rav Shimon said: "Moses did not die. If you ask, yet it is written, 'And Moses [the servant of the Lord] died there....' (Deuteronomy 34:5)" and similarly in every place, death is mentioned by the Righteous. What is death? From our view, it is called so, but from the view of those Above, to the contrary, his life increased. **For we have learned that Rav Shimon taught that one who is in completeness, from whom the Holy Faith is suspended, death is not attached to him and he does not die, as it was with Jacob, who had complete Faith.** Therefore, Jacob the patriarch did not die.

There is no death in perfection.

889. דְּאָמַר ר' שִׁמְעוֹן, לֹא יִקָּרֵא שִׁמְךָ עוֹד יַעֲקֹב כִּי אִם יִשְׂרָאֵל יִהְיֶה שְׁמֶךָ, וַיִּקְרָא אֶת שְׁמוֹ יִשְׂרָאֵל. מַאי יִשְׂרָאֵל. שְׁלִימוּתָא דְּכֹלָּא. דִּכְתִּיב וְאַתָּה אַל תִּירָא עַבְדִּי יַעֲקֹב וְאַל תֵּחַת יִשְׂרָאֵל כִּי הִנְנִי מוֹשִׁיעֲךָ מֵרָחוֹק וְאֶת זַרְעֲךָ מֵאֶרֶץ שִׁבְיָם וְגוֹ'.

889. For Rav Shimon said: "'Your name shall not be called any more Jacob, but Israel shall be your name, and he called his name Israel.' (Genesis 35:10) What does Israel mean? The perfection of everything, which is the lack of death. **It is written, 'Therefore fear you not, My servant Jacob, says the Lord; neither be dismayed, Israel: for I will save you from afar, and your seed from the land of their captivity....' (Jeremiah 30:10)"**

The Holy One came to Jacob's place Below.

890. א"ר יְהוּדָה מֵהָכָא, כִּי אִתְּךָ אֲנִי, דַּיְיקָא, זַכָּאָה חוּלָקֵיהּ, דְּמָארֵיהּ אָמַר לֵיהּ כֵּן. כִּי אִתִּי אַתָּה לָא כְּתִיב, אֶלָּא כִּי אִתְּךָ אֲנִי, דְּמָארֵיהּ אָתֵי לְאִתְחַבְּרָא דְּיוּרֵיהּ עִמֵּיהּ.

890. Rav Yehuda said: "From here it is derived that Jacob did not die, as it is written, **'For I am with you....' (Jeremiah 30:11)** [The word] 'I' **is exact,** since it indicates Malchut that is called 'I.' **Blessed is the portion of him, whose Master speaks thus to him. It is not written, 'For you are with me'** because then it would imply that he was attached to the Holy One, blessed be He, Above but not when he was in his place Below. **Rather 'For I am with you...' (Ibid.)** which indicates **that his Master came to join and dwell with him."**

Shlach Lecha

47. The birth of Moses

A Synopsis

Rav Chizkiyah says that God gave Israel the Torah and also faithful prophets to lead them. All the prophets beheld God's glory from a high place but not as near as Moses, who was closer to God than any of them. Rav Chizkiyah interprets the scripture beginning "And there went a man of the house of Levi, and took to wife the daughter of Levi," (Exodus 2:1) as meaning that Zeir Anpin joined with Malchut. We learn that the Shechinah hid Moses for three months because he was present Above in the Upper Realm before he descended to this world. She allowed Moses to sail among the Angels because he was later destined to go up among them to receive the Torah. We are told that the daughter of Pharaoh came from the Left aspect of Harsh Judgment, and that she saw the child Moses stamped with the impression of Zeir Anpin and Malchut when she found him in the basket of papyrus. From all this, Rav Shimon derives that the souls of the Righteous come from a high place, and that the soul has a father and a mother. Everything comes from and exists from male and female; Malchut is seen to be the Mother of the soul of the first man.

The merit of being given the Holy Torah and faithful prophets.

309. וַיֹּאמֶר יְיָ' אֶל מֹשֶׁה לֵּאמֹר דַּבֵּר אֶל בְּנֵי יִשְׂרָאֵל וְגוֹ' וְעָשׂוּ לָהֶם צִיצִית עַל כַּנְפֵי בִגְדֵיהֶם לְדוֹרוֹתָם וְגוֹ'. ר' חִזְקִיָּה פָּתַח, וַיַּרְאֵנִי אֶת יְהוֹשֻׁעַ הַכֹּהֵן הַגָּדוֹל וְגוֹ'. כַּמָּה זַכָּאִין אִינּוּן יִשְׂרָאֵל, דְּקוּדְשָׁא בְּרִיךְ הוּא בָּעֵי בִּיקָרֵהוֹן עַל כָּל בְּנֵי עָלְמָא, וְיָהַב לוֹן אוֹרַיְיתָא קַדִּישָׁא, וְיָהַב לוֹן נְבִיאֵי מְהֵימְנֵי, דְּמְדַבְּרֵי לְהוּ בְּאוֹרַיְיתָא, בְּאֹרַח קְשׁוֹט.

309. "And the Lord spoke to Moses, saying, 'Speak to the children of Israel, and bid them that they make them fringes in the corners of their garments throughout their generations...'"

(Numbers 15:37-38). Rav Chizkiyah opened: "'And He showed me Joshua the High Priest....' (Zechariah 3:1) How happy are Israel that He desires their glory above all the people, has granted them the Holy Torah and given them faithful prophets that lead them according to the Torah on the true path.

No one was closer to the Holy One, blessed be He, than Moses.

310. תָּא חֲזֵי, כָּל נְבִיאֵי וּנְבִיאֵי דְּאוֹקִים קוּדְשָׁא בְּרִיךְ הוּא לְיִשְׂרָאֵל, כֻּלְּהוּ אִתְגַּלֵּי קוּדְשָׁא בְּרִיךְ הוּא עֲלַיְיהוּ, בְּדַרְגִּין עִלָּאִין קַדִּישִׁין, וְחָמוּ זִיו יְקָרָא קַדִּישָׁא דְּמַלְכָּא מֵאֲתַר עִלָּאָה, אֲבָל לָא קָרִיב כְּמֹשֶׁה, דַּהֲוָה קָרִיב לְמַלְכָּא יַתִּיר מִכֻּלָּא, דְּהָא זַכָּאָה חוּלָקֵיהּ יַתִּיר מִכָּל בְּנֵי עָלְמָא, דְּעָלֵיהּ כְּתִיב, פֶּה אֶל פֶּה אֲדַבֶּר בּוֹ וּמַרְאֶה וְלֹא בְחִידוֹת. וּשְׁאַר נְבִיאֵי, הֲווֹ חָמָאן מֵאֲתַר רְחִיקָא, כְּמָה דְּאַתְּ אָמֵר מֵרָחוֹק יְיָ׳ נִרְאָה לִי.

310. "Come and see, all the various prophets that the Holy One, blessed be He, set up for Israel, the Holy One, blessed be He, revealed Himself to them all on the Supernal Holy levels and they beheld the King's Holy Radiance of Glory from a Supernal Place, but not as near as Moses, who was closer to the King than any of them since his lot was more blessed than that of any other man. About him it is written: 'Mouth to mouth I speak to him, in vision and not in riddles....' (Numbers 12:8) The rest of the prophets saw from a distant place, as you say, 'From afar the Lord appeared to me.' (Jeremiah 31:2)"

The place where Supernal Chochmah and Binah unite.

311. א"ר חִזְקִיָּה, הָכִי אוֹלִיפְנָא, כְּתִיב וַיֵּלֶךְ אִישׁ מִבֵּית לֵוִי וַיִּקַּח אֶת בַּת לֵוִי. וַיֵּלֶךְ אִישׁ: דָּא קוּדְשָׁא בְּרִיךְ הוּא כד"א יְיָ׳ אִישׁ מִלְחָמָה. מִבֵּית לֵוִי: דָּא קוּדְשָׁא בְּרִיךְ הוּא, אֲתַר דְּחָכְמָה עִלָּאָה, וְהַהוּא זוֹהַר מִתְחַבְּרָן כַּחֲדָא, דְּלָא מִתְפָּרְשָׁן לְעָלְמִין. מִבֵּית לֵוִי: דְּאַשְׁרֵי לִוְיָתָן כָּל חִידוּ בְּעָלְמָא, הה"ד לִוְיָתָן

זֶה יָצַרְתָּ לְשַׂחֶק בּוֹ. וַיִּקַּח אֶת בַּת לֵוִי, דָא קוּדְשָׁא בְּרִיךְ הוּא, אֲתָר דְּנְהִירוּ דְסִיהֲרָא נָהִיר.

311. Rav Chizkiyah said: "This is how I learned it. It is written: 'And there went a man of the house of Levi, and took to wife the daughter of Levi.' (Exodus 2:1) 'And there went a man....' (Ibid.) That is the Holy One, blessed be He, Zeir Anpin, **as it says, 'The Lord is a man of war....' (Exodus 15:3) '...the house of Levi...' is the Holy One, blessed be He,** who went from **the place where Supernal Chochmah and that bright radiance,** which is Supernal Binah, **join together and never separate.** He interprets 'Levi' to mean 'cleaving,' derived from *levi'ut* (accompaniment). Another explanation of: **'...of the house of Levi' is that the Leviathan,** that is Yesod of Zeir Anpin, **has inspired all enjoyment in the world** and he interprets 'Levi' as derived from Leviathan, **as it is written: 'There go the [ships and] the Leviathan, whom You have made to play therein.' (Psalms 104:26) '...and took to wife the daughter of Levi' (Exodus 2:1) that is the Holy One, blessed be He, which is the place where the moon is bright,** that being Malchut." The verse is as such: "And there went a man," Zeir Anpin, "from the house of Levi," Supernal Aba and Ima, "and took the daughter of Levi," Malchut. Meaning that Zeir Anpin bestowed Lights of Supernal Aba and Ima to Malchut.

Before and after marriage.

312. וַתַּהַר הָאִשָּׁה וַתֵּלֶד בֵּן. הָאִשָּׁה וַדַּאי, כד"א לְזֹאת יִקָּרֵא אִשָּׁה. בְּקַדְמֵיתָא בַּת לֵוִי, הָכִי הוּא וַדַּאי. וְכִי בַּת לֵוִי בְּקַדְמֵיתָא, וְהַשְׁתָּא אִשָּׁה. אֶלָּא הָכִי אוֹלִיפְנָא, אִתְּתָא עַד לָא אִזְדַּוְּוגַת, אִתְקְרִיאַת בַּת פְּלוֹנִי, בָּתַר דְּאִזְדַּוְּוגַת. אִתְקְרֵי אִשָּׁה, וְהָכָא, בַּת וְאִשָּׁה, כֹּלָּא בְּחַד דַּרְגָּא הִיא.

312. "And the woman conceived, and bore a son...." (Exodus 2:2) Surely, "the woman" is Malchut, **as it says, "...for this (*zot*) she shall be called woman..." (Genesis 2:23)** and *Zot* is the name of Malchut. **At**

first, She is called **"the daughter of Levi" (Exodus 2:1) and certainly it is so.** He asks: **"Why did he first** call Her **'the daughter of Levi' and now a 'woman'?"** He answers: **"This is what we have learned. Before she is married, a woman is referred to as the daughter of so-and-so but after she is married, she is referred to as a woman. Here too, daughter and woman pertain to the same level,** meaning Malchut. However, before he took her in marriage, she was referred to as the daughter of Levi, and after that, a woman.

The Shechinah joined and protected Moses since birth.

313. וַתִּצְפְּנֵהוּ ג' יְרָחִים, אִלֵּין תְּלַת יַרְחִין דְּדִינָא קַשְׁיָא שַׁרְיָא בְּעָלְמָא. וּמַאי נִינְהוּ. תַּמּוּ"ז וְאָ"ב וְטֵבֵ"ת. מַאי קָא מַשְׁמַע לָן. דְּעַד דְּלָא נָחַת מֹשֶׁה לְעָלְמָא, שְׁכִיחַ הֲוָה הוּא לְעֵילָּא, וְעַל דָּא אִזְדַּוְּוגַת בֵּיהּ שְׁכִינְתָּא מִן יוֹמָא דְּאִתְיְלִיד. מִכָּאן אָמַר רִבִּי שִׁמְעוֹן, רוּחֵיהוֹן דְּצַדִּיקַיָּיא שְׁכִיחִין אִינּוּן לְעֵילָּא, עַד לָא יָחֲתוּן לְעָלְמָא.

313. "...she hid him three months." (Exodus 2:2) These are the three months when heavy Judgment rests in the world. Which ones are they? Tamuz, Av, and Tevet. And therefore, the Shechinah hid him. He asks: **"What is it trying to tell us by this?"** He answers: "It lets us know **that before Moses went down to the world, he was Above. Therefore, the Shechinah joined him since the day he was born,** and protected him. **From here Rav Shimon said that the Spirits of the Righteous are found Above before they descend into the world.**

Moses was kept safe from High Angels.

314. וְלֹא יָכְלָה עוֹד הַצְּפִינוֹ וַתִּקַּח לוֹ וְגוֹ' מַאי וַתִּקַּח לוֹ תֵּיבַת גֹּמֶא. דְּחָפַּת לֵיהּ בְּסִימָנָהָא, לְמֶהֱוֵי נָטִיר מֵאִינּוּן נוּנֵי יַמָּא, דְּשָׁאטִין בְּיַמָּא רַבָּא, כְּמָה דִּכְתִּיב שָׁם רֶמֶשׂ וְאֵין מִסְפָּר. וְהִיא חָפַּת לֵיהּ לְמֶהֱוֵי נָטִיר מִנַּיְיהוּ בְּחָפוּ דְּסִטְרָא דְּיוֹבְלָא יַקִּירָא בִּתְרֵי גַּוְונִין, בְּחִוָּור וְאוּכָם, וְאָנַח לֵיהּ לְמֹשֶׁה לְמֵישַׁט

בֵּינַיְיהוּ, לְאִשְׁתְּמוֹדַע בֵּינַיְיהוּ, בְּגִין דְּזַמִּין הוּא לְסַלְּקָא בֵּינַיְיהוּ, זִמְנָא אָחֳרָא, לְקַבְּלָא אוֹרַיְיתָא.

314. "And when she could no longer hide him…." (Exodus 2:3) He asks: **"What is the meaning of: 'She took for him a basket made of papyrus' (Ibid)?"** He answers: **"She coated it with conserving ingredients to keep it safe from these sea fish,** meaning High Angels, **that swim in the great ocean, as it is written: '…wherein are creeping things innumerable….' (Psalms 104:25) She coated it so that he should be guarded from them, with a coat from the precious Jubilee,** Binah, **in two colors, white and black.** This is the secret of clay and tar, which corresponds to the two Columns, Right and Left, since tar is the secret of the left, except that it is blended with Malchut of the attribute of Judgment, and therefore the red in the Left turns to black, which is the secret of the black that is actually red, except that it is defective. **She allowed Moses to sail among them,** the Angels, **and to become known among them because he was destined to go up among them at a later date to receive the Torah."**

The river represents Harsh Judgment.

315. וַתֵּרֶד בַּת פַּרְעֹה. דָּא הִיא, דְּאַתְיָא מִסִּטְרָא שְׂמָאלָא דְּדִינָא קַשְׁיָא, כְּמָה דְּאִתְּמַר לִרְחוֹץ עַל הַיְאוֹר. עַל הַיְאוֹר דַּיְיקָא, וְלָא עַל הַיָּם. וְאִי תֵּימָא, הָא כְּתִיב וּמַטְּךָ אֲשֶׁר הִכִּיתָ בּוֹ אֶת הַיְאוֹר. וּמֹשֶׁה לָא הִכָּה אֶלָּא בַּיָּם, וְקַרְיֵיהּ קְרָא יְאוֹר. אֶלָּא יְאוֹר הֲוָה דִּמְחָא אַהֲרֹן עַל יְדָא דְּמֹשֶׁה, וְשַׁוְיֵיהּ קְרָא דְּאִיהוּ עֲבַד.

315. "And the daughter of Pharaoh came down to wash herself at the River…." (Exodus 2:5) This is the daughter of Pharaoh **who came from the Left aspect of Harsh Judgment, as it is written: "…to wash herself at the River." (Ibid.) "…at the river" is exact, instead of "at the sea,"** since the sea indicates Malchut, but the river is Harsh Judgment from the Left Side, which the Egyptians have made their deity. **If you ask: "It is written: '…and your rod, with which you smote the**

River…' (Exodus 17:5), but Moses only struck the sea yet scripture calls it a river? So we see that 'river' is not exact. He answers: **"It is indeed the River that Aaron struck under Moses' direction, and the scripture assigned it as if Moses himself did the striking."**

Why scripture refers to the Creator and not Aaron.

316. כְּהַאי גַּוְונָא וַיִּמָּלֵא שִׁבְעַת יָמִים אַחֲרֵי הַכּוֹת יְיָ' אֶת הַיְאוֹר, וְאַהֲרֹן הִכָּה, אֶלָּא עַל דָּא דְּאָתָא מִסִּטְרָא דְקוּדְשָׁא בְּרִיךְ הוּא, קַרְיֵיהּ קְרָא הַכּוֹת יְיָ', לְבָתַר קַרְיֵיהּ בִּשְׁמָא דְמֹשֶׁה. וְנַעֲרוֹתֶיהָ הוֹלְכוֹת, אִינּוּן שְׁאַר מַשִּׁרְיָין דְּאַתְיָין מִסִּטְרָא דָּא.

316. Similarly, "And seven days were completed, after the Lord had smitten the River." (Exodus 7:25) Even though **Aaron struck it, it is only because it came from the Holy One, blessed be He,** who commanded him **that scripture referred to it as: "…the Lord had smitten…." (Ibid.) Later on, it was referred to in the name of Moses,** for the same reason. **"…and her maidens walked along…" (Exodus 2:5); these are the rest of the camps that came from that** Left **Side.**

The secret of the words "She saw him."

317. וַתִּפְתַּח וַתִּרְאֵהוּ אֶת הַיֶּלֶד. וַתִּרְאֵהוּ, וַתֵּרֶא מִבָּעֵי לֵיהּ, מַאי וַתִּרְאֵהוּ. וְהָא אָמַר רַבִּי שִׁמְעוֹן לֵית לָךְ מִלָּה בְּאוֹרַיְיתָא, אוֹ אָת וַחַד בְּאוֹרַיְיתָא, דְּלָא אִית בֵּיהּ רָזִין יַקִּירִין וְעִלָּאִין. אֶלָּא הָכִי אוֹלִיפְנָא, רְשִׁימָא דְמַלְכָּא וּמַטְרוֹנִיתָא אִשְׁתְּכַחַת בֵּיהּ, וְאִינּוּן רְשִׁימָא דְוָא"ו הֵ"א, מִיַּד וַתַּחְמוֹל עָלָיו וְגוֹ'. עַד כָּאן לְעֵילָּא. מִכָּאן וּלְהָלְאָה לְתַתָּא, בַּר הַאי קְרָא, דִּכְתִיב וַתֵּתַצַּב אֲחוֹתוֹ מֵרָחוֹק. אֲחוֹתוֹ דְמַאן. אֲחוֹתוֹ דְּהַאי אִיהוּ, דְּקָרָא לִכְנֶסֶת יִשְׂרָאֵל אֲחוֹתִי, כד"א פִּתְחִי לִי אֲחוֹתִי. מֵרָחוֹק: כד"א, מֵרָחוֹק יְיָ' נִרְאָה לִי.

317. "And when she had opened it, she saw him, the child…." (Exodus 2:6) He asks: **"What is: 'she saw him'? It should have said,**

'she saw the child.' **Did Rav Shimon not say that there was nothing in the Torah, or even one letter in the Torah, that does not contain highly valuable secrets?"** He answers: **"Rather, this is how we learned it. The impression of the King and the Matron,** Zeir Anpin and Malchut, the secret of Vav-Hei of Yud-Hei-Vav-Hei, **was found in him, and this is the impression of Vav-Hei (וה)** that were added to 'she saw (*vatere*; **ותרא**),' and therefore it is spelled '*vatir'ehu* (ותראהו; she saw him).' **Immediately, "...she had compassion for him...." (Ibid.) Up to here it relates to the Upper** Worlds. **From here on,** it discusses this world **Below, except for this verse, in which it is written: 'And his sister stood afar off....' (Ibid. 4)** He asks: **"Whose sister?"** He replies: **"The sister of the one who called the Congregation of Israel my sister,** namely Zeir Anpin, **as it is said, '...open to me, my sister....' (Song of Songs 5:2) 'afar off'** is **as in, 'From afar the Lord appeared to me....' (Jeremiah 31:3)"** The verse is read as follows: "And [Zeir Anpin's] sister, [Malchut], stood [on Moses] afar off" in the secret of "From afar the Lord appeared to me," as she appeared to Moses then from afar.

The union from which the soul of Moses was born.

318. מַאי מַשְׁמַע. מַשְׁמַע דְּאִינּוּן זַכָּאִין, עַד דְּלָא נַחְתּוּ לְעָלְמָא, אִשְׁתְּמוֹדְעָן אִינּוּן לְעֵילָּא לְגַבֵּי כֹּלָּא, וכ"ש מֹשֶׁה. וּמַשְׁמַע דְּנִשְׁמָתְהוֹן דְּצַדִּיקַיָּיא, אִתְמְשַׁךְ מֵאֲתַר עִלָּאָה, כְּמָה דְּאוֹקִימְנָא. וְרָזָא דְּמִלָּה אוֹלִיפְנָא, דְּמַשְׁמַע דְּאָב וְאֵם אִית לְנִשְׁמְתָא, כְּמָה דְּאִית אָב וְאֵם לְגוּפָא, בְּאַרְעָא.

318. He asks: **"What does** this passage **teach us?"** He replies: **"It teaches that all these Righteous, prior to their descent to the world, are made known to all that are Above.** This applies to all the Righteous, **and most certainly to Moses. It teaches that the souls of the Righteous are drawn from a lofty Place,** since '...of the house of Levi...' (Exodus 2:1) alludes to Supernal Chochmah and Binah, **as we have explained. We learned that the secret of the matter is that there are a father and a mother to the soul, as there are a father and**

mother to the body on Earth, since 'a man' is Zeir Anpin and 'daughter of Levi' is Malchut. And from their union, the soul of Moses was born.

As Above, so Below.

319. וּמַשְׁמַע דִּבְכָל סִטְרִין, בֵּין לְעֵילָּא, בֵּין לְתַתָּא, מִדְּכַר וְנוּקְבָא כֹּלָּא אַתְיָא וְאִשְׁתְּכַחוּ. וְהָא אוּקְמוּהָ רָזָא דִּכְתִּיב, תּוֹצֵא הָאָרֶץ נֶפֶשׁ חַיָּה. הָאָרֶץ, דָּא כְּנֶסֶת יִשְׂרָאֵל. נֶפֶשׁ חַיָּה, נַפְשָׁא דְּאָדָם קַדְמָאָה עִלָּאָה, כְּמָה דְּאִתְּמַר. אָתָא רִבִּי אַבָּא וּנְשָׁקֵיהּ, אָמַר וַדַּאי שַׁפִּיר קָא אַמְרַת, וְהָכָא הוּא כֹּלָּא.

319. "It teaches that on all sides, both Above, Zeir Anpin and Nukva, **and Below,** father and mother of this world, **are comprised of male and female. This is how they established the secret of the verse: '... "Let the earth bring forth living creatures (*nefesh chayah*)..."' (Genesis 1:24); 'the earth' refers to the Congregation of Israel,** Malchut, **the Living Soul (*Nefesh Chayah*)** is **the Nefesh of Supernal Adam, as we have learned,"** since Malchut is the Mother of the Nefesh of Adam. **Rav Aba approached him and kissed him. He said: "You certainly spoke properly, and it is as you say."**

The Creator raised Moses to His presence.

320. זַכָּאָה חוּלָקֵיהּ דְּמֹשֶׁה נְבִיאָה מְהֵימְנָא, עַל כָּל שְׁאַר נְבִיאֵי עָלְמָא. בְּגִין כַּךְ, לָא אִשְׁתְּדַל בֵּיהּ כַּד אִסְתַּלָּק מֵעָלְמָא, בַּר קוּדְשָׁא בְּרִיךְ הוּא, דְּאַעֲלֵיהּ לְפַרְגּוֹדֵיהּ. וְעַל דָּא סָלִיק מֹשֶׁה בִּנְבוּאָה עִלָּאָה, וּבְדַרְגִּין יַקִּירִין, מִכָּל נְבִיאֵי עָלְמָא, וּשְׁאַר נְבִיאֵי חָמָאן בָּתַר כּוֹתְלִין סַגִּיאִין.

320. Worthy is the lot of Moses, the Faithful Prophet, above all the rest of the prophets in the world. Therefore when he departed, no one else dealt with him besides the Holy One, blessed be He, who raised him to His presence. Thus Moses ascended in lofty prophecy and glorious levels beyond all the prophets in the world, while the other prophets saw as if behind many walls.

Appendix A

Ten Sefirot—Tree of Life

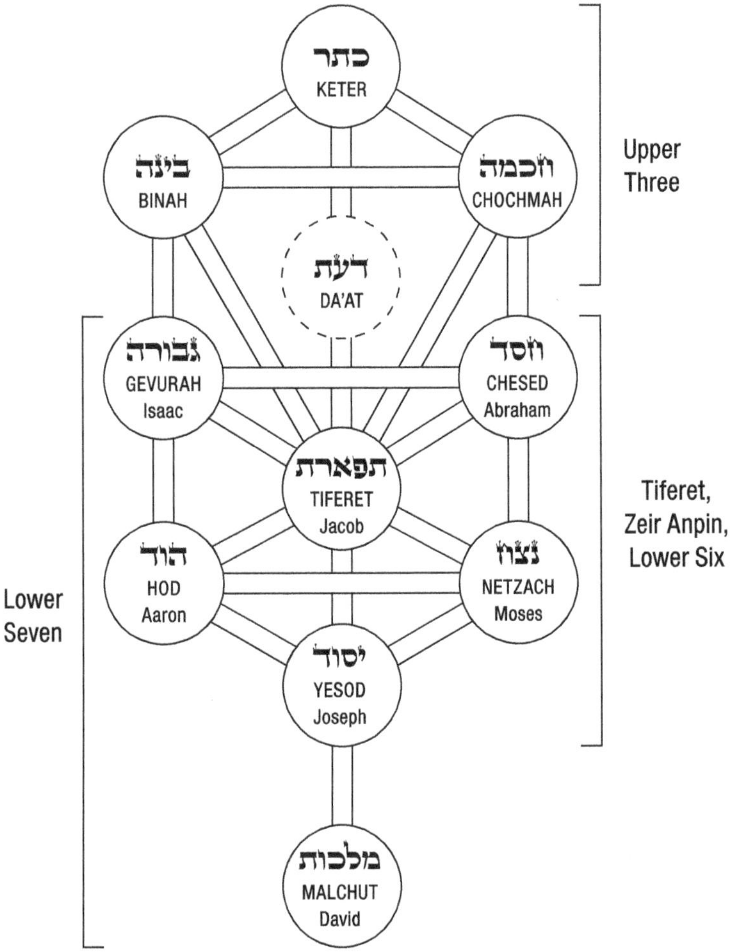

According to kabbalistic teaching, the creation of the universe was made possible by a withdrawal of the Light of the Creator, which was otherwise present everywhere. The reason for this withdrawal was for our own sake. Therefore we are separated from the Light of the Creator by a sequence of ten energy fields known as the Sefirot (singular:

Sefirah), which essentially are packets of bottled-up energies, each with its own intelligence and individual attributes. The Sefirot may be thought of as spiritual transformers, successively downgrading the Creator's infinite Light until it reaches us in a manageable intensity.

Arranged in Right, Left, and Central Columns, these Ten Sefirot make up what kabbalists call the Tree of Life. The Ten Sefirot are not simply external to ourselves as they are both levels to be attained and also are all contained within us in potential form, ready to be awakened and mastered through our transformative spiritual work. As we transform our natures, we increase the capacity of our spiritual vessel to hold more Light, thus giving us the ability to draw ever nearer to the Creator.

1. Keter

Keter is the summit of the Central Column, and is paradoxically both the "crown" and the source. It embodies God as unknown and unknowable and is located just below the endless world of limitless Light, far, far beyond mortal comprehension. Keter is the blazing intelligence that channels the Light of the Creator to the rest of the Tree. It functions as a supercomputer, containing the total inventory of what each of us is, ever has been, or ever will be. As such, it is the genesis not only of our lives in this earthly realm, but of every thought, idea, or inspiration we ever will have while we sojourn here, and that includes lifetimes of the past, the present, and the future. Keter is the source of everything, but only in an undifferentiated potential. The rest of the energy centers on the Tree of Life are needed to turn that potential into something we can perceive as reality.

2. Chochmah

As the highest level of the Right Column, Chochmah is the first Sefirah to receive the power that flows from the Endless World through Keter. Chochmah is recognized as the universal father figure, the primordial point of creation from which all knowable reality originates. It has the property of wisdom "beyond reason," that is, an inspired and pure knowing. But wisdom, existing passively in a kind of warehouse, is of no value on any plane. To be of use, it must be inventoried, shipped out, and supplied to those in need of it. To accomplish that, Chochmah requires connection with its corresponding mother figure, which is the Sefirah of Binah.

3. Binah

Topping the Left Column, Binah is considered to be the universal mother figure, and, complementing Chochmah's knowing, it carries the property of understanding. Binah also contains all energy, ranging from that which motivates human endeavor to that which keeps galaxies spinning. As Chochmah and Binah, universal father and mother, meet, thought becomes manifest in action. Their combined energies are funneled through "the invisible Sefirah" called Da'at, which lies on the Central column below Keter. Even to kabbalists, Da'at is enigmatic, but while not regarded as a true Sefirah, it is thought to unify the energies of Chochmah's wisdom and Binah's understanding, transmitting them to the lower Sefirot of Da'at as knowledge.

4. Chesed

The Sefirah of Chesed, the most expansive of the Sefirot, sits below Chochmah on the right-hand column and represents mercy. Chesed holds the still-undifferentiated seed of all that has taken place between Chochmah and Binah, and since it represents the total desire to share, it can be generous to a fault. We all have seen Chesed run amok. It is the ultra-liberal who weeps more for the criminal than for the victim; it is the parents who cannot ever bring themselves to discipline their children. Fortunately, Chesed does have a balancing counterpart, just across the way, on the left-hand column, right under Binah. It is called Gevurah.

5. Gevurah

The Sefirah of Gevurah represents judgment. Where Chesed expands, Gevurah contracts. Where Chesed says, "Share," Gevurah says, "What's in it for me?" Where Chesed forgives and forgets, Gevurah is a strict and wrathful disciplinarian. Gevurah, run amok, without Chesed's balance, becomes the tyranny of a police state. But even as Chochmah's wisdom cannot become manifest without Binah's energy, neither can the undifferentiated seed that lies in Chesed ever become manifest without Gevurah's strong hand. It is here that the process of differentiation, the beginning of physicality originates. Associated with this Sefirah is the archangel Sama"el (the left hand of God), also known in Kabbalah as "the Adversary." Unrestrained, the energy of Gevurah can become destructive.

6. Tiferet

The Sefirah of Tiferet, representing beauty or the ideal balance of Gevurah (justice) and Chesed (mercy), rests below Keter on the Central Column, and beneath Chesed on the right and Gevurah on the left. Tiferet is the balancing point between right and left columns, and without the symmetry of balance, there can be no beauty. Tiferet may be thought of as the heart of the Tree of Life. As a balance between judgment and mercy, this Sefirah is associated with the patriarch Jacob. Here we find combined wisdom, understanding, and the luminosity of the Light.

7. Netzach

The Sefirah of Netzach, or victory, resides on the Right Column, just below Chesed. A repository of positive energy from Chesed, Netzach radiates the Desire to Share and becomes the channel of that energy as it approaches the physical world in which we live. It is associated with Moses, who as a link between the Creator and humankind, and personifies these enduring qualities. Netzach can be thought of as the sperm that, in union with the egg, ultimately creates the individual human being. Netzach is also known as eternity, and it represents involuntary processes as well as the right brain, where the creative process takes place. Netzach is the artist, the poet, the musician, the dreamer, and the masculine fertilizing principle. Its feminine counterpart, directly across the way on the left-hand column, is Hod.

8. Hod

The Left Column counterpart to Netzach, Hod or glory is analogous to the egg in human conception. Hod is also associated with prophecy, controlling voluntary processes and left-brain activity, as well as channeling the practicality of Gevurah into the human psyche. Hod is the feminine or manifesting principle. It is here that the potentials held in the male aspects of Chesed and Netzach begin to become material. The dreams become concrete.

9. Yesod

At the base of the Tree of Life is Yesod or foundation. This Central Column Sefirah sits like a great reservoir. All the Sefirot above pour their attributes into Yesod's vast basin where they are mixed, balanced, and made ready to be channeled into the World of Action—Malchut. As Binah is the generator of the source contained in Keter, Yesod is the generator of the destination, which is Malchut.

10. Malchut

Malchut or Kingdom is the lowest of the Sefirot, and is the world of our material universe. To understand Malchut and its relationship to the other nine Sefirot, it may be helpful to think of it as a house. The house was conceived of by Chochmah. Binah provided the energy to build it. Chesed provided a loving willingness to build it. Gevurah calculated its measurements. Tiferet provided a lovely and level setting. Netzach supplied a color scheme, while Hod provided the building materials. Yesod dug a foundation. Malchut houses the world in which we live. It is the only Sefirot on the Tree of Life where physical matter exists as a minuscule percentage of the whole, and where the Tree of Knowledge sinks its roots. And it is here that a divergence in human attitude spells the difference between individual lives lived in the Light and those lived in darkness.

Partzuf (Face)

A Partzuf is a complete spiritual structure of the Ten Sefirot. A Partzuf represents the Head—the Upper Three Sefirot or potential, and the Body—the Lower Seven Sefirot or actual. There are five Partzufim (plural of Partzuf) in the metaphysical world:

1. Arich Anpin (Long Face)—also referred to as: Atik, Atik Yomin, Atika Kadisha

2. Aba (Father)—contains two parts:
   a. Chochmah
   b. Yisrael-Saba

3. Ima (Mother)—contains two parts:
   a. Binah
   b. Tevunah

4. Zeir Anpin (Small Face)

5. Nukva (Female)—also referred to as Malchut

The chief Partzufim we interact with are Chochmah, Binah, Tiferet (Zeir Anpin), and Malchut, and they correspond to the four letters of the Tetragrammaton: Yud-Hei-Vav-Hei.

Five Worlds

All of the above Spiritual Structures (Partzufim) create one spiritual world. There are Five Worlds in total that comprise all reality.

Adam Kadmon (Primordial Man) – The fifth and highest spiritual World. There are four spiritual Worlds through which our soul ascends and descends during the course of the day as we make our spiritual connections. However, there is a fifth World that is even higher than these four—a World that we cannot reach through our connections—and this fifth World is called Primordial Man.

Atzilut (World of Emanation) – The second (from above downward) of the Five Spiritual Worlds that appeared after the Tzimtzum (Contraction). In this high and most exalted World, the Vessel is passive in relation to the Light, allowing the Light to flow without any agenda. This World is related to the Sefirah of Chochmah (Wisdom) and is completely protected from the Klipot (shells).

Briyah (World of Creation) – The third (from above downward) of the Five Spiritual Worlds that appeared after the Tzimtzum (Contraction). This World is related to the Sefirah of Binah (Understanding) and is a universal energy store. The World of Briyah is also related to the Shechinah (Supernal Mother) and is almost completely protected from the Klipot (shells).

Yetzirah (World of Formation) – The fourth (from above downward) of the Five Spiritual Worlds that appeared after the Tzimtzum (Contraction). Whereas in the lowest World, the World of Action, evil is the predominant force, in the World of Formation, goodness is the predominant force. Yetzirah is related to the Sefirah of Zeir Anpin (Small Face) and to the energy of the Shield of David.

Asiyah (World of Action) – The lowest of the Five Spiritual Worlds that emerged after the Tzimtzum (Contraction) of the Vessel in the World of the Endless. The World of Action is the dimension where the least amount of Light is revealed. This enables human beings to exercise their free will in discerning between good and evil. This World is also related to the Sefirah of Malchut (Kingdom) and is referred to as the Tree of Knowledge of Good and Evil.

Five Levels of the Soul

Nefesh – The lowest part of our soul, the part that every person is born with. It allows the Klipot to connect to us. Nefesh is usually fueled by the Desire to Receive for the Self Alone; it is the animal instinct and psyche that we all have. The Torah teaches us that the connection to Nefesh is through the blood, and this is why we do not eat or drink anything that has animal blood on it: We do not want to connect to the raw instinct of that animal. At certain age-related milestones in an individual's life, they receives additional parts of the soul.

Ruach (Spirit) – Of the five parts that make up the soul, Ruach is the next level up from Nefesh. It is an additional part of our soul that enters us when we reach Bar/Bat Mitzvah (age 13 for a boy, 12 for a girl), and it activates our free will to choose between Light and darkness.

Neshamah (Soul) – This is the third part of our soul, which we receive when we reach the age of 20. It is called "Soul" because until we receive this third part, our own soul is not yet complete. This third part of the soul allows us to connect directly to the power of the Creator. It is the Light that is contained in Binah.

Chayah (Life-Sustaining) – The fourth part of a person's soul, called Chayah, is very rarely received because it denotes that an individual has achieved such a high level of spirituality that they no longer have the evil inclination within them. Chayah is the Light of the Sefirah of Chochmah, which provides life and sustains the soul.

Yechidah (Oneness) – The fifth and final part of a person's soul, when the individual unites completely with the Light of the Creator.

Names of God

Just as a single ray of white sunlight contains the seven colors of the spectrum, the one Light of the Creator embodies many diverse spiritual forces. These different forces are called Names of God. Each Name denotes a specific attribute and spiritual power. The Hebrew letters that compose these Names are the interface by which these varied Forces act upon our physical world. The most common Name of God is the Tetragrammaton (the four letters of Yud-Hei-Vav-Hei; יְהֹוָה), and because of the enormous power the Tetragrammaton transmits, we do not utter this Name aloud but instead pronounce it as Adonai (Alef-Dalet-Nun-Yud). And since the Name Adonai also reveals a tremendous amount of Light, we only pronounce it when we make a blessing, when we recite a kabbalistic prayer or when we read from the Torah. Other than these instances, we say *HaShem,* which means "the Name" or Yud-Kei-Vav-Kei instead of Adonai.

Below is a list of the Names of God that both the Torah and the Zohar reference, how it is pronounced as well as to which Sefirah each Name corresponds.

Name (Hebrew)	Name (English)	Pronunciation	Corresponding Sefirah
אֶהְיֶה	Alef-Hei-Yud-Hei	Alef-Kei-Yud-Kei	Binah
אֵל	El	Kel	Chesed
אֱלֹהִים	Elohim	Elokim	Gevurah, also Malchut
יְהוָה	Yud-Hei-Vav-Kei	Yud-Kei-Vav-Kei or Adonai	Tiferet, Zeir Anpin
צְבָאוֹת	Tzeva'ot	Tzevakot	Netzach and Hod
שַׁדַּי	Shadai	Shakai or Shin-Dalet-Yud	Yesod
אֲדֹנָי	Adonai	Alef-Dalet-Nun-Yud or HaShem	Malchut/Nukva

Spelled Out (*Milu'i*)

When a Name or a word is spelled out by the letters that comprise its conventionally accepted form, it is called *milu'i*. Rav Isaac Luria (the Ari) explains that each Name of God emanates a different frequency of energy and that changing the Name, even in the slightest way, changes its frequency—similar to changing one atom in a molecule, which will dramatically change the energy and frequency of the molecule. He says that the numerical value of the word *milu'i* is 86, which is the same numerical value of the word Elohim—a name that signifies Judgment. Therefore when a Name is spelled out it makes its energy and frequency coarser or materialized, which is an aspect of Judgment and spiritual thickness. Conversely, when we keep the Name simple, without spelling it out, it is an aspect of Mercy. There are four ways to spell out the

Name of Yud-Hei-Vav-Hei and each corresponds to one of the four Worlds and four Sefirot.

Milu'i of the Name Yud-Hei-Vav-Hei יהוה

Numerical Value	Sefirah	World	Spelled Out			
72 (AV)	Chochmah	Atzilut	הי	ויו	הי	יוד
			Hei-Yud	Vav-Yud-Vav	Hei-Yud	Yud-Vav-Dalet
63 (SaG)	Binah	Briyah	הי	ואו	הי	יוד
			Hei-Yud	Vav-Alef-Vav	Hei-Yud	Yud-Vav-Dalet
45 (MaH)	Zeir Anpin	Yetzirah	הא	ואו	הא	יוד
			Hei-Alef	Vav-Alef-Vav	Hei-Alef	Yud-Vav-Dalet
52 (BaN)	Malchut	Asiyah	הה	וו	הה	יוד
			Hei-Hei	Vav-Vav	Hei-Hei	Yud-Vav-Dalet

Filling (*Milu'i*)

According to the Ari, the word *milu'i* also means "filling." Filling this case means taking an original Name, for example, Yud-Hei-Vav-Hei (26) that is spelled out as AV (יוד הי ויו הי), equaling 72, and removing the first letter from each spelling out as follow: Instead of Yud-Vav-Dalet, we now have Vav-Dalet; instead of Hei-Yud, we now have Yud; instead of Vav-Yud-Vav we now have Yud-Vav; instead of Hei-Yud, we now have Yud, which together equal 46. So the filling or *milu'i* of AV is 46.

Milu'i (Filling) of Yud-Hei-Vav-Hei יהוה:

Numerical Value	Sefirah	World	Spelled Out			
46	Chochmah	Atzilut	י	יו	י	וד
			Yud	Yud-Vav	Yud	Vav-Dalet
37	Binah	Briyah	י	או	י	וד
			Yud	Alef-Vav	Yud	Vav-Dalet
19	Zeir Anpin	Yetzirah	א	או	א	וד
			Alef	Alef-Vav	Alef	Vav-Dalet
26	Malchut	Asiyah	ה	ו	ה	וד
			Hei	Vav	Hei	Vav-Dalet

Milu'i (Spelled Out) of the Name Alef-Hei-Yud-Hei אהיה

Numerical Value	Sefirah	Spelled Out			
161	Chochmah	הי	יוד	הי	אלף
		Hei-Yud	Yud-Vav-Dalet	Hei-Yud	Alef-Lamed-Pei
161	Binah	הי	יוד	הי	אלף
		Hei-Yud	Yud-Vav-Dalet	Hei-Yud	Alef-Lamed-Pei
143	Zeir Anpin	הא	יוד	הא	אלף
		Hei-Alef	Yud-Vav-Dalet	Hei-Alef	Alef-Lamed-Pei
151	Malchut	הה	יוד	הה	אלף
		Hei-Hei	Yud-Vav-Dalet	Hei-Hei	Alef-Lamed-Pei

Milu'i (Spelled Out) of the Name Elohim אלהים:

Numerical Value	Sefirah	Spelled Out				
300	Chochmah	מם	יוד	הי	למד	אלף
		Mem-Mem	Yud-Vav-Dalet	Hei-Yud	Lamed-Mem-Dalet	Alef-Lamed-Pei
300	Binah	מם	יוד	הי	למד	אלף
		Mem-Mem	Yud-Vav-Dalet	Hei-Yud	Lamed-Mem-Dalet	Alef-Lamed-Pei
291	Zeir Anpin	מם	יוד	הא	למד	אלף
		Mem-Mem	Yud-Vav-Dalet	Hei-Alef	Lamed-Mem-Dalet	Alef-Lamed-Pei
295	Malchut	מם	יוד	הה	למד	אלף
		Mem-Mem	Yud-Vav-Dalet	Hei-Hei	Lamed-Mem-Dalet	Alef-Lamed-Pei

Angels

Angels are distinct spiritual energy-intelligences that are part of a vast communication network roaming among us, acting as messengers from the Creator and affecting things that happen in our daily lives. An Angel is a conduit or channel that transports cosmic energy or thoughts from one place to another or from one spiritual dimension to the other. Angels have no free will, and each Angel is dedicated to one specific purpose and responsible for transmitting a unique force of influence into our physical universe. When reading about an Angel in the Zohar, we do no pronounce its name, since saying the name aloud draws the Angel to us and more times than not, our capacity to handle its energy is not large enough. Therefore in the texts the names are broken up as follows: Metatro"n. However, there are a few names of Angels that are also names of humans like: Michael, Gabriel, and Rafael that we can pronounce.

Name (Hebrew)	Name (English)	Pronunciation
מטטרו"ן	Metatro"n	Matat
סנדלפו"ן	Sandalfo"n	Sandal
סמא"ל	Samae"l	Samech-Mem
לילי"ת	Lili"t	Lamed-Yud

Holidays – Days of Power

In the everyday world, our concept of holidays is based on remembering, memorializing, and paying homage to some event in the past. Kabbalah, however, absolutely rejects remembrance or recognition as the basis of these cosmic times of connection known as Holidays. In place of commemoration, a kabbalist focuses on *connection*—that is, the opportunity to tap into the unique energies that exist at the specific points in time that we call Holidays. The holidays are literally power sources we can access using the technology and tools of Kabbalah. The major Holidays or Days of Power are:

- **Rosh Hashanah** – Seed level of the year
- **Yom Kippur** – At-one-ment with the Light
- **Sukkot** – Surrounding ourselves with the Light of kindness, protection and certainty
- **Simchat Torah** – Joy of the Torah and the beginning of the Torah reading cycle
- **Chanukah** – Lighting candles for eight days and connecting to the Or Haganuz (Concealed Light)
- **Purim** – Joy and certainty beyond logic
- **Pesach** – Freedom from the bondage of the ego
- **Shavuot** – Accepting the spiritual system of the Torah, thus breaking free from death

Appendix B

Glossary

248 – There are 248 bone segments of the human body as well as 248 words in the Shema Reading and 248 Positive Precepts. These Positive Precepts are the proactive "to-do" actions, and each one relates to a different part of the body. When we perform these Precepts, we strengthen our body. See also: 365, 613

365 – There are 365 tendons and sinews in the human body as well as 365 Negative Precepts. These Negative Precepts are the proactive "do not do" actions, referring to acts of restriction and refraining from acting on our negative and selfish impulses. Each Precept corresponds to a different sinew and tendon, and to each of the 365 days of the year. See also: 248, 613

613 – The number of Precepts—spiritual actions—that we can do to get spiritually closer to the Light of the Creator. There are 613 Precepts, and all can be found within the Five Books of Moses. These Precepts are divided into two categories: 248 Precepts of positive "to-do" actions, and 365 Precepts of negative "do not do" actions. Performing both types of Precepts will bring us closer to the Creator. See also: Precept, 248, 365

Amen – the word Amen literally means "true" or "trustworthy." When one makes a blessing or says Kaddish, the listeners answer "Amen." The Zohar explains that saying Amen is not really about validating a blessing or a praise, but the word Amen has the numerical value of 91, which is the sum of two names of God: Alef-Dalet-Nun-Yud (65) and Yud-Hei-Vav-Hei (26). Alef-Dalet-Nun-Yud represents the World of Malchut, or the physical world, and Yud-Hei-Vav-Hei represents Zeir Anpin or the metaphysical, Upper World. Saying "Amen" unifies the Upper and Lower Worlds, Light and Vessel, as well as fulfilment with desire. Therefore, the sages said "greater is the one who says 'Amen' than the one who makes the blessing."

Amidah – Literally translates as "standing," the Amidah is the silent prayer we recite standing up. There are 18-19 blessings during the weekday Amidah, and seven during Shabbat and Holidays. We say Amidah three times a day: Shacharit in the morning, Mincha in the afternoon, and Arvit at night.

Central Column – The force that regulates between Right and Left, mercy and judgment. Central Column represents the concept of restricting our reactive nature and regulating mercy and judgment with balance. Jacob the Patriarch was the embodiment of Central Column, and therefore an Israelite is one who aligns themselves with the Central Column concept. Central Column also represents the Sefirot that are in the center of the Tree of Life: Da'at, Tiferet, Yesod.

Chai ha'Olamim –Life of the Worlds or Eternal life; both concepts relate to the Light of the Creator. *Chai* (life) also has the numerical value of 18.

Clothing – All spiritual energy like the Lightforce of the Creator needs to be concealed to be revealed; this concealment is referred to as "clothing." Our thoughts, words, and actions are clothing for the Lightforce of the Creator. Our body is the clothing for our soul. The Torah is the clothing for the Creator. When a Partzuf receives assistance from a lower Partzuf, then the lower one is a garment or clothing to the upper Partzuf.

Ein Sof (Endless) – Before the creation of this world, the endless Light of the Creator filled all existence. There was no lack of any kind. All desires were completely fulfilled, and the Vessel, which is the Desire to Receive, was not blemished by the Desire to Receive for the Self Alone.

Evil Inclination – Each of us always has two inner voices that guide us to do everything, whether positive (proactive) or negative (reactive). The evil inclination is the voice that pushes us to be reactive and negative. It is sometimes referred to as Satan, which in Hebrew simply means "adversary." The evil inclination is our internal opponent that always tells us to act selfishly and reactively.

Exile – The state of existence where we are less connected and less in tune with the Light, a state where chaos rules and miracles are rare. This state was brought about by the destruction of both Holy Temples. The Hebrew word for "exile" is *Galut,* which also means "to reveal," because this state of existence will change permanently once we reveal the wisdom of Kabbalah, spread it to everyone, and thus change the world.

Externals – Both the Zohar and Rav Isaac Luria (the Ari) use the word "Externals" or "Chitzonim" to represent the Negative Side or Klipot. The Externals are negative external forces that block the Light from being revealed.

Gadlut (Maturity/Greatness) – Represents when we have expanded consciousness and are spiritually mature.

Halachah (Law) – Any spiritual law of the universe that is based on the 613 Precepts. The later Talmudic laws along with customs and traditions are collectively referred to as *halachah.* The literal meaning of *halachah* is "the path" because *halachah* is a way of connecting to the path of life through the actions that we do. For those who want to follow a spiritual quest, *halachah* is a system of instructions for what to do, how, and when.

Hell (Gehenom) – A purgatory-like place where souls that have moved on but require cleansing from the negativity they revealed while alive go; here all their negativity is purified. The souls remain in Hell no longer than 12 months to complete the purification process.

Holy One, blessed be He – the Light, the Creator, God. Represents the force of Zeir Anpin, and the male aspect of God that fills the vessel.

Ibur – An additional soul that enters a body and unites with an existing soul either temporarily or permanently. The term Ibur literally means a pregnancy or an impregnation; it is likened to a woman who is pregnant and carries a soul in addition to her own.

Impurity – A term used to describe the level where a person is failing to resist his ego and the Evil Inclination, and thus is sinking lower and lower into selfishness.

Israelite – A code name for anyone following a spiritual path and working on his or her negative traits, and constantly striving to transform them to positive ones. Israelites are people who take upon themselves the responsibility of spreading the Light and for putting other people's needs before their own. They also understand and follow the spiritual rules of cause and effect, and do not take the Torah literally but rather as a coded message.

Katnut (Immaturity/Smallness) – Represents when we have reactive and selfish consciousness and are spiritually immature.

Kavanah (Intention, Meditation) – The act of centering our consciousness with the attention appropriate to a situation or connection.

Klipah, klipot – See "Externals"

Leah – Name of the Partzuf of the Upper part of Nukva, known as the Hidden World.

Left Column – the force that draws energy like a magnet and starts the flow of Light to a vessel or desire. The attribute of Left Column is found in the following characteristics: strength, desire to receive, setting boundaries, discipline and the rejection of that which is bad. Left Column also represents the Sefirot that are on the left side of the Tree of Life: Binah, Gevurah, Hod.

Eruv – So as not to transfer between Domains on Shabbat, the sages established a system of placing a string around sections of the Public Domain, making them one Private Domain, so people could carry objects within this area.

Lower Seven – In each of the Four Spiritual Worlds there are ten levels or Sefirot. The Lower Seven Sefirot are Chesed (Mercy), Gevurah (Judgment/Might), Tiferet (Beauty), Netzach (Eternity/Victory), Hod (Glory), Yesod (Foundation), and Malchut (Kingdom). Collectively, the Lower Seven Sefirot represent the six directions: south, north, east, up, down, and west. See also: *Vav Ketzavot,* Upper Three

Masach DeChirik – Desire to Receive for the Sake of Sharing (Central Column). The pushback and resistance of the Desire to Receive that balances the Right and Left Columns, bringing unity and balance between them so that they can both exist.

Mayin Duchrin (Masculine Waters) – Awakening from Above, in order to give energy for the Unification.

Mayin Nukvin (Feminine Waters) – Awakening from Below, in order to give energy to the Female for the Unification. There are two kinds of Mayin Nukvin: The first is the effort that the Female makes in order to be unified with Her Male. The second is when the Lower Partzuf will make an extra effort in order to give this energy to the Upper Partzuf and thereby the Upper Partzuf will be able to be unified and give back higher illuminations to this Lower Partzuf.

Merit – In Hebrew, this word is *zechut*, which is derived from the root word for "pure," meaning that when we transform our selfish nature into one of selflessness and sharing with others, we become pure. In doing so, we will attain the merit of a spiritual lifeline, which will be there when we most need it to remove the chaos, pain, and suffering we are experiencing.

Messiah (Mashiach) – Often described as a person, the concept of Messiah simply means the collective consciousness of humanity where everyone cares about others' needs ahead of their own, in this way emulating the complete selflessness of the Light. The concept of death (in health, business, relationships, or anything else) cannot exist within the realm of this consciousness.

Mochin – Literally means brains and represents quality of consciousness. When we sleep, our Mochin go up, and that's why we are unconscious. When Zeir Anpin has Mochin, it means Zeir Anpin has attained the Upper Three Sefirot (Chochmah, Binah, Da'at) and is now complete.

Nations – Nations actually represent the inner attributes and character traits of our individual self. The nation of Amalek refers to the doubt and uncertainty that dwells within us when we face hardship and obstacles. Moab represents the dual nature of man. Nefilim refers to the sparks of Light that we have defiled through our impure actions, and to the negative forces that lurk within the human soul as a result of our own wrongful deeds.

Numerical Value – There are 22 Hebrew letters, each with a numerical value ranging from 1 to 400, which when combined produce words and phrases with their own numerical values. Words or phrases that have the same value are usually another form of providing us with spiritual insight for our lives through the Torah. The main sources for deciphering these combinations are the Book of Formation (*Sefer Yetzirah*), the Zohar, and the Writings of the Ari.

Ohr Pnimi (Inner Light) – The Light that we have earned through our proactive actions. This Light is who we are and what we are; it is our life experience and wisdom.

Ohr Makif (Surrounding Light) – The Light that pushes us to grow and reveal our potential Light. Ohr Makif refers to our potential and to everything we were meant to accomplish throughout our lifetime. Ohr Makif is connected to the quantum Light of the Creator that waits to be revealed through our proactive actions.

Patriarchs – Abraham, Isaac, and Jacob, who are the three pillars of the Torah. They are referred to as the chariots and channels for the Sefirot of Chesed (Right Column), Gevurah (Left Column), and Tiferet (Central Column) that we can use to achieve balance in our day-to-day life.

Precept – One of the 613 spiritual actions we can do to connect to the Light of the Creator. There are two types of Precepts: those between man and his fellow man, and those between man and the Creator. In Hebrew, the word for Precept is *Mitzvah,* meaning "unity" or "bonding" because the Precepts create unity between the Creator and us.

Pure – Without spiritual blemish. Someone or something that is completely cleansed of negativity. Someone who has less of a Desire to Receive and more of a Desire to Share. The purer a person is, the more Light can shine through him and illuminate his life and the lives of others around him.

Rachel – Name of the Partzuf of the Lower part of Nukva, known as the "revealed world".

Ribu'a (Squared) – *Ribu'a* is a unique way of writing out a Name of God, where the first letter of the Name is written first, then the first and second letter, then the first, second, and third, and so on. For example, the *Ribu'a* of the Name Yud-Hei-Vav-Hei is Yud, Yud-Hei, Yud-Hei-Vav, Yud-Hei-Vav-Hei.

Right Column – the positive force of Light that wants to fill the vessel. The attribute of Right Column is found in the following characteristics: giving, imparting, mercy, letting go, going with the flow, love, and accepting with love that which is good. Right Column also represents the Sefirot that are on the right side of the Tree of Life: Chochmah, Chesed, Netzach.

Righteous (Tzadik) – A person who is completely devoted to working on transforming his or her negative traits and to sharing unconditionally with others. The Midrash also tells us that this is a person whose positive actions outweigh his or her negative actions. The terms "righteous" and "wicked" also can relate to the righteous and wicked part of us, not necessarily a righteous person or wicked person. Thus, we all have our inner righteous and our inner wicked.

Masters – Kabbalists from the time of the Second Temple who were very wise individuals that left us with deep wisdom and many lessons found in the Mishnah and Talmud.

Shechinah (Divine Presence) – The Light of the Creator when it is on its closest frequency to the physical world. The Shechinah is also the collective soul of all Israelites. The Shechinah corresponds to the female aspect of the Light of the Creator, and many writings refer to the union between God and the Shechinah. In addition, the Shechinah is a protection division of the Creator for the all those who connect to the Tree of Life.

Sitra Achra (Other Side) – According to Kabbalah, the world is made of opposites: positive and negative, good and evil. The Light of the Creator represents the side of positivity, order, and clarity, while the *Sitra Achra* (other side) represents negativity, darkness, and chaos. The *Sitra Achra* needs a source of energy but cannot feed directly from the Light of the Creator. Every time we make a wrong choice or get upset and act reactively, the *Sitra Achra* can take advantage of this and suck the Light away from us.

Teshuvah (Repentance) – Meaning literally "to return," *Teshuvah* is the process of going back to an earlier phase where things were connected to the source. When we "short circuit" (i.e., make a wrong choice) and conduct ourselves with selfishness, we disconnect from the Light of the Creator and attract chaos. *Teshuvah* is designed to reverse our negative consciousness through positive transformation, thus allowing us to reconnect with the Light of the Creator. When we take responsibility and own up to our past mistakes, we preemptively remove whatever chaos and pain we might face in the future as a result of our negativity.

This World – The physical world that we live in, where we are subject to the laws of cause and effect, and bound by the limitations of time, space, and motion. Also called the 1 Percent Reality and the illusionary world. See also: World to Come

Torah – there are 24 books of the Torah, which comprise the Written Torah. The first five books are called the five books of Moses. The Oral Torah is the interpretation of the Written Torah, which the Sages received orally from Moses to Joshua to the Elders, and every generation from teacher to student, until the compilation of the Mishna and the Talmud. The Zohar is part of the Oral Torah, but deals with the soul (secrets) of the Torah and the metaphysical laws, whereas the Mishnah and Talmud deal with the body of the Torah and the corporeal laws.

Tractate (Masechet) – The Talmud and Mishnah are each split into six sections, each of which is further divided into subsections called Tractates. Each subsection is given a name to describe the topic of discussion.

Tzelem **(Image or Shadow)** – The clothing of the Mochin as they go to the Lower Partzuf. This clothing is created by the Returning Light of the Lower Partzuf. The Tzelem is divided into three main aspects: The first and highest is called Mem (ם) of the word *Tzelem;* the second is called Lamed (ל) of the word *Tzelem;* and the third and the lowest is called Tzadik (צ) of the word *Tzelem.*

Upper Three – the head of a Partzuf, represented by Chochmah, Binah and Da'at. The head represents cause and potential, which is more powerful than the Lower Six or body, but the body is what manifests. Similarly, the head or Upper Three represents control, as the body is controlled by the head. A Partzuf or Sefirah without the Upper Three is considered incomplete. The Upper three can also refer to the Mochin. See also: Mochin, Lower Seven

Vav Ketzavot (Six Edges) – Represents the body of a spiritual structure, comprised of the Lower Six Sefirot: Chesed, Gevurah, Tiferet, Netzach, Hod, and Yesod. The head of a spiritual structure is called *Gimel Rishonot* (Upper Three Sefirot), which are: Chochmah, Binah, and Da'at.

Vowels – In Hebrew and Aramaic the vowels of words are marked with dots and lines instead of letters. In the Torah scroll there are only letters, but when one reads from the Torah scroll he must learn the vowels and the cantillation marks in order to consider it a valid Torah reading. See also: cantillation marks

World to Come – A realm where only happiness, fulfillment, love, and joy exist—the 99 Percent Realm of the Light of the Creator. The kabbalists explain that the World to Come exists in each and every moment of our lives. Every action of ours creates an effect that comes back to us either for good and for bad, and through the way we live our lives, we can create worlds according to our design. The World to Come is commonly referred to as "the reality of life after life." See also: This World

Worlds – A term used in the Study of the Ten Luminous Emanations to refer to the Five Spiritual Worlds. There are five channels that bring the Light down to our mundane reality. When these channels are filled with Light, we call them Worlds. Each World represents a different level of consciousness that is related to a level of veil that covers the Light. The word *olam* in Hebrew means "disappearance," referring to the fact that only when the Light is concealed can a reality be revealed. The Five Spiritual Worlds, from highest to lowest, are: Primordial Man (Adam Kadmon), Emanation (Atzilut), Creation (Briyah), Formation (Yetzirah), and Action (Asiyah).

Yaakov – The outer Partzuf of Zeir Anpin and corresponds to the Six Edges (Sefirot) of Zeir Anpin.

Yibum, Chalitzah – The Precept of Yibum (Levirate Marriage) applies when a married man has died before having children. To redeem the soul of the deceased, his brother marries his sister-in-law (the widow).

However, if the brother does not want to perform Yibum, he performs Chalitzah, which removes the obligation to marry his sister-in-law.

Yisrael – The inner Partzuf of Zeir Anpin corresponding to the Mochin of Zeir Anpin

Zivug (Unification) – The Nature of the Supernal Light is to emanate illumination to the Lower Worlds for all eternity. Because of the Masach, the Vessel cannot connect. Therefore, when the Vessel is ready (by Returning Light or by elevating Mayin Nukvin) to connect with the Light it is called Zivug. Zivug literally means "unification," which represents the unification of Light and Vessel, and between Zeir Anpin and Nukva.

Appendix C

Hebrew Letters

Letter	Name	Numerical Value
א	Alef	1
ב	Bet	2
ג	Gimel	3
ד	Dalet	4
ה	Hei	5
ו	Vav	6
ז	Zayin	7
ח	Chet	8
ט	Tet	9
י	Yud	10
כ	Kaf	20
ל	Lamed	30
מ	Mem	40
נ	Nun	50
ס	Samech	60
ע	Ayin	70
פ	Pei	80
צ	Tzadi	90
ק	Kof	100
ר	Resh	200
ש	Shin	300
ת	Tav	400

Five Final Letters

When these five letters appear at the end of a word they change shape:

Letter	Final Letter	Name	Numerical Value
מ	ם	Mem	40
נ	ן	Nun	50
צ	ץ	Tzadi	90
פ	ף	Pei	80
כ	ך	Kaf	20

Tag (Crown) or Tagin (Crowns) on the Hebrew Letters

The special Ashurit font, used to scribe Torah Scrolls, has some letters that have crowns ⩛ or a spike ᵀ on top of them. The letters that have crowns on the them are abbreviated as *Sha'atnez Gatz* or Shin-Ayin-Tet-Nun-Zayin, Gimel-Tzadi שעטנז גץ.

Hebrew Vowels

The letter Alef is used as a demonstration of how the vowels appear on any letter.

Letter	Name	Sefirah
אָ	Kamatz	Keter
אַ	Patach	Chochmah
אֵ	Tzere	Binah
אֶ	Segol	Chesed
אְ	Shva	Gevurah

Letter	Name	Sefirah
אֹ אוֹ	Cholam	Tiferet
אִ	Chirik	Netzach
אֻ	Shuruk	Hod
אוּ	Shuruk Vav	Yesod